Anonymous

History of Grundy County, Illinois

Containing a History from the Earliest Settlement to the Present Time

Anonymous

History of Grundy County, Illinois
Containing a History from the Earliest Settlement to the Present Time

ISBN/EAN: 9783337098476

Printed in Europe, USA, Canada, Australia, Japan

Cover: Foto ©ninafisch / pixelio.de

More available books at **www.hansebooks.com**

HISTORY

OF

GRUNDY COUNTY

ILLINOIS.

Containing a History from the earliest settlement to the present time, embracing its topographical, geological, physical and climatic features; its agricultural, railroad interests, etc.; giving an account of its aboriginal inhabitants, early settlement by the whites, pioneer incidents, its growth, its improvements, organization of the County, the judicial history, the business and industries, churches, schools, etc.; Biographical Sketches; Portraits of some of the Early Settlers, Prominent Men, etc.

ILLUSTRATED.

CHICAGO:
O. L. BASKIN & CO., HISTORICAL PUBLISHERS,
LAKESIDE BUILDING.
1882.

PREFACE.

IN this volume the publishers present the results of their efforts to secure a creditable compilation of the History of Grundy County. In recounting the "short and simple annals" of a community founded in the "piping times of peace," and more in the midst than on the frontier of new settlements, there is little material for a thrilling narrative or a record of interesting exploits, but the authors of this enterprise believe that the essential facts of the early history are here set forth with substantial accuracy. No effort has been made to draw upon the imagination to embellish the story, but as it has been found, it has been given, in a plain, unvarnished tale. The historical matter has been revised by L. W. Claypool, Esq., whose thorough knowledge of the history and wide acquaintance with the people of the county assures its accuracy, and has largely contributed to its completeness, and the publishers take this occasion to acknowledge their indebtedness to him for his valuable assistance in the prosecution of this enterprise. The chapters on Morris were contributed by the Hon. P. A. Armstrong, with whom the undertaking was largely a labor of love, and to his cordial indorsement of the work and interesting contributions to its pages is due much of its success. The chapters on Gardner were contributed by Dr. C. M. Easton, to whom the publishers and patrons are greatly indebted for the intelligent and persevering zeal with which he has discharged the duty imposed upon him. The publishers also desire to thank the people everywhere in the county for the uniform courtesy and assistance tendered our corps of writers, and trust the general accuracy of the work will in some part repay the favors they have shown.

O. L. BASKIN & CO.
Publishers.

CONTENTS.

PART I.

HISTORICAL. PAGE.

The Northwest Territory 11
Early History of Illinois 67

GRUNDY COUNTY.

CHAPTER I.—Topography—Post-Tertiary Formations—Rock-Formations—Carbouiferous Fossils—Economic Geology... 100

CHAPTER II.—Pre-historic Races—Earliest Traces of Man—Mound-Builders and their Remains—Indian Tribes—Relations with the Whites—Waupusee—Shabbona—Nucquette 113

CHAPTER III.—Early French Settlements—Frontier Settlements in La Salle and Grundy Counties—Civilized Life in a New Country—Political Organization—Formation of Grundy County—County Buildings 132

CHAPTER IV.—Social Development—Early Society—Rise of Church and School—Indian Trails and Early Roads—Railroads and the Canal—The Newspapers 146

CHAPTER V.—Grundy County's Share in the War of the Rebellion—The Loyalty of Her Men—The Devotion of Her Women—The Representatives in the Field 164

CHAPTER VI.—Morris City—Introductory—Its Location—First Beginnings—Origin of Name—County Honors—Early Community—Biographical 183

CHAPTER VII.—Morris City—The Second Period—Growth of the Corporation—Official Records—Internal Improvements—1842 to 1850 203

CHAPTER VIII.—Morris Township—Its Organization, Boundaries and Changes—The New Court House—Schools of Morris—Early Teachers—The Board of Education 223

CHAPTER IX.—Morris City—Churches—Early Ministers—The Legal Profession—Business—Pioneers—Secret Fraternities 248

CHAPTER X.—Greenfield Township—Surface—Streams—Timber—Origin of Name—Township Organization—Going to Mill—First Settlers—Incidents—Wolf and Deer Hunting

PAGE.
—Elections—Officers—Improvements and Prospects—What We are To-day, etc., etc 264

CHAPTER XI.—Gardner—Town Platting—Naming—First Buildings—Inhabitants—Improvements—Coal and Mining Interests—Societies—Schools—Churches—Business Firms and Individuals, etc 275

CHAPTER XII.—Nettle Creek Township—First Settlers—Life in a Prairie Country—Schools, etc 285

CHAPTER XIII.—Au Sable Township—Location and Physical Characteristics—Its Early Settlement—Its Natural Attractions—Dresden—Minooka—Churches and Schools 290

CHAPTER XIV.—Saratoga Township—Physical Features—The Early Settlers—The Norwegian Emigration—The Houges Meneghed 297

CHAPTER XV.—Wauponsee Township—Its Material Resources—Early Settlers—Pioneer Life on the Prairie—The Church and School 302

CHAPTER XVI.—Felix Township—Its Topographical Features—Pioneers—Floods—Sickness—Jug-Town—The Silent City 312

CHAPTER XVII.—Erienna—Township 33 North, Range 6 East—Changes of Boundaries—Early Settlement—Hurrom City—Clarkson—Norman—Surface Features—Pioneers—Churches and Schools 321

CHAPTER XVIII.—Mazon Township—Early Topographical Features—Its Pioneers—Growth and Development of the Settlement—New Mazon—Churches and Schools 328

CHAPTER XIX.—Vienna Township—Pioneers of the Prairie—The Changes of Fifty Years—Illinois City—Verona—The Church and School 340

CHAPTER XX.—Braceville Township—Coal Measures—Early Settlement—The Open Prairie 346

CHAPTER XXI.—Goodfarm Township—"The Lay of the Land"—Early Settlement—Pioneer Experiences—Schools—Churches 354

CHAPTER XXII.—Highland Township—Topographical Characteristics—Prairie Bandits—Lawless Law—Settlement of the Township—The Catholic Church 395

CONTENTS.

PART II.

BIOGRAPHICAL.

	PAGE.
Morris City and Township	3
Au Sable Township	41
Mazon Township	62
Wauponsee Township	76
Greenfield Township	82
Braceville Township	105
Felix Township	122
Saratoga Township	124
Nettle Creek Township	132
Erienna Township	134
Norman Township	136
Vienna Township	139
Highland Township	151
Goodfarm Township	154

PORTRAITS.

	PAGE.
S. B. Thomas	45
L. W. Claypool	81
P. A. Armstrong	157
J. C. Lurtz	153
O. J. Booth	169
J. N. Reading	909
Dr. C. M. Easton	261
G. P. Augustine	87
William Stephen	339

THE NORTHWEST TERRITORY,

INCLUDING A BRIEF

HISTORY OF ILLINOIS.

GEOGRAPHICAL POSITION.

WHEN the Northwestern Territory was ceded to the United States by Virginia in 1784, it embraced only the territory lying between the Ohio and the Mississippi Rivers, and north to the northern limits of the United States. It coincided with the area now embraced in the States of Ohio, Indiana, Michigan, Illinois, Wisconsin, and that portion of Minnesota lying on the east side of the Mississippi River. The United States itself at that period extended no farther west than the Mississippi River; but by the purchase of Louisiana in 1803, the western boundary of the United States was extended to the Rocky Mountains and the Northern Pacific Ocean. The new territory thus added to the National domain, and subsequently opened to settlement, has been called the "New Northwest," in contradistinction from the old "Northwestern Territory."

In comparison with the old Northwest this is a territory of vast magnitude. It includes an area of 1,887,850 square miles; being greater in extent than the united areas of all the Middle and Southern States, including Texas. Out of this magnificent territory have been erected eleven sovereign States and eight Territories, with an aggregate population, at the present time, of 13,000,000 inhabitants, or nearly one-third of the entire population of the United States.

Its lakes are fresh-water seas, and the larger rivers of the continent flow for a thousand miles through its rich alluvial valleys and far-stretching prairies, more acres of which are arable and productive of the highest percentage of the cereals than of any other area of like extent on the globe.

For the last twenty years the increase of population in the Northwest has been about as three to one in any other portion of the United States.

EARLY EXPLORATIONS.

In the year 1541, De Soto first saw the Great West in the New World. He, however, penetrated no farther north than the 35th parallel of latitude. The expedition resulted in his death and that of more than half his army, the remainder of whom found their way to Cuba, thence to Spain, in a famished and demoralized condition. De Soto founded no settlements, produced no results, and left no traces, unless it were that he awakened the hostility of the red man against the white man, and disheartened such as might desire to follow up the career of discovery for better purposes. The French nation were eager and ready to seize upon any news from this extensive domain, and were the first to profit by De Soto's defeat. Yet it was more than a century before any adventurer took advantage of these discoveries.

In 1616, four years before the pilgrims "moored their bark on the wild New England shore," Le Caron, a French Franciscan, had penetrated through the Iroquois and and Wyandots (Hurons) to the streams which run into Lake Huron; and in 1634, two Jesuit missionaries founded the first mission among the lake tribes. It was just one hundred years from the discovery of the Mississippi by De Soto (1544) until the Canadian envoys met the savage nations of the Northwest at the Falls of St. Mary, below the outlet of Lake Superior. This visit led to no permanent result, yet it was not until 1659 that any of the adventurous fur traders attempted to spend a winter in the frozen wilds about the great lakes, nor was it until 1660 that a station was established upon their borders by Mesnard, who perished in the woods a few months after. In 1665, Claude Allouez built the earliest lasting habitation of the white man among the Indians of the Northwest. In 1668, Claude Dablon and James Marquette founded the mission of Sault Ste. Marie at the Falls of St. Mary, and two years afterward, Nicholas Perrot, as agent for M. Talon, Governor General of Canada, explored Lake Illinois (Michigan) as far south as the present City of Chicago, and invited the Indian nations to meet him at a grand council at Sault Ste. Marie the following spring, where they were taken under the protection of the king, and formal possession was taken of the Northwest. This same year Marquette established a mission at Point St. Ignatius, where was founded the old town of town of Michillimackinac.

During M. Talon's explorations and Marquette's residence at St. Ignatius, they learned of a great river away to the west, and fancied—as all others did then—that upon its fertile banks whole tribes of God's children resided, to whom the sound of the Gospel had never come. Filled with a wish to go and preach to them, and in compliance with a request of M. Talon, who earnestly desired to extend the domain of his king, and to ascertain whether the river flowed into the Gulf of Mexico or the Pacific Ocean, Marquette with Joliet, as commander of the expedition, prepared for the undertaking.

On the 13th of May, 1673, the explorers, accompanied by five assistant French Canadians, set out from Mackinaw on their daring voyage of discovery. The Indians, who gathered to witness their departure, were astonished at the boldness of the undertaking, and endeavored to dissuade them from their purpose by representing the tribes on the Mississippi as exceedingly savage and cruel, and the river itself as full of all sorts of frightful monsters ready to swallow them and their canoes together. But, nothing daunted by these terrific descriptions, Marquette told them he was willing not only to encounter all the perils of the unknown region they were about to explore, but to lay down his life in a cause in which the salvation of souls was involved; and having prayed together they separated. Coasting along the northern shore of Lake Michigan, the adventurers entered Green Bay, and passed thence up the Fox River and Lake Winnebago to a village of the Miamis and Kickapoos. Here Marquette was delighted to find a beautiful cross planted in the middle of the town, ornamented with white skins, red girdles and bows and arrows, which these good people had offered to the great Manitou, or God, to thank him for the pity he had bestowed on them during the winter in giving them an abundant "chase." This was the farthest outpost to which Dablon and Allouez had extended their missionary labors the year previous. Here Marquette drank mineral waters and was instructed in the secret of a root which cures the bite of the venomous rattlesnake. He assembled the chiefs and old men of the village, and, pointing to Joliet, said: "My friend is an envoy of France, to discover new countries, and I am an ambassador from God to enlighten them with the truths of the Gospel." Two Miami guides were here furnished to conduct them to the Wisconsin River, and they set out from the Indian village on the 10th of June, amidst a great crowd of natives who had assembled to witness their departure into a region where no white man had ever yet ventured. The guides, having conducted them across the portage, returned. The explorers launched their canoes upon the Wisconsin which they descended to the Mississippi and proceeded down its unknown waters. What emotions must have swelled their breasts as they struck out into the broadening current and became conscious that they were now upon the bosom of the Father of Waters. The mystery was about to be lifted from the long-sought river. The scenery in that locality is beautiful, and on that delightful seventeenth of June must have been clad in all its primeval loveliness as it had been adorned by the hand of Nature. Drifting rapidly, it is said that the bold bluffs on either hand "reminded them of the castled shores of their own beautiful rivers of France." By-and-by, as they drifted along, great herds of buffalo appeared on the banks. On going to the heads of the valley they could see a country of the greatest beauty and fertility, apparently destitute of inhabitants yet presenting the appearance of extensive manors, under the fastidious cultivation of lordly proprietors.

On June 25th, they went ashore and found some fresh traces of men upon the sand, and a path which led to the prairie. The men remained in the boat, and Marquette and Joliet followed the path till they discovered a village on the banks of a river, and two other villages on a hill, within a half league of the first, inhabited by Indians. They were received most hospitably by these natives, who had never before seen a white person. After remaining a few days they re-embarked and descended the river to about latitude 33°, where they found a village of the Arkansas, and being satisfied that the river flowed into the Gulf of Mexico, turned their course up the river, and ascending the stream to the mouth of the Illinois, rowed up that stream to its source, and procured guides from that point to the lakes. "No where on this journey," says Marquette, "did we see such grounds, meadows, woods, stags, buffaloes, deer, wildcats, bustards, swans, ducks, parroquets, and even beavers, as on the Illinois River." The party, without loss or injury, reached Green Bay in September, and reported their discovery—one of the most important of the age, but of which no record was preserved save Marquette's, Joliet losing his by the upsetting of his canoe on his way to Quebec. Afterward Marquette returned to the Illinois Indians by their request, and ministered to them until 1675. On the 18th of May, in that year, as he was passing the mouth of a stream—going with his boatmen up Lake Michigan—he asked to land at its mouth and celebrate mass. Leaving his men with the canoe, he retired a shore distance and began his devotions. As much time passed and he did not return, his men went in search of him, and found him upon his knees, dead. He had peacefully passed away while at prayer. He was buried at this spot. Charlevoix, who visited the place fifty years after, found the waters had retreated from the grave, leaving the beloved missionary to repose in peace. The river has since been called Marquette.

While Marquette and his companions were pursuing their labors in the West, two men, differing widely from him and each other, were preparing to follow in his footsteps and perfect the discoveries so well begun by him. These were Robert de La Salle and Louis Hennepin.

After La Salle's return from the discovery of the Ohio River (see the narrative elsewhere), he established himself again among the French trading posts in Canada. Here he mused long upon the pet project of those ages—a short way to China and the East, and was busily planning an expedition up the great lakes, and so across the continent to the Pacific, when Marquette returned from the Mississippi. At once the vigorous mind of La Salle received from his and his companions' stories the idea that by following the Great River northward, or by turning up some of the numerous western tributaries, the object could easily be gained. He applied to Frontenac, Governor General of Canada, and laid before him the plan, dim but gigantic. Frontenac entered warmly into his plans, and saw that La Salle's idea to connect the great lakes by a chain of forts with the Gulf of Mexico would bind the country so wonderfully together, give unmeasured power to France, and glory to himself, under whose administration he earnestly hoped all would be realized.

La Salle now repaired to France, laid his plans before the King, who warmly approved of them, and made him a Chevalier. He also received from all the noblemen the warmest wishes for his success. The Chevalier returned to Canada, and busily entered upon his work. He at once rebuilt Fort Frontenac and constructed the first ship to sail on these fresh-water seas. On the 7th of August, 1679, having been joined by Hennepin, he began his voyage in the Griffin up Lake Erie. He passed over this lake, through the straits beyond, up Lake St. Clair and into Huron. In this lake they encountered heavy storms. They were some time at Michillimackinac, where La Salle founded a fort, and passed on to Green Bay, the "Baie des Puans" of the French, where he found a large quantity of furs collected for him. He loaded the Griffin with these, and placing her under the care of a pilot and fourteen sailors, started her on her return voyage. The vessel was never afterward heard of. He remained about these parts until early in the winter, when, hearing nothing from the Griffin, he collected all his men—thirty working men and three monks—and started again upon his great undertaking.

By a short portage they passed to the Illinois or Kankakee, called by the Indians, "Theakeke," *wolf*, because of the tribes of Indians called by that name, commonly known as the Mahingans, dwelling there. The French pronounced it *Kiakiki*, which became corrupted to Kankakee. "Falling down the said river by easy journeys, the better to observe the country," about the last of December they reached a village of the Illinois Indians, containing some five hundred cabins, but at that moment no inhabitants. The Seur de La Salle being in want of some breadstuffs, took advantage of the absence of the Indians to help himself to a sufficiency of maize, large quantities of which he found concealed in holes under the wigwams. This village was situated near the present village of Utica in La Salle County, Illinois. The corn being securely stored, the voyagers again betook themselves to the stream, and toward evening on the 4th day of January, 1680, they came into a lake, which must have been the lake of Peoria. This was called by the Indians *Pim-i-te-wi*, that is *a place where there are many fat beasts*. Here the natives were met with in large numbers, but they were gentle and kind, and having spent some time with them, La Salle determined to erect another fort in that place, for he had heard rumors that some of the adjoining tribes were trying to disturb the good feeling which existed, and some of his men were disposed to complain, owing to the hardships and perils of the travel. He called this fort "*Crevecœur*" (brokenheart), a name expressive of the very natural sorrow and anxiety which the pretty certain loss of his ship, Griffin, and his consequent impoverishment, the danger of hostility on the part of the Indians, and of mutiny among his own men, might well cause him. His fears were not entirely groundless. At one time poison was placed in his food, but fortunately was discovered.

While building this fort, the winter wore away, the prairies began to look green, and La Salle, despairing of any reinforcements, concluded to return to Canada, raise new means and new men, and embark anew in the enterprise. For this purpose he made Hennepin the leader of a party to explore the head waters of the Mississippi, and he set out on his journey. This journey was accomplished with the aid of a few persons, and was successfully made, though over an almost unknown route, and in a bad season of the year. He safely reached Canada, and set out again for the object of his search.

Hennepin and his party left Fort Crevecœur on the last of February, 1680. When La Salle reached this place on his return expedition, he found the fort entirely deserted, and he was obliged to return again to Canada. He embarked the third time, and succeeded. Seven days after leaving the fort, Hennepin reached the Mississippi, and paddling up the icy stream as best he could, reached no higher than the Wisconsin River by the 11th of April. Here he and his followers were taken prisoners by a band of Northern Indians, who treated them with great kindness. Hennepin's comrades were Anthony Anguel and Michael Ako. On this voyage they found several beautiful lakes, and " saw some charming prairies." Their captors were the Isaute or Santeurs, Chippewas, a tribe of the Sioux nation, who took them up the river until about the first of May, when they reached some falls, which Hennepin christened Falls of St. Anthony in honor of his patron saint. Here they took the land, and traveling nearly two hundred miles to the northwest, brought them to their villages. Here they were kept about three months, were treated kindly by their captors, and at the end of that time, were met by a band of Frenchmen, headed by one Seur de Luth, who, in pursuit of trade and game, had penetrated thus far by the route of Lake Superior; and with these fellow-countrymen Hennepin and his companions were allowed to return to the borders of civilized life in November, 1680, just after La Salle had returned to the wilderness on his second trip. Hennepin soon after went to France, where he published an account of his adventures.

The Mississippi was first discovered by De Soto in April, 1541, in his vain endeavor to find gold and precious gems. In the following spring, De Soto, weary with hope long deferred, and worn out with his wanderings, fell a victim to disease, and on the 21st of May, died. His followers, reduced by fatigue and disease to less than three hundred men, wandered about the country nearly a year, in the vain endeavor to rescue themselves by land, and finally constructed seven small vessels, called brigantines, in which they embarked, and descending the river, supposing it would lead them to the sea, in July they came to the sea (Gulf of Mexico), and by September reached the Island of Cuba.

They were the first to see the great outlet of the Mississippi; but, being so weary and discouraged, made no attempt to claim the country, and hardly had an intelligent idea of what they had passed through.

To La Salle, the intrepid explorer, belongs the honor of giving the first account of the mouths of the river. His great desire was to possess this entire country for his king, and in January, 1682, he and his band of explorers left the shores of Lake Michigan on their third attempt, crossed the portage, passed down the Illinois River, and on the 6th of February, reached the banks of the Mississippi.

On the 13th they commenced their downward course, which they pursued with but one interruption, until upon the 6th of March they discovered the three great passages by which the river discharges its waters into the gulf. La Salle thus narrates the event:

"We landed on the bank of the most western channel, about three leagues (nine miles) from its mouth. On the seventh, M. de La Salle went to reconnoiter the shores of the neighboring sea, and M. de Tonti meanwhile examined the great middle channel. They found the main outlets beautiful, large and deep. On the 8th we reascended the river, a little above its confluence with the sea, to find a dry place beyond the reach of inundations. The elevation of the North Pole was here about twenty-seven degrees. Here we prepared a column and a cross, and to the column were affixed the arms of France with this inscription:

Louis LeGrand, Roi De France et de Navarre, regne; Le neuvieme Avril 1682.

The whole party, under arms, chanted the *Te Deum*, and then, after a salute and cries of "*Vive le Roi*," the column was erected by M. de La Salle, who, standing near it, proclaimed in a loud voice the authority of the King of France. La Salle returned and laid the foundations of the Mississippi settlements in Illinois, thence he proceeded to France, where another expedition was fitted out, of which he was commander, and in two succeeding voyages failed to find the outlet of the river by sailing along the shore of the gulf. On his third voyage he was killed, through the treachery of his followers, and the object of his expeditions was not accomplished until 1699, when D'Iberville, under the authority of the crown, discovered, on the second of March, by way of the sea, the mouth of the "Hidden River." This majestic stream was called by the natives "*Malbouchia*," and by the Spaniards, "*la Palissade*," from the great number of trees about its mouth. After traversing the several outlets, and satisfying himself as to its certainty, he erected a fort near its western outlet and returned to France.

An avenue of trade was now opened out, which was fully improved. In 1718, New Orleans was laid out and settled by some European colonists. In 1762, the colony was made over to Spain, to be regained by France under the consulate of Napoleon. In 1803, it was purchased by the United States for the sum of fifteen million dollars, and the territory of Louisiana and commerce of the Mississippi River came under the charge of the United States. Although La Salle's labors ended in defeat and death, he had not worked and suffered in vain. He had thrown open to France and the world an immense and most valuable country; had established several ports, and laid the foundations of more than one settlement there. "Peoria, Kaskaskia and Cahokia, are to this day monuments of La Salle's labors; for, though he had founded neither of them (unless Peoria, which was built nearly upon the site of Fort Crevecœur,) it was by those whom he led into the West that these places were peopled and civilized. He was, if not the discoverer, the first settler of the Mississippi Valley, and as such deserves to be known and honored."

The French early improved the opening made for them. Before the year 1698, the Rev. Father Gravier began a mission among the Illinois, and founded Kaskaskia. For some time this was merely a missionary station, where none but natives resided, it being one of three such villages, the other two being Cahokia and Peoria. What is known of these missions is learned from a letter written by Father Gabriel Marest, dated "Aux Cascaskias, autrement dit de l'Immaculate Conception de la Sainte Vierge, le 9 Novembre, 1712." Soon after the founding of Kaskaskia, the missionary, Pinet, gathered a flock at Cahokia, while Peoria arose near the ruins of Fort Crevecœur. This must have been about a year 1700. The post at Vincennes on the Oubache river, (pronounced Wa-ba, meaning *summer cloud moving swiftly*) was established in 1702, according to the best authorities.[*] It is altogether probable that

[*] There is considerable dispute about this date, some asserting it was founded as late as 1742. When the new court house at Vincennes was erected, all authorities on the subject were carefully examined, and 1702 fixed upon as the correct date. It was accordingly engraved on the corner-stone of the court house.

on La Salle's last trip he established the stations at Kaskaskia and Cahokia. In July, 1701, the foundations of Fort Ponchartrain were laid by De la Motte Cadillac on the Detroit River. These stations, with those established further north, were the earliest attempts to occupy the Northwest Territory. At the same time efforts were being made to occupy the Southwest, which finally culminated in the settlement and founding of the City of New Orleans by a colony from England in 1718. This was mainly accomplished through the efforts of the famous Mississippi Company, established by the notorious John Law, who so quickly arose into prominence in France, and who with his scheme so quickly and so ignominiously passed away.

From the time of the founding of these stations for fifty years the French nation were engrossed with the settlement of the lower Mississippi, and the war with the Chicasaws, who had, in revenge for repeated injuries, cut off the entire colony at Natchez. Although the company did little for Louisiana, as the entire West was then called, yet it opened the trade through the Mississippi River, and started the raising of grains indigenous to that climate. Until the year 1750, but little is known of the settlements in the Northwest, as it was not until this time that the attention of the English was called to the occupation of this portion of the New World, which they then supposed they owned. Vivier, a missionary among the Illinois, writing from "Aux Illinois," six leagues from Fort Chartres, June 8, 1750, says: "We have here whites, negroes and Indians, to say nothing of cross-breeds. There are five French villages, and three villages of the natives, within a space of twenty-one leagues situated between the Mississippi and another river called the Karkadaid (Kaskaskias). In the five French villages are, perhaps, eleven hundred whites, three hundred blacks and some sixty red slaves or savages. The three Illinois towns do not contain more than eight hundred souls all told. Most of the French till the soil; they raise wheat, cattle, pigs and horses, and live like princes. Three times as much is produced as can be consumed; and great quantities of grain and flour are sent to New Orleans." This city was now the seaport town of the Northwest, and save in the extreme northern part, where only furs and copper ore were found, almost all the products of the country found their way to France by the mouth of the Father of Waters. In another letter, dated November 7, 1750, this same priest says: "For fifteen leagues above the mouth of the Mississippi one sees no dwellings, the ground being too low to be habitable. Thence to New Orleans, the lands are only partially occupied. New Orleans contains black, white and red, not more, I think, than twelve hundred persons. To this point come all lumber, bricks, salt-beef, tallow, tar, skins and bear's grease; and above all, pork and flour from the Illinois. These things create some commerce, as forty vessels and more have come hither this year. Above New Orleans, plantations are again met with; the most considerable is a colony of Germans, some ten leagues up the river. At Point Coupee, thirty-five leagues above the German settlement, is a fort. Along here, within five or six leagues are not less than sixty habitations. Fifty leagues farther up is the Natchez post, where we have a garrison, who are kept prisoners through fear of the Chicasaws. Here and at point Coupee, they raise excellent tobacco. Another hundred leagues brings us to the Arkansas, where we have also a fort and a garrison for the benefit of the river traders. * * * From the Arkansas to the Illinois, nearly five hundred leagues, there is not a settlement. There should be, however, a fort at the Oubache (Ohio), the only path by which the English can reach the Mississippi. In the Illinois country are numberless mines, but no one to work them as they deserve." Father Marest, writing from the post at Vincennes, in 1812, makes the same observation. Vivier also says: "Some individuals dig lead near the surface and supply the Indians and Canada. Two Spaniards now here, who claim to be adepts, say that our mines are like those of Mexico, and that if we would dig deeper, we should find silver under the lead ; and at any rate the lead is excellent. There is also in this country, beyond doubt, copper ore, as from time to time large pieces are found in the streams."

At the close of the year 1750, the French occupied, in addition to the lower Mississippi posts and those in Illinois, one at Du Quesne, one at the Maumee in the country of the Miamis, and one at Sandusky, in what may be termed the Ohio Valley. In the northern part of the Northwest they had stations at St. Joseph's on the St. Joseph's of Lake Michigan, at Fort Ponchartrain (Detroit), at Michillimackinac or Massillimacanac, Fox River of Green Bay, and at Sault Ste. Marie. The fondest dreams of La Salle were now fully realized. The French alone were possessors of this vast realm, basing their claim on discovery and settlement. Another nation, however, was now turning its attention to this extensive country, and hearing of its wealth, began to lay plans for occupying it and for securing the great profits arising therefrom.

The French, however, had another claim to this country, namely, the

DISCOVERY OF THE OHIO.

This " Beautiful " river was discovered by Robert Cavalier de La Salle in 1669, four years before the discovery of the Mississippi by Joliet and Marquette.

While La Salle was at his trading post on the St. Lawrence, he found leisure to study nine Indian dialects, the chief of which was the Iroquois. He not only desired to facilitate his intercourse in trade, but he longed to travel and explore the unknown regions of the West. An incident soon occurred which decided him to fit out an exploring expedition.

While conversing with some Senecas, he learned of a river called the Ohio, which rose in their country and flowed to the sea, but at such a distance that it required eight months to reach its mouth. In this statement the Mississippi and its tributaries were considered as one stream. La Salle, believing, as most of the French at that period did, that the great rivers flowing west emptied into the Sea of California, was anxious to embark in the enterprise of discovering a route across the continent to the commerce of China and Japan.

He repaired at once to Quebec to obtain the approval of the Governor. His eloquent appeal prevailed. The Governor and the Intendant, Talon, issued letters patent authorizing the enterprise, but made no provision to defray the expenses. At this juncture the seminary of St. Sulpice decided to send out missionaries in connection with the expedition, and La Salle offering to sell his improvements at La Chine to raise money, the offer was accepted by the Superior, and two thousand eight hundred dollars were raised, with which La Salle purchased four canoes and the necessary supplies for the outfit.

On the 6th of July, 1669, the party, numbering twenty-four persons, embarked in seven canoes on the St. Lawrence; two additional canoes carried the Indian guides. In three days they were gliding over the bosom of Lake Ontario. Their guides conducted them directly to the Seneca village on the bank of the Genesee, in the vicinity of the present City of Rochester, New York. Here they expected to procure guides to conduct them to the Ohio, but in this they were disappointed.

The Indians seemed unfriendly to the enterprise. La Salle suspected that the Jesuits had prejudiced their minds against his plans. After waiting a month in the hope of gaining their object, they met an Indian from the Iroquois colony at the head of Lake Ontario, who assured them that they could there find guides, and offered to conduct them thence.

On their way they passed the mouth of the Niagara River, when they heard for the first time the distant thunder of the cataract. Arriving among the Iroquois, they met with a friendly reception, and learned from a Shawanee prisoner that they could reach the Ohio in six weeks. Delighted with the unexpected good fortune, they made ready to resume their journey; but just as they were about to start they heard of the arrival of two Frenchmen in a neighboring village. One of them proved to be Louis Joliet, afterward famous as an explorer in the West. He had been sent by the Canadian Government to explore the copper mines on Lake Superior, but had failed, and was on his way back to Quebec. He gave the missionaries a map of the country he had explored in the lake region, together with an account of the condition of the Indians in that quarter. This induced the priests to determine on leaving the expedition and going to Lake Superior. La Salle warned them that the Jesuits were probably occupying that field, and that they would meet with a cold reception. Nevertheless they persisted in their purpose, and after worship on the lake shore parted from La Salle. On arriving at Lake Superior, they found, as La Salle had predicted, the Jesuit Fathers, Marquette and Dablon, occupying the field.

These zealous disciples of Loyola informed them that they wanted no assistance from St. Sulpice, nor from those who made him their patron saint; and thus repulsed, they returned to Montreal the following June without having made a single discovery or converted a single Indian.

After parting with the priests, La Salle went to the chief Iroquois village at Onondaga, where he obtained guides, and passing thence to a tributary of the Ohio south of Lake Erie, he descended the latter as far as the falls at Louisville. Thus was the Ohio discovered by La Salle, the persevering and successful French explorer of the West, in 1669.

The account of the latter part of his journey is found in an anonymous paper, which purports to have been taken from the lips of La Salle himself during a subsequent visit to Paris. In a letter written to Count Frontenac in 1667, shortly after the discovery, he himself says that he discovered the Ohio and descended it to the falls. This was regarded as an indisputable fact by the French authorities, who claimed the Ohio Valley upon another ground. When Washington was sent by the colony of Virginia in 1753, to demand of Gordenr de St. Pierre why the French had built a fort on the Monongahela, the haughty commandant at Quebec replied: "We claim the country on the Ohio by virtue of the discoveries of La Salle, and will not give it up to the English. Our orders are to make prisoners of every Englishman found trading in the Ohio Valley."

ENGLISH EXPLORATIONS AND SETTLEMENTS.

When the new year of 1750 broke in upon the Father of Waters and the Great Northwest, all was still wild save at the French posts already described. In 1749, when the English first began to think seriously about sending men into the West, the greater portion of the States of Indiana, Ohio, Illinois, Michigan, Wisconsin, and Minnesota were yet under the dominion of the red men. The English knew, however, pretty conclusively of the nature of the wealth of these wilds. As early as 1710, Governor Spotswood, of Virginia, had commenced movements to secure the country west of the Alleghanies to the English crown. In Pennsylvania, Governor Keith and James Logan, secretary of the province, from 1719 to 1731, represented to the powers of England the necessity of securing the Western lands. Nothing was done, however, by that power save to take some diplomatic steps to secure the claims of Britain to this unexplored wilderness.

England had from the outset claimed from the Atlantic to the Pacific, on the ground that the discovery of the seacoast and its possession was a discovery and possession of the country, and, as is well known, her grants to the colonies extended "from sea to sea." This was not all her claim. She had purchased from the Indian tribes large tracts of land. This latter was also a strong argument. As early as 1684, Lord Howard, Governor of Virginia, held a treaty with the six nations. These were the great Northern Confederacy, and comprised at first the Mohawks, Oneidas, Onondagas, Cayugas, and Senecas. Afterward the Tuscaroras were taken into the confederacy, and it became known as the SIX NATIONS. They came under the protection of the mother country, and again in 1701, they repeated the agreement, and in September, 1726, a formal deed was drawn up and signed by the chiefs. The validity of this claim has often been disputed, but never successfully. In 1744, a purchase was made at Lancaster, Pennsylvania, of certain lands within the "Colony of Virginia," for which the Indians received £200 in gold and a like sum in goods, with a promise that, as settlements increased, more should be paid. The Commissioners from Virginia were Colonel Thomas Lee and Colonel William Beverley. As settlements extended, the promise of more pay was called to mind, and Mr. Conrad Weiser was sent across the mountains with presents to appease the savages. Col. Lee, and some Virginians accompanied him with the intention of sounding the Indians upon their feelings regarding the English. They were not satisfied with their treatment, and plainly told the Commissioners why. The English did not desire the cultivation of the country, but the monopoly of the Indian trade. In 1748, the Ohio Company was formed, and petitioned the king for a grant of land beyond the Alleghenies. This was granted, and the government of Virginia was ordered to grant to them a half million acres, two hundred thousand of which were to be located at once. Upon the 12th of June, 1749, 800,000 acres from the line of Canada north and west was made to the Loyal Company, and on the 29th of October, 1751, 100,000 acres were given to the Greenbriar Company. All this time the French were not idle. They saw that, should the British gain a foothold in the West, especially upon the Ohio, they might not only prevent the French settling upon it, but in time would come to the lower posts and so gain possession of the whole country. Upon the 10th of May, 1774, Vaudreuil, Governor of Canada and the French possessions, well knowing the consequences that must arise from allowing the English to build trading posts in the Northwest, seized some of their frontier posts, and to further secure the claim of the French to the West, he, in 1749, sent Louis Celeron with a party of soldiers to plant along the Ohio River, in the mounds and at the mouths of its principal tributaries, plates of lead, on which were inscribed the claims of France. These were heard of in 1752, and within the memory of residents now living along the "Oyo," as the beautiful river was called by the French. One of these plates was found with the inscription partly defaced. It bears date August 16, 1749, and a copy of the inscription with particular account of the discovery of the plate, was sent by DeWitt Clinton to the American Antiquarian Society, among whose journals it may now be found.* These measures did not, however, deter the English from going on with their explorations, and though neither party resorted to arms, yet the conflict was gathering, and it was only a question of time when the storm would burst upon the frontier settlements. In 1750, Christopher Gist was sent by the Ohio Company to examine its lands. He went to a village of the Twigtwees, on the Miami, about one hundred and fifty miles above its mouth. He afterward spoke of it as very populous. From there he went down the Ohio River nearly to the falls at the present City of Louisville, and in November he commenced a survey of the company's lands. During the winter, General Andrew Lewis performed a similar work for the Greenbriar Company. Meanwhile the French were busy in preparing their forts for defense, and in opening roads, and also sent a small party of soldiers to keep the Ohio clear. This party, having heard of the English post on the Miami

* The following is a translation of the inscription on the plate: "In the year 1749, reign of Louis XV., King of France, we, Celeron, commandant of a detachment by Monsieur the Marquis of Gallsoniere, commander-in-chief of New France, to establish tranquility in certain Indian villages of these cantons, have buried this plate at the confluence of the Toradakoin, this twenty-ninth of July, near the river Ohio, otherwise Beautiful River, as a monument of renewal of possession which we have taken of the said river, and all its tributaries; inasmuch as the preceding Kings of France have enjoyed it, and maintained it by their arms and treaties; especially by those of Ryswick, Utrecht, and Aix La Chapelle."

River, early in 1652, assisted by the Ottawas and Chippewas, attacked it, and, after a severe battle, in which fourteen of the natives were killed and others wounded, captured the garrison. (They were probably garrisoned in a block house). The traders were carried away to Canada, and one account says several were burned. This fort or post was called by the English Pickawillany. A memorial of the king's ministers refers to it as "Pickawillanes, in the center of the territory between the Ohio and the Wabash. The name is probably some variation of Pickaway or Piequa, in 1773, written by Rev. David Jones, Pickaweke."

This was the first blood shed between the French and English, and occurred near the present City of Piqua, Ohio, or at least at a point about forty-seven miles north of Dayton. Each nation became now more interested in the progress of events in the Northwest. The English determined to purchase from the Indians a title to the lands they wished to occupy, and Messrs. Fry (afterward Commander-in-chief over Washington at the commencement of the French War of 1775–1763), Lomax and Patton were sent in the spring of 1752 to hold a conference with the natives at Logstown to learn what they objected to in the treaty of Lancaster already noticed and to settle all difficulties. On the 9th of June, these Commissioners met the red men at Logstown, a little village on the north bank of the Ohio, about seventeen miles below the site of Pittsburgh. Here had been a trading point for many years, but it was abandoned by the Indians in 1750. At first the Indians declined to recognize the treaty of Lancaster, but, the Commissioners taking aside Montour, the interpreter, who was a son of the famous Catharine Montour, and a chief among the Six Nations, induced him to use his influence in their favor. This he did, and upon the 13th of June they all united in signing a deed, confirming the Lancaster treaty in its full extent, consenting to a settlement of the southeast of the Ohio, and guaranteeing that it should not be disturbed by them. These were the means used to obtain the first treaty with the Indians in the Ohio Valley.

Meanwhile the powers beyond the sea were trying to out-maneuver each other, and were professing to be at peace. The English generally outwitted the Indians, and failed in many instances to fulfill their contracts. They thereby gained the ill-will of the red men, and further increased the feeling by failing to provide them with arms and ammunition. Said an old chief, at Easton, in 1758: "The Indians on the Ohio left you because of your own fault. When we heard the French were coming, we asked you for help and arms, but we did not get them. The French came, they treated us kindly, and gained our affections. The Governor of Virginia settled on our lands for his own benefit, and, when we wanted help, forsook us."

At the beginning of 1653, the English thought they had secured by title the lands in the West, but the French had quietly gathered cannon and military stores to be in readiness for the expected blow. The English made other attempts to ratify these existing treaties, but not until the summer could the Indians be gathered together to discuss the plans of the French. They had sent messages to the French, warning them away; but they replied that they intended to complete the chain of forts already begun, and would not abandon the field.

Soon after this, no satisfaction being obtained from the Ohio regarding the positions and purposes of the French, Governor Dinwiddie of Virginia determined to send to them another messenger and learn from them, if possible, their intentions. For this purpose he selected a young man, a surveyor, who, at the early age of nineteen, had received the rank of major, and who was thoroughly posted regarding frontier life. This personage was no other than the illustrious George Washington, who then held considerable interest in Western lands. He was at this time just twenty-two years of age. Taking Gist as his guide, the two, accompanied by four servitors, set out on their perilous march. They left Will's Creek on the 10th of November, 1753, and on the 22d reached the Monongahela, about ten miles above the fork. From there they went to Logstown, where Washington had a long conference with the chiefs of the Six Nations. From them he learned the condition of the French, and also heard of their determination not to come down the river till the following spring. The Indians were non-committal, as they were afraid to turn either way, and, as far as they could, desired to remain neutral. Washington, finding nothing could be done with them, went on to Venango, an old Indian town at the mouth of French Creek. Here the French had a fort, called Fort Machault. Through the rum and flattery of the French, he nearly lost all his Indian followers. Finding nothing of importance here, he pursued his way amid great privations, and on the 11th of December reached the fort at the head of French Creek. Here

he delivered Governor Dinwiddie's letter, received his answer, took his observations, and on the 16th set out upon his return journey with no one but Gist, his guide, and a few Indians who still remained true to him, notwithstanding the endeavors of the French to retain them. Their homeward journey was one of great peril and suffering from the cold, yet they reached home in safety on the 6th of January, 1754.

From the letter of St. Pierre, commander of the French fort, sent by Washington to Governor Dinwiddie, it was learned that the French would not give up without a struggle. Active preparations were at once made in all the English colonies for the coming conflict, while the French finished the fort at Venango and strengthened their lines of fortifications, and gathered their forces to be in readiness.

The Old Dominion was all alive. Virginia was the center of great activities; volunteers were called for, and from all the neighboring colonies men rallied to the conflict, and everywhere along the Potomac men were enlisting under the governor's proclamation—which promised two hundred thousand acres on the Ohio. Along this river they were gathering as far as Will's Creek, and far beyond this point, whither Trent had come for assistance for his little band of forty-one men, who were working away in hunger and want, to fortify that point at the fork of the Ohio, to which both parties were looking with deep interest.

"The first birds of spring filled the air with their song; the swift river rolled by the Allegheny hillsides, swollen by the melting snows of spring and the April showers. The leaves were appearing; a few Indian scouts were seen, but no enemy seemed near at hand; and all was so quiet, that Frazier, an old Indian scout and trader, who had been left by Trent in command, ventured to his home at the mouth of Turtle Creek, ten miles up the Monongahela. But, though all was so quiet in that wilderness, keen eyes had seen the low intrenchment rising at the fork, and swift feet had borne the news of it up the river; and upon the morning of the 17th of April, Ensign Ward, who then had charge of it, saw upon the Allegheny a sight that made his heart sink—sixty batteaux and three hundred canoes filled with men, and laden deep with cannon and stores. * * * That evening he supped with his captor, Contrecœur, and the next day he was bowed off by the Frenchman, and with his men and tools, marched up the Monongahela."

The French and Indian war had begun. The treaty of Aix la Chapelle, in 1748, had left the boundaries between the French and English possessions unsettled, and the events already narrated show the French were determined to hold the country watered by the Mississippi and its tributaries; while the English laid claims to the country by virtue of the discoveries of the Cabots, and claimed all the country from Newfoundland to Florida, extending from the Atlantic to the Pacific. The first decisive blow had now been struck, and the first attempt of the English, through the Ohio Company, to occupy these lands, had resulted disastrously to them. The French and Indians immediately completed the fortifications begun at the Fork, which they had so easily captured, and when completed gave to the fort the name of Du Quesne.

Washington was at Will's Creek when the news of the capture of the fort arrived. He at once departed to recapture it. On his way he entrenched himself at a place called the "Meadows," where he erected a fort called by him Fort Necessity. From there he surprised and captured a force of French and Indians marching against him, but was soon after attacked in his fort by a much superior force, and was obliged to yield on the morning of July 4th. He was allowed to return to Virginia.

The English Government immediately planned four campaigns; one against Fort Du Quesne; one against Nova Scotia; one against Fort Niagara, and one against Crown Point. These occurred during 1755-6, and were not successful in driving the French from their possessions. The expedition against Fort Du Quesne was led by the famous General Braddock, who, refusing to listen to the advice of Washington and those acquainted with Indian warfare, suffered such an inglorious defeat. This occurred on the morning of July 9th, and is generally known as the battle of Monongahela, or "Braddock's Defeat." The war continued with various vicissitudes through the years 1756-7; when, at the commencement of 1758 in accordance with the plans of William Pitt, then Secretary of State, afterward Lord Chatham, active preparations were made to carry on the war. Three expeditions were planned for this year: one, under General Amherst, against Louisburg; another, under Abercrombie, against Fort Ticonderoga; and a third, under General Forbes, against Fort Du Quesne. On the 26th of July, Louisburg surrendered after a desperate resistance of more than forty days, and the eastern part of the Canadian possessions fell into the hands of the British. Abercrombie captured Fort Frontenac, and when the expedition against Fort Du Quesne, of which Washington had the active command, arrived there, it was found in flames and deserted. The English at once took possession, rebuilt the fort, and in honor of their illustrious statesman, changed the name to Fort Pitt.

The great object of the campaign of 1759, was the reduction of Canada. General Wolfe was to lay siege to Quebec; Amherst was to reduce Ticonderoga and Crown Point, and General Prideaux was to capture Niagara. This latter place was taken in July, but the gallant Prideaux lost his life in the attempt. Amherst captured Ticonderoga and Crown Point without a blow; and Wolfe, after making the memorable ascent to the plains of Abraham, on September 13th, defeated Montcalm, and on the 18th, the city capitulated. In this engagement Montcalm and Wolfe both lost their lives. De Levi, Montcalm's successor, marched to Sillery, three miles above the city, with the purpose of defeating the English, and there, on the 28th of the following April, was fought one of the bloodiest battles of the French and Indian war. It resulted in the defeat of the French, and the fall of the city of Montreal. The Governor signed a capitulation, by which the whole of Canada was surrendered to the English. This practically concluded the war, but it was not until 1763 that the treaties of peace between France and England were signed. This was done on the 10th of February of that year, and under its provisions all the country east of the Mississippi and north of the Iberville river, in Louisiana, were ceded to England. At the same time Spain ceded Florida to Great Britain.

On the 13th of September, 1760, Major Robert Rogers was sent from Montreal to take charge of Detroit, the only remaining French post in the territory. He arrived there on the 19th of November, and summoned the place to surrender. At first the commander of the post, Beletre, refused, but on the 29th, hearing of the continued defeat of the French arms, surrendered. Rogers remained there until December 23d, under the personal protection of the celebrated chief, Pontiac, to whom, no doubt, he owed his safety. Pontiac had come here to inquire the purposes of the English in taking possession of the country. He was assured that they came simply to trade with the natives, and did not desire their country. This answer conciliated the savages, and did much to insure the safety of Rogers and his party during their stay, and while on their journey home.

Rogers set out for Fort Pitt on December 23d, and was just one month on the way. His route was from Detroit to Maumee, thence across the present State of Ohio directly to the fort. This was the common trail of the Indians in their journeys from Sandusky to the Fork of the Ohio. It went from Fort Sandusky, where Sandusky city now is, crossed the Huron river, then called Bald Eagle Creek, to "Mohickon John's Town" Creek, on Mohikon Creek, the northern branch of White Woman's river, and then crossed to Beaver's town, a Delaware town on what is now Sandy Creek. At Beaver's town were probably one hundred and fifty warriors, and not less than three thousand acres of cleared land. From there the track went up Sandy Creek to and across Big Beaver, and up the Ohio to Logstown, thence on to the fork.

The Northwest Territory was now entirely under the English rule. New settlements began to be rapidly made, and the promise of a large trade was speedily manifested. Had the British carried out their promises with the natives, none of those savage butcheries would have been perpetrated, and the country would have been spared their recital.

The renowned chief, Pontiac, was one of the leading spirits in these atrocities. We will now pause in our narrative, and notice the leading events in his life. The earliest authentic information regarding this noted Indian chief, is learned from an account of an Indian trader named Alexander Henry, who, in the spring of 1761, penetrated his domains as far as Missillimacnac. Pontiac was then a great friend of the French, but a bitter foe of the English, whom he considered as encroaching on his hunting grounds. Henry was obliged to disguise himself as a Canadian to insure safety, but was discovered by Pontiac, who bitterly reproached him, and the English for their attempted subjugation of the West. He declared that no treaty had been made with them; no presents sent them, and that he would resent any possession of the West by that nation. He was at the time about fifty years of age, tall and dignified, and was civil and military ruler of the Ottawas, Ojibwas and Pottawatomies.

The Indians, from Lake Michigan to the borders of North Carolina, were united in this feeling, and at the time of the treaty of Paris, ratified February 10, 1763, a general conspiracy was formed to fall suddenly upon the frontier British posts, and with one blow strike every man dead. Pontiac was the marked leader in all this, and was the commander of the Chippewas, Ottawas, Wyandots, Miamis, Shawanese, Delawares and Mingoes, who had, for the time, laid aside their local quarrels to unite in this enterprise.

The blow came, as near as can be ascertained, on May 7, 1763. Nine British posts fell, and the Indians drank, "scooped up in the hollow of joined hands," the blood of many a Briton.

Pontiac's immediate field of action, was the garrison at Detroit. Here, however, the plans were frustrated by an Indian woman disclosing the plot the evening previous to his arrival. Everything was carried out, however, according to Pontiac's plans until the moment of action, when Major Gladwyn, the commander of the post, stepping to one of the Indian chiefs, suddenly drew aside his blanket and disclosed the concealed musket. Pontiac though a brave man, turned pale and trembled. He saw his plan was known and that the garrison were prepared. He endeavored to exculpate himself from any such intentions; but the guilt was evident, and he and his followers were dismissed with a severe reprimand, and warned never to again enter the walls of the post.

Pontiac at once laid siege to the fort, and until the treaty of peace between the British and the Western Indians, concluded in August, 1764, continued to harass and besiege the fortress. He organized a regular commissariat department, issued bills of credit written out on bark, which to his credit, it may be stated, were punctu-

ally redeemed. At the conclusion of the treaty, in which it seems he took no part, he went farther south, living many years among the Illinois.

He had given up all hope of saving his country and race. After a time he endeavored to unite the Illinois tribe and those about St. Louis in a war with the whites. His efforts were fruitless, and only ended in a quarrel between himself and some Kaskaskia Indians, one of whom soon afterward killed him. His death was, however, avenged by the northern Indians, who nearly exterminated the Illinois in the wars which followed.

Had it not been for the treachery of a few of his followers, his plan for the extermination of the whites, a masterly one, would undoubtedly have been carried out.

It was in the spring of the year following Rogers' visit that Alexander Henry went to Missillimacnac, and everywhere found the strongest feelings against the English who had not carried out their promises, and were doing nothing to conciliate the natives. Here he met the chief, Pontiac, who after conveying to him in a speech the idea that their French father would awake soon and utterly destroy his enemies, said: "Englishman, although you have conquered the French, you have not yet conquered us! We are not your slaves! These lakes, these woods, these mountains, were left us by our ancestors. They are our inheritance, and we will part with them to none. Your nation supposes that we, like the white people, can not live without bread and pork and beef. But you ought to know that He, the Great Spirit and Master of Life, has provided food for us upon these broad lakes and in these mountains."

He then spoke of the fact that no treaty had been made with them, no presents sent them, and that he and his people were yet for war. Such were the feelings of the Northwestern Indians immediately after the English took possession of their country. These feelings were no doubt encouraged by the Canadians and French, who hoped that yet the French arms might prevail. The treaty of Paris, however, gave to the English the right to this vast domain, and active preparations were going on to occupy it and enjoy its trade and emoluments.

In 1762, France, by a secret treaty, ceded Louisiana to Spain, to prevent it falling into the hands of the English, who were becoming masters of the entire West. The next year the treaty of Paris, signed at Fontainbleau, gave to the English the domain of the country in question. Twenty years after, by the treaty of peace between the United States and England, that part of Canada lying south and west of the Great Lakes, comprehending a large territory which is the subject of these sketches, was acknowledged to be a portion of the United States; and twenty years still later, in 1803, Louisiana was ceded by Spain back to France, and by France sold to the United States.

In the half century, from the building of the Fort of Crevecœur by La Salle, in 1680, up to the erection of Fort Chatres, many French settlements had been made in that quarter. These have already been noticed, being those at St. Vincent (Vincennes). Kohokia or Cahokia, Kaskaskia and Prairie du Rocher, on the American

Bottom, a large tract of rich alluvial soil in Illinois, on the Mississippi, opposite the site of St. Louis.

By the treaty of Paris, the regions east of the Mississippi, including all these and other towns of the Northwest, were given over to England, but they do not appear to have been taken possession of until 1765, when Captain Stirling, in the name of the Majesty of England, established himself at Fort Chartres bearing with him the proclamation of General Gage, dated December 30, 1764, which promised religious freedom to all Catholics who worshipped here, and a right to leave the country with their effects if they wished, or to remain with the privileges of Englishmen. It was shortly after the occupancy of the West by the British that the war with Pontiac opened. It is already noticed in the sketch of that chieftain. By it many a Briton lost his life, and many a frontier settlement in its infancy ceased to exist. This was not ended until the year 1764, when, failing to capture Detroit, Niagara and Fort Pitt, his confederacy became disheartened, and, receiving no aid from the French, Pontiac abandoned the enterprise and departed to the Illinois, among whom he afterward lost his life.

As soon as these difficulties were definitely settled, settlers began rapidly to survey the country, and prepare for occupation. During the year 1770, a number of persons from Virginia and other British provinces explored and marked out nearly all the valuable lands on the Monongahela and along the banks of the Ohio, as far as the Little Kanawha. This was followed by another exploring expedition, in which George Washington was a party. The latter, accompanied by Dr. Craik, Capt. Crawford and others, on the 20th of October, 1770, descended the Ohio from Pittsburgh to the mouth of the Kanawha; ascended that stream about fourteen miles, marked out several large tracts of land, shot several buffalo, which were then abundant in the Ohio valley, and returned to the fort.

Pittsburgh was at this time a trading post, about which was clustered a village of some twenty houses, inhabited by Indian traders. This same year, Capt. Pittman visited Kaskaskia and its neighboring villages. He found there about sixty-five resident families, and at Cahokia only forty-five dwellings. At Fort Chartres was another small settlement, and at Detroit the garrison were quite prosperous and strong. For a year or two settlers continued to locate near some of these posts, generally Fort Pitt or Detroit, owing to the fears of the Indians, who still maintained some feelings of hatred to the English. The trade from the posts was quite good, and from those in Illinois large quantities of pork and flour found their way to the New Orleans market. At this time the policy of the British Government was strongly opposed to the extension of the colonies west. In 1763, the King of England forbade, by royal proclamation, his colonial subjects from making a settlement beyond the sources of the rivers which fall into the Atlantic Ocean. At the instance of the Board of Trade, measures were taken to prevent the settlement without the limits prescribed, and to retain the commerce within easy reach of Great Britain.

The commander-in-chief of the king's

forces wrote in 1769: "In the course of a few years necessity will compel the colonists, should they extend their settlements west, to provide manufactures of some kind for themselves, and when all connection upheld by commerce with the mother country ceases, an *independency* in their government will soon follow."

In accordance with this policy, Gov. Gage issued a proclamation in 1772, commanding the inhabitants of Vincennes to abandon their settlements and join some of the Eastern English colonies. To this they strenuously objected, giving good reasons therefor, and were allowed to remain. The strong opposition to this policy of Great Britain led to its change, and to such a course as to gain the attachment of the French population. In December, 1773, influential citizens of Quebec petitioned the king for an extension of the boundary lines of that province, which was granted, and Parliament passed an act on June 2, 1774, extending the boundary so as to include the territory lying within the present states of Ohio, Indiana, Illinois and Michigan.

In consequence of the liberal policy pursued by the British Government toward the French settlers in the West, they were disposed to favor that nation in the war which soon followed with the colonies; but the early alliance between France and America soon brought them to the side of the war for independence.

In 1774, Gov. Dunmore, of Virginia, began to encourage emigration to the Western lands. He appointed magistrates at Fort Pitt, under the pretense that the fort was under the government of that commonwealth. One of these justices, John Connelly, who possessed a tract of land in the Ohio Valley, gathered a force of men and garrisoned the fort, calling it Fort Dunmore. This and other parties were formed to select sites for settlements, and often came in conflict with the Indians, who yet claimed portions of the valley, and several battles followed. These ended in the famous battle of Kanawha, in July, where the Indians were defeated and driven across the Ohio.

During the years 1775 and 1776, by the operations of land companies and the perseverance of individuals, several settlements were firmly established between the Alleghenies and the Ohio River, and western land speculators were busy in Illinois and on the Wabash. At a council held in Kaskaskia, on July 5, 1773, an association of English traders, calling themselves the "Illinois Land Company," obtained from ten chiefs of the Kaskaskia, Cahokia and Peoria tribes two large tracts of land lying on the east side of the Mississippi River south of the Illinois. In 1775, a merchant from the Illinois country, named Viviat, came to Post Vincennes as the agent of the association called the "Wabash Land Company." On the 8th of October he obtained from eleven Piankeshaw chiefs, a deed for 37,497,600 acres of land. This deed was signed by the grantors, attested by a number of the inhabitants of Vincennes, and afterward recorded in the office of a notary public at Kaskaskia. This and other land companies had extensive schemes for the colonization of the West; but all were frustrated by the breaking out of the Revolution. On the 20th of April, 1780, the two companies named consolidated under the name of the "United Illinois and Wabash

Land Company." They afterward made strenuous efforts to have these grants sanctioned by Congress, but all signally failed.

When the War of the Revolution commenced, Kentucky was an unorganized country, though there were several settlements within her borders.

In Hutchins' Topography of Virginia, it is stated that at that time "Kaskaskia contained 80 houses, and nearly 1,000 white and black inhabitants—the whites being a little the more numerous. Cahokia contains 50 houses and 300 white inhabitants and 80 negroes. There were east of the Mississippi River, about the year 1771"—when these observations were made—"300 white men capable of bearing arms, and 230 negroes."

From 1775 until the expedition of Clark, nothing is recorded and nothing known of these settlements, save what is contained in a report made by a committee to Congress in June, 1778. From it the following extract is made:

"Near the mouth of the River Kaskaskia, there is a village which appears to have contained nearly eighty families from the beginning of the late revolution. There are twelve families in a small village at la Prairie du Rochers, and near fifty families at the Kahokia Village. There are also four or five families at Fort Chartres and St. Phillips, which is five miles farther up the river."

St. Louis had been settled in February, 1764, and at this time contained, including its neighboring towns, over six hundred whites and one hundred and fifty negroes. It must be remembered that all the country west of the Mississippi was now under French rule, and remained so until ceded again to Spain, its original owner, who afterwards sold it and the country including New Orleans to the United States. At Detroit there were, according to Capt. Carver, who was in the northwest from 1766 to 1768, more than one hundred houses and the river was settled for more than twenty miles, although poorly cultivated—the people being engaged in the Indian trade. This old town has a history, which we will here relate.

It is the oldest town in the Northwest, having been founded by Antoine Lademotte Cadillac, in 1701. It was laid out in the form of an oblong square, of two acres in length and an acre and a half in width. As described by A. D. Frazer, who first visited it and became a permanent resident of the place, in 1778, it comprised within its limits that space between Mr. Palmer's store (Conant Block) and Capt. Perkins' house (near the Arsenal building), and extended back as far as the public barn, and was bordered in front by the Detroit River. It was surrounded by oak and cedar pickets, about fifteen feet long, set in the ground, and had four gates—east, west, north and south. Over the first three of these gates were block houses provided with four guns apiece, each a six pounder. Two six-gun batteries were planted fronting the river, and in a parallel direction with the block houses. There were four streets running east and west, the main street being twenty feet wide and the rest fifteen feet, while the four streets crossing these at right angles were from ten to fifteen feet in width.

At the date spoken of by Mr. Frazer, there was no fort within the enclosure, but a citadel on the ground corresponding to the present northwest corner of Jefferson Avenue and Wayne Street. The citadel was inclosed by pickets, and within it were erected barracks of wood, two stories high, sufficient to contain ten officers, and also barracks sufficient to contain four hundred men, and a provision store built of brick. The citadel also contained a hospital and a guard-house. The old town of Detroit, in 1778, contained about sixty houses, most of them one story, with a few a story and a half in height. They were all of logs, some hewn and some round. There was one building of splendid appearance, called the "King's Palace," two stories high, which stood near the east gate. It was built for Governor Hamilton, the first governor commissioned by the British. There were two guard-houses, one near the west gate and the other near the Government House. Each of the guards consisted of twenty-four men and a subaltern, who mounted regularly every morning between nine and ten o'clock. Each furnished four sentinels, who were relieved every two hours. There was also an officer of the day, who performed strict duty. Each of the gates was shut regularly at sunset; even wicket gates were shut at nine o'clock, and all the keys were delivered into the hands of the commanding officer. They were opened in the morning at sunrise. No Indian or squaw was permitted to enter town with any weapon, such as a tomahawk or a knife. It was a standing order that the Indians should deliver their arms and instruments of every kind before they were permitted to pass the sentinel, and they were restored to them on their return. No more than twenty-five Indians were allowed to enter the town at any one time, and they were admitted only at the east and west gates. At sundown the drums beat, and all the Indians were required to leave town instantly. There was a council house near the water side for the purpose of holding council with the Indians. The population of the town was about sixty families, in all about two hundred males and one hundred females. This town was destroyed by fire, all except one dwelling, in 1805. After which the present "new" town was laid out.

On the breaking out of the Revolution, the British held every post of importance in the West. Kentucky was formed as a component part of Virginia, and the sturdy pioneers of the West, alive to their interests, and recognizing the great benefits of obtaining the control of the trade in this part of the New World, held steadily to their purposes, and those within the commonwealth of Kentucky proceeded to exercise their civil privileges, by electing John Todd and Richard Calloway, burgesses to represent them in the Assembly of the parent state. Early in September of that year (1777) the first court was held in Harrodsburg, and Col. Bowman, afterward major, who had arrived in August, was made the commander of a militia organization which had been commenced the March previous. Thus the tree of loyalty was growing. The chief spirit in this far-out colony, who had represented her the year previous east of the mountains, was now meditating a move unequaled in its boldness. He had been watching the movements of the British throughout the Northwest, and understood their whole plan. He saw it was through their possession of the posts at Detroit, Vincennes, Kaskaskia, and other places, which would give them constant and easy access to the various Indian tribes in the Northwest, that the British intended to penetrate the country from the north and south, and annihilate the frontier fortresses. This moving, energetic man was Colonel, afterward General, George Rogers Clark. He knew the Indians were not unanimously in accord with the English, and he was convinced that, could the British be defeated and expelled from the Northwest, the natives might be easily awed into neutrality; and by spies sent for the purpose, he satisfied himself that the enterprise against the Illinois settlements might easily succeed. Having convinced himself of the certainty of the project, he repaired to the Capital of Virginia, which place he reached on November 5th. While he was on his way, fortunately, on October 17th, Burgoyne had been defeated, and the spirits of the colonists greatly encouraged thereby. Patrick Henry was Governor of Virginia, and at once entered heartily into Clark's plans. The same plan had before been agitated in the Colonial Assemblies, but there was no one until Clark came who was sufficiently acquainted with the condition of affairs at the scene of action to be able to guide them.

Clark, having satisfied the Virginia leaders of the feasibility of his plan, received, on the 2d of January, two sets of instructions—one secret, the other open—the latter authorized him to proceed to enlist seven companies to go to Kentucky, subject to his orders, and to serve three months from their arrival in the West. The secret order authorized him to arm these troops, to procure his powder and lead of General Hand at Pittsburgh, and to proceed at once to subjugate the country.

With these instructions Clark repaired to Pittsburgh, choosing rather to raise his men west of the mountains, as he well knew all were needed in the colonies in the conflict there. He sent Col. W. B. Smith to Holston for the same purpose, but neither succeeded in raising the required number of men. The settlers in these parts were afraid to leave their own firesides exposed to a vigilant foe, and but few could be induced to join the proposed expedition. With three companies and several private volunteers, Clark at length commenced his descent of the Ohio, which he navigated as far as the Falls, where he took possession of and fortified Corn Island, a small island between the present cities of Louisville, Kentucky, and New Albany, Indiana. Remains of this fortification may yet be found. At this place he appointed Col. Bowman to meet him with such recruits as had reached Kentucky by the southern route, and as many as could be spared from the station. Here he announced to the men their real destination. Having completed his arrangements, and chosen his party, he left a small garrison upon the island, and on the 24th of June, during a total eclipse of the sun, which to them augured no good, and which fixes beyond dispute the date of starting, he with his chosen band, fell down the river. His plan was to go by water as far as Fort Massac or Massacre, and thence march direct to Kaskaskia. Here he intended to surprise the garrison, and after its capture go to Cahokia, then to Vincennes, and lastly to Detroit. Should he fail, he intended to march directly to the Mississippi River and cross it into the Spanish country. Before his start he received two good items of information; one that the alliance had been formed between France and the United States; and the other that the Indians throughout the Illinois country and the inhabitants, at the various frontier posts, had been led to believe by the British that the "Long Knives" or Virginians, were the most fierce, bloodthirsty and cruel savages that ever scalped a foe. With this impression on their minds, Clark saw that proper management would cause them to submit at once from fear, if surprised, and then from gratitude would become friendly if treated with unexpected leniency.

The march to Kaskaskia was accomplished through a hot July sun, and the town reached on the evening of July 4. He captured the fort near the village, and soon after the village itself by surprise, and without the loss of a single man or by killing any of the enemy. After sufficiently working upon the fears of the natives, Clark told them they were at perfect liberty to worship as they pleased, and to take whichever side of the great conflict they would, also, he would protect them from any barbarity from British or Indian foe. This had the desired effect, and the inhabitants, so unexpectedly and so gratefully surprised by the unlooked-for turn of affairs, at once swore allegiance to the American arms, and when Clark desired to go to Cahokia on the 6th of July, they accompanied him, and through their influence the inhabitants of the place surrendered, and gladly placed themselves under his protection. Thus the two important posts in Illinois passed from the hands of the English into the possession of Virginia.

In the person of the priest at Kaskaskia. M. Gibault, Clark found a powerful ally and generous friend. Clark saw that, to retain possession of the Northwest and treat successfully with the Indians within its boundaries, he must establish a government for the colonies he had taken. St. Vincent, the next important post to Detroit, remained yet to be taken before the Mississippi Valley was conquered. M. Gibault told him that he would alone, by persuasion, lead Vincennes to throw off its connection with England. Clark gladly accepted his offer, and on the 14th of July, in company with a fellow-townsman, M. Gibault started on his mission of peace and on the 1st of August returned with the cheerful intelligence that the post on the "Oubache" had taken the oath of allegiance to the Old Dominion. During this interval, Clark established his courts, placed garrisons at Kaskaskia and Cahokia, successfully re-enlisted his men, sent word to have a fort, which proved the germ of Louisville, erected at the Falls of the Ohio, and dispatched M. Rocheblave, who had been commander at Kaskaskia, as a prisoner of war to Richmond. In October the County of Illinois was established by the Legislature of Virginia. John Todd appointed Lieutenant Colonel and Civil Governor, and in November General Clark and his men received the thanks of the Old Dominion through their Legislature.

In a speech a few days afterward, Clark made known fully to the natives his plans, and at its close all came forward and swore allegiance to the Long Knives. While he was doing this Governor Hamilton, having made his various arrangements, had left Detroit and moved down the Wabash to

Vincennes intending to operate from that point in reducing the Illinois posts, and then proceed on down to Kentucky and drive the rebels from the West. Gen. Clark had, on the return of M. Gibault, dispatched Captain Helm, of Fauquier County, Virginia, with an attendant named Henry, across the Illinois prairies to command the fort. Hamilton knew nothing of the capitulation of the post, and was greatly surprised on his arrival to be confronted by Capt. Helm, who, standing at the entrance of the fort by a loaded cannon ready to fire upon his assailants, demanded upon what terms Hamilton demanded possession of the fort. Being granted the rights of a prisoner of war, he surrendered to the British General, who could scarcely believe his eyes when he saw the force in the garrison.

Hamilton, not realizing the character of the men with whom he was contending, gave up his intended campaign for the winter, sent his four hundred Indian warriors to prevent troops from coming down the Ohio, and to annoy the Americans in all ways, and sat quietly down to pass the winter. Information of all these proceedings having reached Clark, he saw that immediate and decisive action was necessary, and that unless he captured Hamilton, Hamilton would capture him. Clark received the news on the 29th of January, 1779, and on February 4th, having sufficiently garrisoned Kaskaskia and Cahokia, he sent down the Mississippi a "battoe," as Major Bowman writes it, in order to ascend the Ohio and Wabash, and operate with the land forces gathering for the fray.

On the next day, Clark, with his little force of one hundred and twenty men, set out for the post, and after incredible hard marching through much mud, the ground being thawed by the incessant spring rains, on the 22nd reached the fort, and being joined by his "battoe," at once commenced the attack on the post. The aim of the American backwoodsmen was unerring, and on the 24th the garrison surrendered to the intrepid boldness of Clark. The French were treated with great kindness, and gladly renewed their allegiance to Virginia. Hamilton was sent as a prisoner to Virginia, where he was kept in close confinement. During his command of the British frontier posts, he had offered prizes to the Indians for all the scalps of Americans they would bring to him, and had earned in consequence thereof, the title "Hair-buyer General," by which he was ever afterward known.

Detroit was now without doubt within easy reach of the enterprising Virginian, could he but raise the necessary force. Governor Henry being apprised of this, promised him the needed reinforcement, and Clark concluded to wait until he could capture and sufficiently garrison the posts. Had Clark failed in this bold undertaking, and Hamilton succeeded in uniting the western Indians for the next spring's campaign, the West would indeed have been swept from the Mississippi to the Alleghany Mountains, and the great blow struck, which had been contemplated from the commencement, by the British.

"But for this small army of dripping, but fearless Virginians, the union of all the tribes from Georgia to Maine against the colonies might have been effected, and the whole current of our history changed."

At this time some fears were entertained by the Colonial Governments that the Indians in the North and Northwest were inclining to the British, and under the instructions of Washington, now Commander-in-Chief of the Colonial army, and so bravely fighting for American independence, armed forces were sent against the Six Nations, and upon the Ohio frontier, Col. Bowman, acting under the same general's orders, marched against Indians within the present limits of that State. These expeditions were in the main successful, and the Indians were compelled to sue for peace.

During the same year (1779) the famous "Land Laws" of Virginia were passed. The passage of these laws was of more consequence to the pioneers of Kentucky and the Northwest than the gaining of a few Indian conflicts. These laws confirmed in main all grants made, and guaranteed to all actual settlers their rights and privileges. After providing for the settlers, the laws provided for selling the balance of the public lands at forty cents per acre. To carry the Land Laws into effect, the Legislature sent four Virginians westward to attend to the various claims, over many of which great confusion prevailed concerning their validity. These gentlemen opened their court on October 13, 1779, at St. Asaphs, and continued until April 26, 1780, when they adjourned, having decided three thousand claims. They were succeeded by the surveyor, who came in the person of Mr. George May, and assumed his duties on the 10th day of the month whose name he bore. With the opening of the next year (1780) the troubles concerning the navigation of the Mississippi commenced. The Spanish Government exacted such measures in relation to its trade as to cause the overtures made to the United States to be rejected. The American Government considered they had a right to navigate its channel. To enforce their claims, a fort was erected below the mouth of the Ohio on the Kentucky side of the river. The settlements in Kentucky were being rapidly filled by emigrants. It was during this year that the first seminary of learning was established in the West in this young and enterprising Commonwealth.

The settlers here did not look upon the building of this fort in a friendly manner, as it aroused the hostility of the Indians. Spain had been friendly to the Colonies during their struggle for independence, and though for a while this friendship appeared in danger from the refusal of the free navigation of the river, yet it was finally settled to the satisfaction of both nations.

The winter of 1779-80 was one of the most unusually severe ones ever experienced in the West. The Indians always referred to it as the "Great Cold." Numbers of wild animals perished, and not a few pioneers lost their lives. The following summer a party of Canadians and Indians attacked St. Louis, and attempted to take possession of it in consequence of the friendly disposition of Spain to the revolting Colonies. They met with such a determined resistance on the part of the inhabitants, even the women taking part in the battle, that they were compelled to abandon the contest. They also made an attack on the settlements in Kentucky, but, becoming alarmed in some unaccountable manner, they fled the country in great haste.

About this time arose the question in the Colonial Congress concerning the western lands claimed by Virginia, New York, Massachusetts and Connecticut. The agitation concerning this subject finally led New York, on the 19th of February, 1780, to pass a law giving to the delegates of that State in Congress the power to cede her western lands for the benefit of the United States. This law was laid before Congress during the next month, but no steps were taken concerning it until September 6th, when a resolution passed that body calling upon the States claiming western lands to release their claims in favor of the whole body. This basis formed the union, and was the first after all of those legislative measures which resulted in the creation of the States of Ohio, Indiana, Illinois, Michigan, Wisconsin and Minnesota. In December of the same year, the plan of conquering Detroit again arose. The conquest might have easily been effected by Clark had the necessary aid been furnished him. Nothing decisive was done, yet the heads of the Government knew that the safety of the Northwest from British invasion lay in the capture and retention of that important post, the only unconquered one in the territory.

Before the close of the year, Kentucky was divided into the Counties of Lincoln, Fayette and Jefferson, and the act establishing the Town of Louisville was passed. This same year is also noted in the annals of American history as the year in which occurred Arnold's treason to the United States.

Virginia, in accordance with the resolution of Congress, on the 2d day of January, 1781, agreed to yield her western lands to the United States upon certain conditions, which Congress would not accede to, and the act of Cession, on the part of the Old Dominion, failed, nor was anything further done until 1783. During all that time the Colonies were busily engaged in the struggle with the mother country, and in consequence thereof but little heed was given to the western settlements. Upon the 16th of April, 1781, the first birth north of the Ohio River of American parentage occurred, being that of Mary Heckewelder, daughter of the widely known Moravian missionary, whose band of Christian Indians suffered in after years a horrible massacre by the hands of the frontier settlers, who had been exasperated by the murder of several of their neighbors, and in their rage committed, without regard to humanity, a deed which forever afterward cast a shade of shame upon their lives. For this and kindred outrages on the part of the whites, the Indians committed many deeds of cruelty which darken the years of 1771 and 1772 in the history of the Northwest.

During the year 1782 a number of battles among the Indians and frontiersmen occurred, and between the Moravian Indians and the Wyandots. In these, horrible acts of cruelty were practiced on the captives, many of such dark deeds transpiring under the leadership of the notorious frontier outlaw, Simon Girty, whose name, as well as those of his brothers, was a terror to women and children. These occurred chiefly in the Ohio Valleys. Contemporary with them were several engagements in Kentucky, in which the famous Daniel Boone engaged, and who often, by his skill and knowledge of Indian warfare, saved the outposts from cruel destruction. By the close of the year victory had perched upon the American banner, and on the 30th of November, provisional articles of peace had been arranged between the Commissioners of England, and her unconquerable Colonies. Cornwallis had been defeated on the 19th of October preceding, and the liberty of America was assured. On the 19th of April following, the anniversary of the battle of Lexington, peace was proclaimed to the army of the United States, and on the 3d of the next September, the definite treaty which ended our revolutionary struggle, was concluded. By the terms of that treaty, the boundaries of the West were as follows: On the north the line was to extend along the center of the Great Lakes; from the western point of Lake Superior to Long Lake; thence to the Lake of the Woods; thence to the head of the Mississippi River, down its center to the 31st parallel of latitude, then on that line east to the head of the Appalachicola River; down its center to its junction with the Flint; thence straight to the head of St. Mary's River, and thence down along its center to the Atlantic Ocean.

Following the cessation of hostilities with England, several posts were still occupied by the British in the North and West. Among these was Detroit, still in the hands of the enemy. Numerous engagements with the Indians throughout Ohio and Indiana occurred, upon whose lands adventurous whites would settle ere the title had been acquired by the proper treaty.

To remedy this latter evil, Congress appointed commissioners to treat with the natives and purchase their lands, and prohibited the settlement of the territory until this could be done. Before the close of the year another attempt was made to capture Detroit, which was, however, not pushed, and Virginia, no longer feeling the interest in the Northwest she had formerly done, withdrew her troops, having on the 20th of December preceding authorized the whole of her possessions to be deeded to the United States. This was done on the 1st of March following, and the Northwest Territory passed from the control of the Old Dominion. To Gen. Clark and his soldiers, however, she gave a tract of one hundred and fifty thousand acres of land, to be situated anywhere north of the Ohio wherever they chose to locate them. They selected the region opposite the falls of the Ohio, where is now the dilapidated village of Clarksville, about midway between the Cities of New Albany and Jeffersonville, Indiana.

While the frontier remained thus, and Gen. Haldimand at Detroit refused to evacuate, alleging that he had no orders from his King to do so, settlers were rapidly gathering about the inland forts. In the spring of 1784, Pittsburgh was regularly laid out, and from the journal of Arthur Lee, who passed through the town soon after on his way to the Indian council at Fort McIntosh, we suppose it was not very prepossessing in appearance. He says:

"Pittsburgh is inhabited almost entirely by Scots and Irish, who live in paltry log houses, and are as dirty as if in the north of Ireland or even Scotland. There is a great deal of trade carried on, the goods being brought at the vast expense of forty-five shillings per pound from Philadelphia and Baltimore. They take in the shops flour, wheat, skins and money. There are in the town four attorneys, two doctors, and not a priest of any persuasion, nor church nor chapel."

Kentucky at this time contained thirty thousand inhabitants, and was beginning to discuss measures for a separation from Virginia. A land office was opened at Louisville, and measures were adopted to take defensive precaution against the Indians who were yet, in some instances, incited to deeds of violence by the British. Before the close of this year, 1784, the military claimants of land began to occupy them, although no entries were recorded until 1787.

The Indian title to the Northwest was not yet extinguished. They held large tracts of lands, and in order to prevent bloodshed Congress adopted means for treaties with the original owners and provided for the surveys of the lands gained thereby, as well as for those north of the Ohio, now in its possession. On January 31, 1786, a treaty was made with the Wabash Indians. The treaty of Fort Stanwix had been made in 1784. That at Fort McIntosh in 1785, and through these much land was gained. The Wabash Indians, however, afterward refused to comply with the provisions of the treaty made with them, and in order to compel their adherence to its provisions, force was used. During the year 1786, the free navigation of the Mississippi came up in Congress, and caused various discussions, which resulted in no definite action, only serving to excite speculation in regard to the western lands. Congress had promised bounties of land to the soldiers of the Revolution, but owing to the unsettled condition of affairs along the Mississippi respecting its navigation, and the trade of the Northwest, that body had, in 1783, declared its inability to fulfill these promises until a treaty could be concluded between the two Governments. Before the close of the year 1786, however, it was able, through the treaties with the Indians, to allow some grants and the settlement thereon, and on the 14th of September, Connecticut ceded to the General Government the tract of land known as the "Connecticut Reserve," and before the close of the following year a large tract of land north of the Ohio was sold to a company, who at once took measures to settle it. By the provisions of this grant, the company were to pay the United States one dollar per acre, subject to a deduction of one-third for bad lands and other contingencies. They received 750,000 acres, bounded on the south by the Ohio, on the east by the seventh range of townships, on the west by the sixteenth range, and on the north by a line so drawn as to make the grant complete without the reservations. In addition to this, Congress afterward granted 100,000 acres to actual settlers, and 214,285 acres as army bounties under the resolutions of 1789 and 1790.

While Dr. Cutler, one of the agents of the company, was pressing its claims before Congress, that body was bringing into form an ordinance for the political and social organization of this Territory. When the cession was made by Virginia, in 1784, a plan was offered, but rejected. A motion had been made to strike from the proposed plan the prohibition of slavery, which prevailed. The plan was then discussed and altered, and finally passed unanimously, with the exception of South Carolina. By this proposition, the Territory was to have been divided into states by parallels and meridian lines. This, it was thought, would make ten states, which were to have been named as follows—beginning at the northwest corner and going southwardly: Savlynia, Michigania, Chersonesus, Assenisipia, Metropotamia, Illenoia, Saratoga, Washington, Polypotamia and Pelisipia.

There was a more serious objection to this plan than its category of names,—the boundaries. The root of the difficulty was in the resolution of Congress passed in October, 1780, which fixed the boundaries of the ceded lands to be from one hundred to one hundred and fifty miles square. These resolutions being presented to the Legislatures of Virginia and Massachusetts, they desired a change, and in July, 1786, the subject was taken up in Congress, and changed to favor a division into not more than five states, and not less than three. This was approved by the State Legislature of Virginia. The subject of the Government was again taken up by Congress in 1786, and discussed throughout that year and until July, 1787, when the famous "Compact of 1787" was passed, and the foundation of the government of the Northwest laid. This compact is fully discussed and explained in the history of Illinois in this book, and to it the reader is referred.

The passage of this act and the grant to the New England Company was soon followed by an application to the Government by John Cleves Symmes, of New Jersey, for a grant of the land between the Miamis. This gentleman had visited these lands soon after the treaty of 1786, and, being greatly pleased with them offered similar terms to those given to the New England Company. The petition was referred to the Treasury Board with power to act, and a contract was concluded the following year. During the autumn the directors of the New England Company were preparing to occupy their grant the following spring, and upon the 23d of November made arrangements for a party of forty-seven men, under the superintendency of Gen. Rufus Putnam, to set forward. Six boat-builders were to leave at once, and on the first of January the surveyors and their assistants, twenty-six in number, were to meet at Hartford and proceed on their journey westward; the remainder to follow as soon as possible. Congress, in the mean time, upon the 3d of October, had ordered seven hundred troops for defense of the western settlers, and to prevent unauthorized intrusions; and two days later appointed Arthur St. Clair Governor of the Territory of the Northwest.

AMERICAN SETTLEMENTS.

The civil organization of the Northwest Territory was now complete, and notwithstanding the uncertainty of Indian affairs, settlers from the East began to come into the country rapidly. The New England Company sent their men during the winter of 1787-8 pressing on over the Alleghenies by the old Indian path which had been opened into Braddock's road and which has since been made a national turnpike from Cumberland westward. Through the weary winter days they toiled on, and by April were all gathered on the Yohiogany, where boats had been built, and at once started for the Muskingum. Here they arrived on the 7th of that month, and unless the Moravian missionaries be regarded as the pioneers of Ohio, this little band can justly claim that honor.

General St. Clair, the appointed Governor of the Northwest, not having yet arrived, a set of laws were passed, written out, and published by being nailed to a tree in the embryo town, and Jonathan Meigs appointed to administer them.

Washington in writing of this, the first American settlement in the Northwest, said: "No colony in America was ever settled under such favorable auspices as that which has just commenced at Muskingum. Information, property and strength will be its characteristics. I know many of its settlers personally, and there never were men better calculated to promote the welfare of such a community."

On the 2d of July a meeting of the directors and agents was held on the banks of the Muskingum, "for the purpose of naming the new-born city and its squares." As yet the settlement was known as the "Muskingum," but that was now changed to the name Marietta, in honor of Marie Antoinette. The square upon which the block-houses stood was called "*Campus Martius;*" square number 19, "*Capitolium;*" square number 61, "*Cecilia;*" and the great rough road through the covert way, "*Sacra Via.*" Two days after, an oration was delivered by James M. Varnum, who with S. H. Parsons and John Armstrong had been appointed to the judicial bench of the Territory on the 16th of October, 1787. On July 9, Gov. St. Clair arrived, and the Colony began to assume form. The act of 1787 provided two distinct grades of government for the Northwest, under the first of which the whole power was invested in the hands of a governor and three district judges. This was immediately formed upon the governor's arrival, and the first laws of the Colony passed on the 25th of July. These provided for the organization of the militia, and on the next day appeared the Governor's proclamation, erecting all that country that had been ceded by the Indians east of the Scioto River into the County of Washington. From that time forward, notwithstanding the doubts yet existing as to the Indians, all Marietta prospered, and on the 2d of September the first court of the Territory was held with imposing ceremonies.

The emigration westward at this time was very great. The commander at Fort Harmar, at the mouth of the Muskingum, reported four thousand five hundred persons as having passed that post between February and June, 1788—many of whom would have purchased of the "Associates," as the New England Company was called, had they been ready to receive them.

On the 26th of November, 1787, Symmes issued a pamphlet stating the terms of his contract and the plan of sale he intended to adopt. In January, 1788, Matthias Denman, of New Jersey, took an active interest in Symmes' purchase, and located among other tracts the sections upon which Cincinnati has been built. Retaining one-third of this locality, he sold the other two-thirds to Robert Patterson and John Filson, and the three, about August, commenced to lay out a town on the spot, which was designated as being opposite Licking River, to the mouth of which they proposed to have a road cut from Lexington. The naming of the town is thus narrated in the "Western Annals": "Mr.

Filson, who had been a schoolmaster, was appointed to name the town, and in respect to its situation, and as if with a prophetic perception of the mixed races that were to inhabit it in after days, he named it Losantiville, which being interpreted, means: *ville*, the town; *anti*, against or opposite to; *os*, the mouth; *L.* of Licking."

Meanwhile, in July, Symmes got thirty persons and eight four-horse teams under way for the West. These reached Limestone (now Maysville) in September, where were several persons from Redstone. Here Mr. Symmes tried to found a settlement, but the great freshet of 1789 caused the "Point," as it was and is yet called, to be fifteen feet under water, and the settlement to be abandoned. The little band of settlers removed to the mouth of the Miami. Before Symmes and his colony left the "Point," two settlements had been made on his purchase. The first was by Mr. Stiltes, the original projector of the whole plan, who, with a colony of Redstone people, had located at the mouth of the Miami, whither Symmes went with his Maysville colony. Here a clearing had been made by the Indians owing to the great fertility of the soil. Mr. Stiltes with his colony came to this place on the 18th of November, 1788, with twenty-six persons, and, building a block house, prepared to remain through the winter. They named the settlement Columbia. Here they were kindly treated by the Indians, but suffered greatly from the flood of 1789.

On the 4th of March, 1789, the Constitution of the United States went into operation, and on April 30th, George Washington was inaugurated President of the American people, and during the next summer, an Indian war was commenced by the tribes north of the Ohio. The President at first used pacific means; but these failing, he sent General Harmar against the hostile tribes. He destroyed several villages, but was defeated in two battles, near the present City of Fort Wayne, Indiana. From this time till the close of 1795, the principal events were the wars with the various Indian tribes. In 1796, General St. Clair was appointed in command, and marched against the Indians; but while he was encamped on a stream, the St. Mary, a branch of the Maumee, he was attacked and defeated with the loss of six hundred men.

General Wayne was now sent against the savages. In August, 1794, he met them near the rapids of the Maumee, and gained a complete victory. This success, followed by vigorous measures, compelled the Indians to sue for peace, and on the 30th of July, the following year, the treaty of Greenville was signed by the principal chiefs, by which a large tract of country was ceded to the United States.

Before proceeding in our narrative, we will pause to notice Fort Washington, erected in the early part of this war on the site of Cincinnati. Nearly all of the great cities of the Northwest, and indeed of the whole country, have had their *nuclei* in those rude pioneer structures, known as forts or stockades. Thus Forts Dearborn, Washington, Ponchartrain, mark the original sites of the now proud cities of Chicago, Cincinnati and Detroit. So of most of the flourishing cities east and west of the Mississippi. Fort Washington erected by Doughty in 1790, was a rude but highly interesting structure. It was composed of

a number of strongly-built hewed log cabins. Those designed for soldiers' barracks were a story and a half high, while those composing the officers' quarters were more imposing and more conveniently arranged and furnished. The whole were so placed as to form a hollow square, enclosing about an acre of ground, with a block house at each of the four angles.

The logs for the construction of this fort were cut from the ground upon which it was erected. It stood between Third and Fourth Streets of the present city (Cincinnati) extending east of Eastern Row, now Broadway, which was then a narrow alley, and the eastern boundary of the town as it was originally laid out. On the bank of the river, immediately in front of the fort, was an appendage of the fort, called the Artificer's Yard. It contained about two acres of ground, enclosed by small contiguous buildings, occupied by workshops and quarters of laborers. Within this enclosure there was a large two-story frame house, familiarly called the "Yellow House," built for the accommodation of the Quartermaster General. For many years this was the best finished and most commodious edifice in the Queen City. Fort Washington was for some time the headquarters of both the civil and military governments of the Northwestern Territory.

Following the consummation of the treaty, various gigantic land speculations were entered into by different persons, who hoped to obtain from the Indians in Michigan and northern Indiana, large tracts of lands. These were generally discovered in time to prevent the outrageous schemes from being carried out, and from involving the settlers in war. On October 27, 1795, the treaty between the United States and Spain was signed, whereby the free navigation of the Mississippi was secured.

No sooner had the treaty of 1795 been ratified, than settlements began to pour rapidly into the West. The great event of the year 1796 was the occupation of that part of the Northwest including Michigan, which was this year, under the provisions of the treaty, evacuated by the British forces. The United States, owing to certain conditions, did not feel justified in addressing the authorities in Canada in relation to Detroit and other frontier posts. When at last the British authorities were called to give them up, they at once complied, and General Wayne, who had done so much to preserve the frontier settlements, and who, before the year's close, sickened and died near Erie, transferred his headquarters to the neighborhood of the lakes, where a county named after him was formed, which included the northwest of Ohio, all of Michigan, and the northeast of Indiana. During this same year settlements were formed at the present City of Chillicothe, along the Miami from Middletown to Piqua, while in the more distant West, settlers and speculators began to appear in great numbers. In September, the City of Cleveland was laid out, and during the summer and autumn, Samuel Jackson and Jonathan Sharpless erected the first manufactory of paper—the "Redstone Paper Mill"—in the West. St. Louis contained some seventy houses, and Detroit over three hundred, and along the river, contiguous to it, were more than three thousand inhabitants, mostly French Candians, Indians and half-breeds, scarcely any Americans venturing yet into that part of the Northwest.

The election of representatives for the Territory had taken place, and on the 4th of February, 1799, they convened at Losantiville—now known as Cincinnati, having been named so by Gov. St. Clair, and considered the capital of the Territory—to nominate persons from whom the members of the legislature were to be chosen in accordance with a previous ordinance. These nominations being made, the Assembly adjourned until the 16th of the following September. From those named, the President selected as members of the council, Henry Vandenburg, of Vincennes, Robert Oliver, of Marietta, James Findlay and Jacob Burnett, of Cincinnati, and David Vance, of Vanceville. On the 16th of September the Territorial Legislature met, and on the 24th the two houses were duly organized, Henry Vandenburg being elected President of the Council.

The message of Gov. St. Clair was addressed to the Legislature September 20h, and on October 13th that body elected as a delegate to Congress, Gen. Wm. Henry Harrison, who received eleven of the votes cast, being a majority of one over his opponent, Arthur St. Clair, son of Gen. St. Clair.

The whole number of acts passed at this session, and approved by the Governor, were thirty-seven—eleven others were passed, but received his veto. The most important of those passed, related to the militia, to the administration, and to taxation. On the 19th of December, this protracted session of the first Legislature in the West was closed, and on the 30th of December, the President nominated Charles Willing Bryd to the office of Secretary of the Territory *vice* Wm. Henry Harrison, elected to Congress. The Senate confirmed his nomination the next day.

DIVISION OF THE NORTHWEST TERRITORY.

The increased emigration to the Northwest, the extent of the domain, and the inconvenient modes of travel, made it very difficult to conduct the ordinary operations of government, and rendered the efficient action of courts almost impossible. To remedy this, it was deemed advisable to divide the territory for civil purposes. Congress, in 1800, appointed a committee to examine the question and report some means for its solution. This committee, on the 31 of March, reported that:

"In the three western countries, there has been but one court having cognizance of crimes, in five years, and the immunity which offenders experience attracts, as to an asylum, the most vile and abandoned criminals, and at the same time deters useful citizens from making settlements in such society. The extreme necessity of judiciary attention and assistance is experienced in civil as well as in criminal cases. * * * * To minister a remedy to these and other evils, it occurs to this committee that it is expedient that a division of said territory into two distinct and separate governments should be made: and that such division be made by a line beginning at the mouth of the Great Miami River, running directly north until it intersects the boundary between the United States and Canada."

The report was accepted by Congress, and, in accordance with its suggestions, that body passed an act extinguishing the

Northwest Territory, which act was approved May 7th. Among its provisions were these:

"That from and after July 4th next, all that part of the territory of the United States, northwest of the Ohio River, which lies to the westward of a line beginning at a point on the Ohio, opposite to the mouth of the Kentucky River, and running thence to Fort Recovery, and thence north until it shall intersect the territorial line between the United States and Canada, shall, for the purpose of temporary government, constitute a separate territory, and be called the Indiana Territory."

After providing for the exercise of the civil and criminal powers of the Territories, and other provisions, the act further provides:

"That until it shall otherwise be ordered by the Legislatures of the said Territories, respectively, Chillicothe on the Scioto River shall be the seat of government of the Territory of the United States northwest of the Ohio River; and that St. Vincennes on the Wabash River shall be the seat of government for the Indiana Territory."

Gen. Wm. Henry Harrison was appointed Governor of the Indiana Territory, and entered upon his duties about a year later. Connecticut also about this time released her claims to the reserve, and in March a law was passed accepting this cession. Settlements had been made upon thirty-five of the townships in the reserve, mills had been built, and seven hundred miles of road cut in various directions. On the 3d of November, the General Assembly met at Chillicothe. Near the close of the year, the first missionary of the Connecticut Reserve came, who found no township containing more than eleven families. It was upon the first of October that the secret treaty had been made between Napoleon and the King of Spain, whereby the latter agreed to cede to France the province of Louisiana.

In January, 1802, the assembly of the Northwestern Territory chartered the college at Athens. From the earliest dawn of the western colonies, education was promptly provided for, and as early as 1787, newspapers were issued from Pittsburgh and Kentucky, and largely read throughout the frontier settlements. Before the close of this year, the Congress of the United States granted to the citizens of the Northwestern Territory, the formation of a State government. One of the provisions of the "compact of 1787" provided that whenever the number of inhabitants within prescribed limits exceeded 45,000, they should be entitled to a separate government. The prescribed limits of Ohio contained, from a census taken to ascertain the legality of the act, more than that number, and on the 30th of April, 1802, Congress passed the act defining its limits, and on the 29th of November the Constitution of the new State of Ohio, so named from the beautiful river forming its southern boundary, came into existence. The exact limits of Lake Michigan were not then known, but the territory now included within the State of Michigan was wholly within the territory of Indiana.

General Harrison, while residing at Vincennes, made several treaties with the Indians, thereby gaining large tracts of lands. The next year is memorable in the history of the West for the purchase of

Louisiana from France by the United States for $15,000,000. Thus by a peaceful mode, the domain of the United States was extended over a large tract of country west of the Mississippi, and was for a time under the jurisdiction of the Northwest government, and as has been mentioned in the early part of this narrative, was called the "New Northwest." The limits of this history will not allow a description of its territory. The same year large grants of land were obtained from the Indians, and the House of Representatives of the new State of Ohio signed a bill respecting the college township in the district of Cincinnati.

Before the close of the year, General Harrison obtained additional grants of lands from the various Indian nations in Indiana and the present limits of Illinois, and on the 18th of August, 1804, a treaty at St. Louis, whereby over 51,000,000 acres of lands were obtained from the aborigines. Measures were also taken to learn the condition of affairs in and about Detroit.

C. Jouette, the Indian agent in Michigan, still a part of Indiana Territory, reported as follows upon the condition of matters at that post:

"The Town of Detroit.—The charter, which is for fifteen miles square, was granted in the time of Louis XIV of France, and is now, from the best information I have been able to get, at Quebec. Of those two hundred and twenty-five acres, only four are occupied by the town and Fort Lenault. The remainder is a common, except twenty-four acres, which were added twenty years ago to a farm belonging to Wm. Macomb. * * * * A stockade encloses the town, fort and citadel. The pickets, as well as the public houses, are in a state of gradual decay. The streets are narrow, straight and regular, and intersect each other at right angles. The houses are for the most part low and inelegant."

During this year Congress granted a township of land for the support of a college, and began to offer inducements for settlers in these wilds, and the country now comprising the State of Michigan began to fill rapidly with settlers along its southern borders. This same year, also, a law was passed organizing the Southwest Territory, dividing it into two portions, the Territory of New Orleans, which city was made the seat of government, and the District of Louisiana, which was annexed to the domain of Gen. Harrison.

On the 11th of January, 1805, the Territory of Michigan was formed. Wm. Hull was appointed governor with headquarters at Detroit, the change to take effect on June 30th. On the 11th of that month, a fire occurred at Detroit, which destroyed almost every building in the place. When the officers of the new Territory reached the post, they found it in ruins, and the inhabitants scattered throughout the country. Rebuilding, however, soon commenced, and ere long the town contained more houses than before the fire, and many of them much better built.

While this was being done, Indiana had passed to the second grade of government, and through her General Assembly had obtained large tracts of land from the Indian tribes. To all this the celebrated Indian, Tecumthe or Tecumseh, vigorously protested, and it was the main cause of his attempts to unite the various Indian tribes in a conflict with the settlers. To obtain a full account of these attempts, the workings of the British, and the signal failure, culminating in the death of Tecumseh at the battle of the Thames, and the close of the war of 1812 in the Northwest, we will step aside in our story, and relate the principal events of his life, and his connection with this conflict.

TECUMSEH, AND THE WAR OF 1812.

This famous Indian chief was born about the year 1768, not far from the site of the present City of Piqua, Ohio. His father, Puckeshinwa, was a member of the Kisopok tribe of the Shawanoese nation, and his mother, Methontaske, was a member of the Turtle tribe of the same people. They removed from Florida about the middle of the last century to the birthplace of Tecumseh. In 1774, his father, who had risen to be chief, was slain at the battle of Point Pleasant, and not long after, Tecumseh, by his bravery, became the leader of his tribe. In 1795 he was declared chief, and then lived at Deer Creek, near the site of the present City of Urbana. He remained here about one year, when he returned to Piqua, and in 1798, he went to White River, Indiana. In 1805, he and his brother, Laulewasikan (Open Door), who had announced himself as a prophet, went to a tract of land on the Wabash River, given them by the Pottawatomies and Kickapoos. From this date the chief comes into prominence. He was now about thirty-seven years of age, was five feet and ten inches in height, was stoutly built, and possessed of enormous powers of endurance. His countenance was naturally pleasing, and he was, in general, devoid of those savage attributes possessed by most Indians. It is stated he could read and write, and had a confidential secretary and adviser, named Billy Caldwell, a half-breed, who afterward became chief of the Pottawatomies. He occupied the first house built on the site of Chicago. At this time, Tecumseh entered upon the great work of his life. He had long objected to the grants of land made by the Indians to the whites, and determined to unite all the Indian tribes into a league, in order that no treaties or grants of land could be made save by the consent of this confederation.

He traveled constantly, going from north to south; from the south to the north, everywhere urging the Indians to this step. He was a matchless orator, and his burning words had their effect.

Gen. Harrison, then Governor of Indiana, by watching the movement of the Indians, became convinced that a grand conspiracy was forming, and made preparations to defend the settlements. Tecumseh's plan was similar to Pontiac's, elsewhere described, and to the cunning artifice of that chieftain was added his own sagacity.

During the year 1809, Tecumseh and the prophet were actively preparing for the work. In that year, Gen. Harrison entered into a treaty with the Delawares, Kickapoos, Pottawatomies, Miamis, Eel River Indians and Weas, in which these tribes ceded to the whites certain lands upon the Wabash, to all of which Tecumseh entered a bitter protest, averring as one principal reason that he did not want the Indians to give up any lands north and west of the Ohio River.

Tecumseh, in August, 1810, visited the General at Vincennes and held a council relating to the grievances of the Indians. Becoming unduly angry at this conference he was dismissed from the village, and soon after departed to incite the Southern Indian tribes to the conflict.

Gen. Harrison determined to move upon the chief's headquarters at Tippecanoe, and for this purpose went about sixty-five miles up the Wabash, where he built Fort Harrison. From this place he went to the prophet's town, where he informed the Indians he had no hostile intentions, provided they were true to the existing treaties. He encamped near the village early in October, and on the morning of November 7th, he was attacked by a large force of the Indians, and the famous battle of Tippecanoe occurred. The Indians were routed and their town broken up. Tecumseh returning not long after, was greatly exasperated at his brother, the prophet, even threatening to kill him for rashly precipitating the war, and foiling his (Tecumseh's) plans.

Tecumseh sent word to General Harrison that he was now returned from the South, and was ready to visit the President, as had at one time previously been proposed. Gen. Harrison informed him he could not go as a chief, which method Tecumseh desired, and the visit was never made.

In June of the following year, he visited the Indian agent at Fort Wayne. Here he disavowed any intention to make a war against the United States, and reproached Gen. Harrison for marching against his people. The agent replied to this; Tecumseh listened with a cold indifference, and after making a few general remarks, with a haughty air drew his blanket about him, left the council house, and departed for Fort Malden, in upper Canada, where he joined the British standard.

He remained under this Government, doing effective work for the Crown while engaged in the war of 1812 which now opened. He was, however, always humane in his treatment of the prisoners, never allowing his warriors to ruthlessly mutilate the bodies of those slain, or wantonly murder the captive.

In the summer of 1813, Perry's victory on Lake Erie occurred, and shortly after active preparations were made to capture Malden. On the 27th of September, the American army, under Gen. Harrison, set sail for the shores of Canada, and in a few hours stood around the ruins of Malden, from which the British army, under Proctor, had retreated to Sandwich, intending to make its way to the heart of Canada by the Valley of the Thames. On the 29th Gen. Harrison was at Sandwich, and Gen. McArthur took possession of Detroit and the Territory of Michigan.

On the 2d of October, the Americans began their pursuit of Proctor, whom they overtook on the 5th, and the battle of the Thames followed. Early in the engagement, Tecumseh who was at the head of the column of Indians was slain, and they, no longer hearing the voice of their chieftain, fled. The victory was decisive, and practically closed the war in the Northwest.

Just who killed the great chief has been a matter of much dispute; but the weight of opinion awards the act to Col. Richard M. Johnson, who fired at him with a pistol, the shot proving fatal.

In 1805 occurred Burr's Insurrection. He took possession of a beautiful island in the Ohio, after the killing of Hamilton, and is charged by many with attempting to set up an independent government. His plans were frustrated by the general government, his property confiscated and he was compelled to flee the country for safety.

In January, 1807, Governor Hull, of Michigan Territory, made a treaty with the Indians, whereby all that peninsula was ceded to the United States. Before the close of the year, a stockade was built about Detroit. It was also during this year that Indiana and Illinois endeavored to obtain the repeal of that section of the compact of 1787, whereby slavery was excluded from the Northwest Territory. These attempts, however, all signally failed.

In 1809 it was deemed advisable to divide the Indiana Territory. This was done, and the Territory of Illinois was formed from the western part, the seat of government being fixed at Kaskasia. The next year, the intentions of Tecumseh manifested themselves in open hostilities, and then began the events already narrated.

While this war was in progress, emigration to the West went on with surprising rapidity. In 1811, under Mr. Roosevelt of New York, the first steamboat trip was made on the Ohio, much to the astonishment of the natives, many of whom fled in terror at the appearance of the "monster." It arrived at Louisville on the tenth day of October. At the close of the first week of January, 1812, it arrived at Natchez, after being nearly overwhelmed in the great earthquake which occurred, while on its downward trip.

The battle of the Thames was fought on October 6th, 1813. It effectually closed hostilities in the Northwest, although peace was not fully restored until July 22d, 1814, when a treaty was formed at Greenville, under the direction of General Harrison, between the United States and the Indian tribes, in which it was stipulated that the Indians should cease hostilities against the Americans if the war were continued. Such, happily, was not the case, and on the 24th of December, the treaty of Ghent was signed by the representatives of England, and the United States. This treaty was followed the next year by treaties with various Indian tribes throughout the West and Northwest, and quiet was again restored in this part of the new world.

On the 18th of March, 1816, Pittsburgh was incorporated as a city. It then had a population of 8,000 people, and was already noted for its manufacturing interests. On April 19th, Indiana Territory was allowed to form a State government. At that time there were thirteen counties organized, containing about sixty-three thousand inhabitants. The first election of State officers was held in August, when Jonathan Jennings was chosen Governor. The officers were sworn in on November 7th, and on December 11th, the State was formally admitted into the Union. For some time the seat of government was at Corydon, but a more central location being desirable, the present capital, Indianapolis (City of Indiana), was laid out January 1, 1825.

On the 28th of December, the Bank of Illinois, at Shawneetown, was chartered, with a capital of $300,000. At this period all banks were under the control of the States, and were allowed to establish branches at different convenient points.

Until this time Chillicothe and Cincinnati had in turn enjoyed the privileges of being the capital of Ohio. But the rapid settlement of the northern and eastern portions of the State demanded, as in Indiana, a more central location, and before the close of the year, the site of Columbus was selected and surveyed as the future capital of the State. Banking had begun in Ohio as early as 1808, when the first bank was chartered at Marietta, but here as elsewhere it did not bring to the State the hoped-for assistance. It and other banks were subsequently unable to redeem their currency, and were obliged to suspend.

In 1818, Illinois was made a State, and all the territory north of her northern limits was erected into a separate territory and joined to Michigan for judicial purposes. By the following year, navigation of the lakes was increasing with great rapidity and affording an immense source of revenue to the dwellers in the Northwest, but it was not until 1826, that the trade was extended to Lake Michigan, or that steamships began to navigate the bosom of that inland sea.

Until the year 1832, the commencement of the Black Hawk War, but few hostilities were experienced with the Indians. Roads were opened, canals were dug, cities were built, common schools were established, universities were founded, many of which, especially the Michigan University, have achieved a world-wide reputation. The people were becoming wealthy. The domains of the United States had been extended, and had the sons of the forest been treated with honesty and justice, the record of many years would have been that of peace and continuous prosperity.

BLACK HAWK AND THE BLACK HAWK WAR.

This conflict, though confined to Illinois, is an important epoch in the Northwestern history, being the last war with the Indians in this part of the United States.

Ma-ka-tai-me-she-kia-kiah, or Black Hawk, was born in the principal Sac village, about three miles from the junction of Rock River with the Mississippi, in the year 1767. His father's name was Py-e-sa or Pahaes; his grandfather's, Na-na-ma-kee, or the Thunderer. Black Hawk early distinguished himself as a warrior, and at the age of fifteen was permitted to paint, and was ranked among the braves. About the year 1783, he went on an expedition against the enemies of his nation, the Osages, one of whom he killed and scalped, and for this deed of Indian bravery he was permitted to join in the scalp dance. Three or four years after, he, at the head of two hundred braves, went on another expedition against the Osages, to avenge the murder of some women and children belonging to his own tribe. Meeting an equal number of Osage warriors, a fierce battle ensued, in which the latter tribe lost one-half their number. The Sacs lost only about nineteen warriors. He next attacked the Cherokees for a similar cause. In a severe battle with them, near the present City of St. Louis, his father was slain, and Black Hawk, taking possession of the "Medicine Bag," at once announced himself chief of the Sac nation. He had now conquered the Cherokees, and about the year 1800, at the head of five hundred Sacs and Foxes, and a hundred Iowas, he waged war against the Osage nation and subdued it. For two years he battled successfully with other Indian tribes, all of whom he conquered.

Black Hawk does not at any time seem to have been friendly to the Americans. When on a visit to St. Louis to see his "Spanish Father," he declined to see any of the Americans, alleging as a reason, he did not want *two* fathers.

The treaty at St. Louis was consummated in 1804. The next year the United States Government erected a fort near the head of the Des Moines Rapids, called Fort Edwards. This seemed to enrage Black Hawk, who at once determined to capture Fort Madison, standing on the west side of the Mississippi above the mouth of the Des Moines River. The fort was garrisoned by about fifty men. Here he was defeated. The difficulties with the British Government arose about this time, and the War of 1812 followed. That government, extending aid to the Western Indians, by giving them arms and ammunition, induced them to remain hostile to the Americans. In August, 1812, Black Hawk, at the head of about five hundred braves, started to join the British forces at Detroit, passing on his way the site of Chicago, where the famous Fort Dearborn Massacre had a few days before occurred. Of his connection with the British Government but little is known. In 1813, he with his little band descended the Mississippi, and attacking some United States troops at Fort Howard, was defeated.

In the early part of 1815, the Indian tribes west of the Mississippi were notified that peace had been declared between the United States and England, and nearly all hostilities had ceased. Black Hawk did not sign any treaty, however, until May of the following year. He then recognized the validity of the treaty at St. Louis in 1804. From the time of signing this treaty in 1816, until the breaking out of the war in 1832, he and his band passed their time in the common pursuits of Indian life.

Ten years before the commencement of this war, the Sac and Fox Indians were urged to join the Iowas on the west bank of the Father of Waters. All were agreed, save the band known as the British Band, of which Black Hawk was leader. He strenuously objected to the removal, and was induced to comply only after being threatened with the power of the Government. This and various actions on the part of the white settlers provoked Black Hawk and his band to attempt the capture of his native village now occupied by the whites. The war followed. He and his actions were undoubtedly misunderstood, and had his wishes been acquiesced in at the beginning of the struggle, much bloodshed would have been prevented.

Black Hawk was chief now of the Sac and Fox nations, and a noted warrior. He and his tribe inhabited a village on Rock River, nearly three miles above its confluence with the Mississippi, where the tribe had lived many generations. When that portion of Illinois was reserved to them, they remained in peaceable possession of their reservation, spending their time in the enjoyment of Indian life. The fine situation of their village and the quality of their lands incited the more lawless white settlers, who from time to time began to encroach upon the red men's domain. From one pretext to another, and from one step to another, the crafty white men gained a foothold, until through whisky and artifice they obtained deeds from many of the Indians for their possessions. The Indians were finally induced to cross over the Father of Waters and locate among the Iowas. Black Hawk was strenuously opposed to all this, but as the authorities of Illinois and the United States thought this the best move, he was forced to comply. Moreover other tribes joined the whites and urged the removal. Black Hawk would not agree to the terms of the treaty made with his nation for their lands, and as soon as the military, called to enforce his removal, had retired, he returned to the Illinois side of the river. A large force was at once raised and marched against him. On the evening of May 14, 1832, the first engagement occurred between a band from this army and Black Hawk's band, in which the former were defeated.

This attack and its result aroused the whites. A large force of men was raised, and Gen. Scott hastened from the seaboard, by way of the lakes, with United States troops and artillery to aid in the subjugation of the Indians. On the 24th of June, Black Hawk, with 200 warriors, was repulsed by Major Demont between Rock River and Galena. The American army continued to move up Rock River toward the main body of the Indians, and on the 21st of July came upon Black Hawk and his band, and defeated them near the Blue Mounds.

Before this action, Gen. Henry, in command, sent word to the main army by whom he was immediately rejoined, and the whole crossed the Wisconsin in pursuit of Black Hawk and his band who were fleeing to the Mississippi. They were overtaken on the 2d of August, and in the battle which followed the power of the Indian chief was completely broken. He fled, but was seized by the Winnebagoes and delivered to the whites.

On the 21st of September, 1832, Gen. Scott and Gov. Reynolds concluded a treaty with the Winnebagoes, Sacs and Foxes, by which they ceded to the United States a vast tract of country, and agreed to remain peaceable with the whites. For the faithful performance of the provisions of this treaty on the part of the Indians, it was stipulated that Black Hawk, his two sons, the prophet Wabokieshiek, and six other chiefs of the hostile bands should be retained as hostages during the pleasure of the President. They were confined at Fort Barracks and put in irons.

The next spring, by order of the Secretary of War, they were taken to Washington. From there they were removed to Fortress Monroe, "there to remain until the conduct of their nation was such as to justify their being set at liberty." They were retained here until the 4th of June, when the authorities directed them to be taken to the principal cities so that they might see the folly of contending against the white people. Everywhere they were observed by thousands, the name of the old chief being extensively known. By the middle of August they reached Fort Armstrong on Rock Island, where Black Hawk was soon after released to go to his countrymen. As he passed the site of his birthplace, now the home of the white man, he was deeply moved. His village where he was born, where he had so happily lived, and where he had hoped to die, was now another's dwelling place, and he was a wanderer.

On the next day after his release, he went at once to his tribe and his lodge. His wife was yet living, and with her he passed the remainder of his days. To his credit it may be said that Black Hawk always remained true to his wife, and served her with a devotion uncommon among the Indians, living with her upward of forty years.

Black Hawk now passed his time hunting and fishing. A deep melancholy had settled over him from which he could not be freed. At all times when he visited the whites he was received with marked attention. He was an honored guest at the old settlers' reunion in Lee County, Illinois, at some of their meetings, and received many tokens of esteem. In September, 1838, while on his way to Rock Island to receive his annuity from the Government, he contracted a severe cold which resulted in a fatal attack of bilious fever which terminated his life on October 3d. His faithful wife, who was devotedly attached to him, mourned deeply during his sickness. After his death he was dressed in the uniform presented to him by the President while in Washington. He was buried in a grave six feet in depth, situated upon a beautiful eminence. "The body was placed in the middle of the grave, in a sitting posture, upon a seat constructed for the purpose. On his left side, the cane, given him by Henry Clay, was placed upright, with his right hand resting upon it. Many of the old warrior's trophies were placed in the grave, and some Indian garments, together with his favorite weapons.

No sooner was the Black Hawk war concluded than settlers began rapidly to pour into the northern parts of Illinois, and into Wisconsin, now free from Indian depredations. Chicago, from a trading post, had grown to a commercial center, and was rapidly coming into prominence. In 1835, the formation of a State Government in Michigan was discussed, but did not take active form until two years later, when the State became a part of the Federal Union.

The main attraction to that portion of the Northwest lying west of Lake Michigan, now included in the State of Wisconsin, was its alluvial wealth. Copper ore was found about Lake Superior. For some time this region was attached to Michigan for judiciary purposes, but in 1836 was made a Territory, then including Minnesota and Iowa. The latter State was detached two years later. In 1848, Wisconsin was admitted as a State, Madison being made the capital. We have now traced the various divisions of the Northwest Territory (save a little in Minnesota) from the time it was a unit comprising this vast territory, until circumstances compelled its present division.

OTHER INDIAN TROUBLES.

Before leaving this part of the narrative, we will narrate briefly the Indian troubles in Minnesota and elsewhere by the Sioux Indians.

In August, 1862, the Sioux Indians living on the western borders of Minnesota fell upon the unsuspecting settlers, and in a few hours massacred ten or twelve hundred persons. A distressful panic was the immediate result, fully thirty thousand persons fleeing from their homes to districts supposed to be better protected. The military authorities at once took active measures to punish the savages, and a large number were killed and captured. About a year after, Little Crow, the chief, was killed by a Mr. Lampson near Scattered Lake. Of those captured thirty were hung at Mankato, and the remainder, through fears of mob violence, were removed to Camp McClellan, on the outskirts of the City of Davenport. It was here that Big Eagle came into prominence and secured his release by the following order:

"Special Order, No. 439.   "WAR DEPARTMENT,
   "ADJUTANT GENERAL'S OFFICE,
        "WASHINGTON, Dec. 3, 1864.

"Big Eagle, an Indian now in confinement at Davenport, Iowa, will, upon the receipt of this order, be immediately released from confinement and set at liberty.

" By order of the President of the United States.
"Official: "E. D. TOWNSEND,
                    Ass't Adj't Gen.
"CAPT. JAMES VANDERVENTER,
        Com'y Sub. Vols.
"Through Com'g Gen'l, Washington, D. C."

Another Indian who figures more prominently than Big Eagle, and who was more cowardly in his nature, with his band of Modoc Indians, is noted in the annals of the New Northwest: we refer to Captain Jack. This distinguished Indian, noted for his cowardly murder of Gen. Canby, was a chief of a Modoc tribe of Indians inhabiting the border lands between California and Oregon. This region of country comprises what is known as the "Lava Beds," a tract of land described as utterly impenetrable, save by those savages who had made it their home.

The Modocs are known as an exceedingly fierce and treacherous race. They had, according to their own traditions, resided here for many generations, and at one time were exceedingly numerous and powerful. A famine carried off nearly half their numbers, and disease, indolence and the vices of the white man have reduced them to a poor, weak and insignificant tribe.

Soon after the settlement of California and Oregon, complaints began to be heard of massacres of emigrant trains passing through the Modoc country. In 1847, an emigrant train, comprising eighteen souls, was entirely destroyed at a place since known as "Bloody Point." These occurrences caused the United States Government to appoint a peace commission, who, after repeated attempts, in 1864, made a treaty with the Modocs, Snakes and Klamaths, in which it was agreed on their part to remove to a reservation set apart for them in the southern part of Oregon.

With the exception of Captain Jack and a band of his followers, who remained at Clear Lake, about six miles from Klamath, all the Indians complied. The Modocs who went to the reservation were under chief Schonchin. Captain Jack remained at the lake without disturbance until 1869, when he was also induced to remove to the reservation. The Modocs and the Klamaths soon became involved in a quarrel, and Captain Jack and his band returned to the Lava Beds.

Several attempts were made by the Indian Commissioners to induce them to return to the reservation, and finally becoming involved in a difficulty with the commissioner and his military escort, a fight ensued, in which the chief and his band were routed. They were greatly enraged and on their retreat, before the day closed, killed eleven inoffensive whites.

The nation was aroused and immediate action demanded. A commission was at once appointed by the Government to see what could be done. It comprised the following persons: Gen. E. R. S. Canby, Rev. Dr. E. Thomas, a leading Methodist divine of California; Mr. A. B. Meacham, Judge Rosborough, of California, and a Mr.

Dyer, of Oregon. After several interviews, in which the savages were always aggressive, often appearing with scalps in their belts, Bogus Charley came to the commission on the evening of April 10, 1873, and informed them that Capt. Jack and his band would have a "talk" to-morrow at a place near Clear Lake, about three miles distant. Here the Commissioners, accompanied by Charley, Riddle, the interpreter, and Boston Charley, repaired. After the usual greeting the council proceedings commenced. On behalf of the Indians there were present: Capt. Jack, Black Jim, Schac Nasty Jim, Ellen's Man, and Hooker Jim. They had no guns, but carried pistols. After short speeches by Mr. Meacham, Gen. Canby and Dr. Thomas, Chief Schonchin arose to speak. He had scarcely proceeded when, as if by a preconcerted arrangement, Capt. Jack drew his pistol and shot Gen. Canby dead. In less than a minute a dozen shots were fired by the savages, and the massacre completed. Mr. Meacham was shot by Schonchin, and Dr. Thomas by Boston Charley. Mr. Dyer barely escaped, being fired at twice. Riddle, the interpreter, and his squaw escaped. The troops rushed to the spot where they found Gen. Canby and Dr. Thomas dead, and Mr. Meacham badly wounded. The savages had escaped to their impenetrable fastnesses and could not be pursued.

The whole country was aroused by this brutal massacre; but it was not until the following May that the murderers were brought to justice. At that time Boston Charley gave himself up, and offered to guide the troops to Capt. Jack's stronghold. This led to the capture of his entire gang, a number of whom were murdered by Oregon volunteers while on their way to trial. The remaining Indians were held as prisoners until July, when their trial occurred, which led to the conviction of Capt. Jack, Schonchin, Boston Charley, Hooker Jim, Broncho, *alias* One-Eyed Jim, and Slotuck, who were sentenced to be hanged. These sentences were approved by the President, save in the case of Slotuck and Broncho whose sentences were commuted to imprisonment for life. The others were executed at Fort Klamath, October 3, 1873.

These closed the Indian troubles for a time in the Northwest, and for several years the borders of civilization remained in peace. They were again involved in a conflict with the savages about the country of the Black Hills, in which war the gallant Gen. Custer lost his life. Just now the borders of Oregon and California are again in fear of hostilities; but as the Government has learned how to deal with the Indians, they will be of short duration. The red man is fast passing away before the march of the white man, and a few more generations will read of the Indians as one of the nations of the past.

The Northwest abounds in memorable places. We have generally noticed them in the narrative, but our space forbids their description in detail, save of the most important places. Detroit, Cincinnati, Vincennes, Kaskaskia and their kindred towns have all been described. But ere we leave the narrative we will present our readers with an account of the Kinzie house, the old landmark of Chicago, and the discovery of the source of the Mississippi River, each of which may well find a place in the annals of the Northwest.

Mr. John Kinzie, of the Kinzie house,

established a trading house at Fort Dearborn in 1804. The stockade had been erected the year previous, and named Fort Dearborn in honor of the Secretary of War. It had a block house at each of the two angles, on the southern side a sallyport, a covered way on the north side, that led down to the river, for the double purpose of providing means of escape, and of procuring water in the event of a siege.

Fort Dearborn stood on the south bank of the Chicago River, about half a mile from its mouth. When Major Whistler built it, his soldiers hauled all the timber, for he had no oxen, and so economically did he work that the fort cost the Government only fifty dollars. For a while the garrison could get no grain, and Whistler and his men subsisted on acorns. Now Chicago is the greatest grain center in the world.

Mr. Kinzie bought the hut of the first settler, Jean Baptiste Point au Sable, on the site of which he erected his mansion. Within an inclosure in front he planted some Lombardy poplars, and in the rear he soon had a fine garden and growing orchard.

In 1812 the Kinzie house and its surroundings became the theater of stirring events. The garrison of Fort Dearborn consisted of fifty-four men, under the charge of Capt. Nathan Heald, assisted by Lieutenant Lenai T. Helm (son-in-law to Mrs. Kinzie), and ensign Ronan. The surgeon was Dr. Voorhees. The only residents at the post at that time were the wives of Capt. Heald and Lieutenant Helm and a few of the soldiers, Mr. Kinzie and his family, and a few Canadian voyageurs with their wives and children. The soldiers and Mr. Kinzie were on the most friendly terms with the Pottawatomies and the Winnebagoes, the principal tribes around them, but they could not win them from their attachment to the British.

After the battle of Tippecanoe it was observed that some of the leading chiefs became sullen, for some of their people had perished in that conflict with American troops.

One evening in April 1812, Mr. Kinzie sat playing his violin and his children were dancing to the music, when Mrs. Kinzie came rushing into the house pale with terror, exclaiming, "The Indians! the Indians!" "What? Where?" eagerly inquired Mr. Kinzie. "Up at Lee's, killing and scalping," answered the frightened mother, who, when the alarm was given, was attending Mrs. Burns, a newly-made mother, living not far off. Mr. Kinzie and his family crossed the river in boats, and took refuge in the fort, to which place Mrs. Burns and her infant, not a day old, were conveyed in safety to the shelter of the guns of Fort Dearborn, and the rest of the white inhabitants fled. The Indians were a scalping party of Winnebagoes, who hovered around the fort some days, when they disappeared, and for several weeks the inhabitants were not disturbed by alarms.

Chicago was then so deep in the wilderness, that the news of the declaration of war against Great Britain, made on the 19th of June, 1812, did not reach the commander of the garrison at Fort Dearborn till the 7th of August. Now the fast mail train will carry a man from New York to Chicago in twenty-seven hours, and such a declaration might be sent, every word, by the telegraph in less than the same number of minutes.

PRESENT CONDITION OF THE NORTHWEST.

Preceding chapters have brought us to the close of the Black Hawk war, and we now turn to the contemplation of the growth and prosperity of the northwest under the smile of peace and the blessings of our civilization. The pioneers of this region date events back to the deep snow of 1831, no one arriving here since that date taking first honors. The inciting cause of the immigration which overflowed the prairies early in the '30s was the reports of the marvelous beauty and fertility of the region distributed through the East by those who had participated in the Black Hawk campaign with Gen. Scott. Chicago and Milwaukee then had a few hundred inhabitants, and Gurdon S. Hubbard's trail from the former city to Kaskaskia led almost through a wilderness. Vegetables and clothing were largely distributed through the regions adjoining the lakes by steamers from the Ohio towns. There are men now living in Illinois who came to the State when barely an acre was in cultivation, and a man now prominent in the business circles of Chicago looked over the swampy, cheerless site of that metropolis in 1818 and went southward into civilization. Emigrants from Pennsylvania in 1830 left behind them but one small railway in the coal regions thirty miles in length, and made their way to the Northwest mostly with ox teams, finding in Northern Illinois petty settlements scores of miles apart, although the southern portion of the state was fairly dotted with farms. The water courses of the lakes and rivers furnished transportation to the second great army of immigrants, and about 1850 railroads were pushed to that extent that the crisis of 1837 was precipitated upon us, from the effects of which the Western country had not fully recovered at the outbreak of the war. Hostilities found the colonists of the prairies fully alive to the demands of the occasion, and the honor of recruiting the vast armies of the Union fell largely to Gov. Yates, of Illinois, and Gov. Morton, of Indiana. To recount the share of the glories of the campaign won by our Western troops is a needless task, except to mention the fact that Illinois gave to the nation the President who saved it, and sent out at the head of one of its regiments the general who led its armies to the final victory at Appomattox. The struggle, on the whole, had a marked effect for the better on the new Northwest, giving it an impetus which twenty years of peace would not have produced. In a large degree this prosperity was an inflated one, and with the rest of the Union we have since been compelled to atone therefor. Agriculture, still the leading feature in our industries, has been quite prosperous through all these years, and the farmers have cleared away many incumbrances resting over them from the period of fictitious values. The population has steadily increased, the arts and sciences are gaining a stronger foothold, the trade area of the region is becoming daily more extended, and we have been largely exempt from the financial calamities.

At the present period there are no great schemes broached for the Northwest, no propositions for government subsidies or national works of improvement, but the capital of the world is attracted hither for the purchase of our products or the expansion of our capacity for serving the nation at large. A new era is dawning as to transportation, and we bid fair to deal almost exclusively with the increasing and expanding lines of steel rail running through every few miles of territory on the prairies. The lake marine will no doubt continue to be useful in the warmer season, and to serve as a regulator of freight rates; but experienced navigators forecast the decay of the system in moving to the seaboard the enormous crops of the West. Within the past few years it has become quite common to see direct shipments to Europe and the West Indies going through from the second-class towns along the Mississippi and Missouri.

As to popular education, the standard has of late risen very greatly, and our schools would be creditable to any section of the Union.

More and more as the events of the war pass into obscurity will the fate of the Northwest be linked with that of the Southwest.

Our public men continue to wield the full share of influence pertaining to their rank in the national autonomy, and seem not to forget that for the past sixteen years they and their constituents have dictated the principles which should govern the country.

In a work like this, destined to lie on the shelves of the library for generations, and not doomed to daily destruction like a newspaper, one can not indulge in the same glowing predictions, the sanguine statements of actualities that fill the columns of ephemeral publications. Time may bring grief to the pet projects of a writer, and explode castles erected on a pedestal of facts. Yet there are unmistakable indications before us of the same radical change in our great Northwest which characterizes its history for the past thirty years. Our domain has a sort of natural geographical border, save where it melts away to the southward in the cattle raising districts of the Southwest.

Our prime interest will for some years doubtless be the growth of the food of the world, in which branch it has already outstripped all competitors, and our great rival in this duty will naturally be the fertile plains of Kansas, Nebraska and Colorado, to say nothing of the new empire so rapidly growing up in Texas. Over these regions there is a continued progress in agriculture and in railway building, and we must look to our laurels. Intelligent observers of events are fully aware of the strides made in the way of shipments of fresh meats to Europe, many of these ocean cargoes being actually slaughtered in the West and transported on ice to the wharves of the seaboard cities. That this new enterprise will continue there is no reason to doubt. There are in Chicago several factories for the canning of prepared meats for European consumption, and the orders for this class of goods are already immense. English capital is becoming daily more and more dissatisfied with railway loans and investments, and is gradually seeking mammoth outlays in lands and live stock. The stock yards in Chicago, Indianapolis and East St. Louis are yearly increasing their facilities, and their plant steadily grows more valuable. Importations of blooded animals from the progressive countries of Europe are destined to greatly improve the quality of our beef and mutton. Nowhere is there to be seen a more enticing display in this line than at our state and county fairs, and the interest in the matter is on the increase.

To attempt to give statistics of our grain production would be useless, so far have we surpassed ourselves in the quantity and quality of our product. We are too liable to forget that we are giving the world its first article of necessity—its food supply. An opportunity to learn this fact so it never can be forgotten was afforded at Chicago at the outbreak of the great panic of 1873, when Canadian purchasers, fearing the prostration of business might bring about an anarchical condition of affairs, went to that city with coin in bulk and foreign drafts to secure their supplies in their own currency at first hands. It may be justly claimed by the agricultural community that their combined efforts gave the nation its first impetus toward a restoration of its crippled industries, and their labor brought the gold premium to a lower depth than the government was able to reach by its most intense efforts of legislation and compulsion. The hundreds of millions about to be disbursed for farm products have already, by the anticipation common to all commercial nations, set the wheels in motion, and will relieve us from the perils so long shadowing our efforts to return to a healthy tone.

Manufacturing has attained in the chief cities a foothold which bids fair to render the Northwest independent of the outside world. Nearly our whole region has a distribution of coal measures which will in time support the manufactures necessary to our comfort and prosperity. As to transportation, the chief factor in the production of all articles except food, no section is so magnificently endowed, and our facilities are yearly increasing beyond those of any other region.

The period from a central point of the war to the outbreak of the panic was marked by a tremendous growth in our railway lines, but the depression of the times caused almost a total suspension of operations. Now that prosperity is returning to our stricken country we witness its anticipation by the railroad interest in a series of projects, extensions, and leases which bid fair to largely increase our transportation facilities. The process of foreclosure and sale of incumbered lines is another matter to be considered. In the case of the Illinois Central road, which formerly transferred to other lines at Cairo the vast burden of freight destined for the Gulf region, we now see the incorporation of the tracts connecting through to New Orleans, every mile co-operating in turning toward the northwestern metropolis the weight of the interstate commerce of a thousand miles or more of fertile plantations. Three competing routes to Texas have established in Chicago their general freight and passenger agencies. Four or five lines compete for all Pacific freights to a point as far as the interior of Nebraska. Half a dozen or more splendid bridge structures have been thrown across the Missouri and Mississippi Rivers by the railways. The Chicago and Northwestern line has become an aggregation of over two thousand miles of rail, and the Chicago, Milwaukee and St. Paul is its close rival in extent and importance. The three lines running to Cairo *via* Vincennes form a through route for all traffic with the States to the southward. The trunk lines being mainly in operation, the progress made in the way of shortening tracks, making air-line branches, and running extensions does not show to the advantage it deserves, as this process is constantly adding new facilities to the established order of things. The panic reduced the price of steel to a point where the railways could hardly afford to use iron rails, and all our northwestern lines report large relays of Bessemer track. The immense crops now being moved have given a great rise to the value of railway stocks, and their transportation must result in heavy pecuniary advantages.

Few are aware of the importance of the wholesale and jobbing trade of Chicago. In boots and shoes and in clothing, twenty or more great firms from the East have placed here their distributing agents or their factories; and in groceries Chicago supplies the entire Northwest at rates presenting advantages over New York.

Chicago has stepped in between New York and the rural banks as a financial center, and scarcely a banking institution in the grain or cattle regions but keeps its reserve funds in the vaults of our commercial institutions. Accumulating here throughout the spring and summer months, they are summoned home at pleasure to move the products of the prairies. This process greatly strengthens the northwest in its financial operations, leaving home capital to supplement local operations on behalf of home interests.

It is impossible to forecast the destiny of this grand and growing section of the Union. Figures and predictions made at this date might seem ten years hence so ludicrously small as to excite only derision.

EARLY HISTORY OF ILLINOIS.

The name of this beautiful Prairie State is derived from *Illini*, a Delaware word signifying Superior Men. It has a French termination, and is a symbol of how the two races—the French and the Indians—were intermixed during the early history of the country.

The appellation was no doubt well applied to the primitive inhabitants of the soil whose prowess in savage warfare long withstood the combined attacks of the fierce Iroquois on the one side, and the no less savage and relentless Sacs and Foxes on the other. The Illinois were once a powerful confederacy, occupying the most beautiful and fertile region in the great Valley of the Mississippi, which their enemies coveted, and struggled long and hard to wrest from them. By the fortunes of war, they were diminished in numbers, and finally destroyed. "Starved Rock," on the Illinois River, according to tradition, commemorates their last tragedy, where, it is said, the entire tribe starved rather than surrender.

EARLY DISCOVERIES.

The first European discoveries in Illinois date back over two hundred years. They are a part of that movement which, from the beginning to the middle of the seventeenth century, brought the French Canadian missionaries and fur traders into the Valley of the Mississippi, and which at a later period established the civil and ecclesiastical authority of France, from the Gulf of St. Lawrence to the Gulf of Mexico, and from the foot-hills of the Alleghenies to the Rocky Mountains.

The great river of the West had been discovered by De Soto, the Spanish conqueror of Florida, three quarters of a century before the French founded Quebec in 1608, but the Spanish left the country a wilderness, without further exploration or settlement within its borders, in which condition it remained until the Mississippi was discovered by the agents of the French Canadian government, Joliet and Marquette, in 1673. These renowned explorers were not the first white visitors to Illinois In 1671—two years in advance of them—came Nicholas Perrot to Chicago. He had been sent by Talon as an agent of the Canadian government to call a great peace convention of Western Indians at Green Bay, preparatory to the movement for the discovery of the Mississippi. It was deemed a good stroke of policy to secure, as far as possible, the friendship and co-operation of the Indians, far and near, before venturing upon an enterprise which their hostility might render disastrous, and which their friendship and assistance would do so much to make successful; and to this end Perrot was sent to call together in council, the tribes throughout the Northwest, and to promise them the commerce and protection of the French government. He accordingly arrived at Green Bay in 1671, and procuring an escort of Pottawatomies, proceeded in a bark canoe upon a visit to the Miamis, at Chicago. Perrot was therefore the first European to set foot upon the soil of Illinois.

Still there were others before Marquette. In 1672, the Jesuit missionaries, Fathers Claude Allouez and Claude Dablon, bore the standard of the Cross from their mission at Green Bay through western Wisconsin and northern Illinois, visiting the Foxes on Fox River, and the Masquotines and Kickapoos at the mouth of the Milwaukee. These missionaries penetrated on the route afterwards followed by Marquette as far as the Kickapoo village at the head of Lake Winnebago, where Marquette, in his journey, secured guides across the portage to the Wisconsin.

The oft repeated story of Marquette and Joliet is well known. They were the agents employed by the Canadian government to discover the Mississippi. Marquette was a native of France, born in 1637, a Jesuit priest by education, and a man of simple faith and of great zeal and devotion in extending the Roman Catholic religion among the Indians. Arriving in Canada in 1666, he was sent as a missionary to the far Northwest, and, in 1668, founded a mission at Sault Ste. Marie. The following year he moved to La Pointe, in Lake Superior, where he instructed a branch of the Hurons till 1670, when he removed south and founded the mission at St. Ignace,
on the Straits of Mackinaw. Here he remained, devoting a portion of his time to the study of the Illinois language under a native teacher who had accompanied him to the mission from La Pointe, till he was joined by Joliet in the spring of 1673. By the way of Green Bay and the Fox and Wisconsin Rivers, they entered the Mississippi, which they explored to the mouth of the Arkansas, and returned by the way of the Illinois and Chicago Rivers to Lake Michigan.

On his way up the Illinois, Marquette visited the great village of the Kaskaskias, near what is now Utica, in the county of La Salle. The following year he returned and established among them the mission of the Immaculate Virgin Mary, which was the first Jesuit mission founded in Illinois and in the Mississippi Valley. The intervening winter he had spent in a hut which his companions erected on the Chicago River, a few leagues from its mouth. The founding of this mission was the last act of Marquette's life. He died in Michigan, on his way back to Green Bay, May 18, 1675.

FIRST FRENCH OCCUPATION.

The first French occupation of the territory now embraced in Illinois was effected by La Salle in 1680, seven years after the time of Marquette and Joliet. La Salle, having constructed a vessel, the "Griffin," above the falls of Niagara, which he sailed to Green Bay, and having passed thence in canoes to the mouth of the St. Joseph River, by which and the Kankakee he reached the Illinois, in January, 1680, erected Fort Crevecœur, at the lower end of Peoria Lake, where the city of Peoria is now situated. The place where this ancient fort stood may still be seen just below the outlet of Peoria Lake. It was destined, however, to a temporary existence. From this point, La Salle determined to descend the Mississippi to its mouth, but did not accomplish this purpose till two years later —in 1682. Returning to Fort Frontenac for the purpose of getting materials with which to rig his vessel, he left the fort in charge of Tonti, his lieutenant, who during his absence was driven off by the Iroquois Indians. These savages had made a raid upon the settlement of the Illinois, and had left nothing in their track but ruin and desolation. Mr. Davidson, in his History of Illinois, gives the following graphic account of the picture that met the eyes of La Salle and his companions on their return:

"At the great town of the Illinois they were appalled at the scene which opened to their view. No hunter appeared to break its death-like silence with a salutatory whoop of welcome. The plain on which the town had stood was now strewed with charred fragments of lodges, which had so recently swarmed with savage life and hilarity. To render more hideous the picture of desolation, large numbers of skulls had been placed on the upper extremities of lodge-poles which had escaped the devouring flames. In the midst of these horrors was the rude fort of the spoilers, rendered frightful by the same ghastly relics. A near approach showed that the graves had been robbed of their bodies, and swarms of buzzards were discovered glutting their loathsome stomachs on the reeking corruption. To complete the work of destruction, the growing corn of the village had been cut down and burned, while the pits containing the products of previous years, had been rifled and their contents scattered with wanton waste. It was evident the suspected blow of the Iroquois had fallen with relentless fury."

Tonti had escaped, La Salle knew not whither. Passing down the lake in search of him and his men, La Salle discovered that the fort had been destroyed, but the vessel which he had partly constructed was still on the stocks, and but slightly injured. After further fruitless search, failing to find Tonti, he fastened to a tree a painting representing himself and party sitting in a canoe and bearing a pipe of peace, and to the painting attached a letter addressed to Tonti.

Tonti had escaped, and after untold privations, taken shelter among the Pottawattomies near Green Bay. These were friendly to the French. One of their old chiefs used to say, "There were but three great captains in the world, himself, Tonti and La Salle."

GENIUS OF LA SALLE.

We must now return to La Salle, whose exploits stand out in such bold relief. He was born in Rouen, France, in 1643. His father was wealthy but he renounced his patrimony on entering a college of the Jesuits, from which he separated and came to Canada a poor man in 1666. The priests of St. Sulpice, among whom he had a brother, were then the proprietors of Montreal, the nucleus of which was a seminary or convent founded by that order. The Superior granted to La Salle a large tract of land at La Chine, where he established himself in the fur trade. He was a man of **daring genius, and outstripped** all his

competitors in exploits of travel and commerce with the Indians. In 1669, he visited the headquarters of the great Iroquois confederacy, at Onondaga, in the heart of New York, and obtaining guides, explored the Ohio River to the falls at Louisville.

In order to understand the genius of La Salle, it must be remembered that for many years prior to his time the missionaries and traders were obliged to make their way to the Northwest by the Ottawa River (of Canada) on account of the fierce hostility of the Iroquois along the lower lakes and Niagara River, which entirely closed this latter route to the UpperLakes. They carried on their commerce chiefly by canoes, paddling them through the Ottawa to Lake Nipissing, carrying them across the portage to French River, and descending that to Lake Huron. This being the route by which they reached the Northwest accounts for the fact that all the earliest Jesuit missions were established in the neighborhood of the Upper Lakes. La Salle conceived the grand idea of opening the route by Niagara River and the Lower Lakes to Canadian commerce by sail vessels connecting it with the navigation of the Mississippi, and thus opening a magnificent water communication from the Gulf of St. Lawrence to the Gulf of Mexico. This truly grand and comprehensive purpose seems to have animated him in all his wonderful achievements and the matchless difficulties and hardships he surmounted. As the first step in the accomplishment of this object he established himself on Lake Ontario, and built and garrisoned Fort Frontenac, the site of the present city of Kingston, Canada. Here he obtained a grant of land from the French crown, and a body of troops by which he beat back the invading Iroquois and cleared the passage to Niagara Falls. Having by this masterly stroke made it safe to attempt a hitherto untried expedition, his next step, as we have seen, was to advance to the Falls with all his outfit for building a ship with which to sail the lakes. He was successful in this undertaking, though his ultimate purpose was defeated by a strange combination of untoward circumstances. The Jesuits evidently hated La Salle and plotted against him, because he had abandoned them and co-operated with a rival order. The fur traders were also jealous of his superior success in opening new channels of commerce. At La Chine he had taken the trade of Lake Ontario, which but for his presence there would have gone to Quebec. While they were plodding with their bark canoes through the Ottawa he was constructing sailing vessels to command the trade of the lakes and the Mississippi. These great plans excited the jealousy and envy of the small traders, introduced treason and revolt into the ranks of his own companions, and finally led to the foul assassination by which his great achievements were prematurely ended.

In 1682, La Salle, having completed his vessel at Peoria, descended the Mississippi to its confluence with the Gulf of Mexico. Erecting a standard on which he inscribed the arms of France, he took formal possession of the whole valley of the mighty river, in the name of Louis XIV, then reigning, in honor of whom he named the country LOUISIANA.

La Salle then went to France, was appointed Governor, and returned with a fleet and immigrants, for the purpose of planting a colony in Illinois. They arrived in due time in the Gulf of Mexico, but failing to find the mouth of the Mississippi, up which La Salle intended to sail, his supply ship, with the immigrants, was driven ashore and wrecked on Matagorda Bay. With the fragments of the vessel he constructed a stockade and rude huts on the shore for the protection of the immigrants, calling the post Fort St. Louis. He then made a trip into New Mexico, in search of silver mines, but, meeting with disappointment, returned to find his little colony reduced to forty souls. He then resolved to travel on foot to Illinois, and, starting with his companions, had reached the valley of the Colorado, near the mouth of Trinity river, when he was shot by one of his men. This occurred on the 19th of March, 1687.

Dr. J. W. Foster remarks of him: "Thus fell, not far from the banks of the Trinity, Robert Cavalier de la Salle, one of the grandest characters that ever figured in American history—a man capable of originating the vastest schemes, and endowed with a will and a judgment capable of carrying them to successful results. Had ample facilities been placed by the King of France at his disposal, the result of the colonization of this continent might have been far different from what we now behold."

EARLY SETTLEMENTS.

A temporary settlement was made at Fort St. Louis, or the old Kaskaskia village, on the Illinois River, in what is now La Salle County, in 1682. In 1690, this was removed, with the mission connected with it, to Kaskaskia, on the river of that name, emptying into the lower Mississippi in St. Clair County. Cahokia was settled about the same time, or at least, both of these settlements began in the year 1690, though it is now pretty well settled that Cahokia is the older place, and ranks as the oldest permanent settlement in Illinois, as well as in the Mississippi Valley. The reason for the removal of the old Kaskaskia settlement and mission, was probably because the dangerous and difficult route by Lake Michigan and the Chicago portage had been almost abandoned, and travelers and traders passed down and up the Mississippi by the Fox and Wisconsin River route. They removed to the vicinity of the Mississippi in order to be in the line of travel from Canada to Louisiana, that is, the lower part of it, for it was all Louisiana then south of the lakes.

During the period of French rule in Louisiana, the population probably never exceeded ten thousand, including whites and blacks. Within that portion of it now included in Indiana, trading posts were established at the principal Miami villages which stood on the head waters of the Maumee, the Wea villages situated at Ouiatenon, on the Wabash, and the Piankeshaw villages at Post Vincennes; all of which were probably visited by French traders and missionaries before the close of the seventeenth century.

In the vast territory claimed by the French, many settlements of considerable importance had sprung up. Biloxi, on Mobile Bay, had been founded by D'Iberville, in 1699; Antoine de Lamotte Cadillac had founded Detroit in 1701; and New Orleans had been founded by Bienville, under the auspices of the Mississippi Company, in 1718. In Illinois also, considerable settlements had been made, so that in 1730 they embraced one hundred and forty French families, about six hundred "converted Indians," and many traders and voyageurs. In that portion of the country, on the east side of the Mississippi, there were five distinct settlements, with their respective villages, viz.: Cahokia, near the mouth of Cahokia Creek and about five miles below the present city of St. Louis; St. Philip, about forty-five miles below Cahokia, and four miles above Fort Chartres; Fort Chartres, twelve miles above Kaskaskia; Kaskaskia, situated on the Kaskaskia River, five miles above its confluence with the Mississippi; and Prairie du Rocher, near Fort Chartres. To these must be added St. Genevieve and St. Louis, on the west side of the Mississippi. These with the exception of St. Louis, are among the oldest French towns in the Mississippi Valley. Kaskaskia, in its best days, was a town of some two or three thousand inhabitants. After it passed from the crown of France its population for many years did not exceed fifteen hundred. Under British rule, in 1773, the population had decreased to four hundred and fifty. As early as 1721 the Jesuits had established a college and a monastery in Kaskaskia.

Fort Chartres was first built under the direction of the Mississippi Company, in 1718, by M. de Boisbraint, a military officer, under command of Bienville. It stood on the east bank of the Mississippi, about eighteen miles below Kaskaskia, and was for some time the headquarters of the military commandants of the district of Illinois.

In the Centennial Oration of Dr. Fowler, delivered at Philadelphia, by appointment of Gov. Beveridge, we find some interesting facts with regard to the State of Illinois, which we appropriate in this history:

In 1682 Illinois became a possession of the French crown, a dependency of Canada, and a part of Louisiana. In 1765 the English flag was run up on old Fort Chartres, and Illinois was counted among the treasures of Great Britain.

In 1779 it was taken from the English by Col. George Rogers Clark. This man was resolute in nature, wise in council, prudent in policy, bold in action, and heroic in danger. Few men who have figured in the history of America are more deserving than this colonel. Nothing short of first-class ability could have rescued Vincennes and all Illinois from the English. And it is not possible to over-estimate the influence of this achievement upon the republic. In 1779 Illinois became a part of Virginia. It was soon known as Illinois County. In 1784 Virginia ceded all this territory to the general government, to be cut into States, to be republican in form, with "the same right of sovereignty, freedom, and independence as the other States."

In 1787 it was the object of the wisest and ablest legislation found in any merely human records. No man can study the secret history of

THE "COMPACT OF 1787,"

and not feel that Providence was guiding with sleepless eye these unborn States. The ordinance that on July 13, 1787, finally became the incorporating act, has a most marvelous history. Jefferson had vainly tried to secure a system of government for the northwestern territory. He was an emancipationist of that day, and favored the exclusion of slavery from the territory Virginia had ceded to the general government; but the South voted him down as often as it came up. In 1787, as late as July 10th, an organizing act without the anti-slavery clause was pending. This concession to the South was expected to carry it. Congress was in session in New York City. On July 5th, Rev. Dr. Manasseh Cutler, of Massachusetts, came into New York to lobby on the northwestern territory. Everything seemed to fall into his hands. Events were ripe.

The state of the public credit, the growing of Southern prejudice, the basis of his mission. his personal character, all combined to complete one of those sudden and marvelous revolutions of public sentiment that once in five or ten centuries are seen to sweep over a country like the breath of the Almighty. Cutler was a graduate of Yale—received his A. M. from Harvard, and his D. D. from Yale. He had studied and taken degrees in the three learned professions, medicine, law, and divinity. He had thus America's best indorsement. He had published a scientific examination of the plants of New England. His name stood second only to that of Franklin as a scientist in America. He was a courtly gentleman of the old style, a man of commanding presence, and of inviting face. The Southern members said they had never seen such a gentleman in the North. He came representing a company that desired to purchase a tract of land now included in Ohio, for the purpose of planting a colony. It was a speculation. Government money was worth eighteen cents on the dollar. This Massachusetts company had collected enough to purchase 1,500,000 acres of land. Other speculators in New York made Dr. Cutler their agent (lobbyist). On the 12th he represented a demand for 5,500,000 acres. This would reduce the national debt. Jefferson and Virginia were regarded as authority concerning the land Virginia had just ceded. Jefferson's policy wanted to provide for the public credit, and this was a good opportunity to do something.

Massachusetts then owned the Territory of Maine, which she was crowding on the market. She was opposed to opening the northwestern region. This fired the zeal of Virginia. The South caught the inspiration, and all exalted Dr. Cutler. The English minister invited him to dine with some of the Southern gentlemen. He was the center of interest.

The entire South rallied round him, Massachusetts could not vote against him, because many of the constituents of her members were interested personally in the western speculation. Thus Cutler, making friends with the South, and, doubtless, using all the arts of the lobby, was enabled to command the situation. True to deeper convictions, he dictated one of the most compact and finished documents of wise statesmanship that has ever adorned any human law book. He borrowed from Jefferson the term "Articles of Compact," which, preceding the Federal constitution, rose into the most sacred character. He then followed very closely the constitution of Massachusetts, adopted three years before. Its most marked points were:

1. The exclusion of slavery from the territry forever.

2. Provision for public schools, giving one township for a seminary, and every section numbered 16 in each township; that

is, one thirty-sixth of all the land, for public schools.

3. A provision prohibiting the adoption of any constitution or the enactment of any law that should nullify pre-existing contracts.

Be it forever remembered that this compact declared that "Religion, morality and knowledge being necessary to good government and the happiness of mankind, schools and the means of education shall always be encouraged."

Dr. Cutler planted himself on this platform and would not yield. Giving his unqualified declaration that it was that or nothing—that unless they could make the land desirable they did not want it—he took his horse and buggy, and started for the constitutional convention in Philadelphia. On July 13, 1787, the bill was put upon its passage, and was unanimously adopted, every Southern member voting for it, and only one man, Mr. Yates, of New York, voting against it. But as the States voted as States, Yates lost his vote, and the compact was put beyond repeal.

Thus the great States of Ohio, Indiana, Illinois, Michigan and Wisconsin—a vast empire, the heart of the great valley—were consecrated to freedom, intelligence and honesty. Thus the great heart of the nation was prepared for a year and a day and an hour. In the light of these eighty-nine years I affirm that this act was the salvation of the republic and the destruction of slavery. Soon the South saw their great blunder, and tried to repeal the compact. In 1803, Congress referred it to a committee of which John Randolph was chairman. He reported that this ordinance was a compact, and opposed repeal. Thus it stood a rock, in the way of the on-rushing sea of slavery.

With all this timely aid, it was, after all, a most desperate and protracted struggle to keep the soil of Illinois sacred to freedom. It was the natural battle-field for the irrepressible conflict. In the southern end of the State, slavery preceded the compact. It existed among the old French settlers, and was hard to eradicate. The southern part of the State was settled from the slave States, and this population brought their laws, customs and institutions with them. A stream of population from the North poured into the northern part of the State. These sections misunderstood and hated each other perfectly. The Southerners regarded the Yankees as a skinning, tricky, penurious race of peddlers, filling the country with tinware, brass clocks and wooden nutmegs. The Northerner thought of the Southerner as a lean, lank, lazy creature, burrowing in a hut, and rioting in whisky, dirt and ignorance. These causes aided in making the struggle long and bitter. So strong was the sympathy with slavery, that in spite of the ordinance of 1787, and in spite of the deed of cession, it was determined to allow the old French settlers to retain their slaves. Planters from the slave States might bring their slaves, if they would give them a chance to choose freedom or years of service and bondage for their children till they should become thirty years of age. If they chose freedom they must leave the State in sixty days or be sold as fugitives. Servants were whipped for offenses for which white men are fined. Each lash paid forty cents of the fine. A negro ten miles from home without a pass was whipped. These famous laws were imported from the slave States just as they imported laws for the inspection of flax and wool when there was neither in the State.

These Black Laws are now wiped out. A vigorous effort was made to protect slavery in the State Constitution of 1817. It barely failed. It was renewed in 1825, when a convention was asked to make a new constitution. After a hard fight the convention was defeated. But slaves did not disappear from the census of the State until 1850. There were mobs and murders in the interest of slavery. Lovejoy was added to the list of martyrs—a sort of first fruits of that long life of immortal heroes who saw freedom as the one supreme desire of their souls, and were so enamored of her, that they preferred to die rather than survive her.

The population of 12,282 that occupied the Territory in A. D. 1800, increased to 45,000 in A. D. 1818, when the State Constitution was adopted, and Illinois took her place in the Union, with a star on the flag and two votes in the Senate.

Shadrach Bond was the first Governor, and in his first message he recommended the construction of the Illinois and Michigan Canal.

The simple economy in those days is seen in the fact the entire bill for stationery for the first Legislature was only $13.50. Yet this simple body actually enacted a very superior code.

There was no money in the Territory before the war of 1812. Deer skins and coon skins were the circulating medium. In 1821, the Legislature ordained a State Bank on the credit of the State. It issued notes in the likeness of bank bills. These notes were made a legal tender for every thing, and the bank was ordered to loan to the people $100 on personal security, and more on mortgages. They actually passed a resolution requesting the Secretary of the Treasury of the United States to receive these notes for land. The old French Lieutenant Governor, Col. Menard, put the resolution as follows: "Gentlemen of the Senate: It is moved and seconded *dat de notes of dis bank* be made land office money. All in favor of dat motion say aye; all against it say no. It is decided in de affirmative. Now, gentlemen, I bet you one hundred dollar he never be land-office money!" Hard sense, like hard money, is always above par.

This old Frenchman presents a fine figure up against the dark background of most of his nation. They made no progress. They clung to their earliest and simplest implements. They never wore hats or caps. They pulled their blankets over their heads in the winter like the Indians, with whom they freely intermingled.

Demagogism had an early development. One John Grammar (only in name), elected to the Territorial and State Legislatures of 1816 and 1836, invented the policy of opposing every new thing, saying, "If it succeeds, no one will ask who voted against it. If it proves a failure, he could quote its record." In sharp contrast with Grammar was the character of D. P. Cook, after whom the county containing Chicago was named. Such was his transparent integrity and remarkable ability that his will was almost the law of the State. In Congress, a young man, and from a poor State, he was made Chairman of the Ways and Means Committee. He was pre-eminent for standing by his committee, regardless of consequences. It was his integrity that elected John Quincy Adams to the Presidency. There were four candidates in 1824, Jackson, Clay, Crawford, and John Quincy Adams. There being no choice by the people, the election was thrown into the House. It was so balanced that it turned on his vote, and that he cast for Adams, electing him; then went home to face the wrath of the Jackson party in Illinois. It cost him all but character and greatness. It is a suggestive comment on the times, that there was no legal interest till 1830. It often reached 150 per cent., usually 50 per cent. Then it was reduced to 12, and now to 10 per cent.

PHYSICAL FEATURES OF THE PRAIRIE STATE.

In area the State has 55,410 square miles of territory. It is about 150 miles wide and 400 miles long, stretching in latitude from Maine to North Carolina. It embraces wide variety of climate. It is tempered on the north by the great inland, saltless, tideless sea, which keeps the thermometer from either extreme. Being a table land, from 600 to 1,200 feet above the level of the sea, one is prepared to find on the health maps, prepared by the general government, an almost clean and perfect record. In freedom from fever and malarial diseases and consumptions, the three deadly enemies of the American Saxon, Illinois, as a State, stands without a superior. She furnishes one of the essential conditions of a great people—sound bodies. I suspect that this fact lies back of that old Delaware word, Ilini, superior men.

The great battles of history that have been determinative of dynasties and destinies have been strategical battles, chiefly the question of position. Thermopylæ has been the war-cry of freemen for twenty-four centuries. It only tells how much there may be in position. All this advantage belongs to Illinois. It is in the heart of the greatest valley in the world, the vast region between the mountains—a valley that could feed mankind for one thousand years. It is well on toward the center of the continent. It is in the great temperate belt, in which have been found nearly all the aggressive civilizations of history. It has sixty-five miles of frontage on the head of the lake. With the Mississippi forming the western and southern boundary, with the Ohio running along the southeastern line, with the Illinois river and canal dividing the State diagonally from the lake to the lower Mississippi, and with the Rock and Wabash rivers, furnishing altogether 2,000 miles of water front, connecting with, and running through, in all about 12,000 miles of navigable water.

But this is not all. These waters are made most available by the fact that the lake and the State lie on the ridge running into the great valley from the east. Within cannon-shot of the lake, the water runs away from the lake to the gulf. The lake now empties at both ends, one into the Atlantic and one into the gulf of Mexico. The lake thus seems to hang over the land. This makes the dockage most serviceable; there are no steep banks to damage it. Both lake and river are made for use.

The climate varies from Portland to Richmond; it favors every product of the continent, including the tropics, with less than half a dozen exceptions. It produces every great nutriment of the world except bananas and rice. It is hardly too much to say that it is the most productive spot known to civilization. With the soil full of bread and the earth full of minerals; with an upper surface of food and an under layer of fuel; with perfect natural drainage, and abundant springs and streams and navigable rivers; half way between the forests of the north and the fruits of the south; within a day's ride of the great deposits of iron, coal, copper, lead and zinc; containing and controlling the great grain, cattle, pork and lumber markets of the world, it is not strange that Illinois has the advantage of position.

This advantage has been supplemented by the character of the population. In the early days when Illinois was first admitted to the union, her population were chiefly from Kentucky and Virginia. But, in the conflict of ideas concerning slavery, a strong tide of emigration came in from the East, and soon changed this composition. In 1870 her non-native population were from colder soils. New York furnished 133,290; Ohio gave 162,623; Pennsylvania sent on 98,352; the entire South gave us only 206,734. In all her cities, and in all her German and Scandinavian and other foreign colonies, Illinois has only about one-fifth of her people of foreign birth.

PROGRESS OF DEVELOPMENT.

One of the greatest elements in the early development of Illinois is the Illinois and Michigan Canal, connecting the Illinois and Mississippi Rivers with the lakes. It was of the utmost importance to the S ate. It was r co mended by Gov. Bond, the first governor, in his first message. In 1821, the Legislature appropriated $10,000 for surveying the route. Two bright young engineers surveyed it, and estimated the cost at $600,000 or $700,000. It finally cost $8,000,000. In 1825, a law was passed to incorporate the Canal Company, but no stock was sold. In 1826, upon the solicitation of Cook, Congress gave 500,000 acres of land on the line of the work. In 1828, another law—commissioners appointed, and work commenced with new survey and new estimates. In 1834-35, George Farquhar made an able report on the whole matter. This was, doubtless, the ablest report ever made to a western legislature, and it became the model for subsequent reports and action. From this, the work went on till it was finished in 1848. It cost the State a large amount of money; but it gave to the industries of the State an impetus that pushed it up into the first rank of greatness. It was not built as a speculation any more than a doctor is employed on a speculation. But it has paid into the treasury of the State an average annual net sum of over $111,000.

Pending the construction of the canal, the land and town-lot fever broke out in the State, in 1834-35. It took on the malignant type in Chicago, lifting the town up into a city. The disease spread over the entire State and adjoining States. It was epidemic. It cut up men's farms without regard to locality, and cut up the purses of the purchasers without regard to consequences. It is estimated that building lots enough were sold in Indiana alone to accommodate every citizen then in the United States.

Towns and cities were exported to the Eastern market by the ship-load. There was no lack of buyers. Every up-ship came freighted with speculators and their money.

This distemper seized upon the Legislature in 1836-37, and left not one to tell the tale. They enacted a system of internal improvement without a parallel in the grandeur of its conception. They ordered the construction of 1,300 miles of railroad, crossing the State in all directions. This was surpassed by the river and canal improvements. There were a few counties not touched by either railroad or river or canal, and those were to be comforted and compensated by the free distribution of $200,000 among them. To inflate this balloon beyond credence, it was ordered that work should be commenced on both ends of each of these railroads and rivers, and at each river crossing, all at the same time. The appropriations for these vast improvements were over $12,000,000, and commissioners were appointed to borrow the money on the credit of the State. Remember that all this was in the early days of railroading, when railroads were luxuries; that the State had whole counties with scarcely a cabin; and that the population of the State was less than 400,000, and you can form some idea of the vigor with which these brave men undertook the work of making a great State. In the light of history I am compelled to say that this was only a premature throb of the power that actually slumbered in the soil of the State. It was Hercules in the cradle.

At this juncture the State Bank loaned its funds largely to Godfrey Gilman & Co. and to other leading houses, for the purpose of drawing trade from St. Louis to Alton. Soon they failed and took down the bank with them.

In 1840, all hope seemed gone. A population of 480,000 were loaded with a debt of $14,000,000. It had only six small cities, really only towns, namely: Chicago, Alton, Springfield, Quincy, Galena, Nauvoo. This debt was to be cared for when there was not a dollar in the treasury, and when the State had borrowed itself out of all credit, and when there was not good money enough in the hands of all the people to pay the interest of the debt for a single year. Yet, in the presence of all these difficulties, the young State steadily refused to repudiate. Gov. Ford took hold of the problem and solved it, bringing the State through in triumph.

Having touched lightly upon some of the more distinctive points in the history of the development of Illinois, let us next briefly consider the

MATERIAL RESOURCES OF THE STATE.

It is a garden four hundred miles long and one hundred and fifty miles wide. Its soil is chiefly a black sandy loam, from six inches to sixty feet thick. On the American bottoms it has been cultivated for one hundred and fifty years without renewal.

About the old French towns it has yielded corn for a century and a half without rest or help. It produces nearly everything green in the temperate and tropical zones. She leads all other States in the number of acres actually under plow. Her products from 25,000,000 of acres are incalculable. Her mineral wealth is scarcely second to her agricultural power. She has coal, iron, lead, copper, zinc, many varieties of building stone, fire clay, enma clay, common brick clay, sand of all kinds, gravel, mineral paint—everything needed for a high civilization. Left to herself, she has the elements of all greatness. The single item of coal is too vast for an appreciative handling in figures. We can handle it in general terms like algebraical signs, but long before we get up into the millions and billions the human mind drops down from comprehension to mere symbolic apprehension.

When I tell you that nearly four-fifths of the entire State is underlaid with a deposit of coal more than forty feet thick on the average (now estimated by recent surveys, at seventy feet thick), you can get some idea of its amount, as you do of the amount of the national debt. There it is! 41,000 square miles—one vast mine into which you could put any of the States; in which you could bury scores of European and ancient empires, and have room all round to work without knowing that they had been sepulchered there.

Put this vast coal-bed down by the other great coal deposits of the world, and its importance becomes manifest. Great Britain has 12,000 square miles of coal; Spain, 3,000; France, 1719; Belgium, 578; Illinois about twice as many square miles as all combined. Virginia has 20,000 square miles; Pennsylvania, 16,000; Ohio, 12,000. Illinois has 41,000 square miles. One-seventh of all the known coal on this continent is in Illinois.

Could we sell the coal in this single State for one-seventh of one cent a ton, it would pay the national debt. Converted into power, even with the wastage in our common engines, it would do more work than could be done by the entire race, beginning at Adam's wedding and working ten hours a day through all the centuries till the present time, and right on into the future at the same rate for the next 600,000 years.

Great Britain uses enough mechanical power to-day to give to each man, woman, and child in the kingdom, the help and service of nineteen untiring servants. No wonder she has leisure and luxuries. No wonder the home of the common artisan has in it more luxuries than could be found in the palace of good old King Arthur. Think if you can conceive of it, of the vast army of servants that slumber in the soil of Illinois, impatiently awaiting the call of Genius to come forth to minister to our comfort.

At the present rate of consumption England's coal supply will be exhausted in 250 years. When this is gone she must transfer her dominion either to the Indies, or to British America, which I would not resist; or to some other people, which I would regret as a loss to civilization.

COAL IS KING.

At the same rate of consumption (which far exceeds our own), the deposit of coal in Illinois will last 120,000 years. And her kingdom shall be an everlasting kingdom.

Let us turn now from this reserve power to the *annual products* of the State. We shall not be humiliated in this field. Here we strike the secret of our national credit. Nature provides a market in the constant appetite of the race. Men must eat, and if we can furnish the provisions we can command the treasure. All that a man hath will he give for his life.

According to the last census Illinois produced 30,000,000 of bushels of wheat. That is more wheat than was raised by any other State in the union. She raised in 1875, 130,000,000 of bushels of corn—twice as much as any other State, and one-sixth of all the corn raised in the United States. She harvested 2,747,000 tons of hay, nearly one-tenth of all the hay in the republic. It is not generally appreciated, but it is true that the hay crop of the country is worth more than the cotton crop. The hay of Illinois equals the cotton of Louisiana. Go to Charleston, S. C., and see them peddling handfuls of hay or grass, almost as a curiosity, as we regard Chinese gods or the cryolite of Greenland; drink your coffee and *condensed milk;* and walk back from the coast for many a league through the sand and burs till you get up into the better atmosphere of the mountains, without seeing a waving meadow or a grazing herd; then you will begin to appreciate the meadows of the Prairie State, where the grass often grows sixteen feet high.

The value of her farm implements is $211,000,000, and the value of her live stock is only second to the great State of New York. In 1875 she had 25,000,000 hogs, and packed 2,113,845, about one-half of all that were packed in the United States. This is no insignificant item. Pork is a growing demand of the old world. Since the laborers of Europe have gotten a taste of our bacon, and we have learned how to pack it dry in boxes, like dry goods, the world has become the market.

The hog is on the march into the future. His nose is ordained to uncover the secrets of dominion, and his feet shall be guided by the star of empire.

Illinois marketed $57,000,000 worth of slaughtered animals—more than any other State, and a seventh of all the States.

Be patient with me, and pardon my pride, and I will give you a list of some of the things in which Illinois excels all other States.

Depth and richness of soil; per cent. of good ground; acres of improved land; large farms—some farms contain from 40,000 to 60,000 acres of cultivated land, 40,000 acres of corn on a single farm; number of farmers; amount of wheat, corn, oats and honey produced; value of animals for slaughter; number of hogs; amount of pork; number of horses—three times as many as Kentucky, the horse State.

Illinois excels all other States in miles of railroads and in miles of postal service, and in money orders sold per annum, and in the amount of lumber sold in her markets.

Illinois is only second in many important matters. This sample list comprises a few of the more important: Permanent school fund (good for a young State); total income for educational purposes; number of publishers of books, maps, papers, etc.; value of farm products and implements, and of live stock; in tons of coal mined.

The shipping of Illinois is only second to New York. Out of one port during the business hours of the season of navigation she sends forth a vessel every ten minutes. This does not include canal boats, which go one every five minutes. No wonder she is only second in number of bankers and brokers or in physicians and surgeons.

She is third in colleges, teachers and schools; cattle, lead, hay, flax, sorghum and beeswax.

THE NEW YORK
PUBLIC LIBRARY

ASTOR, LENOX AND
TILDEN FOUNDATIONS
R   1922   L

She is fourth in population, in children enrolled in public schools, in law schools, in butter, potatoes and carriages.

She is fifth in value of real and personal property, in theological seminaries and colleges exclusively for women, in milk sold, and in boots and shoes manufactured, and in book-binding.

She is only seventh in the production of wood, while she is the twelfth in area. Surely that is well done for the Prairie State. She now has much more wood and growing timber than she had thirty years ago.

A few leading industries will justify emphasis. She manufactures $205,000,000 worth of goods, which places her well up toward New York and Pennsylvania. The number of her manufacturing establishments increased from 1860 to 1870, 300 per cent.; capital employed increased 350 per cent., and the amount of product increased 400 per cent. She issued 5,500,000 copies of commercial and financial newspapers—only second to New York. She has 6,759 miles of railroad, thus leading all other States, worth $636,458,000, using 3,245 engines, and 67,712 cars, making a train long enough to cover one-tenth of the entire roads of the State. Her stations are only five miles apart. More than two-thirds of her land is within five miles of a railroad, and less than two per cent is more than fifteen miles away.

The State has a large financial interest in the Illinois Central railroad. The road was incorporated in 1850, and the State gave each alternate section for six miles on each side, and doubled the price of the remaining land, so keeping herself good. The road received 2,595,000 acres of land, and pays to the State one-seventh of the gross receipts. Add to this the annual receipts from the canal, $111,000, and a large per cent. of the State tax is provided for.

THE RELIGION AND MORALS

of the State keep step with her productions and growth. She was born of the missionary spirit. It was a minister who secured for her the ordinance of 1787, by which she has been saved from slavery, ignorance, and dishonesty. Rev. Mr. Wiley, pastor of a Scotch congregation in Randolph County, petitioned the Constitutional Convention of 1818 to recognize Jesus Christ as king, and the scriptures as the only necessary guide and book of law. The convention did not act in the case, and the old covenanters refused to accept citizenship. They never voted until 1824, when the slavery question was submitted to the people; then they all voted against it and cast the determining votes. Conscience has predominated whenever a great moral question has been submitted to the people.

But little mob violence has ever been felt in the State. In 1817 regulators disposed of a band of horse-thieves that infested the Territory. The Mormon indignities finally awoke the same spirit. Alton was also the scene of a pro-slavery mob, in which Lovejoy was added to the list of martyrs. The moral sense of the people makes the law supreme, and gives to the State unruffled peace.

With $22,300,000 in church property, and 4,298 church organizations, the State has that divine police, the sleepless patrol of moral ideas, that alone is able to secure perfect safety. Conscience takes the knife from the assassin's hand and the bludgeon from the grasp of the highwayman. We sleep in safety, not because we are behind bolts and bars—these only fence against the innocent; not because a lone officer drowses on a distant corner of a street; not because a sheriff may call his posse from a remote part of the county; but because *conscience* guards the very portals of the air and stirs in the deepest recesses of the public mind. This spirit issues within the State 9,500,000 copies of religious papers annually, and receives still more from without. Thus the crime of the State is only one fourth that of New York and one half that of Pennsylvania.

Illinois never had but one duel between her own citizens. In Belleville, in 1820, Alphonso Stewart and William Bennett arranged to vindicate injured honor. The seconds agreed to make it a sham, and make them shoot blanks. Stewart was in the secret. Bennett mistrusted something, and unobserved, slipped a bullet into his gun and killed Stewart. He then fled the State. After two years he was caught, tried, convicted, and, in spite of friends and political aid, was hung. This fixed the code of honor on a Christian basis, and terminated its use in Illinois.

The early preachers were ignorant men, who were accounted eloquent according to the strength of their voices. But they set the style for all public speakers. Lawyers and political speakers followed this rule. Gov. Ford says: "Nevertheless, these first preachers were of incalculable benefit to the country. They inculcated justice and morality. To them are we indebted for the first Christian character of the Protestant portion of the people."

In education Illinois surpasses her material resources. The ordinance of 1787 consecrated one thirty-sixth of her soil to common schools, and the law of 1818, the first law that went upon her statutes, gave three per cent of all the rest to

EDUCATION.

The old compact secures this interest forever, and by its yoking morality and intelligence it precludes the legal interference with the Bible in the public schools. With such a start it is natural that we should have 11,050 schools, and that our illiteracy should be less than New York or Pennsylvania, and only about one half of Massachusetts. We are not to blame for not having more than one half as many idiots as the great States. These public schools soon made colleges inevitable. The first college, still flourishing, was started in Lebanon in 1828, by the M. E. church, and named after Bishop McKendree. Illinois College, at Jacksonville, supported by the Presbyterians, followed in 1830. In 1832 the Baptists built Shurtleff College, at Alton. Then the Presbyterians built Knox College, at Galesburg, in 1838, and the Episcopalians built Jubilee College, at Peoria, in 1847. After these early years, colleges have rained down. A settler could hardly encamp on the prairie but a college would spring up by his wagon. The State now has one very well endowed and equipped university, namely, the Northwestern University, at Evanston, with six colleges, ninety instructors, over 1,000 students, and $1,500,000 endowment.

Rev. J. M. Peck was the first educated Protestant minister in the State. He settled at Rock Spring, in St. Clair County,

1820, and left his impress on the State. Before 1837 only party papers were published, but Mr. Peck published a Gazetteer of Illinois. Soon after John Russell, of Bluffdale, published essays and tales showing genius. Judge James Hall published *The Illinois Monthly Magazine* with great ability, and an annual called *The Western Souvenir*, which gave him an enviable fame all over the United States. From these beginnings, Illinois has gone on till she has more volumes in public libraries even than Massachusetts, and of the 44,500,000 volumes in all the public libraries of the United States, she has one thirteenth. In newspapers she stands fourth. Her increase is marvelous.

This brings us to a record unsurpassed in the history of any age.

THE WAR RECORD OF ILLINOIS.

I hardly know where to begin, or how to advance, or what to say. I can at best give you only a broken synopsis of her deeds, and you must put them in the order of glory for yourself. Her sons have always been foremost on fields of danger. In 1832-33, at the call of Gov. Reynolds, her sons drove Blackhawk over the Mississippi.

When the Mexican war came, in May, 1846, 8,370 men offered themselves when only 3,720 could be accepted. The fields of Buena Vista and Vera Cruz, and the storming of Cerro Gordo, will carry the glory of Illinois soldiers long after the causes that led to that war have been forgotten. But it was reserved till our day for her sons to find a field and cause and foemen that could fitly illustrate their spirit and heroism. Illinois put into her own regiments for the United States government 256,000 men, and into the army through other States enough to swell the number to 290,000. This far exceeds all the soldiers of the Federal government in all the war of the Revolution. Her total years of service were over 600,000. She enrolled men from eighteen to forty-five years of age when the law of Congress in 1864—the test time—only asked for those from twenty to forty-five. Her enrollment was otherwise excessive. Her people wanted to go, and did not take the pains to correct the enrollment. Thus the basis of fixing the quota was too great, and then the quota itself, at least in the trying time, was far above any other State.

Thus the demand on some counties, as Monroe, for example, took every able-bodied man in the county, and then did not have enough to fill the quota. Moreover, Illinois sent 20,844 men for ninety or one hundred days, for whom no credit was asked. When Mr. Lincoln's attention was called to the inequality of the quota compared with other States, he replied: "The country needs the sacrifice. We must put the whip on the free horse." In spite of all these disadvantages Illinois gave to the country 73,000 years of service above all calls. With one thirteenth of the population of the loyal States, she sent regularly one tenth of all the soldiers, and in the peril of the closing calls, when patriots were few and weary, she then sent one eighth of all that were called for by her loved and honored son in the White House. Her mothers and daughters went into the fields to raise the grain and keep the children together, while the fathers and older sons went to the harvest fields of the world. I knew a father and four sons who agreed that one of them must stay at home; and they pulled straws from a stack to see who might go. The father was left. The next day he came into the camp, saying: "Mother says she can get the crops in, and I am going, too." I know large Methodist churches from which every male member went to the army. Do you want to know what these heroes from Illinois did in the field? Ask any soldier with a good record of his own, who is able to judge, and he will tell you that the Illinois men went in to win. It is common history that the greater victories were won in the West. When everything else looked dark Illinois was gaining victories all down the river, and dividing the Confederacy. Sherman took with him on his great march forty-five regiments of Illinois infantry, three companies of artillery, and one company of cavalry. He could not avoid

GOING TO THE SEA.

If he had been killed, I doubt not the men would have gone right on. Lincoln answered all rumors of Sherman's defeat with, "It is impossible; there is a mighty sight of fight in 100,000 Western men." Illinois soldiers brought home 300 battle-flags. The first United States flag that floated over Richmond, was an Illinois flag. She sent messengers and nurses to every field and hospital, to care for her sick and wounded sons. She said, "these suffering ones are my sons, and I will care for them."

When individuals had given all, then cities and towns came forward with their credit to the extent of many millions, to aid these men and their families.

Illinois gave the country the great general of the war—Ulysses S. Grant— since honored with two terms of the Presidency of the United States.

One other name from Illinois comes up in all minds, embalmed in all hearts, that must have the supreme place in this story of our glory and of our nation's honor; that name is Abraham Lincoln, of Illinois.

The analysis of Mr. Lincoln's character is difficult on account of its symmetry.

In this age we look with admiration at his uncompromising honesty. And well we may, for this saved us. Thousands throughout the length and breadth of our country, who knew him only as "Honest Old Abe," voted for him on that account; and wisely did they choose, for no other man could have carried us through the fearful night of the war. When his plans were too vast for our comprehension, and his faith in the cause too sublime for our participation; when it was all night about us, and all dread before us, and all sad and desolate behind us; when not one ray shone upon our cause; when traitors were haughty and exultant at the South, and fierce and blasphemous at the North; when the loyal men here seemed almost in the minority; when the stoutest heart quailed, the bravest cheek paled, when generals were defeating each other for place, and contractors were leeching out the very heart's blood of the prostrate republic; when every thing else had failed us, we looked at this calm, patient man, standing like a rock in the storm, and said: "Mr. Lincoln is honest, and we can trust him still." Holding to this single point with the energy of faith and despair we held together, and, under God, he brought us through to victory.

His practical wisdom made him the

wonder of all lands. With such certainty did Mr. Lincoln follow causes to their ultimate effects, that his foresight of contingencies seemed almost prophetic.

He is radiant with all the great virtues, and his memory shall shed a glory upon this age, that shall fill the eyes of men as they look into history. Other men have excelled him in some point, but, taken at all points, all in all, he stands head and shoulders above every other man of 6,000 years. An administrator, he saved the nation in the perils of unparalleled civil war. A statesman, he justified his measures by their success. A philanthropist, he gave liberty to one race and salvation to another. A moralist, he bowed from the summit of human power to the foot of the Cross, and became a Christian. A mediator, he exercised mercy under the most absolute abeyance to law. A leader, he was no partisan. A commander, he was untainted with blood. A ruler in desperate times, he was unsullied with crime. A man, he has left no word of passion, no thought of malice, no trick of craft, no act of jealousy, no purpose of selfish ambition. Thus perfected, without a model and without a peer, he was dropped into these troubled years to adorn and embellish all that is good and all that is great in our humanity, and to present to all coming time the representative of the divine idea of free government.

It is not too much to say that away down in the future, when the republic has fallen from its niche in the wall of time; when the great war itself shall have faded out in the distance like a mist on the horizon; when the Anglo Saxon language shall be spoken only by the tongue of the stranger; then the generations looking this way shall see the great president as the supreme figure in this vortex of history.

CHICAGO.

It is impossible in our brief space to give more than a meager sketch of such a city as Chicago, which is in itself the greatest marvel of the Prairie State. This mysterious, majestic, mighty city, born first of water, and next of fire; sown in weakness, and raised in power; planted among the willows of the marsh, and crowned with the glory of the mountains, sleeping on the bosom of the prairie, and rocked on the bosom of the sea; the youngest city of the world, and still the eye of the prairie, as Damascus, the oldest city of the world, is the eye of the desert. With a commerce far exceeding that of Corinth on her isthmus, in the highway to the East; with the defenses of a continent piled around her by the thousand miles, making her far safer than Rome on the banks of the Tiber; with schools eclipsing Alexandria and Athens; with liberties more conspicuous than those of the old republics; with a heroism equal to the first Carthage, and with a sanctity scarcely second to that of Jerusalem—set your thoughts on all this, lifted into the eyes of all men by the miracle of its growth, illuminated by the flame of its fall, and transfigured by the divinity of its resurrection, and you will feel, as I do, the utter impossibility of compassing this subject as it deserves. Some impression of her importance is received from the shock her burning gave to the civilized world.

When the doubt of her calamity was removed, and the horrid fact was accepted, there went a shudder over all cities, and a quiver over all lands. There was scarcely a town in the civilized world that did not shake on the brink of this opening chasm. The flames of our homes reddened all skies. The city was set upon a hill, and could not be hid. All eyes were turned upon it. To have struggled and suffered amid the scenes of its fall is as distinguishing as to have fought at Thermopylæ, or Salamis, or Hastings, or Waterloo, or Bunker Hill.

Its calamity amazed the world, because it was felt to be the common property of mankind.

The early history of the city is full of interest, just as the early history of such a man as Washington or Lincoln becomes public property, and is cherished by every patriot.

Starting with 560 acres in 1833, it embraced and occupied 23,000 acres in 1869, and having now a population of more than 600,000, it commands general attention.

The first settler—Jean Baptiste Pointe au Sable, a mulatto from the West Indies—came and began trade with the Indians in 1796. John Kinzie became his successor in 1804, in which year Fort Dearborn was erected.

A mere trading-post was kept here from that time till about the time of the Blackhawk war, in 1832. It was not the city. It was merely a cock crowing at midnight. The morning was not yet. In 1833 the settlement about the fort was incorporated as a town. The voters were divided on the propriety of such corporation, twelve voting for it and one against it. Four years later it was incorporated as a city, and embraced 560 acres.

The produce handled in this city is an indication of its power. Grain and flour were imported from the East till as late as 1837. The first exportation by way of experiment was in 1839. Exports exceeded imports first in 1842. The Board of Trade was organized in 1848, but it was so weak that it needed nursing till 1855. Grain was purchased by the wagon-load in the street.

I remember sitting with my father on a load of wheat, in the long line of wagons along Lake street, while the buyers came and untied the bags, and examined the grain, and made their bids. That manner of business had to cease with the day of small things. One tenth of all the wheat in the United States is handled in Chicago. Even as long ago as 1853 the receipts of grain in Chicago exceeded those of the goodly city of St. Louis, and in 1854 the exports of grain from Chicago exceeded those of New York and doubled those of St. Petersburg, Archangel, or Odessa, the largest grain markets in Europe.

The manufacturing interests of the city are not contemptible. In 1873 manufactories employed 45,000 operatives; in 1876, 60,000. The manufactured product in 1875 was worth $177,000,000.

No estimate of the size and power of Chicago would be adequate that did not put large emphasis on the railroads. Before they came thundering along our streets, canals were the hope of our country. But who ever thinks now of traveling by canal packets? In June, 1852, there were only forty miles of railroad connected with the city. The old Galena division of the Northwestern ran out to Elgin. But now, who can count the trains and measure the roads that seek a terminus or connection in this city? The lake stretches away to the north, gathering into this center all the harvests that might otherwise pass to the north of us. If you will take a map and look at the adjustment of railroads, you will see, first, that Chicago is the great railroad center of the world, as New York is the commercial city of this continent; and, second, that the railroad lines form the iron spokes of a great wheel whose hub is this city. The lake furnishes the only break in the spokes, and this seems simply to have pushed a few spokes together on each shore. See the eighteen trunk lines, exclusive of eastern connections.

Pass round the circle, and view their numbers and extent. There is the great Northwestern, with all its branches, one branch creeping along the lake shore, and so reaching to the north, into the Lake Superior regions, away to the right, and on to the Northern Pacific on the left, swinging around Green Bay for iron and copper and silver, twelve months in the year, and reaching out for the wealth of the great agricultural belt and isothermal line traversed by the Northern Pacific. Another branch, not so far north, feeling for the heart of the Badger State. Another pushing lower down the Mississippi—all these make many connections, and tapping all the vast wheat regions of Minnesota, Wisconsin, Iowa, and all the regions this side of sunset. There is that elegant road, the Chicago, Burlington & Quincy, running out a goodly number of branches, and reaping the great fields this side of the Missouri River. I can only mention the Chicago, Alton & St. Louis, *our* Illinois Central, described elsewhere, and the Chicago & Rock Island. Further around we come to the lines connecting us with all the Eastern cities. The Chicago, Indianapolis & St. Louis, the Pittsburg, Fort Wayne & Chicago, the Lake Shore & Michigan Southern, and the Michigan Central and Great Western, give us many highways to the seaboard. Thus we reach the Mississippi at five points, from St. Paul to Cairo and the Gulf itself by two routes. We also reach Cincinnati and Baltimore, and Pittsburg and Philadelphia, and New York. North and south run the water courses of the lakes and the rivers, broken just enough at this point to make a pass. Through this, from east to west, run the long lines that stretch from ocean to ocean.

This is the neck of the glass, and the golden sands of commerce must pass into our hands. Altogether we have more than 10,000 miles of railroad, directly tributary to this city, seeking to unload their wealth in our coffers. All these roads have come themselves by the infallible instinct of capital. Not a dollar was ever given by the city to secure one of them, and only a small per cent. of stock taken originally by her citizens, and that taken simply as an investment. Coming in the natural order of events, they will not be easily diverted.

There is still another showing to all this. The connection between New York and San Francisco is by the middle route. This passes inevitably through Chicago. St. Louis wants the Southern Pacific or Kansas Pacific, and pushes it out through Denver, and so on up to Cheyenne. But before the road is fairly under way, the Chicago roads shove out to Kansas City, making even the Kansas Pacific a feeder, and actually leaving St. Louis out in the cold. It is not too much to expect that Dakota, Montana, and Washington Territory will find their great market in Chicago.

But these are not all. Perhaps I had better notice here the ten or fifteen new roads that have just entered, or are just entering, our city. Their names are all that is necessary to give. Chicago & St. Paul, looking up the Red River country to the British possessions; the Chicago, Atlantic & Pacific; the Chicago, Decatur & State line; the Baltimore & Ohio; the Chicago, Danville & Vincennes; the Chicago & La Salle Railroad; the Chicago, Pittsburgh & Cincinnati; the Chicago and Canada Southern; the Chicago and Illinois River Railroad. These, with their connections, and with the new connections of the old roads, already in process of erection, give to Chicago not less than 10,000 miles of new tributaries from the richest land on the continent. Thus there will be added to the reserve power, to the capital within reach of this city, not less than $1,000,000,000.

Add to all this transporting power the ships that sail one every nine minutes of the business hours of the season of navigation; add, also, the canal boats that leave one every five minutes during the same time—and you will see something of the business of the city.

THE COMMERCE OF THIS CITY

has been leaping along to keep pace with the growth of the country around us. In 1852, our commerce reached the hopeful sum of $20,000,000. In 1870 it reached $400,000,000. In 1871 it was pushed up above $450,000,000, and in 1875 it touched nearly double that.

One half of our imported goods come directly to Chicago. Grain enough is exported directly from our docks to the old world to employ a semi-weekly line of steamers of 3,000 tons capacity. This branch is not likely to be greatly developed. Even after the great Welland Canal is completed we shall have only fourteen feet of water. The great ocean vessels will continue to control the trade.

The schools of Chicago are unsurpassed in America. Out of a population of 300,000, there were only 186 persons between the ages of six and twenty-one unable to read. This is the best known record.

In 1831 the mail system was condensed into a half-breed, who went on foot to Niles, Mich., once in two weeks, and brought back what papers and news he could find. As late as 1846 there was often only one mail a week. A post-office was established in Chicago in 1833, and the post-master nailed up old boot-legs on one side of his shop to serve as boxes for the nabobs and literary men.

The improvements that have characterized the city are as startling as the city itself. In 1831, Mark Beaubien established a ferry over the river, and put himself under bonds to carry all the citizens free for the privilege of charging strangers. Now there are twenty-four large bridges and two tunnels.

In 1833 the government expended $30,000 on the harbor. Then commenced that series of maneuvers with the river that has made it one of the world's curiosities. It used to wind around in the lower end of the town, and make its way rippling over the sand into the lake at the foot of Madison street. They took it up and put it down where it now is. It was a narrow stream, so narrow that even moderately small crafts had to go up through the willows and cat's tails to the point near Lake street bridge, and back up one of the branches to get room enough in which to turn around.

In 1844 the quagmires in the streets were first pontooned by plank roads, which acted in wet weather as public squirt-guns. Keeping you out of the mud, they compromised by squirting the mud over you. The wooden-block pavements came to Chicago in 1857. In 1840 water was delivered by peddlers in carts or by hand. Then a twenty-five horse-power engine pushed it through hollow or bored logs along the streets till 1854, when it was introduced into the houses by new works. The first fire-engine was used in 1835, and the first steam fire-engine in 1859. Gas was utilized for lighting the city in 1850. The Young Men's Christian Association was organized in 1858, and horse railroads carried them to their work in 1859. The alarm telegraph adopted in 1864. The opera-house built in 1865. The city grew from 560 acres in 1833 to 23,000 in 1869. In 1834, the taxes amounted to $48.90, and the trustees of the town borrowed $60 more for opening and improving streets. In 1835, the Legislature authorized a loan of $2,000, and the treasurer and street commissioners resigned rather than plunge the town into such a gulf.

One third of the city has been raised up an average of eight feet, giving good pitch to the 263 miles of sewerage. The water of the city is above all competition. It is received through two tunnels extending to a crib in the lake two miles from shore. The first tunnel is five feet two inches in diameter and two miles long, and can deliver 50,000,000 of gallons per day. The second tunnel is seven feet in diameter and six miles long, running four miles under the city, and can deliver 100,000,000 of gallons per day. This water is distributed through 410 miles of watermains.

The three grand engineering exploits of the city are: First, lifting the city up on jack-screws, whole squares at a time, without interrupting the business, thus giving us good drainage; second, running the tunnels under the lake, giving us the best water in the world; and third, the turning the current of the river in its own channel, delivering us from the old abominations, and making decency possible. They redound about equally to the credit of the engineering, to the energy of the people, and to the health of the city.

That which really constitutes the city, its indescribable spirit, its soul, the way it lights up in every feature in the hour of action, has not been touched. In meeting strangers, one is often surprised how some homely women marry so well. Their forms are bad, their gait uneven and awkward, their complexion is dull, their features are misshapen and mismatched, and when we see them there is no beauty that we should desire them. But when once they are aroused on some subject, they put on new proportions. They light up into great power. The real person comes out from its unseemly ambush, and captures us at will. They have power. They have ability to cause things to come to pass. We no longer wonder why they are in such high demand. So it is with our city.

There is no grand scenery except the two seas, one of water, the other of prairie. Nevertheless, there is a spirit about it, a push, a breadth, a power, that soon makes it a place never to be forsaken. One soon ceases to believe in impossibilities. Balaams are the only prophets that are disappointed. The bottom that has been on the point of falling out has been there so long that it has grown fast. It can not fall out. It has all the capital of the world itching to get inside the corporation.

The two great laws that govern the growth and size of cities are, first, the amount of territory for which they are the distributing and receiving points; second, the number of medium or moderate dealers that do this distributing. Monopolists build up themselves, not the cities. They neither eat, wear, nor live in proportion to their business. Both these laws help Chicago.

The tide of trade is eastward—not up or down the map, but across the map. The lake runs up a wingdam for 500 miles to gather in the business. Commerce can not ferry up there for seven months in the year and the facilities for seven months can do the work for twelve. Then the great region west of us is nearly all good, productive land. Dropping south into the trail of St. Louis, you fall into vast deserts and rocky districts, useful in holding the world together. St. Louis and Cincinnati, instead of rivaling and hurting Chicago, are her greatest sureties of dominion. They are far enough away to give sea-room—farther off than Paris is from London—and yet they are near enough to prevent the springing up of any other great city between them.

St. Louis will be helped by the opening of the Mississippi, but also hurt. That will put New Orleans on her feet, and with a railroad running over into Texas and so West, she will tap the streams that now crawl up the Texas and Missouri road. The current is East, not North, and a seaport at New Orleans can not permanently help St. Louis.

Chicago is in the field almost alone, to handle the wealth of one fourth of the territory of this great republic. This strip of seacoast divides its margins between Portland, Boston, New York, Philadelphia, Baltimore and Savannah or some other great port to be created for the South in the next decade. But Chicago has a dozen empires casting their treasures into her lap. On a bed of coal that can run all the machinery of the world for 500 centuries; in a garden feed the race by the thousand years; at the head of the lakes that give her a temperature as a summer resort equaled by no great city in the land; with a climate that insures the health of her citizens; surrounded by all the great deposits of natural wealth in mines and forests and herds, Chicago is the wonder of to-day, and will be *the city of the future*.

MASSACRE AT FORT DEARBORN.

During the war of 1812, Fort Dearborn became the theater of stirring events. The garrison consisted of fifty-four men under command of Captain Nathan Heald, assisted by Lieutenant Helm (son-in-law of Mrs. Kinzie) and Ensign Ronan. Dr. Voorhees was surgeon. The only residents at the post at that time were the wives of Captain Heald and Lieutenant Helm, and a few of the soldiers, Mr. Kinzie and his family, and a few Canadian *voyageurs*, with their wives and children. The soldiers and Mr. Kinzie were on most friendly terms with the Pottawatomies and Winnebagoes, the principal tribes around them, but they could not win them from their attachment to the British.

One evening in April, 1812, Mr. Kinzie sat playing on his violin and his children were dancing to the music, when Mrs. Kinzie came rushing into the house pale with terror, and exclaiming: "The Indians! the Indians!" "What? where?" eagerly inquired Mr. Kinzie. "Up at Lee's, killing and scalping," answered the frightened mother, who, when the alarm was given, was attending Mrs. Barnes (just confined) living not far off. Mr. Kinzie and his family crossed the river and took refuge in the fort, to which place Mrs. Barnes and her infant not a day old, were safely conveyed. The rest of the inhabitants took shelter in the fort. This alarm was caused by a scalping party of Winnebagoes, who hovered about the fort several days, when they disappeared, and for several weeks the inhabitants were undisturbed.

On the 7th of August, 1812, General Hull, at Detroit, sent orders to Captain Heald to evacuate Fort Dearborn, and to distribute all the United States property to the Indians in the neighborhood—a most insane order. The Pottawatomie chief who brought the dispatch had more wisdom than the commanding general. He advised Captain Heald not to make the distribution. Said he: "Leave the fort and stores as they are, and let the Indians make distribution for themselves; and while they are engaged in the business, the white people may escape to Fort Wayne."

Captain Heald held a council with the Indians on the afternoon of the 12th, in which his officers refused to join, for they had been informed that treachery was designed— that the Indians intended to murder the white people in the council, and then destroy those in the fort. Captain Heald, however, took the precaution to open a port-hole displaying a cannon pointing directly upon the council, and by that means saved his life.

Mr. Kinzie, who knew the Indians well, begged Captain Heald not to confide in their promises, nor distribute the arms and munitions among them, for it would only put power into their hands to destroy the whites. Acting upon this advice, Heald resolved to withhold the munitions of war; and on the night of the 13th after the distribution of the other property had been made, the powder, ball and liquors were thrown into the river, the muskets broken up and destroyed.

Black Partridge, a friendly chief, came to Captain Heald and said: "Linden birds have been singing in my ears to-day; be careful on the march you are going to take." On that night vigilant Indians had crept near the fort and discovered the destruction of their promised booty going on within. The next morning the powder was seen floating on the surface of the river. The savages were exasperated and made loud complaints and threats.

On the following day when preparations were making to leave the fort, and all the inmates were deeply impressed with a sense of impending danger, Capt. Wells, an uncle of Mrs. Heald, was discovered upon the Indian trail among the sand hills on the borders of the lake, not far distant, with a band of mounted Miamis, of whose tribe he was chief, having been adopted by the famous Miami warrior, Little Turtle.

When news of Hull's surrender reached Fort Wayne, he had started with this force to assist Heald in defending Fort Dearborn. He was too late. Every means for its defense had been destroyed the night before, and arrangements were made for leaving the fort on the morning of the 15th.

It was a warm, bright morning in the middle of August. Indications were positive that the savages intended to murder the white people; and when they moved out of the southern gate of the fort, the march was like a funeral procession. The band, feeling the solemnity of the occasion, struck up the Dead March in Saul.

Capt. Wells, who had blackened his face with gun-powder in token of his fate, took the lead with his band of Miamis, followed by Captain Heald with his wife by his side on horseback. Mr. Kinzie hoped by his personal influence to avert the impending blow, and therefore accompanied them, leaving his family in a boat in charge of a friendly Indian, to be taken to his trading station at the site of Niles, Michigan, in the event of his death.

The procession moved slowly along the lake shore till they reached the sand hills between the prairie and the beach, when the Pottawatomie escort, under the leadership of Blackbird, filed to the right, placing those hills between them and the white people. Wells, with his Miamis, had kept in the advance. They suddenly came rushing back, Wells exclaiming, "They are about to attack us; form instantly." These words were quickly followed by a storm of bullets which came whistling over the little hills which the treacherous savages had made the covert for their murderous attack. The white troops charged upon the Indians, drove them back to the prairie, and then the battle was waged between fifty-four soldiers, twelve civilians and three or four women (the cowardly Miamis having fled at the outset) against five hundred Indian warriors. The white people, hopeless, resolved to sell their lives as dearly as possible. Ensign Ronan wielded his weapon vigorously, even after falling upon his knees weak from the loss of blood. Capt. Wells, who was by the side of his niece, Mrs. Heald, when the conflict began, behaved with the greatest coolness and courage. He said to her, "We have not the slightest chance for life. We must part to meet no more in this world. God bless you." And then he dashed forward. Seeing a young warrior, painted like a demon, climb into a wagon in which were twelve children, and tomahawk them all, he cried out, unmindful of his personal danger, "If that is your game, butchering women and children, I will kill too." He spurred his horse towards the Indian camp, where they had left their squaws and papooses, hotly pursued by swift-footed young warriors, who sent bullets whistling after him. One of these killed his horse and wounded him severely in the leg. With a yell the young braves rushed to make him their prisoner and reserve him for torture. He resolved not to be made a captive, and by the use of the most provoking epithets tried to induce them to kill him instantly. He called a fiery young chief a *squaw*, when the enraged warrior killed Wells instantly with his tomahawk, jumped upon his body, cut out his heart, and ate a portion of the warm morsel with savage delight!

In this fearful combat women bore a

conspicuous part. Mrs. Heald was an excellent equestrian and an expert in the use of the rifle. She fought the savages bravely, receiving several severe wounds. Though faint from the loss of blood, she managed to keep her saddle. A savage raised his tomahawk to kill her, when she looked him full in the face, and with a sweet smile and in a gentle voice said, in his own language, "Surely you will not kill a squaw!" The arm of the savage fell, and the life of the heroic woman was saved.

Mrs. Helm, the step-daughter of Mr. Kinzie, had an encounter with a stout Indian, who attempted to tomahawk her. Springing to one side, she received the glancing blow on her shoulder, and at the same instant seized the savage round the neck with her arms and endeavored to get hold of his scalping knife, which hung in a sheath at his breast. While she was thus struggling she was dragged from her antagonist by another powerful Indian, who bore her, in spite of her struggles, to the margin of the lake and plunged her in. To her astonishment she was held by him so that she would not drown, and she soon perceived that she was in the hands of the friendly Black Partridge, who had saved her life.

The wife of Sergeant Holt, a large and powerful woman, behaved as bravely as an Amazon. She rode a fine, high-spirited horse, which the Indians coveted, and several of them attacked her with the butts of their guns, for the purpose of dismounting her; but she used the sword which she had snatched from her disabled husband so skillfully that she foiled them; and, suddenly wheeling her horse, she dashed over the prairie, followed by the savages shouting, "The brave woman! the brave woman! Don't hurt her!" They finally overtook her, and while she was fighting them in front, a powerful savage came up behind her, seized her by the neck and dragged her to the ground. Horse and woman were made captive. Mrs. Holt was a long time a captive among the Indians, but was afterward ransomed.

In this sharp conflict two thirds of the white people were slain and wounded, and all their horses, baggage and provision were lost. Only twenty-eight straggling men now remained to fight five hundred Indians rendered furious by the sight of blood. They succeeded in breaking through the ranks of the murderers and gaining a slight eminence on the prairie near the Oak Woods. The Indians did not pursue, but gathered on their flanks, while the chiefs held a consultation on the sand-hills, and showed signs of willingness to parley. It would have been madness on the part of the whites to renew the fight; and so Capt. Heald went forward and met Blackbird on the open prairie, where terms of surrender were agreed upon. It was arranged that the white people should give up their arms to Blackbird, and that the survivors should become prisoners of war, to be exchanged for ransoms as soon as practicable. With this understanding captives and captors started for the Indian camp near the fort, to which Mrs. Helm had been taken bleeding and suffering by Black Partridge, and had met her step-father and learned that her husband was safe.

A new scene of horror was now opened at the Indian camp. The wounded, not being included in the surrender, as it was interpreted by the Indians, and the British general, Proctor, having offered a liberal bounty for American scalps, delivered at Malden, nearly all the wounded men were killed and scalped, and price of the trophies was afterward paid by the British government.

This celebrated Indian chief, Shabbona, deserves more than a passing notice. Although he was not so conspicuous as Tecumseh or Black Hawk, yet in point of merit he was superior to either of them.

Shabbona was born at an Indian village on the Kankakee River, now in Will County about the year 1775. While young he was made chief of the band, and went to Shabbona Grove, now De Kalb County, where they were found in the early settlement of the county.

In the war of 1812, Shabbona, with his warriors, joined Tecumseh, was aid to that great chief, and stood by his side when he fell at the battle of the Thames. At the time of the Winnebago war, in 1827, he visited almost every village among the Pottawatomies, and by his persuasive arguments prevented them from taking part in the war. By request of the citizens of Chicago, Shabbona, accompanied by Billy Caldwell (Sauganash), visited Big Foot's village at Geneva Lake, in order to pacify the warriors, as fears were entertained that they were about to raise the tomahawk against the whites. Here Shabbona was taken prisoner by Big Foot, and his life threatened, but on the following day was set at liberty. From that time the Indians (through reproach) styled him "the white man's friend," and many times his life was endangered.

Before the Black Hawk war, Shabbona met in council at two different times, and by his influence prevented his people from taking part with the Sacs and Foxes. After the death of Black Partridge and Senachwine, no chief among the Pottawatomies exerted so much influence as Shabbona. Black Hawk, aware of this influence, visited him at two different times, in order to enlist him in his cause, but was unsuccessful. While Black Hawk was a prisoner at Jefferson Barracks, he said, had it not been for Shabbona the whole Pottawatomie nation would have joined his standard, and he could have continued the war for years.

To Shabbona many of the early settlers of Illinois owe the preservation of their lives, for it is a well-known fact, had he not notified the people of their danger, a large portion of them would have fallen victims to the tomahawk of savages. By saving the lives of whites he endangered his own, for the Sacs and Foxes threatened to kill him, and made two attempts to execute their threats. They killed Pypeogee, his son, and Pyps, his nephew, and hunted him down as though he was a wild beast.

Shabbona had a reservation of two sections of land at his Grove, but by leaving it and going West for a short time, the Government declared the reservation forfeited, and sold it the same as other vacant land. On Shabbona's return, and finding his possessions gone, he was very sad and broken down in spirit, and left the Grove forever. The citizens of Ottawa raised money and bought him a tract of land on the Illinois River, above Seneca, in Grundy County, on which they built a house, and supplied him with means to live on. He lived here until his death, which occurred on the 17th of July, 1859, in the eighty-fourth year of his age, and was buried with great pomp in the cemetery at Morris. His squaw, Pokanoka, was drowned in Mazon Creek, Grundy County, on the 30th of November, 1864, and was buried by his side.

In 1861 subscriptions were taken up in many of the river towns, to erect a monument over the remains of Shabbona, but the war breaking out, the enterprise was abandoned. Only a plain marble slab marks the resting-place of this friend of the white man.

HISTORY OF GRUNDY COUNTY.

CHAPTER I.*

TOPOGRAPHY—POST-TERTIARY FORMATIONS—ROCK-FORMATIONS—CARBONIFEROUS FOSSILS—ECONOMIC GEOLOGY.

THE relation of the physical features of a country to its development is an important one, and he who would learn the hidden causes that make or mar a nation at its birth must seek in these " the divinity that shapes its ends." Here is found the *elixir vitæ* of national life; the spring from whence flow those forces that on their broader current wreck the ship of state or bear it safely on to its appointed haven. It is in these physical features that are stored those potent industrial possibilities that make the master and the slave among the nations. From the fertile soil comes fruit-laden, peace-loving agriculture; from the rock-bound stores of mineral wealth springs the rude early-time civilization of the Pacific slope, or the half savage clashing of undisciplined capital and labor in the mining regions; from the rivers rises, fairylike, the commercial metropolis, which "crowned with the glory of the mountains," and fed with the bounty of the plains, stands the chosen arbiter between the great forces that join to make a nation's greatness. The influence of this subtle power knows no bounds. Here it spreads the lotus plant of ease and binds the nation in chains of indolent effeminacy; here, among the bleak peaks of a sterile land,

"The heather on the mountain height
Begins to bloom in purple light,"

type of a hardy and unconquered race; here it strews the sand of desert wilds, and man without resource, becomes a savage.

The manifestations of this potent factor in human economy are scarcely less marked in the smaller divisions of the State, and in them is found the natural introduction to a consideration of a county's social, political and military history.

Grundy County, situated in the northeastern part of the State of Illinois, is bounded on the north by Kendall, on the east by Will and Kankakee, on the south by Livingston, and on the west by La Salle. It includes twelve townships, or about 420 square miles, forming a rectangle of twenty-four miles long and about seventeen and a half miles wide. Of this, about two thirds is slightly rolling prairie, and the balance mostly well timbered creek banks and river bottoms.

The Illinois River divides the county near the middle of its northern half, running

* By J. H. Battle.

a W. S. W. course, with but little variation. Its principal affluent on the south is Mazon Creek, which drains fully one third of Grundy, and portions of Livingston, Kankakee and Will Counties. Its principal water supply is from surface drainage, but few springs being found along its course. From this character, one would readily predicate the truth that a very wet season often causes it to overflow its banks, though twenty feet or more in height, while a dry one leaves its bed bare, except where deep pools have formed.

A few miles west of the Mazon is the Waupecan, draining a comparatively small extent of country; but in an ordinary season, carrying nearly as much water, the product of several strong springs on the lower part of its course—some of them from the drift, others from the sandstones and shales of the Coal Measures, which show a small outcrop here. Still farther to the westward, are Billy Run, Hog Run, and Armstrong Run, which are simply prairie drains, and show no outcrop of rocks. Nettle Creek, on the north side of the river, is principally of the same character; but in the lower part of its course, there are a few springs, and two or three outcrops of the shales and sandstones which overlie the lower coal. Finally, in the northeast corner of the county is the Au Sable Creek, with a comparatively large amount of water, partly derived from springs and partly from drainage of this and Kendall County.

Of the post-tertiary formations, the beds of the alluvium formation are very largely developed in the terraces of the river valley and the beds of the smaller streams. From the west line of the county nearly to Au Sable Creek, the Illinois and Michigan canal follows the north bank of the present river valley pretty closely, while the second terrace varies from half a mile to two miles to the northward. On the south side of the river the high, gravelly banks of the second terrace hug the river banks very closely, as far as the Waupecan Creek. Here they lose much of their elevation, and have as their continuation a low ridge about a mile distant from the present bank. East of Mazon Creek this declines still more and becomes the heavy sand ridge which bears still farther southward and then eastward, south of Wilmington into Kankakee County. This sand ridge forms the water shed between Mazon Creek and Kankakee River, so that, where it strikes the bank of the latter stream, to the southward of Wilmington, the water flows from within two hundred yards of the river, through swamps and sloughs and finds its way through the Mazon, into the Illinois, opposite Morris.

The flats of the old river valley, back of the present banks, show in many places plain evidence of the comparatively recent date of their formation. On section 11, (in Erienna) town 33 north, range 6 east, a layer of thin slabs of fissile sandstone of the Coal Measures is found a short distance below the surface. They were evidently distributed here by the current of the river, not long before it became so contracted as to leave this level dry. When this old channel was the outlet of Lake Michigan, a large body of water must have flowed through here, and appearances seem to indicate that its diversion toward Niagara must have been sudden rather than gradual; otherwise the present valley would probably have been wider, and the descent to it less abrupt.

A topographer would take peculiar pleasure in studying the various islands of the old valley, especially at the confluences with the Illinois of the Au Sable and Nettle Creeks, both of which streams, apparently, were much larger than at present. Upon one of these islands stands Morris, the county seat. Another, and far the largest in the county, is the high land lying between the head of the Illinois, the lower part of the Kankakee, and the slough which contains Goose Lake, and runs thence to Pine Bluff, near the embouchure of the Mazon, upon the Illinois valley.

The following level points within this county, are gathered principally from the notes of the Illinois River Survey. The figures indicate distances below the established "datum of six feet below the lowest registered water of Lake Michigan":

			Feet.
Bluffs at Morris, north side (level of town)			55.938
"	"	south "	59.48
"	"	" lower terrace.	78.00
Level of river, at head of the Illinois			87.892
"	"	" mouth of Au Sable creek	92.664
"	"	" Morris, under roadbridge	95.13
"	"	" Marseilles, La Salle Co., above dam	99.808
"	"	" " " below "	103.256
"	"	" Goose Lake, about	60.
"	"	" Minooka, as per railroad survey above datum	35.

These levels show that the elevation of first terrace above the river, opposite Morris, is a little over seventeen feet, and that the elevation of the second bluff or gravel ridge above the first terrace is about eighteen and one half feet.

The coarser portion of the beds of river gravel consists mostly of fragments of the Niagara group limestone, which forms so heavy beds, from below Joliet to Chicago and beyond. Much of the sand is probably due to the disintegration of the Coal Measure sandstones, while some of it may have come from the northward. There is, however, in these beds, but a very small proportion of the metamorphic material from Canada, which forms so large a part of the true drift, but upon the *surface* of the soil, and often partially buried, are great numbers of small boulders of quartzite, gneiss, granite and trap, unquestionably of northern origin. These are especially abundant south of Goose Lake, over the surface of the valley which starts from the Kankakee, near the county line, includes Goose Lake, and joins the Illinois valley near where the Mazon first strikes the bottoms. This was probably a shallow channel, in which floating fields of ice lodged, melted and dropped the loads of stone which they had brought from the northward. Similar aggregations of boulders occur in the adjacent parts of Will County, at points where eddies would have been likely to detain the ice floes. It is suspected that this Goose Lake channel was formerly the main channel of the Kankakee, which there met the Des Plaines only four miles above Morris.

The bed of "potter's clay," worked near the southwest bank of Goose Lake, and lying "near the level of the fire clay," owes its origin and deposition to river action, though principally consisting of the decomposed shales and fire clays of the Coal Measures.

During the autumn of 1868 the remains of a *Mastodon* were found at Turner's strippings, about three miles east of Morris, under eighteen inches of black mucky soil, and about four feet of yellowish loam, and resting on about a foot of hard blue clay, which covered the coal. The bones were badly decayed, and most of them were broken up and thrown away by the miners; a portion were saved, however, of which a fragment of a lower jaw, a part of a thigh bone, three teeth, and a few small bones were presented to the State Cabinet. The locality is a portion of the old river bottom, but it is uncertain, from the lack of scientific investigation at the time, whether to believe that the presence of the bones indicates that the animal was mired and died here, or to suppose that the carcass was deposited here by the river.

The Coal Measure rocks of this county are too soft and too readily disintegrated to allow of the preservation of any scratches that may, at any time, have been impressed upon their surface; so that, although we find in the gravel very numerous scratched and polished pebbles and boulders, it is within only a very small area that striated and polished rock surfaces have been noticed. In the S. E. quarter of Sec. 23, township 34 north, range 7 east, (Saratoga) at Walter's quarry of Trenton limestone, smoothly polished surfaces have been frequently met with; so in one or two other localities. As these localities, however, are all within the old river valley, we can not, with certainty, predicate upon these facts the conclusion that those scratchings and polishings are attributable to glacial action. In fact, these and some other circumstances give some reason for assuming that they are results of river action alone. At Petty's shaft, the outer portion of the shale next to the creek banks, is found broken up for several feet, and thoroughly mingled with the drifted materials which here form an overlying bank of about fifteen feet. This disturbance, as well as the grinding of the surface, may fairly be attributed to the action of the creek while at its former level. But, while allowing that, in these particular cases, river agencies are sufficient to account for all observed phenomena, the frequent occurrence in the Drift of gravel of large and small boulders unquestionably planed and striated by glacial action must also be recorded. These are especially abundant along the Mazon.

The True Drift, in the western part of the county consists, mainly, of the tough blue "boulder clay," with pebbles and boulders, sometimes also including fragments of wood, overlaid but slightly, or not at all, with gravel, and underlaid, so far as known, with a bed of "hard-pan," and a water-bearing quicksand which has thus far prevented any knowledge of the underlying materials. The eastern part of the county, on the contrary, shows but little boulder clay, this being replaced by a heavy layer of sand and gravel. Township 34 north, range 6 east, (Nettle Creek) has no known outcrop of rock, and wells near its south line have reached depths of forty-eight, fifty and fifty-two feet, before meeting the quicksand. Townships 31 and 32, (Highland and Vienna) of the same range, and so much of 33 as lies south of the river, (Norman) together with townships 31 and 32, range 7 east, (Goodfarm and Mazon) possess no outcrop of rock, but the depth of the Drift is not known. At Gardner, in section 9, township 31 north, range 8 east, (Greenfield), the Drift is said to be one hundred feet deep at the coal shaft. At Braceville, section 25, township 32 north, range 8 east, it was found to be forty-four feet deep. Going northward into township 33, in ranges 7 and 8, (Wauponsee and Felix,) it rapidly thins out, owing partly to the downward slope of the surface, partly to the upward slope of the underlying rocks, which come to the surface in the northern part of these townships. Much of the "coal land" in the immediate neighborhood of Morris is bare of drift, having been stripped by the old river. To the northward, however, through township 34 north, range 7 east, the gravel and boulder clay lie, in some places, forty feet deep. Township 34 north, range 8 east, is deeply buried in Drift; at Minooka, on the line between sections 1 and 2, a well-boring found one hundred feet of gravel overlying the shaly limestone of the Cincinnati Group.

Of the rock formations, the beds of the coal measures occupy far the larger part of the surface of the county. The outcrops, however, are so disconnected, and the beds so irregular, that it has been found practically impossible to construct any general section to represent connectedly all the outcrop. Apparently the higher beds exposed in the county are those which outcrop near the old coal openings on the Waupecan, in the southeast quarter of section 20, township 33 north, range 7 east, (Wauponsee). No outcrop of beds above the coal has been discovered, nor has any been seen in the deeper parts of the mine. Near the outcrop a foot of coal was left as a working roof. The seam is now five feet thick, resting on a bed of fire clay. It is coal No. 4 of the Illinois section. The connection below is not exposed, but at a short distance from the floor of the seam, not over ten feet, there is a coarse, ferruginous, shaly sandstone, filled with fragments of *Lepidodendron, Calamites, Neuropteris hirsuta*, etc., with an occasional streak of coaly matter. Of this bed, there is a low, nearly continuous outcrop for a mile up the stream, the last spot observed being at "Hog-grove quarry," in the southwest quarter of section 28. At the road crossing, about half a mile down the creek from the coal mine, the sandstone rises a little, and exposes about six feet of blue and black shales filled with a variety of small mollusca. The lower part of the blue shale holds two thin layers of rusty brown nodules of carbonate of iron, which often, partially or wholly, include shells of these mollusca. The upper part of the black shale also contains nodules of the same material (with probably some phosphate of lime) but smaller and less evenly distributed; the smaller of these contain comminuted scales and bones of fishes, and judging from both form and contents, are probably the fossil excrement of larger fishes. These beds, with others, outcrop at intervals for about a mile along the right bank of the stream; and the following section will fairly represent the whole:

	Feet.
1. Sandy shale	5
2. Blue clay	3
3. Fissile sandstone	15
4. Blue clay shale, with iron nodules	2 to 5
5. Black shale, top slaty, with small nodules, bottom very fragile	2 to 3
6. Cone-in-cone, locally becoming solid sandstone	½ to 1¼
7. Soft olive shale	1½
8. Solid gritty sandstone	1

Another outcrop, on nearly the same horizon, occurs on Mazon creek from the center of the south line of southwest quarter of section 6, township 32 north, range 8 east (Braceville), to near the center of the south line of section 25, (Wauponsee). The strata are here very irregular in thickness, but the following section gives an average representation of the exposed outcrop:

	Feet.	Inches.
1. Ironstone conglomerate, (local)		6
2. Sandstone		8
3. Black shale, some slaty, with large ironstones	3 to 4	
4. Cone-in-cone running into massive limestone	2	to 6
5. Olive shales, changing into concretionary argillaceous limestone	5 to 7	
6. Soft black shale	2 to 3	
7. Blue Clay shale		9
8. Coal No. 3	2	
9. White fire-clay		7

Small quantities of coal have been mined at this seam at several points along the limited outcrop. The coal is said to be good house-fuel, but rather soft. The argillaceous limestone of No. 5, of this section generally contains numerous shells of the genera *Productus*, *Athyris*, *Terebratula*, etc., and some fragments of criniods. The coal apparently holds the position of the thin coal which locally underlies No. 56 of the La Salle County section.

The outcrop along the Mazon appears nearly continuous, but still I have not been able to satisfy myself as to the connection of the above beds with those of the lower part of the stream. The strata, there developed, consist of very variable sandy clay shales and sandstones, in some places becoming nearly pure clay shales, but containing many nodules of carbonate of iron. Pine Bluff, at the lowermost crossing of the Mazon, is composed of about forty feet of heavily bedded, but rather fissile sandstone, partly nearly white, partly highly ferruginous. Less than a mile up the creek the lower part of this bed changes to highly argillaceous sandy shales with occasional streaks and nodules of sandstone. The section is not quite continuous, but there is no distinct line of demarcation to separate these latter beds from the ferruginous sandy shales, twenty to thirty feet thick, of section 24, of township 33 north, range 7 east (Wauponsee), which contain large numbers of fossiliferous nodules of carbonate of iron, for which this locality has become famous. Besides a large variety of ferns mentioned in the State Geological report, these nodules also contain a large number of fossil insects, marking this as one of the richest deposits of Carboniferous Articulates ever discovered, if not *the* richest. These nodules range from about two to about ten feet above the main coal seam of all this region, the intervening space being occupied by the soft, blue clay shales, filled with fossil plants, which, at most points, overlie this seam.

About a mile farther up this stream coal has been dug in the beds and banks of the stream, but is now abandoned. Still further south, near the southeast corner of section 19, township 33 north, range 8 east (Felix), a shaft was sunk upon the creek bottom, starting at about twenty-five feet below the general level of the prairie. The section is as follows:

	Feet.	Inches.
1. Blue clay and sandy shale, with ferns	20	
2. Coal	20	
3. Soft black shale		6 to 8
4. Fire clay with rootlets		6 to 8
5. Hard, sandy clay		8
6. Fire clay	2	6

At this place the coal is about eight feet below the bed of the creek. Near the water level, an offshoot from the main seam, about seven inches thick, is exposed in the bank; the shales immediately over it afforded a few plants.

Near the center of section 18, township 33 north, range 8 east (Felix), Mr. John Holderman's artesian well furnishes the following section:

	Feet.
1. Gravel	15
2. Sandstone	74
3. Coal	3
4. Sandy shale	88
5. Limestone	105

It will be noticed that this section gives the sandstone as immediately overlying the coal. This condition of the seam has been elsewhere noticed, so far as I can learn, only in a shaft sunk near the southeast corner of section 9 of the same township, and in one shaft in the adjoining part of Will County.

On the north side of the Illinois River, in the neighborhood of Morris, the coal outcrops in the bank of the canal, and in the stre ch of low land, about one mile to the northward. The overlying beds are here mostly blue clay shales, with occasional irregular layers of sandstone. The iron nodules, above mentioned, occur here at the same level, but not in so great numbers as at the Mazon locality. The shales immediately above the coal frequently yield magnificent specimens of fossil ferns and other plants. In the north part of township 33 north, range 6 east (Erienna), the shaly sandstones overlying this seam are exposed in the bottom of every little run which cuts away the soil from the edge of the second terrace, and fragments of them are found scattered just below the surface over the whole lower flat.

It has long been a favorite theory with miners that another seam of coal could be found by sinking shafts in the bottom of the present working. This is not impossible, at points distant from the outcrop; but at Morris, and to the eastward, the coal lies directly upon lower Silurian rocks, with only four or five feet of firm clay to separate them. This is shown at several points.

It was supposed that the coal seam extended, in its full thickness, much further northward; but two wells, one in section 27, and the other in section 13, township 34 north, range 7 east, (Saratoga) after passing through fossiliferous shales which overlie the coal, met with only about ten inches of soft coaly shale, underlaid by a few inches of greenish clay shale, with small rounded grains of calcareous (?) matter, (probably belonging to the Cincinnati group) which rested upon the solid limestones of the Trenton. From these and similar facts is derived the conclusion that the present line of workings corresponds very nearly with the original outline of deposit of the true coal seam, while beyond this line, only occasional small outlying patches will ever be found, though thin layers of coaly shale may be met with some miles further northward. On the Au Sable Creek, a few miles north of the county line, small quantities of coaly shale and cannel-coal have been found, but they are probably of no practical value, and have no direct connection with the Morris seam.

Upon the lower part of the Au Sable, however, in the southeast quarter of section 19, township 34 north, range 8 east (Au Sable). there is a peculiar outcrop of probably the lower seam. We have here a seam of coal twenty-eight inches thick, with a floor of fire clay at least six feet thick, and a roof of black shale, which is, at the outcrop, quite solid and a foot thick, but at the shaft, perhaps fifty yards distant, it thickens to between five and six feet and becomes quite soft. This shale has yielded a few small *Discinæ Lingulæ*, and a few fragments of fish scales; but these are not sufficient to determine its position in the series. The bed seems to be but a small outlier, covering only a few acres, as borings to the southward and westward have failed to find any continuation of the bed in these directions, while to the northward and eastward the shales and limestone of the lower Silurian outcrop within a few hundred yards. It seems to be still uncertain whether this is a locally peculiar condition of the main seam, or lies above or below it. If it be the main seam, the black roof shales are probably the equivalent of the bed mentioned in the La Salle County section, as lying there about eighteen feet above the coal; but no other outcrop of it has been seen in this part of Grundy, though it appears in a shaft in the southeastern corner of the county.

Another peculiar outcrop of uncertain connections is along the Kankakee, from the east line of the county to the "Head of the Illinois," in section 36, township 34 north, range 8 east (Au Sable), where the river has cut through some fifty feet of shales and sandstones of the coal measures, including a thin seam of coal, and has reached the underlying shaly limestone of the Cincinnati group. A few indistinct plants have been met with in the sandstone, but in too poor condition for specific determination. In conclusion, the outline of the Coal Measure in Grundy County may be roughly stated as a line running from near the northwest corner of the county, with some variations in an east-southeast course to the mine on Au Sable Creek, just above the railroad; thence southeasterly to the Goose Lake slough, and easterly to the east end of the lake; thence northerly to the mouth of the Kankakee.

The shales and shaly limestones of the Cincinnati group outcrop in the northeastern part of the county, showing most prominently upon the high ground between Goose Lake and the head of the Illinois. This outcrop consists of coarse granular, highly fossiliferous, ferruginous limestones, readily disintegrated by the weather, which have been used, to some extent, for fences. This outcrop continues southward for about a mile, and forms the bottom of the north half of Goose Lake, the south half being underlaid with coal. At the ford of the Kankakee, in the northwest quarter of section 36, in Au Sable township, beds of soft blue shaly limestone, which probably lie near the base of this group, outcrop in the bed of the river, but show little upon the bank, and contain but few and indistinct fossils.

From the bed of the canal, a half mile west of Dresden, there were thrown out considerable quantities of a heavy, but rather cellular ferruginous limestone, in heavy layers, probably belonging below the beds mentioned. The outcrop at this point did not quite reach the surface. Over most of the country, north of the Illinois, the alluvial and drift deposits cover the country so as to allow of outcrops only along the streams. In ascending the Au Sable Creek from the railroad, the scattered fragments of the shaly limestones of this group are frequently seen, but no outcrop is met until the middle of section 3 in Au Sable township is reached, where small quantities of stone have been quarried for wells and foundations. From this point there is a nearly continuous outcrop to some distance above the county line.

A small outcrop of rock of this age is exposed in the bed of Collins' run, a branch of the Au Sable, in the southwest quarter of section 18, of the same township. The rock here is a rather more solid limestone, breaking irregularly, and containing but few fossils. It is reported that similar small outcrops occur farther up this run, but they have not been opened, so as to know whether stone of any value can be obtained. Similar outcrops were observed in the bottoms of ditches near the middle of the north line of Saratoga township. In the borings about Morris, only a few feet of beds which can be referred to this group are found between the Coal Measures and the underlying Trenton limestone, and to the northward of that place no such beds have been found.

The two remaining outcrops of rock in this county are limestones of the Trenton group, probably near its top. The principal one is near the center of section 24, township 34 north, range 7 east (Saratoga); this rock has been quarried for building purposes and for making lime. The top layers of the quarry are thin, and somewhat stained with iron. Below these, the rock is heavily bedded, gray or light drab, fine grained, clinking limestone, not very rich in fossils, but yielding some good specimens of several varieties. This rock has been penetrated to the depth of twenty feet without exposing any other layers; but it is said that at one point the drill passed into a pocket of a softer black material. Possibly this may have been a small deposit of carbonaceous material analagous to the petroleum which this rock has yielded in small quantities in the adjoining county of La Salle. These beds contain small portions of pyrite (*sulphide of iron*) disseminated through the whole mass. There were also occasional streaks of soft clay. The quarry has exposed two sets of crevices, one trending south 45° west, and the other south 35° east. These crevices are filled with a fine clay of very nearly the same color as the limestone, through which are sparsely disseminated small crystals of blende (*sulphide of zinc*) with occasional pyramidal crystals of pyrite; no galenite has been observed. The remaining outcrops of this rock are in the bed of the Au Sable, on the two sides of the yoke-like bend of the stream, in the east half of the northeast quarter of section 19, in Au Sable township, and consists of small patches of a thin bedded, fine grained limestone, containing but few fossils. In the Morris boring, the Trenton limestone is two hundred feet thick.

St. Peter's sandstone has been struck at the railroad station in Morris, at a depth of 370 feet, and here, as elsewhere in this region, has furnished a constant and abundant supply of artesian water.

The economic geology of this county is quite an important feature, coal, brick and potters' clay, building stone and sand, lime and water being found in abundance, beside hydraulic lime and iron ore in smaller quantities. Coal underlies fully three fourths of the county, the seam averaging about three feet, except on the borders of the field. It has been very largely worked in the immediate vicinity of Morris, upwards of one hundred openings having been made, though a larger part of them at this writing have been abandoned. These are principally shafts from thirty to sixty feet deep, though there are several extensive strippings. Some of the latter uncover coal thirty inches thick, which is about the average thickness in this neighborhood; while others on the borders of the outcrop, find not more than eighteen inches. A smaller cluster of shafts and strippings is found to the south and west of Goose Lake, with average thickness of full thirty inches. At a stripping in the southwest corner of section 12, in Felix township, the bed is locally thickened to over four feet, but contains, near its center, a heavy band of crystalline carbonate of iron and lime, with much disseminated pyrite.

This seam is also worked at Braceville, by a shaft ninety-eight feet deep, and in section 26, of the same township, by a shaft of 110 feet. At Gardner, it is worked by a shaft 160 feet deep. In the southeast corner of this township, three or four shafts, of about sixty feet each, work this seam in its usual condition; but one in the northeast corner of section 25, finds a roof of black slaty shale, with heavy ironstone concretions covering about three feet of a very pure "block coal," with much mineral charcoal in the partings. Both the coal and the accompanying beds, at the mine on the Au Sable Creek, closely resemble the conditions found here; and at both points the indications leave it uncertain whether they represent a local change of the main seam, or are portions of a lower seam which is only occasionally present. The weight of opinion seems to favor the former view.

The upper seams, which have been worked upon the Waupecan Creek, and upon the Mazon, near the mouth of Johnny run, apparently occur over only small areas at either locality; and elsewhere, wherever met with, they have proved to be irregular seams, locally quite thick, but of the running out to a mere streak of coaly matter, and even disappearing altogether. The Mazon seam is, apparently, the equivalent of a stream, which, on the eastern side of the coal field, in the Wabash valley, is usually too thin to work, except at a single point, where it reaches twenty-two inches.

The outcrops are not sufficient to give any exact data as to dips, but there seems to be no reason to believe that the main seam lies at a greater depth than 250 feet in any part of the county, if indeed it be anywhere so deep. Whenever, therefore, any portion of the southern part of the county becomes so thickly settled as to create any considerable demand for coal, it can be obtained on the spot without much difficulty. This seam is of pretty constant thickness, at every point where it has been opened, and the miner can rely upon finding a paying thickness of coal at almost any point in this part of the county. At many points, also, one or more of the upper seams would be found much nearer the surface, with from two to nine feet of coal.

In the openings of this county, as elsewhere, the miner is often troubled with "faults" and "rolls," which interrupt the regularity and even the continuity of the seam. Upon the outer edge of the field, near Morris, and to the eastward, the dip of the seam is very variable and irregular, which greatly interferes with the drainage of the mines in many cases. Much of this seems to have resulted from the irregularity of the denuded surface of the Silurian rocks upon which the coal was deposited; but in one or two cases, the indications seem to prove that these contortions are the result of the removal of the subjacent limestone by solution in subterranean streams after the deposition of the coal. This seems to be the only explanation of the condition of the seam, in a shaft a short distance east of the Jugtown pottery. In this neighborhood, the seam is generally about twenty feet below the surface; but in the shaft referred to, it was found forty feet down, and after yielding about 300 bushels, the coal ceased abruptly, on all sides.

So far as known, all coal mined in the county contains more or less pyrite—"sulphur" of the miners—and streaks of calcite; but this is so variable, even in neighboring portions of the same mine, that it would be useless to attempt to discriminate between the products of the various localities. As a whole, the product of the main seam is a fine steam and grate coal, and is largely shipped to the Chicago market, the distance being only sixty-two miles.

The best clay for brick making is not found here, though there are several large brick yards in the county. The materials used are the decomposed shales which overlie the lower coal. As these beds contain considerable calcareous matter, the brick are not very firm and do not stand the weather well. It would appear probable that the fire clay below the coal would make a better article. This has been tried with some success at Gardner. The fire clay, and soft clay shales underlying it, are said to be thirty-five feet deep and so much of these beds as may be convenient, in mining the coal, is dug out and used promiscuously. Without thorough grinding, therefore, in the pugmill, the bricks are variable in character and irregular in burning.

The only bed of Potter's clay known and worked is that near the west end of Goose Lake, and extensively used at Jugtown, in the manufacture of a fair grade of domestic earthernware, together with drain tile and sewer pipes. The bed consists of more or less thoroughly decomposed clay shale and fire clay of the Coal Measures, containing many fragments of coal, thoroughly mingled and deposited in a low part of the old river channel, which contains Goose Lake, by the current of the river which formerly flowed there. The bed has been worked to a depth of fifteen or twenty feet, but the mixed character of the materials has given much trouble to the potters.

The principal source of building stone in this county is the quarry of Trenton limestone in Saratoga township, about four miles northeast of Morris. This yields an abundance of light gray or drab massive limestone, which has been extensively used for foundation walls, and in a few cases also for the superstructures. It appears fitted to stand the weather as well as any ordinary stone, and is said to dress well. The Cincinnati group along the Au Sable Creek near the county line, yields small quantities of stone for wells and foundations, but nothing suitable for superstructures. Beds of the same group upon the northern side of Goose Lake, have been quarried slightly, for similar purposes. Upon the bank of the Waupecan Creek in the southeast quarter of section 18, in Wauponsee township, small quantities of a very solid limestone —No. 6, of the Waupecan section—have been quarried. A sandstone, representing Nos. 1 and 3 of the same section, has been quarried to some extent for foundations on the upper part of the stream, at "Hog Grove Quarry," and has given good satisfaction; though when exposed to the weather it crumbles rapidly. The same defect exists in the sandstone of Pine Bluff.

Lime is obtained from the Saratoga quarry, where considerable quantities of the stone are annually burned, though some care has to be exercised to exclude from the kiln the ferruginous layers. The only hydraulic limestone found in the county occurs in nodules along the Kankakee River, and in small quantity. The abundant supply from an adjoining county renders these deposits of no commercial value.

Builders' sand is obtained in unlimited quantities from the sand ridges of the river valley. From one of these ridges, about one mile south of Morris, large quantities of road gravel are also obtained.

Iron ore is found in form of ironstone nodules (carbonate of iron) on the Mazon and Waupecan Creeks, but not in sufficient quantities to supply a furnace. Bog ore is found near the quarries in Saratoga, but its quality or quantity has not been tested.

The natural supply of water through this county is quite variable. In a dry season, large portions are very scantily supplied. In ordinary seasons, however, wells running ten or fifteen feet into the top of the drift in the eastern part, supply all needs. In the western part of the county, reliable wells can be obtained only by passing through the boulder clay to the underlying quicksand. The lower seam of coal is everywhere accompanied by an abundance of water, which is pure and good, until the working of the coal exposes the accompanying pyrite to decomposition. A well bored at the tile factory in Jugtown some years ago, struck coal at about thirty feet, and gave exit to a strong stream of water, highly charged with sulphurated hydrogen. Small springs of similar character are said to accompany the supposed line of outcrop of this coal seam, along the foot of the first terrace, from Mazon Creek, nearly to the Morris bridge. A very strong spring of this character flows from beneath the drift gravel, over the black shale, No. 3, of the upper Mazon section, in the southwest quarter of section 6, in Braceville township, leaving a heavy white deposit of sulphur on the surface of the shale.

The artesian boring on the northeast quarter of section 3, in Felix township, brings to the surface a small but constant supply of slightly sulphurous water from the upper part of the Trenton limestone, at a depth of about 137 feet. On section 18 of the same township, a boring of 325 feet failed to secure flowing water, after penetrating 185 feet of the Trenton limestone. The boring for the railroad well at Morris, shows this limestone to be 200 feet thick, and that in this county the underlying St. Peter's sandstone is full of pure water, which is ready to flow to the surface wherever it is tapped. This abundant supply can be reached anywhere in the northern part of the county at about 400 feet, and in the southern part, at probably nowhere more than 600 feet, and in part of it much less than that.

"Gas" wells in the boulder clay are known at two localities. Near the northeast corner of section 3, in Vienna township, a well at twenty feet, gave off so much carbonic acid gas, as to prevent farther excavations. Probably this flowed from some ancient soil, like the muck beds encountered in Livingston and other counties. On section 35 in Nettle Creek township, a well at forty-seven feet, gave off light carburetted hydrogen with so much noise as to be heard at a considerable distance, and in such quantity as to blaze "as high as the house," for some minutes after being approached with a lighted candle. The gas still flows freely, though it is several years since the well was dug, and a load of gravel has been thrown in, to act as a filter for the water, which was at first filled with quicksand, brought up by the ebullition of the gas. Similar phenomena have been observed in other wells in this vicinity. A large spring on section 22 of the same township, constantly gives off bubbles of this gas. Springs of similar character have been found along the outcrop of the lower coal seam in the adjoining county of La Salle, and it is generally accepted as a partial indication of the coal outline, when the depth of drift prevents actual observation.

CHAPTER II.*

PREHISTORIC RACES—EARLIEST TRACES OF MAN—MOUND BUILDERS AND THEIR REMAINS—INDIAN TRIBES—RELATIONS WITH THE WHITES—WAUPONSEE—SHABBONA—NUCQUETTE.

ROBINSON CRUSOE'S unexpected discovery of a human footprint upon the sands of his solitary island, was hardly more startling than have been the discoveries of antiquarians in Europe within the past twenty-five years. Scientific followers of Usher and Petarius, had placed the various migrations of men, the confusion of tongues, the peopling of continents, the development of types—the whole evolution of human society, within the narrow compass of little more than four thousand years, when the discoveries of the geologist and ethnologist developed the trace of human existence dating back to a possible period, 30,000 years ago. Nor are confirmatory evidences to the truth of these discoveries entirely wanting in the *new* world. The gold-drift of California has supplied abundant testimony to the high antiquity of man, and notably the "Pliocene Skull," the popular conception of which is derived more widely, perhaps, from a characteristic poem by Bret Harte than from scientific publications. Explorations in Illinois, Missouri and South Carolina, have yielded similar testimony, and while it should be stated, that in many cases these evidences rest upon the testimony of single observers, and that there is not that recurrence of "finds" which would render "assurance doubly sure," yet there seems to be no doubt in the minds of scientists that the "elder man" was also an inhabitant of this *new* world.

Descending to a later time and one probably falling within the historic period,* we find the more tangible traces of an early race of men. Of this race, named from the character of their remains, the Mound Builders, we find the evidences vastly multiplied, and of such character as to afford means of forming a reasonable conjecture as to their mode of life, their advancement in civilization, and final destiny. These evidences, though first accepted with great distrust, have been so amplified and confirmed by more recent researches, as to leave no room for reasonable doubt as to the former existence of this race. The remains upon which this conclusion is based, "consists," says Mr. Foster, "of tumuli symmetrically raised and often enclosed in mathematical figures, such as the square, the octagon and circle, with long lines of circumvallation; of pits in the solid rocks, and rubbish heaps formed in the prosecution of their mining operations, and of a variety of utensils, wrought in stone or copper, or moulded in clay."† To the

*By J. H. Battle.

* Foster's "Prehistoric Races of the United States."
† "Prehistoric Races, etc."

uninstructed mind these mounds doubtless seem a very slight foundation upon which to construct the fabric of a national existence, and yet to the archæologist they furnish "proofs as strong as Holy Writ;" in them they find as distinctive characteristics as mark the prehistoric remains of the Pelasgi, the "wall-builders" of Europe, a not dissimilar race in many respects, and one who long ago found a place in the realities of history; and while they differ in external form and are scattered over a wide scope of territory, — characteristics in marked contrast with those of the aboriginal race found here in possession of the country, yet the scientist finds in each mound the never failing marks of a race peculiarity.

The widest divergence from the typical mound is found in Wisconsin. Here instead of the circular or pyramidal structure are found forms, for the most part, consisting of rude, gigantic imitations of various animals of the region, such as the buffalo, bear, fox, wolf, etc.; of the eagle and night hawk, the lizard and turtle, and in some instances the unmistakable form of man. These, though not raised high above the surface, and even in some cases represented intaglio, attain the largest dimensions; one representing a serpent extending 700 feet and another representing a turtle, had a body 56, and a tail 250 feet long. The significance of these peculiar forms has not been determined, but unmistakable evidences have been discovered which mark them as the work of the same race whose structures are found elsewhere, so numerous throughout the Mississippi valley. Typical structures are sometimes classified with reference to their purpose as "Enclosures—1. For defense; 2. Sacred; 3. Miscellaneous. Mounds—1. Of sacrifice; 2. For temple sites; 3. Of sepulture; 4. Of observation." Of the first class, the enclosures for defense seem to have been constructed simply for protection against hostile attack. The locations chosen are those best adapted naturally to repel a military attack. The only approach is generally by a steep and narrow way, requiring the assailant to place himself at immense disadvantage, while the garrison provided with parapets often constructed of rubble stone, could fight under cover and may be found in these stones, his store of ammunition. The "sacred" enclosure included within its lines, the mounds of the three leading classes, as the uses to which they were put, were all sacred to this people, and yet in the "American Bottom" in Illinois, where the mound system reaches, perhaps its highest development, the mounds of these classes are not enclosed. The mounds of sacrifice or altars, as they are variously termed, are generally characterized by the fact " that they occur only within the vicinity of the enclosures or sacred places; that they are stratified; and that they contain symmetrical altars of burned clay or stone, on which were deposited various remains, which in all cases have been more or less subjected to the action of fire."* In relation to this latter characteristic it should be said, that it is not at all plain that the use of fire was intended for the purpose of cremation. A thin coating of moist clay was applied to the body nude, or wrapped in cloth, and upon this a fire was maintained

---
* Squier and Davis' "Ancient Monuments," etc.

for a more or less prolonged period, but in many cases the heat was not sufficient to destroy the cloth sometimes found in a good state of preservation. This evidently did not result from a lack of knowledge, as cremation and urn burial was also practiced.

Temple mounds are described by Squier and Davis as "distinguished by their great regularity of form and general large dimensions. They consist chiefly of pyramidal structures, truncated and generally having graded avenues to their tops. In some instances they are terraced or have successive stages. But whatever their form, whether round, oval, octangular, square, or oblong, they have invariably flat or level tops," and upon these were probably constructed their temples, but which, constructed of perishable materials, have left no trace of their existence. This class of mounds are not found along the lake region or that line which seems to mark the farthest advance of this people. The principal structures of this class are found at Cahokia in Illinois, near Florence and Claiborne in Kentucky, at Seltzertown, Mississippi, at Marietta, Newark and Chillicothe in Ohio, and at St. Louis, Missouri. The mound at Cahokia, "the monarch of all similar structures in the United States," may well serve as a type. When in all its integrity, this mound formed a huge parallelogram with sides at the base, respectively 700 and 500 feet in length, towering to the height of 90 feet. On the southwest there was a terrace 160 by 300 feet, which was reached by a graded way, and the summit was truncated, affording a platform 200 by 450 feet. This structure, upon which was probably reared a spacious temple, perhaps the principal one in the empire, covered an area of about six acres, while in close proximity were four elevated platforms, varying from 250 to 300 feet in diameter. The great mound of St. Louis reached a height of thirty-five feet, and that at Marietta to about the same height.

"Sepulchral mounds," says Mr. Foster in his volume on the Prehistoric Races, "consist, often, of a simple knoll, or group of knolls, of no considerable height, without any definite arrangement. Examples of this character may be seen at Dubuque, Merom, Chicago, and Laporte, which, on exploration, have yielded skulls differing widely from the Indian type. * * * The corpse was almost invariably placed near the original surface of the soil, enveloped in bark or coarse matting, and in a few instances fragments of cloth have been observed in this connection. Sometimes a vault of timber was built over it, and in others it was enclosed in long and broad flags of stone. Sometimes it was placed in a sitting position, again it was extended, and still again it was compressed within contracted limits. Trinkets were often strung about the neck, and water jugs, drinking cups, and vases, which probably contained food, were placed near the head. Over the corpse thus arrayed, a circular mound was often raised, but sometimes nothing more than a hillock." Other mounds have been found that favored the theory that many of these structures were used for miscellaneous burial. A notable example is the "Grave Creek Mound," in West Virginia, twelve miles below Wheeling. This mound is something over 70 feet high, of circular form, with a circumference at the base of about 900 feet. In the center of this mound, on a level with the original surface, was found a vault with twelve human skeletons, and thirty-four feet above this was found a similar vault, enclosing a skeleton which had been decorated with a profusion of shell-beads, copper rings, and plates of mica. In a mound at Vincennes "a bed of human bones, arranged in a circle eighteen feet in diameter, closely packed and pressed together." In another at Merom, three tiers of vaults were found, in each of which were found from five to seven human skeletons. Mounds of observation is a rather fanciful classification intended to mark mounds found on elevated points of land. The authors of this classification think that these may have been used as platforms on which to build signal fires, and such is their elevation and outlook that such signals could have been seen at great distance. This theory of a special purpose, however, has not been accepted, as supported by any special evidence. They may have been so used, or simply as an eligible site for residence.

There is in addition to these mounds a large number which are not embraced in this classification, which following Mr. F. W. Putnam, whom Mr. Foster quotes at length, may be called "Habitation Mounds." A large number of these are described as located at Merom, Indiana, and "a group of fifty-nine mounds" at Hutsonville, Illinois, a few miles above the former place and across the Wabash River. These mounds were carefully examined "to ascertain if they were places of burial," without discovering a single bone or implement of any kind, but, on the contrary, the excavations "showed that the mounds had been made of various materials at hand, and in one case ashes were found which had probably been scraped up with other material and thrown upon the heap." In the ancient fort at Merom, in *depressions* found within the earthworks, were found striking evidences of food having been cooked and eaten there, and the conclusion drawn by Mr. Putnam is, "that these pits were the homes of the inhabitants or defenders of the fort, who were probably further protected from the elements and the arrows of assailants, by a roof of logs and bark, or boughs." Another writer,[*] in a paper read before the American Association for the Advancement of Science at their Boston meeting, August, 1880, says: "There is in this region a peculiar class of mounds that was for a long time a puzzle to me. They are usually found in groups of from two or three to twenty or thirty, and even more, and are generally on some pleasant knoll or rising ground in the vicinity of a spring or watercourse, especially in the vicinity of our prairies or level areas of land. These mounds are from one to three, and in a few instances, even four feet in height, and from twenty to fifty feet in diameter. One mound of the group is always larger than the rest, and always occupies the commanding position. Sometimes the group is arranged in a circle; other groups have no apparent design in arrangement. Numbers of these mounds can be seen in the cultivated fields.

"Although I have made excavations in them, and dug trenches entirely through them, I have found nothing but ashes, charcoal, decayed portions of bones of fishes and animals partially burned, shells from the adjacent streams, flint chippings, and

---

[*] Hon. Wm. McAdams, Jr., of Otterville, Ills.

in one or two instances a flint implement of a rude character.

"After examining many of these structures I am induced to believe that they are possibly the remains of ancient dwellings, made by placing in an upright position the trunks of young trees in a circle, or in parallel rows, the tops of the poles inclining inward and fastened together, the whole being covered with earth and sod to form a roof, or in the same manner as many Indian tribes make their mud lodges; as for instance, the Mandans and the Omahas. Such a structure, after being repaired from time to time by the addition of more earth on top, would finally, by the decay of the poles, fall inward and the ruins would form a slight mound.

"Conant and Putnam describe such mounds in Missouri and Tennessee, some of the largest of these ancient towns being provided with streets and highways. They are also found in Southern Illinois, Indiana and Ohio. Putnam has described an enclosed town in Tennessee, in which were many low mounds, or rather, as he calls them, earth circles, that he has pretty conclusively shown to be sites of the lodges or houses of the people."

To which of these classes the mounds found at Morris shall be referred, is difficult to determine. There were nineteen of these mounds, circular in form, from two to four feet high, and from seventeen to thirty in diameter at the base. These were superficially explored and evidences of the *intrusive* burials of Indians found, but nothing bearing upon their ancient origin. The growth of the village has encroached upon these ancient relics and their site so obliterated as to afford little inducement for any scientific investigation. There are mounds along the southern margin of the river that offer better prospects of reward to a properly conducted research, but at best such exploration is likely to develop little more than to connect their origin with this ancient people.

These mounds, with the implements formed in stone, metal and pottery (of which the scope of this work allows no mention), form the data upon which is founded the historical speculation concerning this people. Once having reasonably established the former existence of this extinct race, the absorbing question presents itself—who were the Mound Builders? The limited space devoted to this subject, however, forbids any extended consideration of the interesting scientific deductions made from this data, though the conclusion arrived at may be briefly stated in the language of Mr. Foster,* as follows: "Their monuments indicate that they had entered upon a career of civilization; they lived in stationary communities, cultivating the soil and relying on its generous yield as a means of support; they clothed themselves in part at least, in garments regularly spun and woven; they modeled clay and carved stone, even of the most obdurate character, into images representing animate objects, even the human face and form, with a close adherence to nature; they mined and cast copper into a variety of useful forms; they quarried mica, steatite, chert, and the novaculite slates, which they wrought into articles adapted to personal ornament, to domestic use, or to the chase; unlike the Indians who were ignorant of the curative proper-

---

*"Prehistoric Races," etc., p. 350.

ties of salt, they collected the brine of the salines into earthen vessels moulded in baskets which they evaporated into a form which admitted of transportation; they erected an elaborate line of defense, stretching for many hundred miles, to guard against the sudden irruption of enemies; they had a national religion, in which the elements were the objects of supreme adoration; temples were erected upon the platform mounds, and watchfires lighted upon the highest summits; and in the celebration of the mysteries of their faith, human sacrifices were probably offered up. The magnitude of their structures, involving an infinitude of labor, such only as could be expended except in a community where cheap food prevailed, and the great extent of their commercial relations reaching to widely separated portions of the continent, imply the existence of a stable and efficient government, based on the subordination of the masses. As the civilizations of the old world growing out of the peculiar conditions of soil and climate developed certain forms of art which are original and unique, so on this continent we see the crude conception in the truncated pyramid, as first displayed in Wisconsin, Ohio and Illinois, and the accomplished result in the stonefaced foundations of the temples of Uxmal and Palenque. And finally, the distinctive character of the Mound Builder's structures, and also the traditions which have been preserved, would indicate that this people were expelled from the Mississippi Valley by a fierce and barbarous race, and that they found refuge in the more genial climate of Central America, where they developed those germs of civilization, originally planted in their northern homes, into a perfection which has elicited the admiration of every modern explorer."

The obvious inquiry suggested by these conclusions is, who succeeded this extinct race? To this question science offers no answer. Two hypotheses are entertained as to the origin of Mound Builders here, the one supposes them to be of autothionic origin, and that semi-civilization originating here flowed southward and culminated in the wonderful developments of the Toltecs of Mexico; the other supposes to have originated in the South American continent or in Central America, and to have emigrated northward from natural causes, and later to have returned to Mexico, driven from their northern empire by an irresistible foe or by a powerful political irruption among themselves. Upon any theory, the line of their most northward advance is pretty clearly defined, and writers upon this subject generally agree that the line of defenses "extending from sources of the Alleghany and Susquehanna, in New York, diagonally across the country, through central and northern Ohio, to the Wabash," accurately indicates the region from whence attacks were made or expected, and marks the farthest extent of the Mound Builders' empire. But what was the character of the foe, what his action on the retreat of the Mound Builders, and what his final destiny, is an unwritten page of science, and for which there exists no known data. It is a late suggestion, that the North American Indian may be a degenerate but legitimate descendant of the dominant race, but there is a broad chasm to be bridged before the Mound Builder or his successful assailant can be linked with these aboriginal tribes. Without making any such attempt, however, the Indian naturally succeeds this people in regular historical order, and passing over the vexed question of his origin, it is sufficient for the purposes of this work that the whites found him everywhere in full possession of the country.

With the advent of the white man in America, began an "irrepressible conflict" which was destined never to cease so long as the red man retained a vestige of power. In this struggle, the absence of national organization or affiliations on the part of the Indians, made the final success of the whites inevitable from the beginning. Taking each tribe or section of country in succession, the little band of adventurers conquered this vast country in detail, and planted here one of the mighty nations of the world. It was due to this lack of any bond of union that the Illinois tribes were allowed to rest so long undisturbed in their fancied security. Rumors of the conflict waging on the Atlantic border were borne to their ears by chance visitors from other tribes, and later by remnants of vanquished tribes who sought with them an asylum from their foes, but still no apprehension of impending disaster dawned upon their superstitions ignorance, while the reflection that the Iroquois, the enemy which their experience had taught them most to fear, had met an overpowering foe, gave them no little satisfaction.

The great family to which these tribes were allied by language, physical and mental peculiarities, was the Algonquin. Before the encroachments of the whites the numerous tribes of this family occupied most of the territory now embraced in the United States, between the 35th and 60th parallels of latitude, and the 60th and 105th meridians of longitude. According to Davidson,* the starting point in the wanderings of the Algonquin tribes on the continent as determined by tradition and the cultivation of maize, their favorite cereal, was in the southwest. Passing up the western side of the Mississippi valley, they turned eastward across that river, the southern margin of their broad tract reaching about to the 35th parallel, while the center probably covered the present territory of Illinois. On reaching the Atlantic coast they seem to have moved northeasterly along the seaboard to the mouth of the St. Lawrence; thence ascending this river and the shores of the great lakes, they spread northward and westward to Hudson Bay, the basin of Lake Winnipeg and the valley of the upper Mississippi; and thence the head of the migratory column circling around the source of the great river, recrossed it in a southeasterly direction above the Falls of St. Anthony, and passing by way of Green Bay and Lake Michigan came into the present limits of Illinois, Indiana and Ohio. Thus after revolving in an irregular ellipse of some 3,000 miles in diameter, they fell into the original track eastward. This extended course of migration induced by a variety of causes and circumstances, continued through a long period, the original stock probably receiving considerable accessions from the nomadic tribes of the Pacific slope, and leaving behind large numbers at each remove, until the head of the column came to rest from sheer lack of momentum or other moving influences. Thus scattered over a large

---

*Davidson and S. ueve's "History of Illinois."

expanse of country, and broken into numerous tribal organizations, they lost much of their family affiliations and characteristics, and the early whites found the Algonquins everywhere possessing the border lands, and waged with them their first and bloodiest wars. Situated within the ellipse above described, were the nations of the Iroquois family, who held together by circumstances and posted advantageously on the inner side of the circle, able at any time to mass their forces upon a single point of the circumference, soon proved a devastating scourge to the Indian world, and especially so to the Algonquins.

Of the tribes of this latter family this history has to do only with the tribes of the "Illinois Confederation." This was made up of the Tamaroas, Michigamies, Kaskaskias, Cahokias and Peorias. The name of the confederation, as explained by Gallatin, one of the ablest writers on the structure of Indian languages, is derived from the Delaware word Leno, and variously written Leni or Illini, meaning "superior men." Its present termination is of French origin. The Algonquin family, so far as cranial indications, were marked by a larger intellectual lobe than their great adversaries, the Iroquois, and their whole history adds force to these indications. While not so ferocious or fiendish in their warfare, they exhibited no less bravery and skill in their savage encounters, and were rewarded with no less success when circumstances admitted an equal contest. In courageous resistance to the superior numbers and arms of the whites and in savage strategy and diplomacy, the history of our Indian wars bears ample testimony to their high mental and physical qualities. Of the Illinois Confederation, however, this can not be said without qualification. Exposed like the rest of the Algonquin family to the powerful attacks of their ferocious enemy, though gaining some notable victories, they had been forced to leave their earlier location near Lake Michigan and settle west of the Mississippi, from whence, about 1670-73, they migrated to the Illinois River. Here they seem to have stood in great fear of their hereditary foe, and while proving their warlike superiority to *other* tribes, their only sure defense against the Iroquois appeared to be in flight. The early association of this confederacy with the whites was of an unusually peaceable and pleasant nature and did much to confirm their unwarlike character. As early as 1670, the Jesuit Missionary, Marquette, stationed at the western extremity of Lake Superior, mentions the visit of members of these tribes who earnestly requested that missionaries might be sent among them. When, therefore, Joliet and Marquette, returning from their exploration of the Mississippi, found the tribes on the banks of the Illinois in 1673, they were hailed with joy by the natives, who from that day never wavered in their allegiance to the French. In 1675, Marquette returned and established the "Mission of the Immaculate Conception" at their village, located near the present site of Utica. In December of 1679, La Salle* with his little band of adventurers found here a town of 460 lodges temporarily deserted, and passing on to where the city of Peoria now is, found another village of about eighty lodges, where he landed and soon established amicable and permanent relations. With the consent of the tribes, La Salle soon built the fort of

---

* Réné—Robert Cavelier, Sieur de la Salle.

Crevecœur, a half a league below, and then early in March of 1680, set out for Fort Frontenac in Western New York, and thence to Montreal to repair the loss of his vessel, the Griffin.

In the meanwhile the Jesuit faction, engaged in fierce competition with him in securing the peltry trade of the Indians, and jealous of La Salle's success, and the English of the Atlantic border, striving to overreach the French in securing both territory and trade, united in stirring up the Iroquois to assault La Salle's Illinois allies in his absence. "Suddenly," says Parkman, "the village was awakened from its lethargy as by the crash of a thunderbolt. A Shawanoe, lately here on a visit, had left his Illinois friends to return home. He now reappeared, crossing the river in hot haste with the announcement that he had met on his way an army of Iroquois approaching to attack them. All was panic and confusion. The lodges disgorged their frightened inmates; women and children screamed; startled warriors snatched their weapons. There were less than five hundred of them, for the greater part of the young men had gone to war." Here Tonti, La Salle's able lieutenant, left in charge of the fort, found himself weakened by the early desertion of most of his force, and now an object of suspicion to his allies, in an awkward and dangerous predicament. Undaunted by the untoward circumstances, he joined the Illinois, and when the Iroquois came upon the scene, in the midst of the savage melee, faced the 580 warriors and declared that the Illinois were under the protection of the French King and the Governor of Canada, and demanded that they should be left in peace, backing his words with the statement that there were 1,200 of the Illinois and 60 Frenchmen across the river. These representations had the effect of checking the ardor of the attacking savages, and a temporary truce was effected. It was evident that the truce was but a ruse on the part of the Iroquois to gain an opportunity to test the truth of Tonti's statements, and no sooner had the Illinois retired to their village on the north side of the river than numbers of the invading tribes, on the pretext of seeking food, crossed the river and gathered in increasing numbers about the village. The Illinois knew the design of their foe too well, and, hastily embarking, they set fire to their lodges, and retired down the river, when the whole band of Iroquois crossed over, and finished their work of havoc at their leisure. The Illinois, in the meanwhile, lulled into a false security, divided into small bands in search of food. One of their tribes, the Tamoroas, "had the fatuity to remain near the mouth of the Illinois, where they were assailed by all the force of the Iroquois. The men fled, and very few of them were killed; but the women and children were captured to the number, it is said, of seven hundred," many of whom were put to death with horrible tortures. Soon after the retreat of the Illinois, the Iroquois discovered the deception of the Frenchmen, and only the wholesome fear they had of the French Governor's power restrained their venting their rage upon Tonti and his two or three companions. As it was, they were dismissed, and bidden to return to Canada.

It was in the wake of these events that La Salle returned in the winter of 1680 and found this once populous village devastated and deserted, surrounded by the frightful evidences of savage carnage. Disheartened but not cast down, he at once set about repairing his fortunes. Discerning at once the means and object of his enemies he set about building up a bulwark to stay a second assault. Returning to Fort Miami on the St. Joseph, by the borders of Lake Michigan, he sought to form a defensive league among the Indians whom he proposed to colonize on the site of the destroyed village of the Illinois. He found ready material at hand in remnants of tribes fresh from fields of King Phillip's war; he visited the Miamis and by his wonderful power won them over to his plans; and then in the interval, before the tribes could arrange for their emigration, he launched out with a few followers and hurriedly explored the Mississippi to the Gulf. Returning to Michillimackinac in September, 1682, where he had found Tonti in May of the previous year, La Salle, after directing his trusty lieutenant to repair to the Illinois, prepared to return to France for further supplies for his proposed colony, but learning that the Iroquois were planning another incursion, he returned to the site of the destroyed village and with Tonti began in December, 1682, to build the Fort of St. Louis on the eminence which is now known in history as "starved rock." Thus the winter passed, and in the meanwhile, La Salle found employment for his active mind in conducting the negotiations which should result in reconciling the Illinois and the Miamis and in cementing the various tribes into a harmonious colony. The spring crowned his efforts with complete success. "La Salle looked down from his rocks on a concourse of wild human life. Lodges of bark and rushes, or cabins of logs, were clustered on the open plain, or along the edges of the bordering forests. Squaws labored, warriors lounged in the sun, naked children whooped and gamboled on the grass. Beyond the river, a mile and a half on the left, the banks were studded once more with the lodges of the Illinois, who, to the number of six thousand, had returned, since their defeat, to this their favorite dwelling-place. Scattered along the valley, among the adjacent hills, or over the neighboring prairie, were the cantonments of a half score of other tribes, and fragments of tribes, gathered under the protecting aegis of the French,—Shawanoes, from the Ohio, Abenakis from Maine, and Miamis from the sources of the Kankakee."* In the meanwhile, a party was sent to Montreal to secure supplies and munitions to put the colony in a state of defense, which to the disappointment and chagrin of the sorely beset leader, he learned had been detained by his enemies, who by a change of Governors had come into official power. Devolving the com-

* "Discovery of the Great West." Third part. Franquelin's map finished in 1684 and reproduced in part in this work, adds some further particulars which may be of local interest. From the location of the tribes on this map, it is ascertained that the Indian colony of La Salle, numbering, according to his representation to the French ministry, "about four thousand warriors or twenty thousand souls," occupied the country bordering both sides of the Illinois, from the present site of Morris to the junction of the Big Bureau Creek. Of the tribes represented, the Illinois proper numbered 1,200 warriors; the Miamis, 1,300; the Shawanoes, 200; the Weas, 500; the Pepikokia, 160; the Kilatica, 300; Onabona, 70; the Piankishaws, 150; in all, 3,880 warriors. This latter tribe occupied the present site of Morris village, while northeastwardly to the margin of the lake, the country was occupied by the Kickapoos, and other friendly tribes.

mand of the enterprise upon his faithful lieutenant, La Salle set out in November, 1683, for Canada and France, where he hoped to thwart his enemies and snatch success from the very jaws of defeat. Triumphant over his enemies, he returned to America in 1685, and after wandering ineffectually for two years in the inhospitable wilderness of Texas, fell dead, pierced through the brain by the bullet of a treacherous desperado of his own band. It was not until the latter part of 1688, that Tonti with grief and indignation learned of the death of La Salle. In 1690, Tonti received from the French government the proprietorship of Fort St. Louis on the Illinois, where he continued in command until 1702, when by royal order the fort was abandoned and Tonti transferred to lower Louisiana. This fort was afterward re-occupied for a short time in 1718, by a party of traders, when it was finally abandoned.

Hitherto, the Indians, faithful to the French, found vent for their savage nature in warfare upon their fellows, but events were rapidly hurrying forward the time when this state of affairs should be reversed. In turn the French power here gave way to the English, and they to the Americans; these momentous changes manifesting themselves to the Indian world in little more than the change of the national ensign on Fort Chartres. Upon the savages, however, a subtle change had been wrought. Unwillingly released from their fealty to the French, they became the fatal cats-paw of the warring whites. Incited by the French to hostilities against the English, they easily turned against the Americans under the influence of British goods and gold. Other influences were powerfully moving them to fulfill their destiny. The success of the American colonies in their war with the mother country, brought them in contact with the natives of the "far west." The whole Indian world viewed their conquests with alarm, and when the restless tide of emigration reached the natural boundary of the Ohio, tribal animosities were forgotten in the united struggle to hold the insatiable pale-faces at bay. In the meantime, the abandonment of Fort St. Louis followed by the removal of Kaskaskia and the erection of Fort Chartres had drawn the remnant which their savage enemies had left of the Illinois Confederation, to the southern part of the State, while their deserted lands were occupied by the Sacs and Foxes, Pottawattomies and other tribes which the success of the Americans had forced to find a new home.

The first cession of territory demanded of the tribes here was made by the treaty of Greenville, O., in 1795, consisting of "one piece of land, six miles square, at the mouth of Chicago River, emptying into the southwest end of Lake Michigan, where a fort formerly stood;" one piece 12 miles square near the mouth of the Illinois River; and one piece 6 miles square, at the old Peoria Fort and Village, near the south end of the Illinois Lake, on the said Illinois River."* In 1803 by a treaty at Vincennes the greater part of southern Illinois was ceded by the Illinois Confederation and other tribes; and by a treaty in the following year signed at St. Louis, the Sacs and Foxes ceded a great tract of country on

---

*At these points the National Government subsequently erected Forts.

both sides of the Mississippi, extending on the east bank from the mouth of the Illinois River to the head of that river, and thence to the Wisconsin River. In 1816 a treaty was concluded with the "united tribes of Ottawas, Chippewas and Pottawattomies," at St. Louis. The treaty recites: "Whereas, a serious dispute has for some time existed between the contracting parties relative to the right to a part of the lands ceded to the United States by the tribes of Sacs and Foxes, on the third of November, 1804, and both parties being desirous of preserving a harmonious and friendly intercourse, and of establishing permanent peace and friendship, have for the purpose of removing all difficulties, agreed to the following terms:" etc. The boundaries established by this treaty are the only ones that have found a place upon the published county maps of the State. The territory ceded is marked by lines drawn from a point on Lake Michigan ten miles north, and south of the mouth of Chicago Creek, and following the general direction of the Desplaines to a point north of the Illinois on the Fox River, ten miles from its mouth, and similarly on the south on the Kankakee River. This treaty, it will be observed, ceded only that part of Grundy County north of the river. In 1818, however, the Pottawatomies ceded the larger part of their remaining possessions in Illinois, and with other territory, the balance of Grundy County. The Indians did not at once abandon the territory thus ceded, but under a provision of these treaties lived and hunted here for years, while numerous reservations in favor of individuals and families made these relics of a peculiar race, like the dying embers of a great fire, a familiar sight for years to many of the present generation.

The Indians found in and about Grundy County by the first settlers, were bands of the Pottawatomie tribe, and while owning but little allegiance to any chief, recognized in Shabbona and Wauponsee the representatives of tribal authority. The band of the latter made their home at one time on the Illinois River, near the mouth of Mazon Creek, in Grundy County, but in 1824 they moved to Paw Paw Grove. Wauponsee is represented as a large, muscular man, fully six feet and three inches in height. His head presented an unusual feature for an Indian, being entirely bald save a small scalp lock at the crown. In manner he was markedly reserved and gave frequent evidences of an untamed savage disposition that needed only an opportunity to lapse into the cruel barbarity of earlier years.

He was a war-chief and claimed to be one hundred years old, though this statement was but little credited by the whites. With the rest of his nation he was engaged in the battle of Tippecanoe and other Indian demonstrations in the following years. He is credited by some as being the *Waubunsee* who befriended the family of Kinzie after the massacre at Fort Dearborn, but while such action, inconsistent as it is with the part he would naturally take in the attack upon the retreating garrison, it is not without parallel in Indian history. However, the strong impression is that these are two individuals. He moved with his band to the government reservations in the "far West" in 1839, signalizing his departure with a deed of barbarous cruelty that characterizes his memory here. This occurred in October, 1839, and is described by L. W. Claypool, who had ample facilities for learning the truth, as follows: "James McKeen residing on the north bank of the Kankakee River, a mile above the mouth, with a hired man, John Byers, had been burning logs in the afternoon. Some Indians asked the privilege of camping there for the night, which was readily granted. In the evening they gathered in to the camp to the number of some fifty, bringing a supply of whiskey. Soon Wauponsee and his family came, having camped the night before near our place (S. W. ¼ Sec. 20, 33, 7). My father and visited his camp, as he was leaving in the morning, and curiously observed their preparations for moving. His family consisted of one wife, of middle age—very attentive to his wants, adjusting pillows on his pack-saddle and assisting him on a stump to mount his pony; an old squaw—a wife evidently not in favor; a son, sixteen or eighteen years old; son-in-law with wife and two or three children; and two slave squaws, poor, miserable, forlorn-looking wretches in every respect.

"After supper McKeen and Byers went out to the fires where the Indians were having a drunken frolic. On approaching the Indians, they found a crowd of savages about a log heap, with one of the slave squaws lying on the ground near the fire, Wauponsee stooping over her and talking in a low voice. Immediately after he gave a signal when the other slave came up, and buried a squaw-ax into the brains of the unfortunate victim. The body was removed to a pile of rails lying near, and being joined by other Indians the orgie was continued far into the night. In the morning the Indians broke camp and went on their way, when McKeen and Byers buried the unfortunate squaw on the banks of the Kankakee.

"The prevailing opinion here as to the reason for the deed, was that Wauponsee, realizing the truth of the old adage, 'Dead men tell no tales,' and that as their new reservation in the west joined that of the Winnebagos, to which tribe the squaw originally belonged, fearing that her relatives might be moved to avenge her ill treatment received at his hands, ordered her execution, and thus 'took a bond of fate.'" Waubonsie is said to have been killed by a party of the Sacs and Foxes for opposing them in the "Black Hawk War." "His scalp was taken off, the body mutilated, and left on the prairie to be devoured by wolves."*

Shabbona, who shares with Shakespeare the distinction of having his name spelled in an endless number of ways, was born of Ottawa parents, on the Kankakee river in Will County, about 1775. In his youth he married the daughter of a Pottawatomie chief, who had his village on the Illinois a short distance above the mouth of the Fox River. Here at the death of Spotka, his father-in-law, he succeeded to the chieftainship of the band, which soon sought a more salubrious spot, and settled in De Kalb County, where he was found by the early settlers. Shabbona seems to have lacked none of those qualities which were required to command the respect and confidence of his band and yet he was possessed of rare discernment and decision of character, which led him early to see that war with the whites was hopeless, and that the only hope

---

*"Memories of Shaubena," by N. Matson.

of the savage was to make the best terms possible with the inevitable. To this policy, he was one of the first of his people to give earnest support, and once committed to this line of action, he allowed no influence, however strong, to swerve him from it for a moment.

He was easily influenced by the eloquence of Tecumseh, and became an ardent admirer and devoted personal attendant of that celebrated warrior. He was absent from the battle of Tippecanoe with Tecumseh, and returned only to hear of the massacre at Fort Dearborn, and to assist in the defense of Kinzie on the following night. Believing that his nation would join the British in the war of 1812, he joined his hero-warrior, and acted as aid to Tecumseh until the latter was killed. In the general pacification of the tribes after this war, Shabbona seems to have imbibed his peace policy, to which he ever afterward adhered. While not gifted as an orator, his reputation for honesty, fidelity to his nation, and good judgment, gave him a wide influence among the more warlike of his people, and in 1827, he rendered valuable service to the whites in dissuading the Pottawatomie nation from joining the Winnebago war. In 1832, when Black Hawk strove to unite the Indian nations in a combined attack upon the whites, he met a fatal obstacle in the influence of Shabbona for peace. Notwithstanding every influence and inducement brought to bear upon him, the "white man's friend" stood firm, and was largely influential in bringing the aid of the Pottawatomies to the white forces. Subsequently, when "Black Hawk was betrayed into hostilities, and the news of the Indians' first blow and success reached him,

he sent his son and nephew in different directions, while he went in still another, to warn the settlers of the impending danger, thus saving the lives of many in the isolated settlements, a service for which he suffered the loss of his son and nephew at the hand of the enraged Sacs and Foxes years afterward. In the military operations which followed with Waubonsie, "Billy Caldwell" and a considerable number of warriors, he enlisted with the army under Gen. Atkinson, who at once placed him in command of the Indian contingent. After performing valued service, he retired with his band at the close of the war, to his village in De Kalb County, where they remained to the date of their removal to the West in 1836.

In consideration of his services the national government, beside many other tokens of esteem, reserved a tract of land for his use at Shabbona's Grove, and granted him a pension of $200 per annum. In the summer of 1836, however, the Indian agent notified him that his band must go to the lands assigned them in the West, as none but himself and family could remain on the reservation. Much as he regretted to leave the scenes of his manhood, about which gathered his dearest memories, he could not consent to a separation from his band, and so in September, the whole band came to Main Bureau Creek, and camping at the crossing of the Peoria and Galena road, they remained here about six weeks hunting and fishing. The government proposed to bear the expense of their removal as in the case of other tribes, but Shabbona rejecting this offer, set out one October day with his band of about one hundred and forty-two souls and one hundred and sixty ponies, for their lands in Western Kansas.

Not long after this the government moved the Sacs and Foxes from the reservation in Iowa to lands adjoining the Pottawatomies. These tribes entertained the bitterest hostility against Shabbona for the part he took in the Black Hawk War, and Neopope, a chief of these tribes, had sworn to accomplish the destruction of the "white man's friend," together with his son and nephew. In the fall of 1837, Shabbona with his son and nephew and a few hunters went out on the plains to hunt buffalo, when without the slightest apprehension of danger they found themselves attacked by a band of the Sacs. Shabbona with his son Smoke and four hunters escaped, but knowing that a relentless Nemesis was on his track, he left his band and returned with his family to his reservation in De Kalb County; this consisted of 1,280 acres, most of which was fine timbered land. A clause of the treaty conveyed this, and other reservations granted them in fee simple, but the Senate struck out this clause making the property only a reservation. This fact escaped the notice of Shabbona, and in 1845 he sold the larger part of his land and returned to Kansas to visit his band. It was soon discovered by designing persons that this transfer was illegal, and on the strength of representations made at Washington, the authorities declared the reservation vacant and the transfer void. On his return in 1851, he found his whole property sequestered and himself homeless. This grove had been his home for nearly fifty years; here he had made the grave of his first squaw and two papooses, and here he had expected to lay his own bones. It was natural that he should feel a deep sense of injury at this ungrateful requital of devotion to the white race; but this was a new generation, the reservation had been technically abandoned, and none were greatly wronged save the Indian, who had not yet excited the romantic or humanitarian interest of a later day, and brokenhearted he went out to a retired place to implore the Great Spirit, after the fashion of his tribe.

The case excited the interest of his early friends, who purchased a small tract of improved land, with house, out-buildings and fencing, situated on the bank of the Illinois near Seneca in Grundy County. Here he lived in a wigwam, his family occupying the house, until his death, at the age of eighty-four, on July 17, 1859. His remains were laid in lot 59, block 7, in the Morris cemetery with elaborate ceremony and grateful regard of the whole county. Here rest also eight of his family, five of whom were his children or grandchildren.

Shortly after his death his family removed to their nation in the West, and while his land is held by the County Court in trust for the benefit of his heirs, there is no monument to mark the memory* of one whom General Cass once introduced to a distinguished audience at Washington as, "Shabbona, the greatest red man of the

---

*There is in the Court House at Morris, a fine life sized oil portrait of Shabbona, representing him standing and arrayed in a dress coat, presented to him at Washington —— supplemented by Indian finery, which gives him a picturesque but noble appearance. This picture is still the property of the artist, and it is to be regretted that the State or National authorities do not see fit to place it in a position to which its artistic merit and the high character of the subject richly entitle it.

West." His grandson, Smoke, is supposed to be acting as chief of his nation at this time.

An Indian relic which has given rise to many conjectures, is a cedar pole about six inches in diameter at the base, and from twenty to twenty-five feet in height standing in the center of the largest of the ancient mounds found in the village of Morris. The pole stands at the lower end of Wauponsee street, its base protected by a close fitting piece of flagging, and surrounded by an iron fence. The universal respect on the part of the citizens for this monument of the past is, however, its surest protection. None of the Indians with whom the early settlers came in contact could give satisfactory accounts of its erection (indeed they did not claim to know), until the engineers who surveyed the line of the canal made some investigations in this mound. Some members of this party made some unauthorized explorations, and were rewarded by the discovery of some interesting Indian remains. The engineering party was subsequently joined by an Indian named Clark, who evidently belonged to the extinct Illinois nation, and of him Mr. A. J. Matthewson, the engineer in charge, obtained much valuable information, which he has embodied in a letter to L. W. Claypool, of Morris. By permission, the portion bearing upon matters of interest to this county is given as follows: Speaking of Clark, "when asked, he said—'Yes, the bones dug up at the cedar pole belonged to Nucquette, a celebrated chief who was killed upon the ground and buried in a dug-out'—a kind of rude trough which our boys found in 1837, and from which they took the bones, a bit of red rust which had once been a knife blade, and circular ornaments in silver. His squaw, who died years after, lay beside him, her blanket intact, with a profusion of silver brooches and silver rings with green glass sets, upon the bones of two or three fingers of each hand. The threads of the blanket would crumble upon touch, and yet the teeth and hair seemed nearly perfect. The pole, a red cedar, was very old, full of curious cuts and marks, giving in a rude way, as Clark said, the exploits of Nucquette. This brute had a story of his cruelties noted upon that pole, but the poor slave of a squaw lay there without a word being said of her. *She* was laid in her blanket,—nothing more.

"I had found a curious mound at the west side of a small grove, north of the old river stage road and a little west of south from Seneca, and upon asking Clark about the stones carelessly thrown about it he said: 'Oh, yes, that was a very bad Indian! Steal horses, etc. They killed him; put him in this old mound by himself,' and then when any Indian passed the mound he felt bound to show his contempt for the outcast who would not, or did not take *scalps*—but *horses* (he was a *horse fancier*), and before reaching the place they would pick up finger stones and cast them upon the mound and spit upon it, showing their utter contempt for his want of good taste while living.

"Clark said Nucquette was killed in battle—that the fight began at Blue Island. The Illinois tribe retreated, and again had a fight three miles east of Joliet, at a village on north bank of Hickory Creek, where Oakwood cemetery now is, then a retreat and a hard fight at Nettle Creek (Morris), the Indian name for which has escaped me; then a retreat and pursuit as far as Starve Rock, where Clark gave a description of the siege and the daring conduct of the devoted band, rushing up to the very edge of the cliff to challenge the foe to combat. Of course, these were the acts of a few men in a desperate situation, but when relating these things the eyes of Clark, usually mild enough, would assume a ferocious appearance quite shocking. He was evidently a friend of the weaker party. He gave also the exploits of a very few who escaped down the Illinois River in a skiff and were pursued for days, though finally escaping. Those left upon Starve Rock generally perished. * * *

"In regard to the cedar pole, Clark told me the tribe or some of them came at times, as late as 1837-8, to replace the white flag upon the pole, when the winds had blown it away. Our men went on the sly to dig about the cedar pole in the mound, and upon their return to camp were told decidedly to go back and fix the mound and the pole, and to leave everything as they found it or there would be trouble; that the savages were then about, and that they would miss their top-knots by delay. I went back with them to see the order executed, and it was. We had no trouble with the Indians on account of the act."*

---

* Mr. Matthewson adds: "The death of Nucquette was probably between 1680 and 1700, and the cedar pole may have been placed there at that time." This date is not probably derived from the narrative of Clark. The description of the series of Indian engagements and the incident of Starve Rock corresponds with the historical account of the exterminating war waged by the Pottawatomies and their allies against the Illinois to avenge the murder of Pontiac by one of the latter nation at Cahokia in 1769. It is possible that Nucquette fell in a series of conflicts with the Iroquois, and that Clark confused the traditions of these fights with those which terminated at Starve Rock. Even the later date gives the pole a respectable antiquity.

CHAPTER III.*

EARLY FRENCH SETTLEMENTS—FRONTIER SETTLEMENTS IN LA SALLE AND GRUNDY COUNTIES—CIVILIZED LIFE IN A NEW COUNTRY—POLITICAL ORGANIZATION—FORMATION OF GRUNDY COUNTY—COUNTY BUILDINGS.

"IN southern Illinois near the Mississippi, a hundred miles or more above the mouth of the Ohio, is situated the ancient village of Kaskaskia, supposed to be the oldest permanent European settlement in the valley of the Father of Waters,"† but while thus attaining an unparalleled eminence in one particular, it must not be supposed that the whole State permanently shared in this distinction. Though thus promised with an early dawn of civilization in the latter part of the 17th century, the promise proved illusive before the march of greater events, and the bright flush of a hoped-for day paled into the darker obscurity of a more savage barbarism.

In 1700, the settlement of the French and Indians at old Kaskaskia was removed to the spot where the village of that name now stands; two years later followed the abandonment of Fort St. Louis on the Illinois; and in 1718, the erection of Fort Chartres on the Mississippi, sixteen miles above the former village, confirmed the tendency of the white population to concentrate in the southern part of the State. About the fort, rapidly sprang up a village

*By J. H. Battle.
†Paper read before Chicago Hist. Soc., by Edward G. Mason, 1879.

which was subsequently called New Chartres ; five miles away the village of Prairie du Rocher became a growing settlement, while all along the river between Kaskaskia and the fort a strong chain of settlements was formed within a year after the fort was finished. The erection of Fort Chartres, at this point, however, was dictated by national considerations rather than by fear of the savages. The colonization of Louisiana consequent upon the exploration of the Mississippi and the influx of colonists who found a home at Cahokia and Kaskaskia, made this section the key to the French possessions in America, the connecting link between Canada and Louisiana. Here the French settlers, but little disturbed by the forays of the Sacs and Foxes, pushed their improvements up to the Illinois, while lands were granted, though perhaps never occupied, some distance up this stream. The military force found occupation in supporting the friendly Illinois tribes against the Iroquois and Sacs and Foxes, and in unsatisfactory or disastrous campaigns against the Chickasaws. In the meantime this "neck of the woods" was rapidly becoming a spot of national importance. From the southwest the Spaniards were jealously watching the French colonists, while the British gradually pushing westward were building forts near the Ohio and Mississippi Rivers. The European war of 1741-6, in which France and England were opposed, was echoed in these Western wilds, and it was found that the fort must be strengthened or abandoned. The former course prevailed, and in 1750 the old fortress of wood was transformed into one of stone, and garrisoned by a full regiment of French grenadiers. It was from this point that an important contingent went out to the capture of George Washington and his forces at Fort Necessity, July 4, 1754, and thus furnished to George II one of the causes for a declaration of hostilities and a beginning of the "Old French War." In the ensuing war a detachment burned Fort Granville, sixty miles from Philadelphia; another party routed Major Grant near Fort Duquesne, but compelled to abandon that fortress, set it on fire and floated down the river in the light of its destroying flames; again a large detachment augmented by a considerable number of friendly Indians, assisted in the vain attempt to raise the British siege of Niagara, leaving dead upon the field, the flower of the garrison. The fort was no longer in condition to maintain the offensive, and learning that the British were preparing at Pittsburgh to make a hostile descent upon him, the commandant writes to the Governor-General: "I have made all arrangements, according to my strength, to receive the enemy." The victory on the Plains of Abraham decided the contest, but the little backwoods citadel, knowing but little of the nature of the struggle, dreamed that it might be the means of regaining, on more successful fields, the possessions thus lost to the French crown. The news that this fort, with all territory east of the river, had been surrendered without so much as a sight of the enemy, came like a thunder-clap upon this patriotic colony. Many of the settlers with Laclede, who had just arrived at the head of a new colony, expressed their disgust by going to the site of St. Louis, which they supposed to be still French ground.

Though transferred by treaty to the English in 1763, the fort was the last place in North America to lower the white ensign of the Bourbon King, and it was not until the latter part of 1765 that the British formally accepted the surrender of Fort Chartres. Pontiac, the unwavering friend of the French, took upon himself, unaided by his former allies, to hold back the victorious English. Major Loftus, Captains Pitman and Morris, Lieutenant Frazer, and George Crogan, some with force, some in disguise, and others with diplomacy, sought to reach the fort to accept its capitulation, but each one was foiled and turned back with his mission unaccomplished, glad to escape the fate of that Englishman for which Pontiac assured them, he kept a "kettle boiling over a large fire." Wearied out with the inactivity of the French, the Indian sought an audience with the commandant, and explained his attitude. "Father," said the chieftain, "I have long wished to see thee, to recall the battles which we fought together against the misguided Indians and the English dogs. I love the French, and I have come here with my warriors to avenge their wrongs." But assured by St. Ange that such service could no longer be accepted, he gave up the struggle, and the flag of St. George rose in the place of the fair lilies of France.

Thus another nationality was projected into this restricted arena, a situation which was immediately afterward still further complicated by the secret Franco-Spanish treaty, which made the west bank of the Mississippi the boundary of the Spanish possessions. "It is significant of the different races, and the varying sovereignties in that portion of our country," says a writer, "that a French soldier from the Spanish city of St. Louis should be married to an Englishwoman by a French priest in the British colony of Illinois."

The effect of this political change upon the growth of the Illinois settlements was disastrous. At the first announcement of the treaty, the natural hostility of the people to the English induced large numbers of the colonists to prepare to follow the French flag, and a hegira followed which swept out of the colony fully one-third of its three thousand inhabitants. There was still a large number left, forming the largest colony in the west; but there were forces constantly at work which gradually depleted its numbers. Under the British rule an abnormal activity among traders and land speculators was developed. The natives were constantly overreached in trade by unscrupulous persons, protected by the dominant power, and representatives of land purchasing organizations were acquiring vast tracts of country from ignorant savages, who had little comprehension of the meaning or consequences of these transactions. These schemes and practices, though happily brought to naught by the Revolution, rendered the Indians, for a time, savagely hostile, and left their blighting influence long after their removal. The lack of proper sympathy between the governing race and the governed, the hostility of the savages in which they were involved with the British, induced many of the Old French colonists to leave their old homes as rapidly as they could make arrangements to do so. Unfortunately there was at this time no emigration to repair this depletion constantly going on; few English or Americans even visited this region, much less settled here.

The British garrison had hitherto occupied the old French Fort Chartres, but one day in 1772, the river having overflowed its banks, and swept away a bastion and the river wall, the occupants fled with precipitate haste to the high ground above Kaskaskia, where they erected a palisade fort. This was the principal achievement of the British forces, up to the beginning of the war with the colonies. In this struggle, removed from the scene of active operations, the commandant, resorting to the favorite means of the British during the entire early history on this continent, furnished supplies and munitions of war to the savages, and thus equipped, incited them to war upon the unprotected frontier settlements in Pennsylvania, Kentucky and Virginia. So disastrous in their consequences, and distracting in their influence, were these attacks, that Col. George Rogers Clark early set about procuring the means to effectually check them. Recognizing the British post at Kaskaskia as the source of the Indians' supplies and inspiration, he directed his efforts toward the capture of this point, and enlisting the interest of Patrick Henry, governor of Virginia, securing such help as he could give, Clark was able on June 24, 1778, to start from the falls of the Ohio with one hundred and fifty-three men for lower Illinois. So skillfully did he manage his movements that he caught the garrison napping, and captured on the 5th of July, both force and fort without the spilling of a drop of blood. Cahokia fell in like manner without a blow, and in the following October, the Virginia Assembly erected the whole country secured by Clark's several victories, into the county of Illinois; a territory now divided into five States.

This county thus erected was at once placed under control of civil authority, John Todd representing the sovereignty of Virginia as County Lieutenant. His instructions were broad enough to meet the whole case; he was to conciliate the French and Indians; to inculcate on the people the value of liberty, and to remove the grievances that obstruct the happiness, increase and prosperity of that country. These certainly were the great ends to be achieved if possible, but in the nature of things their accomplishment was *not* possible. The French population were easily conciliated, but the education of a life-time, and the hereditary characteristics of the race rendered them incapable of appreciating the value of liberty. They had grown up under the enervating influence of the most arbitrary manifestations of monarchial government, and self-government involved too great a risk for this simple folk. The result was a lack of sympathy with the new order of things, more decided perhaps than under British rule. To this was added a business competition, to which they were unaccustomed; more frequent hostile incursions of the Indians in which the savages gradually forgot the old-time love for the French, and repeated losses by the inundations of the river, made up a sum of discouragement which gradually depleted this country of the French inhabitants. This loss was but imperfectly repaired by the immigration which came in from Virginia and Maryland. Notwithstanding the fertility of the soil had been widely published, and a considerable number had already found much better advantages here than the older colonies afforded, yet the Indian depredations that followed the Revolutionary war, deterred others from following until the general pacification at Greenville in 1795.

In 1787, the whole country northwest of the Ohio was erected into the Northwest Territory, and in February, 1789, General Arthur St. Clair arrived at Kaskaskia as first Territorial Governor. Among the earliest acts of his administration was the erection of the first county, including all of the present State extending north as far as the mouth of Little Mackinaw Creek (now in Tazewell County), and named St. Clair after the governor. May 7, 1800, Ohio was set off and the balance of the territory called Indiana; on February 3, 1809, the Illinois territory was constituted, including the present State with the State of Wisconsin, and on April 18, 1818, the present State of Illinois was admitted into the union. These dates are approximate indications of the advance of settlements in the State. The population in 1809 was estimated at 9,000; in the census of the following year a total population of 12,282 was returned. The frontiers had been steadily advanced by the adventurous pioneers. To the north, the settlement had extended to the Wood River country, in the present Madison County; eastward on

Silver Creek and up the Kaskaskia River; south and east from Kaskaskia, some fifteen miles out on the Fort Massac road; a family had also located at the mouth of the Ohio, and at old Massac and Shawneetown were the remains of old colonies. The new settlements were very sparse and all feeble, and from 1810 to the close of the war, four years later, immigration was almost at a standstill.* With the close of hostilities, however, and the cessation of Indian aggressions, stimulated by the passage of the act granting the right of pre-emption to settle upon the public lands, the tide of emigration set in toward this State with unequaled volume.

At the time of the admission of the State, fifteen counties had been organized, embracing about one fourth of the territory of the State. The settled portions were all south of a line drawn from Alton via Carlyle to Palestine, on the Wabash, but within this area were large tracts of unsettled country, several day's journey in extent. At this time there were some 40,000 inhabitants, of whom scarcely a twentieth part were descendants of the old French colonists. Nineteen-twentieths of the balance were Americans from the Southern states, with the exception of some from Pennsylvania. In 1820, the population was returned at 157,447, while the political organization represented fifty-six counties, though some of the northern ones were large and thinly settled. The territory lying between Galena and Chicago, extending southward to the Kaskaskia, the headwaters of the Vermillion, along the Rock River, and far down into the "Military Tract," was a trackless waste occupied by various Indian tribes. The results of emigration had been shown in the interior of the southern part of the State, and the country bordering the Embarrass, the Sangamon and their tributaries, where the hitherto unoccupied wilderness had been made to blossom with the harvest of the frontier farmer. The advanced settlements still clung to the edge of the timber lands that fringed the streams, and along the Illinois to Chicago—which was just then beginning to attract attention—were found at this time a few scattered settlements, weak in numbers and situated long distances apart. The tide of emigration which continued to sweep into the State—somewhat changed in character—coming largely from the Eastern States, and comprising a considerable percentage of foreigners, followed the old channels, and gradually spread over the northern part of the State until it met the tide which came latterly by way of the lake region. The rapidly increasing demand for the organization of new counties at this period, gave sure indication of this rapid development of the State.

Up to 1812, St. Clair and Randolph Counties had sufficed, but for the purposes of better representation in the territorial council, three more counties were added at this time. In 1815, two more were added; in 1816, five; in 1818, three; and in 1821, seven. Of the latter were Sangamon and Pike, the latter including all of the State north and west of the Illinois, and what is now Cook County. Sangamon included the territory east of the river to the boundary of Pike on the north. In 1825, the county of Peoria was formed of the north-

---

*Hist. of Ill., Davidson & Stuvé, pp. 245-246.

ern part of Sangamon, and in 1831, Peoria was divided and La Salle formed, which then included what is now Grundy County, and the larger part of Kendall.

The advancing tide of emigration coming up along the river made its first permanent settlement on the territory of the present county of La Salle, near the present site of South Ottawa, in 1823-4-5. As early as 1821, Joel Hodgson came in the interest of several families resident in Clinton County, Ohio, to seek a place suitable for the founding of a colony. Crossing Indiana, he entered the State of Illinois near the present site of Danville, and guided only by his compass and an occasional Indian trail, he reached the Illinois, near the mouth of the Kankakee, and following the larger stream down to the mouth of the Fox River, he, for the first time since he entered the State, recognized his position on the map with which he was provided. He carefully explored the land along the Illinois and its tributaries in this region, making his way finally to the settlement at Dillon's Grove, where he met the first white men after leaving Danville. It is not a flattering consideration to those who now rejoice in pleasant homes and fruitful farms in this section, to recall that this explorer returned to his principals only to report that there was no land here suitable for the purposes of the proposed colony. But there were not lacking those who could see beyond the present forbidding aspect, and who had the courage to dare and do. In 1827, there were some fifteen or eighteen families within the present territory of La Salle, situated some distances apart on both sides of the river. The colony located south of the river, included a considerable part of this number, and when the news of the Winnebago outbreak reached them, although the scene of action was a long distance off, they realized that they were on the frontier, and at the mercy of a horde of savages whose motives and impulses could not safely be conjectured, and they at once set about building a fort which served as a rallying point for the pioneers in this section. The speck of war, however, soon vanished, and emigration, temporarily stayed, began again to push its way up the Illinois. In 1828, the first settler on the present territory of Grundy County made his appearance in the person of William Marquis. He came untrammeled by contingencies, and upon no uncertain mission; he came here to stay, and settling on the banks of the Illinois, above the mouth of Mazon Creek, he reared his cabin and was found here by those who reached this country after the Black Hawk War. During these hostilities, the brunt of which fell upon the settlements of La Salle County, Marquis, although a trader and on the best of terms with the natives, found greater security in the protection of the fort at Ottawa than in the friendly disposition of his patrons, and spent the interval at the settlement. He did not return to his place on the Mazon, but settled further north in the county, and later left for the more unsettled parts, where trading with the Indians was more profitable.

The second family in the county was that of William Hoge, who settled north of the river in what is now Nettle Creek township, in the fall of 1831. Here the first white child of the county, James B. Hoge, was born, May 6, 1834. In 1833 a number of families came in and settled on both sides of the river; John Beard, Sr., and his son-in-law, James McKeen, settled near the Kankakee north of the river, the latter building the first house in Morris, a log structure, for John P. Chapin, in May, 1834. Col. Sayers built a cabin in Wauponsee, which was occupied in the following year by W. A. Holloway; W. H. Perkins built his cabin in Au Sable; Zachariah Walley settled in the same township, and A. K. Owen in Mazon. The latter in a published autobiography says: "At the close of the war (Black Hawk) I sold my claim on Corille Creek to a man by the name of Moore, and in the following spring Edwin Shaw, Dr. S. S. Robbins, Sheldon Bartholomew, John Hogoboom and myself fitted out an exploring expedition, and on the second day arrived safe and sound at the celebrated Sulphur Spring on Mazon Creek, and proceeded to make claims as follows, to wit: Dr. Robbins at the Sulphur Spring, John Hogoboom at John Grove, Shaw and Bartholomew at Parers' Groves, and myself on the south branch of the Mazon, one mile below Mazon Town.

"While we were exploring we made headquarters at Johnny Grove, and on leaving we organized a meeting for the purpose of naming the different points selected. Dr. Robbins proposed that from its location, it should be called Center Grove, but I proposed that it should be called John Grove, in honor of John Hogoboom, the wealthy proprietor, and my name was adopted, so the name is John Grove in place of Johnny Grove. Wauponsee—tradition had it that the old chief had, in a drunken fit, taken his butcher knife and killed six wives in one day, so from this and the fact that he had lived here during the Black Hawk War, we gave the name of Wauponsee Grove. Parer's Grove was christened Spring Grove, in honor of a big spring I found just at the foot of the grove, but as these claimants failed to put in an appearance, it was subsequently claimed by an Englishman by the name of Parer, hence the name. Sulphur Spring was called Robbins' Sulphur Spring, and my claim Owen's Spring, with reference to a spring at the top of the bank and a small point of timber running into the prairie, which I subsequently cleared off. I think this was in the spring of 1833." In the following year Robbins alone moved onto his claim. Early in the same spring also came James McCarty, an old bachelor, who took two or three acres in Wauponsee Grove. He built him a little camp and raised a crop of corn which he put in with a hoe. In the fall he erected a shelter out of the stalks, in which he passed the winter. About this time came also the families of Claypool, Collins, Cryder, Tabler, Chapin, Cragg, Hollands, Kent, Millers, Griggs, Ewing, Adkins, Newport, Taylor, Robbs, Eubanks, Snowhill, Samuel and Isaac Hoge and others. These were the principal families here before the government land sale of June 15, 1835.

The early settlers here found the public lands in a very unsatisfactory shape. Congress, in 1827, had granted to the State in aid of a proposed canal, the alternate sections found in the space of five miles on each side of the proposed line of its construction. These lands were resurveyed by the State in 1829; the "odd sections" selected, Chicago and Ottawa laid off, and in 1830, some lots brought into market. Under this sale, the only property bought in Grundy County, was the purchase of Mr. William Hoge on

Nettle Creek. Up to 1834, the Congress lands were subject to pre-emption, and those who came prior to that date found no difficulty in securing the property upon which they had made improvements. The larger number of Grundy County's pioneers, however, came subsequent to 1833 hoping that the privilege of pre-emption would be extended. This, the government did not do, but ordered a sale of the lands. In the meanwhile, considerable improvements had been made; each man striving to include all the land that the old pre-emption law would allow. In February, 1835, the lands were advertised to be sold; Ranges 1, 2 and 3 east, and all west of them from the southern line of township 13, to the northern boundary of the State, at Galena; and from range 3, to the eastern border of the State, at Chicago. The sale began at Chicago, on June 15, the land being offered at auction, and sold to the highest bidder above $1.25 per acre. The sale at the latter place was the one in which the settlers of this county were interested, and they soon found their worst fears realized. The town of Chicago was full of land speculators, who were ready to bid against the settlers for lands upon which they had "squatted" and improved. The sale was made by ranges, and matters went quietly forward until a spirited contest arose over some land at Marseilles, on which Ephraim Sprague had erected a saw-mill. That night there was a meeting of settlers and speculators, and finding that the land-holders were bound to assert their prior claim by force if need be, the speculators made a virtue of necessity, and agreed that the actual settlers should have the privilege of purchasing a quarter-section without competition. To carry out this arrangement, a committee of three from each township was appointed, who should certify to the actual settlers, and appoint a man who should bid off the property. Instead of several persons, Dr. Goddard was chosen to bid off the property in the region covering La Salle County, as then constituted. This arrangement greatly discouraged the foreign land speculators, and it is said $500,000 left the town on the following morning. Thus weakened and discouraged, the speculators conceded to the settlers the privilege of peaceably bidding off more than a quarter-section, provided their improvements covered more land, and on reaching range 8, Salmon Rutherford claimed the right to bid off in this way, all he had money to buy, and this being conceded, became the rule of the sale. This land auction, which continued for upwards of two weeks, was held for a day or two on the steps of a store which stood where 121 Lake street now is, this spot proving to be too muddy for comfort, the sale was adjourned to Garrett's new auction rooms near South Water street, where the weight of the crowd, breaking down some part of the structure, the sale was finished in a store room on South Water street. On the second of August following, the books were opened for entries and then the speculators, having little opposition, bought every available piece of timber in the northeast part of the State.

As this section of the country gradually became settled and less dependent upon the older settlements, the county seat at Ottawa was felt to be at too great distance from the northern limits of the county. The demands of a frontier farm rendered the loss of several days on the occasion of every necessary visit to the county capital a serious burden, while the tedious character of traveling facilities aggravated the burden by the discomfort of the journey. In addition to this it was felt that those portions of the county which had readier access to the county seat had an undue influence, which acted to the prejudice of the less represented limits. These motives, whatever else may have entered into the movement, were sufficient to create a desire for a division of the county. Jacob Claypool, in settling in Wauponsee, with shrewd forecast, had satisfied his mind that the distance between Ottawa and Joliet—the latter not then a county seat, but of such growing importance that he believed it could not be ignored in the formation of a county—left space for another county with its center near the present location of Morris. The natural discontent of this section of the county was therefore first crystallized by the efforts of Mr. Claypool and G. W. Armstrong, who, though not so far distant from Ottawa, became interested in the movement. It was a year or two before the idea secured supporters enough to challenge the serious attention of the lower part of the county, but when it did there was considerable opposition manifested. However, the unwieldy size of La Salle was manifest, and the opposition finally addressed itself to the effort to confine the surrender to as small a territory as possible. The supporters of the proposition for a new county, while united against those who opposed the division, were by no means united as to the line of division. The friends of the Grundy County plan were surrounded by those who desired a different division with reference to other interests, giving rise to a conflict of interests that afforded scope for diplomatic management and rendered the issue by no means certain. The supporters of the Kendall County division, having "pooled their issues" with those of Grundy, the prospects of success visibly brightened. In the fall of 1840, Wm. E. Armstrong, a man of energy and ability, seeing that the formation of Grundy might be turned to speculative account, interested himself in the project, and securing in addition to others a numerously signed petition for the two counties, presented it to the General Assembly in the winter of 1840-41; by which bills erecting the counties of Kendall and Grundy were passed, the latter being approved by the Governor Feb. 17, 1841, and the Kendall bill two days later.

At this time the public interest was centered in the building of the Illinois and Michigan Canal, the construction of which was being delayed by lack of funds, and all public measures were made more or less subsidiary to this object. It was therefore required in the act erecting Grundy County, that the "Seat of Justice" should be located "on the line of the Illinois and Michigan Canal, on canal lands," of which territory, not to exceed ten acres, was to be laid off "as a town site, embracing lots, streets, alleys and a public square;" the lots thus formed to be assigned one half to the State and one half to the county, "in alternate lots of equal value." For the lots assigned to the State, the county was to pay ten dollars an acre, and this revenue devoted by the Canal Commissioners to the purposes of the canal. A board to carry out these provisions of the act was constituted, to be composed of the Canal Commissioners,

Hon. Newton Cloud and Gens. Thornton and Fry, and William E. Armstrong, R. S. Duryea and Gen. W. B. Burnett, the latter an engineer on the canal. A glance at the situation demonstrated the fact that to secure anything near a central location, the county seat would necessarily be placed on section 7 or 9, in township 33, range 7. Section 9, was objectionable to the Canal Commissioners, as there was but a fraction of its northeast corner north of the river, and this was the only portion suitable for a town site. Section 7 was objectionable to the local members of the board, principally because their lands were located in the vicinity of the other position, and that the approach to the site from the south, would be over the low bottoms which would oblige travel to make a considerable detour. Such a conflict of interests left no room for compromise, and the result of a vote was a dead-lock," Gen. Burnett voting with the local members.

Under the organizing act an election was held at the cabin of Columbus Pinney, May 24, 1841, with Perry A. Claypool, Robert Walker and John Beard, Sr., as judges of election. One hundred and forty-eight votes were cast, which, as there was a spirited contest over these first offices, represented the entire population. It should be noted, however, that about one third of these votes represented an Irish element brought here by the work on the canal, and stayed here but a short time. In this election, Henry Cryder, Jacob Claypool and James McKeen were made county commissioners; James Nagle, clerk; L. W. Claypool, recorder; Isaac Hoge, sheriff,*

Joshua Collins, probate justice; † and J. L. Pickering, treasurer.‡ On June 14, 1841, the commissioners elect with James Nagle as clerk, met at the house of William E. Armstrong, and after attending to the preliminary duties in relation to oaths and bonds, proceeded to organize the county. On the organization of La Salle County ranges 1 and 2 constituted Vermillion Precinct; ranges 3 and 4 Ottawa Precinct, and ranges 5, 6, 7 and 8 the Eastern Precinct. In June, 1834, a "Northern Precinct" was erected including Au Sable Grove and vicinity, and a year later, in June, 1835, Wauponsee was erected, embracing the whole of what is now Grundy County. In the following December that part of Wauponsee and the county north of the river was divided into two precincts, the dividing line starting at the river on the line between sections 3 and 4, township 33, R. 7, and going to section 21, 36, 7. The territory east of this line was known as Franklin, and west of this line as Grafton. The newly formed county was in this shape when the first Board of Commissioners sat down to arrange its political divisions. At their first session they formed the first precinct, composed of all of township 34, in range 8, north of the Illinois and Desplaines Rivers, and called it Dresden; the second, composed of all territory north of the river in ranges 6 and 7, they called Jefferson; the third composed of all territory comprised in range 6, and the west half of range 7 south of the river, they called Wauponsee; and the fourth, composed of all territory south of the river, and east of the middle line of

---

*Mr. Hoge refused to qualify, and at a special election held Sept. 25, 1841, William E. Armstrong was elected.

†L. S. Robbins was elected subsequently, in place of Mr. Collins who failed to qualify.

‡Sidney Dunton was elected first treasurer but failed to qualify.

range 7, they called Kankakee. Subsequently, on December 6, 1841, Grundy Precinct was erected out of the east side of Jefferson, and comprised all of range 7, north of the river. On September 8, 1847, Mazon Precinct was erected out of the Territory of Kankakee, lying south of an east and west line drawn through the middle of sections 25 and 30, in township 33, range 8, and continued through sections 25 and 27, in township 33, range 7. There were no further changes until March 2, 1850, when under the new Constitution, the Board of Supervisors through George H. Kiersted, Phillip Collins and Robert Gibison acting as commissioners, made the precinct lines to coincide with the township lines, save where the rivers made a deviation necessary. The present names and lines are those fixed at that time save in the case of the boundaries of Felix which was attached to Wauponsee, and was named and given a separate existence Nov. 22, 1854. The present boundaries between the two townships were arranged on petition of their citizens, September 9, 1856. The original names of Fairview, Addison and Dover were changed by the request of the State auditor, respectively to "Arianna," Braceville and Goodfarm.

One of the first duties imposed upon the County Commissioners by the act creating Grundy County, was to " prepare a place for holding courts in said county." The county at this time possessed neither buildings nor land, and it was ordered that the house of Wm. E. Armstrong be used for the court. This seemed to be the most available place for the purpose, and continued to be so used, notwithstanding a formal protest by Mr. Cryder, until the May term in 1843, when Mr. Armstrong, having erected a frame wooden building 20 by 40 feet and two stories high, on the northwest corner of the present court house lot, the court was transferred to this new temple of justice. In the meanwhile the "dead-lock" on the question of locating had been broken, and the matter decided in favor of its present location. The commissioners, therefore, finding this building suitably located, bought the building which, after having it " lathed and plastered," cost a total of $485.36. The county offices were in the upper story, the east room being assigned to the Clerk, and the southwest room to the Recorder. As the court room was the most available hall in the town, it found considerable demand for this object other than that to which it had been devoted, and its use was finally restricted to religious, political and court purposes. This modest edifice survived until the erection of the present court house which cost $22,760, and was accepted April 26, 1858. The " Commissioners' Court," as it was called, rivaled the Circuit Court in importance. It provided for court and jury, for prisoner and pauper; it ordered roads and licensed ferries, regulated the early tavern's bill of fare and laid its paternal hand on trade; it was in that day the sole arbiter of the county's destiny. The difficulties under which this executive board of the county labored have been long forgotten and now find expression only in the musty records of that time. The oft recurrence of the same names in the list of juries, the claims made for "guarding prisoners," and sums paid for the care of paupers, suggest a lack of resources in both means and men, which was characteristic of pioneer days. An incident, published by Mr. Perry Armstrong, "points the moral." Michael D. Prendegast, a man of fair scholastic acquirements, but of inordinate self-esteem, in August, 1847, was elected Probate Justice of the Peace by the large Irish vote which was then an important element in county politics. His success stimulated his vanity, which he betrayed by signing his name "Michel De Prendegast," and adorning his person with a Catalonian cloak, stove-pipe hat and a fancy ivory headed cane. His wife expressed the family pride by remarking to a friend: "My husband is none of your common justices like Pat Hynds; he is the reprobate justice of the peace."

The greatness thus thrust upon him could not satisfy all the demands of his earlier tastes, and the "De Prendegast" was found, one Sunday evening, wending his way to one of the saloons with his judicial cloak about him. His entrance was greeted by a numerous and noisy crowd, and as he produced a bottle from the folds of his cloak, ordering it filled with port wine, Owen Lamb, noted no less for his strength and size than for his love of fun and adventure, stepped up to the justice, saying: "Judge, we will all drink with you, and I'll have the best in the house; give me some brandy." This was too much for the self-complacent dignity of the "judge," and he burst out with: "The likes of you, Owen Lamb, insulting me! Why, I'll blow your brains out on the spot;" and carried away with his anger, he instantly presented an old horse pistol to carry out his threat. The weapon was instantly knocked to the other side of the room, when the judge precipitately left the field.

The wits saw fun in this incident, and at the suggestion of Wm. Armstrong and George Kiersted, Lamb brought action against Prendegast for assault. The instigators of the action represented the prosecution, and the defendant, aided by the only lawyers in the place, E. H. Little and C. M. Lee, appeared on the part of the defense. The proofs in behalf of the prosecution were positive, clear and unquestioned, hence the defendant confined his efforts to prove his good character. Among other witnesses, L. W. Claypool, deposed substantially that he had known the defendant a long time; his reputation as a law abiding citizen was good; he did not consider him a willful or malicious man; not half so dangerous as a little black dog the judge owned. Dr. Curtis testified that he had never considered the judge a malicious or dangerous man, but rather as a d—d fool. This was the tenor of the testimony for the defense.

In the meanwhile, news of the trial had come to the ears of the devoted wife as she was engaged in "wiping the dishes." Her impetuosity knew no method, but rushing out with a cup and towel in her hand, she entered the court room, just as Kiersted was addressing the court. Without a word of parley or protest she rushed up to him saying: "So you have turned lawyer, Mr. Kiersted, take that!" at the same time accompanying her words with a blow of the teacup on his breast, which shivered her missile to atoms. Utterly surprised by the attack he drew back his fist to strike, when he recognized his assailant and gallantly apologized for threatening a woman.

During the progress of the trial, the defendant was pelted with eggs and subjected to other personal indignities. As he rose to "sum up" the evidence, an egg struck him squarely in the ear. Throwing his hand up to the smitten organ, he exclaimed: "I'm kilt! I'm kilt!" and instantly feeling the soft material oozing out of his stunned ear, he displayed his hand covered with the meat of the egg, and with a horrified ejaculation, "See me brains!" broke with the speed of a quarter horse for his residence, declaring as the hope of a longer existence dawned upon his mind, "I'll demand protection from the Governor and his posse comitatus." Esquire Barber, before whom the trial was had, discovered the whole matter was intended for a joke, and discharged the defendant.

The first jail was built on or near the site of the old brick structure south of the court house. There is no record of this, but tradition has it that it was a two-story log house with a square excavation in the ground, with an entrance in the center of the lower apartment. The prisoner was dropped in and secured by an iron grate over the opening and shielded from the bare earth walls by hemlock logs. From the numerous "claims for guarding prisoners" it is surmised that this jail was not much used. Indeed the early sheriffs declared it unfit for human beings, and occasionally employed the prisoners in the business affairs of the jailor. It is said, but not fully credited, that Wm. Armstrong fastened one Cottrell, arrested for numerous thefts, with a chain and padlock to a whisky barrel. At any rate, the prisoner served the sheriff as bartender and ferryman for some time, and served himself so good a turn that on coming to trial the jury acquitted him in the face of the most explicit evidence of his guilt. So marked was this action of the jury that it was for some time afterward sufficient to show that a man had been on the Cottrell jury to exclude him from the jury box.

The old jail was subsequently sold for fourteen dollars, when the brick was erected. This was built at a cost of $3,237.13, and accepted April 17, 1855. On July 14, 1875, after the brick jail had been officially and repeatedly called a nuisance the Board of Supervisors decided to build a new one, the result of which decision is the present stone structure. erected at a cost of $16,190.60, and accepted Sept. 14, 1876.

The last, and perhaps the least satisfactory of the county institutions is the "Poor Farm." The first farm consisted of 160 acres (the N. E. quarter section No. 24, 33, 6), in Norman township. This land cost $2,400; was high land, and while not presenting its greatest attractions to the road, was considered well adapted to the purposes for which it was bought. It was found to be too large for practical purposes, and portions of the farm were sold. Later it was thought a smaller farm could be made nearer self-supporting, and another farm was finally bought October 27, 1879; eighty acres (the south half of S. W. quarter, section No. 33, 7) in Wauponsee were bought at forty-five dollars an acre. This selection was very much opposed, and a special committee appointed by the Board after examining the property reported as follows: "It is too low and flat, with no building place above level of prairie, and no drainage suitable for such a cellar as the wants of a poor-house require—wholly unfit for the erection of such buildings as this county will require in after years." The purchase was persevered in, however, and subsequently a brick building erected at a cost of $3,800. What remained of the old farm was sold for $2,510.

Under the statute of 1849 the probate business was transferred to the county judge, while that of the commissioners was transferred to a county court composed of a county judge and two associates. At the election in April of the following year the township organization was adopted by a vote of the people, and under this arrangement the first Board of Supervisors organized June 12, 1850.

CHAPTER IV.*

SOCIAL DEVELOPMENT—EARLY SOCIETY—RISE OF CHURCH AND SCHOOL—INDIAN TRAILS AND EARLY ROADS—RAILROADS AND THE CANAL—THE NEWSPAPERS.

THE pioneers of Grundy County came principally from southern Ohio, with a number from the southern States, and later, a few from Pennsylvania and other more eastern States. Most of these families had been pioneers in older settlements in the States from which they came, or had grown up in frontier colonies which their fathers had founded, and had been trained in the stern school of experience to meet and conquer the difficulties of a new country. But the problem here, nevertheless, presented features and difficulties entirely different from that with which their earlier experience had acquainted them. The timber that skirted the margin of the river and sent out spurs here and there along the banks of the creeks and ravines, divided the vast open sea of grass and flowers into two great divisions. On either side the broad expanse of verdant meadow, marked here and there by a stray clump of under-sized trees, stretched away from the river, unbounded save by the horizon, and the pioneer with his little retinue of wagons was lost in this luxuriant wilderness like a convoy of sloops in mid ocean.

A party of pioneers came on foot by way of Chicago, in May, 1835, and one of them presents this picture:† "There had been heavy showers for several days, and the low prairie around Chicago was more like a lake than dry land. For seven miles before reaching Berry's Point, the water was from three to fifteen inches deep, through which we worked our weary way. When within about two miles of dry land, one of our companions gave out, and two of us, one on either side, placed our arms around and under his opposite arm, while he placed his on our shoulders, and thus we bore him through.

"The next day we walked about forty miles to Plainfield. It gave us our first view of a rolling Illinois prairie. We strained our eyes to take in its extent, till the effort became painful. We descanted again and again upon its beauty and richness, and wondered why such a country had remained so long in the hands of the savage. It was a wonderful country. All was new. Strange sights and sounds greeted us. The piping note of the prairie-squirrel, as he dropped from his erect position, and sought the protection of his hole close by our path; the shrill notes of the plover, scattered in countless numbers, fitfully starting and running over the prairie; the constant roaring of the prairie cock; the mad scream of the crooked-bill curlew, as we approached its nest; the distant whoop of the crane; the pump sounding note of

---

* By J. H. Battle.

†Elmer Baldwin's Hist. of La Salle County, p. 124.

the bittern; the lithe and graceful forms of the deer, in companies of three to five, lightly bounding over the swells of the prairie;—it seemed a new creation that we had entered."

Every immigrant supplied his own means of reaching his destined home. The pioneer from Pennsylvania, Ohio, or the Southern States, betrayed his nativity and prejudice in the schooner-shape wagon box, the stiff tongue, the hinder wheels double the size of the forward ones, and closely coupled together, the whole drawn by a team of four or six horses which were guided by a single line in the hands of a teamster riding the "nigh wheeler." His harness was of gigantic proportions. What between the massive leather breeching, the heavy hames and collar, the immense housing of bear skin upon the hames, the heavy iron trace chains, and the ponderous double-tree and whiffletrees, the poor beasts seemed like humanity in a chain gang, or some terrible monsters that human ingenuity could scarcely fetter securely. The eastern immigrant, from New York or farther east, was marked as far as his caravan could be seen, by a long coupled, low boxed, two horse wagon, provided with a seat, from which with double lines the driver guided his lightly harnessed pair of horses. There was about each part of the outfit, evidences of the close calculation of means to an end, and an air of utility which left no room for doubt as to the purpose of the maker in every part of it. This strange contrast in these early outfits suggests that they may not unfittingly be taken as types of two civilizations that met here on this middle ground, and in many a sterner contest waged an "irrepressible conflict." In the end, these "wooden-nutmeg Yankee wagons," as they were called, prevailed.

This prairie country undoubtedly offered opportunities to the pioneer occupant, far superior to those of a timbered country, but the early settlers, imbued with the logical deductions of their early experiences, looked with distrust upon the open prairie. The general impression was that only the timber belts would ever be inhabited; the prairie swept by the fires of summer, and by the piercing blasts of winter, seemed little better than a desert, and for several years there was not a cabin in Grundy County built more than one hundred yards from the timber. The necessity of the early cabins similar in size, style and materials, confirmed this impression, and made it a conviction.

The pioneer having selected a site on some prospecting tour, or being attracted to a certain region by the report of friends, came with all his worldly possessions on wagons, and making selection of a farm, chose a site for his cabin, and set at once to build it. Trees were felled; logs of the proper length chopped off and drawn to the chosen site, and willing neighbors for miles about invited to the raising. Rude as these structures were it needed no little handicraft to rear them, and it was not long before the special ability of each member of the community, entailed upon him his special duty on these occasions. The logs trimmed, "saddled," and properly assorted, were placed in the pen shape of the cabin; the gable ends were run up with regularity, shortening logs shaped at the ends, to allow for the slope of the roof; on these the long roof poles two feet apart, stretched from end to end, served as foundation for the roof, which was made up of clapboards, riven by the froe from bolts of oak laid in place and held secure by "weight poles" made firm by pegs or stones. Then followed the sawing out of the door-way and windows, the chinking of the cracks with pieces of riven timber; the caulking with a mixture of mud and chopped hay; the construction of floors and a door from puncheons, and the building of the chimneys of "cat and clay." Hinges were supplied from rawhide, and the wooden latch, reached from the outside by means of an attached leather latch-string passing through a hole in the door, was often the only protection against forcible entrance. Later experiences introduced the use of heavy wooden bars, but the proverbial expression of early hospitality was the hanging out of the latch-string. The local characteristics of the early settlers found their expression in the construction of the chimneys. Few early cabins were more than one story high, and the chimney placed on one side, was constructed in the case of the southerner or the Indianian on the outside of the cabin, while the rest built inside, the top in all cases scarcely reaching the height of the ridge.

The interior of the cabin was marked by the same general similarity. In each the wide fire-place shed abroad its genial warmth of hospitality or aided in the preparation of the table's cheer. The "crane," hung with iron pots and kettles, and the Dutch oven, half submerged in coals, were in all cabins the "evidence of things not seen," and furnished forth, under the guidance of the deft housewife, a meal which is still sighed for as the "grace of a day that is dead." The "corn pone," or when so exceptionally fortunate as to be able to use flour, the hop-yeast or salt-rising bread, the "chicken-fixings," the game, the fresh, luscious vegetables,—are memories that more pretentious days have not dimmed in the hearts of the pioneers. The latter-day inventions of saleratus and baking powder had their prototype in the pearlash, which was prepared by burning the potash, so common then, upon the lid of the "bake kettle;" the sputtering, greenish flame produced by the process, in the meanwhile enforcing upon the childish minds of the household the stern doctrines of the hereafter. The frontier cabin, as a rule, contained but one room, which served all the domestic and social purposes of the family alike, unchanged. Curtains arranged about the beds suggested the retirement of sleeping apartments, while the cheerful blaze of the fire-place afforded an unstinted glow to the whole establishment.

The women of those days ate not the bread of idleness. They were indeed the helpmates of father, brother and husband, and nowhere in the world did man prove such an unbalanced, useless machine as the unmarried pioneer in this western wild. While the man, with masterful energy, conquered the difficulties of a new country and asserted his sovereignty over an unsubdued wilderness, it was woman's hand that turned its asperities into blessings, and made conquered nature the handmaid of civilization. The surplus product of the frontier farm sufficed to supply a slender stock of tea, coffee, sugar and spices, with an occasional hat for the man and a calico dress for the woman;—all else must be derived from the soil. How this was accomplished, the occasional relics of a flax-wheel, brake, spinning-wheel or loom, suggest. To card and spin, to dye and weave, were accomplishments that all women possessed. Housekeeping was crowded into the smallest possible space, and the preparation of linen, of "linsey woolsey," and stocking yarn, with their adaptation to the wants of the family, became, to vary the catechism, the chief end of woman. About these homely industries gathered all the pride of womanly achievement, the mild dissipations of early society, and the hopes of a future competence; a social foundation, of which the proud structure of this great commonwealth bears eloquent testimony.

But with all this helpful self-reliance indoors, there was plenty to engage the vigorous activity of the male portion of the family out of doors. The exigencies of the situation allowed no second experiment, and a lifetime success or failure hung upon the efforts of the pioneer. The labor of the farm was carried on under the most discouraging circumstances. The rude agricultural implements and the too often inadequate supply of these, allowed of no economical expenditure of strength, and for years rendered the frontier farmer's life a hand to hand struggle of sheer muscle and physical endurance with the stubborn difficulties of nature. The location of the cabins along the lowlands that formed the margin of the streams, exposed the early settlers at their most vulnerable point. During a considerable part of the year the almost stagnant water of the sluggish streams filled the air with a miasmatic poison that hung in dense fog over stream and grove like a destroying spirit. The difficulty experienced in securing good water often rendered it necessary for the farmers to drink from stagnant pools, "frequently blowing off the scum and straining the wigglers from the sickening, almost boiling, fluid through the teeth." That the "fever and ague" should stalk through the land, a veritable Nemesis, was inevitable under such circumstances, and many a hardy pioneer was cowed and fairly shaken out of the country in the chilly grasp of this grim monster. But having withstood these discouragements and secured a harvest, the greatest disappointment came in the utter lack of markets. After a year of labor, privation, and sickness, the moderate crop would hardly bear the expense of getting it to market. How this country was settled and improved under such circumstances can be explained upon none of the settled principles of political economy. Retreat there was none; and that homely phrase, "root, hog, or die," was borne in upon the pioneer by his daily experience with a benumbing iteration that must have wrought ruin to any class of people of less hardy mental and physical health.

In such a community where "The richest were poor and the poor lived in abundance," there was no chance for the growth of caste, and families for miles around were linked together as one neighborhood, by the social customs of the time, which in the spirit of true democracy, drew the line at moral worth alone. The amusements of a people taking their character from the natural surroundings of the community, were here chiefly adapted to the masculine taste. Hunting and fishing were always liberally rewarded, while log cabin raisings, the opening of court with its jury duty, and the Saturday afternoon holiday with its scrub horse race, its wrestling match, its jumping or quoit pitching, and perhaps a fight or two, afforded entertainments that never lost their zest. It was a common remark, however, that "Illinois furnished an easy berth for men and oxen, but a hard one for women and horses."* Outside of "visiting" and camp meetings, the diversions in which women participated at that early day were very few; husking and spinning bees, and "large" weddings where the larger part of the night was spent in dancing, did not have the frequent occurrence so characteristic of the Eastern States, and nothing here seemed to offer any substitute. So long as the community gathered here lacked easy communication with the outside world this state of things continued. There was a market at Chicago at this time, where a fair price could be had for the surplus crop, and the growth of the older settlements further south brought the advantages of civilization nearer to these outlying communities, but the lack of roads prevented the early enjoyment of these privileges.

The early lines of travel were along the Indian trails. These were clearly defined paths about a foot or eighteen inches wide, cut into the sod of the prairie, sometimes to the depth of ten or twelve inches. A portion of one of these trails can be seen now on the farm formerly belonging to Jacob Claypool, where it has been carefully protected by a furrow plowed up on either side of it. There were three of these following the general course of the river through the county, and terminating at Chicago, which was at an early time a great resort of the Indians. One of these ran along the north side of the river, between

*History of La Salle County

it and the present site of the canal up to near the five mile bridge then passing north of the line of the canal, but south of the Catholic cemetery, it crossed both branches of Nettle Creek near where the stone bridges now stand, thence recrossing the canal line near the Peacock bridge, and passing on the ridge through to the Protestant cemetery, it crossed the Au Sable below the aqueduct, and thence through Dresden it took its course over the bluffs toward Channahon. Another on the bottoms south of the river crossed the Waupecan Creek at the quarter corner of the east line of section 18, in Wauponsee township, thence nearly in a straight line, passing twenty rods north of the center of section 17, it continued to Spring Creek which it crossed at its mouth, and thence it led across the Mazon on section 16, and up the river, crossing the Kankakee one half mile above its mouth. There was a second trail on the south side of the Illinois river, which skirted the points of timber, passed a little north of the present residence of Jonathan Wilson on section 4, 32, 6, and entered Wauponsee about the center of the west line of the southeast quarter section 20, continuing thence in a direct line and intersecting the first trail at the crossing of the Mazon River. There was a "high prairie trail" through Holderman's Grove north of Grundy County, which came to be an important line of travel.

There were of course no fences at first to interfere with the choice of road or to serve as guides, and these trails were followed until a wagon path, pretty clearly defined, made traveling between well established points no very difficult matter in the day-

time, or on moonlight nights. But the belated traveler on a dark night, or one a little unfamiliar with the fords, found it advisable to make an unexpected bivouac on the open prairie. Even some of the older settlers, when near at home, had some experience of this, as an incident related of Mr. Jacob Claypool, very forcibly illustrates:

He and his boys, Perry A. and L. W., had husked corn for Holderman, for one and a half bushels per day. Late in November (1834) they set out from home with two teams, one of horses and the other of oxen, to bring home their hard earned corn. On their return they reached the Indian trail near the west line of section 7, 33, 7, just about dark. To add to the difficulties of the situation, a heavy fog arose as night set in, and knowing that there was no escape from an open air camp, they made the best of their situation by carefully feeling their way along the trail to a point near the present residence of Isaac Hoge, where there were some hay-stacks. Here the party remained until about four o'clock in the morning, when the fog rising and the moon coming out, they started for the ford of the Illinois River, on the west line of section 8. Perry Claypool with the horses led, and fortunately striking the right place passed over safely, but the ox team failed to follow closely, and becoming unmanageable, began to swim out of the difficulty with the wagon and passengers. By daylight the party reached their cabin home wet, cold and hungry, and worst of all, with one load of their hard earned corn floating down the river.

Such experiences were not uncommon and stimulated the pioneer to the earliest possible efforts to secure roads and bridges.

The northern part of the State had settled up so slowly that there was no thoroughfare through Grundy County at all until about 1833. About this time the Bloomington and Chicago road began to be outlined by the droves of live stock going to market, and the return teams hauling salt and supplies. This soon became the principal route of travel, and crossed the county through the northern part of Highland, passed old Mazon and crossed the Mazon River at Sulphur Springs, on section 6, Braceville. From this point it led to the Kankakee River at "Cousin John Beard's ford," about a mile and a half from its mouth. This road was not officially laid out or worked until after the county of Grundy was formed, when the commissioners at one of their earliest meetings ordered it run out from "Lone tree point to Cousin John Beard's ford at the crossing of the Kankakee." It was subsequently worked, and in 1843 a bridge was erected over the Mazon, where the road crossed, but it was soon destroyed. It was the earliest and greatest thoroughfare of its time, but it did not reach the dignity of a mail route, and has long since been abandoned. In December of 1834, the commissioners of La Salle County appointed Henry Green, Benjamin Bloomfield and Sam'l S. Bullock to lay out a road from Marseilles toward Joliet. This was laid out as near as practicable along the Indian trail nearest the north bank of the river. This was afterward divided into three divisions, and Wm. Ruhey appointed supervisor of the western division, Wm. Hoge, of the middle division, and Joshua Collins of the eastern. On July 3, 1839, the "Shaking Bridge" was erected near where the present stone bridge spans the west branch of Nettle Creek on Jefferson street in Morris. To raise this early bridge required the united energies of most of the men in the country about, and was probably the first bridge erected in the county. It was hoped that this road would prove to be the route for the north and south travel of the State, and upon such expectations Lovell Kimball of Marseilles laid out the village of Clarkson on the southeast quarter 12, 33, 6, with a double log cabin hotel as a nucleus about which to gather the expected city. This village aspired to county honors, until the construction of Grundy blighted all such hopes, and remained even then the principal village in this region until the location of the county seat at Morris, when it rapidly went to decay. At Dresden, on the other end of this road in Grundy County, Salmon Rutherford erected a large "framed" hotel, where, by license of the court he was allowed to charge the following scale of prices:

"For each meal, common ....25 cents.
"   "   "   extra..37½   "
"   "   lodging ....12½   "
"   "   horse or ox, hay over night..................12½   "
"   8 quarts corn or oats...................................25   "
"   each glass of spirits.....................................6¼   "
"   "   "   extra spirits..................................12½   "

For this privilege he paid $6 and gave a bond of $100 for the faithful performance of his obligations. Another of these early hostelries was erected about this time on the west fork of the Mazon, and was kept by James McKean, and was for a considerable time the resort of drovers on their way to market with stock.

The division of the large northern counties and the demands of the local communities led to great changes in these early highways. Roads were run with some reference to the farmers who lived along the lines of these "through routes," which led, not without an occasional serious struggle, to their abandonment. The result of these changes was to establish the main line of through travel along the high prairie trail by way of Holderman's Grove, etc., on which Frink and Walker subsequently established a line of coaches running between Chicago and Peru. From four to eight four-horse coaches left each terminal point daily, connecting at Peru with a steamboat from St. Louis. Neil, Moor & Co., an Ohio firm, ran a line of coaches between the same points following a route south of the river, but it proved but a short-lived competition, though vigorous while it existed. The latter firm failed and withdrew its coaches in a short time. But with all these improvements, Chicago, which had become the market for this section, was too far off for the means of transportation possessed by the farmers. Everything was hauled in wagons and the roads were stern autocrats of the pioneer's destiny. The treacherous sod that covered the long stretch of swamp about the city would bear up only a moderate load, and thus restricted the amount of produce to be taken by a single wagon. Add to this the rude construction of the best roads and there is a sense of discouragement that might have worked despair if it had not incited to improvement. It may be noticed here that the civilization of the broad tread wagon and that of the narrow-tread, met at the eastern line of Grundy County. With all the other inconveniences, the farmers of this section found that their wagons had a hard road to travel even where it was well constructed, one wheel being on the unbroken or unsettled roadway all the time. This was soon remedied by the adoption of narrow tread wagons, but the other difficulties still remained.

The project of connecting the waters of Lake Michigan with the navigable waters of the Illinois River had been talked of since 1812, and urged from time to time on the ground of its military as well as its commercial importance, but it was not until July 4, 1836, that ground was first broken for its construction. The line surveyed for its construction, connecting with the eastern arm of the south branch of the Chicago River, followed the general line of the Desplaines and Illinois Rivers to Peru, where it was proposed to pass by locks into the river. The estimate of its cost varied from $6,640,000 to $10,000,000, the latter being nearer the actual cost when constructed. There was an urgent demand for greater transportation facilities, and scarcely a year passed without a recommendation on the subject by State or national official, but here the matter seemed to end until 1825. In this year the "Illinois and Michigan Canal Association" was formed with a capital of $1,000,000, which received a charter granting most extraordinary privileges. At this time Daniel P. Cook, the only Representative of the State in the lower House of Congress, was earnestly seeking to secure a grant of public lands in aid of the canal, and he felt that this charter would defeat his plans. He therefore used every effort to have it annulled, publishing an able argument against the association scheme and sending it throughout the State. The "Association" did not seem to prize its privileges; no stock was ever subscribed, and the charter was voluntarily surrendered soon after its receipt. In 1827, came the grant of public lands, but this was not easily turned into money, and in 1833 the advisability of devoting the grant to the building of a railroad between the terminal points was seriously discussed. "Up to January 1, 1839, the gross expenditure on the canal, derived from the various sources of loans, lot and land, amounted to $1,400,000. All of it, but about twenty-three miles between Dresden and Marseilles, was contracted, and the jobs let were roughly estimated at $7,500,000."* In the meanwhile the public and Legislature had been carried away with a vast scheme of public improvement, and the State involved in great financial embarrassment. After negotiating several loans on account of the canal which involved the State's finances without proportionately aiding the canal, there was a general collapse. The breaking of the State bank in 1842 added to the general distress, and gave rise to an agitation in favor of repudiating the State debt, which then amounted to $14,000,000. It was about this time that the unlet section of the canal was contracted, Jacob Claypool taking section 126 about where the aqueduct is placed. The failure of funds, however, brought the work here to an early close. The effort to secure a loan of $1,600,000 to finish the canal was protracted through some three years, in which the work came to a standstill, but in 1845 its construction was renewed, and "finally, by the opening season of 1848, the Illinois and Michigan canal, a stupendous public work,

---

* Hist. of Illinois, Davidson and Stuve.

urged for thirty years, and in course of actual construction for twelve, after many struggles with adverse circumstances, was completed."

The influence upon Grundy County was felt at once; warehouses were erected, and a good market for grain of all kinds was brought within easy reach, while goods and supplies of all sorts were as easily secured. Its effect in another way was quite as marked. When the work ceased in 1843 a large number of those employed on the canal, thrown out of work, took up land here, and, industriously engaging in farming, have become well-to-do, and are still here, or represented by their descendants. During the progress of the work the transient Irish element outnumbered the residents of the county, and worked their will for a year or two at the polls. The village of Morris suddenly changed from a rather quiet town to a place "where whiskey and Irish were plenty," together with what such a combination implies, but with the completion of the canal this element passed away, leaving Morris and Grundy County to work out its own destiny untrammeled by outside influences.

Closely related with the canal was a scheme for the construction of a railroad from Chicago to the mouth of the Illinois. But the completion of the former and its being placed in trust with all its property and revenues to secure the payment of the English capitalists who had loaned the $1,600,000, discouraged the granting of a charter for the upper part of such a road. The slight dependence to be placed upon the river for through transportation had been demonstrated, and had proved very disappointing to the great expectations entertained of the canal. Through freight shipped by the canal was occasionally seriously delayed because of the inability of boats of ordinary draught to come up the river far enough to make connections. A charter had therefore been granted for a railroad from La Salle to Rock Island. The country through which it was proposed to build this road was not thickly settled, and capital was therefore slow in taking up this enterprise. In the meanwhile, as it languished, Senator Douglas, impressed with the advantage of a railroad from Chicago to Rock Island, began urging his views upon others, and among the rest upon Norman C. Judd, who then represented Cook County in the State Senate. He suggested that the charter for the La Salle & Rock Island road be amended, so as to allow an extension of the road to Chicago. Mr. Judd entered into the project at once, and had no difficulty in enlisting the interest of Wm. Reddick, State Senator from La Salle, Bureau, Livingston and Grundy Counties, and the late Governor Matteson, Senator from Will County. The citizens along the route of the proposed extension were easily enlisted in the cause, and frequent consultations were had. At a conference of the supporters of this scheme, held in the old American House in Springfield, Senators Judd, Reddick, and Matteson, with P. A. Armstrong as clerk, were appointed a committee to prepare a bill for the purpose of amending the charter. This was immediately done, Armstrong drawing up the bill at Mr. Judd's dictation, which was then put upon its passage on the next day. It was obstinately contested by the English interest, but notwithstanding the apparent demands of equity, the bill passed both houses, and went to the Governor for his approval. This was the critical point, as it was understood that Governor French had assured the canal trustees that he would veto the measure. Mr. Reddick, who had been of considerable service in the passage of a bill championed by a brother of the Governor's wife, at once proposed to see Mrs. French, who had the reputation of being a good deal of a politician, and no mean power behind the Governor's throne. The bill was already in the hands of the Governor, and a veto was feared in the morning. So, late as it was in the evening, Mr. Reddick proceeded to the gubernatorial mansion. The Governor's salary was then $1,500 a year, and Mrs. French was her own door-girl. Recognizing her guest, she congratulated him on the passage of his railroad bill. "I am afraid we are not out of the woods yet," he responded. "Why so?" said Mrs. French, "I read in the *Register* this morning that your bill had passed both houses and gone to the Governor for his approval." "True," replied Mr. Reddick, "but we are informed that Governor French will veto it." Springing to her feet, and looking Mr. Reddick straight in the face, she said, stamping her foot to enforce her words, "But Governor French shall not veto this bill!" The next morning the bill was returned *approved*.

The provisions of this charter which authorized the construction of a railroad from Rock Island "by way of Ottawa and Joliet to Chicago," and changed the name to "Chicago & Rock Island R. R. Company," were peculiar, and explain its success in the Assembly. It was skillfully drawn to "catch votes" and served its purpose. It provided: 1. That the road should pay toll to the canal board upon all freights carried, with the exception of (a) all live stock; (b) on freight carried after the close of canal navigation; (c) on freight carried during the cessation of canal navigation caused by any casualty or otherwise; (d) on freight received from or destined to a point on said road twenty miles west of the southern termination of the canal. 2. These tolls should cease when the interest and payment of the $1,600,000 should be paid. 3. That the canal trustees should grant the right of way free of cost. 4. If the trustees should refuse their assent to this provision on the first Monday in June after the passage of the act, the tolls imposed should be remitted, and the company have the right to construct the road untrammeled. It was further required that the road should be built within a year. It is needless to add that the canal board made a virtue of necessity and yielded. The act was passed February 7, 1851, and the work begun with energy. The route was surveyed in the early summer and before the following January the whistle of the locomotive was heard in Grundy County. At the time this charter was granted, there were only about one hundred miles of railroad in the State, and the "Kingdom of Grundy," as it was jocosely called, considered itself on the royal road to prosperity and fame. This road follows the general line of canal through the county, and has 106,747 feet of main track, 106,747 feet of second main track, and 8,015 feet of side track in the county.

The Chicago & Alton road is the second railroad of the county in importance and in the order of construction. It was built in response to a demand for a closer connection between Chicago and St. Louis. It crosses the southeast corner of the county, and affords an outlet for the coal found in that region, which, however, was discovered subsequent to the construction of the road. It was opened in 1854, and has 106,737 feet of main track, 63,641 feet of second main track, and 15,102 feet of side track in the county. In 1874 the Chicago & Illinois Valley Railroad was laid to within a few feet of the Mazon Creek in Braceville Township, and in the following year it was continued through the county by the Chicago, Pekin & Southwestern Company. These roads are separate in their organization and are likely to become the prey of more important roads. The former has 39,230 feet of track, and the latter 76,992 feet. The Kankakee & Seneca Railroad is one of local interest, connecting these two points and crossing the county diagonally through the southwestern part of the county, having about 107,000 feet of track in the county. The Wabash, St. Louis & Pacific Railroad appears on the tax duplicate as having 26,740 feet of track in Greenfield Township, the Wilmington Mining & Manufacturing Company some 6,000 feet of track, used to reach the mines of this company in Braceville Township, and the Milwaukee & St. Paul about a mile of track for the same purpose. The railroad interest of Grundy County, however, centers in the two leading roads.

Closely following the advent of the first railroad in Morris came the pioneer newspaper, the harbinger of democratic civilization. This was in 1852; arriving in the village on the verge of winter, accompanied with an almost helpless wife, and possessing barely enough material to answer the requirements of his modest office, J. C. Walters began the publication of an anti-slavery paper, the *Morris Yeoman*. The citizens recognizing the value and importance of having an "organ" contributed such support as they could, and about Oct. 1, 1852, the first number appeared. It was a seven column folio, printed on a sheet 24 by 36 inches in size, and dealt in general topics of news and politics. The "office" was in an adobe hut (an old mud-house is the name by which it is referred to now); the stands and other furniture were home made, and the old "Franklin press," shipped from Ann street, New York, struck off the edition. The editor was unique in appearance, surroundings, and in his literary style. He wore long hair and a cadaverous countenance emphasized by a pair of very dark eyes; his old fashioned press was surmounted, it is said, by an Indian's skull, the eye socket of which served to hold a tallow candle; and his editorials—"philippics" his friends called them—were full of such personal attacks as only the untutored taste of that day could admire. In 1854, the paper passed into the hands of Buffington & Southard and the name changed to the *Herald*. Subsequently, Mr. Buffington retired and Mr. Southard continued its publication until March 30, 1864, when he was called away and sold the paper to C. G. Perry, who subsequently took Mr. Turner in partnership. On Southard's return after about a year's absence, the proprietors of the *Herald*, having accomplished some political ends in which they were interested, offered to sell the paper to him again. This was agreed upon, but when the transfer was about to be made, a political consideration was attached to the bargain which defeated the sale. Angered at this turn of affairs, some of Mr. Southard's friends insisted on his starting up a new paper, and the *Morris Advertiser* was started with Southard as editor and proprietor. It did not take long to demonstrate which was the "fittest," and in accordance with Darwin's formulation of a natural law, the *Herald* sold out, and the two consolidated were conducted by Mr. Southard under the name of *Herald and Advertiser*. It had in the meanwhile been enlarged to a nine column folio, and its name simplified to the *Herald* alone. In October, 1874, the paper was purchased by General P. C. Hays, an Ohio editor of ability, but a native of an adjoining county, who conducted it alone until July 1, 1876, when Mr. Fletcher was added to the firm. It is now a seven column quarto.

The Morris *Gazette* was a six column folio printed on a sheet 21 by 29 in size. It was begun by Andrew J. Ashton in July, 1853. It was Democratic in politics, and of a sharply personal character in all its effusions. The projector of the paper had little or no means, and depended upon party friends to establish the paper. The paper did not succeed, but in 1855, the material was sold to the *Herald*, leaving a deficit to be paid by those who had aided in its establishment. Another paper of the same political faith was established about 1860 by Matt. Parrott, but it was not a success, and failed in a few months. The next paper was the *Reformer*, started in 1872, by "Joe" Simpson. This paper was anti-Republican, principally Democratic, but considerably tinctured with greenbackism. In 1876, this paper passed into the hands of A. R. Barlow, but soon coming back to Mr. Simpson it was closed out. Again, in March, 1880, Col. Blackmore revived Democratic journalism in Morris by issuing the *Morris Democrat*. The paper added a considerable vigor to the campaign of that year, but its energies were soon spent and it died before the issue was decided. It seems to be simply a question of demand and supply, and there being no demand, any paper of pronounced Democratic tendencies gluts the market and necessarily fails.

The *Independent* is a semi-weekly paper, independent in matter as well as in name. Its first number was issued March 1, 1878. It was established by Messrs. Perry, Crawford & Kutz, who leased the material of the *Edwards' Directory* office, Morris. It started as a seven column folio, but was increased one column in March, 1881. The business has fallen into the hands of J. A. Kutz, the other members having dropped out. It is the only semi-weekly paper in the Congressional district.

The other papers of the county are the Gardner *Weekly News*, *Braceville Miner*, and *The Independent*. The first named is a weekly paper published at Gardner, an 8-column folio, printed on a sheet about 26 by 40 inches. It was established September 29th, 1881, by C. M. King, when the "boom" in coal promised a rapid growth to the village. Mr. King, the editor and proprietor, is a busy, energetic man, and publishes editions of his paper adapted to the locality where issued, for Essex, Reddick and Braceville. *The Braceville Miner* is one of these editions, and was begun in 1882. It is the same size of *The News*, but is devoted especially to the interests of the miners, who form the leading part of the paper's patrons. It is

Republican in sentiment upon all political matters, but aims more particularly at furnishing the families of this part of the county with the county news. The office of these publications at Gardner is well equipped with material and presses. The *Independent*, a 6-column folio, printed on a sheet about 22 by 32 inches, is published at Gardner by J. H. Warner. It was established about 1880, as an edition of the paper at Braidwood, in the adjoining county. It aims at local news, and serves its purpose with success.

But deeper than all these elements, more important than markets, or railroads, or newspapers, the foundation of social progress, is the church and school. Whatever success the individual lacking these influences, may achieve, a community can never prosper without them, and much that Grundy County may be proud of is due to these benign forces. The early settlements were considerably scattered, and it was for years a difficult matter to get more than two families together for religious services. The pioneer preachers were men of slender education and homely address, but were wonderfully effective in their self-denying earnestness. They visited from cabin to cabin, exhorting, counseling, reproving, as the occasion might demand; they became in every house a welcome guest, and many a weary heart and feeble hand was stayed by these simple hearted servants of the cross. Among the earliest names familiar to this vicinity were those of Adam and Aaron Payne, Stephen Beggs, William Royal and Isaac Scarrett. These were all of the Methodist church which established an early mission at the mouth of Fox River, in La Salle County. It was from this point that the Rev. Scarrett was brought to solemnize the first wedding within the present boundaries of Grundy County—that of James Galloway to Martha Matilda Stype, at the house of Mr. Isaac Hoge. The introduction of a considerable Irish element here brought with it the Catholic church and its earliest representative, Father Dupontaris, who was a worthy man and proved himself an efficient shepherd of a wayward flock. He was at any time ready to administer "extreme unction" or quell a riot, and did either with equal skill. The Mormons were also represented by their itinerants, but the people of Grundy did not seem to take kindly to their peculiar doctrines and gave them little encouragement. In the meantime, while the country part of the county was being molded and modified by these influences, the principal village was rapidly gaining an unenviable notoriety for its boisterous incivility and it required no little moral and physical courage for the first ministers to attempt to hold services in the old Court House. Several ministers were broken down by the rude participation of the audience in the proceedings of the meeting and left in disgust. The Rev. James Longhead, who founded the first Protestant church in the county, was attracted to Morris, principally by a missionary spirit. On his first entrance into town his vehicle was assailed by a huge foot-ball kicked into it by a boisterous crowd of men and boys who occupied the main street for their game, while ruder oaths from every side assailed his ears. It was the roughest town he had met on his travels from the East, and most in need of gospel influence. Thirty-five years of such influence have wrought great changes; "this was the Lord's doing, and it is marvelous in our eyes."

Hand in hand with the church is found the school. The early library was made up of the Bible, Pilgrim's Progress, the Columbian Orator and Webster's Speller. Out of these the members of the family too young for service in or out of doors drew mild draughts of mental exhilaration. Reading came by the devotion of odd moments from the mother's otherwise crowded life, and once in possession of this magic power, the trials and triumphs of Christian with the eloquence of the "Orator" proved both entertainment and instruction. There were very few private schools in the county before the establishment in this county of the "District Schools," about 1851. Since then there has been a rapid development of school facilities and Grundy County with the rest of the State may pride itself on the possession of educational advantages second to none.

CHAPTER V.*

GRUNDY COUNTY'S SHARE IN THE WAR OF THE REBELLION—THE LOYALTY OF HER MEN—THE DEVOTION OF HER WOMEN—THE REPRESENTATIVES IN THE FIELD.

THE war! What memories, at that magic word, crowd the mind!

"Of most disastrous chances,
Of moving accidents by flood and field;
Of hair-breadth 'scapes i' the imminent deadly breach;
Of being taken by the insolent foe!"

of woman's devotion, and of all the nation's sacrifice during those woeful years! And yet, how our fancy fails. Time's kindly touch has dulled the anguish of those days; fame's "ineffectual fire" is but a misty halo in the intervening shadows, and children read with proud surprise of gallant deeds on unfamiliar fields.

The Senatorial campaign of 1858, with the succeeding Presidential contest in 1860, in which the great citizen of Illinois had been the prominent figure, served to fix the undivided attention of this county, with the rest of the State, upon the political storm which seemed to be gathering with portentous mutterings over the southern portions of the country. It is doubtful whether hope or fear predominated in the minds of the people as the day approached when Lincoln was to be inaugurated, and the universal hope and expectation was that in his grasp the serpent of secession would be strangled, as Jackson had done before in the case of the "nullifiers." It was in this state of vacillation between hope and fear, that the reverberations of Fort Sumpter's guns assailed the ears of the eager North. It was this explosion, echoing round the world, that united the various elements and made men Union or non-Union. Niceties of political distinctions were lost sight of at once, and to the credit of Grundy County be it said, there was but one party here, and that for the support of the Union. Fort Sumpter capitulated on Saturday, April 13, 1861, and on the 15th, the Secretary of War telegraphed to the Governor of Illinois, the apportionment of that State under the President's call for 75,000 men to put down the insurrection at Charleston. The call was made under the authority granted to the President of the United States to call out the militia when the laws of the general government were opposed and the execution thereof obstructed, and required the Governor of Illinois to "detach from the militia" 225 officers and 4,458 men. The militia thus called upon had no actual existence in this State. Here and there through the State were half-filled companies of holiday troops, but even these in a majority of cases had no efficient organization or equipment. On the 15th, the Legislature was called to convene on the 23d inst., and an order issued from the Adjutant General's office to the various militia officers to hold themselves in readiness for actual service. On the following day an order was issued for

---

* By J. H Battle.

the immediate organization of the six regiments called for by the general government. The response from every part of the State was prompt and unanimous, and in ten days over ten thousand men tendered their services to the government for the defense of the Union. In the meanwhile such companies as had an organization and partial equipment were hurried forward, under General Swift, to Cairo. This force amounted to 908 officers and men, including among others the Ottawa Light Artillery from this section of the State. Of the ten thousand men that gathered at Springfield in response to the Governor's call, the majority were in company organization, clothed and equipped by the communities which sent them forth. Of these Grundy County sent out the "Grundy Tigers," with W. T. Hopkins, Capt.; Sam'l Elton, 1st Lieut.; G. S. Doane, 2d Lieut., and Capt. Hulburd's Company which was mustered in June as Company E. of the Twenty-Third Regiment of Infantry.

The response from this county to the governor's call, was prompt and enthusiastic. On the 20th inst., the Board of Supervisors voted $5,000 for the equipment of volunteers and the aid of their families, while ladies very soon after organized a "Soldier's Aid Society" which enlisted for the war. The record of the disbursement of the fund thus provided by the Supervisors, is quite amusing in the light of subsequent events. The people here, as everywhere else, were impressed that the war would be over in sixty days, and that the business in hand was little more than a squirrel hunt in which there might be accidents, or at worst not more serious than putting down a mob. With this view the country and town was scoured for guns, the men were provided with boots, and the ladies prepared such additions to a soldier's bill of fare, as would make his temporary absence from home less irksome. But the war did not end in sixty days, and the first draft came and found the people of Grundy County relying on their first effort. This was a rude awakening, and from that time to the end of the war, the county was alive to the exigencies of the occasion. In August, 1862, a bounty of $60 was offered, of which one hundred and seventy-six men availed themselves. On December 30, 1863, the Board offered to pay $110.00 ($100 with interest at ten per cent. in bonds payable in one year) to all soldiers "who now, have been, or hereafter may be regularly mustered into the service of the United States, as Grundy County volunteers." Under this resolution eighty-five men were paid as new volunteers, and in 1881, under this resolution, $2,750 additional was paid on old claims. In May, 1864, under the call for "one hundred days" men a bounty of twenty-five dollars was offered and paid to sixty-four volunteers. The war had by this time become a very serious business, and while there was no lack of loyal regard for the cause of the Union, the burden began seriously to be felt, and there was less alacrity manifested in volunteering. Those who had lighter claims upon them at home, had either felt some of the severities of soldier life, or were disposed to take their chance of being drafted, while those whose families and business seemed to demand their staying at home were anxious to avoid the necessities of a draft. There was in addition to all this, an unselfish desire to avoid the draft as a reflection upon the county's loyalty to the cause, and in September, 1864, the Board of Supervisors impelled by these various motives, offered a bounty of $300 to each volunteer under the call of July of that year. Under this action of the Board one hundred and ninety-five persons were paid this bounty at a gross expense of something more than $64,000. The revised enrollment of persons in the county subject to military duty, made January, 1865, placed the number at 1,622. The total quota under the various calls during the war was 1,364 men, of which 1,343 were credited to the county. This would leave a deficit in the number of men required of the county, but in such a vast undertaking, with the necessary official machinery to originate and put in motion, it was impossible to avoid all errors; and while Grundy County appears to have fallen short of her quota by the official records, it is susceptible of proof that she furnished many more than her quota, which were unfortunately credited elsewhere.*

In the matter of bounties it is equally difficult to get an accurate statement of all the county expended in putting troops into the field. The records show, however, that the county authorities expended $112,175, and the various townships, in their separate capacity, over $27,000, to which should be added private subscriptions and subsequent payments by the county, which would bring the total up to the amount of $145,000.

The Soldiers' Aid Society of Morris was auxiliary to the society in Chicago over which Mesdames Hoge and Livermore presided with such efficiency. Every expedient which would bring an honest dollar into the treasury was successfully tried, and the fund thus accumulated was religiously expended here, or sent to the society at Chicago for the benefit of the boys in the field. It would be a tedious recital to recall the various expedients resorted to by the ladies to extort the last dollar in aid of their enterprise. The regular plan was to collect gifts of money, under-clothing, etc., make up a box and send it to some company or hospital. To vary the monotony of this plan, and to approach the public on a more susceptible side, balls were given and fairs held. One of the most important of these was the "Sanitary Fair," held on the grounds, and in connection with the Agricultural Society of this county. In a spacious dining hall, one hundred feet long, dinner was served to large crowds on each day of the fair. The supplies were contributed by the various townships interested in the Agricultural Fair, and the proceeds, beside a large number of the entries, were contributed to the purposes of the society. Canned fruits, vegetables and pickles, were among the donations from the farmers' wives—one lot of twelve half-barrels of pickles coming from the ladies of Minooka. Others gave hay, coal and cattle, which were sold, free of charge, on the grounds, and we may believe the bidding was not less spirited because it was known the proceeds were to be devoted to the army hospitals. But this dry recital does

---

*In October, 1862, a list of volunteers furnished by the different townships of the county was as follows: Erienna, 13; Au Sable, 76; Braceville, 53; Felix, 20; Goodfarm, 52; Greenfield, 51; Highland, 68; Mazon, 91; Morris, 1; Nettle Creek, 63; Norman, 24; Saratoga, 62; Vienna, 38; Wauponsee, 52; City of Morris—1st ward, 38; 2d ward, 43; 3d ward, 78; 4th ward, 17; a total of 855.

woman's work during the period of the war scant justice. The value of her moral support and courageous self-sacrifice can never be adequately estimated, nor its appreciation placed too high.

> "The wife who girds her husband's sword,
> 'Mid little ones who weep or wonder,
> And bravely speaks the cheering word,
> What though her heart be rent asunder,
> Doomed nightly in her dreams to hear
> The bolts of death around him rattle,
> Hath shed as sacred blood as e'er
> Was poured upon the field of battle."

The law provided that in token of respect to the Illinois regiments in the Mexican war, the six regiments organized under the first call of the President should begin their designating number at seven, and that these regiments when organized should constitute the "First Brigade Illinois Volunteers." The *Eleventh*, therefore, was the fifth regiment organized, of which the Grundy Tigers constituted Company F. This regiment was mustered in at Springfield, April 30, 1861, and on May 5th was ordered to Villa Ridge, in this State, in the vicinity of Cairo. In the following month the regiment was ordered to Bird Point on the other side of the river, where the regiment served out its term of enlistment in garrison and field duty. While not seeing any active service during this time the regiment, with others assembled at this point, did excellent duty in warding off the danger which the overwhelming forces of the rebels on the river below threatened, and at the same time gained that discipline which made them such efficient soldiers during the war. On July 30th, its term of enlistment having expired, the regiment was mustered out of service, and having re-enlisted for three years, it was on the following day mustered in for three years. The old number was retained, but the arrangement of companies was considerably changed, the Grundy County Company taking the letter C. The membership of the regiment was greatly changed as well. Out of 916 mustered out only 288 were mustered in again on the following day, but during the months of August, September, October and November, it was recruited to about 801 men. During this time the regiment doing garrison and field duty, participated in several unimportant expeditions, among others, the one to Charleston, Mo., where they got into a spirited skirmish with the enemy. February 2d, the regiment embarked on transports for Fort Henry, participating in the campaign against that place, and on the 11th inst. moved toward Fort Donelson. Here the regiment got their first "baptism of fire." The regiment came in sight of the fort about noon of the 12th, and here Wallace's brigade, composed of the 11th, 20th, 45th and 48th Ill. Volunteers, Taylor's and McAllister's batteries of light artillery, and Col. Dickey's cavalry, halted and drew up in line of battle. Col. Oglesby's brigade took up its position on the right of Wallace, and in this position but little occurred save occasional shots at the enemy and a change of position, until the 15th. Grant had in the meanwhile strengthened his line of investment, so that but little hope of escape remained to the garrison. On the morning of the 15th, therefore, the enemy, to the number of 7,500, emerged from his works and in separate columns hurled himself on the right of the federal line, seeking to break through and escape. The first blow dealt upon Oglesby's brigade, was followed by a second on Wallace's brigade and then upon Morrison's and McArthur's brigades constituting the extreme right. One of the "Grundy Tigers" writes as follows of this engagement: "The rebels fought well but not fairly—like Indians, they sought shelter of stumps and trees. The first attack on the 11th regiment was made by a regiment of Mississippi riflemen. We suffered them to advance to within 100 yards, when we opened upon them with terrible effect and drove them back to their trenches, where they were reinforced and advanced again, this time within fifty yards, but were again forced to retire. We suffered severely, but not a soldier fell back unless wounded. At this time we had lost about eighty men, killed and wounded. The rebels withdrew their troops from our front and concentrated them on our right, and very soon we knew by the firing that Oglesby's brigade was giving way. It proved worse than we expected. First came the 18th in full retreat, followed by the rest of the brigade. By great exertion Col. Logan rallied the 31st on our right, forming two sides of a hollow square, and here for half an hour these two regiments held the enemy in check, the 31st giving way and rallying twice, only to retreat in utter confusion at last. The 11th still held its own, Lieut. Col. Ransom, though wounded, remaining cool and firm. We changed our front by the right flank, where the 31st had been under a most galling fire, firing as we moved around by the side step, until ordered to halt. The rebels, exultant at the retreat of the 31st, pressed forward to within forty yards of our line, but they were mistaken in their men, and soon fell back to a ridge, 150 yards distant, leaving the ground strewn with their dead and wounded.

"There, by a little ravine, we remained for half an hour, fighting three times our number, outflanked on either side, waiting for reinforcements, which did not come. Suddenly a body of rebel cavalry charged across the ridge, on our left, and gained our rear. There was but one way of escape, and that lay through the body of cavalry, and through we went, the bayonet opening the way. Two hours afterward, the remnant of our regiment drew up to receive Col. Wallace, who, being in command of the brigade, had seen us but once since the battle began. It was no fault of his that we were left unprotected. When Oglesby's brigade gave way, he sent an order to Col. Ransom to fall back on the 20th, but the messenger was killed. The tears streamed down Col. Wallace' face as he scanned his regiment. Over 600 had engaged the enemy, and 115 muskets were all we had left to show. Our flag still waved over us, though shot to ribbons. Early next morning we marched into the fort, the 11th being allowed to lead the van, on account of its having suffered the most severely. The loss in this regiment, so far as we can learn, is 329 killed, wounded and missing. Of the Grundy Tigers, but one is missing." In this battle, Grundy County suffered severely. Out of sixteen men who enlisted from the southern part of the county in another company, every man was wounded.

Early in March, the regiment went by Fort Henry to Savannah, Tenn., and thence to Pittsburgh Landing, where it took part in the bloody battle of Shiloh, of April 6th and 7th. The 11th, incorporated in the division of McClernand, was on the right of the federal line, near where the line touched the lower point of the river, and with its division supported Sherman in the first onset of that memorable battle. Here the regiment suffered cruelly, as they did in the second day's fight, losing 27 killed and wounded out of 150 engaged. After participating in the protracted siege of Corinth and in the engagements near Trenton, Tenn., the regiment was finally ordered back to Cairo to recruit. In the latter part of August the 11th proceeded once more to the front, taking part in various expeditions, reporting in the latter part of November to Gen. McArthur, at Lagrange, Tenn., when it was assigned to the 13th Army Corps. During the early part of 1863, the regiment took part in the campaign in northern Mississippi; later, resting for a time in Memphis, it was assigned, in February, to the 17th Army Corps, reinforced by a consolidation with the 109th Ill., and ordered to Vicksburg, where it arrived May 18th. On the 19th and 22d, the regiment was engaged in the assaults upon the enemy's works; then in the advance siege works up to July 4th, when the city surrendered. In these engagements the regiment lost its colonel, three line officers, and forty men. The regiment subsequently took part in the Natchez expedition, returning to Vicksburg in October, where it remained till the latter part of July, 1864, engaging in various minor expeditions from that point. At this time, the 11th was assigned to the 19th Army Corps, and after taking part in several minor expeditions, took part in the reduction of Mobile, Ala., participating in the investment and siege of Spanish Fort and Fort Blakely, and in the assault upon the latter. This ended its active service, and, moving from one point to another, it was mustered out of the service, July 14th, 1865, at Alexandria, La., when the regiment left for Springfield, Ill., for payment and final discharge.

Among the early volunteers from Grundy County was Capt. Hulburd's company. This company was among those that were crowded out of the earlier regiments, but was accepted by the State, and finally authorized by the Secretary of War during the month of June and on the 15th was mustered into the service as Company E of the 23rd regiment, but better known as the "Irish Brigade," under command of Col. Mulligan. The regiment enlisted under the call for "three months" volunteers, and spent an uneventful career, first at Quincy, Ill., and then at the St. Louis arsenal, until the latter part of July, when the regiment was moved to Jefferson City, Mo. In the latter part of August the regiment was re-enlisted, a large part, however, returning to Chicago and being mustered out. In the reorganization which followed the re-enlistment of the regiment, 21 men of Company E., 52 men of Company G., and 25 men of Company H, were consolidated and called Company G, which, by an order of Jan. 3, 1865, was changed to Company C. The movement of Gen. Price toward Jefferson City caused Col. Mulligan, who had been engaged in several minor expeditions, to move to Lexington as soon as possible after the reorganization, and arriving at the place on the 9th of September he set at once to fortifying his position. His command consisted of the 23d Ill. infantry, 1st Ill. cavalry, and about 1,200 Missouri "home guards," the entire force numbering less than 3,000 men. Gen. Price set down before the works on the 11th, with a force estimated at 20,000. An assault was made on the following day, but so determined was the resistance that the rebel General was forced to undertake a siege. The nature of the works, however, left no room to doubt the speedy result of such an attack, unless relieved by reinforcements. The besieging force saturated bales of hemp to prevent their ignition from the hot shots of Mulligan's guns, and rolled them in front of the intrenchments, and quietly mounted his guns. Price, who had been waiting for ammunition, on the 18th opened with thirteen guns, posted in commanding positions. Col. Mulligan had but five small brass pieces with which to reply to this fire, and these were charged with rough shot manufactured for the occasion at a neighboring foundry. These pieces were worked, however, with great gallantry, and served to command very considerable respect from the besiegers. Price had previously seized the boats on the river, and fortified the adjacent bluffs, so that the federal troops were entirely cut off from water, and suffered the most intense agonies of thirst. It rained, however, at intervals, and the thirsty men, by spreading their blankets till they became saturated with water, and then wringing them into camp dishes, were enabled to prolong the siege until the 20th, when they surrendered. The Missouri troops, "invincible in peace and invisible in war," left the burden of the defense with the Illinois troops, constituting scarcely more than half of the whole number. A writer in the Chicago *Post* spoke of the 23d regiment as follows: "On the 17th the enemy commenced erecting breastworks of hemp bales, from behind which they continued to fire as they rolled them toward us. About three o'clock of the same day they charged over our entrenchments, upon Col. Peabody's home guards, and planted their flags on the top of our breastworks. The Irish Brigade was ordered to leave its position on the opposite side, and to retake the ground which Peabody had lost. We fired on the run, and continued on the double quick. The rebels scattered and fled like a flock of sheep, but left the top of the breastworks covered with dead and wounded. In this single charge we killed and wounded 55 and lost about 30 killed and wounded." An officer in the rebel service wrote of the capitulation: "This surrender does not cast the slightest discredit upon Col. Mulligan, his officers and men. After having exhausted all their means against an enemy three times their strength they had no choice but capitulation." The regiment was paroled, and by order of Gen. Fremont mustered out of the service in October, but was restored in December by order of McClellan. After remaining at Camp Douglas, near Chicago, guarding prisoners and recruiting until June 14, 1862, the regiment was moved to Western Virginia. Here the regiment found plenty of service, and had repeated encounters with rebel detachments, Company G being captured April 25, 1863, and sent to Richmond. The regiment was mustered out at Richmond, Va., July 24, 1865, and arrived in Chicago six days later.

Grundy County was also represented in the Thirty-sixth regiment by Company G, of that organization. This regiment, like the 23d, was made up of those volunteers who tendered their services just too late to be accepted under the first call of the President. "A meeting of persons interested in the organization of a 'Fox River Regiment' was held at Geneva on the 29th day of July, 1861, and preliminary steps taken for its organization. Fifteen companies, either complete or in an advanced state of formation, were represented and tendered for acceptance, twelve of which were selected, including two cavalry companies."* This regiment was duly authorized by the proper authorities, and Col. N. Grensel was appointed to the command of the "Fox River Regiment," under date of August 14, 1861. The regiment went into camp near Aurora, was mustered into the three years' service September 23d, and uniformed, and on the following day started for St. Louis, where they were armed. The regiment was at once ordered to Rolla, Mo., remaining there until January, 1862, when it took part in the campaign against Price, resulting in the series of engagements ending with the battle of Pea Ridge. In this battle, especially, the 36th took a conspicuous part. It was a part of the Second brigade of Osterhaus' division, and occupied a position on the left of the Federal line. Company G. was the most severely handled, losing thirteen men while in skirmish line. Col. Grensel's report of his part in the engagement describes this action as follows: "My attention was now called to several regiments of infantry in our front, and immediately opposite the 36th Illinois Volunteers, whereupon I threw out Companies B and G of that regiment as skirmishers. These companies crossed the field,

---

*Bennett & Haight's Hist. of 36th Regt.

and on entering the timber discovered the enemy in ambush—three regiments drawn up in line and others formed in square, evidently expecting another attack from our cavalry. A rapid fire was opened up by the enemy and returned by the skirmishers, which was kept up for fifteen minutes. Finding that they were wasting ammunition to no purpose, the skirmishers retired in good order, with a loss of twenty wounded—thirteen in Company G, and seven in Company B."

The regiment was subsequently transferred to the Department of the Mississippi and marched to Cape Girardeau, Mo., and on their arrival was transferred to Gen. Pope's command. September 6, 1862, the regiment was ordered to Cincinnati, O., to defend the city against Gen. Bragg's raid across Kentucky, and joined in his pursuit when that general was forced to retreat. In the battle of Perryville, which followed, the 36th regiment, which formed a part of Sheridan's division, occupied an advanced position in front of Barrett's battery near the center of the federal line. Here the regiment was the object of a fierce attack by three regiments of Hardee's famous troops, and maintained a sharp fight until the ammunition being exhausted the 36th was retired, losing 75 men. They were ordered subsequently to the support of another battery, but did not again become engaged with the enemy. With the rest of the army the 36th went forward to Nashville, where it remained until the latter part of December, 1862, when it moved out with the army under Rosecrans to the bloody encounter of Stone River. In this battle McCook's corps occupied the right of the Union line, Sheridan's division being on the left of this corps. Of the 36th regiment's part in this action Col. Grensel reported: "At daylight on the 31st (December, 1862) the regiment was assaulted by a rebel brigade, under Gen. Weathers, and being supported by the 88th Illinois, on its left, the enemy was soon driven back to the woods; but again and again they were rallied, every time meeting the same fate, until thirty-eight of that fine brigade were all that were left to tell where their rebel comrades had fallen. The 36th charged them at the point of the bayonet twice in succession, driving them back. Forty-one of the poor boys lay dead on their faces on less than an acre of ground. The number of wounded is large, and, in fact, the killed and wounded are the largest in the whole division." Out of this fight the regiment brought only 200 men, Company G losing three men killed and thirteen wounded.

After the battle of Stone River, succeeded a period of more or less inactivity, in which the regiment recruited its wasted energies, losing its colonel in the meanwhile by resignation, his place being supplied by Col. Silas Miller. In September, however, the 36th was called again to face the enemy at Chickamauga. On the 19th, the regiment marched ten miles, from Pond Springs to Gordon's Mills, Sheridan's division occupying at that time the extreme right of the federal line. The attack upon this portion of the line was especially severe. Lieut. Col. Olson's report of this engagement is as follows: "At 2 P. M. went into position near Gordon's Mills, with one company thrown forward as skirmishers. At 5 P. M. fell back to the timber, about 200 yards, and remained during the night. At 4 A. M., 20th, marched two miles and a quarter to the left and formed in the second line. At 11 A. M., after some skirmishing, was ordered forward to the support of the center. Formed on the brow of a hill, under a most terrible fire, but in perfect good order, and engaged the enemy fiercely, checking his advance. At this juncture, the enemy appeared on the left, and, turning the flank, subjected us to a murderous, enfilading fire, against which we could offer but little resistance. The regiment was ordered to fall back. Here the regiment made another stand, but was overwhelmed by numbers, and compelled to fall back." At this juncture, Sheridan's division was relieved, and ordered to Rossville to rescue a train which was in danger of falling into the hands of the enemy. This was skillfully done, the troops going silently within rifle shot of the enemy, securing the train without discovery, and going into camp five miles away. On the 22d, the regiment took up its line of retreat to Chattanooga. In this engagement, Company G lost twenty-two men.

On the following day, the siege and defense of Chattanooga began, the 36th beginning the construction of rifle pits, by five o'clock next morning. Here some two months were spent in watching the enemy on the heights about the city, living on half or no rations, and wondering whether the issue would be starvation or retreat. In the meanwhile the army had changed leaders, the line of supplies had been opened, and Sherman's and Hooker's forces added to the army, which was now under the immediate command of Gen. Grant. About noon of November 23d, 1863, the order was given to the 36th to "fall in," and with Sheridan's division it supported Wood's division, in what was intended as a reconnoisance of the enemy on Orchard Knob. The slight resistance of the enemy changed the character of the movement, and the troops, reinforced by Howard's division, occupied the position gained and fortified, the 36th holding a position on the hill just south of Orchard Knob, where is now the National Cemetery. In the meanwhile, Hooker had taken Lookout Mountain, but his troops, out of ammunition, were forced to remain inactive until their cartridge boxes were replenished, and so passed the day. On the 24th, Sherman renewed his attacks upon the northern summits of Mission Ridge, but finding it impossible to make rapid progress, and Hooker being delayed on the left, Grant determined upon a movement from the center. The plan was to take the rifle pits at the foot of the ridge, by the skirmish line if possible, and the 36th furnished three companies for this service. This was accomplished. From this point a hill rose eight hundred feet out of the valley, swept by a storm of bullets, shot and shell. Along its face, half-way up, stretched a line of works, then 400 feet further up, with the steepness of a gothic roof, rough with rocks and strewn with fallen trees, the summit frowned with all its terrible enginery of war. To stay in the rifle pits already gained meant death, to retreat was as certain destruction, and so without orders the troops struggled up through the deluge of death-dealing missiles. In this fight Company G did not lose a man, though the regiment lost some twenty. In January, 1864, the regiment re-enlisted, and arrived in Chicago on "veteran furlough," at midnight of February 2d. After partaking of the hospitalities of the city, the various companies separated for the localities of their homes, Company G being received at Morris with enthusiastic demonstrations, which was repeated during their six weeks' stay, at the various points where the friends of the regiment resided. During the furlough of the regiment every effort was made by the members to recruit its numbers. Company G took back twenty veterans and eleven recruits. March 19, 1864, the regiment took the cars for Chicago, on their way back to the field. The regiment proceeded at once to Chattanooga, and from thence took part in the actions of Dalton, Resaca, Kenesaw, Atlanta, Spring Hill, Franklin, and Nashville. After the pursuit of Hood, which took the regiment to Lexington, Ala., it returned to Nashville, where it remained until the 15th of June, when orders were received to proceed to New Orleans. Here the 36th was retained for headquarter and special duty until October 8, 1865, when it was mustered out of the service.

In Company I of the 55th regiment, this county was represented by some fifty men, the balance of the company being drawn from La Salle County. The regiment was mustered into the three years' service October 31, 1861, at Camp Douglas. The 55th was ordered January, 1862, to Paducah, Ky., where they remained till March 8, when they were ordered to the Tennessee River to take part in the movements about Corinth. This regiment was finally taken to Pittsburgh Landing, where it was placed on the left of the federal line in that memorable fight. Out of 873 men taken into the fight, 102 enlisted men were killed, and 161 wounded and taken prisoners. It took part in the siege of Corinth, and its colors were the first in the captured city; with Sherman's division the 55th participated in the expedition to Holly Springs, Miss., thence to Memphis; thence to take part in the battle of Chickasaw Bayou, Dec. 29, 1862, losing in this engagement ten men. From this point having re-embarked with the army, it took part in the battle of Arkansas Post; thence to Young's Point early in 1863, and in April joined the army about Vicksburg, taking part in several expeditions against the enemy's outlying posts and in the assaults, 19th and 22d May, upon the main works. Following the fortunes of Sherman's division, the regiment found its way to Chattanooga in November, 1863, and took part in the preliminary movements of the battle of Mission Ridge. In the following winter it re-enlisted and was home on a veteran furlough of thirty days. On its return it rejoined Sherman, took part in the engagements of Kenesaw Mountain, losing 48 men; again in July losing 33 men; in the siege of Atlanta losing 25 men; and in the fight of Jonesboro, losing 23 men. It subsequently joined in the pursuit of Hood through northern Alabama, when it returned to Atlanta, and later with the 15th Army Corps went to Savannah. Marched from Richmond to Washington, took part in the grand review, then moved to Louisville; thence to Little Rock, Ark., where it was mustered out of the service August 14, 1865.

Company I of the 69th regiment was made up principally from Grundy County. This regiment was organized under the call for three months men in 1862, and was mustered into the service June 14, 1862, at Camp Douglas. They were assigned duty of guarding prisoners at this camp and served out their term of enlistment here, being mustered out Sept. 27, 1862.

Company C of the 76th regiment was raised entirely in Grundy County. This company was organized in the summer of 1862, went into camp at Kankakee and was mustered into the service August 22, 1862. The 76th was ordered as soon as mustered to Columbus, Ky., and from thence to Bolivar, Tenn., October 3d. Late in November the regiment joined Grant's forces in the campaign along the Mississippi Central Railroad, and in February, 1863, proceeded to Memphis and thence to Vicksburg, where it took part in the assault of May 22d. This regiment subsequently took part in the movement against Jackson, Meriden, and the expeditions of February and May, 1864, up the Yazoo River. In July, 1864, it was in Slocum's expedition against Jackson, and bore a prominent part in the battle of July 6th and 7th. On the latter day it was cut off from the balance of the command, but cut its way out, losing ninety-eight men. Took part in various minor movements in Louisiana, Mississippi, and Arkansas, and joined in Steele's expedition from Pensacola to Blakely, Ala. May 9, 1865, engaged in the assault and capture of Fort Blakely, losing seventeen killed and eighty-one wounded, but succeeded in being the first to plant the national colors upon the enemy's works. After long marches and tedious encampments at Selden, Mobile and Galveston, the regiment was mustered out and ordered home, July 22, 1865.

In the 91st regiment of Illinois infantry,

Grundy County was represented by Company D. This company was raised in August, 1862, and going to Camp Butler was mustered into the service Sept. 8, 1862. In the following month the regiment was ordered to Louisville and was assigned to duty guarding the Louisville and Nashville railroad. The regiment formed a part of the large force guarding the Louisville and Nashville railroad, and occupied seven detached posts on thirty miles of the line of that road. Three companies were stationed at each of the trestles at Big Run and Sulphur Fork, which are about a mile apart, and seven or eight miles north of Elizabethtown; one company, Capt. Fosha's (Co. D), occupied a stockade at this place; portions of one company, Capt. Hanna's (enlisted in Kendall County), were stationed at two bridges about a mile apart, and nearly two miles south of Elizabethtown; one company at Nolin's Fork, nine miles, and one at Bacon Creek, twenty miles south of Elizabethtown. These detachments had all received orders not to leave their different positions for any cause whatever, but to hold and defend them to the last extremity. For some days before the attack of Gen. Morgan, reports were constantly received at the different stations that the rebels were approaching in large force, and the impression was universal throughout the regiment that under the orders they had received, the small detachments at the different posts would be gobbled up, one after the other, by superior numbers. These reports and impressions were fully confirmed late on Friday night, by the arrival at Elizabethtown of two negroes who had escaped from the companies at Bacon Creek and Nolin's Fork bringing intelligence that both of these companies had been attacked that day by the rebels and compelled to surrender. Capt. Fosha immediately sent a messenger to headquarters at Big Run Trestle, informing Lieut. Col. Smith of the intelligence he had just received by the escaped negroes.

"During the night the rebel scouts were quite active and bold, but our pickets were watchful and alert, and no advantage was obtained. Early in the morning skirmishers were sent out to feel the enemy and retard their advance, and about eight o'clock the six companies at the Trestle, having been relieved by the 71st Indiana volunteers, arrived at Elizabethtown under Lieut. Col. Smith, who immediately ordered Capt. Hanna's company at the bridges below to join him. The command then consisted of eight companies, mustering about 450 effective men, which Col. Smith drew up in line of battle on the west side of the railroad, close by the stockade in which Capt. Fosha's men were left, with orders to hold it. Up to this time, neither the rebel forces nor their commander was known. To ascertain these facts Col. Smith sent out a flag of truce, demanding their immediate surrender. The demand was of course refused, and in about half an hour Col. Smith received a reply signed by John H. Morgan, stating that he had Col. Smith's forces surrounded, and that in ten minutes his batteries would be in position to open upon him, and demanding the surrender of his command. To this Col. Smith replied that it was the duty of United States soldiers to fight, not to surrender. In less than ten minutes allowed by Gen. Morgan, one of his batteries had taken position on some high bluffs to the right of the Nashville pike, and within a thousand yards of the town, and opened fire upon Col. Smith's forces; at the same time, heavy columns of the enemy were observed moving to the right and left of the town, with the evident intention of surrounding our troops. To avoid this it became necessary to change the position of the regiment, which Col. Smith did by moving his men into the town and taking possession of the court house and buildings on the square. On the retirement of the outside forces and before the enemy had advanced on the stockade, Capt. Fosha withdrew his forces and followed the retreat of the rest of the regiment into the town, and occupied a building on the south side of the square. It was now ten o'clock and Col. Smith had determined to hold the buildings to the last extremity. The enemy opened fire upon the town with his artillery, the building from which the regimental colors were flying being struck seventeen times and badly riddled. The men, however, were maintaining their discipline, though several were killed and others wounded, and were returning the musket firing with some effect. As the enemy approached the suburbs of the town, and were dismounting with the evident intention of making an attack upon the regiment's position, numbers of saddles were unceremoniously emptied by the accuracy of our fire, which made the rebels hesitate to advance. The firing had been maintained upward of three hours, and the Union forces were expecting an assault which they confidently expected to repel with heavy loss to the enemy, when a white flag was thrown out of a window in the building occupied by Capt. Fosha's company. It was immediately ordered to be shot down, and when fired upon was withdrawn, but another immediately appeared on the street, and Capt. Fosha's men were seen coming out of the building and throwing down their arms. The firing ceased at once, and the rebels rushing in from the alleys and cover of the houses, captured the whole regiment."* The forces under Morgan numbered some eight or ten thousand with thirteen guns, and the capture of the regiment was a foregone conclusion from the first, but the spirited resistance offered by our troops delayed the rebel expedition and forced them to lose valuable time. When paroled, the regiment was ordered to Benton Barracks, Mo., and in January, 1863, were sent home on furlough. In February, they were ordered back, and subsequently ordered to Vicksburg where they arrived July 14th. They took part in the movements to Port Hudson, Carrollton, La., and Atchafalaya River, arriving at Morganzia, 10th of October. Transferred to the 13th army corps, they went to New Orleans, going into camp October 12th. Later in the month the regiment was ordered to Texas; took part in several minor engagements, and in July, 1864, occupied Brazos Santiago as part of the garrison. About the last of December, the 91st was relieved and transferred to New Orleans and placed on provost duty. In February, it joined the forces at Fort Morgan and subsequently took an active part in the campaign which resulted in the capture of Spanish Fort and Fort Blakely. Following up the retreat of the rebels, the federal forces overtook the enemy at Eight-mile Creek, where a sharp engagement took place, the 91st leading a

---

*Grundy County Herald, January 14, 1863.

bayonet charge, which cleared the field. This was the last engagement of the war east of the Mississippi. The regiment was mustered out of the service, July 12, 1865, at Mobile, and reached Camp Butler on the 22d of the same month.

The 127th Illinois infantry contained nearly a full company from Grundy County, Company D, which was organized about August, 1863, and was mustered at Camp Douglas in September, though the regiment was not organized until October. Early in the following month the regiment was ordered to the field, going by rail to Cairo, and thence by steamboat to Memphis. Taking part in the Talahatchie River expedition, the 127th, on its return to Memphis, was ordered to Vicksburg. The regiment was in Blair's division under Sherman, and after taking their turn at ditching in the various bayous (a line of operations soon abandoned), and the transports having successfully passed the Vicksburg batteries, the 127th, with the rest of the division, steamed up the Yazoo River to divert the attention of the enemy from Grant's real object of crossing the Mississippi. The main army having crossed the river and beaten the enemy back from Fort Gibson and Grand Gulf, a feint was made in the direction of Vicksburg while waiting the return of Sherman's corps, which was ordered to join the main force by a march across the country. Gen. Johnson, who commanded the rebel force in the West, had been apprised of Grant's movements, and was gathering an army to reinforce Pemberton at Vicksburg and to guard against being assailed in the rear. Grant, refraining from moving on the city, attracted Pemberton's attention by a feint, and directed Sherman to follow the eastern side of the Black River to Edward's Station on the Vicksburg railroad, and McPherson to make a detour farther eastward, destroying rebel stores and lines of communication. At Raymond, a few miles south of Edward's Station, a force of the enemy was struck by McPherson, when a short and sharp engagement ensued. The rebels were forced to a second position, and after a severe struggle were driven from the field in disorder, retreating toward Jackson. Fearing the enemy under Johnson at Jackson might prove too numerous for McPherson's force, Sherman and McClernand were directed to follow to Jackson, where, in company with McPherson, they fought the battle of Jackson, forcing the rebels to retreat. Leaving Sherman to destroy bridges, arsenals and other public property, the rest of the army faced about westward to close in upon Vicksburg. Pemberton had moved out to Edward's Station in the meanwhile, and thinking to cut Grant off from his base of supplies, which had been at Grand Gulf, he pushed down toward Raymond, when he found by the Union pickets advancing from the east that Grant had changed his base, and his was a fruitless errand. He now proposed to follow the orders of Johnson, and by retracing his steps to escape by a northeasterly route through Brownsville and join the latter's defeated forces. But his resolution came too late, for the Union forces had occupied this town and were prepared to dispute his advance. As the only alternative the rebel forces were hastily drawn up for action, and then followed the battle of Champion Hills. A courier was sent to

Sherman at Jackson with orders to bring his troops to the scene of conflict. The battle was fought by the troops of McPherson's and McClernand's corps, and the rebel army retreating, these troops pressed rapidly forward in their wake, while Sherman advanced in the direction of Bridgeport, higher up the river, with the intention of crossing at that point. On the following morning, finding the enemy disputing the passage of Black River, McClernand's troops proceeded at once to the attack and soon had the enemy flying. Bridges were placed across the river that night, and Sherman, still on the right of the line, took possession of Haine's Bluffs, while McPherson and McClernand completed the investment of the city. In these operations the 127th, while in active service, enduring severe marching and performing valuable service, was not called upon to do any heavy fighting, though losing a number of men in a number of severe skirmishes. In war, however, there is more drudgery to be done than glory to be gained, and

"He also serves who only stands and waits."

The enemy's forces, rapidly driven into their works about the city, were considerably demoralized, and though the works were skillfully constructed and located, in a naturally strong position, the necessities of the situation seemed to demand quicker results than could be secured by siege. A general assault was therefore made on the afternoon of May 17th, and while no advantage was gained, the 127th had opportunity of showing its metal; this regiment and the 83d Indiana alone succeeding in placing their colors upon the outward slope of the enemy's works. On May 22d they again joined in the general assault, but the works proved too strong and the army sat down to a laborious siege. On July 4, this stronghold capitulated, and on the following day Sherman's corps moved out to Jackson where a force of the enemy had intrenched to dispute the further advance of the victorious federals.

In the meantime the Chattanooga campaign had been fought, ending in Chickamauga and the close surveillance of Chattanooga. Grant had been placed in general command of the west, while Thomas had superseded Rosecrans. After the Jackson expedition the 127th with its corps returned to Vicksburg; in September took transports to Memphis and thence by way of Corinth, Iuka and East Point went to Chattanooga, arriving at the latter place September 23d. After taking part in the movements culminating in Mission Ridge, the regiment made the forced march to Knoxville and having relieved the troops besieged there, returned to Chattanooga. Grant having been made Lieut. General and put in command of the whole field, east and west, Sherman succeeded him in command of the Department of the Mississippi, and at once commenced the campaign of Atlanta. Johnson having succeeded Bragg in command of the rebel forces, had taken a strong natural position at Dalton and greatly strengthened it by fortifications. Here, Sherman finding the position too strong to take by an attack in front, diverted the attention of the enemy by a feint attack and began the flank movements for which he became so famous. The 127th was of the flanking forces, and making a detour to the westward came upon the enemy at Resaca. Here the bearing of this regiment was especially marked by its gallant fighting. On one occasion our men had been ordered back, a movement which evoked exultant shouts from the enemy who supposed we were repulsed. The color bearer of the 127th, becoming exasperated and regardless of danger, returned to an embrasure and defiantly flaunted his flag in the face of the enemy. His life paid the forfeit of his temerity, and others who attempted to regain the colors were shot in the attempt. Then followed the maneuvers ending in the battle of New Hope Church, rapidly followed by that of Kenesaw Mountain and Peach Tree Creek. McPherson's division, to which the 127th was assigned, from this point made a wide detour eastward by way of Decatur, and approaching Atlanta from the east sustained an assault from the whole rebel force. Here the fighting was very severe, the 127th doing its share manfully. Then followed the flank movement by the right, the battle of Jonesboro and the consequent evacuation of Atlanta. From this point Hood, then in command of the rebel forces, went on his ill-starred campaign to Nashville, before whom Thomas retreated, gathering the forces that were destined to crush him in the end. Returning from his pursuit of Hood, Sherman, with the balance of his army, reorganized and rested, set out for his march to the sea, the 127th being in the right wing. From Atlanta to Savannah, thence to Columbia, S. C., Fayetteville, N. C., and Bentonville, to the end, the regiment marched its way through the rebellion, taking part in the "Grand Review," and was one of four regiments complimented by Gen. Sherman for their fine soldierly bearing. The regiment was mustered out of the service May 31, 1865.

The "Mechanical Fusiliers" was a company of mechanics enlisted to aid in the construction of barracks, bridges, etc., for the use of the army. They went out in command of Capt. James Miller of Joliet, assisted in the construction of barracks at Camp Douglas, and were then lost sight of so far as any record exists in this county. The best information to be had is to the effect that this company was organized with others into a pioneer regiment, but of their subsequent career there is unfortunately no information at hand.

In the 60th Infantry, Grundy County was represented by a few men in Company I. This regiment was organized in February, 1862, and took part in the operations of the army of Tennessee. Was at the siege of Corinth, Nashville, Chattanooga, in the campaign about Atlanta, and the battle of Jonesboro. Was a part of the garrison left at Atlanta, and subsequently followed Sherman's army to Savannah and subsequently took part in Sherman's campaign in the Carolinas. Took part in the grand review at Washington; did provost duty at Louisville for a little more than a month and was mustered out July 31, 1865.

The 90th Infantry was organized at Chicago in September and October, 1862. In Company H. of this regiment this county was represented by some fourteen men. The regiment was ordered to Tennessee, arriving at Lagrange December 2d, and on the 4th went to Cold Water, Mississippi. On the morning of the 20th, a detachment of the 2d Illinois Cavalry arrived at Cold Water, having cut their way through Van Dorn's forces, out of Holly Springs. Soon after four companies of the 101st Illinois came in, and were followed by the enemy to our lines. The demonstration made by the 90th deterred the enemy from making any severe attack, although he was 4,000 or 5,000 strong. The regiment was mustered out of service June 6, 1865, at Washington, D. C.

Company B of the 129th Infantry drew some men from Grundy. This regiment was organized at Pontiac, Ill., in August, 1862, and was sent at once to Louisville. After the Buell and Bragg race across Kentucky, the 129th joined in the pursuit via Frankfort and Danville to Crab Orchard, when it returned and did garrison duty at Mitchellsburg, Ky. The regiment was mustered out June 8, 1865, at Washington, D. C.

Company H. of the 138th Infantry also contained some Grundy County men. This was a "hundred day" regiment, organized June 21, 1864. It was assigned to garrison duty at Fort Leavenworth, Kan., where it served out the term of its enlistment. The regiment was mustered out October 14, 1864, at Springfield, Illinois.

Other organizations that numbered one or two men from Grundy County, were Companies E and H of the 144th; Companies C and K of the 147th; Company E of the 153d; Company A of the 156th; Company E of the 2d Cavalry; Naugus Battery, and twelve men in the naval service.

In the above brief survey no attempt has been made to do exact or equal justice to the military career of those who went out from Grundy County to the service of their country. Any such attempt must have failed in the very nature of the case. Such facts as have been given, have been gleaned from various sources of information generally accepted as correct, yet often proving contradictory in essential particulars, and may prove in many instances to fall short of the merits of the case. But however much this sketch may fail of excellence, it will at least serve to show that Grundy County's patriotism found expression "where duty called and danger," and was "never wanting there," and so answers the purpose for which it was conceived.

CHAPTER VI.*

MORRIS CITY—INTRODUCTORY—ITS LOCATION—FIRST BEGINNINGS—ORIGIN OF NAME—COUNTY HONORS—EARLY COMMUNITY—BIOGRAPHICAL.

HE who would attempt to "revive the memories of the past and with feeble pen portray them" in the hope of giving such a chronicle of events as will meet the approval of all, will find his undertaking is a difficult—indeed an impossible one, especially so, if he attempts to write up cotemporary history. What to one seems of importance, to another seems trivial, whilst others are born chronic fault-finders. Fully appreciating these difficulties, and with a desire to show charity to all—malice to none—we shall endeavor to give a faithful narrative of the leading events and incidents connected with the township and city of Morris from their inception down to the present as we now remember them. In our effort we may, indeed we must from the nature of human events and human weakness, omit many, many important incidents and events, and make many mistakes in dates and coloring of those we attempt to describe. We are relying largely upon our memory, indeed we have little other resource to draw from; and as our recollections are most vivid on those events with which we were personally interested, our readers will be charitable enough to excuse what may smack of egotism. Should any of the living who have been participants in the events we shall describe, feel themselves aggrieved at our omission to favorably mention what part they performed, or should the descendants of any of the early settlers of Morris who have "gone before" feel that we have wounded their sensibilities by statements that may be construed to reflect upon the character or habits of the deceased, we in advance disclaim any malice or intention of injuring the reputation of any one. Nor shall we fail to give the habits, customs and characteristics of our early inhabitants, nor "spoil a good tale for relationship." In this way only can we write history whose use, according to Tacitus, "Is to rescue virtuous actions from the oblivion to which a want of records would consign them, and that men should feel a dread of being considered infamous in the opinions of posterity, from their depraved expressions and depraved actions."

Morris (for such is the name given to the county seat of Grundy County), is located on the north or right bank of the Illinois River, some twelve miles below the junction of the Kankakee and Desplaines Rivers, which form the Illinois. Nettle Creek, a considerable stream of pure water approaching from the north, passes through the city and flows into the river about a half mile southwest of the court house. From the south approaches the Mazon, which, in the Algonquin or Indian language, means "River of Nettles," and empties into the

---

* By Hon. P. A. Armstrong.

Illinois directly south of the public square. The Mazon is sometimes called a creek and other times a river. It is a short stream, with decidedly uppish notions. In times of drouth it is an humble creek, but in the spring and fall it is a roaring river. The Illinois & Michigan Canal passes through between the city and the river, at a distance of about forty rods from the river, and runs nearly parallel with it, the general course of the river at this point being nearly from east to west. From the bank of the river, running north to the distance of about one half mile, the surface of the land in Morris gently rises—the apex being some forty feet above the river bank, thus forming a natural drainage into the canal. From the apex north the surface descends for a distance of about one hundred rods to a ravine running southwesterly into Nettle Creek. Sandy loam is the predominating soil, which is admirably adapted to gardening purposes and the raising of fruit, especially grapes. Originally, nearly the entire plat of Morris was studded with forest trees, oak and hickory predominating, with here and there a hazel or plum thicket. Notwithstanding the timber, and many of the trees were giant oaks, there were bowlders scattered over the surface, mute witnesses of the glacier period, and of its great antiquity. Morris is located midway between the cities of Joliet on the east and Ottawa on the west, and sixty-one miles southwest of Chicago. It spreads over parts of four sections of land, viz.: three, four, nine and ten, in township number thirty-three north, range seven, east of the third principal meridian. The Chicago, Rock Island & Pacific railroad, which is one of the foremost railroads of the continent, passes through Morris a half mile north of the court house, thus giving both rail and water highways for the transportation of grain and stock. With our facilities of travel, Chicago is but two and a half hour's ride from Morris by rail.

Few cities are more pleasantly located than Morris. Sheltered on the south and west by heavy groves of timber, with an undulating surface, in the midst of a fine agricultural country, it is no wonder that the Mound Builders, that mysterious yet intelligent prehistoric race, selected the site of Morris for their principal city and cemetery, away back of the historic period. That here was the abode of a large number of these wonderful people is attested by nineteen separate, distinct mounds or cemeteries, for each mound is but a cemetery, pyre, or charnel house, at the center of whose base lie the cremated ashes of their dead. These mounds were constructed in a line on the second rise from the river, and some forty rods to the north of the river bank. The largest of them was located near the south east corner of the present court house square, and was about fifty feet in diameter and ten feet high. There were no moats or ditches surrounding these mounds, hence the material used in their construction must have been carted or carried from a distance. They were constructed of sandy loam, free of clay or gravel.

From whence the Mound Builders came, the period of their existence and the cause or causes of their extermination have not yet been satisfactorily settled. Enough of their history has been delved out of their mounds to establish many very interesting facts, and the ever restless spirit of inquiry and research may yet fix the date of their existence and account for their disappearance. From the knowledge we now have relating to these mysterious people, we deduce among other things: First: They were a very numerous people as evidenced by the great number of tumuli or mounds found in the United States, reaching far beyond a hundred thousand already discovered. Secondly: They built cities and surrounded them with fortifications. Thirdly: They were a religious people and offered up sacrifices. Fourthly: They were an intelligent people and well skilled in some of the arts. Fifthly: They had a knowledge of the use of metals, especially copper, and to some extent of iron and steel. Sixthly: They were experts in the manufacture of earthenware and brick, and used the latter in walling in their cities and in the erection of fortifications. Seventhly: These people must have been as numerous throughout the valley of the Mississippi as the inhabitants along the banks of the Nile or Euphrates in biblical times, with cities rivaling those of Mexico in the days of the Montezumas. Eighthly: They must have been an agricultural and pastoral people, as their cities were too large to subsist on fish and wild game. Ninthly: They well understood the arts of war and civil engineering. Tenthly: They were a wealthy people as well as numerous, or they could not have built the mounds and fortifications which mark their existence and bear testimony to their skill and wonderful works, like those on the Muskingum in Ohio, and Cohokia in Illinois—works in whose construction years of labor and millions of treasure would be required even with the art and skill of the nineteenth century. Eleventhly: They understood and appreciated the precious metals in ornamentation, if not as a circulating medium. Twelfthly: There were at least three separate races of them, Lilliputian, Medium and Giant. Thirteenthly: They were fine judges of soil and natural advantages of locality; always selecting the best lands and most eligible sites for their cities, with a view to natural drainage, abundance of wood and water, and points which could be readily fortified against the attack of an enemy. Fourteenthly: They were probably the descendants of the Israelites, possibly of the lost tribes described by Esdros. Fifteenthly: They were cremators and buried the ashes of their dead, and erected over them tumuli instead of monuments of marble—grand landmarks to point out where their eternity began. Some of them as in Licking County, Ohio, and St. Clair County, Ill., covering acres in area, and rising to the astonishing elevation of one hundred feet; and lastly, and most strangely, they were speculative Masons, as evidenced by finding in their mounds miniature squares, compasses, levels and plumbs cut out of sea shell or imprinted on pieces of pottery. (This last discovery is but quite recent and may not prove general. Hon. William McAdams of Jersey County, Ill., and the writer, vouch for the correctness of the last statement from personal discoveries near Naples, Ill., and Glen-Elder, Kansas.) But as the editor, Mr. Battle, has dwelt at some length upon this subject, we shall simply add that there can be no reasonable doubt but the present site of the city of Morris was once the site of a great city of the Mound Builders, and from specimens of their handiwork found beneath the surface of the prairies we are led to the conclusion that the vast prairies of Illinois were at one time the growing fields of this wonderful race of people whom we only know as Mound Builders.

The numerous human skeletons we find near the surface of these mounds are those of Indians, deposited there probably thousands of years after the mounds were built. The Indians utilized these mounds because they were dry, as burial places for their dead. How many different tribes of Indians have made this their principal village sites is not and never will be known. La Salle found a large one here, on his first trip up the Illinois, in 1679. Prior to the organization of Grundy, La Salle County embraced, in addition to the present large territory, all of Grundy and a portion of Kendall Counties. Ottawa, the county seat of La Salle, is located on Sections 3, 4, 9 and 10, T. 33, R. 3, or just twenty-four miles west of Morris; and as Morris is twelve miles west of the east line of Grundy County, persons living on the eastern side of La Salle County prior to the formation of Grundy would be compelled to travel about forty miles to the county seat; these people soon became dissatisfied, and discussed the feasibility of the division of this monster county as far back as 1836, and in 1839 petitions for the organization of a new county were prepared, and circulated for signers by L. W. Claypool and others, and were very generally signed by the inhabitants of the territory of the proposed new county. The General Assembly (under the State Constitution, adopted Aug. 26, 1818), convened on the first Monday in December in each even numbered year, hence the first session after the commencement of obtaining signatures to said petition would be the first Monday in December, 1840.

During the summer of that year the new county movement received the aid of Hon. Geo. W. Armstrong and his brother, William E., the former then living where he now resides, near the dividing line between La Salle and Grundy, with part of his farm in each county; the latter residing in Ottawa. Wm. E. was a man of great energy and positive character—quick to perceive and prompt to act. Whatever he attempted to do he did, if good management and well-directed efforts could accomplish it. In this movement he saw the necessity of a division of La Salle County, and the erection of a new one, and beyond this he saw an opportunity of making money. Having first surveyed the general topography of the country, out of which the new county was proposed to be organized, his mind settled upon the place where Morris is located, as the most eligible point for the seat of justice. He next conferred with the late John P. Chapin, who then owned the southeast quarter of Section four, T. 33, R. 7, which eventuated in the purchase of an undivided half interest in the south portion thereof, contingent upon the organization of the new county. This done, he pressed forward the petition for the division of La Salle County, with energy and success, and when the Legislature met that fall he went in person to press through his bill for a new county, suggesting the name of Grundy in honor of Tennessee's greatest criminal lawyer and statesman, Felix Grundy. This bill became a law Feby. 17, 1841.

Among its provisions are the following:
"That all that tract of country lying and being in the county of La Salle, in townships thirty-one, thirty-two, thirty-three,

and thirty-four north, of ranges six, seven, and eight, east of the third principal meridian, shall constitute a new county to be called Grundy.

"An election shall be held at the house of C. Piney, on the fourth Monday of May next for the purpose of electing one sheriff, etc., etc., and the said county of Grundy shall be organized so soon as the said officers shall be elected and qualified.

"Ward B. Burnett, Rulief S. Durwyea, and William E. Armstrong be appointed in conjunction with the commissioners of the Illinois & Michigan Canal, to locate the seat of justice of the said county of Grundy.

"It shall be the duty of the said commissioners to locate the said seat of justice on the line of the Illinois & Michigan Canal, on canal lands, and they shall set apart for this purpose any quantity of the canal lands, not exceeding (10) acres, and after doing so shall proceed to lay off the said land as a town site, embracing lots, streets, alleys, and a public square, in such manner as they shall deem proper. They shall divide the said lots in equal number between the State and the said county, and shall allot to the State and the county alternate lots of equal value, or as nearly so as may be practicable.

"It shall be the duty of the canal commissioners to require of the said county, and the inhabitants thereof, in their corporate capacity, shall be liable to them for the payment of a sum equal to ten dollars per acre for one-half of the whole quantity of land to be located as aforesaid, upon the payment of which sum the canal commissioners shall certify the fact to the Governor, who shall thereupon issue a patent to the county commissioners of said county for that portion of the lots by number, which shall be allotted to the county: provided always, that the moneys to be received by the canal commissioners by virtue of this section of the act, shall be applied in aid of the construction of the Illinois & Michigan Canal."

The seat of justice should be located on the line of the canal and on canal land, thus restricting the location virtually to two land points, viz.: Section 7 or 9, T. 33, R. 7; section 9 is centrally located between east and west lines of the county; section 7 is two miles west of the center; both lie on the Illinois river; only a small fraction of 9 lies north of the river, whilst nearly all of 7 does. The lay of the land on the north side of the river at both of these points is high and well adapted for village or city location, and on the south side, low, flat, and subject to overflows in the spring and fall. Only ten acres were to be laid out for the seat of justice, of which the country was to have one half upon the payment to the canal fund of the sum of ten dollars per acre, or fifty dollars for one half of the county seat. But this was not the real consideration on the part of the State. It was the expectation that the locating of the county seat on canal land would enhance the adjacent land in price. Here, then, were two conflicting interests. The one in favor of section 7, the other for section 9. The canal commissioners having the interest of the canal fund only in view were strongly in favor of section 7, whilst the great mass of the people of the county and the other three commissioners were in favor of section 9.

The people, however, could not vote upon

this question, hence the vote upon the location was a tie, and a dead-lock ensued. Great credit is due to General Ward B. Burnett for the stand he took on this question. He was chief engineer of the construction of the canal, in the employment of the State, and subject to removal by the canal commissioners; but he was too much of a man to be swerved or controlled in his action as a commissioner to locate the county seat by fear or favor, hence he stood manfully with Messrs. Durwyea and Armstrong for section 9 first, last and all the time until it was accomplished. Yet, be it said, with shame, that not even a street in the entire city of Morris bears the honored name of Burnett, the gallant soldier and finished gentleman. From the time of this disagreement between the commissioners on the county seat question, which was probably in the forepart of June, 1841 (we have no record of their meeting), up to April 12, 1842, when the plat of Morris was acknowledged by Isaac N. Morris, Newton Cloud, R. S. Duryea and Wm. E. Armstrong (See Book "B," page 39, of Deed Records of Grundy County), Grundy County presented the anomaly of being a fully organized county without a county seat. Mr. Armstrong moved his family from Ottawa, Ills., soon after the passage of the act creating the county, and occupied the log cabin erected by Cryder and McKeen for John P. Chapin in 1834. This cabin stood near the spot where the residence of Judge A. R. Jordan now stands, and contained but one room 16x20 feet. On the 14th of June, 1841, the Board of County Commissioners, consisting of Henry Cryder, Jacob Claypool and James McKeen, held the first meeting for the transaction of county business at this cabin. Among other business transacted at this meeting they approved the official bonds of L. W. Claypool, recorder of deeds; James Nagle, clerk of the county commissioners' court; and Joshua Collins, probate justice of the peace. When this meeting of the board was through with their business they adjourned to meet "at the house of Wm. E. Armstrong, on section 4, July 21, 1841." At this meeting it was "ordered that the Circuit Court be held in the house of Wm. E. Armstrong." Mr. Claypool resigned his office as one of the county commissioners, and Salmon Rutherford was elected to fill the vacancy; and the next meeting was held at the house of Mr. Rutherford, at the village of Dresden, nine miles east of Morris. This was held Sept. 6, 1841, and adjourned to meet at the house of Mr. Armstrong, on section 4, T. 33, R. 7. At this meeting the precinct of Grundy was formed, which embraced what are now the towns of Morris and Saratoga. In the meanwhile Messrs. Chapin and Armstrong proceeded to lay off a village plat, embracing what is now known as Chapin's addition to Morris, but gave it no name, nor did they file it for record. It was, however, generally known as Grundyville, or Grundy, and Mr. Armstrong erected a large frame building upon the spot where the Hopkins House stands and opened it as a hotel under the name of "Grundy Hotel." A petition for a post-office at this point, with the signatures of fully half of the voters of the county, had been forwarded to the Post-Office Department in the fall of 1841, under the name of the "Town of Grundy," but the prayer was not granted because it was not a county seat, and

THE NEW YORK
PUBLIC LIBRARY

ASTOR, LENOX AND
TILDEN FOUNDATI
R   1922   L

the receipts of the office (though postage was then 25 cents per letter), would not defray the expenses of carrying the mail. In the spring of 1842, General Wm. F. Thornton, one of the canal commissioners, was succeeded by Hon. Isaac N. Morris, of Quincy, Ill., when another conference of the County Seat Commission was held—probably about the 1st of March. After inspecting the two competing points, Grundy, on Sec. 9, and Clarkson, on Sec. 7, and conferring with the county officials and people, Mr. Morris cast his vote in favor of Grundy, or Sec. 9. The vote standing as follows: For Sec. 9, Messrs. Morris, Burnett, Durwyea and Armstrong, 4. For Sec. 7, Messrs. Cloud and Fry, 2. Pleased at the independent and manly action of Mr. Morris, and wishing to honor him, the name of the Town of Grundy was changed, first to Morristown, but it was found that there was already a town of that name in the State; Morrisville was then suggested, but to this name Mr. Morris objected, as it suggested a mere village. It was finally named Morris, and the survey was begun (according to the diary of L. W. Claypool, Esq.) March 7, 1842, by Leander Newport, surveyor, with Perry A. Claypool and George W. Armstrong, chainmen. Thus did Grundy County, after months of doubt and uncertainty, obtain her county seat and give it a name. Sometime afterward the Board of County Commissioners attempted to change the name to Xenia, but could not agree upon the orthography of the word; hence they did not make the change.

That the log cabin before referred to as the residence of Mr. Armstrong in 1841, was the first building within the present corporate limits of Morris, there is no doubt, but whether it was built by Mr. James McKeen, who died here only last year, or by John Cryder, who occupied it immediately after it was erected, seems to be in doubt. That it was built for Mr. John P. Chapin, now deceased, is conceded by all, as he was the owner of the land, although the title thereto was then in Mr. Julius Wadsworth, who held it for Mr. Chapin, and for whom John Cryder obtained a pre-emption. Mr. McKeen has frequently told the writer that he built it while Mr. Zachariah Walley, who still survives, is equally positive that Mr. John Cryder built it. We deem it safe to say that both are right, i. e., that each assisted in its erection in the spring of 1834. Mr. Cryder, after moving into said cabin, fenced and broke some ten acres of land lying west of the present Wauponsee street and north of Washington street. He resided there until the fall of 1838, and then went to Beardstown, Cass County, Illinois. The next residents of the town of Morris were John and Thomas Peacock, Englishmen and brothers.

They built a small cabin on the north front of S. ¼ of section 2, just west of the present Morris cemetery, and kept "Old Bach" during the winter of 1834-5. They purchased this land at the land sale in 1835, married and raised families. Many of their descendants are still living there and elsewhere in this county. In the early spring of 1838, Peter Griggs erected a cabin near where the aqueduct now is and moved into it. His widow still survives and is a second time a widow. He left several children who are still living: Jacob, John, Mary, Priscilla and Wilson. Jacob is the only one now living in Morris. On the 3d of July, 1839, all the available force of this section of country assembled at the west branch of Nettle Creek on the west side of the city, to raise what has ever since that time been known as "shaking bridge." The territory, now in Grundy County, was at that time very sparsely settled. The bridge was constructed of green oak logs, and hence they were extremely heavy. Nearly every ablebodied man then in the limits of this county was there. Hayes, Peacocks, Claypools, Warren, Holloway, Tabler, etc. In bridging this stream the people were in hopes of inducing Frink & Walker, who ran a line of stages from Chicago to Ottawa, via Lisbon, to change the line so as to follow the course of the Illinois river, and pass through this locality. That object was not accomplished, however, until 1846, when O. Husteed & Co. became the successors to Frink & Walker in the mail contract between Chicago and Peoria. During the summer and fall of 1841, several new buildings were erected here, but as pine lumber could not be obtained short of Chicago, the greater portion of them were merely log cabins. The first one was probably built by James Nagle, Clerk of the County Commissioners' Court. It was a large sized, heavily built log cabin, and stood near the old Kinsted homestead, on the S. W. ¼, section 3, near the N. W. corner thereof. In this cabin Mr. Nagle kept his office containing the books, papers and archives of the county. He was a highly educated *Irishman*, which means one of Nature's noblemen, for as a general rule, an *educated Irishman* is a *finished gentleman*. He was a most splendid penman and very agreeable man. An invalid, he fell a victim to that fell destroyer—consumption—in the spring of 1843. James Hart, father of John Hart, Esq. and widow Reynolds, of this city, built a small house near the Indian pole, and occupied it for a residence and saloon. He was a partner with Mr. Armstrong in one or more contracts to dig the canal. Andrew Kinchella, a man of energy and means, built and occupied a log cabin near the present residence of L. P. Lott, Esq. He afterward purchased and improved a farm near Minooka, and died several years since, leaving quite a property. Anthony Horan, who always appeared in white pants and vest on St. Patrick's Day, no matter what the weather was, built and occupied a cabin near where the present fine residence of L. W. Claypool stands. In a fit of anger at his wife he is said to have set fire to it in 1846. Whether this was true or not, the cabin was burned, and he was arrested for the incendiarism, but as we had no suitable jail, Deputy Sheriff P. Kelly started with him in a buggy for the Ottawa jail. On reaching a point this side of Marseilles where the road approached the Illinois River, he complained of being thirsty and asked permission to get a drink. Having the darbies on, Mr. Kelly deemed it safe, and accompanied him to the river's edge. Horan laid down and drank heartily, but while lying there he worked his hands through his hand cuffs, and as he rose to his feet he sprang into the river, swam across to the other side, and made good his escape, and stayed away until after the next term of court, at which no indictment was found, as his wife refused to go before the Grand Jury to testify against him. She died soon afterward, and Anthony returned to Morris, where he remained until some years afterward, when he went to the State of Pennsylvania, and was living at last advices. Perry A. Claypool built a cabin about where Ray's store now stands, in 1842, and occupied it with his family for about a year, when Samuel Ayres and family took possession of the cabin and kept boarders. During the residence of Mr. Ayres here he held the office of coroner and deputy sheriff. He was a capital good fellow and had an interesting family. He left about the year 1848 and went to Texas, much to the regret of our people. With full confidence that this point would ultimately be the county seat, Mr. Armstrong, of his own volition and at his own expense, commenced the erection of a frame building near the northwest corner of the public square, for a court house, in the winter of 1841-2. This building was probably 20x40 feet, two stories high. As there was no pine lumber to be had short of Chicago, and then it would have to be hauled by teams, he used hardwood lumber. It was an old fashioned heavy frame, thoroughly braced, with oaken floors and siding. The siding was undressed and hence could never be painted. This siding was sawed from a very independent kind of trees and had a decidedly snarlish disposition, and little regard for the confining influence of nails; hence, the clapboards or siding turned up their noses or heels in the most provoking manner—resembling somewhat the bristles of the hedgehog. This building was virtually accepted by the county commissioners as and for a court house in the fall of 1842, and forty dollars were paid to Mr. Armstrong as part pay, and in June, 1843, they paid him another county order for $310.06, making a total of $350.06. This was for the building, before it was lathed and plastered. That cost $175.30, making the total cost of the court house $525.36. Rather a cheap building for such a purpose, yet it served the purpose for which it was erected until superseded by the present fine stone one in 1856, a period of thirteen years. The lower story was done off for a court room, with a door on each side near the center and opposite each other, for ingress and egress, and the upper story was divided into three rooms of nearly equal size, with stairway at southeast corner. In the upper story were the offices of the clerks of the Circuit and County Commissioners' Courts and recorder's office, but not used as such.—L. W. C. Our sheriff, Mr. Armstrong, had charge of the court room, and being a very liberal man in his religious views, this court room was always free for religious services, no matter of what denomination. It was equally free for temperance meetings, singing schools, Sabbath schools, lectures, legerdemain, or for the exhibition of learned pigs, bears, natural monstrosities, or that greatest of humbugs, mesmerism.

During the winter and spring of 1841-2 Robert Peacock' erected a small frame building for a hotel on the spot where the Clifton House now stands and christened it the "Plow Inn." His sign was the representation of a plow painted upon a board, and underneath the letters "Inn." Mr. Peacock was a man of fair education, honest and fair but slightly addicted to gossip; hence he was very liable to be occasionally duped. He was a justice of the peace and a good one. In the absence of the coroner, a justice of the peace of the precinct where a dead body may be found was required to hold an inquest. In the summer of 1842 P. P. Chapin (a natural wag) was running a brick yard near where the Gas Factory is located on the bank of East Nettle Creek. An English family, of the name of Bandly, with three or four daughters, ranging from six to fourteen years of age, lived near by his brick yard. These little girls had an enormously large rag doll baby, and while playing on the bank of the creek which is very abrupt and high, either by accident or intent, they let this doll fall into the creek, and as they could not reach it to pull it out, they left it floating down stream. Mr. Chapin rescued it from its watery grave and carefully laid it out to dry upon a large stump close by. Here was a rare chance for "Pete" (as he was called, although his Christian name was Paschal) to gratify his ever ready wit and propensity for fun, even at the expense of friendship. A couple of elderly maidens lived "all alone" in a cabin near by, with whose reputation the busy tongue of scandal was dealing insidious innuendoes—though in all human probability very unjustly. It was therefore an easy matter to start the inference of infanticide in that locality, and Squire Peacock—good, honest soul, would be among the very first to jump at a conclusion from the most obscure hint or gesture. With a serious countenance he approached the Squire, and in a solemn voice informed him of the *corpus delicti*. How his attention was attracted to the creek by the high bluff, near the residence of these old maidens; how he saw the dead body of a babe in the water; how he had carefully drawn the body out all dripping with water, and carefully laid it on a stump awaiting an inquest. All confidingly the Squire was entrapped, exclaiming, "I told you nothing good would come of those two women living there alone." He consulted the statute relative to holding inquests, and then proceeded to summon a jury. L. W. Claypool and Samuel Ayers had been let into the secret by Chapin. The former declined to serve on the jury, but the latter wanted to see the fun. Having obtained his jury of twelve "good men and true," he repaired to the stump to examine the corpse, when lo! there was nothing there but a bundle of rags. The Squire laid up a hickory in oil for Chapin's use, but really never got quite even with him.

On the 15th of April, 1842, having reached the age of nineteen, with all our worldly goods and possessions, consisting of a few home-made clothes and Blackstone "done up in two volumes," all ensconced in a "cotton bandana," with two Spanish quarters in our pocket like "Japhet in search of a father," we struck out from the paternal nest in the town of Deer Park, La Salle County, Illinois, and "on foot and alone like the girl that went to get married" we wended our way to the new town of Morris, with great expectations of achieving a fortune and of building up a name that would be the envy of the old and the emulation of the young. We toiled along cheerily and manfully for the first half of the road—some fifteen miles. From thence on, those ponderous words of Blackstone, or the amount of paper used to print them, grew in weight step by step until each seemed to outweigh a common sized anvil. Night spread her sable wings over woodland and prairie long ere we reached our goal. On striking the point where Messrs. Kenrick & Kennedy now live we gave com pletely out. The roads were in a horrid condition and the mud was half leg deep. The arguments of the legal sage were too heavy for us and hence we deposited them in a hollow oak tree and covered them over with leaves and mud, to be exhumed at a more convenient season. At about nine P. M., we reached the Grundy Hotel, though it was then far from being finished. Here we received a hearty welcome, with many proffers of a drop of whisky, with the assurance that it would do us good. We received the welcome without the whisky. Morris had been located and christened just three days before we cast our lot within its precincts. We have been inseparable companions since that time and have grown old together. It has grown larger, stronger and better. We, too, have grown larger, but alas, weaker and more wicked. Hope deferred for forty years, and still our expectations seem no nearer realization than when we came. Some days after our arrival here we returned to the hollow tree for our books. They were safe and uninjured. Our first day in Morris as a citizen was full of adventure and decidedly discouraging. We came here ostensibly to keep the books of account of the firm of Armstrong & Hart, who were canal contractors and built the canal through Morris, but our main object was to study law, and as we were informed before coming that the book-keeping would occupy but a small portion of our time, we expected to literally absorb the contents of Blackstone. We were to board at the Grundy Hotel, of which Mr. Armstrong was proprietor. On the day after our arrival we were placed in charge of said hotel as well as of the books of the firm, while Mr. Armstrong and family started to Ottawa for a short visit. Early in the day we were informed by the cook of the boarding house for the canal hands that he was "out of meat," and as none could be obtained short of Dresden, we mounted a horse and went thither and made a purchase of several barrels of pork from Antoine Peltier and returned towards evening. There was a cubby-hole under the stairway of the hotel in which was stored a barrel of cheap brandy, the door to which we locked and put the key in our pocket. During our absence some thirsty soul broke open this door to get at the brandy. Having taken a few drinks he imagined that he was the owner of the entire barrel. Soon it was known all over the village that brandy was free at the Grundy Hotel. Once fairly started, brandy was carried in pails, dippers, pitchers and tin cups to the men on the work, and as a natural result a sober man was the exception and fighting was general.

As we approached the hotel the engineer in charge of the construction of the canal and the boss carpenter on the erection of the court house were stripped for a fight, each insisting that he would knock the other over the Alleghany mountains if he could only get a fair lick at him. They had a scratch across the road, which they vainly endeavored to toe, but were so drunk that when they attempted to straighten up, they lost their equilibrium, and were forced to step back, so a collision was impossible, so long as they respected the road mark. We had seen but little drunkenness thus far, and were horrified and pained at the sight. Here was a man of intellect and education, a first-class gentleman, so muddled with the accursed liquor that he forgot who he was and what he was trying to do. By the joint use of persuasion and physical strength we got the engineer in bed, when he soon went to sleep, and came out the next day humiliated and humble and eschewed cheap brandy ever after, as a beverage. Having thus disposed of the engineer, we started in search of a sober man, but failed in the effort. As we left the hotel a fight was in progress between Mat Catlin, the plasterer, and Johnnie May, a teamster. They were of the banty order and fought lively with the advantage in favor of May, who soon got Catlin down and was pummelling him in the most approved style. We went to the rescue of Catlin and released him from his perilous condition, and for this kindly act he became highly incensed at us and turned the vials of his wrath upon our poor head. The result was a slight conflict, with a pair of badly-damaged eyes to the plasterer. We then went into the office to post up books when Kurtz, the carpenter, came in and demanded more brandy. We had none to give him if we had wished to do so, as the barrel had been completely emptied before our return from Dresden, and had we had it to give we should most certainly have declined to give him any, as he was still quite tipsy. Our refusal roused him to a towering rage. We ordered him out of the room, to which he replied: "I know you are the boss here, but you are too small for a boss. I will go out if you can put me out, but not otherwise." We thereupon went for him and rushed to the door when he caught hold of the door jambs with his hands. This we expected, but were in no way disconcerted by it. We had seen such tricks before and well knew how to defeat them. We seized him around the legs and ended him over, when he fell on the flat of his back into the bar room. He sprang quickly to his feet and came at us for fight, striking out with both fists wildly. We dodged the blows and gave him a hip lock, landing him across the flared edge of an old-fashioned Franklin stove, which settled him, and at the same time broke one of his ribs, when he was ready—yes, anxious, of being put in his "little bed." Gilman, the teamster, was the next to make trouble. He got up in the night to interfere with the cook whose room was down stairs. We heard him getting up and knew his design. Stealing to the head of the stairway in the dark hall we were ready for action. As he reached the first step we gave him a violent push. He had no time to count the steps or open the door at the foot of the stairs. He stopped very suddenly with his head in the bar room and his body in the stairway. The stairway door, however, was demoralized, and minus a panel. He was satisfied that "the way of the transgressor is hard," and very willingly returned to his bed. When Mr. A. returned from Ottawa, he found the work on the court house suspended and his team idle for want of a driver. Upon inquiring the cause of Mr. Catlin, he was informed that "we got on to a bit of a tantrum, when Picayune like to have kilt the whole of us."

This was the way a new name was given to us. Not a very elegant one, but one that stayed by us for several years. Thus we had a busy day, even though it was our first day in Morris. We established our reputation as a "*fighter*" and have rested since.

WILLIAM E. ARMSTRONG, the founder of Morris, was born in Licking County, Ohio,

Oct. 25, 1814, and died Nov. 1, 1850. With his mother's family he moved overland from Ohio to Illinois in the spring of 1831, and located near where Lacon now stands, in April of that year. In August, of the same year, the family moved to the present town of Deer Park, La Salle County. A man of great mental and physical strength, he was a born leader of men. In September, 1841, he was elected sheriff, and was re-elected several times thereafter. So great was his influence that he was generally called "the emperor of Grundy." He always had a host of friends, who looked upon him as their leader. Yet he never appeared to seek their leadership. It was accorded him. In energy, perseverance and business tact, he had few equals. He could plan and execute great undertakings, where the common man and mind could see nothing to do. He was probably the ablest man Grundy County ever had. He with his wife and two daughters moved from Ottawa here in March, 1841, and took possession of the Chapin log cabin before described. With him came GEORGE H. KIERSTED, a graduate of South College, Kentucky. Mr. Kiersted was a man of liberal education and magnificent physical form, a man who would attract attention and admiration among a crowd of hundreds of fine looking men. There was a peculiar dignity—yea, majesty in his very step, whilst every motion of his fine form was graceful and easy. About six feet in height, with broad shoulders and powerful limbs, yet he was as active as a cat; even up to the time of his death, which occurred but a few years since, he could turn a handspring on the barn floor. With clear blue eyes, finely shaped head and remarkably pure complexion, he was a very handsome man. Fond of music, poetry and flowers, and a poet himself of no common type, yet too modest to let his poetry see the light of publication. Possessed of a fine tenor voice, and master of the flute, and of great conversational powers, he was a welcome guest and leader of society. His life and history here are parts and parcels of the history of Morris. He was generous to a fault, and acquired money only for its use. Next to Mr. A. no man ever excelled him in influence in Grundy County. He was defeated for the office of recorder by Mr. L. W. Claypool, May 24, 1841, and then accepted a position as assistant engineer on the canal, making his home still here. He married Miss B. Kelley, the accomplished sister-in-law of James Nagle, and upon the death of Mr. Nagle succeeded him as clerk of the county commissioners court, June 5, 1843, which office he continued to hold until the office was changed to county clerk, in 1849. He also held the office of clerk of the circuit court from 1842 to 1853, and postmaster a short time under Polk's administration, but resigned it in favor of the writer in the spring of 1864. He died poor, leaving a large family—all daughters. The eldest, Anna, is the wife of D. C. Huston, Esq.; the second, Abbie M., is the wife of Alexander Burrell, Esq., both of Morris. Both are ladies of fine physique and intelligence. PASCHAL PAOLA CHAPIN, before mentioned, was a brother of John P. Chapin, one of the proprietors of Morris and came here in 1842 to look after his brother's interest. A natural wag, yet handsome and accomplished. We find him acting as, clerk *pro tem.* of the county commissioners court in the fall of 1842. He was the first clerk of the circuit court of the county and "a hale fellow well met," in all the public gatherings of the time. He went by the name of P"Flora P"Nellie or P. Chapin, and left here about the year 1845 and died in Wisconsin lately. He was "a gay and festive old bach," ever ready for sport and fun. Of medium size, dark complexion, jet black hair and whiskers, he was decidedly handsome. JAMES HART came here with his family in the fall of 1841 and located his cabin near the Cedar Pole on Wauponsee street. He was a giant in size and strength and possessed of good executive ability. In company with Mr. Armstrong he took one or two contracts on the canal, one of them being that portion which passes through Morris. Teams and scrapers in digging canals had not come into use at that time, and if they had, they could not have been obtained, for they were not in the country. The work was done with the shovel and barrow, a very slow and expensive mode of digging a canal. In this slow mode of canal building, Mr. Hart was well educated, and would have made money on their contracts if the State had not gone into practical bankruptcy and paid their estimates in scrip, worth only about 33¼ cents on the dollar. Notwithstanding this ruinous depreciation in the funds, Messrs. Armstrong & Hart finished up their contracts at a heavy financial loss. At the regular election, Aug. 7, 1843, Mr. Hart was elected school commissioner of the county and qualified as such Sept. 4th, giving a $12,000 bond, which office he held to the time of his death, which occurred in 1844. He left quite a family, of whom Mrs. Thomas Reynolds, Mrs. Wm. Telfer and John Hart, our popular blacksmith, still reside in Morris. MICHAEL DEPRENDEGAST came here from Ottawa in the winter of 1843-4 and built a double log cabin where the First National Bank of Morris now stands. Elected to the office of justice of the peace soon after coming here, he held that office up to August, 1846, when he was elected probate justice of the peace. For him nature did but little, education much. He made a good justice of the peace and by no means a bad probate judge. He had been admitted to the bar, but never practiced as a lawyer. A man of inordinate vanity, he was extremely susceptible to flattery, but his honesty and integrity were never questioned. He built the fine brick block at the corner of Washington and Wauponsee streets, known now as the Bank Block, but during his life-time as the "Pendegrass Block." It was asserted by some that his name when he came from Ireland was Pendegrass and that for style he changed it to "DePrendegast" to make it Frenchy and aristocratic. He died about the year 1870, leaving his widow and one son surviving; both of whom died shortly after, leaving an estate for litigation without direct heirs. LUTHER S. ROBBINS, M. D., moved to Morris from the Sulphur Springs, south of this city, in 1842, and took possession of the Chapin cabin when Mr. Armstrong moved to the Grundy Hotel. Dr. Robbins was doubtless the first regular physician of Grundy County, having located at the Sulphur Springs, now owned by George Harold, in 1834. He was elected probate justice of the peace in 1843 which he held to the time of his death, April 1, 1845. He was a man of good acquirements with considerable skill as a physician.

BARTHOLOMEW MCGRATH came here from Dresden and built the "Morris Hotel" in 1843, which stood at southwest corner of Main and Liberty streets where the Gibbard brick block now stands. A natural mathematician and fine business man, he had been engaged for several years preceding as a canal contractor, and was elected one of the county commissioners to succeed Henry Cryder, Esq., Aug. 7, 1843. This office he filled with credit to himself, and satisfaction to the county for several years, and died of consumption, very generally regretted, in 1846, leaving a widow and three children, two of whom now survive, viz.: Thomas E. and Samuel D. McGrath, the former of this city, the latter a compositor on the Chicago *Times*. His widow became the wife of Col. James H. O'Brien, and died here in 1850.

JOHN MCNELLIS, or black Jack, as he was sometimes called, came here from Ottawa in 1844, and built a frame house, on the spot now occupied by Brown's drug store, for a boarding house and saloon. Unable to read or write, yet nature supplied this defect by giving him a large, well balanced and active brain. He did a good business, and accumulated some means so that when the canal was opened in 1848 he was able to purchase a fine canal boat, and christened it the General Shields. With this boat and the exercise of good judgment in the purchase and sale of grain, he made considerable money. What would have seemed to others a misfortune not unfrequently proved to him fortunate. For instance, on one occasion he bought several thousand bushels of wheat, which were shipped on the General Shields for the Chicago market; while on its way a break in the canal detained the boat some fifteen days, during which time the price of wheat went up several cents per day, so that he nearly doubled his money on this venture. When the canal trustees held their public sale here, Mr. McNellis purchased sixty acres of land, all now within the corporate limits of the city of Morris. He also purchased at that sale several other tracts of land. Honest in his dealings with the farmers he gained their confidence and good will to such a degree, that, other things being equal, he got their grain. Erecting a warehouse where the McEwen warehouse now stands, he did the leading grain business for many years. Having purchased the fine farm lying northwest of Morris, now owned by William Stephens and occupied by his son Charles, he built the fine brick dwelling thereon, and otherwise improved the place so as to make it one of the best farms of the county. A devout Catholic in religion, and feeling the want of education himself, he erected a fine four story brick building, and with ten acres of land surrounding it, he donated it for a "*Catholic School forever.*" Thus was St. Angela's Convent, which is an honor to our city—founded. It was the munificent gift of John McNellis. Nor were his church donations confined to his own church; having also given to the Catholic church two acres of land for a church building and parsonage, he also subscribed and paid $3,000 toward the erection of the splendid Catholic Church edifice, and then gave $250 to the Congregational, $100 to the Presbyterian, $100 to the Baptist, and $250 to the Episcopal Churches of Morris. Donations whose aggregate amount would make a moderate fortune to any individual. But he met with reverses and is now old and poor. Highwines, at one time during the war, went up to a high figure, which induced him to erect a distillery at the Au Sable, some six miles east of Morris. This proved his downfall. Of the practical working of a distillery he had no knowledge whatever. He tried to operate it awhile, but finding it was proving a heavy loss, he then leased it to parties who ran "crooked," when his property was seized by the government and virtually confiscated. What, between litigation and hope of the property being restored to him by the government, he has become broken down, mentally and physically, and is compelled to live on small means and cheaply. No man has done more toward the material prosperity of Morris, than John McNellis.

His brother-in-law, JUDGE PATRICK HYNDS, came here also in 1844, built and started a blacksmith shop (the first in the place) on the lot just north of the present residence of his widow. He was elected Justice of the Peace soon after coming here, and such was his fine sense of even-handed justice that he gave very general satisfaction as such. Indeed, his decisions were seldom if ever reversed on appeal. His fine judgment pointed him out as a suitable person to fill the vacancy in the office of County Judge on the resignation of Judge Henry Storr, in 1851. In that year he was elected County Judge at a special election and re-elected in 1853 at the regular election. Notwithstanding the County Court had a common law jurisdiction to the amount of $1,000, and exercised certain chancery jurisdiction, he discharged the duties thereof very satisfactorily to the bar and the people, though he was not a lawyer, nor indeed had he ever read law. He died of consumption in 1860, leaving a widow and three children, all of whom are still living. Judge Hynds was in many respects a remarkable man. He was a warm true friend, of positive character, generous impulses and high-toned honor. What he promised, that he did. There was no halfway business in his composition. His rule of life and conduct were based upon this thought: Whatever is honest must be right—whatever is dishonest is a crime that should be punished.

MAHLON P. WILSON, whose adz and driver have been heard from early morn to dewy eve for nearly forty years, was the first cooper of Morris. Indeed, we may say the only one, except his brother Alexander, who came many years later. On the 10th of May, 1844, Mahlon P. with his wife and one child moved into the double log cabin erected for a boarding house for canal hands, on the spot now occupied by the fine residence of S. S. Strong, Esq. Here he opened his shop and commenced the manufacture of barrels, firkins, etc., which he has carried on continuously in Morris for over thirty-eight years. In 1845 he erected a small frame house on the spot now occupied by the McCann brick building on Washington street, and moved his family into it and opened a boarding house. This building was but 16 by 24 feet, if we remember aright. When Messrs. LeRoy & Hannah built the brick building, this house was removed and is still standing as a part of the Clifton House (forming the kitchen, we believe). For many years past, his shop has been on Canal street, east of the court house, where from morn till late at night his driver and adz are in constant motion.

Industrious, and by no means extravagant, yet he never made a fortune. He, however, succeeded in keeping out of debt, raising and educating a large family. He is now sixty-five years of age, hale and hearty and as slim as a shad, yet tough as sole leather. Though not an Episcopalian, he is decidedly neutral in politics and religion. He never sought nor held an office, and seldom attended a church, but for all that he is a moral man and a good citizen.

PATRICK KELLEY, a man of large size and great physical strength, opened a saloon— or grocery as then called—in a shanty on the corner of Main and Wauponsee streets. He was deputy sheriff under Mr. Armstrong, and at the election of 1846 he was elected recorder over Henry Storr, although he received few or no votes outside of the laborers on the canal. In those days the canal vote was by no means an uncertain or doubtful element in elections of county officers in Grundy County. They constituted a clear majority of the legal voters of the county, and when united they "licked the platter clean." In 1846 the canal vote swept the boards, except for sheriff. Mr. Armstrong succeeded in diverting a part of their vote, and was re-elected. Mr. Kelley, by the assistance of Dr. A. F. Hand, managed to do the recording passably well. The doctor in those days was slightly given to the spread eagle, and decorated several pages of the records with counterfeit presentments of that famous bird. Mr. Kelley was a mason by trade and a good one. He died in this city some years since, leaving two highly educated and accomplished daughters.

ADAM LAMB, or more generally known as Scotch Lamb, was a canal contractor and came here in 1844 and built what was known as the "Mud House," for a store. This house stood on Washington street nearly opposite the present Normal School building. It was merely an adobe building—the first and last of its kind. The clay would not resist the rain; it simply melted. To protect it a coat of lime and sand mortar had to be spread outside. The cohesion of the mud was insufficient to hold the mortar, hence the latter fell off in patches, leaving the surface irregular and decidedly resembling a clear case of small pox. It stood, however, for many years and was the regular "catch basin" for new-comers to tarry in for a time until they could do better. Its last use was for the printing office of the *Morris Yeoman*, the first newspaper published in Morris. This was too weighty and the poor old adobe caved in and its debris was hauled away. Mr. Lamb was not only a ripe scholar but a finished Scotch gentleman; at one time a member of the club of Edinburgh critics. He was a bachelor with jet black hair and whiskers, with fair complexion and symmetrical form; he was remarkably handsome. He left here for Chicago on business, and never returned, leaving a large amount of property and unsettled business. He was free from debt and had considerable money on his person when he started to Chicago. He was heard from in New York city, where all trace of him ceased. It was supposed that he took a sudden notion to return to "Bonnie Scotland" for a visit, but he never reached there; he was probably killed and robbed in the city of New York. This was in 1846, and his brother closed up his business here and sold out the store to the writer. We are uncertain whether this stock of goods or that of Col. Wm. L. Perce, was the first brought to Morris. They were both opened in 1845 and were mere supply stores for the accommodation of the canal hands.

Col. William L. Perce took the contract of building the aqueduct across Nettle Creek on the west side of the city, and came here with his family in 1845, occupying a frame house built by Geo. H. Kiersted where the residence of John F. Hamilton now stands. He was an elderly man of considerable means and large experience as a contractor. With him came Charles H. Goold, now president of the Grundy County National Bank, as book-keeper, and Alexander Morrison, now a member of the State Senate of Michigan and a leading capitalist of that State, as foreman. The stone for this aqueduct was quarried some seven miles below Morris, near the river bank and hauled by teams. It was a reddish sandstone of inferior quality and disintegrated so that the aqueduct had to be rebuilt. Col. Perce opened a stock of dry goods in a room in the American House, with C. H. Goold as manager, in the fall of 1845, which was probably the first store in Morris. He left here when the canal was finished and has been dead many years. Passionately fond of euchre he was a good partner if you understood his signs, and a dangerous rival in a four-handed game. He was bald headed and had large ears, which he could move forward or backward at will, and by means of his ears he could indicate to his partner whether he had one or more trumps, and in case the dealer turned down the trump card he told his partner what he desired for trump, by the motion of his ears. To those who did not know of this peculiarity his playing and luck were marvelous. Elijah Walker opened a boot and shoe shop in a log cabin where Alex Miller's residence now stands, in 1841. He was the first president of the board of trustees, under the special charter of the town of Morris in 1853, and served one term as sheriff of the county and was supervisor of the town in the county board. Defeated for re-election as sheriff, by John Galloway, in 1856, he became disgusted with politics and went to Iowa.

CHAPTER VII.*

MORRIS CITY—THE SECOND PERIOD—GROWTH OF THE CORPORATION—OFFICIAL RECORDS—INTERNAL IMPROVEMENTS—1842 TO 1850.

FROM April 12, 1842, to August 15, 1850, Morris was a kind of go-as-you-please town organization, under general act and special charter. As before shown, the county seat of Grundy County was located and named April 12, 1843. It remained without being incorporated into a municipality a little over thirteen years. On the 15th of August, 1850, an election in conformity with chapter 25 of the statute then in force, was held at the old court house in Morris, to vote upon the question of incorporation, under the section of the statute referred to: " the *free white male* residents of lawful age, * * who may have resided six months in said proposed incorporation, as a freeholder therein," were entitled to vote provided that said town or village contained 150 inhabitants. At this election L. P. Lott was chairman or president, and P. A. Armstrong, clerk of said election, who certify that " there were in favor of incorporation forty-nine votes, and against it no vote; a beggarly vote for a city, but it was all that were cast. On the 22d day of that month an election was held for five trustees, with the same election board, when there were seventy-six votes cast. As party lines were drawn at this election, this vote was very nearly a full one. Orville Cane, Ezra P. Seeley, Wm. S. Woolsey, Jacob Jacoby and Robert Kelley were the successful ones, each receiving about fifty votes, while their opponents received only about half that number.

On the 2d of September of that year, the first village council met and organized by the election of E. P. Seeley, President of the Board of Trustees, and Henry Storr, Clerk. Beyond being sworn in and organizing the board, and defining the boundaries as follows: " Ordered that the jurisdiction be extended over and embrace the following territory, viz.: The southwest quarter of section 3; S. E. ¼ of Sec. 4; N. fr. of N. E. ¼ Sec. 9; N. fr. N. W. ¼ Sec. 10, in town 33, R. 7 east, 3d P. M., and also that portion of the Illinois River lying opposite to the N. fr. N. E. ¼ Sec. 9, and the N. fr. N. W. ¼ Sec. 10 as aforesaid, and extending four rods on the margin of the south bank of said river, to be measured from the top of the bank," no business was transacted at this first meeting of the Town Council of Morris.

Of these five trustees Mr. Cane only survives. Old, yet hale and hearty. He has retired from business and is spending his time in reading and conversing with his olden time friends. An old settler of the county, he was its second sheriff, and has lived on his farm, a few miles west of the city, for many years past, and returned to Morris some two years ago.

---
* By Hon. P. A. Armstrong.

The second meeting of the Board of Trustees was held at the court house January 13, 1851, when they passed an ordinance establishing the boundaries of the board as in the previous order, and fixed the regular meeting of the board for second Monday of each month at 6 P. M., creating the appointive officers of the board as follows: One constable, pound master, street commissioner, fire warden, clerk and treasurer, defining their duties, and then appointed George Gillett, constable, Charles L. P. Hogan, street commissioner, A. W. Newell, treasurer, and Robert Peacock, fire warden. At this meeting they passed a general code of ordinances for the police regulations of the town, many of which are still in force with but little alteration, and ordered them published by posting up three copies in public places in Morris. The next meeting of this board was held at the court house February 10th, 1851, when Capt. Charles L. Starbuck was elected clerk of the board, to fill the vacancy of Henry Storr, resigned.

Under the impression that the charter granted by the Legislature to the late Wm. E. Armstrong, February 27, 1841, to establish a ferry across the Illinois River on section seven or nine, T. 33, R. 7, and granting him, his heirs and assigns the exclusive right to cross said river within a mile of the point where he may establish said ferry for ten years, was either inoperative or had expired, the board passed an impracticable, long ordinance to license and regulate the running of a ferry across the river here. There are seven sections in this ordinance prescribing the duties of ferrymen, and the running of the boats, their kind and size, and giving precedence to physicians, surgeons and midwives, prescribing fines and penalties for the violation of any provisions of said ordinance.

Upon the passage of this ordinance, Col. Eugene Stanberry, Byron Stanberry and George H. Kiersted, submitted to the incipient city fathers a proposition to pay into the town treasury for a license to run a ferry across the river at Morris during the period of three years, $305, viz.: for the first year $100, second $101, and third $104, subject to the terms and conditions of the ordinance on that subject. For the consideration of this proposition a special meeting of the trustees was held March 1, 1851, when the offer was accepted, and petitioners executed and delivered to the board a $500 bond for the faithful observance of the ordinance and performance of the duties therein prescribed. Big with expectation of golden rewards from this ferry license, Col. Stanberry ordered La Salle County's popular rope maker, Ole Johnson, to make him a ferry rope, some 700 feet in length, at a large cost, purchased an old flat boat and started his ferry. They kept it running just three days when they discovered that they had one lawsuit on their hands with a fine prospect for several others. Geo. W. Armstrong as the administrator of Wm. E. Armstrong, brought suit against the firm of Stanberry & Kiersted, for damages for intruding upon his " 'tater patch," and received judgment; while several parties whom the company had ferried over and charged the regular rates of toll allowed under the Armstrong charter, when the license only allowed them to charge one fifth of that toll, were threatening to bring suit for extortion. Indeed, the Colonel came to the conclusion that five cents for ferrying a double team and wagon, and taking them back free on the same or succeeding day, was rather too small a business to ever be remunerative. He and his company became sad, melancholy, disheartened and abandoned it. Thus was Morris robbed of the services of three Charons, and the ferry license was "consigned to the tomb of the Capulets." It died of neglect and was buried without a mourner, and the Board of Trustees never after attempted to run a ferry.

At the April meeting of the board several licenses to vend spirituous and vinous liquors were granted, the price being $25 per year, with a $500 bond. Four saloons were granted licenses at this meeting. An election for trustees was held August 22, 1851. At the meeting of the board August 11, each member of the board had been paid three dollars for his services as trustee for one year preceding. An exceedingly modest board was this. At this election the old board (except that James B. Jones was elected in place of Mr. Kelley) was re-elected, and Mr. Seeley was elected president. The treasurer's report for the preceding year showed the sum of $160 collected as grocery and circus license, and $74.30 paid out as the expenses of running the "city government" per year. A corporation tax of fifteen cents on each $100 worth of taxable property was levied at their meeting Sept. 8, 1851, "for establishing a grade of the town and defraying the other expenses of the corporation." Oliver S. Newell was re-appointed treasurer on bond of $200. Dr. Newell died a few days later, and L. P. Lott was appointed his successor Nov. 10th, and the bond raised to $300. The board did not meet again until January 27, 1852, when the only business transacted was the drawing of the per diem of the board and town officers, amounting to $17. This was rather a cheap town board. The next meeting was held April 7th, when printed hand-bills were ordered to the value of $1.50, " cautioning a'l persons against the danger of small-pox at the Franklin House in Morris." Only this and nothing more was done. The first sidewalk ordinance was passed April 17, 1852. At this meeting Mr. Kiersted made a written proposal "to establish grades on all the streets and alleys of the town of Morris, and additions placing stones of grade at the intersection of the several streets, and making profiles and a map of the same for $50." The record says:

"After mature consideration the above proposition was accepted and a contract entered into," etc., and an order was drawn on the treasurer in favor of Mr. Kiersted, as an advance payment, for $6. But as Mr. K. was rather backward in coming forward with his grade, this contract was rescinded August 9, 1852. At this meeting the salaries of the town officers for the past six months were ordered paid, amounting to the sum of $13. Thus the total expense of the municipal government of Morris for one year was just $30. The clerk of the board received $7 for his year's salary, whilst the street commissioner and fire warden were paid by the *honor* conferred by the title. The election for a new board was held Aug. 23, when George Fisher, Eugene Stanberry, Henry Benjamin, Orville Cane and James Barrett were elected trustees—a new board except Mr. Cane. Mr. Fisher was made President, and Wells F. Stevens, Clerk. We do not now remember what were the issues in this election, but from the clean sweep of the old board, there must have been some cause of complaint. Some political petard or bomb which over-slaughed and retired them to private life. This new board held its first meeting Sept. 21. 1852, and appointed a committee, consisting of Messrs. Fisher, Cane and Stanberry, " to prepare and report an amendment to the charter more fully defining the limits of the corporation of the Town of Morris." Messrs. Fisher, Stanberry, Cane and Barrett were appointed as a committee to procure a " buring " ground. The latter committee reported an ordinance for the purchase of the E. ½, S. W. ¼, Sec. 27, T. 34, R. 7, on Sept. 27, which was passed. At this meeting Geo. Parmelee was appointed fire warden, and John Galloway, town constable; and a tax of fifteen cents on each $100 of taxable property for municipal purposes was levied. The treasurer's report submitted and approved, showed $180.28 received the past year from all sources, and $31.50 paid out on orders drawn. Surely these were economical times. Up to this date not a dollar had been expended to enforce police regulations or for assessing or collecting revenue.

At a special meeting of the board, Oct. 2, 1852, James Jacoby in company with the street commissioner and town constable were appointed to kill and destroy all dogs running at large contrary to the form and effect of this ordinance. This committee were probably inefficient, as no pay was provided for their services, nor were the kind of dogs to be " killed and destroyed " very clearly defined—whether biped or quadruped. On the 23d of October Thomas Reynolds was appointed street commissioner, and it was " ordered that the fees of the street commissioner be the same as those of town constable for like service." Now what similarity there could be between the duties of street commissioner and constable we will not attempt to point out. If it is meant to apply to the amount of fees or salary paid to the town constable then the whole thing " is clear as mud," for from Sept. 13, 1850, to the date of this meeting the town constable worked for nothing and boarded himself so far as drawing any money from the town treasury is concerned. At this meeting the town clerk's salary was fixed at one dollar per meeting for recording the proceedings and ordinances. At a special meeting, Dec. 13, 1852, Eugene Stanberry was appointed street commissioner (Mr. Reynolds not qualifying), and was paid by an order of the treasurer $15 for services, cleaning streets, etc. This was the first money paid by the board for work on the streets of Morris. At this meeting the land purchased for a cemetery (being what is known as the Old Catholic Cemetery, north of Morris) was ordered sold and $20 was appropriated toward a hook and ladder for the Fire Company. In February, 1853, there was a mad dog scare, and a proclamation issued on that subject. This appears to have been the first scare of that kind. Liquor licenses were raised to $50 at the March meeting of the board, 1853, and four licenses granted. On February 12, 1853, a special charter, incorporating the town of Morris, was passed, submitting the same to the people of Morris for adoption. This election was held May 2, 1853, and the record says " Eugene Stanberry was *Juge*, and W. F. Stevens, Clerk," who certify that there were 141 votes cast at said election, of which 101 were for and 40 against said charter.

This new charter did not change the name or style of the corporation, but increased the number of trustees to six instead of five, and cut off their per diem. It divided the town into three wards. All south of Washington street constituted the First; north of Washington and west of Liberty, the Second; and north of Washington and east of Liberty, the Third ward; each ward to have two trustees, the president to be elected on general ticket; so the council would consist of seven instead of five members. Under this charter the treasurer and town constable were elected by the people. The treasurer was ex-officio assessor, and the town constable was collector. The old board, however, remained in office until Sept. 26, 1853, when they canvassed the votes cast at an election held Sept. 24th under the new charter, and declared Elijah Walker elected president, Geo. E. Parmelee, treasurer and assessor; James B. Jones, constable and collector; L. P. Lott and George Turner, trustees of the 1st ward; Geo. W. Lane and Charles H. Goold of the 2nd; David LeRoy and John Antis of the 3rd. The retiring board, not one of whom had been re-elected, audited their own accounts for services for the past year at $5 each, and a like sum to their clerk for his year's services. The record book of the board of trustees, in which were kept the proceedings and ordinances of the board for three years, was a two-quire paper-back ledger, costing as per price mark 75 cents, and the record covers 42 pages, while the entire cost of running the municipal government for the three years was less than $100, all told. One of the last official acts of this old board reads as follows: "Ordered, that an order for three and $\frac{75}{100}$ dollars be drawn in favor of L. P. Lott for paper and candles furnished the board." This was before the days of kerosene or gas, or indeed of camphene, and yet but twenty-nine years have elapsed.

At the first election under the new charter there were only 136 votes cast, all of which Mr. Walker received. Indeed there was little or no opposition to those elected from president to constable. The new board met at the office of C. H. Goold Sept. 27, 1853, and elected Nathan B. Dodson, clerk, and Messrs. Lott, Lane and Goold were appointed a committee on "Rules of Order." Messrs. Goold, Lott and Lane were appointed as a committee to receive the books and papers of the former board, examine the same, and make a condensed report thereon." Their first regular meeting should have been held Oct. 10, 1853, but there was not a quorum present, and they adjourned to Oct. 15th to meet at the office of Drs. Hand & LeRoy. No quorum present at that time, and adjourned to the 17th, when a full board were present, when Mr. Lott, from committee on rules of order, reported a series containing twenty-four rules of order, which was adopted. Messrs. Lott and Lane, from the committee to receive and examine the books of the late board of trustees, submitted a report accompanied with a resolution, which was also adopted. Among the suggestions of this report they say, "We carefully inspected said books, etc., and find nothing contained therein that will need any action of this board for the present. The books and papers have been kept in a somewhat careless and loose manner," etc. Mr. Lott, as late treasurer, submitted his report of receipts and disbursements, showing total receipts from January 15, 1852, to Sept. 28, 1853, to be $473.71, with the sum of $420.61 paid out, leaving a balance of $53.10. He also reports the receipt of notes from Patrick Terry (now Dean Terry, of Chicago) amounting to $162.59, for sale of forty acres of cemetery land sold him, and a note for $25 given by Dominic Henry for liquor license. Here the old board was very obliging to the liquor vender, granting a license "on tick." At a meeting of the board Nov. 28th an ordinance was passed selling the west half of the southwest ¼ of township 27, 3, 4, and 7, to Patrick Terry, for $300, and the money to be derived therefrom was appropriated to the purchase of a Potter's field to bury the poor in the Morris cemetery. They also passed two other ordinances at this meeting, the one entitled "Hogs," the other "Dogs."

Though a body politic, the town of Morris had no official seal until the spring of 1854. Nor did the Board of Trustees have a finance committee until Jan'y, 1854. Messrs. Lott, Antis and Le Roy being the first. It would seem that absenteeism in the board was becoming a serious question about this time, and at a meeting Jan'y 12 the record says: "Mr. Lane offered his excuse for absence at last meeting; Mr. Goold came in; Mr. Turner was, by order of the president, summoned to appear before the board immediately; John Antis was deputized to serve the summons." At this meeting an ordinance entitled "Compensation of Town Officers" was passed containing nine sections. Messrs. Goold, Lott and Lane were also appointed to suggest amendments to the charter. At the next meeting Feb'y 13, this committee reported "that they had taken legal advice, and got Col. Bennett to draw up a code of amendments, and submitted the same to our member, Captain Starbuck, who had requested to have the whole matter left to him." This report was adopted and committee discharged. At this meeting one "Henry Fay applied for a license to sell liquor by the small, which was unanimously refused." The clerk presented his bill for services, $38.53—a sum larger than any previous year's entire expenses of the officers of the corporation. At the March meeting, on motion of Mr. Lane, the board purchased blocks nine and twelve, in the Morris Cemetery for the sum of $200 for "burial purposes." J. M. Goold was paid "fifty cents for killing a dog." Mr. Le Roy moved that the president and clerk be authorized to provide a supper to be given to the present board, and the new members elected at the coming election, and that an order be drawn on the treasurer for the cost thereof." But the board sat down *on* the *motion* instead of sitting down to the supper.

On the 1st of March, 1854, the charter of the town of Morris was amended by the General Assembly, fixing the time of election on the first Monday in April. At this election the following were elected: B. M. Atherton, president; Levi Hills, assessor and treasurer; Alban Bennett, police magistrate; John Galloway, constable and collector; N. B. Dodson, clerk; and the old aldermen, Lott, Turner, Lane, Goold, LeRoy, and Antis. At a meeting of the board April 10th, for the organization of the new board, six standing committees were appointed as follows: Finance and claims,

L. P. Lott; Fire department, G. W. Lane; Streets and alleys, George Turner; Health, David Le Roy; Judiciary, C. H. Goold; License, John Antis.

These were the first set of standing committees in the town council of Morris. There were one hundred and sixty-nine votes cast at this election, and in the 3d ward David Le Roy and E. P. Seeley each received thirty-two votes for alderman. Instead of deciding which was elected, by drawing cuts, it was referred to the board, and by the board referred to its president. At the second meeting of this new board April 17, 1854, the record says: "The president issued an order for the attendance of Antis, Turner and Goold, served by E. Stanberry, who reported Mr. Goold sick, Mr. Turner absent from town, and Mr. Antis present, which formed a quorum." Whether this order was a summons, notice, attachment, or *capias ad respondendum*, the record fails to show. At this meeting President Atherton submitted a long report upon the tie vote between Messrs. Le Roy and Seeley, finding in favor of Le Roy on the ground of a failure to elect his successor. This report was laid on the table on motion of Mr. Lott, and no further action seems to have been taken on the subject. Mr. Le Roy continued in the council during the year. At this meeting C. R. Parmelee, Patrick Hynds and H. P. Gillett were elected street commissioners, and P. A. Armstrong, city surveyor. This was a somewhat noted board in the introduction and passage of ordinances, and then enforcing or suspending them by resolution, they were never excelled if equaled. Indeed, this board assumed legislative jurisdiction over everything animate or inanimate within the limits of the corporation, and put on more style, "than a country school ma'm." Let us give a little copy from their record, viz.: "Mr. Le Roy asked leave to present a bill. On motion of Mr. Lott the bill was read by its title, and referred to the last named committee. The committee appointed to draft an ordinance on revenue reported with a bill which was read for the first time. On motion, the second reading was by its title. The bill was then referred to a committee of the whole, and made the order of to-morrow." We suppose to-morrow meant the next regular meeting of the board, but can only guess at it. It was a monster ordinance covering 21 sections, and was passed April 24, 1854. At a special meeting April 29, the board by a vote of five to one refused to grant liquor licenses; what was the effect of that action we do not remember, but are inclined to the belief that whisky was about as free as usual that year. At the May meeting the record says: "It was ordered by the board that Mr. Turner be fined for absence at the meeting of May 6th; Mr. Turner came in quarter to nine o'clock." But we are giving too much in detail, and must hurry along with our chronicle. A corporate seal was not adopted until May 29, 1854. The revenue collected this year was $1,274.97. The city surveyor completed a general system of trade, and an ordinance establishing the same was passed July 10, 1854.

There seems to have been a coolness about this time between President Atherton and the trustees, and at the August meeting "President Atherton tendered his resignation. Mr. Antis called for ayes and nays. Messrs. Le Roy and Lane voted aye, Messrs. Lott, Antis and Turner nay, whereupon the president withdrew his resignation." At the October meeting Chapin Park was ordered to be inclosed. It is now known as the Public Park. Mr. Dodson resigned and Alban Bennett was elected clerk, Nov. 13, 1854. At the April election, 1855, there were 227 votes cast, and the following were elected: Wm. T. Hopkins, president; B. F. Hall, A. H. Bishop, Robert Longworth, Nathan B. Dodson, James N. Reading and E. B. Hanna, trustees; H. B. Atwater, clerk; Geo. E. Parmelee, assessor and treasurer, and Abel Longworth, constable and collector. This was another clean sweep of the old board and a new deal throughout—except assessor and treasurer. Mr. Atwater, however, did not accept the office of clerk and Mr. Bennett held over. Before the next election a new charter had been granted by the Legislature, creating another ward. The election was held April 7, 1856, and resulted in the election of the following: W. T. Hopkins, re-elected president; L. P. Lott, B. F. Hall, S. C. Bliss, Geo. W. Lane, J. B. Jones, Patrick Hynds, A. Kirkland and Samuel Fatsinger, trustees; J. W. Woodrow, clerk; W. S. Gibson, constable and collector, and Hiram Mallory, assessor and treasurer. Another clean sweep except on president. This retiring board had learned to vote aye on appropriations and salaries, the clerk's fees allowed being $128.54, for the year; the treasurer reported receipts for the year, $2,877.29; disbursements $2,456.25, and his fees for collecting and paying out the same, $53.33. During this year another charter was obtained, creating Morris a city with a mayor and common council, a police magistrate, street commissioner, etc.

At the April election, 1857, the following officers were elected: F. S. Gardner, mayor; Elijah Walker, marshal; Patrick Hynds, treasurer; Wm. Skehan, collector, T. A. Henry, street commissioner; A. Clark, J. B. Davidson, Wm. B. Grenell, S. W. Harris, Philip Hart, S. Fatsinger, L. P. Lott and L. Ashton, aldermen. This council elected J. M. P. Butler, clerk. At the April election, 1858, the following officers were elected: C. R. Parmelee, mayor; F. S. Goold, marshal; George Selleck, treasurer; H. P. Gillett, collector; J. L. Dow, street commissioner, J. P. Southworth, police justice, and one alderman from each ward, viz.: Miles Gordon, C. H. Goold, Geo. F. Brown, E. S. Webber and C. Storr were elected: Jno. W. Woodrow, was elected city clerk; Oscar Baugher, city attorney. The collector collected $3,588.19 of taxes this year. At the next election, April, 1859, the following were elected: J. W. Newport, mayor; F. S. Goold, marshal; F. K. Hulburd, treasurer; J. L. Dow, street commissioner; John Barr, collector; H. C. Goold, J. W. Massey, Jno. G. Armstrong and David Pratt, aldermen.

The taxes collected this year were $3,777.70. L. P. Lott was elected city clerk by the council. At the April election, 1860, the officers elected were Wm. C. Hammill, mayor; Alex Bushnell, marshal; James McWilliams, collector; Geo. W. Lane, treasurer; James H. Oliver, street commissioner; E. B. Hanna, Hiram Plimpton, Daniel Matteson, Wm. A. Kiersted and C. Storr, aldermen. Messrs. James Reardan, H. C. Goold and J. W. Massey, holding over.

The council at their meeting of April 23d elected L. P. Lott, city clerk; David Le Roy city attorney; Nathaniel McBride, surveyor ; and C. H. Goold, assessor, who declined, and H. P. Gillett was elected in his place. Samuel B. Thomas and Calquhann Grant were designated as police justices. George Fisher was appointed health officer. Drs. Mathews, Hand and Antis, health commissioners, and James Miller, chief of the fire department, and for the first time in the history of the municipal government of Morris, standing committees of three members each were appointed. May 14, 1860: six standing committees were established, finance and claims, streets and alleys, licenses, judiciary, fire and water, and health. The fiscal report of the finance committee shows total receipts for the year ending April 15, 1860, were $4,098.68, of which $855.00 was for liquor licenses, and $80.00 for billiard table licenses. The expenditures were fire department, $811.26 ; streets and alleys, $827.05 ; street commissioner's services, $256.29 ; city marshal, $56.00 ; city clerk, $212.34 ; printing charter ordinances, etc.. $364.32, etc. The same committee reported $1,475.81 in hands of the late treasurer. This city council seem to have gotten down to business and reduced everything to rule, while their records were well kept, and are very full. Alderman H. C. Goold having moved out of his ward, L. B. Ray was elected in June of that year as his successor. The late treasurer's bond, if any he ever gave, could not and never has been found. The city, however, obtained some Iowa land for the $1,475.81 in his hands, but were the losers. In the early spring of 1861 a new charter for the city had been obtained. It was very long, and indeed a copy of the charter of Chicago. It was, however, submitted to a vote of the people March 23d, and literally snowed under, there being 224 votes against and only 26 for its adoption.

At the city election, April 2, 1861, there were 440 votes cast. This was by far the largest vote ever cast before that time and resulted in the election of John Antis, mayor; Geo. W. Lane, treasurer; F. M. Robinson, (now member of the Legislature) marshal; Wm. A. Rogers, street commissioner; William McFarland, Jr., collector; and L. P. Lott, Eli F. Johnson, Charles Comerford, and C. G. Conklin, aldermen. The fiscal report for the year ending April 15, 1861, shows total receipts, $4,667.83, of which liquor licenses furnished $1,385; show licenses, $61; ball alley licenses, $48; billiard tables, $40, and fines, $76. Total liabilities of the city, $4,422.19, with assets of $10,943.05, which was certainly a fair showing. Charles Turner was elected city clerk; John P. Southworth, city attorney ; H. P. Gillett, assessor, and C. Grant and Samuel B. Thomas were designated as city justices; James Miller was elected chief engineer of the fire department, with Daniel Matteson and John Barr, assistants.

On the 1st of April, 1862, there were 462 votes cast and Uri B. Couch was elected mayor; Geo. F. Brown, treasurer; John C. Jones, marshal; Jacob Gorich, street commissioner; John Vesly, collector; with the following aldermen: E. B. Hanna, Hiram Plimpton, M. K. Keller, and Alex. Bushnell. The receipts for the year were $4,300.77 of which liquor licenses were but $650.00, a falling off of one half from the previous year. The city clerk got $169.30 for his year's service, an income of $162.30 over Capt. Starbuck for like duties ten years before. Charles Turner was re-elected clerk; William Grant, city attorney; A. M. Cleveland, surveyor, and Thomas Reynolds, assessor; Jno. W. Woodrow was elected chief engineer of the fire department, with David Conlong and John Gunlock, assistants. The officers for 1863 were Geo. F. Brown, mayor; Wm. McFarlan, Jr., collector; Jacob Gorich, street commissioner; Geo. W. Lane, treasurer; Wm. Zimmerman, marshal; and S. B. Thomas, D. O. Goodrich, Geo. Fisher and Charles Comerford, aldermen. The retiring Council for the first time in the history of the corporation tendered a vote of thanks to retiring Mayor Couch "for the impartial, prompt and efficient manner in which, he has presided over the deliberations of the Council during the past year." C. Turner was re-elected city clerk; Hiram C. Goold was elected assessor; James N. Reading, city attorney, and Jno. W. Woodrow chief of the fire department, with David Conlong and Charles B. Ingersoll, assistants. B. M. Atherton and Thomas Alford were designated as city justices. This new council seem to have been one of great ability in *auditing accounts* and drawing orders on its treasurer. It was also pretty heavy on dogs, as a large number of bills were presented for "burial of dogs," and allowed at fifty cents each.

At the next election, April 5, 1864, E. B. Hanna was elected mayor; Charles Sparr, treasurer; E. T. Hopkins, marshal; J. H. Oliver, collector; Wm. H. Rogers, street commissioner, and H. E. Reinhart, W. H. Parmelee, N. C. Petteys and T. Donnovan, aldermen. The finance committee report receipts by the treasurer for past year $4,687.82. Expenditures $4,502.84. The amount received for liquor licenses was $1,055;

shows $83.00. Bridge stock dividends, $441.00; fines, $75.00. This was a good year for the city attorney, as he got $212.00; city clerk, $151.57. The fire department cost $323.72, and the sum of $1,254.49 was expended on street repairs. The administration of justice this year was expensive. In addition to the $312.00 paid to the attorney, there were $331.70 paid to justices and constables for fire and police services. W. H. Parker was elected city clerk ; T. B. Rice, attorney ; J. W. Massey, assessor ; Jno. W. Woodrow, chief of the fire department, with D. Conlong and Jacob Meyer, assistants, and Nathaniel McBride, inspector of weights and measures. Whether Me ever performed service in this office or not the record fails to state. George H. Kiersted was elected surveyor. Mr. Parker, the new clerk, kept a very full and well-arranged record of the council proceedings. At the meeting of the council, Dec. 19, 1864, a bill of two dollars and fifty cents was paid for "removing" five dogs, and one dollar for hauling them to the boneyard. Did the assassin Guiteau steal this term from the common council of the city of Morris ? Page 358 of the record is as follows : "To the memory of Timothy Donnovan, who received injuries from the explosion of an anvil while firing a national salute on the 22d Feb'y, of which injuries he died Feb'y 26, 1865." Mr. Donnovan was an alderman, and while endeavoring to fire off an anvil on the news of the evacuation of Richmond, on the 22d of Feb'y, he was fatally injured, and John P. Mannahan, one of our best business men, was instantly killed by the bursting of the anvil. Many other people stood near the spot, but fortunately no others were injured.

The writer stood within a few feet of Mannahan when he was instantly killed by a piece of the anvil striking his head. Mr. Donnovan was a blacksmith, and it was his own anvil that killed him.

The total receipts by the city treasurer for the year were $5,450.10. Of this sum $1,275 were from liquor licenses, $215.44 from fines and judgments. The clerk's salary was $195.32; attorney's, $103; marshal's, $170.21; fire department cost $556.14, and police $188.04. At the April election, 1865, E. B. Hanna was re-elected mayor, and Geo. W. Granby, Geo. W. Lane, Geo. Fisher and C. G. Conklin were elected aldermen. Colquhann Grant was elected clerk; J. W. Massey, assessor; J. N. Reading, attorney; and Geo. H. Kiersted, surveyor. Judge Grant made an excellent city clerk. David Conlong was elected chief of the fire department, with Miles Gordon and Jacob Geisen, assistants. Our friend Geisen must have been many pounds lighter then than now. He would make a decidedly weighty fireman now. Deacon Bross was elected collector. The assessor, Mr. J. W. Massey, gave a bond in the sum of $10,000, conditioned that he would well and faithfully perform the duties of assessor, etc. Under no circumstances could the assessor handle the money of the city,—not a dollar came to his hands,—hence we fail to see any reason, good or bad, requiring a $10,000 bond from a town assessor. At the next city election, April 3, 1866, E. B. Hanna was again elected mayor; E. T. Hopkins, marshal; Charles Sparr, treasurer; J. R. Combs, collector; Abram Bogart, street commissioner; N. McBride, police magistrate; and James Miller, Edward Sanford, Wm. Sheehan, aldermen. This council elected F. C. Mayo, clerk; A. Bennett, attorney; Thomas Reynolds, assessor; and Joseph Hicks, health officer.

Total receipts of the treasurer for past year were $9,436.51; disbursements, $8,167.30; liquor licenses, $1,150; expended on streets, $2,380.89; gutters, $2,339.41. This was a year of taxes and improvements. Mr. Mayo did not qualify as city clerk, and Judge Grant seems to have held over.

The receipts for the year ending April, 1867, were $10,240.80, and expenditures, $9,717.10. The liquor license money this year was $1,614.30. The total assets of the city were reported as follows:

In hands of Treasurer	$ 523 70
Bridge stock	6,300 00
S. W. Harris' note	4 33
Fire King engine, hose and carriage	2,500 00
Niagara do do	1,200 00
Lots in Morris Cemetery	200 00
Furniture in Council room	50 00
Tools in Street Commissioner's hands	50 00
Real estate—Iowa lands, 160 acres	880 00
Engine building and lot	700 00
Total	$9,306 03

Liabilities were stated at "outstanding orders, $209.50." This was surely a fine showing. The city clerk received for his year's services $299.75.

At the election April 2, 1867, S. B. Thomas was elected mayor; E. T. Hopkins, marshal; C. Sparr, treasurer; J. R. Combs, collector; and A. Bogart, street commissioner; with Wm. B. Field, Charles H. Goold, D. R. Holmes, James B. Jones, Joseph Hicks, Wm. Selleck, and Samuel Jordan, aldermen. A fifth ward having been added, thus increasing the number of aldermen to ten—Mr. Holmes having been elected to fill a vacancy in the second ward.—Judge Grant was unanimously re-elected clerk; Charles Turner was elected attorney; L. Whitney, assessor; A. M. Cleveland, surveyor; and E. T. Hopkins, health officer. At this city election nearly 500 votes were cast. The total receipts of the year ending April, 1868, were reported to be $12,839.50; expenditures, $8,111.27; leaving a balance in treasury, $5,251.93. Total assets are given at $9,141.26, with liabilities for outstanding orders, $80.03. At the election April 7, 1868, E. B. Hanna was again elected mayor; John Unfred, marshal; Nelson Carpenter, collector; Abram Bogart, street commissioner; and L. P. Lott, George Galloway, and B. Olin, aldermen, with a tie between E. Pyle and B. F. Hall in the second ward, and between John Vesley and Jacob Gouch in the third ward. These gentlemen "cast lots" for the position, when Pyle and Gouch were the successful ones.

This council elected Lucius Whitney, clerk; Gen. Wm. Birney, city attorney; Thomas Reynolds, assessor. The total receipts of the treasurer for the past year were $12,843; disbursements, $8,246.21. The sum of $1,937.08 was expended on street repairs, and $736 for night watch services. The amount received from liquor licenses was the large sum of $3,126.47. The amount of fines collected was $473.55, which was probably the largest amount ever collected in one year in Morris.

On the 10th of August, 1868, Alderman Olin resigned, and Edward Sanford was elected to fill the vacancy. Mr. Unfred, the city marshal, resigned in October of that year and E. T. Hopkins was appointed by the council to fill the vacancy.

At the council meeting of the 8th of March, 1869, the committee on fire and water submitted a long report on the expense of the fire department, from which we glean the following items. That Shabonch steam engine cost $1,500; necessary hose, $2,925. That the city hall building together with engine, hose and fire apparatus cost $14,927.82.

This committee was composed of Aldermen Lott, Selleck, Field and Jones, with Mayor Hanna. To raise the means to meet these expenditures, interest-bearing bonds to the amount of $9,250 were issued and sold. At the election of April 6, 1869, E. B. Hanna was again elected mayor; E. T. Hopkins, marshal; Joel W. Ellis, collector; Jacob Geisen, treasurer; Alex. Bushnell, street commissioner, and the following named aldermen: Oliver Hanlen, A. M. Cleveland, J. S. R. Scovill, and Charles Wilkins. There being a tie in the 3d Ward, between James Honie and George Baum, lots were cast and Honie won.

The financial statement shows the total receipts for the past year were $16,575.66, of which "spirit licenses" were $2,625.68, and show licenses $309.00 with $5,251.03 in the treasury at commencement of the year, making a total of $21,837.59, with disbursements of $20,408.70, leaving in the treasury $1,430.89. This was a large sum of money for one year's municipal transactions. J. H. Pettit was elected clerk; A. R. Jordan, attorney; H. Plimpton, assessor.

The city election of April 5, 1870, was a warm one, and nearly 600 votes were cast, resulting in the election of David D. Spencer, of State Savings notoriety, Major E. T. Hopkins, marshal; C. W. Card, collector; Jacob Geisen, treasurer; Wm. Mason, Jr., street commissioner; N. McBride, police magistrate, with E. Gifford, A. P. Buckley, A. F. Hand, Geo. W. Rossiter and E. Sanford, aldermen; J. H. Pettit was re-elected clerk; A. R. Jordan, attorney; Thos. Reynolds, assessor; E. Ridgeway, chief engineer of the fire department, with H. L. Miller and Geo. Green, assistants. The fiscal report of the year ending April 11, 1870, shows receipts, $11,189.91, with amount in treasury at commencement of the year, $1,430.89, making a total of $12,620.80. The liquor licenses for the year were $2,706.99; show licenses, $334.33. The disbursements were $9,491.07, leaving $3,129.73 in the treasury. Among the expenditures were $956.75 for repairs on Lisbon road, and $350 for Waupousee road, south of the bridge across the Illinois river, and $1,107.82 on street repairs.

At the next election, April 4, 1871, John S. R. Scovill was elected mayor; E. T. Hopkins, marshal; O. W. Card, collector; Leander Irons, treasurer; Alex. Bushnell, street commissioner; with D. W. Burry, James McKeen, George Banm, Wm. M. Collins, and Wm. Mason, aldermen.

This was the most hotly contested election our little city ever had, and the judiciary committee assumed judicial functions in canvassing the aldermanic vote, and reported that neither Mr. Burry nor Mr. McKeen, aldermen elect, was eligible to the office—Mr. Burry, "because he is not a naturalized citizen. The papers under which he claims citizenship, were issued about the last days of March, 1871, by the county court of Grundy County, Illinois," citing *Mills et al.* v. *McCabe*, 44 Ill. Reports, 195, which, upon examination, it will be found, has no sort of bearing upon the case whatever. Hence, the opinion of the judiciary committee of the common council of the city of Morris, that county courts under the statute laws of Illinois, have no jurisdiction over naturalization of aliens, was a little "too previous." In the case of Mr. McKeen, the committee say he has not resided in the city limits one year next preceding his election as required by the city ordinance. Now, it so happened that Mr. McKeen had been a resident of the county nearly forty years, and of the second ward in the city, from which he was elected, several years, having purchased a lot and built a nice residence there, but had been temporarily absent with his wife visiting his son in the town of Mazon, on his old homestead. This report was however, adopted by the old council, and Aldermen-elect Burry and McKeen, by a vote of five to four, were declared ineligible, and Messrs. Coy and Bliss, by a like vote, were declared elected, though both were defeated at the polls. Mayor Scovill, having qualified as such, called a special meeting of the council April 17, 1871, for the purpose of electing city clerk, attorney, assessor, etc. The record of this meeting, as kept by the clerk, shows a want of accord between the mayor and the clerk. We give one extract to show the general tenor. It says: "The meeting was called to order by J. S. R. Scovill, mayor, who immediately commenced calling the names of individuals, some of whom, as appears from the record, are aldermen, and others not, omitting the names of Aldermen Hamlin and Bliss, and substituting the names of Messrs. Burry and McKeen. The mayor proceeded to read a paper, no copy of which has been handed the clerk, and then proceeded to read the appointments of certain persons as the several committees, some of whom appear from the records to be aldermen, and some do not, but no copy of said appointments has been filed with the clerk." The record of this meeting shows a first-class wrangle covering two full pages, and at a meeting of the council, May 15, 1871, the entire record of this meeting was ordered to be expunged, and the words, "Expunged by resolution passed by the common council of the City of Morris, May 15, 1871. George W. Howard, City Clerk." Mr. Howard gives his version of that celebrated meeting of April 17th on the following page of the record. It is a very different record. At this meeting Messrs. Burry and McKeen were admitted to their seats, and Geo. W. Howard was elected clerk, W. T. Hopkins, attorney, and Thomas Reynolds, assessor. The fiscal report for year ending April, 1871, shows receipts of $10,279.75, with balance over from previous year, $3,129.73, making total of $13,409.48. The spirit licenses amounted to $2,724.00; shows, $322.50; expenditures, $12,679.78; leaving in the treasury, $729.70. Mayor Scovill was re-elected April 2, 1872. E. T. Hopkins was elected marshal; Valentine Zimmerman, collector; Jacob Geisen, treasurer; Alex. Bushnell, street commissioner; and Henry Rutherford, L. Irons, A. F. Hand, Geo. W. Rossiter and A. Harrison, aldermen. Mr. Howard was elected clerk; P. A. Armstrong, attorney; T. Reynolds, assessor. The receipts for year ending April 8, 1872, were $8,661.62, including amount from former treasurer ($729.70); disbursed, $8,648.71, leaving $1,291 in treasury.

On April 1, 1873, Mayor Scovill was re-elected; Mr. Hopkins was also re-elected marshal; Geisen, treasurer; Bushnell, street commissioner, and L. P. Lott, T. W. Tupper, J. C. Carr, Wm. Handwork and Michael Gormley were elected aldermen; F. B. Handwork was elected clerk; P. A. Armstrong, attorney. The financial report for year ending April 7, 1873, shows receipts $7,549.18, of which spirit licenses furnished only $1,500.00. The expenditures were $6,917.61, leaving $631.57 in the treasury; the total assets of the city are given at $20,847.39, with liabilities for outstanding orders, $1,009.10; Mr. Handwork made a very fine clerk; his record is clear and full. At the April election, 1874, Mr. Scovill was again elected mayor, and E. T. Hopkins, marshal; Thomas Mernan, treasurer; T. Reynolds, assessor; Val Zimmerman, collector; Alex. Bushnell, street commissioner; N. McBride, police magistrate, and the following aldermen: H. Rutherford, H. C. Gifford, J. Gorich, G. A. Acton and A. Harrison; F. B. Handwork was elected clerk, and A. R. Jordan, attorney. The fiscal report of the clerk shows total receipts, including $631.57 on hand, at beginning of the year, $33,535.81, of which liquor licenses furnished $1,716.16; other licenses $390.00; expenditures, $28,940.57, leaving balance in treasury, $4,086.14; among the items of expenditures are two entries of permanent improvements amounting to $18,200.00; this was for investment in the Sherwood School Furniture Manufacturing Company, and bonus to obtain its location here. We find there were expended this year upon street repairs, $3,216.41, and $990.50 in the fire department. The assets of the city are given at $24,815.01, and liabilities $20,049.49; among the assets are engine house, $5,786.43; fire department, $10,961.95; real estate, $1,301.50, and $4,086.14 in the treasurer's hands, and $877.16 in hands of F. K. Hulburd, late treasurer; outstanding bonds, $18,000.00, the last eight of which ($4,000.00) mature Feb'ry 1, 1884. Alderman Carr having moved out of the 3d ward, P. A. Armstrong was unanimously elected to fill the vacancy in November, 1874.

At the next election of city officers in April, 1875, Mayor Scovill was re-elected; E. T. Hopkins was again elected marshal; Alex. Bushnell, street commissioner; Thos. Mernan, treasurer; T. Reynolds, assessor, and Geo. M. Jones, collector, with the following named aldermen: John W. Miller, Ono Earnshaw, Geo. Baum, J. O. Levitte and John Barr; M. S. Prindle was elected clerk; P. A. Armstrong, attorney; Dr. E. Ridgeway, who had been for several years chief engineer of the fire department, was again appointed to that office, with H. S. Reading and James Johnson, as his assistants. Mr. Handwork, the retiring city clerk, submitted an elaborate trial balance of the books; from this and the report of the finance committee, a very clear statement of the financial standing of the city is made; the total receipts were $12,474.24, expenditures, exclusive of permanent improvements and interest on bonds and loan orders, $9,073.70. The assets of the city are given at $22,136.24, and liabilities at $21,169.03; of this latter amount city bonds make the sum of $19,000.00, and outstanding orders, $2,169.03.

Amount in the treasury $1,357.72; again was Mayor Scovill re-elected at the April election, 1876; E. T. Hopkins, marshal; T. Mernan, treasurer; Geo. M. Jones, collector; Thomas Reynolds, assessor, and Geo. Taylor, street commissioner, with R. L. Schofield, C. J. I. Murray, Henry Fey, Thomas Owen and Wm. Rolley, aldermen; Mr. Prindle was re-elected clerk; Armstrong, attorney; E. Ridgeway, chief engineer of the fire department, with H. A. Cleveland and L. Irons as his assistants. Mr. Prindle prepared and submitted a full and detailed statement of the fiscal year, showing receipt for the year $17,879.86, with amount in treasury at close of previous year, $1,357.72, total, $19,237.58; paid out on orders, $17,865.02; leaving on hand, $1,372.56. The saloon licenses amounted to $2,117; other licenses, $471.10. The expense of the fire department this year was $2,496.30, and for street repairs, $640.47. The city assets are given as $23,181.52, and liabilities at $19,107.09; being for city bonds, $19,000; orders outstanding, $107.09. At the next election, April, 1877, Dr. John Antis was elected mayor; Timothy Rodd, marshal; Wm. Jones, treasurer; and Fred Johnson, street commissioner; with Wm. Humble, James McHoran, Dr. A. E. Palmer, O. J. Nelson, J. McCambridge and Wm. Mason, aldermen.

The fiscal report shows receipts, $18,198.20; with amount from former treasurer, $1,372.56; total, $19,570.82. Disbursements, $18,659.27, leaving a balance in treasury of $911.56. Total assets, $24,503.48; liabilities, $16,183.97; outstanding city bonds, $16,000. This was a discordant council. L. Irons was appointed and confirmed as chief engineer, with H. S. Reading and James W. Willard, assistants. His Honor the mayor's appointments of clerk and attorney were not concurred in, whereupon he issued a manifesto to the council, whereupon the council adjourned without action. Geo. W. Lane was finally confirmed as clerk, and C. Grant as attorney, when matters moved along smoothly. At the November meeting a petition signed by 99 legal voters of Morris was presented to the council, praying that an election be called to vote for or against abandoning the special charter and organizing under Chapter 24 of the Statute entitled "Cities, Villages and Towns." The petition was granted, and an election held for that purpose on the 18th day of December, 1877. The vote resulted in favor of the reorganization under the general law by sixty majority in a light vote cast. Minority representation in the council was defeated by a larger majority.

At a special meeting of the council Jan'y 21, 1878, Aldermen Rolley, Humble and Fey, a committee to divide the city into wards as required by law. This committee reported to the council at their next regular meeting Feb'y 11, 1878, dividing the city into four instead of five wards, when an ordinance was passed entitled "An ordinance dividing the city into wards," as follows: "All that part of the said city which lies south of the south line of Main street and east of Nettle Creek shall constitute the First Ward.

"All that part of the said city which lies west of Liberty street, south of the Chicago, Rock Island and Pacific railroad, and included in the First Ward, shall constitute the Second Ward.

"All that part of the said city which lies east of Liberty street, and between the south line of Main street and the Chicago, Rock Island and Pacific railroad, shall constitute the Third Ward.

"All that part of the said city which lies north of the Chicago, Rock Island and Pacific railroad shall constitute the Fourth Ward."

At the regular March meeting of the council, an ordinance was passed making the marshal and superintendent of streets (as called in the statute) elective by the people annually, on the third Tuesday of April, being the time fixed under the statute for city elections. By the reorganization Mayor Antis held over another year while an entirely new council had to be elected. At this election, April, 1878, N. McBride was elected police magistrate; Fred Johnson, superintendent of streets; E. T. Hopkins, marshal; and Geo. M. Jones, Francis Hall, Wm. Mason, L. W. Claypool, O. J. Nelson, Henry Fey, T. Owen and J. O. Levitte were elected aldermen. The fiscal report of the preceding year shows receipts including amount from former treasurer, $12,839.32, disbursements, $11,897.85, leaving balance in treasury $941.47. During this year there was a general revision of the ordinances made, so as to conform more nearly to the provisions of the statute.

At an adjourned meeting of the council April 21, 1879, an ordinance was passed fixing the salary of the mayor at $100 per year payable quarterly and allowing aldermen $2.50 for each meeting actually attended by them.

At the election April 15, 1879, John Barr was elected mayor; Geo. W. Lane, clerk; Wm. Jones, treasurer; Thomas Murray, marshal; Fred Johnson, superintendent of streets; A. L. Doud, attorney, and A. E. Palmer, Wm. Mason, O. J. Nelson and Charles Canahan, aldermen. At a meeting of the council April 30, 1879. Mayor Antis read a veto of the ordinance allowing the mayor and aldermen compensation for their official services. Thereupon the vote by which said ordinance was passed at the last meeting was reconsidered, and the ordinance again put upon its passage notwithstanding the mayor's objections. But it failed to pass, ayes 5, noes 3. Not a two-thirds vote, as required to pass an ordinance over the mayor's veto.

The receipts for the year were $13,459.15, disbursements $11,604.07, leaving $1,855.08 in the treasury. The expense of the police were unusually heavy, being $686.25. Geo. W. Lane was re-appointed clerk, and Henry S. Reading chief of the fire department, with H. L. Miller and Wm. Gibbard assistants. This city council was a "go-as-you-please one." It was harmonious, though by no means orderly or dignified. At the next election Fred Johnson was re-elected superintendent of streets, Thomas Murray marshal, and Geo. M. Jones, Wm. Stephens, Henry Fey and R. M. Wing, aldermen, the mayor holding over (under the law the mayor is elected for two years). The mayor re-appointed Mr. Lane clerk, H. S. Reading chief, and H. L. Miller and Wm. Gibbard assistants of the fire department. The receipts of the year were $9,993.59, of which spirit licenses furnished $2,258.70; billiard tables $150.00. The expenditures were $8,880.16. Of this the police department cost $1,127.20. An amount which is startlingly large, and makes a bad showing for the peace and order of our really quiet and orderly city.

This brings us down to the election of our present mayor, Hon. John S. R. Scovill in April, 1881, who is now on his ninth year's service in that capacity. We close this branch of our history with an apology for its length. Indeed, we bit off a larger slice than we intended, when we started on this subject. It was rather more than we could chew. Quite too much to be easily digested or profitably swallowed. Mr. Prindle is again the clerk, and is one of the best the city ever had.

CHAPTER VIII.*

MORRIS TOWNSHIP—ITS ORGANIZATION, BOUNDARIES AND CHANGES—THE NEW COURT HOUSE—SCHOOLS OF MORRIS—EARLY TEACHERS—THE BOARD OF EDUCATION.

TURN we now from the noise, bustle and confusion, of the city to the country. The question of adopting township organization having been submitted to a vote of the people and carried by a large majority, the county court at its December term, 1849, appointed George H. Kiersted, Philip Collins and Robert Gibson, commissioners, to divide the county into towns or townships. This committee submitted their report in writing to said county court at its March meeting, 1850, which report was approved by said county court, March 4, 1850. Under and by virtue of this report, and its approval, the township or town of Morris embraced the following territory: "The whole of the north fraction of Congressional Township No. thirty-three (33) north, of Range No. seven (7) east, together with that portion of Section No. six (6) in Township No. thirty-three (33) north, Range eight east, lying north of the Illinois River; also the island in said river, with the exception of that portion of Waupecan Island lying on the south half of Section No. seven (7) in Township No. thirty-three (33) north, Range No. seven (7) east, etc. to constitute one division to be known by the name of Morris." The territory embraced in the township of Morris, as established by the commissioners, contained about 4,000 acres of land as follows: All that portion of Sec. 6, T. 33, R. 8, lying north of the Illinois River; also so much of Sections 1, 2, 7, 8, 9 and 10, as lie north of said river, with Sections 3, 4, 5 and 6 entire. But since then Morris has been badly shorn of her territory by taking from the Sections 5, 6, 7, and 8, and attaching or adding them to the town of Erienna, leaving Morris but a small town in point of territory. The fraction on Section 6, T. 33, R. 8, and the north fractions of Sections 1 and 2, and a part of the east half of Section three, compose, with the lands embraced in the city, our entire territory as a township. The town of Morris was fully organized by the election of town officers, on the first Tuesday in April, 1850. At this election P. A. Armstrong was elected supervisor; E. W. Hulburd, town clerk; Thomas Reynolds, assessor, etc. The first board of supervisors of the county convened at the old court house in Morris, June 12, 1850, and organized by the election of Philip Collins, chairman. At this meeting of the county board, George H. Kiersted and Robert Gibson were each paid $11.00, and Philip Collins $1.25, for their services as commissioners in dividing the county into towns. Why the services of Messrs. Kiersted and Gibson were worth so much more than those of Mr. Collins the record fails to disclose.

---

*By Hon. P. A. Armstrong.

This was a very economical board. At their November meeting they appointed a committee consisting of P. A. Armstrong, Geo. H. Kiersted and L. W. Claypool "to count the assessment rolls and carry out in appropriate columns the several amounts of taxes in dollars and cents, and also to prepare the collector's warrants for the different towns of this county," fixing the compensation at one dollar and a half per day. Thus the board took from the county clerk, Mr. E. W. Hulburd, about the only paying work of his office. The books used by this committee for collector's books are a curiosity. They are small sized account books costing about twenty-five cents each, and are laid away among the archives as a witness to the over zealous disposition manifested by this first county board to be very economical. They never repeated the experiment. This board also attempted to make each town maintain its own paupers, and passed a resolution to that effect; but as it was diametrically opposed to the statute, the resolution was "more honored in the breach than in the observance." At the November meeting, 1850, Mr. Armstrong presented a petition of Jacob and L. W. Claypool for a license to establish a ferry across the Illinois river at Morris, accompanied with a resolution granting the same for a period of five years, upon condition that they execute a bond in $500, to keep the same in accordance with the statute, and pay into the county treasury ten dollars per year as tax, establishing the rates of toll at fifteen cents per team over and back the same day, and ten cents for crossing one way. For man and horse over alone on the flat boat, ten cents, all owing double ferriage after 8 P. M., etc., which was, after various attempts were made to raise the amount of tax payable to the county, adopted, without amendment, by a vote of six to three.

Fearing that the county officers might be extravagant in the purchase of stationery, on motion of Supervisor Jacob Claypool, Mr. Armstrong was appointed "special agent to purchase and provide stationery for those officers entitled to the same, and that the board would audit no bills for stationery presented by any other person." Mr. Jacob Claypool, a member of the first County Board in 1841, and the first Board of Supervisors in 1850, has been dead several years, but his grandson, Henry C. Claypool, now wears the toga and represents the town of Wauponsee so long represented by his grandfather in the Board of Supervisors. What, between Jacob Claypool, L. W., his son, John and Henry, his grandsons, Wauponsee has been represented in the County Board by a Claypool, the greater portion of time, for thirty-two years past. At the fall election, 1853, P. A. Armstrong was elected county clerk, and as in his judgment the old court house had no suitable place to keep the books and papers of the office, or afford comfortable quarters, he rented the north room on the second story of a frame building standing where the Claypool block now stands, and then known as Goold's bank building, and moved the office to that room. This was a severe shock to the nerves of the economical Solons of the County Board. There was a special meeting of the board April 17, 1854. They met at the old court house instead of the county clerk's office. The clerk alone had the right to organize them. After some parleying the mountain went to Mahomet, and held their meeting, as the motion was "to Mr. Armstrong's office." When the rent for the use of the office fell due, they paid it, however. At the September meeting that fall, Mr. E. Walker, supervisor of the town of Morris, offered a resolution declaring in favor of building a new court house. On the passage of which, the ayes and nays were called, and it was adopted, ayes, 9, nays, 2. Messrs. Augustine, Walker and Renne, were appointed a committee to prepare plans, etc., who reported in favor of building a court house forty by seventy feet, at a cost not exceeding $8,000. On motion of Supervisor Justice Renne, " the clerk of the board was appointed to procure from some good architect a plan and specifications of a building for a court house, of nearly the dimensions of the one proposed by the building committee, to be presented for action at the next meeting of the board." But the clerk enlarged the plan or size of building to fifty-four by eighty-four, and obtained from J. M. Van Osdell, of Chicago, the plan of the present court house, which was adopted by the board, April 17, 1855, and a loan of $5,000 was ordered to raise funds to help build the same. The building committee, having advertised to let the contract to build such a building of brick, found the lowest bid was over $18,000.00, and therefore was afraid to let the contract.

A special meeting of the board was called June 15, 1855, when Supervisor L. W. Claypool offered a resolution, limiting the amount to $18,000, exclusive of superintendence. Supervisor Walker offered an amendment to strike out $18,000 and insert $20,000, which amendment was carried by ten to four, and the resolution of Mr. Claypool, as amended, was adopted by a like vote. The old court house was ordered to be sold; the log jail had already been sold for $14. Mr. Miles Hills having resigned, as a member of the building committee, Mr. L. W. Claypool was appointed in his place, which committee consisted of Supervisors C. Grant, E. Walker, and L. W. Claypool. This committee awarded a contract, to build said court house of brick, to R. J. Cunningham & Co. for $19,360, who built the foundation and commenced on the brick walls. The brick were of an inferior quality. The clerk becoming disgusted with the appearance of the work, called a special meeting of the board Oct. 9, 1855.*

* Mr. L. W. Claypool adds: "After various preliminaries, the board decided on building the court house of brick with stone trimmings; and in June, 1855, the building committee, consisting of C. Grant, Miles Hills and E. Walker, let the contract to Cunningham, Foster and Williams for $19,360 ($20,000 being the limit).
At the September meeting, 1855, Superintendent Grant tendered the resignation of Miles Hills, and L. W. Claypool was elected to fill the vacancy.
At this time the foundations were all built to the top of the water table, and the brick were being delivered for the main walls. Mr. Claypool at once declared that he would have nothing to do with the building if such brick were to be used, and being ably assisted by County Clerk Armstrong, Superintendent Watkins, E. P. Seeley, and particularly Mr. Dubreil, one of the contractors for, and then engaged in building the piers for the Morris bridge, being an expert in stone work, in computing the difference in cost between stone and brick, on a careful estimate, found that the additional cost of stone would not exceed $3,400.
The board was called together by the clerk, with the advice of the building committee, no doubt, to meet Oct. 9, 1855, when Superintendent Claypool offered the following resolution:
Resolved, That the court house building committee be, and they are hereby authorized, to change the plan of the court house with the contractors thereof, so that said building shall be built of stone on exterior walls, after the manner and of similar stone and dimensions as the Joliet court house; provided, however, that the cost thereof shall not exceed $3,400, the original contract price, and that any order of

The record reads as follows: "Tuesday, October 9, 1855. The Board of Supervisors met at the county clerk's office this day pursuant to a call from the county clerk, for the purpose of considering the propriety and expediency of using stone entirely in lieu of brick in the construction of the court house." Mr. L. W. Claypool offered a resolution for such change, " provided the cost should not exceed $3,400 over the original contract price and that any order of the board previously passed *limiting* the cost of the court house to $20,000 be and the same is altered to $23,400, to suit the above proposed change, if made by the committee"—

the board heretofore passed, limiting the entire cost of court house to $20,000, be, and the same is altered to $23,400, to suit the above proposed change, if made by the committee; and if not made, the committee are hereby instructed to have the exterior walls of said court house built of first-class common brick, such as are, or should be used, in constructing buildings of that dimension and cost, being in accordance with plan and specifications now on file. And should said committee make such change, the contractors are hereby allowed until the 25th of September (next) to complete said building." Adopted without division.

At this time no good brick were being made in or near Morris; the contractors would be obliged to ship them quite a distance, at great expense; hence were quite willing to accept the proposition of the committee, to construct of stone at the cost of $3,400.

Nov. 19, 1855, board met. E. Walker resigned as member of the committee, and F. S. Watkins was elected to fill the vacancy. Nov. 20, Superintendent Walker moved to retire Grant from the building committee, on account of ill health, and nominated Superintendent Renne in his place; adopted.

April 22, 1856, Mr. Renne was retired, and L. P. Lott substituted.

The building committee, now consisting of Claypool, Watkins and Lott, completed the building, and March 6, 1858, made final settlement with contractors, and accepted the building; entire cost, $22,760; and as the contract was missing, it was stipulated in the settlement that if found at any time thereafter, all errors should be corrected, and money over-paid to be refunded, the committee believing that the contract price was $22,360. The contract was never found, and no money refunded.

Miles Gordon assisted the committee as superintendent and his bill was $44.50."

which resolution was adopted by the board, and the building committee succeeded in effecting a change from brick to Joliet stone in the contract without increasing the cost but three thousand four hundred dollars. Thus, by the action of the county clerk, Mr. L. W. Claypool, and a few other liberal men, did Grundy County obtain a building 54 by 84, instead of 40 by 70, and at a cost of $22,760, instead of not exceeding $8,000 and lastly, a permanent stone building, instead of a tumble-down soft brick structure—for at that time no good brick had ever been made at or near Morris. We confess that it required a good deal of finessing and skill to work the country Solons up to the liberal point required to vote for so large an appropriation at that time. An appropriation equal to $100,000, now. It was accomplished, however, and the county has a court house that will serve all the purposes required for half a century. The old court house was in the way of building the new one, hence it had to be taken away, leaving the county with no place to hold courts. The clerks of the circuit and county courts had taken possession of the two offices of the brick jail, which had been built in the fall and winter of 1854, at a cost of $3,180. The Court House Committee had sold the old court house to Messrs. Foster & Williams (who had the contract for the carpenter work of the new court house) for $255, and they had sold it to H. L. Smith (better known as Husband Smith), who had moved it to his farm, W. ¼, S. W. ¼, S. 31, T. 34, R. 7, some three miles northwest from Morris, when after re-clothing and painting, it presented quite a respectable appearance as a farm dwelling, and where it still stands as a painted ghost of former times. The building committee rented the carpenter shop, now occupied by the Morris Cutlery Company, for the purpose of holding the fall and spring terms of the circuit court, and said court was there held. The first jail of the county was ordered built by the county commissioners at their December meeting, 1845. Jacob Claypool and George H. Kiersted were appointed as a special committee to prepare plans and specifications, and let the contract to build a jail to be located on the southeast corner of the court house square. They were men of genius as well as ability, with a keen sense of the ludicrous. They knew that the county board expected a jail to be built which would cost not to exceed $200 when completed. Both had a strong prejudice against building a jail independent of a court house, or before building a court house. Hence they decided to make the thing as ridiculous as they conveniently could, and accordingly decided to build a jail of green logs, with the bark on. The size, as we now remember, was 14 by 16. The bottom logs were placed some ten feet below the surface, a hole having been first dug and the bottom covered with logs, as nearly straight as possible, so that they could be placed closely side by side. Then the log walls were carried up to the surface, when another log floor was laid and then extended up some ten feet above ground. A trap-door (iron lattice work) was placed in or near the center of the upper floor, hung at one side with heavy iron hinges and a heavy staple and clasp on the opposite side, to be fastened by a mammoth padlock. The underground compartment was to form the cells, where the prisoners were to be put at night, and the upper part was for corridors. To put the prisoners in the cell, the jailor, after throwing back the trap-door, would cause the prisoner to let himself down by suspending himself through the trap hole the length of his arms, and then letting go, alighting on his feet. To get them out in the morning, the jailor, who was physically very powerful, would reach down, and taking hold of their wrists, pull them up by main strength. True, they had a ladder, which, however, was seldom used. This jail was let to the lowest bidder, and our old friend, Dominic McGrath, was the successful one. His bid was $202.60, just $2.60 more than the county commissioners felt like investing in the jail business. But as it was so near to it, the committee let the contract, to be paid for in county orders. Mr. McGrath used hickory logs in the construction of the jail, and soon had it completed, but when he applied for his county order, the county board cut him down to $162.60, simply on the ground that the contract price was too high. Rather than go to litigation, "Old Dom," accepted this price and was paid in county orders, worth about 75 cents on the dollar. This jail was sold for $14 in 1855.

As a place to keep prisoners, this jail was a dead failure. Capt. Jeremiah Cottrell, who had been charged with the larceny of almost everything, from a trace chain to a threshing machine, in Cook county, took a change of venue to this county. Complaining of rheumatism, Sheriff Armstrong was too humane to put him down in the underground cell, where there was no light, save that which came through the grated trap-door, hence he was put in the corridor or upper part. He soon managed to get out and report himself for duty at the ferry across the river at Morris, telling the sheriff that he was an old and experienced boatman and could and would, if permitted, make himself useful in that capacity. Struck with the impudent boldness of the man, and his unquestionable desire to be of use, the sheriff trusted him, not only with his entire liberty, but soon entrusted the entire management and control of the ferry to him. This trust he never attempted to betray, but he used his position as the trusted agent of the sheriff to manage the ferry, in making friends, and protesting his innocence of the crime charged against him, so that when his trial came off he was acquitted, notwithstanding the proofs of his guilt were clear and overwhelming. Hon. B. C. Cook was the prosecutor, and ever after held that the fact of a juror being on the Cottrell jury was a better cause for challenge than any defined in the statute. His first question to a juror was, "Were you a juror on the Cottrell trial?" If the answer was in the affirmative, Mr. Cook's reply was, "stand aside." And this he kept up as long as he practiced law in our court.

THE SCHOOLS AND EDUCATIONAL FACILITIES OF MORRIS.

That Mrs. Ann Nagle, widow of James Nagle, the first clerk of the commissioners' court of Grundy County, opened and taught the first school in Morris, there is no doubt. After the death of her husband in 1843, she opened a private school (for in those days we could have no other as we had no school fund) in her double-log cabin, which stood a little southeast of the present depot of the C. R. I. & P. R. R. in Morris. Of her scholars several survive, among whom are Thomas Mernan, John Hart, widow Reynolds, Jacob Griggs, John Claypool, etc., all living now in Morris. She continued her school for a year or over. The next school was taught by Miss Adelia Wilkes, now the widow of E. P. Seeley, deceased, and residing on Washington street. The next was Miss Mary Hyslap, now Mrs. J. Blanding, and also living on East Washington street in this city. The next was Charles M. Lee, afterward county judge of Livingston County, Ills. The next was Charles R. Starr, who has since been judge of the circuit court of Kankakee County. All of whom, except Mrs. Nagle, occupied the old court house. Of course, there was a school vacation during court weeks. The first record we can find of any school board bears date Dec. 21, 1843, when Peter Griggs, Perry A. Claypool and William Brown (who signed his name by making a cross) met at the recorder's office in Morris, and divided township 33, R. 7, as follows: "Ordered, that the E. ¼ of T. 33, of R. 7 E. 3d P. M., on the south side of the Illinois River, shall compose one school district to be known and designated by the name of the Mazon District, and that the west ½ of said township on south side of the Illinois River shall compose one school district, to be known and designated by the name of the Waupecan District, and all that portion of said township lying north of the Illinois River shall compose one school district, to be known and designated by the name of Nettle Creek District. Ordered, that William White, Sen., Barton Halderman and Edmund Brown be appointed trustees of schools in the Mazon District. Ordered, that James Robb, William Patteson and James Thompson be appointed trustees of schools in Waupecan District." In January, 1844, E. Warren was appointed "Treasurer of School Lands," on bond of $200. The first school money received by the treasurer of the board of trustees, seems to have been a warrant issued by the Auditor of Public Accounts on the State Treasury for $18.12, which the treasurer was "directed to sell at ten per cent. discount, and pay Waupecan District $4.89, Mazon District $4.46, Nettle Creek District $8.27, in auditor's warrants or cash, if sold at ten per cent. discount, and that he retain 50 cents auditor's warrants to purchase a book for the use of the treasurer." It would seem from this that auditor's warrants on the State Treasury were divisible *ad infinitum*. At the regular meeting of the board, Oct. 5, 1846, we find the following entry:

"Whereas it appears that no returns were made in said township except in Waupecan district for the year 1845, and the treasurer reporting $35.34 auditor's warrants, therefore ordered that Waupecan district receive the sum of $35.34, and the treasurer is ordered to pay out the money to school teachers in said district, entitled to it according to law, and that the treasurer sell the auditor's warrants on hand at not more than 20 per cent. discount." This, then, was the condition of the obligations of the great State of Illinois thirty-seven years ago. Twenty per cent. discount.

On the 8th of January, 1848, at a regular election held at the house of James Berry, P. A. Armstrong, John Antis and A. G. Barber were elected trustees. This board selected L. W. Claypool as their treasurer. This board changed the names of the three school districts from Nettle Creek to District 1; Waupecan to District 2, and Mazon to District 3, Jan'y. 11, 1848.

At the April meeting, 1848, the treasurer, Mr. Claypool, reported the receipt " from the school commissioners, the school, college and seminary fund appropriated to town 33, R. 7, for 1847, in cash $16.34, auditor's warrants $5.90. Also same fund for $18.45, in auditor's warrants $1.91; total $24.15." He was ordered to sell the auditor's warrants at not more than ten per cent. discount, and distribute the same in direct ratio on returns of Dist. No. 1, filed Jan'y 20, 1848—95 scholars; Dist. No. 2—22 scholars; Dist. No. 3—48 scholars," total number of scholars in the township, 165. This embraced Morris, Wauponsee and part of Erienna. One hundred and sixty-five persons between the ages of five and twenty-one years. The apportionment of the school fund was made April 5, 1848, as follows: To District 1, $16.68; District 2, $3.17; District 3, $6.91. At the January (1849) meeting of the board, Mr. Claypool, as treasurer, reported that he had on hand eighty-four cents, being one year's interest on Thompson's note. Ordered, that it remain on hand until next meeting. This note seems to have been for ten dollars and eighty-four cents. At the March meeting, 1849, the treasurer reported the receipt of $19.60 in auditor's warrants, which he sold at ten per cent. discount. This with other funds on hand amounted to $31, for the year, and was apportioned as follows: Dist. No. 1, $17.85; Dist. No. 2, $4.14, and Dist. No. 3, $9.01. At the March meeting, 1850, Dist. No. 1 reported 123; No. 2, 20;

No. 3, 42 school children, and the sum of $14.51 was apportioned. Morris got $9.20 of it.

Dr. Antis went to California, and Mr. C. L. P. Hogan was elected to fill the vacancy. In 1851 L. W. Claypool succeeded Mr. Barber as trustee, and there were $29.07 distributed to the various school districts, of which Morris got $18.32. L. P. Lott succeeded Mr. Claypool as treasurer. There is no record in 1852 to be found. In 1853 the amount distributed was $140.65, of which Morris got $93.90, on 227 school children. In 1854 Messrs. Hogan, Claypool and C. H. Goold were the trustees, with Mr. Lott as treasurer. We find a plat of a subdivision of Sec. 16, T. 33, R. 7, being the school section donated by Congress to each township for the support of schools posted in the record as of May 10, 1854, certified by Geo. H. Kiersted, county surveyor; by P. A. Armstrong, deputy. A Mr. Jenkins did the surveying. He was afterward killed by Gen. Jim Lane, in Kansas, over a claim difficulty. By this plat said school section was divided into fourteen lots, containing in the aggregate 642 21-100 acres, which were sold by Geo. Fisher, then school commissioner, for $9,470.08. This was the foundation of our fine schools of Morris. In October, 1854, the number of school children in Dist. No. 1 (Morris) was 711, and the amount distributed for the year ending Oct. 1, 1854, was $79.67, of which Morris got $59.95. In 1855 the distribution was $419.96, of which $315.97 went to Dist. No. 1. The law was changed in 1855, so the distribution was made upon the actual school attendance. At the October meeting of that year $520.19 was apportioned, and Morris got $433.35 of this amount. In January, 1856, Messrs. Claypool, Goold and C. R. Parmelee were elected trustees, who re-elected Mr. Lott, treasurer. In 1856 there were $2,013.65 apportioned or distributed, and Morris got $1,661.93. In 1857 the amounts were about the same as for 1855. The school census for 1858 showed that the total number of children between five and twenty-one years was 701; under five years, 419; total, 1,120. School Dist. No. 1 was divided in 1849, forming Dist. No. 5, composed of Sections 5, 6, 7 and 8, which now are attached to and form part of the town of Erienna, or Acrienna, as more generally spelled.

Hon. L. B. Ray was elected treasurer Jan'y 21, 1864, and has continued in office ever since, except the years 1876 to 1878, when L. F. Beach was treasurer; Mr. C. H. Goold was one of the trustees from 1854 to 1878, a period of twenty-four years of continuous service. The increase of school children in the county from 1856 to 1858, was 774; at the March meeting of the Board of Supervisors, 1858, Supervisors L. W. Claypool, L. P. Lott and Wm. Pierce, special committee to settle with the school commissioner, submitted a report in which they use the following language in relation to the increase of school children in T. 32, R. 8: "Your committee are also of the opinion that there must, from the nature of the case, be some errors in the returns of the children as returned to the school commissioner; the most glaring of which is in town 32, 8; in their return of 1854 there appears but 192 children, whereas in 1856 it is 492; this is an *alarming* increase in the short space of two years, and if it continues in the same ratio for a few years longer, it will make this town one of the most thickly populated towns in Illinois." We are inclined to the opinion that friend Claypool had not read Fox's Book of Martyrs, or if he had read it he had forgotten John Rogers with his "nine small children, and one at the breast." Braceville may have been settled by the descendants of this self-same John Rogers, which would explain the "alarming increase." Indeed this town of Braceville (32, 8) is in many respects a wonderful one; it has more high priced poor land, more railroads, more coal and more children to the acre than any other town in the county, and is ready to take a contract to double discount 492 children on short notice, but we are drifting from our subject,

THE MORRIS SCHOOLS.

Unable to find the early school records we must depend on our memory largely for facts up to 1859.

The last teacher mentioned by us was Judge Starr. Mrs. W. S. Woolsey, who still lives in Morris, taught a private school at the court house for several months. Mr. Oliver E. Parmelee, a druggist (and who was drowned in the canal here while bathing in June, 1850), erected the building now occupied by Francis Hall, as a saloon, in 1849; the upper part was in one room, known as "Parmelee Hall;" this room was rented by the school board, and B. M. Atherton, the father-in-law of Mr. Parmelee, was engaged to teach school in this room; he was a man of education and talent; one leg was several inches shorter than the other, hence he used crutches; naturally of a domineering disposition and irascible temper, he was anything but a pleasant man, yet his fine intelligence and legal ability (for he was a lawyer by profession) gave him a good standing in the community; barring his severity of manner, he was a very fine teacher, and did much in "teaching the young ideas how to shoot;" indeed, his school was a sort of County Normal, to which pupils from all over the county came. Parmelee Hall was used as a school room from 1850 to the fall or winter of 1853, when the district erected the main part of what is now known as the Old Center School House.

In August, 1851, a vote of the district was taken upon the question of building a school-house and purchasing lots 1 and 2, B. 11, Chapin's addition to Morris, as a school-house site, which resulted favorably to both propositions, and on the 3d of September of that year, said lots were purchased from Geo. W. Armstrong for $175, and a deed was executed by Mr. A. to School District No. 1, T. 33, R. 7. A contract for the erection of a school-house was awarded to R. S. Jones (as we remember) to build a school-house on said lots thirty by sixty feet, two stories high. There was a deal of fault finding at what was then considered by some the enormous size of this building. So general was this feeling that the people refused to vote the necessary amount of tax to complete the building the next year, so that work was suspended. But at the next vote upon the subject the appropriation or tax was carried and the building completed. If our memory is correct a Mr. Brooks—better known as Bully Brooks—a young man with very red hair and prominent nose, taught, or tried to teach, school in the then new school-house in the winter of 1853-4, but was forced to abandon the enterprise by the big boys before his term was out. Miss Sarah Parmelee, or "Aunt Sarah," as she was called, taught a school in one of the rooms in the spring of 1854.

In September of that year Edward Sanford, A. B., a graduate of old Yale, was induced to accept the position of principal of the Morris public school. A man of magnificent executive ability and a perfect model of systematic order, he made a great success of the school. However, he could not be induced to teach but two years, and closed his duties as such principal July 31, 1856, to enter the law office of E. P. Seeley, since deceased, as a law student. Having been admitted to the bar he became the law partner of Mr. Seeley, and remained as such until the death of the latter. He is now one of our wealthiest citizens. A little fussy fellow by the name of Smith, from somewhere in Wisconsin, succeeded Mr. Sanford. He had as an assistant a woman, supposed to be his wife, but Dame Rumor said she was some other man's wife, and like the "Heathen Chinee, they had to go."

In 1859 H. K. Trask, A. B., was principal, with John Trask, Anna Trask, Eliza Baldwin, Sarah Parmelee, and Kate Grant, assistants. Their salaries were as follows: H. K. Trask, $900; John Trask, $750; and $270 to each lady. The same corps of teachers had charge in 1860 at the same salaries, with Gertrude Vincent as an additional assistant. In August, 1860, the people voted down the proposition to levy a tax to extend schools beyond six months the ensuing year. This caused Mr. Trask, who was, besides being a first-class teacher, a first-class gentleman, to decline a re-appointment here. He left Morris, and went to Wisconsin, where he has remained ever since, and is president of a college there.

At a meeting of the directors, Sept. 14th, it was ordered to have six months school with seven teachers, fixing the salary of the principal at $400 for the six months, and placing the assistants' pay at $25 per month. School to commence Oct. 7, 1861. John Trask was made principal, Kate Frame, Anna Trask, Sarah Parmelee, Kate Grant, Fannie A. Hale and Celia Frary were selected as assistants. B. H. Streeter and B. F. Matteson, two of the directors, resigned April 2d, 1862. Robert Longworth and C. G. Conklin were elected to fill the vacancies April 14, 1862. Mr. Trask was re-engaged with Kate Frame, C. Vanvalkenburgh, S. Wright, K. Morley, C. Frary and A. A. Hennessey, assistants. School commenced Oct. 6, 1862. Andrew Kirkland succeeded Mr. Conklin as director this year. In 1863, Mr. McVay was principal, but the record fails to show what his initials or first names were, what wages he received, or who were his assistants when the school began or closed, or indeed that we had any school. We find under date of Nov. 16, 1863, Mr. Longworth moved to increase the salary of McVay five dollars per month; whether the motion was carried or lost, the record fails to state. In 1864, W. T. Hopkins succeeded Mr. McBride as director and clerk of the board. This board selected L. B. Searles, principal, on salary of $900, with Misses Morley (now Mrs. Hamilton), Longworth, Hennessey, Wright, Hale, Bross and Vincent, at $30 per month each. On April 1, 1865, a petition signed by C. Grant, G. W. Lane,

D. D. Spencer, and thirty others was presented to the school board praying the removal of Mr. Searles. The record says: "After hearing the defenses, it is ordered that Mr. Searles be discharged." This discharge was clearly irregular and illegal. He left but collected his salary.

It appears that a Mr. Fisher was employed to finish the year's school as principal. There is no record of it except of the payment of schedules, July 15, 1865, when "Fisher and Miss Morley were allowed $440. Misses Tinkham, Bross, Bean, Harrison, Hale and Wright, each $120. Mr. Kirkland resigned, when at the election to fill vacancy, and elect a successor to Mr. Longworth, E. B. Hanna and L. P. Lott were elected. Of this board, Judge Hopkins was made president, and L. P. Lott, secretary, and this was the starting point of keeping a record of the board. Zorodus Trask of Beaver Dam, Wisconsin, was selected principal at $1,200 per annum, with Misses Bross, Bean, Harrison, Tinkham and Hale, assistants, at $300 per annum each. The school-house now was too small to accommodate the scholars, and outside rooms were engaged, with Miss Riordan as an additional teacher. In December of that year, the wages of the female teachers were raised to $360 per annum. We find by the schedules paid, that a Miss Wheaton was Mr. Trask's first assistant. We have no personal recollection of the lady. Additions were built to the main building this year.

E. B. Hanna was again elected director in 1866. It was also voted to build a brick school-house in the 3d ward. At the August meeting, 1866, of the board the school year was fixed at forty weeks. This has been the rule ever since. Henry K. Trask was elected principal, with Misses Jennie Bross, Belle Grant, Sarah Tinkham, Alida Bliss, Fannie Hale, Alice Riordan and Gertrude Vincent, assistants, for year commencing in Sept., 1866.

The school rooms were so crowded that on the 13th Oct., 1866, the board made a contract with Mrs. Bailey, wife of Rev. G. S. Bailey, to teach from forty to fifty small scholars at their residence, for $400 for forty weeks. Mr. H. K. Trask declining to accept the offer of principal, Mr. Stetman E. Massey was selected as such at $1,000 per annum. Miss Riordan did not accept the position offered, and Miss Mary E. McQueston took her place. Miss Vincent also resigned in March, 1867, when a Miss Fitch was appointed to the place. Aug. 5, 1867, C. Grant was elected to succeed Judge Hopkins. It was also voted to build a brick school-house in the 4th ward north of the railroad. The site for 3d ward school was purchased Aug. 8th, 1867, for $850. The board also bought from Thomas Hynds ninety feet south end of lot 3, B. 11, Chapin's addition to Morris, adjoining the old school-house, for $200 at this meeting. The school was opened again in Sept., 1867, with S. E. Massey, principal, Belle Grant, Jennie Bross, Fannie Hale, Alida Bliss, Sarah Tinkham, Mary McQueston and E. B. Fitch, assistants. Gouch & Smith received the contract to do the mason work on 3d ward school for $1,250. F. H. Williams & Co., the carpenter work for $1,500, selecting the Oliver brick as the material. At a meeting of the board July 11th, 1868, lots 6 and 7, B. 9, in Edwards' addition to Morris, were purchased for a school-house site for a brick school-house in the 4th ward at the sum of $600. The first mistake we note in the action of this board, one of the very ablest the city ever had, is in ordering the building of "a one story brick school-house 30 by 40 feet." On the 3d of August, 1868, Geo. W. Lane was elected to succeed Mr. Lott as director. It was also decided to purchase a site, and erect a brick school-house, in the then 5th, now 2d ward. At a meeting of the new board August 12, 1868, Mr. Grant was elected president and Mr. Hanna secretary, and Mr. Massey was reappointed principal of the schools, with Misses Bross, Bliss, Hale, McQueston, Grant, Hennessey, Harrison, Barstow and Mrs. Phillips, assistants. The principal to be paid $1,000, and each assistant $300. At this meeting the board ordered that the proposed school-house in the 4th ward be of brick and one story high and 30 by 40 feet in size; and the contract was let to Messrs. Kutz and Storr for the carpenter work at $960. The brick and stone work was let to Wm. Stage at $679. At a meeting of the board September 7, it was decided to make the 4th ward school building two stories instead of one. The lower story 14, the upper 12 feet high. The old teachers were re-employed for ensuing year at same salaries. Mary Grant was added to the list of teachers at the next meeting of the board.

On the 28th of July, 1870, Prof. H. H. C. Miller was elected principal, on a salary of $1,300. His selection proved a very good one. He is a man of fine executive ability and scholastic acquirements. On the 1st of September the clerk submitted a system of grading the schools, which was adopted, and has been but slightly changed since, strange as it may seem, yet it is true that this was the first effort ever made to establish graded schools in Morris, so far as appears of record.

At a meeting of the board Sept. 3d, 1870, on motion of the clerk, the salaries of the assistant teachers were raised from $300 to $340, and the following were selected and assigned:

Center School.
Room No. 2—Miss Emma Green.
"   "   3—"   Carrie Barstow.
"   "   4—"   Dora Schoonmaker.
"   "   5—"   Jennie A. Bross.
"   "   6—"   Jennie Wing.
"   "   7—"   Myra Massey.

In 3d Ward Brick School House.
Room No. 1—Miss Mary Hubbard.
"   "   2—Miss Lizzie Hennessey, principal.

4th Ward Brick.
"   "   1—Miss Carrie Bullis.
"   "   2—Miss M. A. Rippan, principal.

5th Ward Brick.
"   "   1—Miss Alida C. Bliss.
"   "   2—Miss Minnie Barstow, principal.

Much feeling sprang up over this assignment of teachers, but it proved a very judicious one, and never did the Morris public schools do better than this year. Prof. Miller proved to be "the right man in the right place," while he was ably assisted in all the departments. This school board adopted the single seat system and rendered the principal active support in building up a first-class graded public school. In January, 1871, Mr. Brown resigned, and Mr. F. Caspori was elected his successor. At the regular April election of that year, Mr. Lane was re-elected director without opposition.

On the 21st of June, 1871, "Prof. Miller submitted his annual report of the workings of the several schools under his charge, which showed a very flattering condition, and, on motion, it was ordered that said report be published in pamphlet form and that 300 copies be printed for distribution."

This was the first report of the Morris public schools ever printed.

On the 23d of June, 1871, on motion of Mr. Caspori, Prof. Miller's salary was raised to $1,500 per annum, and on motion of Mr. Armstrong, the following assignment and salaries of the assistants were made:

Miss Bliss, assistant to principal, $375
Center School.
Miss Jennie M. Wing, Room 6, 375
" Myra Massey, - " 5, 375
" Dora Schoonmaker, " 4, 375
" Emma E. Green, - " 3, 340
" Gracie Peirce, - " 2, 300
3d Ward School.
Mrs. L. Thayer, principal, Room 2, 375
Miss Mary L. Hubbard, " 1, 340
4th Ward School.
Miss Ella C. Harrison, No. 2, principal, - - - - 340
Only one room ready for use.
5th Ward School.
Miss Minnie Barstow, No. 2, principal, $375
" Jennie A. Bross, " 1 " 375

The teachers' salaries paid for previous year was $5,253. The total cost of the year's school was $7,828.17, as appears from the clerk's report. The whole number of persons under 21 years residing in the district was given at 1,730, and those between 6 and 21 were 1,200, of whom 18 were colored. The whole number of enrolled scholars was 852; number of teachers, 13—12 females and 1 male; with 4 graded schools, with 112 volumes in the public school library.

This was truly a fine showing. But we are extending this article too long. The teachers selected for the year commencing in September, 1871, were Prof. Miller, principal, Ada Brumback as his assistant, and Misses Bross, Bliss, Green, Peirce, Harrison, Mary Foster, Mary J. Henry, Emma Card, Schoonmaker, Hubbard, and Mrs. M. L. Thayer. In March, 1872, Miss Card resigned on account of poor health, and Miss Julia McFarland succeeded her as a teacher. At the April election, 1872, Mr. Armstrong was unanimously re-elected director. On the 15th of June that year, the salary of the teacher of the grammar school was raised to $400. Prof. Miller was again chosen as principal at $1,500; Miss Lizzie Winters, as his assistant, $400. The salaries of the other teachers were not changed. The old teachers were re-engaged except Misses Brumback, Greene, Hubbard, M. J. Henry, and Mrs. Thayer, who declined to re-engage. Misses Irene Henry and Elsie F. Hare were employed in their stead. The wages were substantially the same as the prior year.

On the 3d of April, 1869, Lot 3, B 2, C. H. & H. C. Goold's addition to Morris, was purchased of Mr. Caspori for the site for 5th ward school at $1,030, and contracts were awarded for the erection of a two-story brick building, 30x46 feet, to Messrs. Massey & Jackson, carpenter work and blinds $1,600; Wm. Stage, brick, stone and plastering for $1,878.50. The following teachers were selected Sept. 13, 1869: S. E. Massey, principal; Myra Massey, Susan A. Phillips, Carrie Barstow, Mary Mc-

Queston, Emma Harrison, Minnie Barstow, Jennie A. Bross, Alida C. Bliss, Lizzie Hennessey, Nellie Hall, and Ada Harrison. Their salaries were fixed at $1,000 to principal, and $300 to the assistants. On the 1st of Jany., 1870, Mrs. M. W. Loyd was made principal of 5th ward school, and Mrs. Harrison was selected to take the place made vacant by the resignation of Miss McQueston, Miss McQueston having elected to take a school of one scholar for better or for worse—for life. The school law having been amended or altered so as to bring the election in April instead of August, the election was held April 4, 1870, for two directors. This was an exciting election, and resulted in the election of Messrs. John Brown and Benjamin Olin to succeed Messrs. Hanna and Grant. This new board organized by electing Mr. Lane, president, and Olin, secretary. Miss Kate Prideaux was selected April 9, 1870, to succeed Mrs. Harrison who had resigned in Center School. Judge Olin resigned June 1, 1870, and moved to Joliet, and at a special election June 7, 1870, P. A. Armstrong was elected to fill the vacancy, and was elected clerk of the board. The total number of scholars attending the public schools at this time was 601. While the total number of males under the age of twenty-one years was 786, females, 787: total 1,573. The division of the sexes was close—one majority for the girls. Between 6 and 21 years there were 1,052.

The school law again being changed, requiring the election of a board of education, of six members, at the election held April 5, 1873, Wm. A. Jordan, John Duckworth, J. C. Carr, F. Caspori, Geo. W. Lane and P. A. Armstrong were elected as such

board. Messrs. Lane and Armstrong drew the short term of one year, Messrs. Jordan and Carr the middle term of two years, and Messrs. Caspori and Duckworth the long term of three years. Geo. W. Lane was elected president of the board, and Mr. Armstrong, secretary. In May, 1873, Miss Lizzie Winters having married, resigned, and Miss T. H. Briggs was appointed to the vacancy, as principal of the grammar school, at $45 per month salary. At the June meeting of the board, Prof. Miller was again appointed principal, on the same salary as before. Miss Dora E. Schoonmaker was appointed as assistant principal at $500, Misses Bliss, Bross, Hare and Gill at $400, Misses Harrison, Foster and M. E. Hare, $375 each. The census report showed the whole number of persons under 21 years of age, 1,715, of whom 11 were colored. Whole number of pupils enrolled in the Morris public school, 858. It also showed an excess of 102 females. Miss Gill declined and Miss E. F. Hare was made principal of the grammar school, and Miss Julia Pomeroy was placed in 3d ward brick in place of Miss Hare, and Miss Alice A. Conlong was also employed as a teacher that year; also Miss Lizzie A. Hock as assistant in 4th ward school, at $300 per year. On the 3d of January, 1874, Miss Maggie Brown was assigned to the 4th ward school in place of Miss Hock, resigned, and [Miss Damon to the 3d ward school in place of Miss Foster. On motion of the secretary, the following was adopted as an additional rule, viz.: "Those teachers who are most successful in governing their pupils without resorting to corporal punishment, other qualifications being sufficient, shall be awarded by the board a higher degree of appreciation, and receive the preference over all others in promotion and appointments." Miss Damon, being unable to manage her school, was transferred to Center school, and Mrs. Dukes was employed as principal of 3d ward school, in February, 1874. At the April election, 1874, for two members of the board of education, Stilman E. Massey and Mr. Armstrong were elected (Mr. Lane refusing to serve any longer). Mr. Jordan was elected president, and Mr. Armstrong secretary of the board. In June, Prof. Miller was again selected principal, on salary of $1,500. Lizzie Royce, assistant, $500. Miss Bliss, grammar school, $450. The older teachers were allowed $400 each and the newer ones $300 to $340. The new teachers were Misses Lizzie Massey and Mary J. Noble. The fiscal report of the clerk for year ending June 30, 1874, shows total receipts, $7,707.54. Expenditures, $8,203.54. The number of teachers employed, 13—1 male; 12 females. On the 7th of January, 1875, Prof. Miller tendered his resignation as principal, to take effect at the close of the school year. The board assured him that if the only reason for his leaving the school was insufficiency of salary, that should be raised. At a meeting of the board, June 9, 1875, Prof. Miller was again elected principal by a unanimous vote, and his salary increased to $2,000 per year. But he had already agreed to take charge of the public schools of Pittsfield, Ill., and declined the position here.

By the secretary's fiscal report, the receipts from all sources, from June 30, 1874, to June 30, 1875, were $10,066.70. Disbursements, $9,001.33. Balance in treasury $1,065.37. The board of education, in parting with Prof. Miller, say among other things, June 19, 1875:

"As an organizer of a thorough system, both of studies and discipline, and a thorough educator, we consider him second to no man in the State. * * He adds to a thorough classic education a fine understanding of the law as well as a practical education. A man of sound judgment, quick discernment and admirable temperament." He is now practicing law in Chicago.

At the same meeting the old corps of teachers, except principal and assistant, were re-elected with a slight increase in salaries. On the 6th of July, 1875, Prof. Mathew Waters was unanimously elected principal on a salary of $1,500. On the 25th of June, a petition signed by C. H. Goold and some sixty tax payers of the district was presented to the board, praying the erection of a new school-house which had been referred to the committee on grounds and buildings, and at the July meeting this committee by Mr. Caspori made a verbal report relative to eligible sites, etc., when it was ordered to submit the question of building a new school-house to a vote of the people. Miss Flora Trumbull was elected assistant principal, at $600, July 20, 1875. On the 2d of August, 1875, on motion of Mr. Carr, the series known as the "Independent series," published by A. S. Barnes & Co., were adopted to be introduced, as classes were formed, etc. This, in the opinion of the writer, was the most foolish act of this Board of Education, notwithstanding we voted for it. We consider the Independent series the poorest of all the recent series of school books published. But there is and always will be serious objections to frequent changes in school books; with all their pretended improvements, we have not been able to find among the vast number of new Readers any one that equals the old time "Columbian Orator," or "National Reader." On the 23d of August, a vote was taken on the new school-house proposition, the new school-house to cost not exceeding $30,000, which resulted in favor of such new school-house 193 votes, and 120 votes were cast against the proposition. The law simply requiring a majority of the votes cast to make it obligatory on the board to act, said proposition was declared carried.

In October of that year the schools were so full that two rooms in the city hall were procured, and schools opened there. On the 30th of October, a vote of the people was had upon the proposition to purchase the east half of block eighteen, Chapin's 2d addition to Morris, for $7,000, which resulted 191 for, and 61 against said proposition; this resulted in the selection of the present beautiful site of the best and among the finest public school buildings of this State.

The committee on grounds and buildings having visited many of the best school-houses in the State, reported verbally to the board, Nov. 20, 1875, recommending the plan of the new Jones school-house of Chicago, with slight changes. Mr. Bigelow, who was the architect of the Jones school-house, came before the board with the plans and specifications of said Jones school, and fully explained the same. On Dec. 1, on motion of Mr. Carr, the committee on grounds and school-houses were instructed " to procure plans, specifications, and working drawings for a building nearly similar to the new Jones school of Chicago as to internal arrangements, with exterior something like the Rochelle school building." Mr. Duckworth moved, " that the new building be constructed of brick with stone trimmings." Mr. Armstrong moved to amend this motion by striking out the words " brick with stone trimmings," and insert the words " Au Sable stone," upon which motion the ayes and nays were called; those voting aye were Messrs. Massey and Armstrong, two; those voting nay were Messrs. Caspori, Carr and Duckworth, three; hence, the amendment was lost; the vote recurring on the original motion of Mr. Duckworth, it was carried; Mr. Armstrong alone voting nay; Mr. Jordan, the president, was in favor of a stone building, but could not vote except upon a tie vote, which never can occur with a full board of six.

Bonds bearing not exceeding ten per cent. interest were ordered to be issued to pay for the school-house site, at this meeting, to the amount of $7,000, the purchase price thereof. The next meeting of the board was on the 5th of January, 1876, when J. H. Bigelow, the architect, presented plans and specifications which were accepted. It was also decided to advertise in the Morris papers for sealed proposals up to the first Monday in February, 1876, to furnish material and perform the labor in the erection of a school-house in conformity with the plans and specifications prepared by the architect, now in the office of the secretary. The first plan provided for a slate roof. Bids were solicited for a brick building with stone trimmings, and also for a stone building. On Monday, February 7th, the board met, opened and examined the bids, thirty-three in all, and as there were many bids for some special parts that required time to arrange and compare, the board adjourned to the 9th of February, 1876. At this meeting it was found that the lowest bid, even for a brick building, was $31,000, which was above the limit of the appropriation. The board having reserved the right to reject any or all bids, by their advertisement, on motion of Mr. Armstrong it was: "*Resolved*, That each and every bid submitted to this board on the 7th inst., pertaining to the erection of the new school-house in said District No. 1, be and are hereby rejected; that the roof of said proposed building be changed to near an eighth pitch, and standing groove iron be substituted for slate; and that tin be substituted for galvanized iron for the valleys and gutters; and that the architect be, and hereby is required to make such alterations in the plans and specifications as he may deem necessary to fully carry out the above named changes and alterations; that the board re-advertise for sealed proposals, to be opened Feb'y 21, 1876; that bids be invited for the erection of a brick school-house with stone trimmings, also for a stone school-house, etc.

On the 21st of February there were some thirty-five proposals opened and examined. The difference between the cost of a stone building and a brick one as shown by the bids, was less than two thousand dollars. The bids of Messrs. Gordon, McGaveny, Boyer, Stage, and Gorich, who were finally awarded the contract, made but $1,650 difference in their bids between stone and brick. Their bids were for stone $28,977, for brick $27,327. After comparing the bids and discussing the question as to whether the building should be of brick or stone, the board adjourned to February 22d, when Mr. Armstrong submitted the following resolution upon the passage of which he called for the ayes and nays : "*Resolved*, That the action of this board at their meeting of December 1, 1875, relative to the material for the outside walls be and the same is hereby amended by striking out the words 'brick with stone trimmings,' and inserting in lieu thereof the words 'Au Sable sandstone,' in accordance with the plans and specifications prepared by the architect," which was carried. Those voting aye were Messrs. Jordan, Duckworth and Armstrong, and Messrs. Carr and Caspori voting no. Mr. Armstrong had induced the architect to make plans for a stone building, pledging himself to pay for the extra labor the sum of $35, if the board should not finally adopt stone. Messrs. Jordan and Massey were in favor of stone all the time.

The contract for a stone building was awarded to our fellow townsmen Miles Gordon, Andrew J. Boyer, Thos. G. McGaveny, William Stage and Jacob Gorich, together with two wooden privies, for the sum of $28,977.00. They furnishing all materials and keeping an insurance on the building as it progressed. The work was well done. Indeed, every one of the contractors lost their time and some of them considerable money on their parts of the contract, but they did their work and did it well, and the best school house in the State stands a monument to the skill and perseverance of the builders. The entire cost of this building which is a stone building 74 by 84, three stories and basement, incluing superintendence, was $30,030, with $7,000 for site, making a total of $37,030, which is probably the cheapest school-house, in proportion to its real value, in the State; it has 12 rooms large enough to accommodate 63 scholars each, with a single desk; well may our people feel proud of our public school building and of our public schools. At the April election, 1877, John Duckworth and George Woelfel, were elected members of the board. Prof. Waters with Miss Mosier as his assistant, and very nearly the same corps of teachers, were selected for the school year commencing Sept. 3, 1876; Miss Mosier's salary was raised to $700; she was a very fine teacher and an accomplished young lady. The new teachers were Misses Hattie Hall, Carrie Rogers, Hettie McFarlane and Abbie M. Kiersted; Miss Irene Henry, being the only old teacher, dropped out; she preferred a school of one scholar, and changed her name to Patt; the lowest wages paid this year was $340, and the total aggregate of the fifteen teachers' salaries was $7,280.

The census report for this year shows whole number of males under 21, 876; whole number of females under 21, 914; between 6 and 21, males, 584; females, 655; males between 12 and 21 who can not read and write, 12; females, 6.

The winter term was opened Jan'y 8, 1877, in the new building; Miss M. E. Hare having resigned, her place was filled by the selection of Miss Myra Woods, Dec. 27, 1876; Miss E. F. Hare resigned April 2, 1877, and her sister, Sarah A., was selected in her place, and on the next day Miss Lizzie Massey resigned, and Miss Anna E. Harvey succeeded her; at the April election for members of the Board of Education, Messrs. Lott, Comerford and Stephen were elected to succeed Messrs. Armstrong, Massey and Jordan, the latter having resigned, and Mr. Wm. Stephen was elected to fill the unexpired term; Mr. Stephen was elected president, and Mr. Carr secretary of the new board. On the 31st of August, 1877, the old corps of teachers, except Misses Mosier, Woods, Kiersted and Rogers, all of whom declined a re-engagement; the new teachers were Misses Alforetta Clute (assistant principal), Lillie H. Fyfe, Sadie T. Hall, Ella M. Pasegate and Lizzie E. Cody; their salaries were slightly reduced, but not materially so; at the April election, 1878, Messrs. E. Ridgeway, L. W. Claypool, and R. B. Strong, were elected members of the board vice Mr. Carr, (who declined a re-election), Mr. Stephen and Mr. Duckworth who "got lost and never was founded." This new board organized by electing Mr. Lott president and Mr. Claypool secretary, who still hold their positions respectively; Miss Clute "all the way from York State," a maiden lady of uncertain age, assistant principal on a salary of $600 per year, proved to be much abler in teaching the arts of wooing than the sciences; this compelled Prof. Waters to do a large amount of extra labor; a fine teacher and ambitious, he neglected his health, and finally broke completely down during the spring term, 1878; his nervous system was destroyed; he was confined to his bed here all that summer, and is now an inmate of the Home of the Incurables in Chicago; his limbs are all drawn up into a rigid, crooked shape; unable to feed himself, yet his mind and memory are as strong and active as they ever were, but there is absolutely no hope of his recovery. S. E. Massey, A. M., took his place as principal for the unexpired year for Mr. Waters, whose salary was paid him in full by the board, June 24, 1878.

The Morris high school graduated nine scholars this year, which, in addition to the former graduates, made the full number of twenty-eight. In the class of graduates for 1873 were Miss Alice A. Conlong, who has been for many years a popular teacher in the Morris public schools, and Miss Maggie Brown, now the wife of Henry C. June, Esq., of Oak Park, Illinois. In class of 1874, Miss Mary J. Noble, also for many years last past a popular teacher in the Morris schools. Miss Hattie Coy, since married, Miss Emma E. Jones, now wife of F. Starr, Esq., of Streator, Illinois, and Miss Carrie E. Rogers, for awhile one of the teachers in Morris school.

In class of 1876, Miss Kate A. Horrie and Miss Eliza Jones, now the wife of Benedict Zens, Esq., of this city.

In class of 1877, Misses Della Robinson, Ettie F. Johnson, Mary H. Shaffer, Lizzie E. Comerford (now a teacher in the school), Lizzie E. Cody, now the wife of E. H. Quigley, Esq., railroad agent at Morris, Mary Comerford, Fannie Lane (since married), Gertie Nelson, Susie C. Brown, Nora Marshall (now one of the teachers), and Charles J. Reed, since then a graduate of the Ann Arbor University, and now principal of the Princeton (Illinois) schools.

In class of 1878, Miss Nellie Barr, Hattie E. Parker, Lulu Ross, now Mrs. T. P. Bailey, Nellie F. Cody, now wife of Mr. Davis, of the firm of Cody & Davis, Emma E. Leacock, Abbie C. Woods, Minnie D. Porter, Ida Caspori and Wm. J. Leacock. In August, 1878, Prof. L. T. Regan was elected principal, and has continued as such up to the present, and has been engaged for the ensuing year; and the only changes in the board of education are, Mr. Wm. Stephen and J. S. R. Scovill have succeeded Messrs. Strong and Comerford. This brings the public school history down to the time when the memory of our people is fresh, and as our chronicle is growing too long we stop here with our history of the Morris public schools, of which we feel a just pride.

ST. ANGELA'S ACADEMY.

On the 12th of March, 1858, John McNellis and wife executed a conveyance of out lot 8, in the Canal Trustees' subdivision of the S. W. ¼, Sec. 3, T. 33, R. 7, containing ten acres (less the streets), with a large three story brick building at a consideration expressed at one dollar to "Rev. E. Sorin, Provincial, of the congregation of the Holy Cross, resident of Notre Dame University, of the county of St. Joseph, and State of Indiana, and to his successor in office * * on condition that a Catholic school shall be kept on said premises forever." Father Sorin immediately established and opened thereon and therein St. Angela's Academy, with Mother Frances—a sister-in-law of Senator John Sherman of Ohio, as Mother Superior, for the thorough and practical education of young ladies. This school is second to no academy in this State. Its attendance has been large from its inception up to the present, and we can commend this school to all persons wishing a first-class boarding school for young ladies, whether Catholic or Protestant, as no effort is allowed to be made toward proselyting. It is a model of good order, and is supplied by the very best of teachers. Of course the teachers are all nuns; Mother Frances was taken further West to open other convents, but a competent Lady Superior has taken her place. This convent has been much enlarged, and the Sisters of the Holy Cross are doing their good work as silently as the dew falls, yet thoroughly and intelligently. The only effort they make at public notoriety is their annual commencements.

They have students from all over the northern part of the State. Being an adjunct of Notre Dame, it is essentially a preparatory department to that leading Catholic University. In painting and music St. Angela's Academy stands high, while its curriculum is practical and well selected. With commodious buildings and extensive grounds highly cultivated and adorned with exotics, plants and flowers, St. Angela's is a very pretty place as well as a pleasant one.

THE MORRIS NORMAL AND SCIENTIFIC SCHOOL

is the outgrowth of the "Morris Classic Institute," started by N. C. Dougherty, A. M., over the office of Mr. Sanford, in 1869. Mr. Dougherty, now principal of the Peoria schools, came here an entire stranger, rented a room and opened a private school under the above title, and made a decided success of it. A man of push and energy, with a large degree of self-confidence, he soon established the Morris Classic Institute upon a firm basis. So rapid was its growth that his quarters were too small. He then rented a portion of the present Normal School building, and employing assistant teachers, transferred the Institute to that building where he soon established a fine reputation as an educator. He, however, did not remain long at his new quarters. Having received many offers of positions in other schools, he finally accepted the position of principal of the Mount Morris Seminary, and sold his interest in the Morris Classic to a Mr. Ross, who proved a failure. He in turn sold out to a Rev. Mr. Sloat, who imagined himself a natural-born Demosthenes and Spurgeon combined. But with all his supposed ability, the Morris Classic went into a rapid decline. It had a consumptive cough; hollow-eyed and feeble it lingered a short time and "gave up the ghost." Several efforts were made to revive the "Morris Classic Institute," but they proved unavailing or spasmodic.

In October, 1875, J. J. Kinkaide, A. M., of Oil City, Pa., rented the building and tried to resuscitate it. Although a teacher of many years experience, he found he had undertaken a difficult task. He succeeded in injecting some little life into the defunct institute, but did not restore it to full life and vigor.

He was succeeded in his efforts by A. W. Bulkley, A. B., and he in turn by Prof. Beatie, with about the same result—a sickly kind of disappointment. In the fall of 1878, Messrs. Cook & Stevens rented the entire building and changed the name to "Morris Normal and Scientific School." Comparatively young men, full of energy and push, with unbounded confidence in their own ability as organizers and educators, they soon commanded success and placed the Morris Normal on a sure foundation as one of the very best preparatory schools in the State. This school brings to our city talented young gentlemen and ladies from all over the country—not only from Illinois but from other States. The curriculum is a judicious one, whilst the energy and perseverance of the entire corps of teachers have been such as to win the confidence and command the respect of all. We notice the sale of the interest of Messrs. Cook & Stevens to Messrs. Kean & Forsythe. They are no strangers here. Prof. Kean has been a successful teacher for many years, and for over a year past he has been one of the principal teachers in this school, while Mr. Forsythe has also had considerable experience as a teacher, and was one of the regular teachers of the school before purchasing. And whilst many may regret that Messrs. Cook & Stevens have sold out their interest in the school, none need fear of its complete success under the new management. With four separate fine brick and stone public school buildings, with fifteen school rooms, well filled with scholars, under a competent superintendent, with fifteen assistants, with a population of 4,200 people, Morris is well prepared to educate her own children. Add to this St. Angela's Academy and the Morris Normal and Scientific School, we may well be proud of our educational facilities. No city in the State can excel Morris in that line. We now turn to our

SABBATH SCHOOLS.

The first Sabbath school of Morris antedates the organization of the first church here. About the 30th of June, 1847, Messrs. E. P. Seeley, A. F. Hand and P. A. Armstrong posted up written notices for a Sabbath school, to be held at the old court house in Morris, on the following Sabbath. Dr. Hand and Mr. Armstrong were on hand at the time designated, but the other signer failed to put in an appearance. The court house was filled, literally packed, by the most heterogeneous crowd imaginable. Old and young, rich and poor, gray headed men and women, barefooted and hatless urchins, county officials, canal contractors, professional men, mechanics and common laborers; while the ladies, ever first in sympathy and ready to do battle in the cause of religion and reformation, were there in force, ready, yea eager, to assist in so laudable an enterprise. Previous to this time the children had run riot in the streets and woods, the older boys spending their Sundays in hunting, fishing and ball playing, while the lesser boys and girls made mud pies or played blackman, with no one to teach them to "remember the Sabbath day, and keep it holy." Prominent among the good ladies who favored this enterprise were Mrs. Abigail Hull, now the widow Atwater, Mesdames Wm. E. and P. A. Armstrong, both deceased and Mrs. Alex. Peacock, still living. It was a trying situation for the originators, Messrs. Hand and Armstrong; neither of them were professed Christians. Propriety demanded that the exercises should be opened with prayer; no minister of the gospel or professed Christian gentleman was present. A prayer had to be offered up to the Infinite, to keep up at least the semblance of piety. Mr. Armstrong with fear and trembling called on the doctor for a short prayer. To the great relief of the expectant crowd Dr. Hand was equal to the occasion, and made, if not his only, at least his first public prayer, and it was a good one. A prayer that was fine in conception and impressively delivered. This broke the ice and the Sabbath school was inaugurated. This was the nucleus of our present magnificent system of Sunday schools.

Having inaugurated this school Messrs. Hand and Armstrong rested upon their laurels and gave place to the ladies and professed Christian gentlemen as managers.

The Congregational church was organized about that time, and assumed the charge of this embryo Sabbath school. Whether the Sabbath school records contain any reference to the organizers or not we are not advised, but that this was the origin of the school is true beyond a question. Nor was there any hypocrisy on the part of these men in organizing this movement. They were both sons of pious mothers, who taught them while "little toddlers," to keep the Sabbath day holy. That influence had not deserted them, and we trust, never will. Our only religious books were the Bible and John Bunyan's Pilgrim's Progress. Sabbath school books had not yet reached this locality. Those capital singers, Geo. H. Kiersted and Thomas A. Henry, led the singing in fine style. Which of us acted as superintendent we do not now remember, but are inclined to the belief that we yielded the leadership to the ladies, and that either Mrs. Hall or Mrs. P. A. Armstrong took the lead as teachers. We are quite certain that we left the field early and ceased from our labors in that noble cause.

CHAPTER IX.*

MORRIS CITY—CHURCHES—EARLY MINISTERS—THE LEGAL PROFESSION—BUSINESS—PIONEERS—SECRET FRATERNITIES.

THAT the first religious services in Morris were held by the Catholics there is no question, and that Father Dupontaris was the first to celebrate Mass at this place, is equally true. He was in charge (as we now remember), of the Catholic churches at Ottawa and Dresden (the latter being then by far the largest village in Grundy County, having a Catholic church, two good-sized hotels and several dry goods stores). He commenced to celebrate Mass here in the fall of 1841, ere Morris had a name. He was a Frenchman or of French descent; rather small in stature with fine physical form, dark complexion, and a very fine orator, with ability equal to any emergency. He was peculiarly well suited to the times and circumstances surrounding him. With the patience of a Job and energy of a Cæsar, which were so admirably combined that he was able to meet and overcome every obstacle in his way. And when physical force was required to quell or disperse a mob, he not only had it, but used it. He was equally brave and humane. His charge extended from Ottawa to Dresden—a distance of over thirty miles, and as we had neither canal, railroad or stage route, he had to travel overland—mostly on horseback; hence, he was forced to labor long and hard. This he did uncomplainingly and successfully. From here he went to St. Louis, Mo., and died of cholera in 1848, contracting the disease while visiting and shriving the dying of his parish. Deeds he did worthy of being perpetuated in monuments of gold. We believe he was succeeded here by Father O'Donnell. Dean Terry came later and built the present magnificent Catholic church, which is the largest in our county, and assisted in inaugurating St. Angelas Academy. The Catholics of Morris are the most numerous of any of the churches and have the largest and finest church edifice.

PROTESTANT CHURCH SERVICES.

Next to the Catholics came the Methodists in holding religious services in Morris. In the winter of 1842-3, John F. Devore, a tall, spare young man, with far more zeal than brain, and who was on his first charge as a Methodist minister, his circuit embracing what was then called South Ottawa Circuit, extending from South Ottawa to Wash. Halliday's, being the late "Sam" Habberman farm, commenced and carried on religious services in the court house in Morris. His meetings were held about once in four weeks. He had some tough cases among his Morris audience, and though he was quite a revivalist, he could not revive the Morrisites worth a cent. What between P. Chapin, Bill Armstrong

---
* By Hon. P. A. Armstrong.

and Sam Ayres, he had a tough time of it, and concluding that "Ephraim was joined to his idols," gave them up as a stiff-necked and hopeless people, and turned his attention to a more susceptible community.

The next effort made by this church was by a Mr. Humphrey, who was also the minister in charge of South Ottawa circuit. He made an effort at the court house about the 10th of January, 1846. There were but few professed Christians here of the Protestant faith—not even a "baker's dozen." In view of this fact the effort of Rev. Humphrey was looked upon as an attempt to "beard the lion in his den, the Douglas in his hall." Indeed, the few Protestant Christian men and women looked forward to this effort with fear and trembling, the ungodly with curiosity rather than interest, whilst others were not all serenity in their feelings. There was a silent monitor tugging away at their consciences, which said or seemed to say, "You have not kept my commandments and lived holy lives." To others this unseen monitor said, "Unless ye repent of your sins ye shall not enter the Kingdom of Heaven," whilst the gamins and urchins anticipated lots of fun from going to hear a sermon—a something the meaning of which had never entered their heads. Thus matters stood in feverish excitement on the arrival of the eventful Sabbath on which Mr. Humphrey was to preach at the court house. At that time there was no law upon our statute against keeping tippling houses open on Sunday. About three-fourths of our inhabitants were canal laborers. Sundays were their holidays, and above all other days this was their drinking and gambling day. All the saloons were open and running at full speed. On the Sabbath in question all the drinking hells in Morris were run to their utmost capacity to get ready to hear what Rev. Humphrey might have to say that evening. Indeed the proposed sermon was often mentioned during the day in ribaldry and ridicule. When the time came for the meeting the court house was lighted up with "tallow dips" and was densely filled by the most incongruous mass of human beings possible to imagine, many of whom were maudlin drunk. The preacher was rather a weak cistern to hold much Methodism, yet he had zeal and was promptly on hand with Bible and hymn book. Standing fully six feet, straight and slender, in faltering voice he announced his hymn commencing,

"O, for a thousand tongues to sing
My great Redeemer's praise,"

followed by the request: "Will some brother start the tune?" But alas! no brother was present, and no outsider volunteered, so the singing had to be abandoned, and prayer followed next. But there were too many inopportune "Amens" and "bless Gods," to suit his invocation. He then announced his text: "Walk about Zion, mark well her bulwarks, and tell the towers thereof." But the fellows felt more like walking about Morris, finding the saloons and testing the whisky thereof, and hence they kept interjecting: "It's time to splice the main brace," "Cut him short, young fellow"; "We are all getting dry," etc. He did cut it short, and dismissed his hearers, or such of them as had not already gone, without the benediction. Bro. Humphrey was very much discouraged. This, we believe, was his last effort at missionary work—certainly it was his last effort among the heathen of Morris. What his report was to the church we were never able to learn, but doubt not that it was graphic, if not glowing. About this time the Rev. W. S. Strong, a leading minister of the Protestant Methodist Church, was en route for Joliet from Princeton, Ill., and traveled overland in his own conveyance, and reached Morris in the evening, and stayed over night with us. We had heard him preach many times in Putnam County, Ill., and knew him to be a man of towering ability. Before leaving here we got his promise to preach for us at the court house on his return trip. Due notice was given of the time and place of the meeting, and when the time came, the court house was crowded. But when, instead of a gawky looking young fledgling, a man of giant size, middle age, and commanding presence, rose, and with a fine, full voice read his hymn, and asked the congregation to help him sing, all mirth was hushed, and a profound stillness, if not awe, settled over the audience. Indeed, if any there were "who came to scoff" (and there doubtless were many such), "they remained to pray." From this time on there were no efforts made to interrupt religious services in Morris.

The next Methodist preacher to try his hand was Alonzo Kenyon, also of the South Ottawa circuit. He succeeded in organizing a class, and preached in the court house once a month for several months. He was, or is, for he is still living, a man for whom nature did much, but illiterate. He abandoned the pulpit, went to California, made some money and then turned lawyer and went to the Legislature from Lee County, Ill., and afterward was elected judge of the city court of Amboy, Illinois.

In the summer of 1846 Rev. James Langhead, deceased, a Congregational minister of the Gospel, commenced to preach at the court house—a man of fair ability and practical common sense. He continued to preach about twice a month for some time. The canal was finished in 1848, when a better class of people took the place of the canal laborers. In July, 1848, a society of nine members was formed, known as the "Congregational Society," yet its membership was composed of other Protestant denominations, Presbyterian, Methodist and Baptist. The organization of the Congregational Society was of the most liberal character and upon an accommodating plan. It was only intended for temporary purposes, and left its members free to unite with an organization of their own churches when formed. Thus did Mr. Langhead organize the first Protestant church society in Morris. He became the pastor and moved his family to Morris, where he died some years later leaving a widow, since deceased, and a daughter, now Mrs. L. Whitney. We are not sure whether his son Storrs was killed in the army before or after his death.

About the year 1850 this society erected a small church edifice just north of the present fine stone church, and called Rev. A. W. Henderson, a Presbyterian minister, as its preacher. Thus we had the anomaly of a Congregational church with a Presbyterian pastor, for several years. Mr. Henderson finally resigned his position and accepted a call elsewhere. He was succeeded by Rev. E. B. Turner. This society has for its pastor Rev. Montgomery, one of the very ablest men ever in the ministry here, and embraces in its membership a large number of our best and most influential citizens. In the short space we can possibly give to the different churches of Morris, we can not take time to consult the church records and must speak of them in a general way only, and will not attempt to give the names of the various good men who have endeavored to point the way to heaven and God.

THE METHODIST CHURCH.

Following close upon the Congregational church came the Methodist church edifice, on the corner of Jefferson and Kiersted streets, now occupied by the Reformed Lutheran church. In 1849 Morris was attached or united with Lisbon, nine miles north of Morris, as a circuit, with Rev. J. W. Flowers—afterward a presiding elder—as the minister in charge. He was a man of fine forensic ability and a good organizer. Under his able management the membership increased so rapidly that in 1850 steps were taken to erect a church. This was pressed to speedy completion and was at the time of its erection the most spacious church building of the place. Morris was established as a station or circuit in August, 1850, with a settled minister. We do not remember the order of the Methodist ministers, but the early ones were Denning, Linn, Adams, Prince, Davidson, Reeder, Stover, etc. This society grew to such proportions that before the year 1868 their church was too small, when steps were taken to erect their present fine church on Jackson between Liberty and Wauponsee streets, which is the most commodious church edifice in Morris, except that of the Catholics, and its membership is much larger than either of the other Protestant churches of Morris. Among its many pastors some were men of fine pulpit talent. Notably so were Revs. W. P. Gray, J. W. Phelps, J. H. Alling and Geo. S. Young. As a popular preacher none have surpassed Mr. Young. The management of this church has been liberal, indeed. In point of courtesy and Christian fellowship the ministers and members of the various Protestant churches of this city have been a model, well worthy of imitation and commendation. No spirit of jealousy or improper rivalry has ever existed among them, and when the Methodist church was partially burned a few years ago, the other churches so arranged their services as to give that congregation the free use of their churches to hold their regular worship in, thus manifesting a beautiful Christian spirit of kindness and good will.

THE PRESBYTERIAN CHURCH.

As early as 1855 a goodly number of members of the Presbyterian faith had settled here, and in that year they extended a call to Rev. W. T. Paterfield, who then resided in the State of Ohio. He came here and held services at the court house, Parmelee Hall and other places. Immediate steps were taken for the erection of the first brick church of Morris, now standing at the corner of Jackson and Franklin streets, of which Rev. Mr. Killen is the present pastor. This congregation embraces quite a membership, and its pulpit has been filled by many able men, none more so than the Rev. McLeod, now in charge of a wealthy church in the State of New York.

THE BAPTIST CHURCH

is a fine frame edifice also on Jackson street, at the intersection of Division street, and was erected about the year 1858. This denomination is rather smaller in numbers than either of the others mentioned, yet it contains many of our good citizens. Their pulpit has been supplied by several men of talent, among whom were Revs. Faslett and De Wolfe.

THE GERMAN LUTHERAN CHURCH

purchased and occupy the old Methodist church building. They have but a small following, but are good people and devout Christians.

THE EPISCOPALIANS

have made many efforts to build a church, but have failed. At one time they seemed in a fair way to build a fine stone edifice on the corner of North and Division streets. This was commenced at the breaking out of the war. The walls were run up one story and work was then stopped and has not since been resumed. Notwithstanding they never had a church edifice here, yet have they had regular service during several years. Some of the clergymen officiating here have gained reputations elsewhere. Among them are Doctor Clinton Locke, of Grace Church, Chicago, Doctors E. A. Gilbert, Benedict, etc.

We now turn to the

DOCTORS, OR PHYSICIANS.

Dr. Luther S. Robbins, before mentioned, was not only the first physician of the county, but also of Morris. He moved to Morris from Sulphur Spring some eight miles south of Morris, in the fall of 1842, and died here a year or so later. Dr. S Ias Miller was the next one. He settled here in 1843, but found the place too painfully healthy for his financial prosperity. Dr. John Antis was the next. He came here in May, 1845. Dr. Thomas M. Reed was the next. He moved here from Waupecan Grove, south of the Illinois River, and was elected sheriff in 1847, and died here before qualifying as sheriff. Dr. A. F. Hand was our next disciple of the pill bags. Drs. David Edwards and Oliver S. Newell came next and at about the same time. Dr. Edwards was well advanced in years, and did but little in his profession. Dr. Newell entered into partnership with Dr. Hand. He was a fine physician and most estimable citizen. He was a charter member of Star Lodge No. 75, I. O. O. F., and its first presiding officer. He died in 1852 and was buried in the Odd Fellows' lot in Morris cemetery. His death was very generally lamented. Dr. Edwards left here some time about 1850, when Dr. Luke Hale purchased his property here, and practiced medicine up to the time of his death, in 1865. Dr. B. E. Dodson came here about the year 1850 and remained several years, and then moved to Elgin; thence to McLeansville, where he died a few years ago. Dr. Roscoe L. Hale, son of Luke Hale, came here about the year 1858, and remained here until after the war, and then moved to Sedalia, Mo., where he still resides. Dr. H. H. De Hart came here in 1852, soon after the death of Dr. Newell, and went into partnership with Dr. Hand, but he soon became tired of so small a town and left. Dr. David Le Roy, a man of some means, now living at Streator, Ill., came here about the year 1855, and entered into partnership with Dr. Hand. He soon embarked in the dry goods business quite extensively with E. B. Hanna, under the firm name of Hanna & Le Roy. They built the brick store building on Washington street, now occupied by Messrs. Levitte & Hughes as a saloon. They afterward built the large brick block now occupied by the Normal school, besides speculating in real estate to a considerable extent. They had just completed this large building when the war broke out, in 1861. But as the war paralyzed business, for a while at least, they were unable to rent the stores to any advantage, or to make any disposition of any part of this immense building, so as to realize from it; together with other bad investments, they were forced to suspend business and make the best compromise they could with their creditors. Their failure was a severe blow to the interests of Morris, for they were our most active and influential business men. Their home creditors were protected. Our next physician was Dr. John N. Freeman, who came here about the year 1857, and remained some ten years, and moved to Rochester, N. Y. Dr. E. Ridgway came here soon after Dr. Freeman, and went into the drug store of Longworth & Ridgway. In 1862, he entered the army as surgeon in the 76th Ill. Vols., and on his return he opened an office and entered into active practice, but has again gone into the drug business with Mr. Enslee, the firm being Ridgway & Enslee. Dr. A. E. Palmer came here from Mazon in 1876, and opened an office, since which time he has had a very large and lucrative practice. Dr. Oaks, his present partner, came here from Minooka this summer. Dr. S. D. Ferguson came here from Minooka some two years ago, and has a fair practice. He had practiced at Minooka many years before coming here. These are all allopathics. Dr. Antis turned homeopathic in 1847, but has not confined his practice to that branch of physics. Dr. A. M. Pierce and Dr. Sturtevant are homeopaths, with a fair practice. And now, "since the law is full of points, we will turn to the points of the law," and briefly mention the

LAWYERS OF MORRIS.

The first was E. H. Little, who came here and opened an office in one of the little upper rooms of the old court house, in the spring of 1845. He accidentally shot himself while gunning near the residence of A. R. Newport, in July, 1847. A whole charge of small shot passed through his left arm, passed into his body, and lodged in his lungs. For all this he lived, and was still living at Montrose, Pa., a short time since. He was a young man of good habits and character, with fair ability. Charles M. Lee read law with Mr. Little, and was admitted to the bar in 1847. Honest and upright, but by no means brilliant, he succeeded in finding out that the "*Law* and the *Profits* did not agree," as he expressed it, so he gave it up and turned peddler for Geo. Turmeyer. The gallant Capt. W. P. Rogers, son of Com. Rogers, came here and stuck out his shingle in the spring of 1847, but only remained a year, and then went to California, where he built up a name and fame worthy of his distinguished father. Ezra P. Seeley was our next limb of the law. He was decidedly a bookworm, and well learned in the law. As an advocate he was not successful. He died, we think, in 1862, leaving a widow and two daughters, still living in Morris. Capt. Charles L. Starbuck was our next disciple of Blackstone. He came here in 1851, and died about the year 1857, leaving a widow and two children. He served one term in the Legislature from Grundy and La Salle. A small, dark complexioned, wiry man, of fine legal and forensic ability. Henry Storr came here about the same time Capt. Starbuck did. He was elected the first county judge, and resigned in 1851, and moved to Sacramento, Cal., where he still lives, and is a prominent California lawyer. Judge W. T. Hopkins came here from Maine in 1849, and has remained here. He was elected captain of the "Grundy Tigers" in 1861, and served out the term of enlistment, and on his return he was elected county judge. He was afterward appointed supervisor of internal revenue—a man of great energy and fine scholastic acquirements. He built the Hopkins House which bears his name. He also first conceived the idea of a bridge across the Illinois River at this place. He procured a charter from the Legislature Feb. 13, 1855, to incorporate the Morris Bridge Company, with W. T. Hopkins, L. W. Claypool, Samuel Hoge, Geo. W. Armstrong and E. P. Seeley, incorporators, and inaugurated steps for the construction of the present bridge. Messrs. Hoge and Seeley did nothing in the matter. But Messrs. Hopkins, Claypool and Armstrong took hold of the matter and pushed it forward to completion in 1856. Mr. Armstrong, we believe, was made president of the organization, and Mr. Claypool, secretary. Judge Hopkins is now, by many years, the earliest lawyer at our bar. He served one term in the Legislature. Judge James N. Reading was the next lawyer here. He came from Missouri in 1855. He too served one term in our State Legislature and two terms as county judge—a gentleman of finish and ability. Being advanced in years, he has practically withdrawn from the profession. Judge Sidney W. Harris came here from Cincinnati, O., about the time Judge Reading came. He was a fine lawyer and powerful advocate, and was elected judge of the circuit court in 1861, and died here about the year 1869.

Edward Sanford read law here with Mr. Seeley and entered into partnership with that gentleman. After the death of Mr. Seeley, Mr. Sanford opened an office and turned his attention more especially to bounty and pension claims, and then to the loan business, in the latter of which he has had great success, and has acquired a handsome fortune.

Geo. W. Watson, John P. Southworth, T. B. Rice and Charles Turner all came here before 1860, and after remaining here awhile left. Judge B. Olin came here in 1863, and in 1865 entered into partnership with the writer under the firm name of Olin & Armstrong. He left here in 1870 and located in Joliet, where he has served nearly nine years as county judge. Judge A. R. Jordan read law with Judge Olin, and was admitted in 1865. Next to the writer, he is the next lawyer in point of time at the Morris bar. Messrs. S. C. Stough, A. L. Doud, county attorney, R. M. Wing (his partner), S. P. Avery, O. N. Carter and J. H. Sampson are of recent date. Judge C. Grant was admitted to the bar in 1861, and died here January 10, 1881. He was a very scholarly man and had served one term as county judge and many years as register in bankruptcy. Leaving the lawyers to plead their own cases, we "go for the"

MERCHANTS.

As early as 1845 Col. Wm. L. Perce and Adam Lamb each had a small stock of goods for the accommodation of their canal hands. In the fall of that year P. A. Armstrong opened a general store in what had been the bar-room of the Grundy Hotel, which then stood where the Hopkins House now stands. He purchased the stocks of goods from Col. Perce and Mr. Lamb, and united them to his other stock, and not having room in his then storeroom, he built the main part of Dr. Hand's residence for a store, and occupied it for a couple of years for a store and post-office. Gov. Mattison having opened a store in the Harvey building, which stood where the Washington House now stands, after operating it about a year with Henry Fish, manager, and, we believe, partner, Mr. Armstrong bought out the goods and moved his store to that building in 1847. He then built the building now occupied by R. Petty, then located where the Geo. M. Jones furniture store stands, and moved his store and post-office to that building. In 1848 Messrs. Hulburd & Lott opened a dry-goods store here. John P. Chapin and C. H. Gould opened a dry-goods store in the Harvey block when Mr. A. left it. But we find that we have undertaken a herculean task and will trace this branch no further.

OUR FIRST WAREHOUSE.

What is known as the Lane Warehouse, just west of the canal bridge, was built by John P. Chapin in 1847, ready for the opening of the canal in 1848. Capt. Hull also built the warehouse now occupied by Messrs. Barr & Philips in the early spring of 1848. E. M. Ross built what is known as the Red Warehouse in 1849.

OUR FIRST GROCER

was Leonard Ashton, deceased. Our next, and, as Samie Reinhart would say, "old reliable," was Miller K. Keller, who has sold more groceries than any man, living or dead—in Morris. For a quarter of a century he has been behind his counter from early morn until late at night, always accommodating, pleasant, and strictly honest. He has been a great blessing to the poor and a comfort to the rich. Indeed, so absorbed is he in his business that he finds no time for pleasure trips or recreation. H. F. Mallory has been very successful in the grocery line and has accumulated quite a fortune at it. Our article is assuming such length that we must pass on without further mention of our merchants.

IN BANKS AND BANKING

we have had a varied and by no means a pleasant experience. As early as 1853 Messrs. C. H. & H. C. Good opened a private banking institution in a building standing where the Claypool Block now stands. This they ran until 1860 when they closed it. They did not fail, but the business ceased to be remunerative. In 1854 Geo. Selleck (decd.) opened a private banking and exchange office in Morris and did a very large business, but failed badly in 1860. In July, 1857, E. W. & F. K. Hulburd opened a private banking and exchange office under the firm name of E.

W. Hulburd & Co. They too did quite a business, but were forced to the wall in 1861 to the injury of their friends as well as others. In 1858 Messrs. F. S. Gardner and C. B. Crumb, without capital or experience, opened a banking and exchange office, but it was "no go." Weak at its birth, it did not grow strong, and died in a few short months. Nobody had confidence in the concern, hence their deposits amounted to nothing or substantially so. We never held their checks over night. The next were T. Hatten & Son, who succeeded C. H. & H. C. Goold, in February, 1860, and failed the next year leaving many mourners. Then came D. D. Spencer, of State Savings notoriety, who in company with Mr. W. C. Hammell opened an exchange and deposit bank, which eventuated in the Grundy County National Bank. The bank opened a branch bank at Seneca, the stock of which was purchased by the Cunneas and the bank moved to Morris under the name of the First National Bank of Morris. These two banks proved to be "solid Muldoons."

From banks we turn to

GRAVEYARDS.

For many years the question of a suitable spot for cemeteries was a serious one. Our first dead were interred on the elevated ground near the residence of R. M. Wing, but the subsoil proved to be clay, and the graves would fill with water so that the coffin was deposited in mud and water. We next tried the bank of Nettle Creek near the residence of Judge Hopkins, but found the same difficulty there. Another attempt was made on the A. W. Telfer farm, late Oliver farm, west of the canal and east of Morris, with like result.

The board of trustees of Morris then purchased, in conjunction with Father Terry, of the Catholic church of Morris, the E. ¼ of the S. W. ¼ of Sec. 27, T. 34, 7, where the old Catholic cemetery is located, but the same difficulty was found there and it was abandoned by the city and their interest therein was sold, as before shown, to Father, now Dean, Terry in 1853. He located a cemetery there but it has been abandoned and the greater portion of the remains deposited there have been exhumed and reburied in the beautiful new Catholic cemetery near the residence of Messrs. Kennedy and Kenrick. On the 12th of February, 1853, The Morris Cemetery Association was chartered by the Legislature with Geo. Fisher, Geo. W. Lane, Charles H. Goold, L. P. Lott and Eugene Stanberry, incorporators.

On the 25th of August of that year this association purchased from Thomas Peacock, since deceased, about five acres, and from John Peacock, now deceased, about five acres of land, on the N. fr. of Sec. 2, T. 33, R. 7, lying nearly two miles east of Morris, and adjoining each other, for a cemetery, and on the 14th of September following, authorized and appointed P. A. Armstrong to survey and subdivide said land into suitable sized lots with appropriate drives, alleys, etc. Owing to the course of the public road running along the north side of the land, the ten acres so purchased, while a parallelogram in shape, the long side being from east to west, it does not lie with the cardinal courses of the compass, hence there are many triangular lots, but this adds beauty to the general features of the cemetery. The subsoil is gravel, whilst the general lay of the surface is high yet undulating. The work of subdividing and driving the stakes was done with great care and precision, Mr. Armstrong driving every stake with his own hands, to the end that they should be in their exact place, and driven in the ground perpendicularly. Originally free from tree or shrub, the directors caused evergreens and other nice shrubs and trees to be planted so that it is now a most beautiful "silent city of the dead." Additional land has been purchased by the association. "God's half acre," the Potter's field, has proved insufficient to bury the poor. The number of unknown dead huddled side by side with naught but a rough unlettered stone to mark the place is surprising. A new and larger plat will be assigned to bury the poor. Many fine monuments have been erected there, and the Morris cemetery is one of the finest in the country. Among other distinguished dead slumbering here, is Shaubc-nay, the great Sanzanath, or white man's friend. By his side lie the remains of his wife, one daughter and one grandchild. No stake or stone marks the spot where slumber the remains of this once mighty king of the red men—a triple chief—on whose will hung the destinies of three great Indian tribes—Chippewas, Ottawas and Pottawatomies. Will the descendants of these early white settlers, whose lives were saved during the Black Hawk War, do anything to honor the memory of the man who risked life and standing with his own people to befriend and protect their ancestors? But this is a grave question and we turn to

OUR MANUFACTURERS.

The first manufacturing establishment of Morris was the Morris Plow Factory, in 1857. They made an excellent plow, and why it was abandoned we never could learn. The large brick building west of the court house, now carried on by H. L. Miller as a blacksmith and carriage shop, planing mill, etc., was the building occupied as the plow factory. In 1873, the city gave a bonus to encourage manufactures. There were some $10,000 invested by the city within a couple of years which eventuated in the establishment here of the Sherwood School Furniture Company's Works near the canal on the west side of the city, which has since been converted into the Ohio Butt Company. The buildings and machinery of this concern are large and valuable and give employment to about 150 hands. The Anderson Paper Car Wheel Manufacturing Company on the east side of the city, have fine buildings and splendid machinery, and while they do not employ many hands to run it because nearly everything is run by machinery, yet they furnish a ready market at a high price for all the rye and oat straw of the county.

The Morris Cutlery Company's Manufactory stands at the corner of Wauponsee and Fulton streets. The building is the one mentioned as being used for a court room while building the new one. This is a new enterprise here; indeed, but few of the people of Grundy County know of its existence. It is a regularly incorporated company under the statute with $15,000 capital stock. The stockholders are men of action, not of boasting. They are practical business men with means and energy. M. W. Steiner, Geo. Riddle, L. F. Beach, Drs. Palmer and Ferguson, M. K. Keller, J. H. Pettit, A. W. Crawford, Albert and William Smith, are the stockholders, the latter two being thoroughly educated cutlers from Sheffield, England. The officers are Geo. Riddle, president, Albert Smith, superintendent, and M. W. Steiner, secretary and treasurer. They have the very best of machinery, and can employ and successfully operate 150 hands. They already have twenty-one skilled laborers in their establishment, and have up to the present manufactured eighty-four varieties or kinds of pocket knives, equal in style and finish to the celebrated Wostenholm and Sons of England. No better finished knife is made in the United States, if indeed in the world, than by the Morris Cutlery Company. So fine is their work that they have more orders than they can possibly fill with the force of workmen they now have. They employ none but skilled workmen, hence they experience some difficulty in obtaining all the workmen they need. They intend to do none but first class work. This is made apparent upon inspection of their goods. To all who wish a first class pocket-knife either for ornament or use, we commend them to try one of home manufacture. Try a Morris knife.

IN THE BREWERY LINE.

Louis Gibhard, at his large brewery at the foot of Washington street on the east bank of Nettle Creek, manufactures a first class article of lager and ale and in large quantities.

We have some three or four manufactories of cigars, besides boot and shoe makers, etc.

THE MORRIS ACADEMY OF SCIENCE

occupy the room over the court house, where they have a large collection, especially so of fossil botany, of which this locality is the most prolific of any yet discovered in the civilized world. The Mazon fossils are known and readily recognized in every civilized country. This fine collection is open to inspection at all times. The officers are, P. A. Armstrong, president; F. T. Bliss, secretary; J. C. Carr, treasurer; Prof. Kern, corresponding secretary. In addition to the fine collections in geology, there is a fair display in natural history, engravings and pre-historic relics, etc.

OUR SECRET BENEVOLENT SOCIETIES.

Star Lodge, No. 75, I. O. O. F. was instituted by the late James T. McDougal, of Joliet, under a dispensation from the R. W. Grand Master of the Grand Lodge of Illinois, October 17, 1851. L. P. Lott, N. G.; E. M. Ross, V. G.; O. S. Newell, deceased, T., and A. H. Bishop, also deceased, secretary. On that night several of our best citizens were initiated, among whom were Geo. W. Lane, Henry Benjamin, deceased, W. S. Woolsey, deceased, Miles Gordon and P. A. Armstrong. This lodge still exists, and is in a very prosperous condition. It has never failed to hold its regular weekly meetings, or in visiting the sick, comforting its widows, educating its orphans or burying its dead. Shabonch Encampment was organized in 1871, with P. A. Armstrong, C. P., F. B. Handwork, H. P., etc. It, too, is in a flourishing condition.

Cedar Lodge No. 124, A. F. and A. M., was instituted Feby. 26, 1852, with B. M. Atherton, W. M.; C. L. Starbuck, S. W.; John Gibson, J. W.; Geo. Fisher, T.; James Gibson, sec'y; Leonard Ashton, S.

D.; and Lawrence Wilkes, J. D.; all of whom are now dead, except James Gibson who now resides in San Francisco, Cal. A charter was granted Oct. 3, 1853; L. P. Lott was one of its first initiates, and has served as Master over a dozen years in all. Cedar Lodge embraces in its membership a very large portion of our leading citizens, and has been a prosperous and harmonious organization.

ORIENT ROYAL ARCH CHAPTER, NO. 31,

was constituted Oct. 23, 1856; the charter members were Franklin K. Hulburd, L. P. Lott, B. M. Atherton, Nathan B. Dodson, E. W. Lusk, C. R. Parmelee, Leonard Ashton, Geo. Riddle and Geo Fisher; of these nine charter members, Companions Lott, Dodson, Riddle and Parmelee alone survive. Companions Hulburd and Lusk lost their lives in the Union service; F. K. Hulburd was High Priest of this chapter up to the time of his death; since that time Messrs. Lott, Armstrong and Irons have filled that position, Companion Irons being the present chief officer. Up to the year 1858 there were but three Commanderies of Knights Templar in this State, viz.: Apollo, No. 1, at Chicago; Belvidere, No. 2, at Alton, and Peoria, No. 3, at Peoria. F. K. Hulburd had taken the orders of knighthood in Mt. Vernon Commandery, No. 1, under the jurisdiction of the Grand Commandery of Ohio, before coming here to live. E. W. Lusk had also taken the orders in Kalamazoo Commandery, under the jurisdiction of the Grand Commandery of the State of Michigan. These two Sir Knights conceived the idea of establishing a Commandery at Morris, being midway between Joliet and Ottawa, so as to render the chapters of these two cities tributary to the Morris Commandery; but there were serious difficulties to encounter; it either required nine Sir Knights of the jurisdiction of Illinois, or three Sir Knights hailing from different jurisdictions, to open a Commandery for work; they had neither, but they had two hailing from other jurisdictions, and must have a third; this they obtained by procuring Rt. Eminent Sir Hosmer A. Johnson, of Apollo, No. 1, and since R. E. Grand Commander of the Grand Commandery of Illinois. They were extremely anxious to keep the matter a profound secret from the resident Sir Knights at Joliet and Ottawa, at both of which places there were a few Sir Knights, and right here another difficulty arose; they were compelled under the rules and regulations of the Grand Commandery, to obtain the consent and recommendation of the nearest Commandery; this was Apollo at Chicago, of which some of the Sir Knights of Joliet were members, and in that way the secret got out, and immediate steps were taken by Sir Knight Nelson D. Elwood and others, of Joliet, to counteract and check the Morris movement; they, with equal secrecy, prepared a petition for a dispensation to open and organize a Commandery at Joliet, and like the Morris Sir Knights, they, too, were short of the requisite number of Sir Knights resident there; to obviate this they passed by Morris and went to Ottawa and procured the signatures of Sir Knights Oliver C. Gray and J. W. Stone, and then procured the consent and recommendation of Apollo to open and organize a Commandery at Joliet, and when Sir Knight Hulburd presented his petition and recommendation for a Commandery to be established at Morris, to Grand Commander James V. L. Blaney, on the 17th of February, 1858, he found Sir Knight Elwood there with his petition in favor of Joliet; the secret then became an open one; the result was that Grand Commander Blaney decided to grant a dispensation to both, when it was agreed by and between Sir Knights Elwood and Hulburd, that the former should take precedence in number, and the latter in the name when in power of the decision of the Grand Commander. Sir Knight Hulburd selected Blaney as the name; hence, dispensations were granted on the same day to open and organize Joliet Commandery, No. 4, at Joliet, and Blaney, No. 5, at Morris; these two Commanderies having been born on the same day, were not inaptly called twin sisters; the kindliest feeling has ever existed between these Commanderies; a rivalry has existed between them, but it has only been a rivalry of courtesy and good will. Joliet Commandery was constituted by Grand Commander Blaney, March 18, 1858, and Blaney on the following day. Grand Commander Blaney was assisted in constituting

BLANEY COMMANDERY, NO. 5,

by the following Sir Knights: N. D. Elwood (deceased), T. Hatton, Jr., W. W. Mitchell (deceased), E. W. Lusk (deceased), E. Wilcox, C. E. Munger (since G. C.), F. K. Hulburd, E. Bean, James H. Miles, T. Hatton, Sr., and E. J. Higgins. On the day of the constitution of the Commandery the following Companions of Orient R. A., Chapter No. 31 received the orders of Christian Knighthood conferred in said Commandery: Geo. Fisher (deceased), E. W. Hulburd, L. P. Lott, P. A. Armstrong,

Wm. B. Grenell, J. W. Massey, Charles H. Goold, Uriah B. Couch (deceased), Geo. Dimon, Charles R. Parmelee, John Gibson, Jr. (deceased), and B. M. Atherton (deceased). Sir Knight F. Hulburd was installed as Commander, which office he held to 1861, when P. A. Armstrong succeeded him. He was succeeded by Arnold M. Cleveland, and he by P. A. Armstrong again, who held the office some ten years and was succeeded by Charles H. Goold, who served some five years and was succeeded by L. F. Beach, present Commander, who is on his third year. During the war Blaney Commandery (having received its charter Oct. 28, 1858, it having worked under a dispensation up to that date) had a hard struggle for existence, and was kept alive by a few of the surviving Knights, P. A. Armstrong advancing Grand Commandery dues for eight years; but it is now in a very prosperous condition, and occupies an enviable position in Templar Masonry. In addition to those receiving the orders March 19, 1858, the following named Templars received the orders during that year, viz.: N. B. Dodson, April 26; A. M. Cleveland and Wm. Stanhope (deceased), April 27; Rev. W. G. Johnson, May 18; Miles Gordon, May 28; Gen. Wm. H. L. Wallace (deceased), June 1. (It will be remembered that this gallant officer lost his life while leading his brigade in the battle of Shiloh.) Hiram Mallory (dec'd) and Samuel Jordan, June 8; F. C. Mayo and J. P. M. Butler, June 11; J. S. Dyke (dec'd), June 30; Joh Antis and A. J. Hutchinson, Dec. 30; and in 1859, S. E. Massey, March 7; B. H. Streeter (dec'd), June 7; in 1860, E. C. Hollands, Aug. 29; Rev. Seaman Stover, afterward Grand Prelate, Dec. 13; C. S. C.

Crane, Dec. 20. In 1861, Q. D. Whitman, S. E. Miner, R. N. Goodsell and Daniel H. Ashton, Jan'y 29. This was the last work done until 1870. E. T. Hopkins (killed while performing his official duty, by the ruffian Miller), June 14; H. D. Hitchcock (dec'd), Oct. 31. In 1871, Geo. W. Ashton and R. L. Tatham, Feb'y 8; H. H. Holtzum and A. W. Telfer, Feb'y 27; Edward Sanford and H. H. C. Miller, May 10; Judge S. B. Thomas (dec'd) and Dr. W. P. Pierce, May 18; R. B. Horrie and W. W. Phillips, May 25; F. Caspori and A. J. Boyer, June 9; Geo. Mann and J. H. Pettit, June 15; in 1872, John Jacob Gorich, March 11; John, Geo. and Charles Woelfel, March 18; Leander Irons, March 25; Geo. R. Beach, April 18; Charles K. Charlton, Oct. 11; C. E. Daniels, Oct. 18; Dr. A. E. Palmer, Oct. 28; H. B. Elliott, Nov. 25. In 1873, F. Dirst, Feb'y 20; Geo. Gaskill, Feb'y 24; J. W. Tatham, June 9; C. S. Beach, June 16. In 1874, C. E. Halbert, Jan'y 15; Jacob Geisen, Jan'y 15; A. Van Riper, April 6; Israel Cryder, May 4th; A. F. Rodgers, May 7th; G. Dahlem, May 15th; E. W. Weis, May 22d; A. K. Knapp, June 10th; E. L. Stevens, Oct. 26th; A. Stauffer, Nov. 30th; A. F. Mallory, Dec. 7th. In 1875, Dr. S. T. Ferguson, Jan'y 18th; Geo. Mason, May 17th; L. E. Daniels, May 24th; John Vandyke, May 31st; O. W. Weston, June 10th; David Nickel, June 14th. In 1876, Daniel Shaide, April 24th; J. F. Peck, May 1st. In 1877, Geo. Riddle, Jan'y 29th; Geo. N. Widney, Feb'y 5th; Wm. B. Cogger, Feb'y 27th; A. W. Crawford, Sept. 8th; Henry G. Gorham, Oct. 29th; C. D. Ferguson, Nov. 12th; Nicholas Quadland, Nov. 26th. In 1878, H. C. June, Nov. 18th; Henry Long, Dec. 2d; A. Kimple, Dec. 9th; J. F. Cobleigh, Dec. 16th. None in 1879. In 1880, C. H. Overocker, Feb'y 16th; J. J. Widney, Feb'y 23d; T. H. Ross, March 15th; Nathan Small, July 15th; C. O. Barker, July 22d. In 1881, J. G. Colleps, April 25th. In 1882, Wm. Mason and D. W. McEwen, May 1st; John A. Gouch, May 15th; Wm. Gebhard, May 29th; and John Ray, Oct. 6th. The present Commander E. Sir Knight L. F. Beach, united by card, March 27th, 1871, and Sir Knight R. C. Auld, Dec. 26th, 1881. These are the men who compose the membership of this higher branch of masonry in Morris. Good men, and true to their obligations.

"For a chain sweetly twined by humanity's hand,
 Is bound like a circlet of diamonds around them,
And fearless and strong as a legion they stand
 In the battle of life when the chain hath been there.
For its love knotted links have a magical charm,
 Earth's trials to meet and its woes to disarm;
Every stranger finds a friend his sorrows to share,
 While no heart beats alone where Knight Templars are."

Having spent several weeks in collecting reliable dates and facts for the history of Morris, we confess that we are tired and weary. Many things have been omitted that might have proved of interest, while other matters have received but a lick without a promise. If we have succeeded in laying the foundation for a more able pen than ours at some future day to write a fuller history of our town, then we shall have accomplished much.

CHAPTER X.*

GREENFIELD TOWNSHIP—SURFACE—STREAMS—TIMBER—ORIGIN OF NAME—TOWNSHIP ORGANIZATION—GOING TO MILL—FIRST SETTLERS—INCIDENTS—WOLF AND DEER HUNTING—ELECTIONS—OFFICERS—IMPROVEMENTS AND PROSPECTS—WHAT WE ARE TO DAY, ETC., ETC.

Greenfield! the land of grass and flowers,
Of pleasant homes and happy hours;
Where richest lands her treasures yield,
To every tiller of the field.

Here hill and vale are never seen,
But an endless plain forever green;
No rivers here go rushing o'er
A rocky bed with ceaseless roar.

No lakes are here extending wide,
Inviting travelers to their side;
But those who came could easy tell,
That with earnest work they might do well.

Wealth was here for all who'd come,
To till the earth and make a home;
So here we write this story, true,
Of what our fathers used to do.

FOR several years before the dividing of the county into townships, the territory, afterward called Greenfield, belonged to Mazon Precinct. In the year 1850, a township organization was effected, the first "town meeting" being held the first Tuesday in April of that year. In order of business came the "naming of the township." Seventeen voters were present and nearly every one had a name for his new home—a name dear to him because it belonged to "the old home in the East." Each pressed his claim with all the enthusiasm at command; but after a noisy canvass and several ballots, a choice was not made. Finally a committee of three—

*By Dr. C. M. Easton.

Robert Wood, Robert Finley and Milo Wilcox, was appointed to choose a name. Wilcox proposed "Greenfield" after Thomas R. Green, a land speculator of Chicago, who then owned several tracts in the township. The name was sent in and adopted with a hurrah!

Greenfield township occupies the southeast corner of Grundy County, and includes an area of six miles square. Braceville township bounds it upon the north, Goodfarm upon the west, Round Grove (Livingston Co.) upon the south and Essex (Kankakee Co.) upon the east. The surface is very level, with gentle undulations along the banks of creeks and sluices. The highest land is in the southern part with a gradual descent as you go northward. Unfortunately for drainage, the banks of the streams are generally a little higher than the lands some distance back; so in order to get rid promptly of the superfluous water, it is needful to cut drains through these rolls.

The soil is a rich black loam from one to two feet in depth, and with proper drainage and cultivation, its productiveness can not be excelled.

The timber originally consisted only of a few groves, scattered along the banks of the Mazon. One of these on the south line of the township, known as Currier's Grove, was widely known among the early settlers, receiving its name from a family who settled in the immediate neighborhood during the early years. As we go down the stream we find another fine timber lot on section fourteen, now the premises of L. C. Fuller. On sections one and twelve was another grove of considerable size, probably the largest in the township. The varieties were such as were indigenous to this part of the State, namely; oak, hickory, walnut, elm, basswood, etc.

The Mazon Creek, the largest of our water courses, has its origin in Broughton, Livingston County, and running north enters Greenfield upon the south line, a half mile east of the center. Bearing to the northeast to the south line of section one, on the farm of F. O. Andrews, it turns to the northwest, and runs out on section two.

Cranery Creek, a stream of considerable size, draining a portion of Essex, comes into our town from the east and unites with the Mazon on section one. Another creek coming from the south, and draining a goodly portion of the southeast part of the town, empties into the Mazon a little farther up, near the residence of the late Robert Wood. Two creeks rising in Round Grove enter Greenfield, one near the southwest corner, the other a mile farther east, and running to the northeast, coalesce on section twenty-two, and on section fourteen, pour their united waters into the Mazon. These streams, like all others dependent entirely for supplies upon surface water, get very low in dry seasons, and, perhaps, all except the Mazon, at times go dry. Though insignificant at low water, when swollen with heavy rains they are very torrents; and in the years gone by, when bridges were not, they were sources of embarrassment and often danger to the inhabitants.

"HOW WE WENT TO MILL."

The winter of 1858-9 was one of those wet, open winters that has always wrought ruin to Illinois roads, and ruffled the sweetest tempered souls that tried to travel them. The streams were full and covered with ice, but not strong enough to bear a team. Then flour was not kept in the markets as it now is; but farmers grew their own wheat and got it ground as needed. In our neighborhood we had been borrowing one of another, waiting for a "harder freeze," until all were out and something must be done. D. R. Doud, still living four miles northwest, started to Wilmington to mill, but striking one of these treacherous streams, his horses broke through the ice and went down, wagon following. With considerable difficulty he got his horses out and across; carried the sacks of wheat—about fifteen—across; took off the wagon box, slid it across; uncoupled the running gears and tugged them over; so after long hours of fearful labor and exposure, he found himself again upon *terra firma*, and on his "way to mill." After reaching Wilmington he found he could not get his grinding done and must at last return home empty. The novel part of our story remains to be told. Governor Madison at that time held control of the Chicago & Alton Railroad, and for some reason no trains were run for several days, coming to Gardner. Doud secured a handcar, a dummy without gearing, with platform about four by five feet, and he and Allen Slyter, a local preacher, and the writer, got aboard. Holding aloft a couple of boards to catch the southwest breeze, we rattled down the track, and across the raging Mazon.

Here we were joined by John Booth, now in Kansas, riding a little bay mare owned by Doud and known as "Queen." As our story proves, Queen was one of the most sensible and docile of her race. The old mare was hitched to the car by a long rope and away "we all went to mill." To get old Queen over the cattle-guards and bridges, all we had to do was to lay down our boards and lead her over. Upon the return trip to make room for grist and passengers, we laid the boards upon the sides of the car, stood the sacks thereon, while the passengers stood between the rows of bags, or perched on top. Coming home we had about fifteen hundred pounds of flour and bran, and two extra passengers— one a woman who left the car at the first station. We pushed the dummy across the Kankakee River, and then attached our locomotive (old Queen) with plenty of steam and a wide "open throttle" we made good time for home.

When we reached the first cattle-guard, we were for a little time nonplussed; our sacks were upon the boards that had served for a bridge going over, and could not well be moved. Between the sacks was a space, when the "train hands" were off, the length of the car, some five feet in length by one foot and a half in width. Here was just barely room for a horse to stand, and at Doud's word, Queen took and was pushed over. This was repeated again and again, until we reached the Mazon; here we halted for a hasty council. The bridge was 280 feet in length, and some 25 feet above low water; to undertake to cross it as we had the small ones seemed perilous; to swim the faithful mare through the stream full of running ice would be cruel indeed. Queen stepped "on board" with her usual promptness and was safely wheeled across the eddying mass of ice and waves. The old bridge long since went down under a freight train, and a fearful wreck was the result. Without further adventure we reached home "in good order," with an abundance of "stuff" to make the "staff" upon which to lean for many weeks.

The first to settle in this part of Mazon Precinct (two years later named Greenfield) were Dr. James Miller and Nelson La Force, who moved here from Chicago, April 8, 1848. They bought the northeast quarter of section three and put up a house on the north line. This was the first building on the thirty-six square miles of which we write, and is yet standing, sheltering a tenant. In this house the Doctor with his family lived for many years, and here George Miller, now in Florida, was born, the first birth in our territory. Doctor Miller had a crippled leg and always went on crutches; yet during the early years he attended to quite an extensive practice among the pioneers besides overseeing the farm. After a time he moved to Gardner and kept a drug store on the west side; here he ministered in medicine until about four years since, when he closed out and moved to Florida; here, in unending summer, amid the orange groves and everglades, we leave him to while away his declining years. The old farm is now owned by J. C. Lutz, who bought it a year ago of Miller, paying $60 per acre.

Nelson La Force was born in New Jersey and drifted to New York city in his youth, from there to Chicago, which was then only a small town without a railroad. Stopping there for a couple of years he concluded the quickest way to fortune would be over some "government land," and so persuaded Dr. Miller to come onto this prairie with him; when the quarter section was divided he (La Force) took the south half. He went back to New York and was married in 1852; a year later returned with his wife and settled down on the little farm in the west. Here was their home until a year ago when he sold to Taylor Williams of Sterling, and moved to Gardner. Here, fixed in a pleasant home, although bearing down the "shadowy side of life," they are enjoying well the fruits of their labor.

Taylor Bradfield built the second house in our precinct in the spring of 1849, near the northeast corner of section ten, for many years the home of Robert Glass. He came here from Trumbull County, Ohio, remained here a few years on section ten, sold out to Joseph Robinson and built a new house on the farm now owned by F. O. Andrews, on the Mazon. The house was afterward moved to Gardner, Jackson street, and is known as the Blake place. Bradfield moved from here to Iowa.

Robert Glass moved here from Guernsey Co., Ohio, in April, 1849, and bought the northwest quarter of Sec. ten, and erected a cabin on the west line, opposite the Fielder place. He afterward bought the northeast quarter of the same section, built a good house and continued to reside there until the spring of the present year (1882) when he sold to Mr. Taylor Williams and moved to Sedgwick County, Kansas, where he now lives. Mr. Glass sojourned here for a third of a century, and through all these years he enjoyed the full confidence and esteem of all who knew him. A son, Frank Glass, is at this writing, a resident of Braceville. The old farm has this summer been tested for coal and is found to be underlaid with a valuable vein of the dusky diamonds, varying in thickness from two feet ten inches to six feet. Three drillings gave each three feet and a half.

Robert Finley, another of the pioneers, came here from Guernsey Co., Ohio, in June, 1849, and settled upon the northeast quarter of section nine, having a land warrant. The tract cost him $134. A little later he bought the northwest quarter for $175. During the building of the Chicago & Alton railway, in 1854, one of the teamsters employed jestingly told Mr. Finley that his "land would some day be worth $200 per acre." Since that Gardner village has spread over quite a proportion of the original purchase, and he has lived to see small lots of less than one-fourth acre sell for more than the money named. Mr. Finley built his first cabin a little west of where Mrs. Purvis now lives, on Jackson street. It was constructed of slabs cut at a horse saw-mill, on the West Mazon. Later, he put up a frame house on the site where John Allison now lives. The old farm (N. E. qr.) has long since been divided—the north half laid off into town lots and decked with comfortable dwellings, while here and there a residence of costly and elaborate finish varies the scene. Father Finley is now in his eighty-sixth year, and is living near where he built his first rude cabin, thirty-three years ago. Sickness and financial reverses have years since robbed the pioneer of his broad fields, and forever blighted the hopes of his early manhood; but, for bread he wanteth not, till the last inn is reached, where all must lie down and forever sleep. Daniel Fuller came from the State of New York in 1849, and first located on the northeast quarter of section six. After a little time he moved onto the southwest quarter of section eight, now owned by Mike Bookwalter. He sold out here in 1854 and moved to Iowa, from there to Nebraska. He is represented as being a shrewd fellow and a skilled hunter; that the timid deer, which were then plenty upon the prairies, fell before his unerring rifle at long range.

Robert Wood, one of our first settlers, was born in Wayne Co., N. Y., moved from there to Quincy, Michigan, from there to Illinois; came here in 1849, or the early part of 1850, and located on the southwest quarter of section 22, now owned by Thos. Crooks. He lived here five or six years, and sold out to C. K. Snyder and his brother, and moved to Missouri; soon tiring of that country, he came back and bought out John Kelso, on the east bank of the Mazon, section 12. Here he resided until three years since, when, ripe in years, rich in experience, his brow furrowed with many cares, his hair whitened by the frosts of seventy winters, he lay down " to sleep with the Eternal."

Another to anchor upon this prairie in the early years was George Willis. He arrived here from Guernsey Co., Ohio, May 10th, 1850, and bought the southwest quarter of section four, built a cabin out of split logs on the site where J. W. Hull now lives, on Main street. He lived in the little house the first summer without a floor; in the fall he went to the timber and split out slabs and put one down. Mr. Willis lived here about ten years, when he sold out and moved back to Morrow Co., Ohio. From there he went to Lynn Co., Kansas, where he now lives. S. V. Hartley, a well-to-do farmer living a mile west of Gardner, came here with George Willis in 1850. He (Hartley) was then a lad of eleven summers. (See biography.) The east half of Mr. Willis' old farm has been divided and subdivided, and now a score of village lots have taken the place of the old wide fields. The west half still serves the purposes for which intended, and is owned and cultivated by A. M. Bookwalter.

Franklin Morgan came here from the State of New York in April, 1849, and bought the southeast quarter of section five, now owned and cultivated by B. D. Parker, and the northeast quarter of section eight, now owned by Mrs. Arnold, west half, and A. Easton, east half. Mr. Morgan built his house—probably the second one in our territory—upon the place where Mrs. Arnold now lives, but just on the east side of the sluice. He remained here until 1854, when he sold out, and after several moves brought up at Plymouth, Indiana, where he now lives. Mr. Morgan was quite a scholarly fellow, and much given to putting up jokes upon his neighbors.

Joseph Elliot came to Illinois from near Boston, Mass., and for a time stopped in Du Page County. He came to Mazon Precinct, and in 1849, took up a quarter section—one eighty on section 24, and the adjoining eighty on section 23. He lived for awhile in a rough shanty upon the farm now owned by Mrs. Henrietta Dodge. His shanty experience was unpleasant; the winter was exceedingly cold, and the bleak unbroken winds of the prairie whistled through every crevice of the rude dwelling, making a music for the benumbed occupants not at all inviting. He afterward built a house upon his own premises, where he lived for about twenty-five years, when he sold out and moved with his son—Henry Elliot—to California. Two years since he contracted small pox and died, and his sacred dust forever sleeps on the slope beyond the mountains. Henry Leach now owns and cultivates "the old farm" and it is one of the best kept places in Greenfield. Upon an unlucky day some four years since, the humble cottage, for a quarter century the home of "Uncle Joe" Elliot, went up in flame and smoke, and the imposing farm house of Mr. Leach now marks the spot.

John Kelso, one of the early settlers, came here from Indiana in 1849, and located on the east bank of the Mazon—on section 12. After a few years he sold to the late Robert Wood and moved to South-eastern Kansas, where he died some ten years ago. The farm was sold a year since to James Mix, a speculator in coal lands from Kankakee.

Milo Wilcox came to this county at an early date, and for a few years lived near the West Mazon; in 1849 he took up the southeast quarter of section 15, and put up a little house on the bank of the creek. He lived here but a short time when he sold to Charles Roe, a Methodist preacher. Mr. Wilcox finally moved down onto the northeast quarter of section 12, now a part of the Wilson estate, where he died. George Wilcox, a son, is now a well-to-do farmer in Pilot township, Kankakee County. Myron, another son, was married three years since in Chicago, to quite a noted woman, and taking his wife he went to China as a Methodist missionary. With all that vital force begotten by early life and training upon these Western prairies, he now pours salvation into the untutored ears of the "heathen Chinee."

George F. Spencer came from Monroe County, New York, and located upon the southeast quarter of section one, putting up a house on the east bank of Cranery Creek, where he still lives.

Mr. Spencer brought with him from the East a good constitution and good habits; these were his stock in trade, and these have won him a competency. He had another quality and a virtue too, a contented mind. Of the sixteen tax payers that were here when Mr. Spencer came, he is the *only* one now residing upon the original purchase, and *one* of three, to remain in the township. Mr. Spencer has made himself a fine home, large orchard, fine shade and ornamental trees, good fences, good buildings and all that belong to a well-ordered farm. He has lived here through thirty-two eventful years; thriving villages have sprung up around him, railroads have been built on every side. The rank grasses of the early years have given way to golden grain; where the wild deer roamed unalarmed and the wolf dug his hole unscared, he sees a harvest of ripening corn. The lonely hut of the pioneer has been replaced with homes of luxury and splendor, and Lazarus with his rags has made room for Dives in his golden armor. School-houses have been built around him, and the children of education are pressing back the tribes of the ignorant.

Nelson Clapp came here in 1849, and built a little house on the bank of the sluice, on the northwest quarter of Sec. 22. He lived there a short time when he sold out and moved out on Grand Prairie. About ten years ago, when on his way home from Gardner, he was taken suddenly ill—we think with cholera morbus, and stopped at C. K. Snyder's, where he died.

Benjamin Banister came the same year as Clapp and built on the east line of section fifteen. The place is now the north half of Wm. Kewin's farm.

Thos. McCartney came here from Ohio about the same time, and lived a half mile north of Banister's, late the home of Frank Glass.

We have now briefly noticed about all that were here at the time of township organization, April, 1850. Prominent among those who came a little later, were Alexander and Kennedy Brown, J. W. Hull and Robert Atkinson. Brown sold out several years since and moved away. Hull and Atkinson are both citizens of Gardner, the latter a dealer in grain and coal.

We are under obligations to Nelson La Force, J. W. Hull and Robert Atkinson for most of the facts connected with the first settlement of Greenfield.

ROADS AND BRIDGES.

The Greenfield highways are generally laid out upon the section lines; there are a few exceptions, to wit: the road running south from Snyder's mill in Gardner to the Livingston County line—five miles, passes through the center of five sections, and the road running south from the iron bridge, known as Nason's, passes through sections 14 and 53, eighty rods from the east line.

During the early years, while travelers could keep upon the native prairie sod, but little attention was paid to roads; but as the years went by and travel increased and was concentrated by the fencing of the farms, throwing up grades and opening ditches became a necessity. Although considerable work had been done and quite a sum of money expended, our roads, where much traveled, were in wretched condition. Three years ago James Cook bought a grading machine and began operation upon our highways, and the work has been kept up since, until now nearly all our roads are well graded. Under the thorough work of our highway commissioners for three years, our roads have steadily improved; but in wet seasons they continue the bane of this otherwise delightful country. It is a fact, well demonstrated, that prairie muck is a poor material for constructing roads. Macadamized roads are expensive, but something of the kind must be made before we can have good roads in wet seasons.

The first *bridge* to span the Mazon in Greenfield, was a wooden structure at Nason's ("three mile house"), built by John F. Peck, of Gardner, in the winter of 1867-8. It was 200 feet in length and 20 feet above low water; this bridge stood the ravages of flood and time until 1878, when it was condemned by the commissioners, and replaced by an iron bridge 150 feet in length. There were two spans of 75 feet each, supported by stone butments with a middle pier. The structure of stone and iron, looking as permanent as the stream itself, was taken from its moorings by a cyclone the following summer, and the present one, of heavier iron, put in its place. Bridges were built across the creeks at Goodson's and Snyder's on "Snyder's Lane," some time before the first bridge at Nason's; both of these were wood; the latter was replaced a year since ('81) by stone butments and iron superstructure; the former at this writing (September, 1882), is being torn down to make room for stone and iron. An iron bridge—stone butments—was put in across the creek, four miles south of town on the "mill road" last year, and this year one is going in at Andrews of the same material. Many of the bridges over the smaller streams being "worn out in the service," are being replaced this year by iron. The Greenfield highway commissioners will expend this season, five thousand dollars for iron bridges.

FIRST BIRTH, DEATH AND MARRIAGE.

Greenfield's first birth was George Miller, born in spring of 1850, to Dr. and Mrs. James Miller. George grew to maturity, worked some on the farm, clerked in his father's drug store in Gardner; was married four years since and moved to Florida, where he now resides.

The first death, was that of George Beal, who came here from Guernsey County, Ohio, with Robert Finley's family in the spring of 1849. He was a young man yet in his "teens"—full of hope and promise; but a hot season, undue exposure, and surface water, brought on dysentery, from which he died before the first summer in the west had ended. The obsequies were conducted in Mr. Finley's log cabin, where he had died. A neighbor offered a prayer, three or four chanted a mournful hymn, and two or three rude wagons followed the remains to Wheeler burying ground, where they were interred; there still he sleeps, the first of *our* " sacred dust."

The first marriage was that of Henry Brown to Amanda —— (we have failed to get the whole name), a sister-in-law of Daniel Fuller, the officiating justice. The marriage was solemnized at Fuller's house, now owned by M. Bookwalter, and known as the " Bachman farm."

The date of this, the first nuptial tie was June or July, 1851. The magic words which made the twain one, are said to have been these: " Henry do you love Amanda? 'Yes.' Amanda do you love Henry? 'Yes.' Then I pronounce you man and wife by God."

EARLY ELECTIONS AND OFFICERS.

In another place we have noticed the organization of township and origin of name. This was at first "town meeting" held at the house of Milo Wilcox, where Calvin Cotton now lives, first Tuesday in April, 1850.

At this meeting seventeen votes were polled, and the following officers elected: Supervisor, Franklin Morgan; town clerk, Nelson La Force; assessor, Robert Glass; overseer of poor, Taylor Bradfield; collector, Nelson La Force; highway commissioners, Robert Finley, Robert Wood, and John Kelso: constables, Thomas McCartney and Jachin Banister; justice of the peace, Daniel Fuller; path-master, Taylor Bradfield. At the next town meeting, April 1, 1851, the same officers were re-elected, except Robert Finley, highway commissioner, who was replaced by Daniel Fuller, and Thomas McCartney, constable, by Daniel Otis. Two path-masters were elected: Taylor Bradfield and Joseph Elliot. Twenty-three votes were polled at this election. During this year La Force concluded to go back to New York—thinking, no doubt, that the pleasure that a wife could give was preferable to the honors of office. Oliver Williams was appointed his successor and held both offices (clerk and collector) until April, 1853. A. J. Brown was elected clerk to succeed Williams, but failing to qualify, James W. Snyder was appointed. In addition to those mentioned who officiated during the early years, were Dr. James Miller, supervisor and, later, justice of the peace; William B. Royal, supervisor; Chester K. Snyder, town clerk; Milo Wilcox, justice of the peace; D. B. La Force, assessor. The present town officers are: Louis Germain, supervisor; John H. Coles, town clerk; Henry Leach, assessor; H. K. Lovejoy, collector; C. K. Snyder, G. W. Melbourn, and A. W. Root, commissioners of highways; Isaac B. McGinnis and J. H. Coles, justices of the peace; Isaac C. Persels and Fred. G. Thompson, constables; J. H. Coles, B. D. Parker and Wm. Kewin, school trustees. From seventeen voters in 1850, we have increased to about 325 in 1882. At the last Presidential election we cast 305 votes. Politically Greenfield is most emphatically Republican —at the election of the lamented Garfield the "tally-sheet" showed 39 Greenback tickets, 41 Democratic and 225 Republican.

Our township residents of to-day are, as regards place of birth and nationality, thoroughly mixed. The "Scully prairie" in the southwest, embracing over two thousand acres, owned by Wm. Scully in Ireland, is cultivated almost entirely by Danes and Norwegians. The northern and central parts are generally settled with people from the New England and Middle States. In the southeast are quite a number of well-to-do Irish families. Every State east of us to the Atlantic has sons and daughters upon the prairie. They have come from the classic towns of Massachusetts and the "back woods" of Ohio, from the malarious bottoms of the Wabash and the Dominion across the lakes, from the White mountains of New Hampshire and the fruitful gardens of little Jersey, from the green hills of Vermont and the historic valley of the Mohawk. Nor is this all; many countries across the sea are represented here. Out of Scandinavian snows they have come, and from the shores of the Baltic; from the busy marts of old England, and Scotland's Grampian hills; from the bogs of the Emerald Isle and the slopes beyond the Rhine. These are the people that are here to-day. They came with little means—poor in purse but rich in hope. In the bosom of our virgin soil they plowed deep furrows and scattered good seed, and the yield has been "an hundred fold."

In the settlement of every new country there is commonly more or less of the "eventful;" some "wonderful adventures" and "hair-breadth escapes" that enter into the warp and woof of its history, that give spice and aroma to what must otherwise be a dry and insipid literature. Unfortunately for the writer, and for the reader who has a taste for tragedy, our chronicles reach not back to the remote past. Our first settlements are within the memory of the middle aged. The cruel wars with the Black Hawk chief and his allies had years been over. The death song of the relentless savage and the wail of his helpless victim were forever hushed. The smoke of peace had curled up to heaven, and quiet reigned throughout the border. The council fires had gone out upon the shores; the cabins of the red men were in the dust, and their war-cry had faded away in the untrodden West.

The prairie wolves were here, and while no one was ever injured by them, many a belated traveler was badly scared. They howled in the darkness along the lonely pathways, and men of good courage were startled by their unwelcome nearness, and were only too glad to reach home and shut back their noisy company. Plenty of deer were here in the early years, and venison at the farmer's board frequently figured largely in the bill of fare. In those days a drove of a dozen were sometimes seen in close proximity to the settler's cottage. At night in winter they would seek the groves along the creeks for shelter. C. K. Snyder relates how he and his cousin, a young Wood, hunted them one cold winter's night. A drove was known to come every night to a certain clump of trees for shelter. Wood having had more experience was master of ceremonies. He proposed that each climb a tree, a little distance apart, and keep breathlessly still until the wild ruminants should seek their accustomed retreat, when they would fire upon them from their elevated positions. Snyder climbed his tree, fixed himself astride a limb, and Wood passed up his gun, telling him under no consideration must he speak, but if likely to freeze he might whistle. S. found his perch a desperate cold one, but being "gamey" and after game he proposed to wait.

The night being bitter cold and his position such that he could not move, he was soon chilled to the bone and thought to whistle; but he could not, his mouth would not pucker! his lips were mute. His tongue, however, loosened lively! Wood came to his rescue. The deer that were afar off heard his voice and stood well aloof. Mr. S. was often afterward reminded of his tree top experience, and the little episode is still fresh in his memory.

The first *mowing machine* ever used in Greenfield was made in Ottawa, and was brought by Alexander and Kennedy Brown in the fall of 1852.

The first *tile draining* was done last year by C. K. Snyder, upon the Nason farm S.E. ¼. Sec. 7, and by J. C. Lutz on N. W. ¼, same section. Mr. Lutz has laid this season over three miles of drain and will add to it as fast as tile can be procured. George Goodson will put in two car loads upon his farm this year; J. S. Small one car load and Dr. Taxis one car load each. This is the extent of underdraining in Greenfield up to date; so far as tested it has proven eminently satisfactory; so much so that doubtless hundreds of miles will be laid in the near future. For these lowlands, by nature so poorly drained, stigmatized "frog ponds" and "mortar beds," despised by many and forsaken by few, tile draining is our hope. No enterprise in which our farmers can engage promises so well. With this well done, we have nothing to wish, nothing to fear, no country can bear our laurels. Our fields will blossom like the rose, and our granaries will be the pride of our commonwealth.

A *wolf hunt* in which one of the best of our early settlers very nearly lost his life, will be of sufficient interest to warrant its publication here. Although our hero was a little outside of our precinct, we are in possession of the facts which will not likely reach the ears of the other historians, and hence we take the liberty to write them. John Wheeler, with his family, came to Mazon Precinct from Pennsylvania in 1846 and located in what was, four years later, named Goodfarm,—northeast quarter, section two, now Goodrich estate. At the time of which we write his place was upon the outskirts of the settlement. To the south there was not a mark of civilization short of the Vermillion River, a distance of twenty-five miles. In December,'47, there having been a fall of snow, Mr. Wheeler and one or two others started out to hunt wolves which were plenty. Being well mounted they struck out boldly to the south, across the snowy plain. After going quite a distance they struck a wolf track which they continued to follow for several miles, when all but Wheeler were tired of the chase and turned about and rode home. He, being more determined than the others, rode on in pursuit of his game, but by this time snow was falling thickly, the tracks were obscured and he, too, thought to return. He was now many miles from home, the winds were sweeping wildly about him and cheerless darkness was coming on apace. Chilled by the cold and storm he alighted from his horse, thinking to warm a little by walking. The horse was startled at something, and with a bound pulled the rein through Wheeler's benumbed fingers, and sped away like an arrow through the storm. The unfortunate man following the tracks of his steed, pressed on as fast as he could through the heavy drifts. However it was to no purpose; soon every footprint was obliterated; night closed in around him her sable pall, and in a desert of shifting snows, he was alone. Through the pitiless storm he plodded his weary way, knowing not whither he was tending. On and on, breasting the huge drifts, until his very vitals seemed frozen within him. Exhausted with ceaseless effort he sank down in the snow. Digging for himself a little pit in the drift, he found the cold was less severe, and getting a little rest he raised himself up and made another struggle for home. Again his chilled and weary limbs succumbed; again he pitted his body in the drift. This process was repeated eight or nine times; as the night wore on the cold increased; at last he could not stand. He planted his rifle in the drift, pressing the snow about it, that it might stand erect, and serve as a guide to those who might come in search. His very blood seemed frozen in his veins, the last ray of hope had fled his breast, and with a prayer for wife and babes upon his mute lips he lay down to die. He did not die; with the morning light he spied the cabin of John Brown, and began crawling toward it. Mrs. Brown was the first to see him; his clothes frozen and covered with snow alarmed her. Mr. B. helped him to the house and when sufficiently recovered, to his own home, about five miles west. Brown lived where H. Jackman does now—center sec. 33, Braceville.

CHAPTER XI.*

GARDNER—TOWN PLATTING—NAMING—FIRST BUILDINGS—INHABITANTS—IMPROVEMENTS—COAL AND MINING INTERESTS—SOCIETIES—SCHOOLS—CHURCHES—BUSINESS FIRMS AND INDIVIDUALS, ETC.

GARDNER was laid out immediately after the completion of the Chicago & Alton railway in 1854. The first town plat covered an area of 160 acres, namely: The southeast quarter of section four, Greenfield. The original town site belonged to Henry A. Gardner, J. C. Spencer and C. H. Goold. Gardner was chief engineer of the C. & A. railroad company during the construction of their line. He did the surveying of the original town, and for him the village was named. Gardner did a great deal of engineering afterward upon lines running in and out of Chicago; died some five years since. Goold and Spencer, who was also a railroad engineer, were then dealing in lands and town lots; the former is still a resident of the county, residing in Morris. The territory first platted was divided into blocks, twenty-seven in number; but owing to the railroad running diagonally across the site, they were not uniform in shape nor size. About ten years later the town had reached such proportions that more room was in demand, and a part of the north half of section nine was laid out in lots and described as Price's first and second addition, Peck's addition, Hyatt's addition and Finley's addition. The east part of the southwest quarter of section four was quite early platted and is known as Willis' addition to Gardner. The south half of sec. 4 and the north half of 9—one mile square, is the territory now incorporated.

Gardner was incorporated in February, 1867, containing at that time about four hundred inhabitants. The first village trustees were John H. Coles, Amos Clover, W. W. McMann, F. Lathrop and Louis Germain. George Milner, the village school master, was the first clerk of the board, and J. H. Coles the first president, and also first police magistrate.

The first dwelling house built in town was the home of the "section boss" on the east side of the C. & A. track. The house has undergone some repairs and still serves the purpose for which erected. The building in the north part of town, known as the "barracks," was the second house in order of construction. It was built by Absalom Gleason, the first postmaster, and served as the first post-office. It has served the town as post-office, store, dwelling and boarding house, paint shop, etc. The old house still stands, but tenantless; the marks of advancing years are clear, and speedy decay is sure. Gleason is now living in Rose County, Kansas.

The *first hotel* was the "Eagle," 18x36, a story and a half high, built by G. R. Taxis and Scott Armitage during the summer of 1855. While building, the carpen-

---

* By Dr. C. M. Easton.

ters slept on shavings in a box car, on the C. & A. side track; this was the best the young town could give. During the night they were bunted hither and thither by passing trains; never knowing when retiring, where they would find themselves in the morning. The builders, Taxis and Armitage, have laid away the jack plane and hammer—the former is now circuit clerk, and the latter for many years has served the U. S. Express company as their Gardner agent. George Allen, for whom the little tavern was built, and who provided the first *menu*, now lives in Chebanse, Iroquois County. Allen, as caterer, was succeeded by J. W. Hull, he by Chas. Royal, and he by S. N. Underwood, who conducted the business for many years. Four or five years ago the hotel was remodeled and more than doubled in size; the name was changed to the "Gardner House" and James Cook entered as proprietor. Mr. and Mrs. C. still provide the "bill of fare."

The *first store* was kept by Chas. & Wm. Royal, opened in 1855, in a little building on the West side, where O. P. Stumph's building now stands. The store room was a diminutive affair and the stock of goods never exceeded the capacity; upon nail kegs and shoe boxes were seated a number of the "first settlers," who in point of gossip have not been outdone in these later years. The Royals are now living near Portland, Oregon. They were succeeded in the store by Chas. E. Gardner, who looked after the trade for a number of years, and was finally elected sheriff of the county. He died at his home in Gardner in 1866. I. F. Benson was one of our first merchants, coming here and going into business in the fall of 1856. He commanded quite a trade here for several years, but financially was not successful. During his last years he speculated considerably in coal lands. He died suddenly two years ago in Chicago, in the bath-room of his hotel. He put up the brown building on the West side, which is known as the "Benson store." The first warehouse built in town was put up by Charles Booth, east side of C. & A. track, where Atkinson's elevator lately stood. It was built in 1857, Taxis & Armitage doing the carpenter work as usual. A. V. Eversoll bought the building and moved it up the track to where it now stands. It was afterward fitted up for a grist-mill, and for a few years did considerable grinding. Corn is still ground there in considerable quantities. A few years since it was generally overhauled and converted into an elevator, while the milling apparatus was improved. It is now owned by Snyder & Son, who are running it to a good purpose.

Charles Johnson, a tinner, from Kentucky, built the first sidewalk in Gardner, on the north end of Liberty street. Joseph Hall built the first garden fence, and Virginia M. Hawley planted the first flowers, on Washington avenue, where Henry Donaldson now lives.

The country being sparsely settled, the growth of the town was slow up to the time of the sinking of the Gardner coal shaft in 1864, when it started up with new life. At that time Morgan & Hart put up a store on the West side, now owned by John Allison, occupied by Truesdell & Wylie, and put in quite an extensive stock of general merchandise. Business was entirely confined to the West side until the spring of 1867, when Lutz & Foote opened up a general store on the East side, in the building now occupied by H. C. Goold as a drug store.

The *first brick* building put up in town was by McMann's drug store in 1869. The Commercial House, 50 by 60, three stories, was begun August 2d of the same year and completed the winter following. R. R. Stone was the first landlord. He was succeeded by Wm. Smith, John Southcomb, A. K. Stiles, Rowland Price, James Wilson and one or two others. Mrs. Nancy A. Wilson, widow of James Wilson, is now owner of the property and provider of the *menu*. The hotel was built, and for some time owned by A. K. Stiles and Rowland Price. No. 3 Commercial block was built a year later. In 1872 the brick row, numbers 4, 5, 6, 7 and 8 Commercial block was built by Jones, Price, McClure and Kloft. The five stores were destroyed by fire Christmas night, 1878. This was the most destructive fire the town has known; besides the loss of building, the destruction of goods amounted to many thousands of dollars. The losers on stocks were: O. P. Stumph, No. 4, drugs; R. B. Huss, No. 5, dry goods and groceries; C. E. Parker, clothing, and T. F. Lippengood, boots and shoes, No. 6; Pratt, Martin & Phelps, dry goods and groceries, No. 7; Wm. Kloft, saloon fixtures, No. 8.

The "city hall" was built by A. S. Martin and Louis Germain in 1868, and was first occupied by Lebrecht, a Jew, with boots, shoes and groceries. The elevator in front of the Commercial House was built in 1869 by E. W. Cole, of Chicago, and is one of the best buildings of its kind in this part of the country. It is now owned and operated by Lutz & Germain. The brown elevator, which is now being moved to the north part of town onto the line of the K. & S. railroad, owned and operated by Robert Atkinson, was built in the winter of 1872-73 by R. Turner.

RAILROADS.

Gardner has two railroads, the Chicago, Alton & St. Louis and the Kankakee & Seneca. The first was built in 1853-54, the first passenger train over the line, passing through Gardner upon the morning of the 24th of August, 1854. The line through here is double tracked; runs five passenger trains each way daily and takes rank with the best thoroughfares in the State. The second was built last year, 1881, and the first regular trains were put on the 1st of February of this year. The K. & S. is a short line connecting the Cincinnati, Indianapolis & Chicago, with the Chicago & Rock Island. It is a well constructed road, now running two trains daily each way. The people of Gardner and immediate vicinity gave $3,000 for right of way. C. K. Snyder was the first ticket agent of the Chicago & Alton at this station, receiving his appointment about two weeks after the completion of the road. The company provided no building for an office, but gave Snyder a tin trunk in which to carry his tickets, books and valuable papers. Gardner was then a "town without houses" and the agent boarded with his uncle, two miles south. Going home at night after the "eleven o'clock train," on foot and alone, wading through wet grass breast high, hearing the bark of the prairie wolves almost within reach of a walking stick, was the experience of the "first agent." B. N. Haslett was the first agent of the Kankakee & Seneca road.

COAL INTERESTS, SHAFTS, ETC.

In 1862 the Gardner people began to take interest in the coal product, with which the town and vicinity were thought to be under-laid, and by subscriptions, money was raised and drill tests made. These were satisfactory, but it was some time before arrangements could be made for sinking a shaft. December 1, 1863, James Congdon and Wm. H. Odell leased of H. A. Gardner, J. C. Spencer, J. R. Reese, T. C. Meyer and C. H. Goold, the north part of the village plat, namely: Blocks 1, 2, 3, 4, 5, 6, 7, 8, 9, 10, 11, 12 and 25, also lots 1, 2, 3, 4, 5, 6, 7, 8 and 9 in block 26, for mining purposes. By the terms of this lease, Congdon and Odell were to have what coal they could raise during the first seven years free, after which they were to pay a royalty of six cents per ton. The Gardner people raised $2,000 by subscriptions for Congdon and Odell, as an inducement to undertake the enterprise. The work of sinking the shaft was begun about the first of January, 1864, but owing to some mismanagement, when down sixty feet, the sides caved in, the hole was abandoned and another begun. The work went on slowly, Congdon selling out his interest to Odell before the coal was reached, which was in the fall of 1864. July 1, 1865, Odell sold to Wm. A. Steel and Thomas Kerr. December 1st, of the same year, Steel sold one half of his interest to D. G. Wells for $7,000. On the 22d day of January, 1867, Steel, Kerr and Wells sold out to Aaron K. Stiles for $25,000. Stiles sold out to the Gardner Coal Company April 17, 1872; it soon after fell into the hands of the C., W. & V. Company, who continued to operate it until the summer of 1874, when they closed it up. The quality of the coal mined at this shaft was pronounced by experts to be fully equal to any in the State.

While Stiles had control of the shaft he started the manufacture of brick out of the fire clay, giving employment to quite a number of men. The most of the brick buildings in town now were made from the brick there and then molded. They were generally rough, but for "staying" qualities they were excellent. The life of this shaft was ten years. The distance from the surface to the top of the coal 180 feet. Thousands of tons of the "dusky diamonds" were brought to the surface and sent to Chicago and other markets. The mining gave employment to lots of hands, and business of all kinds was brisk. An accident at the shaft which cost the lives of two employes, will be of sufficient interest to justify its record. E. L. Sutton, Alex. McKinzie, Wm. Harwood and Harry Watts had just stepped upon the cage to go below when the rope broke and all went crashing to the bottom, a distance of two hundred feet from the landing where they started. It was in the evening, dark and gloomy, but the knowledge of the accident soon spread through the village, and soon quite a number had gathered at the top of the fatal pit. It was some time before things could be fixed, so the unfortunate men could be hauled up. Those that were at the top were appalled at the moans of distress that came up through the darkness from the helpless victims below. Harwood received internal injuries, from which he died that night; Watts had his spine lacerated; lived twenty days; Sutton got a badly fractured leg, and McKinzie received a dislocated ankle and other injuries. Sutton and McKinzie recovered with slight lameness.

In 1865 a company was organized, called the "Joint Stock Coal Mining Company of Gardner," and on the 8th of June began the sinking of a shaft a little southwest of town, on the line of the C. & A. railway. They got down only forty or fifty feet when they struck a powerful vein of water, and after spending all the means at command, in the vain endeavor to get rid of it, that enterprise was abandoned. In 1874 the railway company laid a pipe under ground from this shaft to their tank in town, since which the iron horses have never wanted for drink. Last fall Taylor Williams, of Sterling, commenced sinking a shaft a mile east of town, was very much delayed by the water, and did not get down until this spring, and when the work was completed all were dismayed in learning that there was no coal there. After spending a large amount of money it, too, was abandoned, and the buildings moved south to near the center of section ten, where, at this writing a shaft is being lowered. We have good reasons for believing that this shaft will not be lowered in vain. Five drill tests have been made near by, showing, at a depth from 156 to 200 feet, a coal vein from two feet eight inches to six feet in thickness.

SCHOOLS AND SCHOOL-HOUSES.

The first Gardner school was taught in a shanty east of the "section house," by Lizzie Russell; the next was in a little house west of the mill, by a Mrs. Brown; after that, school was taught in a little shanty west, across the street from where the Baptist church now stands. Stephen Gray moved the shanty down near the stock yards, and lived there for many years.

The *first school-house* proper, 22 by 36, was built by Taxis and Armitage on the site where J. O. Edmunds now lives, in 1857. J. H. Armitage taught first school; he was succeeded by David Bookwalter, and he by Virginia M. Hawley, who a little later became the wife of Dr. J. B. Taxis. In 1867 a new school-house was built on the east side of town, 28 by 60, two stories, the town having outgrown the first —Peter Hyatt, builder. By 1872 this was found too small and a two story addition, 28 by 44 was put on the rear by J. F. Peck. In February, 1875, the building caught fire from the furnace, and burned to the ground. That summer, the present school building, 52 by 1872, two story brick was erected at a cost, exclusive of furniture, of $8,044. J. F. Peck, architect and builder. Five teachers are now employed, and about 236 pupils enrolled. Miss Elizabeth Baumgardner is principal; Misses Mary A. Bush, Lettie J. Smiley, Mary E. Parker and Belle Overman, assistants.

SECRET SOCIETIES.

Gardner Lodge No. 573, A. F. and A. M. was organized May 24, 1866; received its charter Oct. 6, 1868. The first members were I. F. Benson, W. H. Schoomaker, Ed. Crane, J. W. Hull, Amos Clover, W. W. McMann, Wm. Hart, A. DeNormandie, Henry Elliott and H. V. Whalen. Its present membership is 58, with the following officers: W. M., H. V. Whalen; S. W., Henry Leach; J. W., C. G. Collins; S. D., J. F. Peck; J. D., F. A. Pagle; Treas., James Savage; Sec'y, John McGinnis; Tyler, J. W. Hull. Meetings every alternate

Saturday evening; hall over Dr. McMann's drug store.

Gardner Lodge No. 515, I. O. of O. F., organized Oct. 15 h. 1873; meetings every Wednesday evening in hall, Jones building. Present membership, 50; officers: N G., F. P. Sickels; V. G., F. A. Pagle; Sec'y, R. O. Wood; Treas., C. H. Cotton.

METHODIST CHURCH.

The first preachers in these parts were Methodists, and held services at private houses fifteen years before Gardner was known. Charles Roe was a Methodist preacher; lived on the southeast corner of section 15, where C. H. Cotton now lives. He used to have meetings at his own house and at Daniel Abbot's on the west side of Sec. 5, where Benjamin Bookwalter now lives. Abbot was a Methodist preacher also; he would sometimes preach at home and sometimes at Cotton's. Those who attended these services beside the families of the ministers, were the Bradfields, McCartneys, Browns and J. W. Hull. Abbot moved from here to Iowa, and Roe went back to New York where he died. The Gardner M. E. society was organized in the spring of 1858, and attached to the Mazon circuit, of which Rev. Thomas Watson was minister in charge. The first members were Wm. B. Royal and wife; J. H. Coles and wife; Wm. Hart and wife; Robt. Glass and wife; Joseph Hall and wife, and Mrs. Cynthia W. Hastings. Wm. Hart was appointed the first leader. The pastors in order of succession after Watson, were: John Grundy, J. B. Dillie, A. E. Day, John Cosler, Samuel Hart, H. Tiffany, Wm. M. Collins, D. H. Cridler, A. C. Price, Matthew Evans, B. F. Wonder, J. W. Denning, A. D. Moore, M. C. Eignus, A. Bower, D. W. Brown, T. R. McNair and C. W. Green. "Gardner Circuit" was formed in 1867. The *first church* edifice was built by the Protestant Methodists in 1856, corner of Jackson St. and Washington avenue. Fayette Doud, a local preacher, did the carpenter work and furnished a large amount of the money used in construction. Doud held a lien on the building for $500, which the Protestants were unable to pay; accordingly in Feb'y, 1864 he sold the building to the M. E. Society for the amount of his claim. Under the able ministry of Rev. Eignus in 1875, the congregation outgrew the building, and a new one 34 by 56, was commenced corner of Jefferson and Monroe Sts. The church was dedicated Jan. 9th, 1876; cost about $3,000; Wm. Hastings, contractor and builder. The society now numbers seventy-five members, and our meeting house is free from debt. The old building was sold and moved to Depot St. and converted into a saloon, showing how sometimes a *good* thing is put to a *bad* use. It is now used for harness shop and tin shop.

PRESBYTERIAN CHURCH.

This society was organized September 5, 1858, under the ministry of Rev. L. H. Loss and Rev. S. H. Waldo. The meeting at which the organization was effected was held in the school-house. The society started with six ladies, no gentlemen joining; their names were Mrs. Abbie La Force, Mrs. Phebe Ann Wheeler, Mrs. Sarah M. Wright, Mrs. Susan Sawyer, Mrs. E. C. Benson, Miss Virginia M. Hawley. Rev. Waldo was the first minister in charge.

Of the six original members only two are now known to be living, namely: Mrs. Taxis née Miss Hawley, and Mrs. Wheeler. The pastors, after Rev. Waldo, in order of succession were: Revs. Alvah Day, E. G. Moore, Sextus E. Smith, F. B. Hargraves, J. G. Lyle, Joel Kennedy, S. H. Stevenson and Robert Watt. The school-house served the society for a chapel for several years, and after the school out-grew it and went to new quarters, it was rigged over and still used. After a time this building was moved to Depot street, and converted into a store, and occupied by McClure & Tolman for hardware; then the society used the Methodist church and the city hall. In 1871, under the able pastorate of Rev. Smith, they began the erection of a church edifice, brick, 32 by 56, corner of Elm and Main streets. It was completed and dedicated in the spring of 1872, and is now the society's place of worship. Many of the early members have passed to "the other shore." The number now on record is 35.

BAPTIST CHURCH.

Under the ministry of Rev. W. H. Card this society was organized in 1864 with seven members, namely: W. H. Card, Phillip Spaulding, Albert W. Willard, David M. Griswold, Mrs. L. E. Taxis, Robert Huston and H. J. Edmunds. The names of the ministers, so far as could be learned, are, beginning with the first: Revs. W. H. Card, — Colby, J. Gordon, John Higby, E. G. Sage and F. M. Mitchell. The society built a church 36 by 60 in 1868; in February of 1871 the building took fire in some way unknown, and burned to the ground. The same year a new brick church was begun on the same site, the same in size, with a conference room 24 by 30 added to the rear end, and was dedicated to the service of God, May 11, 1872. The construction of this building plunged the society into debt, and by which they were much embarrassed until Rev. Sage's ministry, two years since, when the obligations were generally paid. The present number of members is sixty-four. Each of the societies supports a Sabbath school with a fair attendance.

THE VILLAGE AS IT IS TO-DAY—ITS TRADE AND TRADERS.

Gardner has thus far achieved very little notoriety as a manufacturing town; its life and business have depended mostly upon the farming country surrounding it. As a grain market, especially for corn, it stands well with other railway towns. During the year 1880 nearly half a million bushels of corn and oats were shipped from this station; the numbers of fat cattle and hogs shipped, were they known, would make a good showing. The census of 1880 gave us a population of 788, which in the two years since has somewhat increased, so that now we number, likely, about 900. The business of to-day is mostly represented by the following gentlemen and firms, carrying stocks of dry goods and groceries: Lutz & Eldred, R. B. Huss, Phelps & Lewis, Truesdell & Wylie—four stores; restaurants, D. L. Strahl, George Hader; grain buyers, Snyder & Son, Lutz & Germain, Robert Atkinson; buyers and shippers of live stock, Germain & Clover; hardware dealers and blacksmithing, Smith & Rogers; blacksmithing, Atkinson & Erwin; hardware, Chas. V. Hamilton; dealer in farm implements, A. S. Martin; ready-made clothing,

Chs. E. Parker; banks—Exchange Bank. John Allison; Bank of Gardner, J. C. Lutz; meat markets, Harpham & Gray, E. I. Briggs; harness makers, Thos. Spiller, H. A. Eversoll; drugs, C. H. Goold, W. W. McMann; Harvey Eldred, dealer in furniture and undertaker; saloons, Mike Kern, E. D. Evans, Andrew Burt, John Schnmm, Joseph Houghton; physicians, J. B. Taxis, W. W. McMann, C. M. Easton and J. Underhill. Dr. Taxis has resided here since 1859, Dr. McMann since 1863; Dr. Underhill came later; Dr. Easton came in 1874. Notaries public, Isaac B. McGinnis and John Coles; attorneys at law, Clover & Clover. The present village trustees are: Harvey Eldred, George Smith, W. W. McMann, R. B. Huss, D. R. Keepers, Arnold Edmunds. Eldred is the president; H. A. Crawford, clerk.

CHAPTER XII.*

NETTLE CREEK TOWNSHIP—FIRST SETTLERS—LIFE IN A PRAIRIE COUNTRY—SCHOOLS, ETC.

NETTLE CREEK is the name applied by the settlers to the principal stream in this township, and from the stream the precinct takes its name. The Indians named the stream Little Mazon, from the number of nettles which were found growing luxuriantly upon the rich bottoms. The township which bears this name, forms the northwest corner of Grundy County, and originally consisted almost entirely of level prairie land. Along the creek from the eastern line of the township to the western line of Section 23, there was a considerable growth of oak and black walnut, but the rest was open prairie. A number of prairie runs, tributary to the main stream, cross the township in a southeasterly direction, but they have no valleys, and farmers till the land right up to the margin of the streams. The population is quite cosmopolitan in its character, Scotland, England, Ireland and Norway, of the European States, being represented, while no State of the Union can claim great preponderance in the number of her sons and daughters here.

The first pioneer was William Hoge. He was of Scotch descent, but was born in Loudoun County, Virginia; married in 1826. He found himself with a family to support and the prospect of acquiring a home in his native State very poor indeed. He resolved on a trip to the West in 1829, and attracted to this region of the country by the canal lands, bought 960 acres in that year. He returned to Virginia, and two years later, with his family and goods in a Winchester wagon, made the tedious journey over hill and stream to what is now Nettle Creek township. His first cabin, which is still pointed out, was a log structure situated within a few rods of his present residence, which was erected in 1845. Here he lived with his family, consisting of his wife and three children, with but one other family in what is now Grundy County. The nearest village was Ottawa. Here he got his mail and bought such supplies as could not be dispensed with and the country did not afford. When the insurrection of Black Hawk's band occurred, alarmed for the safety of his family, Mr. Hoge fled to Pleasant Grove, opposite the present village of Pekin. Happily the Indian trouble was soon over, and in August of 1832 the family returned to their frontier home. Samuel Hoge had come West in 1829 and started a store in Belmont County in company with his brother-in-law, Hendley Gregg, but after the Black Hawk war, selling out to his partner, he joined his brother in Nettle Creek in 1833. William Hoge located his land on Section 25, and later, as he was able, bought Section 24 and other land until he now owns

---

*By J. H. Battle.

something over 3,000 acres of land. Samuel first took up a claim in Erienna, but in 1835 came into Nettle Creek and bought Sections 21 and 22 and lands adjoining until he died in possession of something over 3,000 acres.

In the fall of 1837 John Gray, a Scotchman, and George Brouse, an Englishman, came into Nettle Creek together, the former locating on Section 20 and the latter on Section 17, their lands joining. Gray came on to his land in the following season and began his improvements, but Brouse, who was a bachelor and never married, did not come on for a year or two. In 1837 William Stephen came. He was a young unmarried man, and a native of Scotland. He had known Gray in the old country, and it was through him that he was led to take up his home in Nettle Creek. He was led to emigrate to America, however, by the glowing descriptions of the conutry, given by a Mr. Smith, Chicago's pioneer banker. Smith had gone to Scotland, his native land, to enlist capital in the formation of a stock company to invest in Illinois land, but while prosecuting this scheme the panic of 1837 was precipitated, and he was hurriedly called back to look after his affairs here. Mr. Stephen had intended to accompany Smith on his return, but the latter was obliged to leave so early that Mr. Stephen was obliged to make the trip later and alone. He came to Chicago, but found the banker absent on business, and being free to go where the inclination of the moment prompted, sought out his old friend Gray in Nettle Creek. He took up some land and stayed about one year, when, disgusted with the peculiar disadvantages of the place, he went into Kendall County.

He came right from the civilization of the city to a frontier community without the semblance of a village, and after breaking sod for a day or two, gave up the business here in disgust. He finally bought and improved a fine farm in Kendall County, but has been most of his time identified with Grundy County. About this time George Ballis came from New York and settled on Section 8, where he lived until about 1870, when he moved to Ford County, leaving no descendants here.

About 1840, a Mr. Conp came to Nettle Creek. He had bought a quarter section of land near Chicago, for which he had given his notes. He found it a hard matter to raise the money to make his payments, and his creditors seizing upon some property left on the place, took possession of his land. Giving up hope of prospering in that region he came to this township, entered into contract with Brouse to dig a division ditch, about a quarter section of land for another quarter section. To the fulfillment of this contract he brought an untiring energy, digging when the season permitted until far into the night, and in the meanwhile living in a sod house and practicing all sorts of economy. He achieved his task and started in the nursery business, with a fair prospect of success, but his old time creditors still holding his notes, learned he had got some property here, were about to levy on his land to satisfy his notes, and he was obliged to sell out to one of his neighbors to save anything out of his hard won property. In 1841 or '2, Thomas Loughhead came in from Mercer County, Pennsylvania. He was born of Scotch parents, in the north of Ireland, and emigrated to Canada during the Napoleonic wars. The vessel in which he embarked fell in with a French privateer and barely escaped capture, losing his chest of clothes and the hat from his head. He soon afterward met Mary Donley and married her, a little later coming to Pennsylvania. His wife was the daughter of a lady, the daughter of an Irish nobleman, who had eloped to this country with an Irish teacher. In the war of 1812, Mr. Longhhead was drafted, and served throughout the struggle as a private. His wife died before his coming into Illinois, but he brought a family of two boys and four girls, none of whom were then married. For three or four years he rented the farm of George Brouse, which he bought in 1847. The boys subsequently bought farms near by, and the girls engaged in teaching school. They enjoyed the advantages of liberal study, having attended the seminary at Hudson, Ohio. Another son, James, came to Nettle Creek subsequently, and stayed there about two years, buying the interest of the other heirs in the paternal estate, and finally selling it to a Mr. Moody. A year or two later, James P. Thompson, who had married one of the Loughhead daughters, followed his father-in-law to Illinois, and settled on the northeast quarter of section 19. The head of the Longhhead family died about 1855, and the different members have one by one gone to different parts of the country, leaving no descendants here.

Oliver Dix came here in 1844, from Oneida County, New York, and settled on section 8, and about the same time came Minard Waterman from the same State and settled on land which his father bought of Mr. Stephen, on section twenty. In the following year the Mossmans came into the township, William settling on the southeast quarter of section 17, and Hugh on the northeast quarter of section nine. About the same time came Simon Fry, from Maryland, and settled on section 7, where he is still living. In or about 1848, came Thomas and John Agan, buying land on section 31, where they now reside; in 1849, Isaac N. Brown came from Saratoga County, New York, and settled on section 4, and soon after him David Jamison, from Pennsylvania, and settled on the northwest quarter of section eighteen.

About 1845, the Norwegian element began to come into the township and it is astonishing to observe how rapidly they have supplanted the original settlers. Among the earliest of this class of foreigners were John Peterson, Ben Thornton, Ben Hall, Lars and Erasmus Sheldall, John Wing, G. E. Grunstead and others. In 1849, the population of the township was divided as follows: On section 1, H. A. Ford; on section 3, Baker Knox and R. Carpenter; on section 4, Isaac N. Brown, Lars and Erasmus Sheldall, John Wing and G. E. Grunstead; on section 7, John Peterson, Ben Thornton and Simon Fry; on section 8, Lars Likeness, Ben Hall, Edson Gifford and George Bullis; on section 9, Hugh Mossman; on section 10, Morgan Lloyd and S. H. Rider; on section 12, John Gibson, Alex. Bushnell, Ben Sears and Daniel David; on section 14, Charles McCann; on section 17, John and Thomas Loughhead, Oliver Dix and William Mossman; on section 18, David Jamison; on section 19, James P. Thompson; on section 20, John Gray and Minard Waterman; on section 22, Samuel Hoge; on section 25, William Hoge; and on section 31, Thomas and John Agan.

The first settlers of Nettle Creek were almost to a man of very limited means and cut off by the natural situation from any prospect of a village. The Hoges and Mr. Holderman early went into cattle raising, feeding them on the public lands, wherever water and grass afforded the most eligible site. The scarcity of timber here made fencing an expensive burden to the already sufficiently handicapped farmer, and some quite serious differences arose out of this combination of circumstances. The gradual development of the country, however, has long since removed these causes of irritation. Messrs. Hoge and Holderman still make cattle raising their principal occupation, some of this stock being high grades. Samuel Hoge came to the township rather "full handed," and has given more attention than others to the growing of fine blooded stock.

During the early history of this community, the nearest store and post-office was at Ottawa, and the nearest market at Chicago. As the country settled up, Morris was founded, and with Marseilles on the southwest divided the local trade so that Nettle Creek could not afford sufficient patronage to justify a store here. A log saw-mill was constructed by William Hoge on Nettle Creek, about six rods from his house, which did a moderate business for some ten years, but the dam washed out one winter and the mill was allowed to rot down. Later, during the construction of the canal, a steam mill was erected on canal lands in section 23, which furnished material to the contractors, but passed away with the occasion that brought it. The only approach to a store was attempted in 1876, when Zach. Severson added to his boot and shoe shop on section 8, a small stock of groceries. This was too late a date for such a venture to succeed, and it has been discontinued.

The leading social event which may be noted, is the first white birth in the township, that of James, a son of William Hoge. He is probably the first white child born in the county, and is now living in Saratoga township. The first death in Nettle Creek was a child of Warren Chapin, who lived on section 8, and where in the absence of any cemetery, the child was buried.

In 1835, the Hoge brothers feeling the necessity of a school for their children, built a split log house for the purpose, on the land of William Hoge. It was a neat structure for the time, the roof formed of shakes, the floor of sawed planks, and plank desk and benches. The first teacher here was Maria Southworth, from the Fox River settlement at Milford. She taught two winters and had about nine scholars, receiving for her compensation $2.50 per week, which was paid by William Hoge. The building is still standing about 125 yards from Mr. Hoge's dwelling. Schools were held here until about 1857. The second school-house was erected on section 16. It did not serve long as it was not conveniently located. The next one was built near Mr. Brown's present residence, and this was subsequently abandoned and the single school of the township was taught in the town house, by Oliver Dix. In 1849, the township was divided into four school districts which have been since increased to seven.

The first start for church organization was about 1849 by the Congregational society under the labors of James Longhhead. He came to Illinois in 1845, on a call to the Big Grove church. He was a graduate of the Western Reserve College at Hudson, Ohio, and for several years after his graduation, took part in the slavery agitation, lecturing in favor of emancipation. He subsequently studied theology and preached several years in Ohio, when he accepted the call to Big Grove. Here he preached for two years, but in the meantime acting as an appointee of the Home Missionary Society, and establishing churches in various parts of the county. He had brought his father to Nettle Creek some years before; and was well acquainted with the character of the work needed to be done here. He was a man of great force of character and good practical judgment, and was the originator of the Congregational influence in Grundy County. On his first coming in 1845, he was impressed with the great need of evangelical work in Morris, and determined at the first opportunity to open up a field of labor here. He seems never to have lost sight of this determination, and in 1847 he moved to Morris and began by organizing a church here. While located here he preached in other parts of the county, and was instrumental in establishing churches in Mazon, Au Sable and elsewhere, beside in Nettle Creek. The church in this township was organized by members from Big Grove church, among whom were his brothers and sisters, John, Thomas, Margaret and Hannah, and Mr. and Mrs. J. W. Washburn. The church never built a place of worship, using the school-houses for this purpose until about 1868, when it became extinct as an organization. The church organized a Bible Society, and did good service for years.

The Methodist Church organized a society here about 1850, in which the three Mossman families, Mr. and Mrs. J. P. Thompson, Mrs. Fry and Reuben Aylesworth were leading members. The church used the residence of Oliver Dix as the first place of worship, and later held their meetings in the school-house as they now do. The membership now numbers about thirty persons, and holds services once in each fortnight, depending upon a "supply" from the Rock River Conference.

CHAPTER XIII.*

AU SABLE TOWNSHIP—LOCATION AND PHYSICAL CHARACTERISTICS—ITS EARLY SETTLEMENT—ITS NATURAL ATTRACTIONS—DRESDEN—MINOOKA—CHURCHES AND SCHOOLS.

AU SABLE township forms the northeast corner of Grundy County, and presents some of the finest natural scenery in this region. It is principally a fine rolling prairie, with a fringe of timber along the Au Sable Creek and the Illinois River. The eastern line is marked by a high rise of ground, which forms a watershed of limited extent, the drainage flowing in an easterly and westerly direction from this line. The termination of this ridge at the head of the Illinois is well worth going some distance to see. The high land continues almost to the river brink, affording an outlook over the low land of Felix and the country south for miles. The scene here presented, with its picturesque views along the river and the low meadows dotted with grazing herds, is found nowhere else in this county, and forms the object of many a pleasant drive. The northern tier of sections has a good elevation also, and that part of the town west of the Au Sable Creek. The valley of this creek, which flows a southwesterly course through the township to the northern line of section 30, and then makes a sharp turn to the east and another south to the Illinois in section 32, is low and wet. The soil of the upland is considerably mixed with sand and with a clay substratum, while the lowlands are characterized with a black swamp soil, with murky tendencies. It is a fine grazing country, and is largely used for this purpose, though the staple grains of this section are not overlooked by the farmers. It was here that some of the earliest settlers made their home.

The natural attractions of this township were such as to draw any who might be in the vicinity. It was a favorite winter resort of the Pottawatomies, and the favorite hunting ground of both white and red man. Marquis, though having his cabin at the mouth of the Mazon, could not resist the attractions of this side of the river, and partly to utilize a high and clear piece of ground, and partly to be nearer the natives, spent his summers at the mouth of the Au Sable Creek. In the winter he found the sheltered nook on the Mazon more comfortable. But Marquis could not properly be called a settler, as his purposes in the county were temporary, and he made no permanent improvement in either place. W. H. Perkins, although not the first settler, was one of the earliest to explore the township with that in view, and so well did he like it that as soon as he sought to build up a home of his own, he came back and took up his claim. He was a native of Oneida County, New York, and recognizing that the West was the only place for a young man without capital to get a start, came

---
*By J. H. Battle.

out, after some delays, to Chicago, in 1833. He was accompanied by Levi Hills, and arrived there September 23, 1833, and found characteristic evidence of the newness of the country in a camp of five thousand Indians, who had been gathered on the west side of Chicago. That night these travelers rested at Beaubien's hotel, which, as he expressed it, was kept "like one hell, and made money like dirt," and his guests had no reason to doubt the correctness of the statement in either particular. In the town Perkins met J. D. Caton, James H. Collins and a Mr. Snell, all from Oneida County, New York. On the next day Snell and Collins accompanied Mr. Perkins, all proceeding on foot, to explore the country. On noon of the 26th they reached the cabin of Chester House, located where Seward now is, in Kendall County. Here Mr. Perkins found an old acquaintance of his father, who had come out and settled in the previous May, and gladly volunteered to take his team and pilot the party in a prospecting tour of the vicinity. Under the guidance of Mr. House the party went south across sections 4 and 9, township 34, range 8, and returned. The next day they took the same route, going further south, but finally making an abrupt turn to the west, went to Holderman's grove. Here Mr. Perkins entered into an arrangement with Mr. Holderman to work some of his land. Here for two years, with no company but his three yoke of oxen, he plowed and planted. In 1835, having secured a wife, he came to Au Sable and settled on the northeast quarter of section eight. The first actual settler was Salmon Rutherford, a native of New York. He came in May, 1833, and settled on section twenty-six.

He was a man of an impulsive and determined disposition, and became a leading spirit in this township. He built an early hotel, the first one in the county, and gave its location the name of Dresden. An early stage line made this spot of some importance for a time, but it soon died out, the withdrawal of the stages giving a final blow to any pretensions it may have had.

Following Mr. Rutherford, came three families from Delaware County, Ohio, Henry Cryder, Zach. Walley, and N. H. Tabler. Mr. Cryder was a native of Virginia and came early to Ohio, from whence he came with Walley and Tabler, his son-in-law, and a family of unmarried children. Their goods were packed on a large wagon drawn by three yoke of oxen, while two two-horse wagons furnished the conveyance for the three families, and with these and eight or ten head of cattle, they made the journey across the country. They were not unacquainted with the exigencies of frontier life, and made little difficulty in performing the journey. The attractions of the "Au Sable country" were known for miles around, and its praises began to be sounded as soon as they reached the "Wabash country." Of course one wagon, however large, could bring only the barest household necessities for three families, but among these were the carpenter's tools of Mr. Cryder who was a mechanic. Arriving on the ground the men lost no time in erecting a temporary shelter. Logs were cut and a shed of three sides put up and covered with shakes, while along the open side a huge fire was maintained. These families reached their chosen home in October, and though late in the season for such rude accommodations, they found no trouble in making themselves comfortable with leaves for beds and logs for chairs and tables. Cabins were put up at once for each of the families, Cryder's on the southeast quarter of section eight, Tabler's on the north half of this quarter, and Walley's on section seventeen. This latter location proved unhealthful, and was subsequently changed for a site on the northwest quarter of section eight. These cabins were made in the usual style, with shake roof, puncheon floors and stick and clay chimneys. The floor of the loft was made from lumber which had to be procured at, and hauled across the prairie from Plainfield. The furniture was the product of such skill as the men possessed, and the timber of the basswood trees found here. A section of a good sized log, smoothed with a broad ax and furnished with a rough back and legs, supplied the absence of chairs. Rude bedsteads with the cords brought from Ohio, and "ticks" filled with leaves made a comfortable place to sleep. The manufacture of these household belongings occupied the small part of the fall, which remained after the cabins were completed. The winter proved a remarkably mild, open one, and very favorable for the new settlement.

About the same time with these families came John Beard* and settled on section thirty, where he was soon afterward joined by his son-in-law and his family. In the spring of 1834, Rodney House located on the northeast quarter of section nine, and in the same year three men by the name of McElroy came from Washington County, Vermont, and located on the southeast quarter of the same section. About this time D. M. Thomas came here from Ohio, and Leander Goss, marrying a daughter of Chester House, settled on the northeast quarter of section thirteen. William Lewis and his brothers were the next settlers, coming very soon after Thomas. Of the three brothers, William was a physician and located his claim on section twenty-five, Joseph on the southeast quarter of section thirteen, and Samuel on the southeast quarter of section fourteen, now owned and occupied by William Walter. In 1835, I. W. Rutherford, a physician, settled on the northeast quarter of section twenty-two, and commenced his improvements in the following year. Samuel Randall was an early settler, coming in with Salmon Rutherford as a young man. He afterward married and made a home here where he died. Thomas Carl was another settler who came in about 1836. The township was not slow in filling up. The work on the canal attracted a good many to this vicinity, and when the work stopped many without other resource took up the land which was unoccupied. These were chiefly natives of Ireland who had come from Canada in the employ of a canal contractor, and who now hold the political control of the township.

The land here was one literally "flowing with milk and honey." The great sweep of prairie which extended toward the northeast to the verge of the horizon was the resort of thousands of deer, chickens, and wolves; the river furnished fish in abundance, and the timber echoed with the lively clatter of the small game to which it gave a precarious shelter. The honey bee, the harbinger of civilization, preceded the early settlers here some six or eight

---

* His city at the head of the Illinois River is noted in the chapter on Felix township.

years, and had made the river bluffs famous for the stores of sweetness found in hollow trees along the streams. The Indians were very fond of this delicacy, and never failed to rifle a bee tree of its contents when they discovered it, but from the lack of proper facilities or the number and industry of the bees, vast stores of honey were accumulated to garnish the homely fare of the pioneer.

The winter of 1833-4 was very mild, and in January the weather came off warm and spring-like during the day, but with sharp cool weather at night. The bees deluded by the inviting warmth of the sun sallied from their hives, and becoming chilled, fell dead upon the light covering of snow which lay upon the ground. The new-comers were not at loss to read the meaning of this sign, and the Cryder settlement alone found thirty-three trees and secured their contents. There was, of course, nothing about the e pioneer establishments in which to store this vast amount of honey, and great basswood troughs were made for the purpose and filled. While this raid did not exterminate the bees of this section, the continued ravages of the settlers soon made these "rich finds" much less frequent, and those who enjoyed the sport united pleasure and profit in bee-hunting. An experienced hunter would go out in bright warm day in winter or late fall, and burn some honey-comb, which seldom failed to attract the game to the honey which was provided for them. Loading up with this, the bee would rise circling into the air and then fly straight to its tree, and it was the hunter's business to follow the fleet-winged insect closely and thus discover its secret. To do this required an expert, and there were but few who were marked for their success. Sometimes a number of bees from a single tree are attracted, and the going to and from the bait by these insects makes the line plain enough to be easily followed, but this is rare. In other cases, the best that can be done is to discover the direction of the bee's flight, and taking this—against the sun if possible—to stumble along with upturned gaze, scanning every tree for the tell-tale knot-hole or crack in the tree. But when the tree was found, the battle was but half won. The tree must be felled and the occupants were often found to be no feeble folk. When the hollow of the tree extended down to the point where the ax must penetrate it, the hunter was often obliged to decamp in hot haste as soon as the blows had aroused the swarm. David Bunch, of Norman, was noted for his success as a bee-hunter, and was greatly assisted by a dog which, in some incomprehensible way, had learned the secret of bee-hunting. Indeed, so keen was the animal's interest in the sport, that he occasionally found a tree entirely alone calling his master to the spot by his barking.

The bee was easily domesticated, and many of the settlers captured swarms, placed them in a section of a hollow tree, and in a short time had a constant source of supply for the table and the market. In many cases this was the principal resource for the sweetening used in the culinary work of the cabin, and was the basis of a favorite drink. "Metheglin" was made of steeped honey comb and honey fermented. It was counted an excellent drink and much preferred to cider, and when strengthened by age, became a powerful intoxicant. This, however, has passed away with many other of the homely joys of pioneer days.

The bees, too, have suffered by the advance of the civilization which they seem everywhere to usher in. The destruction of the prairie flowers and the ravages of the bee moth have almost resulted in their annihilation, and it is only by the strictest care that domestic swarms can be profitably maintained.

The earliest settlers in Au Sable found themselves completely isolated, and though in a country abounding in the richest provision of nature, found it necessary to go long distances for such things as the country did not provide. Their first flour was secured at Reed's Grove. A small settlement had been made here a year or two before, and flour had been brought from the Wabash country. Here the Cryder settlement sent for the winter's supply. For their stock they bought some thirty bushels of corn of Marquis, but the open winter allowed the cattle to feed on the prairie most of the season. There was a fall of snow which lay on the ground from early in January to the 10th of February. The cattle had found a choice piece of pasture south of the ox-bow bend of the Au Sable Creek, which they refused of their own will to leave during this snow. They were driven up to the cabins and fed some corn, with the hope that this would reconcile them to the prairie hay which had been provided the previous fall, but in the morning they were found again at their old feeding ground. A considerable band of Indians was encamped at the mouth of the Au Sable, and the cattle feeding in the track of their Indian ponies found plenty to eat where they had pawed off the snow. About 1835 or '6, a log flouring mill was put up on the Desplaines River, near Channahon.

The buhrs were made from "nigger-heads" and turned out very acceptable flour.

The point at which Salmon Rutherford settled early took on the importance and name of a village, though there was little to warrant these pretensions. His log house was very early replaced by a large framed structure, and Rutherford took out the first license for keeping an inn. The stage line which ran in opposition to Frink & Walker's line made this a point for changing horses, and gave Dresden the prestige of a post-office and an occasional glimpse of the outside world. The sharp competition between the rival stage lines, however, diverted the route to a shorter line further north, and the final withdrawal of the stage altogether, left this point with a hotel and a name only. During the construction of the canal, a few temporary buildings gathered about the old hotel and kept it company for awhile, but these passed away with the laborers, and the place lapsed into its original rural simplicity. The building of the Rock Island & Pacific railroad confirmed this decree of fortune, and built up a substitute in the northeast corner of the town.

The village of Minooka was laid out by Ransom Gardner in 1852. He owned some five hundred acres of land at this point, and labored assiduously to secure the location of the line near his property. The little town grew slowly for a year or two, and business was not attracted here until about 1858. Three years previous to this Christopher Tucker put up a store building and brought in a stock of general merchandise, but the venture proved a losing one, and he left the place in the following spring. The most convenient place for making purchases at this time was Channahon, and when, in the fall of 1856, Joseph Lewis rented the old Tucker store, he found the people numerous and willing enough to make a profitable business. In the spring of 1857, Leander Smith, a brother-in-law of Gardner's, came to Minooka and erected the second store in the village. This was located on the corner and is now occupied by Martin Kaffer. In the following year C. V. Hamilton put up a number of business buildings which are now owned by George Comerford and occupied by Wheeler & Saddler, and Barker & Stauffer. Hamilton at the same time erected the first hotel which was known for some time as the Hamilton House, but is now owned by Thomas Sheick. In 1858 a grist-mill was also erected, Gardner & Heiner originating the enterprise. This was a good structure with three run of stone, and proved a great convenience to the farmers about, who gave it a liberal patronage. It stood until 1866 when it was destroyed by fire, and its site subsequently occupied by the elevator which is now the chief business attraction of the place. The first elevator was built in 1868 by Knapp & Griswold, which was burned down in 1880. In the following year A. K. Knapp built the present fine structure, which has a capacity of 100,000 bushels, at a cost of $15,000. Its dimensions are 36 by 70 feet foundation, with an altitude of seventy feet; has a car shed and is provided with all the modern improvements. It is now leased by Henry McEwen, of Morris, who has handled upward of 450,000 bushels of grain. In connection with this business, Mr. McEwen carries on a lumber yard where he has sold some 500,000 feet of lumber in the past year. Connected with the lumber yard is a planing mill, built in 1873 by A. K. Knapp & Griswold, run by McEwen. A hay press is also run by the power of the mill, where about a thousand tons of hay have been handled in a single season. This combination of enterprises makes Minooka a busy little town in the proper seasons, and makes a convenient market for a good many miles around. The village was incorporated December 14, 1869, and now claims about six hundred inhabitants. In the fall of 1870 a considerable fire destroyed four or five business buildings which were replaced during the following winter and spring, improving the appearance of the business quarter. Minooka bears a quiet air of prosperity, which betokens a steady and profitable patronage, if not a large one. The business part of the town is considerably diversified, and numbers three general stores, a drug store, grocery, market, barber shop, pump shop, two blacksmith shops, two wagon shops and two church edifices.

The Catholic church of St. Mary's parish is the stronger organization in Minooka. It was early organized at Dresden where a building was erected and services held for some years. In 1862, the church decided to follow the tendency of business and public interests and removed to Minooka. The Comerfords, Kinsellars and George T. Smith were the leading members who took an active part in the re-establishment of the church. The membership at that time was about fifty, which has since been nearly doubled. The church edifice is a neat wooden structure 40 by 100 feet foundation, with an altitude of 100 feet, and was erected at a cost of about $6,000.

The first Methodist Episcopal Church was organized in 1856 with some nineteen members. Among these were J. G. Smith, Henry Pendleton, S. and A. C. Worthing, Michael Ketcham and their wives. The first sermon was preached in Ferguson's store by Rev. T. L. Olmstead. After this, meetings were held in the school-house until the present place of worship was erected. Mr. Henry Pendleton was an active worker in securing the new church home, which is a pleasant wooden building, 26 by 56 feet. The Sunday school was early established and is still maintained the year round, and has an average attendance of fifty pupils. The church now numbers some fifty members.

The Au Sable Methodist Episcopal Church, whose place of worship is situated on section seven, is really the older organization of the two Methodist churches. It was early organized by Rev. John Devore, an itinerant from the Fox River Mission, at the residence of Henry Cryder. Meetings were held at first in private houses, and later in the school-house as soon as it was built. In 1878 the neat wooden structure on the northern line of section seven was erected at a cost of some $2,500. It is a little out of the ordinary style of rural church architecture, has stained glass windows, and is in every way a credit to the organization to which it belongs. Some of the early members were Henry Cryder, Z. Walley, and their wives, John Craig, D. M. Thomas and others. The church now has a membership of some seventy members.

The first school-house was built about 1837, on section eight, for which the community was largely indebted to Henry Cryder's energy. The first session was taught by a daughter of Rev. Mr. Ashley, from Plainfield. This sufficed for the demands of the little community for some eight or ten years, when a second school house was erected on land belonging to Israel Cryder. This was a log building, and served as a meeting house for some time.

Minooka Lodge of F. and A. Masons, No. 528, was organized in the winter of 1867, and worked under dispensation until the fall of 1868, when the lodge was chartered, with G. Dahlem, A. K. Knapp, G. C. Griswold, Jno. T. Van Dolfson, G. S. Correll, Sam'l Adams, W. H. Smith, E. W. Weese, Jacob Gedelman, John Colleps, Phaley Gedleman, J. E. McClure, C. V. Hamilton and W. A. Jordon as charter members. The first officers were G. Dahlem, W. M.; A. K. Knapp, S. W.; G. C. Griswold, J. W., etc. The lodge is now in a flourishing condition, and holds its meetings on the first and third Wednesdays of each month, in their hall in the third story of Comerford's block.

An effort was made in the fall of 1881 to organize the temperance sentiment of the township for effective work against what was felt to be a growing evil. William Walley was prominent in this movement, and is president of the organization. Members were not required to be residents of the township, and many from Saratoga joined the movement. Since its inauguration, however, the society has taken on a political character, and become pledged to the prohibition party. This organization holds regular meetings in the Methodist meeting house, and numbers about 120 members.

G. P. Augustine.

THE NEW YORK
PUBLIC LIBRARY

ASTOR, LENOX AND
TILDEN FOUNDATIONS
R   1922   L

CHAPTER XIV.*

SARATOGA TOWNSHIP—PHYSICAL FEATURES—THE EARLY SETTLERS—THE NORWEGIAN EMIGRATION—THE HOUGES MENEGHED.

IT was Montesquieu who declared that nation happy whose annals were tiresome; but while this speaks for the peaceful prosperity of a people it furnishes no glowing periods to the historian nor patriotic panegyrics for the citizen. This is especially true in the case of Saratoga. Timber lands were originally very little found here, and Nettle Creek on the west and Au Sable on the east, with pleasant union of timber and prairie, attracted the earlier settlements. Later, as the original location proved unhealthful, or as nearer settlers failed to find eligible timber sites, the prairie land of Saratoga was invaded from either side. The country embraced within the limits of this township was of the most attractive character. Save a spur of timber on the elbow of Au Sable Creek, which crosses the eastern border of Saratoga, and that on Nettle Creek in the southwestern corner of the township, the eye met only a broad expanse of undulating prairie which ended only with the line of the horizon in the north. Through the central portion the Saratoga Creek flowed an easterly course through the township, and the east fork of Nettle Creek, draining the southwestern part, joined the main stream in Morris. There is but little low land here, the most of the township lying north of the second "bench." The southeastern corner, however, is characterized by the low lands which are found between the first and second rises from the Illinois River. The diagonal road which enters the township near the middle of the eastern line of Saratoga, follows upon the margin of the second bench, leaving it at the Concklin road. From this point the line of high ground continues the same general southwesterly direction, deflecting slightly to the west, and passing the southern line of the township about a mile east of Nettle Creek. The rest of the township is admirably situated, and one would expect to find a dry friable soil were it not of prairie origin. As it is, the township is noted for its bad roads, resulting chiefly from the character of the soil, which seems to have a special affinity for water, and the highways, piked never so high, become in the rainy season one quaking bog of impassable mud. This question of roads is a very serious one throughout the county. Considerable expense is annually laid out in "piking" and ditching, but the character of the soil renders these expedients but partially successful even for a twelve-month. There is plenty of accessible limestone which could probably be used profitably in making permanent improvement upon the highways, but the taxpayers have not yet learned that the an-

---

* By J. H. Battle.

nual mud blockade costs the people at large enough to macadamize every principally traveled road in the county.

Saratoga was originally settled by emigrants from New York, who crystallized the memories of their old home in the name which the township bears. The first settlement in this precinct was made by Joshua Collins, in the spring of 1844. His father came from Oneida County, New York, in 1834, following the lead of the Walleys, Tablers and Cryders to Au Sable township. Here he lived and died. His son Joshua married a daughter of Mr. Cryder, and in the following spring set up a home of his own, where his widow now lives. In the same year Phillip Collins came to Saratoga, and Alexander Peacock. The latter was an Englishman, and made his claim on section 33, including in his selection the present Fair Grounds, which he bought some time later. In the southern part also came another Englishman, H. M. Davidson, about the same year. James Cronin, an Irishman, whom the canal work brought to this region, was associated with Peacock on section 33, in the year of 1844. In the northeastern corner a considerable tract of land was secured as early as 1842 or '3, by John B. More, whose cabin, however, was built north of the Grundy County line. Early in 1844, Carpenter Concklin, in whose honor the central road of the township was named, took up a claim on section 9, and was followed very soon by Elias Bartlett, who knew the Concklin family in the State of New York. Bartlett was an unmarried man, and followed school teaching very early. Concklin's daughter had remained behind her father's family engaged in teaching, and after being here a short time, Bartlett, struck by the similarity of their tastes, went to New York and brought back Miss Concklin as his wife. They subsequently engaged in teaching, and for a time conducted the Seminary at Ottawa. Daniel Johnson was another early settler, as was Gersham Hunt.

About 1847 or '8, the immigration of Norwegians began to appear in this township. The first came from La Salle County, with one or two from other sections. They were in poor financial circumstances, but they brought hardy constitutions and abundant energy, and were not long in getting upon an equal footing with their more favored neighbors. Their native tastes inclined them to prefer the timber lands, and here and there, where they could buy an acre or two of timber, their sheepskin coats and calfskin vests could be seen all through the northern and middle part of the county.

"The first emigration from Norway to the United States was in 1825. Cling Pearson, of Hesthamer, in Norway, came over in 1822, and on his return to his native country, gave a glowing picture of America. He found the people of Starvinger, a small town in his neighborhood, dissatisfied with their minister appointed by the government, and desirous of changing their location, and soon persuaded them to emigrate to the new country. They purchased a small vessel, a two-masted fishing sloop, for $1,800, and fifty-two emigrants set sail in their little craft for the Western Continent. They sailed through the North Sea and English Channel to Madeira, where, getting short of provisions, they picked up a pipe of wine, and laid in a stock of supplies. They left Norway July 4th, reached

Funchal August 18th, and New York on the last day of October, 1825, their number having received one accession on the journey.

"In New York they sold the vessel for $400, and the company divided, twenty-eight going with Cling Pearson, who had secured for them a free passage to Orleans County, New York. Here the colony bought land and formed a settlement, the first Norwegian community in America. But the leader of this hegira was a restless spirit, and soon set off to explore the far West. He reached Illinois and struck with its attractions, fixed upon La Salle County as the site for a new settlement of his fellow-countrymen. Cling said that when exploring the country afterward occupied by the Norwegians, that he laid down under a tree to sleep, and in his dreams saw the wild prairie changed to a cultivated region, teeming with all kinds of grain and fruits; comfortable houses and spacious barns dotted the land, which was occupied by a rich, prosperous and happy people. He woke refreshed, and with renewed enthusiasm returned to his countrymen in New York, and persuaded them to emigrate to Illinois. The dream was a natural one and might have been conceived when awake, but however it originated, its most sanguine expectations have been fully realized. The early days of the Norwegian settlement in this country were full of poverty and toil, to which was added the terrible ravages of Asiatic cholera. Happily these days are past, and these difficulties surmounted; those people are now found a wealthy, prosperous and happy people.

"The first Norwegian colony from New York came to La Salle County in 1834, and included some of the original fifty-three who arrived from Norway in 1825. Since that others have followed from the Fatherland, and the members of the original colony have welcomed many of their old neighbors to the land of their adoption. Many of them still adhere to the Lutheran, the national church of Norway, but many are Methodist, and the Mormons have made some converts among them."*

The only church in the township is the Houges Meneghed. This is a Norwegian Lutheran church, and was organized about 1876. The society proceeded at once to build a place of worship on the land of H. Osmonson, which was erected that fall at a total cost of about $4,000, including the price of the lot.

* Hist. of La Salle County.

CHAPTER XV.*

WAUPONSEE TOWNSHIP—ITS MATERIAL RESOURCES—EARLY SETTLERS—PIONEER LIFE ON THE PRAIRIE—THE CHURCH AND SCHOOL.

NEAR the center of Grundy County, abutting on the south bank of the Illinois River, lies Wauponsee Township, or in the technical language of the congressional survey, township 33 north, range 7, east. The name immortalizes that prosaic warrior, better characterized by the closing tragedy on the Kankakee River than the sentiment of the "leather stocking" tales, who once made his home near the western line of the township. This name was early applied to what is now Grundy County, but these extended territorial limits have been curtailed from time to time, until now it contains but little larger area than that assigned to a regular congressional township, six miles square. The surface, considerably broken in the northwestern corner, is generally a rolling prairie, sloping gradually toward the northwest. The natural drainage is fair, the Mazon River, flowing along the eastern border and taking a short turn westward near the northeastern corner and emptying into the Illinois near the middle part of the town; and the Waupecan Creek, entering west of the middle of the southern line of the township, passing in a northwesterly direction to the northwest corner into the Illinois, affording an outlet for the surplus rain-fall. The outline of the highlands, which reach almost to the altitude of bluffs in the northwest corner, gradually recedes from the course of the Illinois as it proceeds eastward, leaving a space of nearly two miles occupied by the first and second bottoms. These are subject to annual overflows which are not an unmixed evil. Skiffs owned and kept by farmers at their residences a mile or two away are suggestive of the inconveniences of a flood, but the luxuriant crops which are annually produced on these lands give sure token of the blessing which comes in this guise. Occasionally a late flood or one accompanied with floating ice does considerable damage, but on the whole these inundations are not unwelcome to the farmers. Along the bottoms the soil is a rich and most alluvial deposit, fertile and of inexhaustible richness. The first and second rises or "benches" are marked by a preponderance of sand, forming a productive loamy soil especially adapted to gardening and certain fruits. The high plateau beyond is more of a clay soil admirably calculated for good results in corn and grass cultivation. Here the timber is principally oak, while in the lower portions of the township black and white walnut, blue ash, hackberry and some maples are found. The original supply of timber was much less than now appears, and differently distributed. Along the margin of

---

* By L. W. Claypool.

the streams, in the bottom and northern sides of ravines there was a considerable growth of trees, which by judicious handling, and the absence of prairie fires has spread, so that the lack of timber is now observable only to the practiced eye. The native prairie grass is yet to be seen here and there, and is prized for hay equal to the finest timothy. The attention of farmers in this township is chiefly devoted to the cultivation of small fruits and vegetables upon the sand ridges, large numbers of melons being shipped from this point, annually. Elsewhere the cultivation of corn, with stock raising, and some dairying, absorbs the farmer's efforts, the product finding a ready and profitable market at Chicago.

The first settlement of the county was made in this township, in 1828, by Wm. Marquis. He came across the country in a wagon from the vicinity of the Wabash. He was of French extraction, of a roving disposition, and being something of a trader, was probably attracted hither by the advertisement of the canal lands and the near location of the Indians. Whatever the reason, he came here and halted his wagon on the south fraction of section 2, 33, 7. Here he erected a building near the banks of the river, of such timber as he could handle, aided only by his wife, children and team. He was more trader than farmer, and made very slight improvements. He cultivated the acquaintance of the Indians that lived and hunted through the contiguous country, and through them some stories of Marquis have come down to a later day. It is said, in dealing on one occasion with Wauponsee for some wild geese feathers, Marquis insisted on paying him in pumpkins, at the rate of *pound for pound*. This was too much for even the indolent credulity of an Indian, and the enraged old chief drove him into his cabin, smashing the pumpkins after him. Marquis threatened to report his actions to the whites—with whom the chief was not in good repute—but the Indian, undaunted, replied, "Whites like Indian more than he like Marquis; he talk nice and smooth, but he d—d rascal." This is said to be not an unfair estimate of his dealings with the Indians, by whom he was not greatly liked. The whites who came to the township subsequently, found in him a good neighbor, but a cunning and dangerous opponent. Here he lived for several years completely isolated, trusting for subsistence upon his own resources alone. The story of the death of his son, about twelve years old, in the winter of 1834-5, and the funeral, gives some idea of the early privations. The father, after placing the body of his child on a scaffold out of doors where it would be safe from the attack of marauding animals, left his family sick in the cabin and walked several miles to get help from the neighbors for the burial. Three of them responded, Jacob and Perry Claypool and William Robb. For a burial case they cut off an old canoe, closing the open end with a piece of board, dressed the body in a clean shirt, and placing it in the extemporized coffin, covered it with a board. To remove it to the place of burial, in the absence of any sort of vehicle, a yoke of oxen was attached to the affair, and the pioneer cortege proceeded in this unceremonious manner through the snow to a ridge at some distance, where the grave had been prepared. The young team, not impressed with the solemnity of the occasion, made a nearly successful attempt to run away, and though the burial was accomplished without any unseemly accident, there was painfully lacking that careful tenderness which so mitigates the pain of the funeral ceremony. This was the first white man's funeral in Grundy County, and is typical of the privations of frontier life—an experience rigorous enough with health and good fortune to support it, but sad beyond expression when sickness and death are added to its miseries. In 1835 Marquis sold out to A. Holderman and removed to the mouth of the Au Sable, where he bought some land and lived a number of years. He subsequently lost the principal part of his property, and left for Texas in 1850.

In 1833 Col. Sayers came from the lower settlements to Wauponsee, and made a claim on the east half of the northeast quarter of section 14, building his cabin near the present residence of J. H. Pattison. He never came here to live or to make further improvements, but sold the claim to W. A. Holloway, who moved into the cabin in March of the following year. The latter was not a long resident of this township, selling his place next year and buying land in what is now Felix township, where he was the first settler.

Mr. S. Crook, who succeeded Holloway in the Sayers cabin in 1835, was a New York merchant. The notoriety which the "canal lands" got through the State agents was such as to create the belief in many minds that there were fine opportunities here for successful speculation in lands, and attracted many who found themselves mistaken, and soon moved elsewhere. Among this number, perhaps, should be placed Mr. Crook. He brought with him several trunks filled with goods, with which to trade with the natives. He never formally opened a store here, but found ready access to his goods when an occasion offered opportunity for trade. He left Wauponsee in the following year, and established a store at Ottawa, where he continued in business for a long time.

The next family to join its fortunes with the little colony in this township was that of Jacob Claypool. He was a Virginian by birth, and moved with his father to Ohio, settling near Chillicothe, in 1799. In the war of 1812 he served in a rifle company which was a part of the first regiment, and in a diary, now in the possession of his son, L. W. Claypool, has left an interesting history of the movements and experiences of that part of the army to which he was attached. He was in the campaign about Detroit, was captured with Gen. Hull and paroled. His observation of the Lake region made a deep impression upon his mind; and when the canal lands were advertised he became possessed with a desire to make his home near the lake on these lands. Mr. Claypool had something of the true spirit of the pioneer, and preferred the isolation and freedom of the frontier to the crowded settlements. On arriving at his majority his first move was to go, with others, to the east fork of the Miami River, in Brown County, Ohio, to establish a new settlement. He was therefore, in 1833, anxious to leave his farm and go further west, and determined, whether he sold his place or not, to go to the lake region; and started this year for the northern part of the State of Ohio. He was forced to return, however, after getting to Dayton, by the sickness of his horse. In the following year, having an opportunity to sell his Ohio farm, he started for the canal lands in Illinois, taking his son, L. W. Claypool, with him, on a prospecting tour. His design was to follow the Illinois River by boat to Peru, and thence to walk to Chicago, the aim of his journey. At Cincinnati they took a boat "bound for the Illinois River," on which they made the journey to Beardstown, where the boat ended its trip. Disappointed, but undaunted, the two started out on foot, and made their way finally to the residence of James Galloway, near Marseilles. Here Mr. Claypool rested for the night, and was advised in the morning to go to Holloway's cabin. Here, tired with his journey and pleased with the prospect, he selected the southwest quarter of section 20 as his future home, and with his son then struck out for home, following the course of the river, determined to take the first boat they could get. They were fortunate enough to find one at Pekin, on which they made the trip to Cincinnati. Mr. Claypool set about preparing for the removal, and in making up a party to accompany him.

In the fall of this year (1834) Mr. Claypool returned with his goods on wagons, accompanied by his family, James Robb and his family, Wm. Brown and family, John Snowhill and Wm. Eubanks. The little company came over the country, and getting into the Chicago trail, Mr. Claypool was then anxious to go to Chicago, notwithstanding he had selected another place. At the point where the road branched off toward Wauponsee the caravan was brought to a halt, and the question of going to the lake was put to a vote, and Mr. Claypool being in the minority, came with the rest to his chosen spot. James Robb located on the southeast quarter, section 18, but subsequently sold out, moved out of the township, and later returned to his homestead on section 28. William Brown erected his cabin on the northwest quarter, section 30, 33, 8, but in 1842 he sold this place, moved to section 13, 33, 7, where he died.

In 1835, Richard Griggs settled on the southeast quarter, section 33, built his cabin and fenced a few acres, but soon sold out and left for parts unknown. In the same year the oldest son of Jacob Claypool, Perry A. Claypool, put up a cabin on the east half of northeast quarter, section 28. He had returned the previous year to Ohio to consummate his marriage to Miss Mary Hollsted, and then brought his bride to Wauponsee to begin life upon the Illinois prairie. The year following, Geo. W. Armstrong, an early settler of La Salle County, and of a very prominent family there, came to Wauponsee, and erected a cabin on the southeast quarter of section 18, and began immediately afterward to erect a saw-mill on the Waupecan Creek, finishing it the next year. He added to this business a few pieces of dry goods and a stock of groceries, which constituted the first regularly opened store in the township, and probably the first in the county. There was but little business in so sparse a settlement, and the venture probably did not yield great returns. The scarcity of timber operated unfavorably to the interests of the mill, though it undoubtedly proved a great convenience to the settlers, who otherwise were forced to split and hew out puncheons as a substitute for boards. The mill changed hands several times, and finally so completely disappeared as to leave no trace by which its actual site can be identified. Mr. Armstrong did not stay long in Wauponsee, returning to his former home in the adjoining county, in a year or two.

Ezekiel Warren, who came to La Salle County in 1832, and where he took part in the Black Hawk War, moved into Armstrong's cabin in 1839. Here he lived two or three years, and then located on the east half of the southeast quarter, section 17, 33, 7. James Thompson and James Berry came into the township about 1841. Both were Irishmen, brought here by interests of the canal, and have proven a valuable acquisition to the growth of the township.

The pioneers who thus formed the little colony that early gathered in this township were familiar with the isolation, and inured to the hardships and privations of frontier life. But with all this, the open prairie presented difficulties to which they had hitherto been strangers. From this point of view, when the adaptability of the prairies has been so abundantly proven, it seems unfortunate that the early experiences of these pioneers led them to cling to the timbered portions of the land, where foul water and miasma aggravated the inevitable discomforts of frontier life. The cabin built, many turned their attention at once to building tight, expensive fences. The Claypools enclosed eighty acres with a stout Virginia fence, "staked and ridered," and others fenced similar fields, but they soon learned that this was an unnecessary expense here. Most of the settlers brought in horses and cows, but the former pretty generally gave way to oxen for working purposes, and hogs were soon introduced from the older settlements on the lower part of the river, as the most available way to supply the table.

These preliminaries accomplished, the most urgent necessity was to secure a crop. The plows were crude affairs, strong and serviceable, but requiring great team power and considerable mechanical skill in the plowman. The sod was found tough, not easily "tamed," and very uncertain in producing a first crop. So tenacious was it, that the furrow turned out one unbroken strip of sod, and occasionally, when not especially careful, the plowman had the disappointment of seeing yards of this leathery soil turn back to its natural position, necessitating the tedious operation of turning it all back by hand. The result of all this labor was generally well repaid the first year, if the sod became thoroughly rotted, though it produced but a small crop. Oftentimes the second and third plowing showed the soil still stubborn and unkind. Few, even among farmers, know much of the labor involved in "breaking prairie," unless they have experienced its obstacles and overcome them. Corn was the only crop planted at first, and this furnished food for man and beast, and a few years later it was a mark of unusual prosperity to be able to furnish wheat bread to especial guests. When these difficulties had been surmounted; when rude barns and stacks of grain began to mark the home of the thriving frontier farmer, his very prosperity made him the readier victim of the desolation that stalked abroad in the prairie fire. Against this evil there was at that time no sure defense, but eternal vigilance. Mr. Baldwin, who has described this so well in his history of La Salle County, says: "From the time the grass would burn, which was soon after the first frost, usually about the first of October, till the surrounding prairie was all burnt over, or if not all burnt, till the green grass in the spring had grown sufficiently to prevent the rapid progress of the fire, the early settlers were continually on the watch, and as they usually expressed the idea, 'slept with one eye open.' When the ground was covered with snow, or during rainy weather, the apprehension was quieted, and both eyes could be safely closed. A statute law forbade setting the prairie on fire, and one doing so was subject to a penalty, and liable in an action of trespass, for the damage accruing; but convictions were seldom effected, as proof was difficult to obtain, though there were frequent fires. These, started on the leeward side of an improvement, while very dangerous to property to the leeward, were not so to the windward, as fire progressing against the wind is easily extinguished. The apprehension, therefore, of a frontier farmer may be readily imagined. Alone, in a strange land, he has made a comfortable home for his family; has raised and stored his corn, wheat, oats, and fodder for his stock, and sees about these, stretching away for miles in every direction, a vast sea of standing grass, dry as tinder, waving in threatening movement as the fierce prairie wind howls a dismal requiem, as over fair hopes doomed to destruction.

"Various means were resorted to for protection. A common one was to plow several furrows around a strip, several rods wide, outside the improvements, and then burn out the strip; or to wait until the prairie was on fire and then set fire outside of this furrowing, reserving the inner strip for a late burn, i. e., until the following summer, and in July burn both old grass and new. The grass would start immediately, and the cattle would feed it close in preference to the older grass, so that the fire would not pass over it the following autumn. This process repeated would soon, or in a few years, run out the prairie grass, and in time would be replaced by blue grass, which will never burn to any extent. But all this took time and labor, and the crowd of business on the hands of a new settler, of which a novice has no conception, would prevent him doing what would now seem a small matter; and all such effort was often futile. A prairie fire driven by a high wind would often leap such barriers and seem to put human effort at defiance.

"A prairie fire when first started goes straight forward with a velocity proportioned to the force of the wind, widening as it goes, but the center keeping ahead; it spreads sideways, but burning laterally, it makes but comparatively slow progress, and if the wind is moderate and steady, this spreading fire is not difficult to manage; but if the wind veers a point or two, first one way and then the other, it sends this side fire beyond control. The head fire in dry grass and a head wind is a fearful thing, and pretty sure to have its own way unless there is some defensible point from which to meet it. A contest with such a fire requires such skill and tact as can be learned only by experience, and a neighborhood of settlers called out by such an exigency at once put themselves under the direction of the oldest and most experienced of their number, and go to work with the alacrity and energy of men defending their homes and property from destruction.

"The usual way of meeting an advancing fire was to begin the defense where the head of the fire would strike, which is calculated by the smoke and ashes brought by the wind long in advance of the fire. A road, cattle path or furrow is of great value at such a place; if there is none such, a strip of the grass is wetted down if water can be procured, which is, however, a rather scarce article at the time of the annual fires. On the side nearest to the coming fire, of such road or path, the grass is set on fire, which burns slowly against the wind until it meets the coming conflagration, which stops of course for want of fuel, provided there has been sufficient time to burn a strip that will not be leaped by the head fire as it comes in. This is called back-firing; but in this method, great care must be exercised to prevent the fire getting over the furrow path, or whatever is used as a base of operations. If it gets over and once under way, there is no remedy but to fall back to a more defensible position. The head of the fire successfully checked, the forces divide, part going to the right and part to the left, and the back-firing continued to meet the side fires as they come up. This must be continued until the fire is checked along the entire front of the premises endangered, and the sides secured.

"Various implements were used to put out a side or back fire, or even the head of a fire in a moderate wind. A fence board, four to six feet long, with one end shaved down for a handle, was very effective when struck flat upon the narrow strip of fire. A bundle of hazel brush, a spade or shovel were often used with effect. The women frequently lent their aid and dexterously wielded the mop, which, when thoroughly wet, proved a very efficient weapon, especially in extinguishing a fire in the fence. When the fire overcame all opposition, and seemed bound to sweep over the settlement, a fear of personal loss would paralyze, for the moment, every faculty, and as soon as that danger seemed imminent, united effort ceased, and each one hastened to defend his own as best he could. It is due to historical truth to say that the actual losses were much less than might have been expected, though frequently quite severe. The physical efforts made in extinguishing a dangerous fire, and in protecting one's home from this devouring element were of the most trying nature, resulting fatally in more than one instance.

"The premises about the residences and yards being trampled down by the family and domestic animals, after a year or two became tolerably safe from fire, but the fences, corn and stubble fields were frequently burned over. When the prairie was all fenced and under cultivation, so that prairie fires were a thing of the past, the denizens of the prairie were happily released from the constant fear and apprehension which for years had rested like a nightmare on their quiet and happiness, disturbing their peace by night, and causing anxiety by day. The early settlers will ever have a vivid recollection of the grand illuminations nightly exhibited in dry weather, from early fall to late spring, by numberless prairie fires. The whole horizon would be lighted up around its entire circuit. A heavy fire six or seven miles away, would afford sufficient light on a dark night to enable one to read fine print. When a fire had passed through the prairie, leaving the long lines of side fires like two armies facing each other, at night the sight was grand ; and if one's premises were securely protected and he could enjoy the fine exhibition without apprehension, it was an awe-inspiring sight well worth going far to see."

The isolation of the Wauponsee community, while not that of many a frontier colony, was such as to command the greatest respect for the patient endurance of the pioneers of this county. The nearest post-office was at Ottawa, while the only "gristmill" was that of a Mr. Green at Dayton. Here the farmers took a wagon load of corn or a year's supply of wheat and often waited a week for their turn, camping out in the vicinity in the meanwhile. This lack of milling facilities led to the adoption of many substitutes, such as grating the corn on a perforated tin or iron, parching and grinding in a coffee mill, or more commonly pulverizing it with a huge wooden mortar and pestle. Sometimes a conveniently placed stump furnished the material for the mortar, otherwise a section of log was hollowed out to form a bowl-like receptacle in which the corn was placed and plied with a heavy wooden pestle. The finest of the product was used for the "corn pone" or "slapjack," while the coarser part furnished forth the characteristic "hominy."

Game consisted principally of wild hogs and wolves. There were some deer to be found in the timber, and smaller game such as squirrels, woodchucks and prairie chickens on the prairie, but the first named animals furnished the principal sport. Wild hogs were such as had wandered off from the older settlements and gone wild in the course of nature. They were of a long-legged, gaunt species, and kept the timber pretty closely. They were no particular damage or annoyance to the early settlers, but furnished capital hunting sport, though of not very long duration. The wolves were of the coyote species and haunted the open prairies. These were of more annoyance to the settlements, and a bounty was early offered by the county for their scalps, and is still paid when claimed by hunters. They were a small undersized breed, and would make the night dismal with their howling, though they never attacked full-sized animals or persons. There were no sheep in the township, but young calves often fell an easy victim to these insatiable beasts, and young pigs when alone or accompanied only by the mother sow were often captured. They were hunted with dogs, and when run down would fall on their backs and fight very much like a cat. On frozen ground and when filled by a recent meal they were run down without much difficulty on horseback, as they seemed to avoid the timber and would risk capture rather than go into it. An instance is related where a wolf was thus run down and suddenly seized by the hinder leg as he lay on the ground ready to fight, was whirled about the hunter's head and killed by bringing him forcibly on the ground. Their nature of late years, however, seems to have undergone a decided change. They now attain a much larger size and inhabit the timber almost exclusively. Occasionally one is still shot and exhibited as quite a curiosity. Prairie chickens are still found, though in decreasing numbers, and serve to attract sportsmen from less favored localities.

Wauponsee was in the line of early travel—one of the principal traveled routes passing through its territory—and the old hotel on the Mazon was for some time a point of considerable importance. But the regulation of the roads, the building of railroads and the location of the county seat so near at hand, have all conspired to discourage the growth of any village within its borders. Its only centers of attraction are the school-houses and a church building, situated rather southeast of the center of the township. There was occasional preaching in the cabins by passing ministers as early as '34 or '35, but the first regular services were held in Wauponsee Grove, just over the township line, in 1837 or '8, by a Rev. Mr. Rogers, of the South Ottawa circuit. In 1839, Harvey Hadley, of the same circuit, officiated, followed by Jno. F. Devore, who was the means of a great revival in 1842 or '3.

The Mormons were also early in the field, and had their preachers out quite regularly until 1844. Elder Pratt is especially remembered as one of these Evangelists of the Latter Day Saints. They made several converts to their peculiar doctrines, some of whom left for Nauvoo, but the majority lost their faith and "slid back." The first church organization in the township, however, was the Wauponsee Methodist Episcopal Church. J. W. and J. P. Riding, though of Congregational proclivities, were prominent in its early organization, but subsequently withdrew. For nearly ten years it held its meetings in the cabins around until about 1872, when, under the lead of Mr. Morgan Button, an effort was put forth for a regular place of worship. The result of these efforts is the neat wooden edifice in which the church now worships. It was dedicated in August, 1873, and cost some $3,000.

Schools were not established until after the formation of the county. The community was small, and there were but few scholars to attend if such had been started. But in 1843 a school was opened in a log cabin erected in the center of section 20, and was kept by Amanda Pickering. This was not a public school, but supported by the patrons, who "swapped" pork, corn. etc., with a little money, for the less materialistic benefit received by their children. This was one of the earliest schools in the county, and the cabin is still pointed out. The second school-house, which was known as the "Satterly School House." was constructed of logs on the east line of section 15, about 1848, where its site is now marked by a modern structure, in which the children of to-day go to school. This old school-house was for years used as town hall for the regular town meetings and occasional religious services. But since then how marked the change! Neat school-houses are found in every quarter of the township, where advanced methods and improved means unite to fit the rich and poor alike for the duties and dangers of life.

NOTE.—The Cicada, or Seventeen-year Locust, has been a visitant of this country, as elsewhere, and since first noticed has been regular in its coming. It was first noticed in 1837, and in June of that year began to attract very general attention. They came out of the ground about the last of May. and by the middle of June seemed to have taken possession of the country. A sudden jar on a small bush would put to flight as many as could be put into an ordinary pail, and during the middle part of the day their noise would drown the tones of a cow-bell a hundred yards away. They took every green thing in their way, and it was estimated that fully one-third of the leaf-bearing twigs on the oak timber on the eastern banks of the Mazon was destroyed by their "prodding" to deposit eggs.

In 1854 the locusts began to appear about the 28th of May. They came out of the ground a large bug, which fastened itself to a twig for an hour or two, when its encasing shell parting along the central line of the back, disclosed the ravaging locust. In a few days the country began to resound with their noise, but a heavy rain early in June seemed to destroy large numbers. By the middle of June they began to deposit their eggs, and becoming fat and enervated by their gorging, fell an easy prey to the birds, which destroyed large numbers. They went away as rapidly as they came, and by July 1st nothing but dried fragments of the insect could be discovered.

In 1871 farmers were expecting the return of the locust invasion, and kept a keen watch for the first appearance of the scourge. On the 20th of May the bug was plowed up, and by the 25th they had become quite numerous above ground. On June 7 these insects killed *sixty* apple trees for L. W. Claypool, though they had been planted three years. By July 2nd there could be heard now and then one in the woods, but all the rest had gone. In the later visits the locusts were much less numerous than in 1837.

CHAPTER XVI.*

FELIX TOWNSHIP—ITS TOPOGRAPHICAL FEATURES—PIONEERS—FLOODS—SICKNESS—JUGTOWN—THE SILENT CITY.

"WHAT'S in a name?" Certainly, not very much when it stands for a designating mark only; as country hostlers are wont to chalk numbers on vehicles to identify them in the payment of the reckoning. "Infelix" would have been more suggestive of impressions derived from an early experience in this section of Grundy County; but the early "powers" held Felix Grundy, Tennessee's brilliant advocate, in high esteem, and this precinct, the youngest of the fourteen, was selected to bear the Christian name of him whom the county honored. There was little appropriateness in this selection and the name serves rather to emphasize the unpleasant peculiarities of the precinct than to do honor to its namesake. This township lies in the eastern tier of the county; is bounded on the north by the Illinois River, on the east by Will County, on the south by Braceville Township, and on the west by the meandering line of the Mazon River and Wauponsee Township. Its outline is quite irregular, and measures seven miles in its widest part, and from the most northerly point on the river to the southern boundary, it stretches out some seven and a half miles. The general surface is low. In the northeast corner the high land abuts upon the river, and from this point gradually recedes, forming bottom lands, nearly two miles in width in some places; the road which follows the general course of the river, marking the general line of the high lands. Immediately south of this line the land sinks somewhat into what was originally low wet meadows, marked by broken outcroppings of limerock and bowlders. On the northern half of sections 9, 10, and 11, is Goose Lake, a relic, probably, of the great watercourse that once overflowed this region and carried the waters of Lake Michigan to the Mississippi River. This body of water is a sedgy lake of swampy tendencies, measuring some three miles from east to west, and little more than a half mile wide. In seasons of high water this lake finds an outlet into the Kankakee. South of this is a ridge extending east and west through the central part of the township, originally covered with a considerable growth of timber; and again, south of this, another space of swamp land succeeds, which in turn is bounded on the south by a sand ridge. Claypool Run drained this swamp into the Mazon, and more recent cultivation has lengthened this run and improved the lands. The natural drainage is slight, the various runs finding their way into the Mazon from the western end of Goose Lake, and the swamp lands, in the southeast corner, and another draining the eastern middle portions of the township into the Kankakee River. These

---

*By J. H. Battle.

runs are but sluggish streams, and scarcely do more than to mark the lowest portion of the low grounds. The soil is principally a low wet clay, a deposit near the western end of the lake proving admirable material for the manufacture of coarse pottery. While a considerable part of the township is un ler a good degree of cultivation, the greater part is devoted to grazing, Mr. Holderman giving especial attention to stock raising.

Among those earliest identified with the interests of this township, was Peter Lampsett. He was a "character" in his way and was a relic of that large and at one t me influential class of pioneers, the Canadian voyageur. He trapped through this country as early as 1820, and this location especially suiting his pursuits, attracted and held him here long after the rest of his class had moved further north. He was known among the earliest settlers as "Specie," a name given him by the residents of the county, beause he invariably refused to accept paper money in his dealings. He seems to have accepted this name good-naturedly, and his descendants, still found in this region, have adopted it as their surname. "Specie Grove" in DeKalb County was named for him, and is likely to prove his most enduring monument. He lived on the Mazon, but never owned any land there, maintaining a homestead by right of his squatter sovereignty, and cultivating only a small patch for gardening purposes. He first discovered coal in the county and picking out such as showed itself where the Mazon uncovered it. sold it to the blacksmiths of the vicinity. W. A. Holloway came into the township from Wauponsee in 1835, bought land on section 12 near where the wooden bridge was put across the Mazon. He was not satisfied with the country here, however, and in 1840 left this county for Bloomington, Wis. Mr. Abram Holderman bought land in the northern part of the township about 1835. He placed his son Henry on the farm, but he stayed only a year or two when he became tired of the place and went further west. Then another son, Barton, took possession, but in a short time he left for Missouri in search of brighter fortunes, and in 1847 or 1848 Samuel Holderman took possession. He found here the materials for building up a fine fortune, and gradually added more land to his place until he owned some five thousand acres on which he pastured droves of some of the finest cattle in the country. This large farm has but recently been sold to Mr. Jerry Collins. In 1839, Abram White, from the Fox River settlements, Mr. Kelso and Martin Luther, came to the township.

Among the earliest settlers of the county, though not so early in Felix, was John Beard. He was a southerner by birth and early emigra'ed from Maryland to Pennsylvania, thence to Indiana, and later to the mouth of the Au Sable. He was a man of about fifty-five years of age when he came to this country, and was probably induced to come here by the bright prospect for speculation which the canal lands promised. To these early pioneers the lands along the route of the proposed canal offered inducements similar to the western lands which now lie along the rapidly constructing railroads in the west. The government sections were no sooner in the market than they were taken up by settlers and speculators, and real estate in this region early rose to fabulous prices for the time and place. The lands were known far and near among moneyed men and many who had means and a taste for pioneer life, put both funds and personal comfort into the speculation. Mr. Beard had a large family, several of his children being married, and though there were few considerations urging him at his age to take upon himself the further privations of frontier life, he could not resist the temptation to try his fortune here. He came overland in a three-horse wagon, without incident, and settled at the mouth of the Au Sable River about 1833. Here he remained one or two years, when he conceived the idea of founding a city at the head of the Illinois between the Desplaines and Kankakee Rivers. This it was hoped would be the head of navigation, and here, situated on a hill with admirable natural advantages, was destined to grow a bubble similar in kind to the South Sea and Great Mississippi schemes. In the meantime Mr. Beard had been joined at the mouth of the Au Sable by his son-in-law, James McKean, with his family. They came from Pennsylvania with a wagon drawn by three yoke of oxen, and driving several cows and 150 hogs. The progress of such a caravan was necessarily slow, making about fifteen miles per day. The Indians were found in large numbers all along their journey, but always friendly and frequently rendering valuable assistance in getting the herd of swine out of the bushes. As it was, some forty were lost on the journey, and it is probable that while the "noble red man" would not steal a hog before the eyes of the owner, these estrays generally turned up in an Indian camp, and furnished a satisfactory meal to the savages. After living at the mouth of the Au Sable for several years, McKean joined his father-in-law on the Kankakee. Here about 1839, the united families put up a large saw-mill, the machinery for which was bought in New York, shipped to Chicago and brought thence with infinite trouble to its destined location.

About 1838, William White with two sons, J. L. and William, came from Marietta, Ohio, and settled in Felix. Mr. White was a soldier in the war of 1812, and now draws a pension. He is still a vigorous old veteran of ninety-four years of age.

The early settlers in this township came into close relations with the Indians, who were here in considerable numbers. The abundance of game attracted them, and the settlers finding them well disposed, encouraged their stay by numberless little courtesies. The earliest families would have found it quite difficult, if not impossible, to put up their log cabins if it had not been for the help of these natives. When hogs or cattle strayed, the Indians could always be trusted to give reliable information concerning them, and would frequently go long distances to bring them back to a favorite white man. McKean seems to have been especially favored in this way. It is related that one day he missed some fifty of his large herd of swine. On inquiry of the Indians he learned where they were. Finding the hogs were his, the natives proposed to go and get them, but wishing to identify them himself, they accompanied him and helped to drive the animals home, for which assistance McKean gave them one of the animals. Subsequently, when the final treaty was made with them, and before their removal, Mc-

Kean's cabin was thronged with Indians, to whom his wife furnished breakfast every morning as regularly as to her own family. At the payment of the sum stipulated in the treaty, the Indians urged McKean to present his bill for their entertainment, but, being satisfied with the return they had made him, he refused altogether. Marquis, of Wauponsee, was more willing to do this, and preferred a claim of $500, which the Indians, who disliked him very much, refused to acknowledge, saying they had paid him for everything they got, and so the commissioners allowed him nothing.

Deer, squirrels, otter, raccoons, muskrats, inhabited the woods and marshes, while prairie chickens, quails and wolves were found in the open country. Deer were unusually plentiful here, and men going out after their cows and taking their guns, seldom failed to bring back the hams of a fine animal as trophies of their marksmanship. It very early became the habit of the pioneers to take only the hams of venison, leaving the rest of the carcass to the wolves and dogs, and it was no unusual thing to see twenty-five hams curing in the smoking-house at once. This abundance of game was a great relief to many of the pioneers. Easy as hogs were kept, and numerous as they became in later years, McKean, who kept a large herd, found ample market for all he could raise among the farmers in this region. Many who could not buy, lived on this abundant game, though it soon became tiresome to the taste and proved a poor substitute for beef and pork.

But there was something to be done beside hunt. This would sustain life, but would not subdue the wilderness nor bring in the happy reign of civilization. The earliest effort was made to get a crop of corn. The first crop was planted by cutting a gash in the inverted sod with an axe, dropping the corn and closing it by another blow beside the first. Or it was dropped in every third furrow and the sod turned on it; if the corn was so placed as to find the space between the furrows, it would find daylight; if not, the result of the planting was extremely doubtful. Of course cultivation in this case was impossible, and if the squirrels and crows gave the crop an opportunity to mature, it generally proved a satisfactory return. At first there was no market for the surplus product, and there was only the household and the limited amount of stock to provide for. Wheat was not cultivated here to any extent; the location was not suited to it, and farmers preferred to buy what they needed for their own use, while giving their whole attention to grazing and corn. The lack of milling facilities was another inconvenience that amounted to a hardship. The nearest place where corn or wheat could be ground was at Green's mill, in Dayton. Here, when the roads were passable, the people brought their corn or wheat, and waited with such patience as they could command until they could be served. This waiting frequently consumed a week, and customers of this mill always went prepared to stay until they got their "grist," as the journey hither was not one to be undertaken lightly. But more discouraging than these were the annual floods which regularly visited this township, and brought in their train destruction and disease, harder to bear than any amount of difficulties which energy and pluck might surmount.

Life, in a new country, is everywhere subjected to the misery of malarious diseases. The clearing off of timber or the breaking up of prairie sod, involving the rapid decay of large quantities of vegetable matter, gave rise to the inevitable miasma, which wrought its sure work upon the human system. "Such sickness was generally confined to the last of the summer and fall. There was but little sickness in winter except a few lingering fall cases that had become chronic; there were but few cases after severe frosts, and the spring and early summer were perfectly healthy. It was commonly remarked that when the bloom of the resin weed and other yellow flowers appeared it was time to look for the ague. The first spring flowers on the prairie were mostly pink and white, then followed purple and blue, and about the middle of August yellow predominated.

"High water in spring, flooding the bottoms and filling the lagoons and low places along the streams, and then drying off with the hot sun of July and August, was a fruitful cause of disease, and in such localities it was often quite sickly, while the high prairie was comparatively exempt." * Felix was especially exposed to these inundations, and hardly a year passed without an extensive overflow. The one of 1837 is especially remembered. In the early spring of this year, a sudden flood broke up the ice, which, forming a gorge, held back the waters until their weight made the ice give way, and the flood of water and ice made its way down the Illinois, submerging the islands in its course and flooding its banks until even the highlands were reached, threatening destruction to homes and stock which were supposed to be out of the reach of anything save another deluge. Huge masses of ice were lodged upon the banks in every conceivable shape, which, gradually melting in the spring suns, kept the soaked earth saturated until the middle of summer, when the hot stifling weather of August gave rise to an unusual amount of sickness all along the river. "That season, exaggerated and fearful stories were sent over the country in relation to the sickness. A correspondent of an Eastern paper stated that he saw in a cemetery at La Salle, 300 graves that had never been rained on, and that in a new country where a settlement was but just commenced. This might have been true, but the cemetery belonged to the Catholics, and was the only one this side of Chicago, and thousands of men were there at work on the canal, and they nearly all came to La Salle for burial; and this was late in the fall when there had been no rain for nearly six months." *

Although there was but little to attract emigration to Felix, and later years have demonstrated its ineligibility as a site for a city, yet two very considerable towns have found a place and varied experience within its limits. Jugtown was what its name implies, a place where pottery interests centered. A bed of good potter's clay was found near the western end of Goose Lake, and in 1853, William White, of Chicago, put up the necessary buildings and machinery for the manufacture of drain tile especially for the Chicago market. Such clay was not to be found

---

*Hist. of La Salle County—Baldwin.

* Baldwin.

readily, and there seemed to be a bright prospect for the enterprise. The business expanded, some forty or fifty men were employed, and gathering about the works with their families made quite a town of their settlement. A great difficulty was met at the very outset in the lack of shipping facilities. The roads were poor at best, and the product of the works had to be hauled to Morris for shipment, though considerable effort was made to utilize the Kankakee feeder to obviate this distance. This did not prove successful, and the enterprise gradually went to decay, and with the business went the town, leaving little but the scarred earth to mark its site.

Kankakee City was a more pretentious aggregation of houses, though hardly so well established in fact. The projected canal was the subject of the most absurd speculations. Its leading advocate in Congress, Daniel P. Cook, declared in a document addressed to his constituents, "that in less than thirty years it would relieve the people from the payment of taxes, and even leave a surplus to be applied to other works of public utility." Such estimates were industriously circulated by the friends of this great scheme among the capitalists of the East, and so little experience was had in such matters then, and so prone were people to believe in the existence of an "El Dorado" in the little known West, that capital forgot its traditional caution, and seemed to struggle to reach its fate. When the government put up its share of these lands for sale there was an excited struggle between the actual settlers and the speculators, which resulted in the victory of the settlers who secured the land which they had improved, and what they could pay for adjoining them. But when these purchasers were satisfied there was a great deal of land left which was subsequently picked up by speculators, who held it at five and ten dollars per acre. These prices were so high as to discourage immigration, and land dealers resorted to every device to stimulate the rage for speculation. The infatuation seemed to be contagious; corner lots, claims, pre-emptions and floats, were the chief subject of conversation. Mr. Baldwin thus describes the situation: "A lodger at any of the rickety hotels at that day, would have to sleep in a room containing four or five beds, and from the bargains and contracts made by the lodgers before going to sleep, might well imagine himself on 'Change, or in Wall street, New York, and his companions all millionaires. The writer called at a log cabin toward evening of a rainy day, where some half a dozen farmers were assembled, who had evidently engaged in high speculation during the day. One of the number, addressing himself to me, said, as he slapped his hand very complacently on his thigh; 'I have made ten thousand dollars to-day, and I will make twice that to-morrow;' and I learned from further conversation with his companions, that he had been the least successful one in the company. Towns and villages were laid out at almost every crossroad, and some, where there had never been any road. I set out some small apple trees on my farm, the only ones to be procured, and stuck a stake by each; a stranger coming past, inquired the name of the town I had laid out."

Kankakee City was an outgrowth of this speculative mania and was pretentious enough to satisfy the most exaggerated announcements. In its palmiest days its population did not reach seventy-five souls, yet it had ten public squares, with public parks and broad streets enough to have formed a nucleus for another New York City. The plat with its numerous additions covered about two thousand acres, and lots were sold at auction in Chicago and New York City, and thousands upon thousands of dollars were invested in this midsummer night's dream. In all the prominent real estate centers were seen highly ornamented plats of this city, beautiful with magnificent buildings, and busy with the traffic of capacious warehouses, and crowded steamboat wharves. In its early history, Mr. Beard, the projector of this city, was offered $35,000 for his property, which he rejected. But the crash of 1837 came, and all this paper prosperity passed away like morning dew. Emigration almost entirely ceased; the work on the canal, which had brought a certain fictitious prosperity to this region, barely struggled on, supported by State scrip.

Wheat went down from two dollars per bushel to fifty cents; pork from twenty-five dollars per barrel to one dollar per hundred; corn to ten cents per bushel, and all this in depreciated scrip or store goods at a profit of one hundred per cent. For many years the large territory embraced in the limits of Kankakee City was assessed as lots and thousands of dollars were loaned upon this property as security, but the burden became too great and the land was finally sold for the accumulated taxes, and whatever titles are now held to this property are based upon tax sales. This famous city has long since reverted back to rustic uses, and serves the purposes of the farm, none the less sedately for having at an early day put on city airs.

NOTE.—The site of Kankakee City, between the forks of the Illinois River, is now a part of Au Sable township, being assigned to that township because the facilities for crossing the Desplaines River are better than for crossing the Kankakee.

CHAPTER XVII.*

ERIENNA TOWNSHIP, 33 NORTH, RANGE 6 EAST—CHANGES OF BOUNDARIES—EARLY SETTLEMENT—HORROM CITY—CLARKSON—NORMAN—SURFACE FEATURES—PIONEERS—CHURCHES AND SCHOOLS.

THE Congressional township 33 north, range 6 east, is divided into nearly equal parts by the Illinois River, which enters the township a little north of the middle point of its eastern boundary, and flows southwestwardly through its territory. The difficulty of passing the river for the purposes of township business, has enforced the natural division by political separation, and though one township by the original survey, these portions have always been in different precincts and borne different names.

Erienna is the elder of these twin townships, and is situated north of the river. The northwest corner is a high plateau, ending on the river front near the western boundary, in an abrupt descent of some eighty feet. From this point the second bottom or bench approaches nearly to the river brink, leaving space for barely two or three hundred acres of alluvial bottom lands. The margin of the plateau from the western line of the precinct follows the trend of the river bank, its margin being marked by the common road north of the railroad till it reaches the eastern line of section 10, where it curves northwardly out of the precinct. South of this line of the highland, with the exception of an oval ridge on which Mr. Hoge's residence is placed, the surface of Erienna is principally a flat sandy soil, underlaid with a coal deposit. Long Point Creek rising in the northwest corner of the precinct, furrows through the plateau and flows to the canal, the course of which it follows out of the precinct under the name of Rat Run. Nettle Creek—the English for Little Mazon of the Indians—rises in the lower ground of the eastern part of the precinct, and takes an eastern course into Morris, where, with a sudden turn south, it joins the Illinois. Along the stream the surface is considerably broken and clothed with some of the finest walnut timber, besides other varieties, to be found in the county. On the highlands the timber was of a scrubby character, a certain indication of the stiff clay soil found here. The greater part of the farmers devote their lands to the cultivation of corn, though Messrs. Hoge & Holderman, who own very extensive farms here, pasture large herds of cattle.

The first settler in Erienna, and one of the earliest in the county, was Isaac Hoge. He was a native of Fauquier County, Virginia, and shrewdly foreseeing that money early invested in Illinois lands would make a large and sure return for the investment, came here very early and bought his lands in this township at the first sale before

---

* By J. H. Battle.

there were any other settlers save Marquis, perhaps. He was a young unmarried man, with considerable capital and impressed with the general belief that the prairie would be taken up only where timber was to be had, entered the most of his lands in the timbered section along the Nettle Creek. Other members of his family settled in Nettle Creek township and for some time after his purchase there was no cabin in Erienna to indicate the presence of the white man. Soon afterward he married and moved onto his land here, and adding to his possessions by further purchase from time to time has now one of the large farms of the county. Another large farm owned by A. Holderman occupies the larger part of the central portion of the precinct, which with that of Mr. Hoge's is devoted largely to pasturage for cattle. The large herds owned by Mr. Holderman at an early date were as remarkable a sight as a herd of buffaloes, and their trails to the watering places during the summer were said to be as conspicuous as those of the buffaloes on the plains. Mr. Holderman, however, was an early settler in Kendall County and bought land here somewhat later.

Columbus Pinney was perhaps the first actual resident of Erienna. He was a native of New York State and came out by the lakes to Chicago and from thence to Marseilles. In the Spring of 1836, he came to section 12, where Datus Kent had put up a log house and barn for Kimball of Marseilles. Here Pinney kept the stage change and hotel which is now known as "Castle Danger." The cabin is destroyed but the stable still serves the purposes of a barn, though it stands on a new location. The origin of its later name is very obscure. After staying here three years Pinney removed to Aurora and the cabin was empty for awhile. It was subsequently inhabited for a short time when it was left untenanted again. It was used occasionally by wayfarers, and perhaps horse thieves and prairie bandits found it a convenient place to stay for a night, but no authentic incident can be learned in which the name could take its rise. Its name is well fixed, however, and generally used, and is probably the outgrowth of the natural respect for the mysterious.

In 1840, O. Cone, a native of Jefferson County, New York, came by the lakes to Detroit. From that point, with his family, he came in wagons across the country to Marseilles, where his brother-in-law, Kimball, was engaged in superintending some public improvements. Cone remained here until 1840, when he rented a farm of Mr. Hoge, on section 6, 33, 7. He was subsequently elected sheriff of the county, and afterward retired to a farm which he purchased on section 2, 33, 6. Messrs. Kennedy and Kendrick were attracted from Ohio by the canal work, and on the stopping of operations, settled, in 1842, on section 7. About 1845 or '6, Peter Griggs settled on section 3, and about the same time Abram Holderman came into the precinct. In 1848, Charles Moody came in from Marseilles and settled near where the road crosses the canal on section 15. After this the settlement of the precinct rapidly increased. The completion of the canal brought in a large number of persons seeking a home, speculators, tired of holding property which did not appreciate fast enough to more than meet the expense of taxes and other charges, began to sell, and the settlement soon became general.

Horrom City was the name of an ambitious plat of ground which was staked out in 1836, by Dr. Horrom, who originally settled south of the river. It did not prove a failure, because it never had any promise of success. A short-lived stage route passed near it, but beyond the imagination of its projector, the location had no relation to it, or anything tangible. Clarkson was the original name of the location of Castle Danger. Kimball, who was interested in the stage line, hoped through the influence of this enterprise to build up a village which should become the county seat, but fate decided in favor of Morris, and Clarkson did not mature. During the construction of the canal a number of temporary shanties gathered about the old log cabin, but they soon passed away, leaving it solitary.

In —— the precinct was extended on the east side to the corporation limits of the county seat. This was done through the influence of the farmers in this part of the county, to avoid the taxation which the extension of the city limits in that direction would involve. This does no injustice to Morris, as there is land remaining in that precinct on which the county capital may expand into a very considerable town.

NORMAN.

This precinct, abutting upon the south margin of the Illinois River, is probably the best timbered and most broken portion of Grundy County. The high land approaches very close to the river bank, leaving not more than five hundred acres of bottom lands on the whole river front. The high, broken land in the northwestern corner of Wauponsee extends into the eastern border of Norman, and forms in this precinct quite a picturesque landscape along the road that enters it from the northeast. A peculiar elevation on Bills' Run at this point is a striking freak of nature, or, as some of its peculiarities suggest, an important relic of the Mound Builders. It is a circular mound, about seventy-five feet high, and some two hundred feet diameter at the base. It stands at the head of a little bayou, isolated from the line of surrounding bluffs, save for the connection of a narrow causeway, which by a gentle descent and ascent bridges the intervening valley. It is entirely bare of trees, save an oak which grows out of the side, half way toward the summit. No excavation has been attempted in this mound, and it is doubtful whether its peculiarities would warrant any considerable expenditure of time and money with the hope of making valuable discoveries, but the difficulty of assigning a plausible theory for its natural construction, has given rise to considerable speculation in regard to it. This is known as "Devil's Mound," and others of less note have a similar nomenclature, though with what appropriateness is perhaps difficult to determine, unless one accepts the statement of the young man who suggested, "because we wonder how the devil it came here."

The middle portion of the river front is less broken, though the ground rises to the final "bench" quite abruptly, until the western third of the river line, where is found the roughest country in the county. Bills' Run, rising near the southern line, in the eastern part, flows north through this precinct and loses itself in the low ground which borders the river. Hog Run takes a westerly course from the center of Norman and flows into the Illinois; and further west Armstrong Run, taking its source near the southern line, flows nearly direct north, and empties into the Illinois a little west of Hog Run. These streams are little more than prairie water-courses that serve to carry off the surplus water of the surface, and are dry a large part of the year. Their names are suggestive of their own origin. The timber is oak, hackberry, walnut and maple. The broken character of the country naturally protected the timber, and the early settlers found here a good field for "foraging," which was largely indulged in at an early date. The soil is largely the black prairie mold, free from bowlders, and rather low and wet in the central parts, with rather strong clay lands on the high ground. The farmers are largely devoted to the exclusive cultivation of corn, and feed more of it to hogs than in other parts of the county. There is some stock-raising, Mr. E. B. James having given considerable attention to the breeding of horses.

The first settler in this precinct was David Bunch, on the southeast quarter of section 21. He was a native of North Carolina, but moved to Tennessee, and from thence came to Illinois, coming to Norman in the winter of 1834-5. It is probable that he was attracted thither by the fine timber here, which had been bought up by the speculators. There was a good market for logs or hewn timber at Ottawa and other points on the river, and as there was none to protect it, large quantities of it were stolen by early settlers, who felt justified in these depredations by the fact that their holding this land prevented the settlement of the county. Mr. Bunch made the cutting and rafting of this timber to market his principal business, and for some years made no effort to make a home here. He afterward cleared up a good farm, on which he lived many years. In the same year Datus Kent joined him here and went into the timber business on the same basis. He had his cabin on the south fraction of section 15, and built the log hotel across the river, which is now referred to as Castle Danger. Kent was from the South, and a winter or two was enough to satisfy him that he was out of his element, and left for Arkansas in 1837, leaving no farm improvements. Henry Norman was another prominent settler, and came in about 1839. He came from Brown County, Ohio, from where he came first to Braceville, about 1836, but subsequently came to Norman and put up his cabin on the east half of the southeast quarter of section 25. Here he stayed until 1842, when he removed to Morris. His son, Thomas J. Norman, remained at the homestead, and was the first supervisor of the precinct under the action of the county in 1850. It is from him that the precinct takes its name. Dr. Timothy Horrom was an early settler here. He was one of that large class of persons who became infected by the speculative mania. He settled on section 20, and with a large family of boys began to make a home. He was a peculiar man; had a taste for whisky, which was not uncommon in that day, but which led him into a great many escapades, and gained for him quite a reputation in the county. His mania for speculation led him to found Horrom City, on the other side of the river, a paper metropolis, which passed through the common experience. He finally moved over to Erienna, where he died about 1860. John Sullivan, an Irishman, who was brought here by the work on the canal, came into Norman about 1841. He came here with no capital but his hands and plenty of pluck, and settled on the southeast quarter of section 13, and has since improved a fine farm. In July, 1847, E. B. James came in from Kendall County. He was a native of Ohio, and came to Kendall County a young man. Here he married, and a little later came to Norman and settled on section 25. In 1848, the canal being finished, the lands rapidly came into market, and Norman shared in the tide of emigration which rapidly filled up the county.

In forming any conception of frontier life, one is apt to be influenced by some preconceived arbitrary standard. The pioneer of to-day goes not into an unknown and unexplored wilderness. The enterprising newspaper has been before him; the soil, the climate, the mineral resources, the agricultural advantages—the whole situation has been exhaustively mapped out, while railroads carry him forward with speed and comfort to the scene of his frontier labors. Nor do the modern advantages cease here. Having fixed upon his field of operations, material ready framed to form his dwelling, improved machinery to till the soil, and a century's experience, unite to rob his experience of much of its difficulties, and to insure a speedily successful outcome of his venture. In ten years he has surrounded himself with more of the luxuries of civilization than the pioneers of Illinois possessed after twenty-five years of effort. And these rapid strides of progress, it should be remembered, have been principally made within the last twenty-five years. While the pioneers of Illinois profited by the momentum acquired in the advance of the previous century, it should not be forgotten that they have placed the weight of their experience and achievement with the forces that now accelerate the advance of the star of empire westward. The large purchases of timber lands by speculators in 1835 greatly retarded the settlement of this section of the State, and Grundy County was as undeveloped and bare of civilizing resources in 1847 as many parts of the State ten years earlier. When Mr. James came to Norman, in this year, there were but five families within its limits, and the general character of the country was that of an untamed wilderness. The completion of the canal, however, was the signal for a mighty change, and from that time forward the county took on a rapid change.

The early settlers brought nothing with them but what the necessities of the situation demanded. One wagon generally sufficed to bring the family, household furniture, farming implements, and frequently one or two months' supplies. It requires no great amount of consideration to believe that luxuries, or even comforts, could find no place in such an outfit, and so the pioneer, after constructing a shelter for his family, found his skill and ingenuity taxed to their utmost to supply this deficiency. It was necessary to manufacture tables, chairs and bedsteads before they could be used, and some of the most striking incidents of frontier cabin life are founded upon this universal dearth of ordinary comforts. The early years of a new settlement were occupied in supplying these wants and in subjecting the land to the payment of its annual tribute. This accomplished, the pioneer, ever mindful of the prosperity of his children and the conservation of society, summoned the church and school to his aid.

The Fox River settlement was early made a base of operations by the Methodist church, and from a missionary plant established here, sent out its itinerants throughout the settlements on the upper part of the Illinois River. The first church organization in Norman was a Protestant Methodist Church, which was built up under the administration of a Rev. Mr. Fowler. John Piatt and E. B. James, with three or four others, constituted the membership, which held its meetings in the different cabins about the neighborhood. About 1854, a Methodist Episcopal church was organized here, which gradually displaced the older society and held its meetings in a school-house which had been erected in the meantime. The church subsequently held its meetings in the Baptist church building until 1870, when it erected a place of worship on the southeast corner of section 35. This is a neat frame structure erected at a cost of about $2,800, and reflects credit upon efforts of the church and the management, Rev. J. W. Odell and Mr. E. B. James, who were prominent in securing it.

The Baptist church was organized here about 1854, and found its main support in the families of Messrs. Haymond, Winters and Manley. This church used the one school-house in the precinct, alternating its services with those of the Protestant Methodist and the Methodist Episcopal churches, until about 1862. Mr. Thos. Haymond, Lewis Winters and the Rev. Mr. Fosket, were prominent in securing a church building at this time, and the frame building, thirty by fifty feet, situated on the southeast quarter of the northeast quarter of section 26, is due to their labors. It was erected at a cost of about $2,700.

The first school-house was a log structure, built in 1853, at Bills' Point. The spot thus designated is a "point of timber" near the center of section 25, the name of which, it is said, originated with Jacob Claypool. Mr. Haymond relates a characteristic story of those times to the effect, that going to Mr. Claypool's on business one day he was accompanied by a friend from the East who was here on a visit. His friend naturally wore his "store clothes," and a linen shirt and collar. This was a remarkable innovation upon the custom of Grundy County at that time and made a decided impression upon Mr. Claypool's mind. Business took the three persons to Bills' Run, when, Mr. Haymond being a new comer to Norman, inquired the origin of the name of the run. His reply was, that some years before a Mr. Bills who had been there, created such a sensation by his civilized attire, that his advent had been commemorated by giving his name to a ford, a stream, and this point of timber. In describing this hero, Mr. Claypool, pointing at Mr. Haymond's friend, said: "He wore a white shirt and collar, and was just such a dandy as he." It may therefore be accepted that the name of Bills' Run and Bills' Point is a frontier compliment to a white shirt and collar. It is certainly appropriate, if not significant, that the first school-house was erected at this point. Here Miss Reniff taught the first school and was succeeded by Mrs. Stoutemyer. This primitive building has been succeeded by a modern structure and the number multiplied, so that whether through the increase of education or the breaking down of frontier isolation, white shirts and collars are now by no means a rarity in Norman Precinct.

CHAPTER XVIII.*

MAZON TOWNSHIP—EARLY TOPOGRAPHICAL FEATURES—ITS PIONEERS—GROWTH AND DEVELOPMENT OF THE SETTLEMENT—NEW MAZON—CHURCHES AND SCHOOLS.

TOWNSHIP 32 north, range 7 east, is situated as near as may be, in the center of Grundy County. Its name, Mazon, was derived from the stream which bears this designation, a branch of which crosses a corner of the township. The Indian signification of the word is nettle, and finds its appropriateness as a name for the township in the fact that this plant was found in considerable numbers on the rich timber bottoms of this section. The Indians and early settlers turned this plant to a useful account, taking its fibre, in the absence of hemp, for twine and a coarse thread. The general surface is very level, with hardly variation enough to afford drainage for the surplus water. The soil is good, strong, black muck, and will prove, when properly drained and cultivated, as good land as there is in the county, but it is readily affected by moisture, which it seems to hold for a long time. This characteristic is the bane of travelers and road-makers, and often causes the farmer expensive delays. The general drainage is toward the northeast, the township being marked by six watercourses running about a mile apart, in a generally parallel course. The principal ones are the Waupecan Creek, Johnny Run, Murray Sluice, and the West Fork of the Mazon. These are all insignificant streams now, generally drying up in the hot months of the summer and assuming a short-lived importance in the spring or on the occasion of a freshet. Their early history, however, was not quite so tame, when from various causes, the water passed off less readily, and swollen with the spring freshet, these streams overflowed their low banks, uniting their waters and giving a large part of the township the appearance of a lake from six inches to two feet deep. The timber was originally found along these streams, the principal bodies being known as Wauponsee Grove, Johnny Grove, and Owen's Spring, on section 24. The farmers give the most of their attention to raising corn, though this is alternated largely with stock-raising, as the corn market proves more or less profitable. There is a gradual increase in the amount of corn fed from year to year, and many of the best farmers believe this to be the most profitable disposition to make of the corn crop. Dairying is becoming a more marked feature here also, the creamery established in Mazon giving quite an impetus to this branch of farming industry.

The first settlement of the township was begun in 1833 by A. K. Owen, who, in company with Dr. L. S. Robbins, John Hogoboom and others, came into the present territory of Grundy County on a prospecting expedition. To this party of explorers the southern portion of the county

* By J. H. Battle.

is principally indebted for its early settlement, and it will doubtless be found interesting to learn something of the history of the leader of this party and at the same time gain some knowledge of the contemporaneous history of the northern part of the State.

Mr. Owen has left an autobiography from which the following is taken: " My first visit to Illinois was in the summer of 1819. I made my way from Syracuse, N. Y., which then contained a population of one family engaged in public entertainment. The next town of any note was Buffalo, which was then being rebuilt after the burning by the Indians and Canadians during the war of 1812-15. The next town was Cleveland, composed of one store, three or four mechanical shops and eight or ten families; next was Columbus, Ohio, containing 300 inhabitants. The first mill was then being built on the Scioto River. The next town was Dayton, composed of about a dozen families; next Eaton, of six or eight families; Conersville, of one family; then two days' journey to Terre Haute, through a wilderness, guided by a blazed trail, but where no wagon had ever passed. The population of Terre Haute consisted of about a dozen families, and here two flatboats had been launched and loaded with goods for trade lower down on the river. From Terre Haute the route lay to Edwardsville, Ill., where a population of 250 or 300 was found. Here I attended a trial for murder—People v. Edwards—for the killing of Daniel D. Smith, the U. S. land agent. After a three days' trial, in which the accused was ably defended by Felix Grundy, of Tennessee, Edwards was acquitted, and Grundy, mounting his horse, took his foe, in shape of a thousand dollar negress, behind him on his horse and paced off for home.

" North and west from Edwardsville there were no settlements whatever. My object had been to hunt up two quarter sections of land upon the bounty tract, but the land agent having been killed and his place not yet supplied, all I could do was to take on a full cargo of fever and ague and return to New York.

" My next visit to Illinois was in the spring of 1827 or 1828. I journeyed from Hazlegreen, Alabama, on horseback to Quincy, Ill. It was a very wet season, and I had creeks to swim more or less every day, carrying my saddle bags on my shoulders. I ferried the Mississippi at Golconda, six miles from the mouth of the Illinois, there being very little settlement thereabouts. The whole of the military tract was then included in Pike County. Some fifteen or twenty miles above the mouth of the Illinois, under the Mississippi bluff, was a little town called Atlas, settled by two Ross families. From there to Quincy were two families, Harrison and Thomas. At Quincy were also two families, Woods and Keys, and one single man, H. H. Snow. The first county election took place a few days after my arrival. Snow was elected circuit and county clerk, recorder and justice of the peace; Wood and Keys held the balance of the offices with the exception of sheriff and constable, which were bestowed upon me. In August of the same year I accompanied the first wagon from Quincy to Galena. The Sac and Fox Indians inhabited Rock Island with two military companies on the island. There were no other whites on the route.

At Galena there were two small trading posts, a few miners, but not a white woman above Quincy. In August of the next year I was again in company with the first wagon from Galena to Chicago, crossing Rock River above Rockford. The population of Chicago was then about 900, with two companies of troops at Fort Dearborn.

"In 1829, we obtained permission to organize a county. At a meeting held for this purpose the name of Daviess was suggested for the new county, but it was objected that there was then a county by that name in the State. At this, John Armstrong jumped up and suggested Jo Daviess, which was accepted. I remained at Galena until the fall of 1830, when I took what was called "the sucker shoot;" went down the river to winter, which was a very common thing with the miners. I put up for winter-quarters on Fancy Creek, eight miles north of Springfield, which then contained just four families and a tread-mill for grinding corn.

"In the spring of 1831, I found myself the wealthy owner of two horses and harness, but no wagon, so I cut a couple of poles for thills, put cross pieces behind the horse, set on my clothes trunk, hitched my other horse in front, and then, whip and single line in hand, set my face northward to seek my fortune. The first good fortune I met was in the person of Chloe, only daughter of Ezekiel Stacey, living on Oxbow prairie. Just there and then we made a life-long contract, got consent of her parents, and next morning I proceeded on my northward journey to locate and prepare a home. That night I reached the cabin of a Mr. Long, three miles south of Ottawa on Coville Creek. Mrs. Long was very low with dyspepsia and had to be fed every half hour. Her husband being exhausted by his unremitting attention, I volunteered to care for her through the night and did so, and the next morning while harnessing my horses, George Walker, the first sheriff of La Salle County, summoned me to appear forthwith to serve on the grand jury, it being the first session of the circuit court of this county. Of course I pleaded non-residence, but the sheriff informed me that he had summoned every eligible man in the county and still lacked one, and I *must* serve. So I went to Ottawa and was appointed foreman of the jury. For want of a better place we held our deliberations under two maple trees on the bank of the river, situated about ten yards apart. Our constable was Moses Booth, and he was kept busy running from one tree to the other to keep the hogs out of hearing distance of our deliberations. The only complaint before the jury was for breach of promise, but the jury brought in no bill. On presentation of this report, the judge complimented the good people of the county as a law-abiding community, from the fact that they had nothing for the grand jury to do. At dinner time we sent the constable to David Walker's, the only cabin in the place, to engage our dinners, and got answer that he had but two rooms, one for the court and one for the kitchen, and that the judge and attorneys had monopolized these accommodations. We got some crackers and cheese, however, at a little trading post kept by George Walker, and was allowed to enjoy this frugal meal only through the indefatigable energy of our constable who kept the hogs at bay. On being dismissed from the grand jury, I returned to Mr. Long's, and at his earnest solicitation bought his claim, giving him one of my horses and two months' work.

"On the 17th of July, 1831, I borrowed a horse and six dollars in cash from Mr. Long, and went to Oxbow prairie and redeemed my vow; then returned and paid my two months' work due on my claim, and on the first of October following, went after my wife. I borrowed a yoke of oxen and wagon of Mrs. Armstrong, living near the mouth of Coville Creek, attached a rope to the horn of the 'near ox,' and went to Oxbow prairie, returning soon after with my wife and little household effects, and set up housekeeping on Coville Creek. The next spring the Black Hawk War broke out, and at its close, I sold my claim, and in the following spring came on an exploring expedition to Sulphur Springs." This party made their headquarters at Johnny's Grove, and claims were made in what are now the townships of Vienna, Braceville and Mazon. Owen was the only one who settled in Mazon, choosing a site on the West Fork of the Mazon Creek, a little below old Mazon Village. This was in the spring or summer of 1833. By the help of one man he succeeded in erecting a log cabin fourteen feet square, into which he moved the following May, and began housekeeping without door, window or floor. For a short time his most accessible neighbors were one family at Ottawa, one at Pontiac, and one at Joliet, each from twenty-six to thirty miles away. But this state of affairs continued but a short time. In this year quite a number of settlers came into Wauponsee and other townships of the county. None came to Mazon until the following spring, when James McCarty moved from Ottawa and took up his abode upon Wanponsee's little corn patch of three or four acres on section five. He was a bachelor, had served in the campaign against Black Hawk, and found no trouble in camping out while he put in his first crop of corn. This he did with a hoe, and in the fall the stalks furnished him the material with which he built his winter quarters. In June of 1835, he bought his land at the "land sale" and lived here until 1845, when he died and was buried in the Claypool burying ground, the first one to occupy it. Following McCarty late in the fall came Jesse Newport, from Belmont County, Ohio. He settled on the southwest corner of section six, secured his land at the public sale in 1835, and improved his place until 1839, when he rented it to Mr. Dewey, an English immigrant, and went to Hennepin where he died in 1840. In the same fall, James C. Spores built a cabin on the east half of the southwest quarter of section five, and improved his claim here for three or four years when he sold out to John L. Pickering, and moved to the "far West."

James P. Ewing came to Mazon in the spring of 1835, building his cabin on the west half of the northeast quarter of section six. The land here was very wet, and greatly discouraged his efforts at making a home. He lived here two or three years, following at times his trade of shoemaker. He finally sold out to Jesse Newport, though not before he had lost a child by the ravages of the miasmatic climate. Pickering, who bought out Spores, was of Quaker extraction, and came from Belmont

County, Ohio. He was one of the early county officers and lived here for many years, but subsequently moved to Bloomington in this State. The marriage of his daughter Sarah to Gales Austin, by Jacob Claypool, J. P., was probably the first wedding in the township.

About the same time with Ewing came John Ridgway, who bought land on the northwest quarter of section five, and built his cabin there. He improved this place until about 1837, when he sold out to Nicholas Summers and went to Indiana. David Spencer became a settler here about this time also, built his cabin just above Pickering, and subsequently married a daughter of Mr. Summers and went to Indiana. In the fall of 1835, Augustus H. Owen, a lawyer, came from New York and took up his residence in the Hogoboom cabin. This was the first lawyer in Grundy County, but he soon discovered that he was considerably in advance of his age, and finding no demand for his legal abilities, he moved in 1836 to Ottawa, where he followed his profession for a year or two and was subsequently drowned in Rock River.

In the summer of 1835, J. C. Murray came to Mazon from Oswego County, New York. He was a brother-in-law of A. K. Owen, and being desirous of getting more land where his growing family could find opportunity of securing homes for themselves, he was induced to come to Mazon on the representations of Mr. Owen. He came with his family by the lakes to Chicago, and was just forty-nine days on the water. He brought with him his household effects two new wagons, but of course, no teams, and leaving his family at Chicago he came to Owen's on foot. The latter at once returned to Chicago with his brother-in-law, taking his own team and hiring another to bring the Murray family to their new home. Owen went to Hennepin subsequently, and Murray rented the farm for awhile, in the meantime looking up an eligible site for a permanent home. He then bought land on the old Chicago and Bloomington trail near the Murray sluice on section 33. His cabin was called the "Half Way House," it being situated about an equal distance—sixty-eight miles—from either terminus of the road. This cabin was one of the earliest in the township to be built out on the prairie. The family was moved in before completed, and a blanket for some time served to close the doorway. There was no floor save the earth, and the only board to be got was finally sawed and spliced so as to furnish a suitable door.

Mr. Murray was drowned in Johnny Run in June of 1844, an accident which affords a striking incident in the life of the early times. Mr. Murray was then on the grand jury, which was in session at Morris, and was a guest of Mr. Armstrong, the pioneer hotel keeper of that place. There had been quite a freshet, and from various causes the landlord found himself out of meat for the morning meal. Murray, who had several pieces of smoked meat at home, volunteered to go in the night and get them to supply the deficiency. He started out on horseback and got home safely, but on his way back to Morris, he missed the ford and was drowned.

James McKeen, an early settler in the county and identified with the early history of several townships, was also an early res-

ident of this township. He first moved to the mouth of the Au Sable, thence to the old "Kankakee city," and later to the old Clover Place near the through trail. Here he kept hotel for awhile, when about 1840, he located on section 23, near the old village of Mazon. Hiram Fuller, a relative of A. K. Owen, came from New York about 1839 and settled in Mazon. In 1840 or 41, the Gibson family came to Mazon from Wauponsee township; the family consisting of Robert and Silas, and two sisters, Ann and Bathsheba, came to Norman township about 1837 or 8. The boys were coopers by trade and found the quality and quantity of speculators' timber a profitable source of supply. The sisters married and Silas died before Robert came into Mazon. He first settled in Wauponsee Grove, but subsequently bought land in sections 10 and 11, on Johnny Run, where he improved a large farm.

Of the early experiences of this settlement there is nothing peculiar to this township to be noted. The nearest post-office was at Ottawa, then Dresden, and later at Morris. The nearest mills were those at Dayton, Wilmington, and Milford, or Millington. In some respects the community in Mazon were less favorably situated than some others in the county. The number of streams across the surface of the township indicates the slow natural drainage, and it was no unusual occurrence for these to join by overflowing their banks. Under these circumstances all traveling was out of the question. Mr. A. O. Murray relates, on such an occasion, his father's family found themselves with a very slender supply of provisions in the house. A man had been engaged to go to mill at Dayton, but the sudden rise of water had cut off his return. The neighbors who were accessible were in nearly as bad a plight, and there was no resort save to take account of stock and wait for the subsidence of the waters. They found their whole stock consisted of some beans and salt, and on these, of which there was no great supply, the family prepared to subsist for an indefinite time. Fortunately they had a new-milch heifer which supplied the family with milk and butter, the latter serving to render more palatable the slippery elm bark which was fried to eke out the meager store. A sharp freeze which rendered a passage through the submerged territory more difficult, protracted this experience for three weeks. This difficulty in getting to mill was felt to be a serious drawback in this section for years, and was not obviated until the county was formed, and bridges built across the principal streams. Mr. Charles Huston relates a tedious experience of this sort as late as 1845. The community in the southern part of the township had been travel-bound for some time, and while each farmer had plenty of wheat and corn, their families were using boiled wheat or grated corn as a substitute for flour. Huston, a newcomer, had neither, and proposed to earn some flour by taking a load to mill for the community. His wagon was soon filled with wheat, and he set out on his journey. He found but little difficulty in getting across streams by ferry or ford, but the frequent sloughs that blocked his way were not so easily surmounted. Four times each way he was obliged to unload his wagon and carry its contents around, while his team used their utmost powers to drag the empty wagon through the quagmires. On his return, his team worn out with the tedious journey, he was obliged to get assistance to get his empty wagon out of one of these places.

There was but little stock in the township save the horses and oxen which served as teams to the farmers. A few cows and hogs were kept, but there was little market for them, and a good cow could be bought for six or eight dollars. The abundance of game relieved the settler of the necessity of buying meat or of using such animals as they had, save for a change or steady supply. Deer, prairie chickens, and wolves were found in great numbers. The latter sometimes proved troublesome to young stock, but the price which the county paid for their scalps more than compensated for their depredations.

The through trail which passed along the southeastern corner of this township gave this section some prestige. A great deal of teaming was done on this trail from as far south as Springfield, while considerable stock was driven along this route to Chicago. The teamsters as a rule were a rough class. They slept under their wagons at night, brought their own provisions and did their own cooking. Their teams were generally turned into the nearest corn-patch, a liberty which settlers learned not to resent. The corn was of but little value, and unless the owner was of a muscular build and willing to take his pay "out of the hide" of the offender there was little chance of redress. Thus the professional teamster, though he got comparatively very little pay, continued to make his trip to Chicago from the south with wheat, and return loaded with salt and store goods, a favorable trip consuming from two to three weeks.

Mr. Huston relates a trip to Chicago, which illustrates a common experience of the time. Some drovers had found it necessary to slaughter some hogs which were unable to travel further, and engaged Mr. Huston to take a load to Chicago for twelve dollars. It was in January, and in company with another team he started on his trip by way of Morris. As they crossed the ice on the river at this place, the rain began to fall with the temperature. The roads gradually became heavier, and little more than half way to the city it was found necessary to leave a part of each load, buried in a hay stack, to prevent the pork from thawing out, and proceed to the city with half a load, which was accomplished only after almost superhuman exertion. On discharging their load, the teams were obliged to get the remainder, and deliver it in Chicago. In the meanwhile the mud of the roads was gradually getting deeper until the last trip was made with the wheels sinking to the hub most of the way. The return trip Mr. Huston utilized by bringing a thousand feet of pine lumber for his building then going up at Mazon. As frequently occurs in an open winter, the weather changed to a cooler temperature as suddenly as it had warmed to a thaw, and the return trip was made through mud, gradually stiffening with the cold, which greatly retarded the progress homeward. On arriving at Morris, the river was found banks full and impassable, and to save time the wagons were loaded with coal from Goold Ridge, and taken to Kendall County where it was disposed of to blacksmiths. On their return the river was found still impassable. Ice had formed in the center of the river, but at either margin was a space of running water which defied passage. After waiting some time and becoming impatient with delay, Mr. Huston conceived a plan to cross the stream. Using his lumber to bridge the margins on either side and after testing the strength of the ice by pushing his wagon on it by hand, and subsequently leading a horse on, he proceeded to cross. Hitching one horse on the end of the tongue of the wagon, and leading the other in the rear, the weight was so distributed as to promise a safe passage. Unfortunately the bridge on the south margin proved defective, and wagon and horses were precipitated into the freezing water. The leading horse proved true, and swam out, bringing the wagon on to solid ground. The led horse, however, refused to swim, and it was only with great exertion and the strength of the other animal, that he was brought to shore. In the meanwhile Mr. Huston had spent an hour or two, waist deep in water getting his team in shape and saving his hard earned lumber. The latter he piled up in a safe place on the bank and reached home nearly frozen after just three weeks' absence.

The early traffic on the Bloomington and Chicago road was very large and seemed to warrant the belief that the canal would not greatly interfere with it. Mr. Charles Huston who had come from Syracuse, N. Y., in 1845, had kept hotel there and doubtless could see no good reason with such advantage as the trail afforded, why a city should not grow up here as readily as elsewhere. At any rate in 1848, urged by a Mr. Hall of Ottawa, who agreed to open a store, he bought land of McKeen and laid out forty acres in streets, squares and lots.

The store was started but subsequently was sold out to Wm. B. Royal. As the country developed all enterprises based on the permanency of trail traffic failed. The railroad and canal put an end to teaming and "droving," and the store here languished. A co-operative store was inaugurated, but this finally failed, passing into private hands and being eventually closed out by fire about 1854. Some years later a temperance society put up a building, renting the under part for a store, but the railroad put a finishing stroke to the declining prosperity of the town and the metropolis was transferred to the "center." The building of the Pekin, St. Louis & Chicago railroad gave a new impetus to the village growth of the township, but transferred it to the location of the depot. A store was begun here about 1875, by McAfee, who was succeeded by Gifford and later by M. Isham. A church, a school-house, a half dozen stores two grain elevators, and a cluster of rather new looking wooden buildings, represent a village of some 500 inhabitants, which is known by the post-office and railroad authorities as Mazon, but is popularly designated by the addition of "New town" in parenthesis, to distinguish it from old Mazon.

An enterprise which does much to build up the village is a creamery which was established at the Miller cheese factory in 1880. In the following winter it was brought to the village and now occupies a building devoted exclusively to its purposes. The project was conceived and put in force by T. Rankin, who found it impossible to profitably handle farmer's butter, which he bought in the course of his business. In starting the creamery he revolutionized the cheese business which had a fair start here, and greatly extended the business of his general store. Nine teams are maintained, each of which makes a daily circuit of twenty-five or thirty miles, skimming the milk of patrons and bringing in the cream to the factory, at the same time taking orders and delivering goods from his store to any who may desire them. The cream is bought by the inch; the milk being placed in cans of a foot in diameter, the thickness of the cream is noted through a graduated glass inserted in the side of the can. An inch of cream is calculated to make a pound of butter, and varies in the price paid with the general changes of the butter market. The capacity of the factory is 1,100 pounds of butter per day, and at certain seasons of the year is crowded to its full capacity, involving an annual outlay of from $25,000 to $35,000 for cream alone.

The Methodist church was the earliest religious organization to gain a foothold in this community. Missionary agents of the Congregational society were early in the township, especially in the southern part, but for various reasons their efforts did not result in any marked permanent achievement. In William and Charles Royal, who came into Mazon about 1847, the Methodist organization had zealous workers, and a society was formed which erected a place of worship at Old Mazon, about 1851. When the new town sprung up, this building was sold, and now serves as a granary, not far from its former site. The present neat, wooden structure at Mazon, was erected about 1877, at a cost of $2,400, and is the only one in the village.

The Wauponsee Grove Congregational Church is a society in the northwestern corner of the township. This church was organized May 6, 1864, with seventeen members, among whom were H. B. Goodrich, William Hotchkiss, F. T. Benton, Abbott Barker, John Sample, and their wives. Rev. James Longhead, of Morris, had been holding Sabbath services here before this, and continued to supply this point and another neighborhood with alternate services. In 1868, a resident pastor was secured, the church holding its services in the school-house in the meanwhile. May 27, 1869, a site was selected, and one acre of land donated for the erection of a church building, and being the jubilee year, the effort to secure a church home was greatly assisted by the enthusiasm evinced by the Congregational membership at large. Memorial offerings were received from various persons and churches abroad, to which was added the enthusiasm of the ladies of the society here, who pledged a thousand dollars toward its erection. The building was erected, dedicated June 3, 1871, and in March of the following year, the church voted itself self-sustaining, having received aid from the American Home Missionary Society since its organization. It has now a membership of some sixty-two members, and a Sunday school of about 106 attendants.

The earliest school-house was probably on section 24, and was built in 1837. In its time it was the finest cabin in the settlement. It was a square structure, built of logs, with windows made of six panes of glass placed in a single horizontal line in an enlarged crack between the logs. Against the log just below this window, supported by pegs driven into the side of the structure, was a rough puncheon which by courtesy was called the desk. Before this, on rude slab benches, the scholars sat and faced about as they copied the epigrammatic wisdom which adorned the top line of the copy-books of a quarter century ago. This cabin had a floor of riven planks, trimmed to lay reasonably still when trod upon, and was the admiration of the community. Mr. Axtell was the first wielder of the birchen scepter.

No trace of these primitive times now greet the eye; the men and women of that early day, with all their toil and privations, have gone and made no sign; they labored, and the present generation has entered into their labors; the present stands upon the shoulders of the past; and, if manfully meeting the duties of the present hour, we lift the world higher by the full stature of a man, the pioneers of this land will not have toiled in vain.

CHAPTER XIX.*

VIENNA TOWNSHIP—PIONEERS OF THE PRAIRIE—THE CHANGES OF FIFTY YEARS—ILLINOIS CITY—VERONA—THE CHURCH AND SCHOOL.

IN following the arbitrary distinctions of township lines, the historian of the early settlement finds himself placed in an unnatural position. The events to which this county was indebted for its first inhabitants, recognized no such limitations. The broad expanse of prairie, radiant with the beauty of the early summer's flowers, or brown with the ripened food for a thousand herds, was unmarked to the pioneer, save by distant groves that indicated the water-courses. The adventurous settler, attracted by the flattering report of friends, or lured on by his love of frontier life and adventure, placed his family and goods in a wagon, and casting off his moorings, became a wanderer, knowing no home but the canvas that served him as shelter by night. His choice of land was dictated by caprice, and generally resulted in an unfortunate selection, though it often took years of sickness, and even bereavement by death itself to convince him of his error. The points of timber were generally chosen, or some spring of water, both of which, experience has proven to be the most insalubrious locations open to choice. But here, patiently enduring toil and privation, the pioneer surmounted the difficulties of his situation, and has left an enduring monument to his memory in these fruitful fields and thriving towns. There seem to have been few indications in that early day as to the points to which subsequent growth would accrue with the greatest advantage. Choice was determined by the most frivolous chance; expectation was at a dead level. This situation was not inconsistent with an almost feverish excitement over the effect which the construction of the canal was expected to have on this whole region. The great consideration which "puzzled the will," was where the "bonanza's" lightning would strike. It is not strange, therefore, that the early settlement of this county, molded by such motives and influences, should be characterized by no definable method. But the later growth of society has long since modified these early traditions. Years of association in the capacity of a political precinct have given rise to a community of interests, out of which have sprung policies and practices plainly apparent even to the stranger, and township lines now bind the country population with as strong a tie as national boundaries.

Vienna lies just west of Mazon, and in its topography and early history is closely related. It is rather of a higher elevation, parts of it being considerably broken and all of it somewhat rolling. It is traversed diagonally in a northeasterly direction, by five unimportant streams, Hog and Bills'

---

* By J. H. Battle.

Runs flowing into Norman, the Waupecan and a nameless stream passing into Mazon, and Thunder Creek joining Johnny Run in the latter township. The character of these water-courses, of the soil and timber is similar to those noted in Mazon. The pursuit of the farmers is similar, save that Mr. Harford, who has given considerable attention to cattle raising, is now turning his effort to breeding horses of the Norman blood.

The first claim made in this township was in 1833. In that year Edwin Shaw and Sheldon Bartholomew came to this section with A. K. Owen, who settled in Mazon. These men selected farms at the point now known as "Parer's Grove," but beyond naming the place "Spring Grove" from a large spring found at one end of it, no attempt was made by them to take permanent possession of it. Not long after the visit of these persons an English family by the name of Grove, took up a claim on section 4 at Hog's Point. Here they built a cabin and cultivated their ground until the fall of 1836, when Jonah C. Newport, a native of Belmont County, Ohio, bought them out. About 1834, or perhaps a year earlier, George W. Armstrong settled on the northwest quarter of section 6, where he resided two years. He then moved to Wauponsee, from whence he subsequently returned, and bought the northeast quarter of section 1, township 33, range 5 (now in La Salle County), where he built a cabin and where his modern residence now is. About the same season, Charles Parer, from Ottawa, came to this region, made a claim near the present residence of Mr. Harford at "Spring Grove."

He cut considerable hay for his stock, and built his cabin, but unfortunately the fire caught in the dry prairie grass and consumed the hay, cabin and fixtures. It is not clear how this accident occurred. It is said, however, that the whole family had gone to Ottawa and in their absence the conflagration took place. On Mr. Parer's return, finding nothing left but blackened ruins, he abandoned the place, his family never coming back to the township. This was the extent of the population in this community until the coming of John Dewey in 1841.

Mr. Dewey was an English mechanic, and attracted by the reports from friends who lived at Vermillion, sent his wife and two children to his American relatives, to spy out the land while he kept his situation. They came in 1837, and sent back so favorable a report, that he came in the following year and decided to cast in his fortunes with this new prairie country. He came to Jesse Newport's in Wauponsee that year and rented the place, bringing his family forward the year following. Here he stayed until 1841, when he came to Vienna and rented the farm of Jonah Newport at Hog Point. Three years later he came to "Parer's Grove." About the same time with Dewey, came John B. Moore, and settled on the southeast corner of section 5. He came from Philadelphia with a young family, made a home here but moved away some years since. About 1845, Henry Hyslop settled on section 22, and his was the pioneer cabin on the prairie. He was soon followed by the Wilks, Curtis and Antis families. The canal also made its contribution to this settlement in the person of Anthony Maloney, who settled on section 7, where he lived many years.

It will be noticed that that part of Grundy County not lying contiguous to the canal, settled very slowly during the first ten years. This is to be accounted for, not so much because of its less desirable character as of the action of speculators. Most of the earliest claims were made on the margin of the river, and the claimants were on the ground to purchase their land at the public sale in 1830. After this sale, speculators bought large tracts in the interior of the county, especially the timbered portion. The price was at once raised above government prices and of course found but little sale. There were here and there sections which were supposed to be less desirable or had been overlooked by general land buyers, and these were gradually picked up. As soon as the settlement grew large enough (and the legal requirements were not severe) a township or precinct organization was effected and after the five years of release, taxes were laid as to force non-resident land owners to pay at least their full share. Their timber was considered free plunder and so little sympathy was felt in any settlement for this class of property holders, that it became unpopular for any one to assist in locating lands for them. This policy, maintained for several years, soon convinced capitalists that the land was not a good investment, and becoming tired of paying comparatively exorbitant taxes, and getting very little protection for what they did pay, they were glad to put the land in the market, getting merely enough to reimburse them for their outlay, and not always getting off so well as that. The result was that up to about 1850, the county was only sparsely settled, but subsequently filled up with remarkable rapidity.

Another feature of the settlement here in contrast with the experience of pioneers of Ohio and the Middle States, may be noted: there seems to have been far less demand here for that invention which is the offspring of necessity. Machinery for mills, though transported over long distances, could be secured; in the older States they were rudely manufactured on the spot. Here the larger part of personal apparel was purchased at stores twenty or thirty miles distant; there everything, from the hat to the shoe, was manufactured at home. Here, though timber was scarce and the country sparsely settled, glass windows were the rule, house hardware not difficult to obtain, and "frame" dwellings early appeared; there these things were the mark of wealth and distinction, and appeared only after the settlement had considerably grown. But history, in early settlements, does not exactly repeat itself. Experience must be taken into the account, and what one generation achieves must accrue to the advantage of its successor. The pioneer experience of the Pilgrims was unique and could not be reproduced in a later day; that of the Middle States modified the early settlement of this western land, and the far West of to-day resembles more the "royal road to fortune" than the "hard road to travel," which the pioneers of other generations found.

But with all this modification of the stern experience of pioneer life, the trials of the first settlers were anything but easy to be borne. The community settled here found the only accessible mills at Vermillionville, Wilmington and Dayton. Here the soil was found to yield fine crops of winter wheat, and flour was not so great a luxury. Fruit did finely, especially peaches, and there was no dearth of orchards, though apples, taking longer to mature, did not yield early, and the change of late years has never made apples so prominent in the county. The severe winter of 1853 or 1854 killed the larger part of the peach trees, and fruit interests have languished here ever since. The ready tact of the pioneer housewives and the unpampered tastes of that early day found a good substitute for fruit in the pumpkin. When frozen they were prepared and stewed down to a syrup, which furnished the sweetening for most of the culinary purposes of the cabin, and mixed with fresh stewed pumpkin formed the coveted sweetmeat. They were planted in large numbers and stored in a vault constructed underneath the hay-stacks to be fed to the cattle during the winter. Well may this "fruit loved of boyhood," be apostrophized by the poet and be honorably placed in a State's coat-of-arms. There was but little weaving done by the women of this township, not a single loom to be found here and only one field of flax. Mrs. Dewey did try to raise silk-worms, and succeeded in securing some return for her efforts, but it was pursued more as a pastime than a means of profit and was soon abandoned. In her early efforts to assist her husband she learned, in Vermillionville, the tailor's trade, and became quite noted in a small circle. In this way she acquired considerable stock. Cattle were cheap, and when a settler was able to have Sunday clothes he was glad to trade off a heifer or yearling for the making of a coat. The other parts of the suit could be made at home, but the outer garment required more skill, and Mrs. Dewey turned her ability to good account.

Game was found here in the usual abundance. Deer passing from one point to another have been counted traveling in single file to the number of one or two hundred, while lynxes and wolves, especially the latter, were "too numerous to mention." An incident is related of the latter animal which, though it occurred outside of the limits of this township, is vouched for by present residents as having happened "just across the river." A country dance had called a knight of the bow some distance from his home and detained him till the early hours of the morning. On his return he heard the hungry howling of the wolves, which seemed to be following on his trail and coming unpleasantly nearer him. Soon convinced that he was in danger, he scrambled, fiddle box in hand, into a tree which stood near by, and was soon surrounded by those miscreants of the prairie. Safe, but annoyed at his detention, the weary musician whiled away the time and "soothed the savage breast" with strains that had served a pleasanter occasion earlier in the night. The dawn released him. If this be true, it is not less strongly authenticated that this was the only case of such boldness on the part of the prairie wolves of this region. They were found troublesome in the destruction of young stock, but otherwise quite harmless. Prairie chickens were found in great abundance, and furnished rare sport as well as a generous supply for the larder. But these, with the deer, have pretty generally disappeared. Many believe the latter left the country about 1845, when it is said vast herds migrated across the Mississippi.

Vienna was rather out of the principal line of through travel, and had little in the circumstances of her business activity or location to encourage the growth of a village, but the mania for founding cities seized a Mr. Bullock, and in 1836 he laid out Illinois City, north of the Waupecan, with a great public square, and streets enough to satisfy a very thriving village. Its only remains is the worn-out plat in records of the county. Verona was an outgrowth of the Pekin, Chicago and St. Louis railroad. It was laid out near the center of section 26, by Martin Finch and Ambrose Kinley. The ground was platted in February, 1877, and in about a year grew to its present dignity. There is really no demand for a large village here, and even now has the appearance of being overgrown. Three or four stores are now doing more or less business, which, with the usual blacksmith and wagon shop, two churches, and some hundred dwelling houses, constitute the village of Verona. Its name may have found its suggestion in the title of the play, as its founders may not inappropriately now be called the "two gentlemen of Verona."

Schools played an early part in this township. Mrs. Dewey was a woman of considerable education, and anxious to turn her various accomplishments to a money account in aid of her husband, began teaching school during her temporary stay at Vermillionville. On coming into Vienna, she opened up in her cabin the first boarding school in the county. She had but a few pupils, and proposed only to teach the rudiments, but children were then so few that they came from five miles away. They stayed during the week, going home Saturday to stay over the Sunday and holiday. This school was not long maintained. The first school-house was soon built near Hog Run, and the pioneer school taught by A. Warnock.

The efforts of the church on the frontier were generally almost as early as the first pioneer. The Methodist church had a station on the Fox River, and no sooner were two or three families gathered in each other's vicinity than a missionary itinerant discovered and preached to them. The size of the audience did not seem to detract from the interest of the occasion, and many an effective sermon has been delivered in a little cabin before two or three auditors. The earliest of these preachers were many times quite illiterate, and others, though scarcely less so, were remarkably successful. The Mormons were here early, but found the people possessed of an independent judgment which was not to be swayed by a latter day revelation. The earliest organization effected, however, was by the Baptist denomination, in 1850. The Fellingham family were among the settlers of this time, and were earnest members of this church. Mr. W. M. Fellingham was a minister, and served the Ebenezer Baptist Society in this capacity until his death, his brothers, George and John, acting as deacons. Until about 1862, services were held in the school-house, but at this time a modest frame building was erected on the northwest corner of section 25, at a cost of about eight hundred dollars. The membership does not now exceed ten members, and services are held only once a month.

The Presbyterian Church of Vienna was organized February 27, 1858, by the Rev. S. H. Loss, a missionary agent of this church, with some fourteen members. For some years they held their services in a school-house, but in 1870 a good frame building was erected as a place of worship. The edifice cost about $3,300, and was placed on the northwest corner of section 36. In 1877, when the town of Verona sprang up, the building was removed to the village, where it now stands. The church has suffered severely from removals, so that it now numbers only some fifteen or sixteen members.

The only other church in Vienna is the Methodist Episcopal. This was organized in 1876, and in the following year erected their present place of worship at a cost of about $2,800. The leading spirits of this church were I. C. Tilden, M. Dix, and J. Kendall. Its membership now reaches about fifty.

CHAPTER XX.*

BRACEVILLE TOWNSHIP—COAL MEASURES—EARLY SETTLEMENT—THE OPEN PRAIRIE.

BRACEVILLE lies just east of Mazon township, and continuing the gradual rise of land in the eastern part of that precinct, becomes quite broken and picturesque along the branch of the Mazon creek. East of this stream the land gradually subsides to a generally level character, and stretches out along the eastern part in an expanse of wild prairie. The trend of the water-courses indicates an elevation in the central part, though it is but slight, and of the character of a plateau. The Mazon Creek enters from the south, a little east of the middle line of the township, and, circling to the west and north, follows the general direction of the western boundary, passing into Mazon and between Wauponsee and Felix at the northwest corner. The soil along the river is good farming land, but in the interior and eastern parts the light covering of sod rests upon a nearly pure, sandy soil, which is profitably available for little more than grazing. The eastern portion, however, is richly underlaid with coal, which more than compensates for the meager productiveness of the surface. This deposit, extending into the adjoining counties of Will and Kankakee, has given rise to considerable business activity in this vicinity, and a number of brisk mining villages have sprung up within some six miles of each other.

The earliest development of coal was made in the counties east of Grundy, but about 1858 some miners opened a co-operative shaft on land belonging to N. Cotton. Water proved a great hindrance and expense here, and the project was about to fail, when some others were induced to give the enterprise assistance. They brought to the work more enthusiasm than capital, however, and the effort was about to prove an entire failure, when Mr. Mehan was enlisted in the work and the shaft pushed down to the coal. At this point Mr. Boyer bought the shaft, and did some mining. Some four or five years later, Mr. Augustine put down a shaft on his land, but the business, crippled by the lack of capital, languished until about 1880, when foreign capital took up the matter and has made this part of the county a busy, thriving section. The principal coal lands are owned and worked by large corporations, of which the Wilmington Coal Mining & Manufacturing Company and the Chicago, Milwaukee & St. Paul Railroad Company are the leading ones. The Chicago *Tribune* last year gave an interesting sketch of these coal-fields in December of 1881, from which the following extract is taken:

"The finest and richest of these coal-fields are now being worked with all the most improved facilities which unrestricted capital can supply. Strange as it may appear, the best veins lie nearest the surface,

---

* By J. H. Battle.

in marked contrast with the vaunted coal-fields of England, where none of the mines are less than 500 feet, and some as low as 3,800 feet below the surface. The coal here is in veins of three feet thickness, much of it not over fifty feet below the surface, and of unexcelled quality; in many respects, excepting for gas and coke purposes, perhaps, excelling the famous Pittsburgh bituminous coal. Here the mineral is found free of clinkers, sulphur and iron, making a charming grate coal, and, for blacksmithing purposes, without equal.

"I began my inspection with the Fairbanks mine in Essex township, of Kankakee County. This mine is twenty miles west of Kankakee, four miles southeast of Gardner, and five miles south of Braceville. At Fairbanks, I found a party of surveyors engaged in running out a line for a railroad from Buckingham to Braidwood, a distance of fifteen miles. At Buckingham this road will connect with the Southwestern Branch of the Illinois Central Railroad, thence crossing the Indiana, Illinois & Iowa Railway, the Wabash, St. Louis & Pacific, the Kankakee & Seneca, and the Chicago, Alton & St. Louis, making three direct lines to Chicago, and three east and west. The name of the new road is the Wilmington Coal-fields Railroad, with which it is designed to form a belt around the coal-fields. It is the intention of the managers of the enterprise to construct this road in a first-class manner, and when it is completed, to transport coal, farm products and passengers.

"The lands owned by the Wilmington Coal-fields Company comprise some 2,600 acres in Grundy and Kankakee Counties. At the invitation of the mining boss I descended into the mine. The surface soil this year yielded a corn crop averaging from forty-five to sixty bushels to the acre, and the grass lands over two tons of hay. The shaft is six by fourteen and a half feet, divided into two compartments of six feet each, two feet and a half being utilized as an air shaft, and a double cage kept running. It is down ninety-five feet. For fifty-six feet two inches, it is built of timbers solidly spiked together, and below that it is made of two by four inches scantling, placed on edge and spiked together, forming the wall casing. This was built in twenty-eight days, and is sufficient for hoisting 1,000 tons of coal per day.

"At the bottom I found no water. The roof was as dry as the interior of a house. The only water which was in sight, and that was very little, was that which came down from the top of the shaft. Below was laid a double track for the cars, which are used in hauling out the coal. There were four rooms being worked, and the weird appearance of the miners digging at the solid coal was a sight to be remembered. The mine ceilings are held in place by timbers, twelve inches square. There is ten feet of solid timber from the lip of the shaft out each way, three feet from the center and two feet space between each. The roof overhead is formed of two-inch planks. All the digging is done with picks, the coal being undermined and dropping down of its own weight, thus obviating the use of gunpowder. The roofing overlying the coal is what miners term 'soapstone,' but is really shale clay, and is impervious to water. Below the coal is a bed of fire clay, which would doubtless make good fire brick.

"Having looked through the new mines, I started over the country to Braceville. This little town is on the Chicago and Alton railroad, and is inhabited by about 1,000 people. Last summer, the Chicago, Milwaukee and St. Paul Railway Company purchased the old Bruce mine, which it is now working. It also bought of James Whitton, 1,680 acres of coal land, paying $168,000 in cash. This land is underlaid with coal of a quality not nearly equal to that of Fairbank. The Milwaukee and St. Paul company is now getting out from 275 to 300 tons of coal per day from the old shaft, which is about the measure of its capacity. The company has a second shaft down now, and is working twenty-five rooms in it. But water is found very troublesome here, and often prevents working the mine to its full capacity. When I was there, No. 2 shaft was working but six rooms out of the twenty-five, and these were not entirely dry. They employ seventy-five miners, but only eighteen of them could work because of water. At present there are four pumps at work in this shaft getting out the water, and they have not succeeded in clearing it out. They run three, four and five-inch pipes to the surface, and the volume of water that is raised can scarcely be computed. In No. 3 shaft, when the company was sinking it, an accident occurred to the pump, and the mine was literally drowned out. The shaft is 117 feet deep, and the water rose to within thirty-five feet of the surface. In this section water overlaps the coal at every point, and streams of it run through the mineral at a number of places.

"In Godley, which is a little east of Braceville, Baird and Hickox have a mine running, and miners told me that there were few dry places there. The standard price paid for mining is $1.05 per ton in winter and 95 cents in summer, but at Godley they are obliged to pay from $1.25 to $1.30, which is from ten to twenty-five cents above the ruling price on the prairie, simply on account of water. The depth of the old Bruce shaft costs the company working it to pay as high as $1.50 per ton for mining in some spots."

The shafts opened along the western border of this township are all of this character, but notwithstanding this drawback, mining in this vicinity is being pushed with renewed vigor of late years. At Coal City, and the Diamond, in the northeast corner, are larger coal interests, and riding along the central part of the township one may imagine the lake not far away, and the distant columns of smoke rising at pretty regular intervals on the eastern horizon to indicate the passage of a fleet of steamers. Many experts believe the coal to be found west of the Mazon will prove a finer quality and much more cheaply mined than at the present scene of operations.

The first settlement of this township was closely allied to that of Mazon, Dr. L. S. Robbins, one of the Owen party of 1833, coming to Sulphur Springs in 1834, and building his cabin on the land he had secured by claim the year before. In the following year the Eslinger family settled north of the Mazon, below the Chicago and Alton railroad. The head of this family was a Methodist preacher, and had a large family of boys. They stayed here some three or four years, made some improvements, but for some reason left for other parts. Soon after, the place was burned over and the buildings and fences destroyed. About 1836 the "West Colony" settled on the Mazon Creek, toward the southeast corner of the township. But little more than this is known of this settlement. What the origin of the enterprise, or name was, is not known, and of their existence but few persons have any remembrance. It is certain, however, that several cabins were built here, and considerable improvement made, but the scheme, for some reason, proved a failure, and the place entirely abandoned after a short time.

In the winter of 1834-5 John Cragg came to Braceville and settled on section 19, where he remained until his death. Cragg was a pattern maker by trade and a fine workman. He was following his trade at Patterson, N. J., when he heard the flattering stories of the Illinois country. But the long journey and the unknown experience to be expected on a frontier farm made him hesitate to come alone. He talked the matter over with his friends and associates, Edward Holland and a Mr. Gates, and with them made a compact to go to the West and settle near each other, agreeing that each should forfeit fifty dollars should he fail to carry out his part of the agreement. Cragg was married and had his wife with him. The others were less fortunate, for while married, their wives were yet in the old country. It was arranged that Cragg and his wife should come on and make a claim for himself and Holland, while Gates returned across the ocean for his own and Holland's wife. Gates found his task a more difficult one to accomplish than was anticipated. His own wife and Mrs. Holland, urged by their family friends, refused to face the perils and privations of the frontier, and Gates, choosing the less of two disappointments, remained at his old home, while Holland, after waiting for his wife in vain for a time, acting on the same principle perhaps, came to Illinois and settled just over the line in Mazon, and set up a blacksmith shop. He was never joined by his wife, and afterward solaced his lacerated feelings with another less afraid of frontier life.

On his journey West, Cragg came by way of St. Louis, where he stayed some time. Here he met a family who had left the vicinity of Ottawa during the Indian troubles of 1832, and who offered him the use of half of a double log cabin they had there. This family was about to return to their claim overland, while Cragg and his family came by the river. It was agreed that when the overland party reached the vicinity of their cabin they should sound a horn, when Mrs. Cragg was to reply with a similar signal. The latter family had been ensconced in their new quarters several days when the expected blast was heard, and had experienced just enough of the isolation of their position to learn of the arrival of companions with no little satisfaction. Mr. Cragg had busied himself in prospecting the country about for a location, and soon fixed upon his place on the Mazon, and after building his cabin moved into it. The log cabin which is still standing was situated near the trail which was principally followed by the travel toward Chicago from the south. In this small building, hardly large enough for the family, they dispensed the courtesies and comforts of a frontier inn. The guests were not less rough than squeamish, and are represented as hardly superior to the Indians in their social accomplishments.

In 1846, came John Kerns from New York and settled in the southern, and E. R. Booth, who settled in the southwestern part. In 1848 came D. R. Dowd, from Trumbull County, Ohio, and settled on the western line of the township near Mr. Booth. He was the first supervisor and gave the name of his Ohio home to this new township. In 1849 came Thomas Martin and Robert Huston. The latter was a weaver by trade, and came from New York by the Erie Canal, the lakes and the Michigan and Illinois Central to Morris. He was from May 1st to 21st in getting to Morris. During the trip the weather had been propitious, but no sooner had he set foot on Illinois soil when a discouraging rain set in. A team was hired to take his goods and family to their destination near where the village of Braceville is located. The rain came down rapidly and they just succeeded in fording the Johnny Run before it became impassable. They reached a deserted cabin near their place that night, though they were obliged to travel much of the way in water from a few inches to two feet deep. Here the team was blockaded, and was forced to wait three weeks before it could return. This sort of an introduction to the new country brought on the usual attack of the fever and ague, and for nine months Mr. Huston was not able to do anything toward putting up a house of his own. In the meantime he located his soldier's warrant, which he had purchased at a cost of $165, and began to invest the balance of his money in getting him a house. After getting a team he made trips to Chicago, teaming for others and bringing a load of lumber back for his house which he erected on the prairie. This was perhaps the first frame building in the township. Other early families were those of B. A. Crisler and H. Cassingham, who settled on the western side of the Mazon.

The larger part of this township was originally prairie land, and enough of it still remains in its natural condition to give one a fair idea of what the whole country once was. The wild grass of these lands made excellent pasture and hay. With the range the early settlers had, their cattle would put on more flesh and in less time than on any other pasture. The sedge which grew along the sloughs was the first to start in the spring, and furnished the earliest pasture. The bent or blue-joint, which was principally found along the sides of the sloughs, or, in the vernacular of the pioneer. "between the dry and wet land," was preferred by stock to all other varieties, especially when mixed with the wild pea vine. This made the best hay, and as its yield was very large, was generally selected for this purpose. But the combined ravages of stock and scythe rapidly exterminated it, so that in many cases the ground where it grew became almost bare of vegetation. The stock and the farmer then resorted to the upland grasses, but before the settlers multiplied so as to limit the range of the stock, the older and more experienced of the herd would go long distances to find their favorite pasture, necessitating on the part of the pioneer a hunt of several days to recover them.

The native grasses were not less marked for their medicinal qualities. Cattle and horses seemed to be remarkably free from diseases so long as they could find plenty of wild hay or grass to feed upon. Horses raised upon the prairie were said never to be afflicted with the heaves, while horses brought here, suffering with this malady, were speedily cured by simply feeding on the native grasses. This advantage, however, was somewhat offset by the colic which this rank feeding frequently produced in horses with fatal effect. The introduction of tame grasses has largely remedied this evil, and most farmers are now able to supply their stock with a mixture of the two kinds. But the wild grass of the present is not found in all its virgin purity. The pea vine is almost if not entirely extinct, while the grass itself is very much modified, and is not valued in the markets equal to good timothy.

The village growth of Braceville township is the result of the mining industry found here. Braceville village was laid out in 1861 by N. Cotton, who did the work himself, using a sixteen foot pole. It may be imagined that as the village grew it was sometimes rather difficult to adjust conflicting claims with the claims of the plat, but that has been regulated, and a village of 1,800 inhabitants is now found here. The recent increased activity among the mines in this vicinity has added a considerable number to the population in the past year. But the large number of cheap, poorly constructed dwellings does not betoken solid prosperity, especially when this is taken in connection with the large number of vacant stores, and lack of public improvement. The Diamond, in the extreme northeast corner, and Coal City, located a little south and west of Diamond, are similar towns but of smaller size.

CHAPTER XXI.*

GOODFARM TOWNSHIP—"THE LAY OF THE LAND"—EARLY SETTLEMENT—PIONEER EXPERIENCES—SCHOOLS—CHURCHES.

GOODFARM, like most of the townships south of the river, is well supplied with prairie water-courses. It lies just south of Mazon township, and contributes to the streams which have been noted there, viz.: Murray sluice, Mazon Creek, Brewster and Wood sluices. The two latter are the most important here, and join the "West Fork of the Mazon" in the township which bears the same name. The direction of these streams are nearly due north, and the general aspect of the land is that of a rolling prairie very liberally supplied with groves. Much of the land is insufficiently drained and has a low wet appearance, though the name of the township pretty correctly characterizes its soil as a whole.

James McKean was the first settler in this township. He seems to have delighted in the isolation of the frontier and to have moved from a neighborhood as soon as it became generally settled. He was here as early as 1841. About 1844, J. M. Clover came from Indiana and bought his place, on section two, in the northern edge of the township. Two or three years later Elijah Saltmarsh came and settled on section five. He was of southern birth and had been a flatboatman on the Ohio River. His life on the river at a time when boating involved a rough, boisterous experience, developed him into a decisive, energetic man, and he became a leading spirit in the township. He had a large family and made a good farm, but in his later years, unsatisfied with this settled country he went to Oregon where some of his family had preceded him. Elnathan Lewis, a native of Vermont, next followed into this township. He had emigrated to New York and from thence to McHenry County in this State, from whence he came to Goodfarm. Other settlers about this time were Elijah Lewis, David Gleason and E. F. Brewster.

In 1849, E. B. Stevens came from Kalamazoo County, Michigan. His route was across the country and his conveyance, a wagon. Michigan was then an old settled State, and the cheap lands of Illinois presented quite an attraction to those of limited means. He came to this present location on section thirty, and bought the claim of Henry Brown who had been here a year or two. Here Stevens found a log cabin, a straw barn and some Lombardy poplars set out, but the rest was left for him to accomplish. After buying his land, a barrel of flour and ten bushels of oats, he had no money left. He came in the spring, and making a good garden he managed to sustain his family until the fall when he got his wheat threshed, and a start for another year.

* By J. H. Battle.

About 1850, a tide of German emigration began to flow into the township, which continued until this nationality constitutes fully one-half of the population. The first of this German element was Leonard Fisher, a native of Bavaria, who came in 1851. In 1852, came Jno. L. Meier, followed by Hoffman Hoag, Pfeiffer and Bucklard. Most of these people came from the same section of Bavaria and settled near each other here. They are good farmers and thrifty both in public and private. The town house is one of the neatest in the county, and has near it a neat tool-house for the protection of the township road implements.

There was but little variety in the early experiences of the first settlers in the different parts of the county. Those who came later, as in Goodfarm, found milling facilities better but no more accessible; stores better supplied with frontier necessities but not much easier to purchase; more neighbors but no better means of communication. Their lives, like those of their predecessors, were a continual struggle with the stubborn, natural difficulties which surrounded them, and none were so completely isolated as to make a few years' later settlement of any appreciable advantage. Those who came after the completion of the canal, enjoyed the benefit of a nearer market than Chicago, and perhaps an increase in the value of farm products, but the roads were not improved and the open prairie wilderness still interposed its difficulties. These obstacles were perhaps the most difficult which the pioneers of this county were called upon to surmount. So long as the paucity of settlements allowed a pretty free selection of route, mud-holes could be evaded, and a worn track avoided. But this practice had also its disadvantages. In a country without continuous fences, and few landmarks save the groves, it required some considerable skill and an intimate knowledge of the county to successfully cross even a small prairie in broad daylight. Mr. Baldwin relates an incident of "a gentleman, fresh from New England, who was viewing the country on the Vermillion and proposed to take a bee line to Ottawa across the prairie on foot. He was advised to take the road, as being easier traveling and decidedly safer; that without any track he might get benighted on the prairie, for although the day was clear he would, for part of the distance, be out of sight of timber, and he might mistake his course and be lost. He foolishly rejected this advice with some indignation, and at noon set out on his journey of some six miles. About twelve o'clock that night, exhausted and nearly famished, he got to a settlement on the Vermillion five miles further from Ottawa than the place from whence he started. In the morning he was willing to follow the road."*

Crossing the uncultivated prairie at night was a very uncertain venture even to the most expert. If the night was clear the stars were a reliable guide and the pioneers became quite proficient in the simpler rudiments of astronomy. In a cloudy night and a snowy or foggy day their resources were less sure. A steady wind often proved the only guide. The traveler, getting his bearings, would note how the wind struck his nose, the right or left ear, and then, keenly alive to these sensations,

---

*History of La Salle County.

would so maintain his course as to keep the bearing of the wind always the same, and regardless of all other guides would generally reach his destination without difficulty. To do this required no little skill and a steady wind. If the latter changed gradually, the better the skill the wider the traveler diverged from home. Without these guides it was a mere accident if a person succeeded in crossing even a small prairie. The tendency is to move in a circle, and when once this is begun and observed by the traveler, the only resource is to camp in the most convenient place and manner and wait for morning. Each family had its signal light which was readily recognized by its members. It was a frequent practice to erect a pole by the chimney of the cabin and place a lighted lantern at the top. Others had a light in the window, which often saved a dreary night's experience on the prairie.

The history of every township is full of misadventures of this sort. A gentleman and his wife were belated on their return home on a cloudy night, and though having some clue to the way, sought in vain for some glimmer of his home signal. His horses seem to have become completely bewildered, and after having urged them forward for some time, the travelers became convinced they were journeying in a confused circle, and were preparing to camp out in their wagon, when a weak flash of light betrayed the location of a residence in the near distance. Getting the direction at the instant, the house was gained in a few minutes, and they found it to be their long sought home. The children had gone to bed, and carelessly removed the light from the window, but a brand falling out of the fire-place had flashed the signal, which saved them from an unpleasant predicament.

A gentleman and his wife, on another occasion, went across an eighty acre field to visit a neighbor. On returning, about eight o'clock in the evening, they lost their way, and notwithstanding there was a fence on one side of this field, the couple became hopelessly bewildered, and would have been obliged to remain out all night, had not their daughter, anxious at their staying so late, opened the cabin door to listen for some evidence of their coming. The light thus flashed out into the darkness, revealed to them their position, which was within calling distance of their home, and where they had been vainly wandering some two or three hours.

Such experiences, unpleasant in the warm weather, were too often fatal in the winter season. The trackless prairie, covered with a deceptive expanse of snow and swept by a fierce blast which pierced the most ample clothing and the hardiest frame, made the stoutest heart waver. Journeys upon the prairie were never undertaken under such circumstances, save under stress of the most urgent necessity. But nearly every early settler can remember some experience in winter season traveling, while some never reached the home they sought, or the end of the journey reluctantly begun.

With the settlement of the prairie, and the regular laying out of roads, traveling became less dangerous, though scarcely less difficult. The amount of labor which could be devoted by the few people in the scattered settlements, made but little effect upon the roads of a country which seemed particularly exposed by the character of the soil, and the conformation of its surface to the unfavorable action of rain. Even now the farming community pays a heavy annual tribute to muddy, impassable roads. Thirty-five years ago, a man caught by high water away from home, was detained for two or three weeks, and many a trip about the county was made more in a boat than in a wagon. Matthew Johnson, who came from Jefferson County, Ohio, in 1852, landed in Morris in April of that year. He had relatives in Felix, and started over to see them. He found a wagon totally inadequate for the undertaking, and had to resort to a boat to reach his friends' house.

The natural outgrowth of a low, wet country, with the "breaking" of a rank soil, was miasmatic disease. During the first forty years of the settlement in Grundy County, the fever and ague reigned supreme, and seemed to mock at quinine and infusions of barks. Doctors were scarce, and the settlers, brought up with a profound belief in the medicinal virtues of sassafras and boneset, preferred to save the expense of a professional visit. Nor did they suffer greatly by this practice. But in the case of accident, the lack of talented surgeons proved a terrible misfortune, resulting in many a misshapen limb, or the loss of it altogether. An incident is related of an early settler, who was accidentally shot by another in handling a gun. A heavy load of shot shattered the bone just below the shoulder. The artery fortunately escaped injury, and the wound was done up to await the arrival of the only two doctors in the county. On coming to the wounded man the doctors disagreed. One declared amputation necessary, but the other refused to consent to an operation, and in the utter lack of any proper instrument for the purpose, the arm was allowed to hang. In this way the wound was left to nature and the simple care of the women folks. A number of pieces of bone were taken out in the process of dressing the wound, but one large piece remained obstinate, and kept the wound unhealed for a year. In the meantime the wounded man, with his arm in a sling, handled his team alone, hauling timber, lumber and farm product. Finally, taken with a throat disease in Chicago, he consulted a physician in the Medical College, when his arm came under observation, and was subsequently gratuitously treated before a class in the college. Similar cases were by no means rare, and serve to indicate some of the unwritten hardships of pioneer life.

The happy commingling of grove and plain marked by numberless streams, made this township a favorite resort of game. The buffalo had left this region before the advent of the settler, but the high prairie bore abundant evidence of his former presence here. Here and there, all over the plain were found skeletons of this animal lying where the hunter's missile had overtaken him or, if Indian tradition is to be believed, where a heavy snow had imprisoned and starved him. There are found in frequent numbers upon the prairie, rings of especially thrifty grass which are explained upon various theories. The Indians represented that in a certain winter long ago, a great fall of snow found the buffaloes scattered about on the prairie. These animals, unwilling to venture out into the untracked deep, kept up an incessant tramp in a limited circle until starvation and death ended the march. Whatever truth there may be in this tradition, it may be said that the position of many of these skeletons favor it very strongly. Deer were found here in great abundance, and to the skillful hunter fell an easy prey. During the wet season when water was to be found in abundance upon the open country, the deer were found here. Getting on the windward side of the animal the hunter found ample shelter in the long grass to approach within easy shot. In the dry hot season the deer frequented the groves. Then the hunter, proceeding against the wind, followed up or down the course of one of the water-courses along which the groves were located. The deer are troubled by a fly at this time of year which attracts so much of their attention that they are easily approached from the proper side. The animal stands feeding for a few minutes until, driven to fury by the insect, it suddenly drops close to the ground to elude its tormentor. Then suddenly rising again it feeds a short time and again as suddenly sinks to the ground. This action gives the hunter peculiar advantages which were never thrown away upon the pioneers. Wild turkeys, wolves, wild bees, and the smaller game that still throng the timber, not only supplied the table and furnished rare sport to the hunter, but often proved a valuable source from which to eke out the meager income derived from the farm crops. One farmer sold wild turkeys and deer-skins enough in Chicago to buy his wife a good winter cloak, at a time when his crops had proved an utter failure.

After the first few years the pioneer had time to plan for something more permanent than present necessities, and the school-house with its molding influences became an institution in every community. In Goodfarm the first school-house was erected in 1850, on the east half of the northeast quarter of section 18. It was built by subscription, some giving lumber, others giving work, and six persons giving one dollar each. The lumber was drawn from Horse Creek in Will County, and with the six dollars was bought all that the country and the labor did not furnish. Elvira Lewis was the first teacher here. About 1856 a second school-house was built near the German cemetery, and the first session of school taught by Philip Ganzert.

The first church organization was of the Free Will Baptist denomination. This society was formed at the cabin of David Gleason, February 5, 1850, with David Gleason, Elnathan Lewis, and their wives, Addison Gleason and Lavinia Brown as members. The church held its meetings in the school-house until about 1868, when the organization was finally abandoned. The Methodist Episcopal church has an appointment here now.

About 1859, the Lutheran church was organized and erected a parsonage on section 27, to which was subsequently added the present church building. Salem Evangelical church was organized about 1857, with Buckhardt and Hoag, Pfeiffer and Hoffman as leading members. In 1877 they built a new place of worship on section 22, at a cost of about $2,400.

The "Church of God," is a recent organization which has a place of worship on the northern line of the township.

CHAPTER XXII.*

HIGHLAND TOWNSHIP—TOPOGRAPHICAL CHARACTERISTICS—PRAIRIE BANDITS—LAWLESS LAW—SETTLEMENT OF THE TOWNSHIP—THE CATHOLIC CHURCH.

HIGHLAND Township, occupying the southwestern corner of the county, is what its name implies, high land—the highest, perhaps, in the "little kingdom of Grundy." The general slope of the surface, similar to most of the southern part of the county, is to the northeast. Johnny Run and Murray Sluice cross the township diagonally in nearly parallel directions, passing out of the township near the northeast corner. The Waupecan crosses the northwest corner and the Mazon the southeast, in the same general direction. The general elevation of the land makes it in this respect, especially in the southern part, among the most desirable for farming purposes. Along the streams, the land is of a decidedly rolling and almost broken character. With the exception of several thousand acres belonging to Wm. Scully, an Irish Lord, the farms are generally small, and the acreage of the township better divided up than elsewhere in the county.

The earliest people who took possession of Highland were some nameless roughs, generally supposed to be connected with a class of thieves and highwaymen, who were known as Prairie Bandits. This part of the State became infested with these desperadoes about 1836 or '7, and while they scrupled at the commission of no form of crime, they were especially annoying in their principal business of horse stealing. The principal scene of their operations was on the Fox River, but no locality in the northern part of the State, where good horses could be had for the stealing, was exempt from these marauders. Their plan was to take the lighter horses of this region to Indiana and sell them, making the return trip with heavy draft horses, which were disposed of in Iowa and Michigan for work in the pineries. For a time these depredations were carried on with impunity. The population, scattered at considerable distances apart, was principally confined to the edge of the timber, leaving the prairie a broad highway for these bandits to pass from one end to the other of the country undiscovered. The early settlers did not submit to this state of affairs without some effort to bring these persons to justice and to recover their property, but singly, the pioneers proved but poor trappers of this game. The bandits were known to be desperate characters and adepts in the use of weapons and in traveling the open prairie, and it often happened that when a party got close upon the thieves, discretion seemed the better part of valor, and the chase was given up. Their success emboldened these robbers, and the early stock and land buyers seldom traveled alone, and never unarmed.

* By J. H. Battle.

A good horse caused many persons to be waylaid and killed, and a large amount of money in the possession of an unprotected traveler, almost inevitably brought him to grief. Burglary soon followed their success on the road. Farmers became more cautious and evaded these foot pads. In this case the cabin was entered and the money taken while the family were kept discreetly quiet by a threatening pistol. The open handed hospitality of a new country made the settlers an easy prey to those who lacked even the traditional respect of the Bedouin freebooter. It was impossible to discriminate between the worthy stranger and the bandit of the prairie, and the stranger taken in was more likely to prove a robber than an angel in disguise. Civil authority seemed hopelessly incapable of remedying the evil. Occasionally a desperado would be apprehended. Legal quibbles would follow and the rascal get free, or justice be delayed until a jail delivery would set him loose to prey upon the public again. This occurred with such monotonous regularity and unvarying success, that the scattered pioneers lost confidence in each other and anarchy seemed about to be ushered in. This general distrust gave rise to many unfounded rumors, and may have been 'the origin of the general belief in regard to the first inhabitants of Highland. But these people were known to be rough, boisterous persons, who did nothing toward making a permanent home, and enough had been stolen in the county to raise suspicion.

Of course such a state of things could not long continue. Deep mutterings of vengeance, portentious of a storm of wrath, were heard, and vigilant societies came into existence at several localities. One of these societies, formed in the northern part of the State, was captained by a man named Campbell. He was a Canadian, and a man of great energy and decision of character. The bandits were alarmed, and resolved to depose him. One Sunday afternoon, two men by the name of Driscoll, called at Campbell's gate and inquired of his daughter for her father; Campbell came to the gate, when, without saying a word, the visitors shot him through the heart, and coolly rode off. The next day the people assembled *en masse*, took three of the Driscolls, tried them by a jury of their own, found two of them guilty, gave them an hour to prepare for death and shot them. They then resolved to serve every thief they caught, in the same way.* The effect of this summary reprisal was salutary in its effect. The gang that had infested this part of the State were struck with terror, and left for a less determined community, and this region was happily relieved of the incubus which had rested heavily upon it. This was about 1836 or '7. Grundy County, as an organization, was unknown, and the community but barely established, did not take an active part in these movements, though sympathizing with and profiting by them. But no communities found difficulty in organizing for its own defense when occasion demanded. Two fellows were suspected of horse-stealing, in the southern part of the county. They were observed to stay at their father's house at day time, and to be abroad at night, and occasionally to be gone for several weeks without any ostensible business. A committee advised them to leave and not re-

* History of La Salle County—Baldwin.

turn, but disregarding this warning they were visited and severely whipped, and the father ordered to move out of the neighborhood, which was a short distance south of the present line of the county. Other organizations were known as "Claim Associations," which did not have so good a reason for their existence. These were combinations by settlers to resist the encroachments of speculators, though their power was exerted against any interloper or new-comer. Certain lands were bought and located near other sections, which the settler intended, as he got the means, to take up. A new-comer was informed that certain sections were open to him, and that others had been assigned to those already on the grounds. The new-comer sometimes saw fit to disregard this intimation, made his own choice and began his improvements. In one such case a large pile of rails, which had been prepared at a considerable expense of time and labor, and drawn to the place where the fence was to be built, was found entirely burned, and a few days later, the wagon left loaded with rails, was found consumed with its load. Such incidents were not frequent, but occurred here and there, and served to illustrate the tendency of very good citizens when the established restraints of society are somewhat relaxed.

A more recent exhibition of the crude administration of justice occurred about 1867, in an adjoining township. Two men were paying attentions to a woman; one was afterward found shot dead, lying in the road near his team. Suspicion was directed toward the rival of the dead man, and he subsequently acknowledged to the grand jury that he had hired his brother to shoot the unfortunate victim for fifty dollars.

The murderer was apprehended and brought to trial, but the witness before the grand jury took refuge behind the plea that his evidence would criminate himself, and the prisoner was discharged, though there was no doubt entertained of his guilt. The two conspirators returned to their homes and conducted themselves in such a way as to inflame the general feeling against them, until the public sentiment crystallized into a "vigilance committee" and an order to leave the country. The one who did the shooting fled, but his brother gave himself to the sheriff for protection. On the following day some two or three hundred men assembled at Morris, forced the jail, and hung the man to a tree on the south side of the river.

The first permanent settlement was made in Highland by James Martin in 1845 or '6. He came from Indiana and located his land in the southeast corner of the township. He was soon followed by his brothers-in-law, John and William Scott, who settled near him. But little more is known of these persons, as they stayed only a short time here. James Funk was the third settler, and William Pierce came soon afterward, taking up land in the northern corner. About 1851 Alvin and Cushman Small, John Empic, and a Mr. Kline came into the northeastern section of the township. In this year also came Paddy Lamb, an Irishman, from New York. He made a claim on section 17, and returned to his home in the East. In 1855 he came back and settled. While at his old home, his project of turning farmer in Illinois was freely discussed among his associates and fellow countrymen, and quite a number were induced to emigrate to this township. A family by the name of Wier, in Vienna Township, had an extensive acquaintance with their countrymen, and it was largely through their influence that the settlement of Highland took its exclusive character. John Weldon, a resident of Vienna, also was an influential factor in the Highland settlement. New-comers were referred to him for advice as to choosing lands, and he soon became known to the Highland people as "Daddy Weldon," a title of respect which still clings to him. With such a beginning, the tendency was to build up a community which was almost exclusively Irish. The settlement was a comparatively late one, there being but fifteen votes in 1856. Of these it is said fourteen were cast against, and only one for, Buchanan for President. Paddy Lamb was the single-handed champion of the successful candidate, and it is said, his was the first Irish or Democratic vote cast in the township. It may be said that the first case of "bulldozing" occurred in the township on this occasion. The majority desired to make the ballot unanimous, and indulged in a good deal of good-natured effort to convert Lamb to the opposition, but he would have none of it, and still glories in the firmness of his convictions.

There is neither village nor post-office in the township. A somewhat pretentious but considerably neglected town-house marks the "center," and a Catholic place of worship, in the northwest corner of section 4, attracts the devout of this township. The latter building was erected in 1868, at a cost of about $2,400.

PART II.

BIOGRAPHICAL SKETCHES.

MORRIS CITY AND TOWNSHIP.

PERRY A. ARMSTRONG, Morris. The publishers have requested us to write a sketch of our life—a difficult and delicate thing to do. We are like the boy who said he was not used to having his teeth pulled and was afraid it would hurt. We have written many obituaries (not our own), but have never written a biography and are afraid it will hurt. But we promised to do it, and therefore make the effort. As all things must have a beginning and should have an ending, we shall endeavor to begin with the beginning whether we succeed in ending or not. We meet with difficulty, however, at the start, because we were born at a tender age, a long time ago, and a long ways off. We had no scratch-back and pencil to make memoranda, and were too much engaged in admiring the wonderful things of this wonderful world to give special attention to our birth, hence, we are remitted to the family tradition for the date, place and surrounding circumstances of our birth. Relying upon that family tradition—and what well-regulated family would be without a tradition, as they are a very handy thing in a family. We were born on the ides of April, 1823, at the homestead of Joseph and Elsie Armstrong, on the East Fork of Licking, in McCain Township, Licking Co., Ohio. Julius Cæsar we believe was born on the same day, A. C., 98. The difference between us was but 1921 years. He became famous from the expression "Et tu, Brute," whilst we have our fame yet to win, hence we have something to do. Our advent to this mundane sphere was not hailed with demonstrations of delight as we have been informed. (Personally, as we said before, we have no distinct recollections on the subject, because we were only a *boy* when they were looking for a *girl*.) They made two more efforts—two more boys. It was too discouraging—they quit. We are told that we came to this world with an empty stomach, wry face and crabbed disposition. To the first count we plead guilty, and admit that we have labored assiduously to fill that self-same empty stomach with indifferent success, lo! these fifty-nine years. To the second count, we enter a special plea of confession and avoidance, admitting that it is true, but allege that they pinched us. We always make a wry face when pinched. To the third count, we would enter a plea of not guilty were we not afraid they will call our wife as a witness against us. If they should do that, we are a gone coon, so we have concluded to enter a plea of guilty, and throw ourself on the mercy of the court. Before coming to this conclusion, we tried to remember whether we had not been called a little angel or cherub some time in our life, but failed, and consoled ourself with the reflection that the good die young, or, in other words, angels are short-lived and ephemeral and we're glad that we never tried to be one. We are told that thumb-sucking was our special delight. No wonder we never got on in the world; this early habit stuck to us like a brother, and has kept us poor all our life. We have also been informed that we took our gruel and catnip like an old soldier at the business, and were intimately acquainted with wind colic, and have been windy ever since, that we were an adept at that other youthful accomplishment—drooling. That our hair was white, eyes hazel and face green looking. The former stuck to us till in our teens, and "tow-head" was our pet name; the latter commenced to sprout when about twenty, and has sprouted ever since. Our complexion was fair, but for a multitude of freckles, which grew into speckles like unto a turkey's egg. The Seventh Son, common report said we were the doctor; Dame Nature had endowed us with the healing art by the "laying on of hands." We always thought Common Report was a common liar, so we took no stock in the doctor theory, but others did, and came from far and near for the removal of warts, wens and other excrescences which rumor said would flee at our approach. We approached, but they didn't flee; they stayed. The days of miracles had passed, and we declined to revive them; hence we worked no miracles. We attended school at a proper age and earned many laurels as a good fighter—few as a good scholar.

In 1831, our mother and brother determined to go West. This was before Greeley's advice, "Young man, go West," was made public. One brother had already gone West, another had crossed the "silent river," leaving seven still at the old homestead. We could not make up our mind to be left like poor Joe all alone, so we concluded to "move on" with the rest of the family. In arriving at this decision, we were not aided by a desire to rival Buffalo Bill in slaying buffalo, or Donald McKay as an Indian-killer, as we had not then read their exploits. Strange as it is true, we had never read a dime novel and were entirely free of sentimentalism. "The household gods" being stowed to the best advantage in the capacious wagon-box of a prairie schooner, with four horses for motor-power, we folded our tent, and "like the Arab, silently stole away," following the Star of Empire westward ho! What between mud and mire, rain, hail and sleet, our four weeks' journey overland were tedious, yet we enjoyed it well, from the fact that our cousin, who was a few months our junior, accompanied us, and we took solid pleasure in trouncing him several times per day just for fun. Occasionally, however, he turned the tables, and trounced us. This was less agreeable. We reached our land of promise—Sand Prairie, near Lacon, Ill., April 28, 1831. Stopping the first night with a paternal uncle, Gen. John Strawn, we got into a bit of an argument ere we had been there fifteen minutes. A controversy arose between our new-found cousin Enoch and myself as to which was the best wrestler. Although 9 P. M., and quite dark, we proceeded at once to try conclusions, which resulted in a fight, and we were banished early the following morning to the shanty on our brother's claim on the prairie. A good fighter was not then appreciated.

The family did not take to sandy land worth a continental, so in July of that year stakes were again pulled, and we migrated north to La Salle County, and located some seven miles southwest of Ottawa. Here we took the ague, or the ague took us, and shook us lively like for six consecutive weeks, despite of all the bouc-set and wangboo teas we could swallow. Quinine was a luxury not to be had, if, indeed, it had yet been discovered. On the day we had our first shake, we ate heartily of mutton and worty squash—our last meal of that kind of fodder. We acquired a distaste, yea, horror, for them, and have never eaten sheep or squash since. The darned ague shook itself weak, and finally abandoned our poor, emaciated anatomy, and has given us a wide berth ever since. True, it has come round occasionally to let us know it still lived, but has never tackled us in real earnest. There was no salt to be had in that vicinity that fall, hence the prospect for meat was like the boy's ground hog. We had to have salt or no meat. Chicago, 100 miles away, was the nearest point where it could be obtained. We had no correspondents there from whom to order it by telegraph or telephone, nor had either of them been invented. We had no railroad, canal or stage line, nor freighter's line, and lastly, we had no roads but Indian trails. Salt must be had and we determined to have it. So, taking an older brother, William E. (or he taking us), we yoked up two yoke of oxen and hitched them to a sled on which was placed the schooner-shaped wagon box, with old Watch, the faithful dog for company and guard, we started for Chicago December 23, 1831, and reached there in four days. We were much surprised at Chicago. Instead of being a respectable village, there were but two white families there (Kinzie and Miller). The soldiers had been ordered from Fort Dearborn, so the place seemed deserted. We got our salt and returned home to rejoice the hearts of all our neighbors, all of whom were, like us, without salt, and must have it. After all this, one of our neighbors, with whom some of our older brothers had difficulty about claims on the Government land, had our mother arrested for selling salt without license. But, as no law could be found in the statute "agin it," she was honorably discharged. Having procured salt, the wild hogs—with which the river bottom was well supplied—had to suffer. How these hogs came there, and in such large quantities, it would be difficult to tell, but we found them there and were glad of the find. Sod corn we had by purchase of a small field of it from T. J. Covell, for whom Covell Creek was named. Too small to use the ax or maul to advantage, to us was assigned the pounding of corn in a wooden mortar during the winter of 1831–32. The finest of the "mash" was sieved through the sieve and made into corn-dodgers. The rest was boiled for hominy or samp. Thus we fared sumptuously on hog and hominy. For "Sabbaday" we ground a little wheat (of which we had a two-bushel bagful) in a coffee-mill, and bolted it through a jaconet cape of our mother's, and made "slapjacks." They were bully. In May, 1832, the Sac and Fox Indians got on a rampage, and did some indiscriminate scalping of women and children, not far distant from our home, hence we emigrated to a fort in Putnam County, and remained until the Indians were tamed. We did not volunteer to assist in their taming. We let our older brothers, Wash and Bill, take our place in that gentle amusement. In the winter of 1832–33, we attended, as we believe, the first school for "pale-faced" children ever opened in La Salle County. The teacher was a Miss Farnam from away down East. This school was taught in a log schoolhouse, 14x16 feet, some four miles southwest of Ottawa, which we believe was the first schoolhouse built in La Salle County. In the summer of 1836, we tried to sell goods at Hidalgo, on the Waupecan, near the road crossing, three miles southwest of Morris. Hidalgo was then the leading village of the county. It boasted a saw-mill, blacksmith-shop and dry goods store, all belonging to G. W. Armstrong. But the Waupecan went dry more than half the year, hence the mill proved a failure, and Hidalgo was deserted. In that winter, we were at school in Ohio. In 1838, we clerked for George W., and tried to keep his books at Utica, Ill., where he had a contract on the canal, and in the winter of 1838–39 we attended school four miles southwest of Utica, and had to cross the Illinois and Big Vermillion Rivers to get there. Gen. William H. L. Wallace, who fell at Shiloh, was our classmate at this old log schoolhouse on the bluff. This was the best school we ever attended, especially in the study of arithmetic. In 1841, we taught our first school at Hollenbeck's Grove, in Kendall County. Hon. George M. Hollenbeck, James L. Haymond and others now living were among our pupils. In April, 1842, we came to Morris on foot and alone—as the girl went to get married—big with expectations. We were to keep books for the Emperor, Bill Armstrong, for our board, and literally chaw old Blackstone. We failed, on account of typhoid fever, and left him in August for our mother's farm in La Salle County. We then entered Granville Academy and prepared to enter Illinois College in September, 1844. But trying to carry the studies of freshman and sophomore together, we broke down in health and returned home in July, 1845, and opened a select school in Mechanic's Hall, in Ottawa, which we sold out to Mr. Hampden, and returned to Morris in October of that year, and have remained here ever since.

Immediately on our return, we opened a general store in the southwest room of the Grundy Hotel, then standing, but was burnt down in 1851 and the Hopkins House erected on the spot. We then built what is the main part of Dr. Hand's residence, in 1846, for a store and post office. There were two other small stocks of goods here, which we purchased and united with our other stock. In the early part of that year, we were appointed Postmaster of Morris, under Polk's administration, and was succeeded by C. H. Gould, under Taylor's administration. December 22, 1846, we married Miss Mary J. Borbidge, of Pittsburgh, Penn., a highly-accomplished and elegant lady, who died of consumption in 1862, leaving three sons—Charles D., Elwood and William E.—all of whom survive and are married. In the Mexican war, we raised a company, and were elected Captain, but the quota being full before our report reached the Governor, hence our company was not received, and we did not go a-soldiering. Owing to a too free use of our name on other people's paper and official bonds, we were forced to the wall financially in 1849, and were elected a Justice of the Peace but did not like the business. We had lots to do, but never had a heart for badgering and brow-beating. In the spring of 1850, we were elected Supervisor of Morris. In the winter of 1851–52, we went to Springfield to get relief on a Collector's bond, and succeeded. While there, we got a position in the State Auditor's office, and selected the lands of the Illinois Central Railroad, and under the dictation of Gov. Bissell and Robert Rantoul, Jr., we drew the charter of that road, forever securing to the State 7 per cent of the gross earnings of said railroad. We also drew the charter of the Chicago & Rock Island Railroad, and when its construction was begun, in the spring of 1852, we secured the position of Assistant Engineer, and ran the transit line from Joliet to Ottawa, and the bench levels over the same line, and also the level from Tiskilwa to Geneseo. Receiving the offer of better wages on the survey of the Chicago, Burlington & Quincy Railroad, we resigned our position on the Rock Island Railroad and accepted the other, and reported to Capt. Whittle at Galesburg for duty. We run experimental levels on that road until we found they had no money in their treasury, when we quit and came home. We then entered the store of Judge Hopkins as general manager and book-keeper, where we remained until the spring of 1853, when we called the attention of Judge Hynds (County Judge) to the necessity of selecting the swamp lands of the county under the act of Congress of September 28, 1850, and was appointed to survey and select the swamp lands of the county. Under this appointment, we surveyed and selected the swamp lands at the salary of $3 per day, "to be in full for all expenses of whatsoever kind," says the law. Our team and driver cost $2 per day, while the law allowed but $1. We did the work and never asked for extra pay. We then prepared and procured its passage by the Legislature a special law authorizing the sale of these swamp lands without draining them, and, being appointed to make sale, we sold them in 1865 for the sum of $23,724.92, and collected from General Government for cash sales made between the passage of the act September 28, 1850, and time of selection in 1853, $1,700, all of which was paid into the county treasury, making a total of $25,424.92 realized from the so-called swamp lands of the county, with a claim on the General Government for some thirteen thousand acres of land entered by individuals by land warrants after the act of 1850, and before their selection in 1853. These swamp lands were selected in the wettest season we have had for a quarter of a century, hence the selections and confirmations were very large. We were the first Supervisor of the town of Morris, and again held that office in 1853, when we were elected County Clerk. Our parents were Democratic, and we followed their prejudice politically and became the same, casting our first vote for Polk, in 1844; Cass. in 1848; Pierce, in 1852; Buchanan, in 1856; Douglas, in 1860; McClellan, in 1864, and was on the electoral ticket for Seymour in 1868; Greeleyized in 1872; for Tilden, in 1876, and Hancock, in 1880. We were re-elected County Clerk in 1857, although Buchanan received but 600 votes to Fremont's 900 in 1856. When Fort Sumter, was attacked by the Confederates in April, 1861, we made the first war speech of the county, and, as Chairman of the Committee on Resolutions, we introduced the first resolutions denouncing secession and in favor of coercion. We were offered the Colonelcy of the Sixty-fifth Illinois Regiment by Gov. Yates, but, owing to the very delicate health of our better half, we were compelled to stay at home. In the fall of 1854, we were elected Grand Master of the Grand Lodge of Illinois, I. O. O. F., and in 1857, Grand Representative to the Sovereign Grand Lodge of the United States for two years. In the fall of 1861, we were elected without opposition a delegate from La Salle, Livingston and Grundy to the State Constitutional Convention of 1862. In 1863, we were elected to the State Legislature from Grundy and Will without opposition, and, in 1872, from Gundy, Kendall and De Kalb without opposition, and were placed on the Judiciary, Railroad and Judicial Department Committees. At this session, the statutes were revised, in which we took an active part. We were the author of several important laws now in force, among which are the jury law, county court law and escheat law, besides materially amending the criminal code and the road and bridge law. Admitted to practice law by the Supreme Court of Illinois February 3, 1865, and by the United States Court June 3, 1868, we entered into a law partnership with B. Olin (now Judge of the County Court of Will County) in 1865, which lasted five years. On the 25th of August, 1863, we married our second wife, Malina J. Eldredge, at Plano, Ill. From this connection, we have two sons—Frank, aged sixteen, Perry, aged eight years. In 1876, we were appointed Master in Chancery, and, in 1877, Trustee of the Illinois Charitable Eye and Ear Infirmary, which position we still hold. In 1870, we were elected to the School Board, and served seven years. During that time, the present fine stone building was erected. We took an active part in building this schoolhouse as Clerk of the Board of Education and agent to negotiate the school bonds. We have spent much time and considerable money in developing the geology of Grundy County, and as the result we have a fine collection, especially in fossil botany. We deposited for safe keeping a carload of fossil trees, or their impressions upon the shale overlying the coal, in the new State House at Springfield some eight years ago, while our home cabinet at the Academy of Sciences in Morris is large and valuable. Tiring of the hard labor required in collecting geological specimens, we have more recently directed our investigation to Indian history, legends, traditions, customs, habits and social relations, occasionally scribbling poetry—a habit we contracted (when we went to see our girl) in our youth, the greater portion of which has been published in the local papers here and at Ottawa. Our last effort, entitled,

A CHILD'S INQUIRY AND MOTHER'S REPLY.

(Suggested by the question of our little son Perry when some five years of age, to his mother, "What is heaven, mother?")

CHILD.

Tell me, mother, what is heaven?
A mysterious retreat,
Where our sins will be forgiven,
And the angels we shall meet?

MOTHER.

Yes, my child, it is the dwelling
Of our Savior and the bless'd,
"Where the wicked cease from troubling,
And the weary are at rest."

CHILD.

Is its beauty in the clothing
Of the brilliant colored sky?
And beyond that is there nothing
Of more awful majesty?

MOTHER.

No, my child, that beauteous clothing
Are but curtains round the throne
Of our Father, ever-living,
Of the Godhead—Three in One.

CHILD.

Is the sun in glory shining,
Mighty monarch of the day?
Or our Father kindly smiling
On His people hereaway?

MOTHER.

He's the agent sent from heaven
To bring light and life to earth;
To inaugurate creation,
And give vegetation birth.

CHILD.

And the moon, whose silent gleaming
Silvers every house and tree—
Is't the Savior's visage beaming
Fondly on mortality?

MOTHER.

No, my child, 'tis but the emblem
Of His precious love and care
For the faithful little children
Of His vineyard everywhere.

CHILD.

And the stars, which silent creeping,
Spring each night to glorious birth,
Are they angels' eyes a-peeping
At the dwellers of the earth?

MOTHER.

Oh, no, my child, each shining star
The heavenly skies unfurl,
Though distant from this world afar,
Is another living world.

CHILD.

Then where is heaven, mother dear?
Where is this heaven of love,
If not within the starry sphere,
Nor in the skies above?

MOTHER.

Heaven, my child, is everywhere;
On land and sea, field and grove;
Pervades creation, fills the air—
Heaven, indeed, is only love.
—*P. A. Armstrong.*

S. P. AVERY, attorney, Morris, was born in Kendall County, Ill., January 13, 1850; son of S. K. Avery, a native of Oneida County, N. Y., born in 1810, a farmer by occupation; he was born, raised and lived on the same farm in New York till 1847, then came to Illinois that fall, and in the spring of 1848, purchased a farm in Kendall County, where he lived till the time of his death, which occurred December 15, 1880. He was a prominent nurseryman and fruit-grower, during the latter part of his life in Illinois. His wife, Asenath (Wilder) Avery, was born at Verona, N. Y., December 16, 1814, and married S. K. Avery, January 20, 1836.

They moved to Kendall County, Ill., in 1847, where Mrs. Avery died November 26, 1874. They raised seven children, six of whom are now living, five sons, of which subject is the fourth, and one daughter. Subject was educated at the common schools of Kendall County, and at Fowler Institute at Newark; he read law two years in Rochester, N. Y., with Jesse Shepard, then one and a half years in Chicago with A. W. Windett. Mr. Avery was admitted to the bar in June, 1876, came to Morris September 13, 1876, and began the practice of his profession; there he has continued since. Mr. Avery was married, in Laddonia, Mo., March 10, 1882, to Kate Wilder, born October 20, 1856, daughter of Judge B. H. Wilder, of Audrain County, Mo. Mrs. Avery is a member of the Baptist Church. Subject was with Judge C. Grant, Register in Bankruptcy, from December, 1877, to January, 1881, when Judge Grant died; from that time, subject has been Acting Register. Mr. Avery is a Republican.

GEORGE BAUM, clothier, Morris, was born in Germany January 20, 1828; son of George Baum, who was born and raised in Germany, and also died there. Subject emigrated to the United States in 1853, landing in New York City on the 16th of August. He was educated in the common schools of Germany, and when twenty-one years of age was put into the regular army, by a law of that country, which compelled all able-bodied young men, to serve six years. Our subject, by good deportment while in the service, was enabled to procure a recommendation from the principal officers over him, which gave him an honorable release two years prior to the expiration of the time for which he had enlisted. From the date of his landing in the United States in 1853 to 1856, he occupied his time principally in laboring as a farm hand in the States of Connecticut and New Jersey, having had but a meager supply of means when he landed. After reaching Morris on the 4th of April, 1856, he began as before in laboring at any kind of work that presented itself, by which he could earn fair wages, and continued in this way some seven or eight years. He and his brother Henry then began in the saloon business, which he followed until 1877. September 1 of that year, he began the clothing business on his own responsibility, and at present is thus engaged, and doing a satisfactory business. He has been Alderman in Morris for seven years, and has been Director for several years for the Cemetery Association. Mr. Baum was married, in Germany, in June, 1853, just before starting for this country, to Elizabeth Keiser. They have raised three children to maturity and lost two sons, one dying in infancy and the other in his thirteenth year. Those living are one son, Henry, and two daughters, viz., Eliza (wife of John Schobert) and Annie. Mr. Baum and wife are members of the Lutheran Church, and he is a member of the I. O. O. F. Mr. Baum owns a handsome and commodious two-story brick residence in Morris, good store-room, a tenement house, and some vacant lots; he is a Democrat.

HENRY BAUM, dry goods and millinery, Morris, was born in New Jersey April 4, 1855, son of George Baum, whose sketch appears in another part of this work. There were three sons, of whom our subject is the eldest, and the only one living, and two daughters. Henry was educated principally at the public schools of Morris, and took a commercial course at Bryant & Stratton's College of Chicago, graduating in that course in the spring of 1872. He began business by clerking in the dry goods establishment of L. F. Beach & Co., of Morris, remaining there nearly two years, then in partnership with Mr. Schobert opened a similar store in 1874, the firm name being Baum & Schobert. This firm continued together till 1881, at which time they divided, and since each of them has run a separate store. Mr.

Henry Baum is a member of the Masonic order at this place, has taken all the degrees of lodge and chapter, and will likely go through the commandery at an early date. Subject has one of the finest stores in the city, and does a good business. He owns a block of tenement houses near the High School building in Morris, and a couple of vacant lots on Main street; he is also interested in several mines in Colorado, prominent among them is the one owned by the Grundy Mining Company.

HENRY BAUM, Sr., saloon, Morris, was born in Lauchroeden, Saxe-Weimar, Germany, October 26, 1834. He was raised and educated in his native country, receiving special training in music. He served three years as apprentice in general masonry. Came to the United States in the fall of 1857, by way of New Orleans. Settled in Morris, where he engaged at his trade, combined with music-teaching, for eighteen months. In 1859, he went to Louisville, Ky., and gave musical instruction, working at his trade, meantime, for one year. Afterward, made a specialty of music, going south with a troupe, and located in Baton Rouge, La., until the breaking-out of the war in 1861, when he returned to Morris, and enlisted in the Thirty-fourth Illinois Volunteers as a member of the regiment band. Served until the band was discharged in 1862. Since his discharge, he has been engaged in keeping a saloon, located on Washington street. He was married, January 14, 1864, to Miss Elizabeth Zeermann. She is a native of Frickenfelt, Bavarian Rheinfels, Germany, born May 16, 1844. They have two children buried and two living—Louise, born in Morris December 9, 1864, died January 31, 1873; Henry B., born January 27, 1865, died September 13, 1873; Willie L., born May 11, 1866; and Birdie, born November 23, 1874. Subject is a member of I. O. O. F., and a Republican. Residence on corner of Washington and Cedar streets, Morris, Ill.

HENRY BURRELL, miner, Morris, is the oldest of three sons of Archie Burrell, of Scotland, and was born in Edinburgh, Scotland, September 30, 1843. When he was nine years old, his parents removed to the United States, and located in Chicago, where his father died of cholera in 1853. In the fall of 1854, his mother and the three sons came to Morris, Grundy Co., Ill. Here the subject and brothers were employed variously for some years by their uncle, Alexander Telfer, a coal merchant. As soon as old enough, they began digging in the mines for support for themselves and mother. At this time (1866), our subject formed a partnership with others, under the firm name of H. Burrell & Co. He is now alone in the coal trade. The mines are one and one-half miles northeast of Morris, between the railroad and the canal. He is also associated with A. W. Telfer in brick-making. The Burrell heirs have a tract of 317 acres of land, which the subject is farming. He was married, May 31, 1870, to Miss Maggie West, then of Morris. She was born in Scotland June 17, 1851. They have a family of four children—two sons and two daughters—Mary E., born May 19, 1871; Lizzie T., April 4, 1874; Henry A., September 19, 1877, and William O., August 29, 1880. Mr. Burrell is a member of the A., F. & A. M. and of the I. O. O. F.; politics, Republican.

ALEXANDER BURRELL, collier, Morris, was born in Edinburgh, Scotland, January 14, 1850. He came with his parents to the United States in 1852, and settled in Chicago. There his father, Archie Burrell, died in 1853. In 1854, his mother, Eliza Burrell, and family, consisting of three sons, removed to Morris, Grundy County, where they have since lived. Subject was married, April 8, 1879, to Miss Abbie Kiersted, daughter of George H. Kiersted, one of the pioneers of Grundy County. They have two children—George, born January 2, 1880, and Alexander, born February 26,

1881. Mr. Burrell is a member of the firm of Gould, Buchanan & Burrell, coal-miners. They have two shafts, situated near the Chicago & Rock Island Railroad, within the city limits; office on Liberty street. Mr. Burrell is a Republican.

JOHN BROWN, druggist, Morris, was born in England September 1, 1825, son of William Brown, who was born in England about 1785. He was a soldier in the English Army the greater portion of his life, and died in 1864. His wife was Margaret (Blease) Brown. The parents had eight children born to them and raised six to maturity—three sons, of which subject is the third, and three daughters. Subject emigrated to the United States in 1851, and settled in this county, where he has lived since. He was educated in the common schools of England, where he began life in the drug business. When he first came to Illinois, he engaged in farming for about fifteen years, and then engaged again in the drug business, and has followed it since. Mr. Brown has been Supervisor for Au Sable Township, and School Director for Morris, besides filling other minor offices not necessary to mention. He bought the hotel known as the Hopkins House, in Morris, in 1875, and ran the hotel business there, in connection with his other affairs, for about five years. He then sold the hotel, and gave his entire attention to his present business. Mr. Brown was married, in England, in 1850, to Ann (Brown) Brown. She was born in 1826. They have nine children, four sons and five daughters. Subject owns a comfortable residence in Morris, and a good store building; carries a large stock and has a very satisfactory trade. He is a Republican.

GEORGE F. BROWN, grain dealer, Morris, was born June 6, 1828, in Madison County, N. Y. In the year 1830, his father removed to the State of Ohio, where he lived eleven years. In 1841, he again moved, and lived two years in Wisconsin. In 1843, he located in Chicago, where he embarked in the mercantile business for eleven years. He then, in 1854, went to Freeport, where he is still engaged in business. George F. was educated principally at Norwalk, Ohio, and Chicago, Ill. In April, 1855, he came to Morris, Grundy Co., Ill., where he has since done an extensive business in grain and lumber. On the 15th day of October, 1855, he was married to Miss Emma Heald, of Freeport, Ill. She was born in Darien, N. Y., on the 1st day of April, 1832, and came to Illinois in 1853. She is a member of the Presbyterian Church. Their family consists of six children, only two of whom are living—Anna H., Emma, George P., Everett R., Isabella G. and Georgie. Mr. Brown is a stanch Republican, and has held several responsible offices in the city and county.

E. L. BARTLETT, musician, Morris, was born in New York September 19, 1821. When he was twelve years old, his father moved to Western New York, where he worked a farm three years. Our subject entered Hamilton College in 1839, from where he graduated in 1843. He was married October 26, 1843, to Miss Rachel A. Conklin, daughter of C. J. Conklin, now living with his daughter, Mrs. Bartlett, in Morris. In July, 1844, they settled in Lisbon, Kendall County, where Mr. Bartlett was for five years Principal of the Long Grove Academy, after which he taught one year in Oswego, Kendall County; he was also called to the Principalship of the Plainfield Academy, of Will County, just then erected, at which place he taught three years. Mr. Bartlett looks with pride upon many of his former pupils, now filling very honorable positions. In 1854, he purchased a farm in Saratoga Township, upon which he lived ten years. At this period of his history, he enlisted in Company G, One Hundred and Forty-six Illinois Volunteers, as Musician, in Hentzleman's Western Division Band, serving till the close of the war. Returning home, he sold his farm and settled in Morris, where he has since lived. He owns a store building on Washington street, where for some years he conducted a music store. Their family numbers ten children—Napoleon B., born in 1846, killed November 11, 1864, at the battle of Duvall's Bluff; Francis E., born in 1848, is a merchant in Morris; Leroy, born in 1850, is a merchant in Chicago; Arabella, born in 1852, and died December 28, 1874; Jessie, born in 1854, married to William J. Davis, of Chicago; Josephine, born in 1856; Lincoln, born in 1859; Sherman, died in infancy; and Stella, born in 1869. Mr. Bartlett has attained an enviable reputation as a musician, having traveled over Illinois and Iowa with a concert company composed of his own family.

JOHN BUCK, coal and tile, Morris, was born in Cork, Ireland, February 1, 1827. When he was three years old, his parents moved to Canada, where he was raised and educated. He came to Illinois in 1849, and to Grundy County in 1850, where he purchased a tract of land of about nineteen acres in the northwest part of the city of Morris, on which he now lives, engaged in the manufacture of drain-tile; he also operates a coal bank on the same site. He was married, December 3, 1861, to Miss Isabella McMinn, of Pennsylvania. She was born November 20, 1832, and died December 29, 1862. Our subject was again married, March 16, 1865, to Miss Susanna Hutchins, of Morris. She was born in Canada September 24, 1843. They have seven children, one of whom is the result of the first marriage—John T., born December 22, 1862. The children of the second marriage are George H., born January 6, 1866; Herbert E., born March 10, 1867; William F., born November 10, 1869; Richard R., born April 29, 1873; Mary E., born November 16, 1874; and Martha, born January 9, 1882. The family residence is on Lincoln street. Mr. and Mrs. Buck are members of the Methodist Episcopal Church at Morris.

OTIS BAKER, livery, Morris, was born in Orleans County, N. Y., June 11, 1834, and educated in the common schools of New York. He was married, June 2, 1855, to Miss Sarah D. Gregory, who was born in New York January 20, 1835. In the fall of 1856, they came to Grundy County, Ill., and settled in Morris, but soon after bought an eighty-acre farm, four miles north of Morris, where they lived until 1866, when they sold their farm and bought another in the same township (Saratoga), where they remained ten years. In 1876, our subject moved to the town of Morris and engaged for two or three years in the dairy business, since which time he has kept a farmers' feed yard. The family consists of two daughters—Minnie G., born February 26, 1857; married, December 1, 1881, to Charles W. Potter, of New York; and Hattie M., born March 24, 1868. Mr. and Mrs. Baker and their oldest daughter are members of the Congregational Church. Mr. Baker is a Republican, and has been repeatedly elected to offices of trust in the community, in which he has lived. His mother, Laura Baker, is a native of Bristol, Vt., born March 16, 1799, and is now living with her daughter, in Milwaukee, Wis.; his father, Otis Baker, was born in Massachusetts November 10, 1795, and died in Orleans County, N. Y., September 23, 1879.

L. F. BEACH, dealer in dry goods, boots and shoes, etc., Morris, was born in North Dansville, New York July 9, 1841; son of Aaron W. Beach, who was also a native of New York, born in December, 1797, was a farmer by occupation, and now in (1882), lives in Chicago in his eighty-fifth year. His wife, Mary A. (Baker) Beach, was also of New York, born in 1802, and died in Chicago, in June, 1882. The parents raised five children; three sons, of whom the subject is the youngest, and two daughters. Mr. Beach was educated in Steuben County, N. Y., and began life as a farmer in his native State. He came to this State in

1869, having merchandized four years before he came; he settled in Morris when he first came to the State, and began merchandising, which he still follows. Mr. Beach is a member of the Masonic order, and has taken all the degrees from E. A. to Knight Templar; he was School Treasurer for this township for two years, and is now a member of the City Council. He was married, in Erie, Penn., in February, 1870, to Amelia A. Hennessey, who was born July 11, 1846. They have four children —three sons, viz., Layton Fayette, Joseph Allen Hunter and James Blaney; one daughter, Maud Amelia. Mrs. Beach is a member of the Episcopal Church. Subject has built up a good trade, carries a large stock, and besides runs a store of general merchandise at Council Grove, Kan.; he is a Democrat.

L. W. CLAYPOOL, whose portrait appears in this work, is a descendant of an old English family.

About 1645, Sir James Claypool, of England, married a daughter of Oliver Cromwell. This is the earliest record of the family obtainable. Some years later, two brothers of the same family emigrated from England to America, and settled in Virginia. One subsequently left for Philadelphia, and joined his fortunes with William Penn, and he or his descendant, James C. Claypool, was a signing witness to Penn's charter in 1682. The other brother remained in Virginia, where his son, William Claypool, was born about 1690, and lived to the extraordinary age of one hundred and two years. William Claypool was the father of three sons—George, John and James, the latter born about 1730, who died leaving three sons—Abraham, Isaac and Jacob. The first, born April 21, 1762, died in May, 1845. He had six sons and five daughters. Of these sons, Jacob was born August 23, 1788, in Randolph County, Va., and died August 17, 1876. His son, Abraham C., moved from Virginia in 1799, and took up his abode in the Northwest Territory, where Chillicothe, Ohio, now is.

The son of Abraham C. and the father of the subject of this sketch, Jacob C., married Nancy Ballard, a lady of Quaker parentage from North Carolina, and had two sons—Perry A., born in Brown County, Ohio, June 5, 1815, and died in Morris, Ill., October 15, 1846; and L. W., born in the same place June 4, 1819.

Mr. L. W. Claypool spent his early years in a new settlement, going with his parents to Indianapolis, where the ague assailed them with such vigor as to drive them back to Ohio. In March of 1834, he set out with his father to explore the canal lands of Illinois for a new home. He was eager to get an education, and, with the meager facilities afforded in frontier settlements, he managed to master the multiplication table and the elements of writing, and he still has in his possession a rudely-constructed diary with the incidents of this journey noted down in his boyish chirography. The story of this trip and the subsequent removal of the family to Wauponsee Township, in Grundy County, Ill., has been told elsewhere in this volume. His life here was one of great activity, but he managed in the meantime to get quite a knowledge of arithmetic by improving days too wet or cold to work out of doors, and he exhibits with some pride a curious record of the days or half days which he devoted to the study of the elements of mathematics. At the first election held in Grundy County, on May 24, 1841, Mr. Claypool was elected County Recorder, a position he held until 1847, in the meanwhile being appointed the first Postmaster in Morris. In 1848, he was appointed by the Canal Trustees Assistant Agent of the canal lands, having in charge the lands situated in La Salle and Grundy Counties. His duties called him to assist in laying out that part of Chicago in and around Bridgeport, and continued until the last of the land was closed out in 1860. Mr. Claypool has always taken a prominent place in the community in which he has lived so long. He was for years the Supervisor of Wauponsee Township, and is now acting in this capacity for Morris Village.

November 15, 1849, he contracted marriage with Caroline B., daughter of John Palmer, of Ottawa, a pioneer of La Salle County, who came overland from Warren County, N. Y., in June, 1834. Mrs. Claypool was born March 12, 1831, before the family left New York. Two sons of the family born of this union are living —H. C., born March 31, 1852, and L. W., Jr., born October 13, 1866.

O. N. CARTER, County Superintendent of Schools, Morris.

JAMES CUNNEA, banker, Morris, was born in Ireland January 6, 1810, and is a son of Patrick and Isabella (Brown) Cunnea. Patrick Cunnea was born in Ireland in 1783, was a farmer and merchant by occupation, merchandized largely, and died in Ireland in 1840, having been sick but six days; his wife died the same year. The parents had sixteen children born to them, twelve of whom were raised to maturity—six sons, of whom subject is the oldest, and six daughters. Our subject received a limited education in the common schools in Ireland. He began for himself by keeping store and farming, which he continued about six years, and then, in 1846, times getting a little hard there, he said to his wife, "We will go to America," and at once sold out his effects and emigrated to the United States, stopping about two years in New York; then he came to Illinois (1848), and, purchasing a large tract of land in Will County, began farming and stockraising, which he followed in connection with his sons till about 1866; from there he came to Morris, and opened a loan office for a few years, and, in 1872, purchased the First National Bank of Seneca, and removed the same to Morris, changing the name to First National Bank of Morris. From that time to the present, he and his sons have run a general banking business here. The officers of the bank are as follows: James Cunnea (subject), President and Director; John Cunnea, Cashier and Director; John McCambridge, Director; George A. Cunnea, Director; James Cunnea, Jr., Director. Subject and sons also own considerable land in this and other States, besides other valuable property. Subject is a Democrat in politics. He was married in Ireland, March 4, 1834, to Ann Glackin, a daughter of Dennis and Catharine (McHugh) Glackin; his wife was born in March, 1817. They had twelve children born to them; eight raised to maturity, one of whom, Thomas, died at the age of twenty-three years. Those living are three sons—John, James and George A., and four daughters, viz., Isabella, Maria (now the wife of John McCambridge), Catharine and Anna. Mr. Cunnea and wife and all the family are members of the Catholic Church. James Cunnea, Jr., was married in 1876, to Estella Smith, daughter of Patrick Smith, of Cleveland, Ohio.

JOHN CUNNEA, banker and cashier, Morris, was born in Ireland, July 22, 1840; is a son of James Cunnea, whose biography appears elsewhere in this history. Our subject came to the United States in 1846; stopped two years in New York City, then came to Illinois, and soon afterward settled in Will County, at what is now called Braidwood. There he attended school, and afterward completed his education at Bryant & Stratton's Business College in Chicago. Mr. Cunnea purchased a considerable tract of land at Braidwood, and remained there engaged in farming for seventeen years. He came to Morris in May, 1866, and about a year afterward, in connection with his brothers, opened a loan office, which they continued till August, 1872, when they purchased of D. D. Spencer his banking business at Seneca. All the appurtenances of the bank they removed to Morris, where they still carry on a general banking business. The bank is known as the First National Bank of Morris, the proprietors being James Cunnea & Sons. September 1, 1875, our subject was married to Jennie A. Hoge, daughter of Samuel and Matilda (Holderman) Hoge. This union has resulted in two children—Samuel James and Charity Isabella. Mr. Cunnea and wife are members of the Catholic Church. He is a Democrat.

DAVID M. COOK, grocer, Morris, was born in Perry County, Penn., January 13, 1837. His father, James Cook, died in Pennsylvania when David was nine years of age, and his mother moved with her family to Miami County, Ohio. Here his mother and one brother died. The three remaining brothers came to Warren County, Ill., in the spring of 1855. In the fall of 1856, they moved to Morris, Grundy County, where he and his brother, John W., established a restaurant and provision store on Washington street. Our subject was married, November 2, 1860, to Miss Jane Claypool, daughter of Perry A. Claypool; she was born in Grundy County, March 7, 1842. The family consists of four children, two of whom are living, viz., Nellie M., born March 25, 1864; Samuel D., December 4, 1870; William M., born December 23, 1875, died July 23, 1880; and John P., born April 5, 1877, died March 18, 1880. Mr. and Mrs. Cook are members of the Presbyterian Church of Morris. Mr. Cook is now proprietor of a grocery and provision store on Liberty street, in a building erected by him in 1861. He is a Republican.

WILLIAM R. CODY, furniture dealer, Morris, was born in Oneida County, N. Y., December 1, 1825, and received his education in his native State. He came to Illinois when eighteen years old, and settled in Lisbon, Kendall County, where he lived for six years, teaching school in various places in the county. He was first married to Miss Martha Hobson, of Naperville, Ill.; October 10, 1854; she died June 28, 1855, and is buried in her native town. September 10, 1856, Mr. Cody was again married, this time to Miss Sarah M. Conant, a native of New York, born December 17, 1835. They have had six children, two of whom are dead—Caroline, born August 24, 1857, died October 5, 1857; Nellie F., born December 21, 1858, married to N. C. Davis, of Morris; Susan E., May 21 1861, married to E. H. Quigley, of Morris; Eddie, July 24, 1843, died November 5, 1870; Annie, born May 7, 1867; and Grace, September 12, 1876. Mr. and Mrs. Cody are members of the M. E. Church of Morris. He is now engaged in the furniture business, in partnership with N. C. Davis; place of business Nos. 94 and 96 Liberty street.

WILLIAM H. CURTIS, retired, Morris. The subject of this sketch is a native of Rutland, Vt., born December 24, 1817, son of Thaddeus and Charlotte (Kimball) Curtis, who came to Grundy County, 1848. His father died in Grundy County, September 3, 1857, in his sixty-sixth year. The mother died in Grundy County, January 9, 1862, in her seventy-fifth year. Subject came to Grundy County in 1846, and bought land in Vienna Township, where he made his home until coming to Morris, January, 1880. Raised and educated in Vermont. Married June 12, 1860, to Mrs. Jane A. Hollenbeck, widow of Abraham Hollenbeck. She is a native of Dutchess County, N. Y., February 13, 1817, and came to Grundy County about 1850. Mr. Curtis is now retired and is living in a beautiful residence on corner of Benton and Spruce streets. Besides his large landed interest in Vienna Township, of this county, he owns a farm of 112 acres in Section 25, of Brookfield Township, La Salle County. "Wolves!" said Mr. Curtis, "I can tell you a big one, but nobody will believe it." "Let us have the benefit of the story," said the interviewer. "I was aroused one morning to find a wolf with a chicken. I had no dog of my own, but Dr. Antis' dog happened to be under my shanty. He gave chase, and was soon joined by William Hinchman's dog. In order to encourage the dogs, I got on a horse, not stopping to put on a bridle, and followed after. They overhauled him on a pond which had a considerable thickness of ice, but they were not equal to the wolf, not being used to his method of defense. Thinking to help the dogs, I got off my horse and caught the wolf by the tail. No sooner had I done so than the dogs left me to engage the wolf while they indulged in a fight with each other. In this dilemma I conceived the idea of killing my game by swinging it over-handed and bringing its head in contact with the ice. This proved a failure, for the first impression broke the ice, letting us into three feet of water. Now my only chance was to drown him, and after several attempts, coupled with the pitchfork in the hands of a boy, the wolf was numbered with the slain."

JOHN B. DAVIDSON, broker, Morris, was born in Beaver County, Penn., January 28, 1815, and spent his boyhood in Eastern Ohio. He resided about twenty years in the towns of Middleton, Poland and Lowellville, fifteen years of which time he was engaged successfully in the dry goods trade, and was five years Postmaster of Lowellville. In 1845, he married Miss Kate Butler, daughter of Mrs. Julia Alford, of the city of Morris; she died April 13, 1858. Before his arrival here in 1854, Mr. Davidson had invested extensively in city real estate and farming lands of the surrounding country. The first year, he engaged in clerical work until he could arrange to go into business. In 1855, he, in connection with Walker and Alford, established the first boot and shoe house in Morris; he soon after bought the interest of Mr. Walker. This store was located where Goold's drug store now is, and in 1858 Mr. Davidson and his partner sold to Edwards & Galloway. Mr. Davidson was elected Alderman of the Second Ward in 1857, and in 1860 was elected Circuit Clerk, which office he held until 1868, declining another term. He was married again, May 28, 1861, to a daughter of the Rev. Reuben Frame, at the time pastor of the Presbyterian Church of Morris. Our subject is now engaged as a banker and broker, being among the leading capitalists of the county. He is a Director and stockholder in the Morris Bridge Company, the Grundy County Bank, and the Morris Gas Company, and is justly regarded as one of the city's leading benefactors. He is a Republican.

PHINEAS DAVIS, retired farmer, P. O. Morris. Mr. Davis was born in Livingston County, N. Y., January 24, 1827. He came to Illinois in 1847, and settled in Kendall County, where he purchased a farm and lived for twenty-seven years. In March, 1874, he moved to Morris, Grundy County, and bought a beautiful location on the corner of Liberty and High streets. He was married, January 22, 1848, to Miss Maria L. Phipps, of New Jersey. She was born in 1822, and died January 29, 1879. The family consists of two sons--James L., born March 28, 1849, married to Elizabeth J. Boyer; and Uriah C., born November 15, 1851, married to Miss Nellie Cody. Our subject was married the second time, February 24, 1881, to Sallie C. Frasee, widow of Barnard Frasee. Mr. and Mrs. Davis are members of the Methodist Episcopal Church of Morris.

OLE ERICKSON, dry goods, boots and shoes, Morris, is a native of Norway; was born October 6, 1850, and came to the United States in 1866. He is a son of Erik Erickson, of Norway, born in 1803; the latter came to the United States July 20, 1880, and settled in Minnesota as a farmer, that being his occupation; he still resides there. His wife, Marit (Svarthaugen) Erickson, was born in Norway in 1812, and died there November 29, 1879. They were the parents of three children, one son, who is the subject of this sketch, and two daughters. Subject was educated at the common schools in Norway; was raised on the farm, and worked at that pursuit a short time after starting for himself, but soon went into a store. When he first came to the Unites States in 1866, he began as clerk at Chicago in a grocery store, where he continued some three years; from there he came to Morris, May 17, 1869, and started a dry goods business with a partner. This he continued for three years, when he sold out, and again engaged as clerk, which he followed about eight years. On the 12th of November, 1880, in partnership with W. B. Hull, he opened a full store of dry goods, boots and shoes, and they are now doing a lively business. Mr. Erickson was married in Morris, September 10, 1871, to Mary M., daughter of William Frey, of this place; she was born November 23, 1851. They have two children, one daughter, Anna M., born November 1, 1872; and one son, Albert E., born March 19, 1875. Subject is a Lutheran, and his wife a Methodist. Mr. Erickson has been Town and City Collector for two years. He is a Republican.

DR. S. T. FERGUSON, Morris, was born in Auburn, N. Y., March 7, 1845, and came to Grundy County in 1854; son of Daniel Ferguson, who was also a native of New York; of Scotch parentage, born about the year 1800; was a blacksmith by occupation, and died of cholera in 1854. Immediately after his death, his wife, Parmelia Fowler, also a native of New York, born in 1802, came to Grundy County with her children, and died in Morris in 1875. The parents raised five children—two sons—of whom our subject is the younger, and three daughters. Mr. Ferguson was educated at the common schools at Morris, afterward taking a medical course at Ann Arbor, Mich., and Chicago, Ill., graduating at the last-named place in the class of 1865. He began business for himself as clerk in a drug store in Morris, which he followed about seven years; thence to Ann Arbor, where he attended the medical school one term, and then to Seneca, in La Salle County, and practiced medicine about one year; next he went into the army, where he was Surgeon of the One Hundred and Thirty-eighth Illinois Infantry for four months. He was then appointed United States Surgeon, and sent to Topeka, Kan., where he remained about a year, including what time was spent at Lawrence. From Topeka, he came back to Morris, and engaged in the drug business; next went to Minooka, and entered into partnership with Dr. William P. Pierce in a general practice, where he remained about thirteen years; from there, subject again returned to Morris, and resumed the practice of his profession. He has had now nearly twenty years practice. While at Minooka, Dr. Ferguson spent two winters at Chicago studying gynecology, which he now makes a specialty of. Dr. Ferguson was married at Seneca, August 2, 1863, to Emma, daughter of Joseph R. Oldycke, of Grundy County. She died April 15, 1881. The Doctor is a Mason, and has taken all the degrees, from E. A. to Knight Templar. He is a Past Master of Minooka Lodge, No. 528, and has filled different offices in the Chapter and Commandery. Subject owns some farm lands in this and Kendall Counties. He is a Republican.

CHARLES D. FERGUSON, Sheriff, Morris, was born near Rochester, N. Y., May 31, 1839, and is a son of Daniel Ferguson, who was also a native of New York, born in 1809, a blacksmith by occupation, who came to Grundy County, Ill., in 1854, and purchased a tract of land, but was taken with cholera and returned to New York, and died in 1854, only living about twenty-four hours after reaching home. His wife, Amelia (Fowler) Ferguson, was born in New York in 1804, and came to Illinois in 1854, shortly after her husband's death, bringing her family, and settling in Morris, where she died in 1874. The parents raised two sons —subject is the oldest—and three daughters. Subject was educated in New York; began business as a blacksmith, which he followed about twenty-five years. In the fall of 1880, he was elected Sheriff of Grundy County, an office he now holds. He has had charge of the steam fire engine for eleven years—from 1869 to 1880. Mr. Ferguson married first in Geneseo, N. Y., April 9, 1861, to Louisa Hall, daughter of John Hall of that place. She died November 24, 1861. His second marriage was in this county, March 25, 1865, to Elizabeth A. Ent, born March 25. 1844, at Stockton, Hunterdon Co., N. J., and is an only daughter of Asa Ent, of New Jersey. The children are as follows: Fred C., born March 31, 1866; Harry M., born September 19, 1870, and Eugene Ray, born January 24, 1874.

JOSEPH FESSLER, saloon, Morris, is a native of Germany, born December 16, 1850. When our subject was two years old, his mother emigrated to the United States, and settled in Chicago, his father having died in Germany in 1851. In 1861, Mr. Fessler went to Minooka, Grundy County, and lived there with his uncle (John Schroeder) until the fall of 1866, when Mr. Schroeder was elected Sheriff of the county, and moved to Morris, where Mr. Fessler has since lived. He was Assistant Warden at the time of the lynching of Alonzo Tibbits in 1868. December 8, 1872, he married Miss Eva Becker, of Morris. She was born in Indiana November 25. 1852. They have three children —Carrie L., born February 14, 1875; Bertha M., July 5, 1878, and Ernest J., May 4, 1880. Subject engaged in the saloon business in 1873, with Charles Wagner, which he continued until April, 1875, when he purchased the interest of Mr. Wagner, and has since conducted the business alone. His saloon is located on Liberty street; his residence on Jefferson street. He is a member of the I. O. O. F.

HIRAM C. GOOLD, druggist, Morris, Ill., was born in Orleans County, N. Y., October 23, 1821, but moved to Ontario County, N. Y., at three years of age, where he attended the common schools during his early childhood. His education was completed at the Wesleyan University, at Lima, N. Y. When twenty years of age, he began teaching, which occupation he followed several years. Came to Illinois in 1845, and located in Putnam County, where he taught one year in the Granville Academy. Went to Michigan and taught two years, and then came to Morris, Grundy County, in 1848. Was in a dry goods store two years as clerk. Then went to California by the overland route, being 100 days on the road. Was engaged in Northern California in mining three years. Then returned to Morris and engaged in the real estate business, and where he eventually went into the drug business. Was elected County Superintendent of Schools in 1852, and filled the office three consecutive terms or ten years, the duties of which office he filled creditably to himself and to the full satisfaction of the people. He was married, at Morris, in the fall of 1853, to Clementine L. Baker, born in Genesee County, N. Y., in 1824. They have one son, Hiram B., who is his father's assistant in the drug business. Mr. Goold has been a member of the Congregational Church since seventeen years of age. Has always taken an active part in the temperance movements of the county, and was one of the charter members of the Sons of Temperance of Morris, organized in 1848. Has been a life-long worker in the Sunday school, and since his residence in Morris has been identified with the Sunday schools of that place, the principal part of the time as Superintendent of the Congregational school.

JACOB M. GRIGGS, farmer, P. O. Morris, is a native of Pennsylvania, born April 12, 1829. He came to the site of Morris in 1837, with his father, who built the second house in the place, in 1838. The father died in Morris in April, 1849. Our subject attended the first school ever organized in Morris. He was married, January 13, 1862, to Miss Emma Cochran, daughter of Samuel Cochran, of Morris, born February 28, 1840. The family consists of seven children, viz., Sigel A., born January 25, 1863; Henry B., February 5, 1866; Helen

J., March 1, 1868; Minnie M., November 14, 1871; Birdie W., September 10, 1875; Archie R., June 2, 1877; Gracie G., November 6, 1879. Mr. Griggs has about seventy-five acres of farm land in Section 9 of Morris Township, and one hundred acres in Section 16 of Saratoga Township, valued at $60 per acre. He is associated in the brick and tile business with Messrs. Martin and Steep, the firm known as Griggs, Martin & Steep. Mr. Griggs is a persistent temperance worker and a Republican.

MILES GORDON, joiner, Morris, was born in Franklin County, Me., January 22, 1820. He came to Morris in 1843, and has been a leading contractor in his line of business during all the years of his residence here. In August, 1844, our subject was married to Miss Betsey Judkins, of Maine; this union has been blessed with five children.

DR. A. F. HAND, Morris. The subject of this sketch may be classed among the early settlers of Grundy County, having come to Morris in the spring of 1847, and resided here ever since. He was born in 1816 in the town of Shoreham, Vt., on the eastern shore of Lake Champlain, directly opposite Fort Ticonderoga, and within a stone's throw of where Ethan Allen embarked to cross the lake in that famous surprise of his on the British forces. At the age of eighteen, he left the home of his parents and came West, stopping for a short time at Logansport, Ind., at the residence of his half-brother, Rev. Martin Post. He next found his way to Jacksonville, Ill., and two years later, entered the Freshman class as a student in Illinois College, graduating in the scientific course of that institution four years afterward. We next find our subject at Louisville, Mo., where he taught school two years, and returning to Jacksonville again, entered the medical department of Illinois College, and three years later obtained his diploma as Doctor of Medicine. He now began the practice of his profession, and spent two years with the distinguished Dr. Charles Chandler, of Chandlerville, Ill. In the spring of 1847, through the influence of Hon. Perry Armstrong, subject was induced to come to Morris, where he has since resided and practiced medicine. Now, at the age of sixty, with a moderate competence in store, he has declared his intention of retiring from the active pursuit of his profession, and enjoying the fruit of his labors. Dr. Hand was married May 1, 1850, in Morris, to Sarah E. Clark, born March 17, 1827, in Philadelphia, a daughter of Job Clark, a boot and shoe merchant of Milford, Conn. They have three children—Eduella Clark, Truman A. and Oliver H. Dr. Hand is a United States Surgeon for examining pensioners. He is a Republican in politics.

C. H. HANSEN, boots and shoes, hats and caps, Morris, was born in Denmark April 1, 1851, son of Hans Christen. Subject emigrated to this country in the spring of 1868 and traveled for two or three years through Southern Missouri, Arkansas, Tennessee, Illinois, Iowa, Wisconsin, and finally settled in Chicago. He began business there in 1870, in partnership with his brother, and in 1873 came to Morris and opened a store, which the brothers have continued since. In 1875, our subject took a trip to Europe, and spent six months, traveling through Germany, Denmark, Sweden and England. In the spring of 1877, he went to the Black Hills, and spent about three years, running a mine and store. Afterward, was in Montana and Wyoming Territories. He came back to Morris in the fall of 1880, and after taking a business trip back to the Territories in the spring of 1881, again returned to Morris, where he has since remained. He was married in Canada, January 25, 1882, to Susan E. Mason, who was born in Canada in 1861. Subject is a member of the Knights of Pythias; has a good stock of goods and a satisfactory trade. R. H. Hansen, brother of our subject, was born in Denmark March 5, 1848, and came to this country in 1867. After traveling for some time, he finally settled and spent one summer in Minnesota. From there, he came to Cook County, Ill., where he was on a farm for some time. He next engaged as clerk at Chicago in a boot and shoe store, where he remained till 1870, and then started a store in that city for himself. This he conducted for six years, and in 1874, opened a branch store in Morris. In 1876, he gave up the store entirely in Chicago and came to this place. He is non-partisan in politics.

WILLIAM T. HOPKINS, attorney, Morris, was born in Maine October 5, 1819, son of David Hopkins, also a native of Maine, born in 1779; he was a farmer by occupation, and died in Maine in 1860; his wife, Esther (Trask) Hopkins, was born in Maine in 1781, and died in 1872, at the old homestead in Maine. The parents raised fourteen children—nine sons, of which subject is the sixth, and five daughters. Subject was educated in the State of Maine, and read law at Bangor, that State. Was admitted to the bar at Morris, Ill., in 1850, and at once began the practice of his profession, which he still continues. Mr. Hopkins was engaged in the mercantile business in Morris from 1853 to 1855. He has been Superintendent of Public Instruction for one term; was elected Judge of the Grundy County Court in 1861, and served one term; in 1864, he was elected Representative to the Legislature from this county for two years; he was also one of the Electors the same year on the Republican ticket, which cast the vote of this State for Abraham Lincoln for President. In 1865 and 1866, Mr. Hopkins was one of the general agents of the Internal Revenue Department of the United States. Was in the three-months service in the late war, and raised a company, of which he was Captain. In 1863–64–65, he was President of the Sanitary and Christian Commission for this district. Subject was married in Maine, in 1846, to Clara H., daughter of Simon Prescott; she was born September 20, 1824. Mr. and Mrs. Hopkins having no children of their own, raised two nieces—Hannah Hopkins, who is now the wife of Allen F. Mallory, and Nora J. Abbott, who is now an invalid at her adopted home with her uncle. Mr. Hopkins is a Mason; has filled most of the offices in Lodge and Chapter, and is at present (1882) Master of the Lodge at Morris. He was a member of the first convention that formed the Republican party in this State. Self and wife are members of the Baptist Church. Subject was an intimate friend of President Lincoln from 1850 to the time of his death, and was at the convention at Chicago that nominated Mr. Lincoln for the Presidency. Mr. Hopkins is still a Republican.

D. C. HUSTON, restaurant and photographer, Morris, was born in Grundy County, Ill., July 13, 1850. Son of Charles and Jane (Enos) Huston, natives of New York State, he born about the year 1809. His parents raised five children—two daughters, one of whom died in her teens, and three sons, of whom our subject was the second. He commenced his education in the country schools, and finished it in the State Normal Institute at Bloomington, Ill. His first work was farming, but after finishing his schooling he began clerking in a dry goods establishment at Gardner. This occupation he continued in different places until in 1874. After clerking again in Gardner for a few months, he began traveling for the Sherwood School Furniture Company, with which firm he continued for about two and one-half years, when he began the photograph business, which he still follows. February 18, 1882, he opened a restaurant, which he still carries on. April 8, 1879, in Ottawa, Ill., Mr. Huston married Annie C. Kiersted, born May 3, 1854, daughter of George Kiersted (deceased), one of the early settlers of this county. This marriage has resulted in one child—Mabel C., born May 9,

1881. Mr. Huston is a member of the Masonic fraternity; has taken the degrees of the Lodge and Chapter; he is a Republican.

H. H. HOLTZMAN, stationery and news depot, Morris, was born in the District of Columbia November 3, 1837, son of James H. and Sophia (Shell) Holtzman, both natives of the District of Columbia. He, born December 7, 1815, was a merchant, and died November 12, 1868; she, born May 22, 1816, died May 28, 1868; they had five sons, of which our subject was the oldest, and six daughters. Mr. Holtzman was educated in the District of Columbia, and, with his father and the family, came to Morris in 1855, where our subject engaged in the same business he follows at present, except that it was on a very limited scale. He has increased his business from year to year until he now has a large and commodious storeroom well filled with goods and controls a good trade. He is no partisan in politics; is a member of the Masonic Order, and has taken all the degrees from E. A. to K. T. Mr. Holtzman was married, in this county, May 9, 1869, to Lucy Hollands, born March 10, 1847. She is a daughter of Joseph and Jane (Smith) Hollands, both born the same year, 1813. She died January 27, 1881. He still lives in this county. Mrs. Holtzman is a member of the Presbyterian Church.

SAMUEL HOLDERMAN, Morris, was born in Marion, Marion Co., Ohio, October 9, 1828. His parents were among the first settlers of Grundy County, settling in Holderman's Grove, then La Salle County, in 1831. The following year (1832), they were compelled to flee to the settlement where Pekin now stands for security from the Indians, then on the war-path. In July, 1852, our subject was married to Miss Martha H. Coke, daughter of Charles H. Coke, of Grundy County. She was born in England September 15, 1830, and died in Felix Township, Grundy County, on the 29th of April, 1866. The result of this union was six children—Charles H., born January 19, 1854, married to Miss Elizabeth Peacock, of Morris; Mary E., born May 22, 1855, died December 25, 1877; Charlotte M., born January 19, 1857, married T. Furgeson in April, 1880; William E., born December 22, 1858; Caroline M., October 22, 1860, and Orville S., December 5, 1863. During the life of his first wife, Mr. Holderman lived on a farm in Felix Township, Grundy County. In January, 1872, he married Mrs. Elizabeth King, widow of Alondas King, and sister of his former wife. Mr. Holderman has, by his enterprise, assisted largely in giving character to the business of his county. He is now engaged, in connection with his two sons, Charles and William, in the stock business in Wyoming and Utah. He also has an interest in three gold and silver mines in Southern Utah. With these, his son-in-law, Furgeson, is connected. Mr. Holderman spends the greater portion of his time in the West, where his business interests call him. His residence is on Fremont avenue, Morris. His politics are Republican.

W. D. HITCHCOCK, County Clerk, Morris, born in Champlain, Clinton Co., N. Y., August 16, 1857; son of H. D. Hitchcock, born at same place in 1827. The father came to Morris in November, 1867, and was Deputy Clerk four years. In 1877, was elected Clerk, in which capacity he served till the time of his death, which occurred April 7, 1880. His wife, Mary J. (Cutting) Hitchcock, was a native of Westport, Essex Co., N. Y., born in 1833. She now lives with her son (subject) in Morris. The parents raised three children—one son (subject), and two daughters. Our subject was educated at the High School at Morris, and began life in the dry goods business as salesman, which he followed some six years. From there, he came into the Clerk's office as Deputy under his father, and after his father's death he was elected to fill the unexpired term. Republican in politics; belongs to the Masonic order.

FRANCIS HALL, saloon, Morris, was born in Clackmannan, Scotland, August 16, 1830. He was raised and educated in Scotland, and came to the United States in June, 1855; settled in Pennsylvania for about one year, then in September, 1856, he came to Morris, Grundy Co., Ill., where he has since resided. He engaged in the coal trade for several years until 1868. In 1861, he sunk the first shaft made on the Conklin road. Since 1868, he has been proprietor of the saloon, corner of Washington and Wauponsee streets; residence on Washington street. He was married, February 3, 1862, to Miss Margaret Rankin, of De Kalb County, Ill. Mrs. (Rankin) Hall was born January 24, 1841. They have a family of nine children, four of whom are dead. They are Thomas Hall, born December 17, 1862; Margaret J., born April 5, 1865, and died July 31, 1866; Christina M., born June 26, 1867, and died October 17, 1868; Francis, born September 11, 1869; Jennie, born February 19, 1872 and died October 22, 1875; Lillie, born August 3, 1874, and died September 30, 1875; Edward, born August 13, 1876; Jessie, born May 27, 1879; Isabel, born June 18, 1882.

JOHN K. HARRISON, mechanic, Morris, is a native of Oneida County, N. Y., born July 7, 1828, and raised in Montgomery County, N. Y. He learned the carpenter trade under his father, serving five years, and afterward served a two-year's apprenticeship as millwright. He was married, December 31, 1847, to Miss Phila Jones, of New York. She was born March 2, 1830. Mr. Harrison came to Morris in 1852, since which time he has been engaged mostly at his trade. August 7, 1862, he enlisted in Company C, Seventy-sixth Illinois Volunteer Infantry, to which regiment he belonged till 1864, when he was transferred to the Sixty-fourth U. S. C. I., acting as Commissary Sergeant. He continued in this regiment until January 1, 1866, when he was discharged. During his entire service, he was employed in the Quartermaster and Commissary Department. After the war, he came home, and remained about eighteen months, when he went South, and engaged in raising cotton in its season, and working at his trade in the winter. The family consists of eight children—only three living. They are William Henry, born in 1854; Thomas Jefferson, born in 1858, and Ida Isabel, born September 23, 1862. Those deceased are Adelphy A., born in 1847; Mary, born in 1849; both died in New York in December, 1857; John J., born in 1863, died in Grundy County in 1863; Josephine, born in 1852, died in Grundy County in 1853, and Eugene M., born in 1867, and died in Mississippi in 1875. Mrs. Harrison is a Methodist; Mr. Harrison is a Democrat.

RICHARD HUGHES, saloon, Morris, is a native of County Mayo, Ireland; was born in June, 1835. His parents emigrated to the United States in 1846, and settled in Portsmouth, Va., where our subject was principally educated. He served an apprenticeship of three years at the trade of confectioner. About 1855, he came to Morris, Grundy Co., Ill., and engaged in farming until the breaking-out of the war. In July, 1862, he enlisted in Company C, Seventy-sixth Illinois Volunteer Infantry. He was appointed Second Lieutenant at the organization of the company; was promoted to the post of First Lieutenant in 1864, and was mustered in as Captain of Company C in 1865, at Blakely, Ala. He participated in about twenty-seven engagements, including the siege of Vicksburg, siege of Blakely, Jackson Cross-Roads, etc. He had six brothers also in the war, all younger than himself; one of them was killed in the battle of Shiloh; three of them, including himself, were wounded at Blakely, Ala., subject receiving two wounds. Since the war, he has been engaged in business in Morris; is now associated with Mr. J. O. Levette, on Washington street; his residence is on the corner of Division and North streets, Morris. He is a member of the I. O. O. F.

EBENEZER HYDE, retired merchant, Morris, was born February 21, 1811, in Berkshire County, Mass., where he was raised and educated, and where he lived until 1852, with the exception of two years spent in Connecticut. During the years 1852-53, he was in Aurora, Ill., in the lumber trade. The year 1854, he spent in Chicago. In the spring of 1855, he moved to Morris, Grundy County, where he has since resided, and for eighteen years engaged in the lumber business, from which he has now retired. He owns a farm ten miles south of Morris, which he rents; his residence is at the corner of Main and Calhoun streets. His sister, Mrs. Louisa Bulkley, widow of A. P. Bulkley, resides with subject; A. P. Bulkley was born October 15, 1812 ; died August 15, 1872. They have one daughter—Mary L. (Bulkley) Gore born March 29, 1858, married to William H. Gore February 2, 1882. William H. Gore was born in Saratoga Township, Grundy County, July 12, 1852. Is now engaged in the drug business at Chicago. Mr. Ebenezer Hyde, our subject, is a Republican.

PHILLIP HART, grocer, Morris, is a native of Hesse-Darmstadt, Germany, born December 17, 1827; received a common school education in Germany and came to the United States in 1846; worked in New York City at the barber business for about six years. In 1850, he removed to Buffalo, where he kept hotel until 1853. In 1854, he settled in Morris, Grundy County, where he has engaged in various kinds of business, principally as proprietor of the American House, and afterward in the grocery business, in which he is now engaged, in Hart's Block, Liberty street. He was married, in May, 1848, to Miss Elizabeth Goering, of Germany; she was born March 7, 1826. They have had six children—Catharine, born February 12, 1851; and Lena, born September 11, 1854; both died in infancy; Mary, born February 16, 1861, died January 16, 1863; Eliza, born September 16, 1857, married, May 31, 1881, to Frederick Harmening ; George, born December 22, 1858, married to Miss Mollie Hynds; and William, born July 10, 1867.

JOHN HART, mechanic, Morris, was born on the 17th of March, 1838, in Elizabeth, Penn. His parents, James and Rebecca Hart, came to Grundy County, his father in 1839 and his mother, with the family, in 1840. His father died in Morris on the 1st of January, 1844. His mother, Rebecca (Simpson) Hart, was born in Ireland in 1803 ; died in Morris November 8, 1846. John, being left an orphan at the age of nine years, early acquired habits of industry. At the age of sixteen, he began the trade of blacksmithing, under Martin Hines, serving as an apprentice three years, since which time he has worked at his trade in Morris, with the exception of three years, from 1859 to 1862, spent in Sacramento, Cal. He is now located on Canal street, between Fulton and Calhoun streets, where he has run a shop for the past fifteen years. He was married, on the 6th of March, 1859, to Miss Ellen Ward, a native of Ireland. They are members of the Catholic Church of Morris. Mr. Hart is among the very first inhabitants of Morris, and attended the first school ever conducted in the town. In politics, he is strictly independent. Residence on the corner of Fremont avenue and Oak street.

JAMES HORRIE, carriage-maker, Morris, was born in the Orkney Islands, Scotland, September 27, 1827, and was raised and educated in the home of his nativity, where he served an apprenticeship of four years at the blacksmith trade, which he still follows. He came from his native place to Grundy County, Ill., and settled in Morris in 1848. August 20, 1850, he married Miss Catharine Anderson, of Scotland. She was born February 26, 1828. The family consists of eight children—Jane, born June 16, 1851, married to William Handwerk January

11, 1876; James A., born July 16, 1853, married to Miss Nina Rolly November 24, 1875; Robert C., born November 7, 1855, married to Miss Mary Baird November 7, 1877; Joseph W., born February 13, 1858; Catharine A., born April 5, 1860; William J., born January 15, 1863; John C., born January 23, 1865, and Minnie, born September 17, 1867. Mr. and Mrs. Horrie are members of the Presbyterian Church of Morris. He is a Republican, and served as Alderman one term. Residence on Main street; carriage manufactory on Canal street.

C. F. HARMENING, tailor, Morris, was born in Germany May 17, 1854, and was there educated; he is the son of Fred Harmening, who was also born in Germany. Our subject emigrated to the United States December 16, 1871, and stopped in New York City for two years, where he followed the tailoring business; from there he went to Rock Island, Ill., where he continued his business about two years; thence to Geneseo, where he remained about three years; then to Morris, in October, 1878, where he has been ever since, and where he controls a good trade. Mr. Harmening was married in Morris, May 31, 1881, to Eliza, daughter of Phil Hart, of this place; she was born in December, 1857. Mr. Harmening and wife are members of the Presbyterian Church; he is a Democrat.

LEANDER IRONS, hardware merchant, Morris, was born in Rhode Island April 4, 1840; son of James Irons, a native of that State, born in 1793, and is now living (1882) in the town of Mazon, in this county. His wife, Phebe (Steere) Irons, was a native of the same State; was born about 1800, and died in 1850. Subject came to this State in the summer of 1861, and was educated at the common schools of Rhode Island; was apprenticed to a jeweler for five years, which time he served out. When he first came to this county in 1861, he taught school one term south of Morris. After returning from the army, he began in the express office, where he remained nearly a year; then began clerking in the hardware establishment of B. C. Church & Co., at Morris; remained there till Church sold out to John Gross, the firm name changing to Geisen & Gross, subject remaining with them a short time; from there subject and Mr. Church, his former employer, purchased the stock of H. C. Pettey's hardware store, and began for himself. This firm changed its name several times afterward, but our subject was a member of each new firm. At the last change, Mr. Riddle bought out J. H. Pettit, the firm name now being Irons & Riddle. They have a very satisfactory trade. Subject has been City Treasurer one term, Alderman two years, Chief of Fire Department one term. Mr. Irons enlisted in the Federal army in July, 1862, in Company C, Seventy-sixth Illinois Infantry; was disabled the following November at Boliver, Tenn., and was discharged in April, 1863, at St. Louis; he enlisted as a private, and was Quartermaster Sergeant of the regiment when discharged. Our subject is a member of the Masonic order, and has taken all the degrees from E. A. to Knight Templar. Has filled the Master's place of his lodge, and has been H. P. of his Chapter for the past six years; also fills prominent offices in the Commandery. He was married in Morris, June 6, 1866, to Mary Stanberry, daughter of Eugene Stanberry, of this place. They have two children--Byron L. and Willie T. Mr. Irons is a Republican.

WILLIAM A. JORDAN, Postmaster and dealer in agricultural implements, Morris, was born at Hudson, Columbia Co., N. Y., July 17, 1829, son of Allen Jordan, a prominent lawyer of that place, who was born February 3, 1798. He came to Illinois with his family in May, 1847, and settled at Plainfield, Will County; from there came to Kendall County, and, after spending quite a number of years in that county, he again returned to Will County, where he now resides. His first wife, Catharine

Dayton, who was the mother of our subject, was born in Rhode Island about 1808, and died in February, 1834, at Hudson, N. Y. There were but two children by the first wife—subject and one sister; she was born in 1831, and died in 1838. Subject was educated at the Hudson Academy. He began life as a farmer in Kendall County, Ill., in 1848, continuing in this till about 1865; then sold his farm and engaged in the agricultural implement business at Minooka, Grundy County, where he carried on a very large trade in this line for quite a number of years. He came from Minooka to Morris in the fall of 1870, and resumed the agricultural business, and is running the leading business in that line at this place, known as the Grundy County Agricultural Warehouse. He was a member of the Board of Education for several years. Was appointed Postmaster at Morris January 19, 1882, by President Arthur, a position he now fills very acceptably. He is Republican in politics. Is a member of the Masonic fraternity. He was married, November 1, 1853, at Ottawa, La Salle Co., Ill., to Annie E. Wing, daughter of Capt. Clifton Wing, of Sandwich, Mass. She was born January 26, 1834. They have had seven children born to them, only four of whom are living—two sons —Clifton and Frank, and two daughters—Kate and Annie..

ALVAH R. JORDAN, lawyer, Morris, is a native of Kennebunk, Me., and was born December 13, 1844. He received a classical education in Schenectady, N. Y. In 1861, he enlisted in Company G, Thirty-sixth Illinois Infantry, and served about six months, when he was discharged in consequence of injuries received at Raleigh, Mo. Soon after recovering, he again enlisted, this time in Company I, of Sixty-ninth Illinois Infantry, holding the commission of Second Lieutenant, and serving the full term of its enlistment. He began the practice of law at Morris in 1869, and has succeeded in building up an enviable reputation in his profession. He is a standard Republican, and has served his county in the capacity of State's Attorney for nine continuous years. He was married, June 18, 1869, to Miss Sarah D. Parmelee, daughter of Charles R. Parmelee, of Grundy County. She was born in Du Page County, Ill., March 20, 1845.

E. F. JOHNSTON, restaurant, Morris, is a native of Pennsylvania, born August 28, 1830, son of James Johnston, who was one of the old settlers of Western Pennsylvania; he was born in 1803; was a farmer by occupation, and died in Pennsylvania in 1876. His wife, Elizabeth (Rigby) Johnston, a Quakeress, was born in 1806, and died about 1865. The parents raised seven children—five sons, of whom subject is the eldest, and two daughters. Subject was educated in the common schools of Pennsylvania, and began in the nail-cutting business, which he followed about three years, when he was forced to leave it on account of failing health. He then learned the mason's trade, which he followed twelve years. He came to Morris in 1855. Mr. Johnston did the mason work of many of the best buildings of Morris, including the court house. He began in the restaurant business in 1860, which he has followed to the present time. He has a good trade, and runs the leading house of its kind in the city. He was married in this place, December 31, 1857, to Jennie M. Wallace, born in Ohio February 27, 1837, daughter of William Wallace, of Scotch descent, born in Pennsylvania in 1812; he is now living in Texas. Alethea Gundy, his wife, was born in Pennsylvania in 1815, and died there in 1850. Mr. and Mrs. Johnston are the parents of two children—Ettie F. and Carrie M. Mr. Johnston is a member of the I. O. O. F., and a Republican.

GEORGE M. JONES, furniture and undertaking, Morris, born at Morris November 25, 1846, son of J. B. Jones (who was born in Pennsylvania about 1816) and Mary (Tyrrell)

Jones, a native of Canada. J. B. Jones was one of the first settlers of this place. He raised two sons, of whom our subject is the older, and one daughter. Subject was principally educated at Morris, finishing, however, at Aurora Seminary. Graduated in the class of 1868. Subject spent his boyhood days in the store which he now occupies, with his father, who was then proprietor. After arriving at the age of maturity, he, in connection with J. W. Lawrence, bought his father out in 1877, and from that time they have carried on the business under the firm name of Jones & Lawrence. Mr. Jones has been Town and City Collector two years, and Alderman four years. He was married in this city, October 29, 1872, to Sophia Hazleton. She was born in Milwaukee June 17, 1853, and is a daughter of C. P. Hazleton, now of Morris. Subject has two children, both girls, viz., Mamie and Bertie. Mr. Jones is a member of the I. O. O. F. and a Democrat.

T. J. KELLY, liquors, grocery, etc., Morris, born in Morris May 8, 1856; son of Patrick Kelly, who was born in Ireland; emigrated to the United States and settled in this town, where he died. There were three children— one son (subject), and two daughters. Subject was educated at the public schools of Morris. Started for himself in 1873, as grocery clerk for N. K. Keller, and was with him seven years. In 1880, he engaged to N. Hanna, as clerk in the same store, in which he now sells goods; was with him two years. On the 4th of April, 1881, he, in partnership with Thomas P. Reynolds, opened a grocery store on Liberty street, where they continued till October 5, 1881, at that date moving to the corner of Washington and Fulton streets, where they now have a flourishing trade. Mr. Kelly was married, at Eureka, Ill., August 14, 1880, to Annie O'Hara, daughter of John O'Hara. She was born in August, 1863. They have one child—a daughter—Mary Theresa. Mr. Kelly is non-partisan in politics. He and wife are members of the Catholic Church.

LEWIS P. LOTT, retired merchant, Morris, was born in 1813, in Covert, Seneca Co., N. Y.; is a son of Zephaniah and Permilla (Phelps) Lott. He was born in Pennsylvania in 1775; pursued farming for sixty years on the same farm in Covert, N. Y., and died July 5, 1855. She was born in Connecticut in 1780; died at Covert, N. Y., April 13, 1863. The parents had thirteen children, eleven of whom grew to maturity. Our subject attended the common schools of New York until thirteen years of age, and then went to Canandaigua where he learned the printer's trade. He worked as a journeyman at Cleveland for about two years, and then, forming a partnership with a friend, commenced a general book business, which he continued at Cleveland for twelve or fifteen years, and then removed to Kirtland, Ohio, where he engaged in the manufacturing business for two and a half years; then for two or three years in the general merchandising business at Warren, Ohio. He next went to Racine, Wis., where he again engaged in the mercantile business for several years; and, in March, 1848, moved to this place, where he still resides. Mr. Lott was married, at Cleveland, Ohio, February 22, 1844, to Delia Lloyd Clark, born in Philadelphia September 29, 1821, a daughter of Job and Sarah Humphrey (Chilcott) Clark. He was born in Connecticut in 1787, and died at Cleveland, Ohio, in 1839. She was born in Pennsylvania in 1787, and died in Ohio in 1849. This union resulted in four children, two of whom died in infancy; one son, Frank Clark, died in his fourteenth year. The eldest son, Edward L., only survives. Mr. Lott owns 200 acres of improved land, besides good town property. He was Deputy Clerk for eight years, and has been Supervisor, Alderman, Superintendent of Public Schools, School Treasurer; for a number of years Chairman of the Board of Supervisors and Justice of the Peace; Master of the Masonic Lodge, and H. P. of his Chapter. Is a member of the I. O. O. F., in which he has passed through the different offices. Mrs. Lott is a Baptist; Mr. Lott is a Republican.

GEORGE W. LANE, retired grain dealer, Morris, was born in Maine April 19, 1817, son of Joshua Lane, born in New Hampshire, February 6, 1788, was a farmer by occupation, a good classical scholar, a zealous member of the Baptist Church, and died December 15, 1859, in Morris. Parents raised two children, one son, our subject, and one daughter. The subject of this sketch was educated in the State of Maine finishing at Kent's Hill Seminary, in Kennebec County. He was raised on the farm.

CHARLES C. MARTIN, molder, Morris, was born October 19, 1848, in Fayette County, Penn., and is a son of J. B. and Sarah (Hamilton) Martin, the latter of whom died in the spring of 1859, in Pennsylvania. In the spring of 1861, the father of our subject removed to Morris, Grundy County, and engaged in brickmaking; he now resides in Ottawa, Ill. Our subject received the greater part of his schooling in Morris. In 1864, when less than sixteen years of age, he enlisted in Company H, One Hundred and Thirty-eighth Regular Illinois Volunteers, in which he served several months. He is now engaged with Messrs. Griggs and Steep in the manufacture of drain-tile and brick, the firm being known as Griggs, Martin & Steep. May 5, 1869, Mr. Martin married Miss Lydia A. Hart, a native of Belmont County, Ohio, born January 23, 1848. She is a daughter of Rev. Samuel and Rachel (Thomas) Hart; he was born June 17, 1817, died January 26, 1882; she was born August 28, 1813, and is now living in Odell, Livingston Co., Ill. Mr. and Mrs. Martin have five children—Leonidas A., born December 19, 1870; Lillie May, August 2, 1872; Charles Wilford, April 11, 1875; Grace M., December 19, 1877; and James Garfield, born May 29, 1880. Mrs. Martin is a member of the Methodist Episcopal Church; Mr. Martin belongs to the I. O. O. F.

T. R. MINKLER, agricultural implements, Morris, was born in New York January 12, 1832; son of Peter Minkler, born in New York in 1788. The latter moved to Illinois, in 1833, with his family, and settled in Specie Grove, Kendall County, where he took a claim of between two hundred and three hundred acres; there he lived till just before the war. He then sold out and moved to Ogle County, where he again bought land, settled on it, and lived there till the time of his death, which occurred in 1881, in his ninety-third year. There were eight children, five boys, of whom our subject is the youngest, and three girls. The subject of this sketch was educated at the common schools of Kendall County, and spent his early life on the farm, which occupation he continued till 1860, since that time he has been engaged in the agricultural implement business, in Morris. For twenty-one years he acted as salesman in this business, and in the fall of 1881 opened an implement warehouse for himself, where he does a satisfactory business. August the 9th, 1863, our subject, while out on a hunting expedition with some friends from Chicago, accidentally let his gun go off, fearfully fracturing his right arm between the elbow and shoulder, rendering it necessary to have the same amputated near the shoulder, which was very successfully done. Mr. Minkler was married first in Saratoga, Grundy County, in 1853, to Sarah A. Conklin, daughter of C. G. Conklin; she died in 1856. He was married the second time to Elizabeth Conklin, a sister of his first wife; she died in 1874. He has one son by his first wife—Henry—and five children by the second wife, viz., one son Horace, and four daughters—Larissa, Carrie, Hattie and Louise. Mr. Minkler is a Democrat in politics.

N. McBRIDE, insurance and surveying, money loaner, etc., Morris, was born in Florence,

Pennsylvania, June 13, 1824; son of James McBride, a native of Pennsylvania, born July 20, 1790; the latter was a farmer by occupation, and died in 1857. His wife, Jane (Wick) McBride, was born in New Jersey in June, 1800, and died in 1859. The parents raised six children, three sons, of whom our subject is the oldest, and three daughters, one of whom is now dead. The subject of this sketch was educated at Mercer, Penn., at Mercer College, and began life as a surveyor, also engaged in engineering and general speculating business. He came to Illinois in 1855, and settled in Morris; has been in the insurance business twenty-seven years, Police Magistrate twenty years, and was County Surveyor ten years. In January, 1881, our subject purchased, in company with several prominent men of Chicago, Morris and other places, what is known as the Keystone Mine, style of the firm being "Keystone Consolidated Mining Co." This mine is located in Summit County, Colo., and promises to be very rich. Mr. McBride was first married in Ohio, to Lydia Davidson, April 29, 1846; she died in 1876, in Morris. His second marriage was May 2, 1877, to A. F. English, of Chicago, daughter of Jacob English, of Lycoming County, Penn. Our subject had by his first wife five children, four of whom are now living, three sons—J. W., T. C. and N. E., the last two live in Chicago, and the first in Colorado, and one daughter, Maggie, wife of H. A. Cagwin, of Gardner, this county. Mr. McBride owns a residence in West Side Morris. He has been a pension and claim attorney, and has given to ex-soldiers $4,000 or $5,000, in reduction of of fees. He is a candidate for County Judge, and a Republican.

DAVID NICKEL, iron molder, Morris, was born in Mercer County, Penn., August 28 1851. His parents removed to Mt. Carroll, Carroll Co., Ill., when he was two years old. Here they remained one year, then moved to Sabula, Iowa, and engaged in milling for five years. In 1859, the father went with his family to Stephen's Point, Wis., where he worked at his trade (iron molder). Here our subject received his education. At the age of fifteen, he began the trade of iron molder, serving an apprenticeship of three years, from which time he followed this work as journeyman until 1880. He has been in the employ of the Sherwood School Furniture Company (now the Ohio Butt Company) since 1874. In August, 1880, he was promoted to the position of foreman of the foundry department. In May, 1881, he was given the position of Assistant Superintendent, and in August, 1881, promoted to General Superintendent of the entire establishment, which position he now hol's. December 27, 1876, he was married to Miss Julia McFarlane, daughter of William McFarlane, of Ohio. She was born in Ohio March 6, 1851, and is a member of the Presbyterian Church. Mr. Nickel is a Republican. His parents are still living, and are among the honored members of the Methodist Episcopal Church of Morris.

N. J. NELSON, grain merchant, Morris, was born in Skaanevig, Norway, on June 24, 1849. In the summer of 1858, his parents emigrated to Canada, and in the same year came to Grundy County, Ill., and settled on the farm on which they lived for seven years, during which time, our subject received a common-school education. In 1869, he came to Morris, where he worked at clerical work and book-keeping until 1872, when he and O. J. Nelson purchased the stock of Undum & Co., Liberty street, where they conducted business until the fall of 1875, when they closed out. Since 1875, he and his brother O. J. have engaged in the grain trade. They have an elevator on Canal street, and, in connection with Mr. M. N. Hull, have an elevator near the railroad depot. In October, 1879, Mr. Nelson was married to Miss Linda Osman, of Grundy County, Ill. She was born December 2, 1856, and died in

Morris January 9, 1881. Joseph Nelson, father of N. J. Nelson, was born in Norway in 1815, and died in Kendall County, Ill., July 22, 1879. Anne Nelson, the mother, was born in Norway in 1822, and is now living in Kendall County, on the old homestead. Besides N. J., there are six children, two older and four younger than himself.

JOSEPH H. PETTIT, Deputy Circuit Clerk, Morris, was born in Hunterdon County, N. J., February 6, 1842; son of Mahlon Pettit, also a native of that State, born in 1803; was a farmer by occupation, and died in 1849. His wife, Amanda (Higgins) Pettit, was born in the same State in 1812, and is now living, adjoining her son, in Morris. The parents raised but one child, our subject, who was educated in the common schools of New Jersey; and came here April 19, 1856, with his mother. He began business as clerk in a general store, where he continued for about fourteen years. He was Cashier of the Grundy County National Bank nearly two years; was in the hardware business here four years; was appointed Circuit Clerk to fill a vacancy for about one year, and since that has acted in the capacity of Deputy Clerk. He enlisted in the Federal army in 1861, and served three months. Was Quartermaster's clerk at Gen. Sherman's headquarters for eight months. Mr. Pettit married in this town, January 30, 1873, to Myra S. Massey, born in La Salle County June 1, 1845, and is a daughter of Jonathan and Nancy B. (Dow) Massey. Mr. and Mrs. Pettit have two children—one daughter, Muriel, and one son, Raymond J. Mr. Pettit and wife attend the Congregational Church. Subject was City Clerk two years in Morris, and was one of the corporators of the Library Association of this place. He is a Mason and a Knight Templar; also a member of the Republican party.

MARSHALL B. PIKE, retired farmer, P. O. Morris, was born in Maine March 25, 1834. He was raised and educated in Maine, coming to Morris when twenty-three years old (1857). He owns a farm of 160 acres of cultivated land in Saratoga Township. He has retired from active labor, and is now living on the old home property of Mrs. Pike's parents, John and Hannah Porter; this property is situated on Main street, between Price and Pine. Our subject was married to Miss Anna Porter March 4, 1858. She was born in Chester County, Penn., March 15, 1829, and came to Grundy County in 1849. The family consists of four children—Lillie E., born March 13, 1859, died May 1, 1862; Edward W., born June 21, 1863; John P., born September 26, 1866; and Clifford L., born April 11, 1873. Joshua Pike, the father of our subject, was born near Portland, Me., February 1, 1809, and came to Grundy County in 1857. He is now living on his farm in Saratoga Township. Caroline (Barker) Pike, mother of M. B., was born in Portland, Me., in June, 1812; and died May 2, 1875, in Saratoga Township. John Porter, father of Mrs. Pike, was born June 2, 1794, in Morris, and died September 14, 1850. Her mother, Hannah Porter, was born January 18, 1793, died in Morris September 8, 1866. Mr. and Mrs. Pike are members of the M. E. Church. Mrs. Pike owns the lots upon which is situated the Goold Block. Mr. Pike has three residence houses on Washington street, east of the court house, and owns the entire eastern frontage of court house square, besides several lots in the southwestern part of the city.

J. H. PATTISON, County Treasurer, Morris, was born in Ohio August 22, 1840; son of William Pattison, also a native of Ohio, born in 1805; was a farmer by occupation; came to this State in 1842, and died in this county March 14, 1882. His wife, Martha (Halsted) Pattison, was born in Ohio, about 1815, and died in this county about 1850. There were ten children, five sons and five daughters, the subject is the third son. He was educated at the common schools in the county. His advantages in this direction were very limited. He began life as a farmer, and has followed that occupation the principal part of his time. In the fall of 1877, he was elected County Treasurer, and took possession of the office in December of that year; he was re-elected in 1879, and still holds the office. He was married in December, 1867, in this county, to Jennie Struble; she was born in New Jersey in 1840, and is a daughter of Elias Struble. Subject has three children, viz., Alice, Mary and Hettie. Mr. Pattison owns a small farm in Wauponsee Township; he is a Republican.

M. S. PRINDLE, book-keeper and City Clerk, born in La Fayette, Ind., January 15, 1846, son of William Prindle, who moved here in 1848, and built the first hotel in Morris, known as the Franklin House, which burned in 1854. Mr. Prindle then built what is now called the Rock Island & Pacific Hotel; ran that several years, and in 1863 retired from the business and never afterward engaged in active business. He died June 20, 1875. His wife, Abigail (Scranton) Prindle, was born in Connecticut June 20, 1812, and is now living with her son, our subject, in Morris. The parents had six children, three sons, of whom subject is the youngest, and three daughters. Subject was educated at the high school in Morris. He began his business life as a book-keeper, which he has followed since. He worked for John Barr for about seven years, and about five years for McEwen & Bros.; was appointed two consecutive terms as City Clerk, and was then elected a third term for some other office. Being a Democrat in politics, and elected to this office in a city that has a Republican majority, speaks well for his popularity. Mr. Prindle was married in this city, July 10, 1870, to Electa A. Lindsay; she was born January 1, 1846, in Wilmington, Ind., and is a daughter of William D. Lindsay, of Wilmington. They have two children, one son—George E., and one daughter, Gracie May. Subject is a member of both Masonic and I. O. O. F. orders and is now filling his second term as Noble Grand in latter order.

WILLIAM A. PARKER, book-keeper, Morris, was born in the State of New York April 3, 1851. His parents came West when he was about one year old, and settled in La Salle County, Ill., where his father engaged in farming for three years, at which time he engaged in mercantile business. In 1860, they removed to De Kalb County, where they remained until 1871. The subject of this sketch was educated at Sandwich, De Kalb Co., Ill. Leaving school at the age of seventeen, he taught school for three years, after which he occupied himself in various employments until 1874, at which time he was employed by the Sherwood School Furniture Company (now the Ohio Butt Company) of Morris. He occupies the position of foreman of the warehouse department, which comprehends the office work of the entire establishment. His father, Andrew Parker, was born August 10, 1822, in New York, and died in Kansas in 1879. The mother, Harriet M. Parker, was born in New York September 22, 1824, and is now living with her son, our subject. Besides William, there are two children—Helen L., born in New York November 3, 1844, married to S. C. Lincoln, of Sandwich, De Kalb County (he is distantly related to Abraham Lincoln); and Harriet E., born in Illinois November 5, 1860, and is living with her mother and brother William. The entire family are members of the Regular Baptist Church. Mr. Parker is a Republican.

E. H. QUIGLEY, railroad agent, Morris. E. H. Quigley was born in Crawford County, Penn. He received a common school education in his native State and in Morris, after which he took a course in the business college of Davenport, Iowa. Came to Grundy County at the age of thirteen. His father,

Henry Quigley, was born in Pennsylvania in December, 1814, and died in Pennsylvania June 3, 1866. Matilda Quigley, mother of subject, was born in January, 1826, and is now living with her son, E. H. Quigley. Mr. Quigley was married, May 21, 1879, to Miss Lizzie S. Cody, daughter of William R. Cody, whose biography appears in this work; she was born in Grundy County May 21, 1861. They have had two children—Freddy W., born March 10, 1880, died August 6, 1881, and Harry H., born September 19, 1881. Mr. Quigley has been in the employ of the Rock Island & Pacific Railroad Company for ten years, as operator, ticket agent, and is now station agent. He is a Republican.

JAMES N. READING, lawyer, Morris, whose portrait appears in this work, was born at the homestead of his maternal grandfather, Dr. John F. Grandin, at Hamden, N. J., where his son, John Grandin, now resides. He was named after his grandmother Grandin's father, Dr. James Newell, whose wife was a Lawrence, and sister of the father of Commodore Lawrence. James N. Reading is the son and eldest child of Joseph Reading, who was the youngest child and only son of John (3), he being the eldest of John (2), who was the eldest son of Gov. John Reading. He commenced his academic course at Flemington, under Charles Bartles, Esq., who then had charge of the academy. He was prepared for college at the Princeton Academy, then entered Nassau Hall in 1827, and graduated in 1829, taking the fifth honor in a class of twenty-six; studied law with Samuel L. Southard in Trenton; was admitted to the bar in 1832, and became a counselor at law in 1836. He married, February 10, 1835, Sarah C. A. Southard, a niece of the Governor. From 1832 to 1850, he practiced law in Flemington, fifteen of which years he was Prosecuting Attorney for Hunterdon County. During his residence in Hunterdon County, he took considerable interest and quite an active part in the military affairs. His first appointment was to the office of Brigade Inspector; resigning that after two years' service, he was appointed Colonel of the Third Regiment of the Hunterdon Brigade, which, with the office of State's Attorney, he held until he moved to the West. In 1850, he removed to Jefferson County, Mo., and for two years was President of a lead mining company. He returned to New Jersey, settled up his private business, and in the fall of 1858 moved to Morris, Grundy Co., Ill., which has since been his place of residence, with the exception of the years 1859-1861, when he resided in Chicago and practiced law, in copartnership with Mr. (afterward Judge) Wallace. He was elected a member of the State Legislature of Illinois in the fall of 1856, and filled the position until the fall of 1858, when he officiated as Clerk of the Circuit Court, filling a vacancy. In June, 1861, his partner having joined the Union army as a Major of the cavalry branch of the service, Mr. Reading closed his law office in Chicago, and returned to Morris. During the war, he was Deputy United States Marshal for Grundy County, and also United States Commissioner, at the same time continuing his legal business. In 1865, he was elected County Judge, which position he held for three successive terms—twelve years—and then declined a re-election. He is an indefatigable worker, having, in addition to his legal practice and official duties, been largely engaged in the real estate business ever since his removal to Illinois. He is an able lawyer and jurist.

GEORGE RIDDLE, hardware merchant, Morris, was born in Blair County, Penn., March 7, 1833, son of John and Jane (McKillip) Riddle, natives of Pennsylvania. He was a farmer by occupation, and died in his native State; she died in Pennsylvania, in 1856. They raised six children, four sons, of whom our subject is the second, and two daughters. Our subject was educated in the common schools of Pennsylvania, and at the age of sixteen began clerking in a dry goods store, in New Castle, where he remained three years. After spending three years more in Mercer County, Penn., he came to Illinois in 1855, and began the foundry business, building the first foundry of this place. He carried on this business two years, and then went into the coal business for three years, after which he pursued farming until 1876, when he opened a hardware store in partnership with Mr. Irons; this firm still continues, and does a good business. Mr. Riddle was married in Morris, November 4, 1856, to Amelia Ferguson, daughter of Daniel Ferguson, spoken of in another part of this work. Our subject has been School Treasurer for fourteen years, in Mazon Township; is a member of the Masonic order, in which he has taken all the degrees from Entered Apprentice to Knight Templar, and is one of the oldest members of the order at Morris. He is President of the Forest City Mining Company, in Summit County, Colo., considered one of the richest mines in that State; he is also Superintendent of the Grundy County Mining Company; President of the Morris Cutlery Company, and a member of the Republican party.

DR. EMANUEL RIDGWAY, physician and druggist, Morris, is a native of Ohio, born October 22, 1831; son of Joshua Ridgway, also of Ohio, where he was occupied in farming until he came to Illinois in 1834, and settled in Grundy County, about six miles northeast of Morris; he died in Channahon, Will County, in 1839. His wife, Sarah (Cryder) Ridgway, was born in Ohio about 1811, and died in this county in 1835. They raised two children, both sons, of whom subject is the youngest. He attended the common schools in Grundy County, from 1835 to 1839, but after the death of his father, in 1839, he was taken back to Ohio in 1840, by his mother's people, and finished his education at South Salem Academy. He began reading medicine with Dr. Wills, of Chillicothe, Ohio, and attended lectures at the University of Pennsylvania, from which institution he graduated in the class of 1855. In 1878, he received an honorary degree of the Chicago Medical College. In April, 1855, he began the practice of his profession at Morris, where he has continued ever since. There he engaged in the drug business in September, 1880; this he still follows, in connection with his practice; he carries a good stock and has a fine trade. He has been Coroner for Grundy County the past sixteen years, Chief Engineer of the Fire Department six years, and has been a member of the Board of Education for the past four years. He enlisted in the Federal army, Seventy-sixth Illinois Regiment, as Assistant Surgeon, in August, 1862, and returned home in August, 1865. Dr. Ridgway was married in this county, in 1869, to Alcinda B. Hoge, born in 1842, daughter of William Hoge, one of the oldest settlers in this county, born July 5, 1801, in Virginia, and is still living at his old homestead in this county. His wife, Rachel (Bowles) Hoge, was born in Virginia in 1807, and died in this county in 1843. Subject has six children, four sons—Frederick William, Henry A., George M. and Franklin S., and two daughters—Mary H. and an infant. Subject is a Presbyterian and a Republican.

THOMAS H. ROSS, miner, Morris, was born in Stark Co., Ohio, May 27, 1845, and here he lived until twenty years old, at which time, being a member of the Ohio National Guards, he, with his regiment, was called into active service. In this enlistment, he served four months in Kentucky and Tennessee, after which he enlisted in Company A, of the One Hundred and Ninety-seventh Regiment Ohio Volunteer Infantry, remaining in the field until the close of the war. He came to Grundy County, Ill., in 1870, and worked in the coal mines of Braceville Township until 1876, when he came to Morris, and associated himself with Mr. Johnson in the mining business, the firm known as Johnson & Ross. He subsequently became owner of the entire mine, but soon sold a half-interest to A. F. Mallory. The partnership continued one year, when Henry Burrell became the successor of Mallory. Since then the firm has been known as Burrell & Ross, now operating on the line of the Chicago, Rock Island & Pacific Railroad. On the 8th of September, 1875, Mr. Ross was married, to Miss Bell Peacock, daughter of John Peacock, one of the first settlers of the county; she was born in Morris September 19, 1844. They have two daughters—Gertrude I., born December 30, 1876; and Lizzie H., born June 4, 1881. Mr. Ross is a member of the Masonic fraternity; his wife is a member of the Episcopalian Church. They own thirty acres of valuable property in the eastern part of the city, adjoining the paper car-wheel manufactory. Their residence is on Fremont avenue, west of Nettle Creek.

HON. J. S. R. SCOVILL, jeweler and Mayor of Morris, was born in Johnstown, Fulton Co., N. Y., May 18, 1832; son of Rev. John Scovill, who was also born in New York, in 1804, and in the same house that our subject was born in; the mother, Clarissa (Young) Scovill, was also born in the same town in 1806. The Rev. Mr. Scovill was a clergyman of the Episcopal Church, and died in December, 1861, and his wife died in 1870. The parents raised four children to maturity—one son, our subject, and three daughters. Subject was educated at Johnstown, common school and academy. He began in the jewelry business in Lyons, N. Y., with a cousin, with whom he learned the trade. He left New York in 1855, and went to Waukegan, Ill., and two years afterward to La Porte, Ind., where he remained five years; thence to Chicago, and remained there till 1866, at which time he came to Morris, and has followed the jewelry business ever since. He now owns not only the leading jewelry establishment of Morris, but of any of the small cities of this part of the State. Mr. Scoville was married at Kenosha, Wis., in January, 1856, to Elmira H. C. Cole, who was born in New York July 20, 1834, and is a daughter of John and Lucy (Hicks) Cole. Mrs. Cole now lives with her son-in-law, our subject, at this place. Subject has four children —two sons, J. S. R., Jr., and De Lancy T. W., and two daughters, Nellie Z. Y. and Fanny Belle Wallace. Mr. Scovill has been Alderman two years; is a member of the Board of Education, and has been elected Mayor seven times, notwithstanding that he is a Democrat, and in general elections the city goes Republican by a handsome majority; this shows the popularity of our subject. He has two maiden sisters living in a house built by his grandfather in New York more than one hundred years ago. Our subject has followed four generations to the grave from his place; first, his great-grandmother, at the age of ninety-two years; next, his grandfather and grandmother; next, his father and mother; and next, a brother and a sister.

CHARLES SPARR, harness shop, boots and shoes, Morris, was born in Germany, April 5, 1836; is the son of Nicholas Sparr, a native of Germany, born in 1800, a harness-maker by trade, died in Germany about 1870. Our subject attended school in his native place until sixteen years of age, when he came to this country; the voyage, which took twenty-eight days, he made alone. He spent two years at Columbus, Ohio, working at the trade of harness-making; from there he came to Oswego, Kendall Co., Ill., where he remained from 1854 to 1856, when he came to Morris, and continued the harness business. In 1868, he formed a partnership with George Woelfel, in the tannery business. This he continued for twelve years, or until January 1, 1880, when he dissolved the partnership, Mr. Sparr taking the harness and boot and shoe departments, and Mr. Woelfel the tannery business. Mr. Sparr does a thriving business; owns several store rooms and a good brick residence at Morris. He was married at Oswego, Kendall County, in 1856, to Catharine Wolf, who was born in Germany in June, 1836. They have had eleven children born to them, ten of whom are still living, viz., Joseph, William, Harry, Frank, Mary, Kittie, Carrie, Hattie, Birdie and an infant. Several years ago, Mr. Sparr was City Treasurer for two years; he also acted as Supervisor for two years. He is a Republican.

WILLIAM STEPHEN, retired farmer, P. O. Morris, is a native of Scotland; was born May 26, 1817, and came to the United States in 1837; he is a son of William and Elizabeth (Cruickshank) Stephen, both natives of Scotland. Subject left Scotland the 24th of April, 1837, and reached New York City some time in the following June, having been on the sea some six weeks. He reached Chicago July 1, 1837; left there the 4th of the same month, arriving at Lisbon, La Salle County, Ill., on the 7th; thence to what is now Nettle Creek, Grundy County, where he made his first purchase of land, one-fourth section, in Section 20. The 22d of November, 1837, Mr. Stephen was caught out in a severe snow storm, and was so badly frozen that it was necessary to amputate two of his toes, and the ends of his fingers were so frozen that they bear the scars to this day; he lived on the aforesaid farm about one year, and afterward settled near Lisbon, Kendall County, where he lived with the exception of two years, till 1869; one of these years was spent in Grundy County, and the other in La Salle County. He next moved on a farm which he purchased near Morris in 1869, where he remained about six years, and in December, 1875, moved to the city of Morris, where he still resides. Subject owns at present about 1,400 acres of good farming lands in this and Kendall Counties, besides city property in the suburbs of Chicago, consisting of about ninety lots, and two good residences in Morris. After his misfortune of getting frozen, when a young man, Mr. Stephen found himself without any means whatever, and what property he now owns is the result of his own efforts, showing what can be accomplished by well directed diligence. Mr. Stephen was married in the town of Big Grove, Kendall County, February 27, 1843, to Margaret Waterman, daughter of Isaiah and Hester (Van Vrankin) Waterman. Mrs. Stephen was born December 16, 1825. They have had ten children born to them, seven living, four sons, viz., William L., Merritt J., Charles M. and Fred L., and three daughters, viz,, Ella, wife of Charles B. Collins; Helen, wife of Albert E. Cogwin, and Hettie J., wife of Frederick Page. Mr. Stephen, wife and one son are members of the Methodist Episcopal Church. Subject has been Justice of the Peace for two terms, Assessor eleven years for the town of Big Grove; is now a member of the Board of Education here, and also Superintendent of Grundy County Poor Farm; he is a Republican.

M. W. STEINER, dentist, Morris, is a native of Pennsylvania; born April 12, 1855; son of Andrew Steiner, born in Pennsylvania in 1822; a bridge-builder by occupation, and is still living in Pennsylvania; his wife, Henrietta (Wiley) Steiner, was born in Pennsylvania in 1824, and died in 1878. The parents had twelve children born to them, nine of whom are living, four sons, of whom our subject is the third, and five daughters. Mr. Steiner was educated principally at Morris; graduated in dentistry at Philadelphia Dental College in 1876. Subject came to this place when eleven years of age, all alone, to visit his married sister, Mrs. Dr. Murray, with whom he made his home till October, 1879. He began the practice of his profession in 1876, and by industry and close attention to business, coupled with a thorough knowledge of his business, he has built up a fine practice. Mr. Steiner was married in this city October 2, 1879, to Miss Lilly Grant born January 15, 1856, daughter of Judge C. Grant, of this place. He was a native of Scotland, born in 1821, and died here in January, 1881. Mr. Steiner is a member of the Congregational Church; subject is a member of the Masonic order, and Secretary of the Morris Cutlery Company; he was City Clerk in 1880; is one of the officers of the fire department, and a Republican in politics.

JOHN SCHOBERT, dry goods, etc., Morris, was born in Germany, July 11, 1847, and came to the United States in June, 1855, with his parents. His father, John William Schobert, was born in Germany, November, 13, 1815, and his mother, Margaretta C. (Zeitler) Schobert was born in Germany, February 16, 1822. The parents raised five boys and three girls, one girl dying when but ten years old, and another when twenty-one years old. Our subject, the eldest son, was educated principally at the public schools in Ottawa, this State, that being the place where his parents settled on their arrival in this country, and where they still reside. Mr. Schobert began business for himself by learning the harness trade, at which he worked at Pontiac, Ill., for about four years, and three years at Ottawa. He next began in the dry goods business, in 1868, as clerk, in Ottawa, which he continued about six years. He came here in September, 1874, and began in the same business, in partnership with Mr. Baum, the firm name being Baum & Schobert. In March, 1881, this firm dissolved, each member opening a store in his own name, in which manner they have continued since. Mr. Schobert is doing a good business at Morris; he is also interested in a store at La Salle, in La Salle County, the firm known as Breuning, Kilduff & Co., which is doing a fine business. Mr. Schobert enlisted in 1863, in the Federal army, Company D, Twentieth Illinois Infantry, and was mustered out in July 1865. He was with Sherman in 1864, when he went through Mississippi. His regiment then came home on thirty days furlough, at the end of which time Mr. Schobert took a trip through Middle Tennessee and Alabama, and joined Sherman at Acworth, Ga. He was in several minor engagements on these raids, and on the 21st of July, 1864, participated in the battle at Atlanta, Ga., where he was severely wounded in the right ankle, from which he still suffers. He was married in this city, January 29, 1878, to Elizabeth Baum, sister of his former partner in business. She was born September 11, 1857, at this place. They have had had two children born to them but one of which is living, a daughter—Jessie B., born October 7, 1880. Mr. Schobert is a Mason and a Republican.

DR. A. D. SMITH, Morris. Mr. Smith was born in Jefferson County, near Watertown. N. Y., August 2, 1847; son of Eleazur Smith, a native of Vermont, born at Rutland September 21, 1807, and was a farmer by occupation. He left Vermont when a young man, and went to New York, where he ran a farm and dairy till 1854, at which time he came to Illinois, selling his property in New York, and purchasing a farm, in 1855, in Saratoga Township, this county, where he still makes his home. His wife, Maria (Darby) Smith, was born in Huntington, Vt., August 24, 1815. The parents raised ten children; eight sons, of whom our subject is the sixth, and two daughters. Dr. Smith was educated in this county, principally, and took a medical course at the university of New York City, from which institution he graduated in 1870. He began life as a telegraph operator, which he followed some three years prior to taking his medical course. Immediately after graduating, our subject began the practice of his profession, in his native county, with an uncle; he remained there but a short time. In the fall of 1870, he came to Morris, where he now enjoys a very lucrative practice. He owns some town lots in Mitchell, this county; he is a Mason and a Republican.

EDWARD STEEP, molder, Morris. Mr. Steep was born in Clinton, Canada, July 5, 1852. His parents, Peter and Mary A. Steep, came to the United States in 1851, and settled in Dayton, Ohio, where his father worked six years at the shoe-maker trade. In 1857, they returned to Canada, where they lived until they came to Grundy County, which they did in 1867. Parents lived in Morris from that date till time of death. The father died in the fall of 1866; the mother died on January 11, 1879. Our subject was principally educated in Morris. Married January 1, 1875, to Miss Margaret A. Longacre, of Morris. She was born February 19, 1857. They have two daughters—Maud W., Isabell, born July 30, 1882. Both Mr. and Mrs. Steep are members of the Methodist Episcopal Church at Morris. Our subject is associated with Messrs. Griggs and Martin in the manufacture of drain-tile. Yard is located in northwest part of city; residence on Liberty street. Henry C. and Hannah Longacre (parents of Mrs. Steep) are living, and among the respected citizens of Morris.

SAMUEL BARBER THOMAS was a native of Pennsylvania, and the second son in a family of five sons and four daughters born to William and Margaret (Evans) Thomas. His father, though born in Chester County, in the same State, was of Welsh descent, and his mother a native of Wales. Until eight years of age, Mr. Thomas lived in Chester County where he was born, when he went with his parents to Center County, in the central part of the State. Here he finished a common school education, and with this capital began life for himself as a clerk in a mercantile establishment at Jacksonville. He followed this line of occupation at various places until about twenty-six years of age, when he entered in partnership with L. W. Irving in a milling and merchandising business. He subsequently went to Clearfield County, and went into the lumber business until 1852, when he removed to Peru, Ind., and for a year and a half engaged with that old-time railroad prince, Andrew DeGraff, in railroad construction. While here at work on the Indianapolis & Peru Railroad, a letter from his friend and former clerk, E. B. Hanna, reached him, urging him to accept a position in Morris, Ill. He at once accepted this offer, and entered the employ of Mr. Hanna as clerk in the mercantile business. Here, as in every position in life, Mr. Thomas formed a wide circle of friends, and paved the way for the long and successful political career which soon followed. In the spring election of 1858, he was elected Justice of the Peace for the town of Morris, and on the 12th of April qualified, and assumed the duties of his office. For four years he amply justified the confidence bestowed upon him by his fellow-citizens, and at the same time so strengthened himself in the regard of a wider circle of friends, that, before the expiration of his term of office, he was called by the popular vote to the position of County Clerk. From 1861 to 1878, he filled this position continuously, and with such satisfaction to the people of the county, that he was elected in November of the latter year to the position of County Judge, a position he held until his death. During his nearly twenty-one years of public service, he held his high place in the public esteem unchallenged, and so marked was his eminent fitness for the position he occupied, that the public voice proclaimed him his own successor so long as he would consent to forego the pleasures of private life. In the fall of 1882, he was urged by various private considerations to refuse the use of his name as candidate for another term as County Judge, and, though persevering in this determination until the near approach of the nominating convention, he was at last overborne by the importunity of friends, and gave a half-hearted assent to his nomination. The convention was held on the 12th of September, and on Monday, the 14th, at 7:15, death intervened. On Saturday evening, he had gone home apparently in good health, although considerably fatigued by the bustle of the convention. A little after 9 o'clock, a physician was summoned, but the patient had passed into an unconscious state from which he never rallied. Shortly after coming to Morris, Mr. Thomas met and married Miss Amanda Ferguson. She was a native of New York; was a daughter of Daniel and Amelia (Fowler) Ferguson, and born October 5, 1828. No children resulted from this union, but devoted entirely to each other their lives so blended that death seemed only partially successful in rending them asunder.

The following account from the Morris *Herald* voices the public grief:

DEATH OF SAMUEL B. THOMAS.

Samuel B. Thomas is dead. Hardly can we realize the truth of this statement, and so sudden was his demise that we cannot reconcile ourselves to the belief that it can be true. On last Saturday at 5:30 o'clock we were in conversation with him, and on Sunday morning came the announcement that he was dying.

On Saturday evening, about 6 o'clock, Mr. Thomas went home and complained of not feeling well, attributing his condition to having been exposed to the heat of the sun too much during the day. His head troubled him. Home remedies were applied, but instead of receiving relief, he grew worse, until it was thought best to send for a physician. At a little after 9 o'clock Dr. Ferguson was summoned, but before his arrival Mr. Thomas had passed into an unconscious state, from which condition he was never aroused. Dr. Ferguson remained with him throughout the night, and the aid of other medical skill was summoned, but without beneficial results. He never spoke after first becoming unconscious. Gradually he sank to rest, and at 7:15 Monday morning he passed away. Words avail nothing at such a time as this. His life has been an open book, read of all men who have looked upon him or came under his influence. He was a true man, devoid of everything unbecoming a gentleman. For over twenty years he has been connected with the political and social history of Grundy County, in that time coming in contact with all of our people, and we have yet to hear of a single person, regardless of his political opinion or social standing, who had ought to say against Samuel B. Thomas. He was the friend of every man, woman and child in the county, and his demise brings mourning to every household.

Samuel B. Thomas was born at St. Marys, Chester Co., Penn., October 20, 1820. At the age of eight years, with his parents he moved to Centre County, where after he arrived at the age of maturity, he was engaged in the lumber business and merchandising until 1852, when he moved to Peru, Ind., and for a year and a half was engaged with Andrew DeGraff in railroading. While there he contracted fever and ague, from which his system was never entirely freed. While at Peru he received a letter from an old time friend and former clerk, Mr. E. B Hanna, inviting him to a situation in Morris. In 1854, Mr. Thomas came here and entered the employ of Mr. Hanna, who was then in the mercantile business in this city.

April 6, 1858, deceased was elected to the position of Justice of the Peace for the town of Morris, and on the 12th of that month he qualified and assumed the duties of his office. From this time commenced his political career. On the 15th of November, 1861, before the expiration of his term of office as Justice of the Peace, Mr. Thomas was elected to the office of County Clerk, which position he filled continuously until December, 1877, when he qualified for the position of County Judge, to which office he had been elected at the November election preceding, his term of office expiring in December next, and would have completed a continuous service of twenty-one years in the court house. What better record could be given to any man. Faithful to every trust, competent for every duty, affable, genial, whole-souled, he won and held the confidence of all people. So strong was his hold upon the people, that when he had declared his intention of retiring from public life, old-time friends would not listen to his protest, but compelled him to signify his willingness to again accept the position of Judge, should the convention which assembled in this city on last Saturday tender him the nomination, with the unstanding always, that he would do no personal work to secure the nomination. At no time did he think seriously of receiving the nomination, and we know from him that he did not want it, and would not have accepted it had he been nominated only as above stated, for the satisfaction of his friends.

Shortly after coming to Morris, Mr. Thomas made the acquaintance of Miss Amanda Ferguson, sister of Sheriff and Dr. Ferguson, of this city, and during his first year's residence here they were married, and for twenty-eight years have lived happily together.

The parents of Mr. Thomas have been dead several years, and are buried in Centre County, Penn. Three brothers are living in Pennsylvania, and one sister in Kansas.

August 13, 1856, Mr. Thomas was inducted into the mysteries of Freemasonry, and was raised from time to time until he reached the Knight Templar degree. He was a devoted member of the order, and filled various offices in the several branches. At the time of his death he was second in rank in the commandery.

The court house and city buildings were clothed in mourning. The flag at the Republican pole, which had proudly flaunted to the breeze, betokening victories in which the deceased had taken an active part to achieve, was hung at half-mast, now the emblem of sorrow for one who had been its friend and defender. Other flags in the city were placed at half-mast, and during the time of the funeral and services, at 2 o'clock Tuesday afternoon the business houses were closed.

Prior to the death of Mr. Thomas, the Knight Templars of this city had been in constant attendance upon him, and after his death they took charge of his remains, and made all arrangements for the funeral services at the request of the widow. Representatives of the fraternity were present from all of the neighboring towns, which together with the county officials and the vast concourse of people from all parts of the county made up one of the largest gatherings for such an occasion ever held in the city.

The floral tributes were profuse and exceedingly appropriate. From the German society of this city came a pillow inscribed "*Unser Freund.*" From the court house an anchor, surmounted by a star; from the Templars, a Maltese cross; from the family, a sickle and sheaf of wheat. There were many handsome bouquets.

The funeral service was held at the residence, Rev. Young, of the M. E. Church, officiating, concluded at the grave by the Blue [Lodge of Masons, followed by the Commandery.

And then was deposited all that was mortal of Samuel B. Thomas, a specimen of God's noblest work—an honest man.

The following resolutions were adopted by Cedar Lodge, A., F. & A. M., of this city:

WORSHIPFUL MASTER, WARDEN AND BROTHERS:

One of the most perfect columns of our superstructure—Past Master Samuel Barber Thomas—has been stricken to earth by that insatiate archer—Death, whose sable wings spread a gloom over this Lodge of Sorrow.

Well has it been said that "the good die young," but our deceased brother was an exception to this rule. He possessed all the elements of a truly good man. Benevolence, courtesy and kindness were his companions; justice, integrity and morality were his rules of action. Therefore be it

Resolved, That in the death of Brother Thomas, Cedar Lodge, No. 124, A., F. & A. M., has lost a just and upright Mason, society an exemplary citizen, his wife a kind and affectionate husband and Grundy County a faithful public servant.

That to his beloved wife we extend our heartfelt sympathy, and commend her to Him who doeth all things well, with the assurance that she will some day go to him in that haven of rest, where all is peace and perfect joy.

That a page in our record book be set apart as sacred to the memory of Past Master Samuel B. Thomas, on which shall be inscribed his Masonic record.

That a copy of the preamble and resolutions be certified and presented to the wife of our deceased brother.
PERRY A. ARMSTRONG,
L. P. LOTT,
LEANDER IRONS,
Committee.

THURSDAY, SEPTEMBER 14, 1892.

Board met pursuant to adjournment; called to order by the Chairman; present, a full Board, except Superintendent Ayers.

Minutes of yesterday's proceedings read and approved.

A motion by Superintendent Germain that the matter of fixing compensation of county officers be set for hearing at 11 o'clock, was carried.

The committee appointed to draft resolutions of respect to the memory of the late Hon. S. B. Thomas, deceased, presented their report as follows, to wit:

Your committee to whom was referred the matter of the death of the Hon. S. B. Thomas, County Judge, would beg leave to submit the following report on the matter before them:

WHEREAS, Death has removed from this community the Hon. Samuel B. Thomas; and, whereas, it is but fitting that we, members of the Grundy County Board of Supervisors, who have known him personally and officially for many years, should express our respect for him as an officer and a man.

Be it resolved, That, in the demise of Judge S. B. Thomas, the people of the county have lost the presence and counsel of a man whose daily life was pure, and whose kindly nature endeared him to all, of an officer who always did his duty fairly and justly, whose sense of justice and equity was strong and constant, and whose memory will long be held in respect and venerance as that noblest work of God, an honest man, and further

Be it resolved, That a page of the record of the Board be dedicated to his memory, and that a copy of these resolutions be certified by the clerk to the widow of the deceased. All of which is respectfully submitted. OREN GIBSON, *Chairman.*

THOMAS TETLOW, mechanic, Morris. The subject of this sketch was born in England February 19, 1832, and was raised and educated in his native country. Having married, July 18, 1852, Miss Sarah A. Haywood, they came to Illinois and settled in Morris in the fall of 1855. Mrs. (Haywood) Tetlow was born March 15, 1825, in Yorkshire, England. In Grundy County, Mr. Tetlow engaged in farming from 1855 to August, 1862, when he enlisted in Company I, One Hundredth Illinois Volunteer Infantry (Capt. Gardner). He continued in this regiment until the battle of Murfreesboro, when he was confined to the hospital for eleven months continuously; when able for duty, he was attached to an invalid corps, Seventeenth Regiment Veteran Reserve, where he remained until discharged, July 1, 1865; his term of service was about three years. He took part in the battles of Perryville, Murfreesboro and others. After the war, he learned the trade of blacksmithing under Oscar Tompkins, of Morris, and he has been running a shop of his own for the past nine years. His shop is situated on the corner of Liberty and Jefferson streets; residence on Jefferson street. Mr. and Mrs. Tetlow have a family of four children—Eliza H., born August 4, 1854, died on shipboard about the 15th of September, 1855; Frances L., born July 22, 1856; Charles S., born July 20, 1858, died August 31, 1861; Joseph E., born July 14, 1860, died September 7, 1861. Mrs. Tetlow is a member of the Congregational Church, of Morris. Frances L. (one of our subject's daughters), was married, December 29, 1875, to Frank W. Edson, of New York, later of Wauponsee Township, and they have three children—Gertie E., born November 21, 1876; Clara B., born July 13, 1878, died November 29, 1879; and Frank T., born June 13, 1881. Thomas Tetlow is a Republican.

A. G. WOODBURY, real estate, loan and insurance agent and Police Magistrate, was born in Putnam County, this State, November 8, 1842; son of A. O. Woodbury, who was born in Franklin County, Mass., August 2, 1813, and came to Illinois first in 1834, and settled in 1836, in Putnam County. He is a farmer by occupation, and came to Grundy County in 1852, remained there till 1875, then moved to Nebraska, where he still lives. His wife, Lydia S. Winters, was born in Miami County, Ohio, November 28, 1812, and is still living. The parents had six children, born to them, but three of them living, two sons and one daughter; one of the sons died at Jefferson Barracks, Mo., during the war. Subject was educated in Grundy County, and began life as a farmer, which he followed from 1866 to 1876, then engaged in his present business, which he has continued since. While living in the country, our subject was Supervisor of his Township, Collector, Township School Treasurer, Assessor, and was elected Magistrate the past spring (1882). Mr. Woodbury enlisted in the Federal army, August 8, 1862, and served three years, lacking a few days; was Sergeant in Company D, Ninety-first Illinois Infantry; participated in many warm engagements; was captured by Gen. Morgan in December, 1862, with the balance of his regiment, at Elizabethtown, Ky., and was exchanged in July, 1863. He was in the Department of the Southwest, operating against Dick Taylor; he was at the siege of Spanish Fort, and at Mobile, Ala. Mr. Woodbury was married in this county, January 4, 1866, to Merinda Mecham, born September 6, 1843, daughter of Sylvester and Delilah (Bunch) Mecham; he died in 1848, she in 1874. Subject has two children, viz.: Susie D. and L. Adella. Mr. Woodbury and wife and older daughter are members of the Baptist Church. Mr. Woodbury owns a comfortable residence in town, and a good farm in the country. Mr. Woodbury is a Republican.

GEORGE WOELFEL, tanner, Morris, was born in Bavaria, Germany, March 25, 1831, and was educated in his native town. At the age of fifteen, he began an apprenticeship as tanner and currier, serving three years. According to the laws of Germany, he traveled and worked at his trade for four years, when, in 1853, he came to the United States, landing in New York, December 1. He worked in Newark, N. J., Pittsburgh, Penn., and Joliet, Ill., as a journeyman workman. Was in business for himself for a time in Lockport, Ill. From 1861 to 1863, he ran a leather store in Ottawa, Ill. In 1863, he settled in Morris and formed a partnership with Fred Caspari, in the Morris tannery; in 1864, they bought a boot and shoe store which they ran in connection with the tannery until October 15, 1865, when the tannery burned. They rebuilt it in the winter of 1865-66. In the fall of 1866, Caspari sold his interest to Charles Sparr, when the new firm added a harness shop to the other business. In this relation, they remained until 1880, when they dissolved partnership, Sparr becoming sole owner of the boot and shoe and harness store, and Woelfel of the tannery. In 1881, our subject erected a large brick building on the site of the old one, at a cost of $5,000. The establishment has a working capacity of thirty hands. Our subject was married November 29, 1861, to Miss Margaret Fleck, who was born in Germany February 12, 1838, and came to the United States in 1851. The family now consists of six children—Edgar H., born October 28, 1862; George L., July 11, 1864; Annie L., August 12, 1867; Albert, October 19, 1871; Ernest, September 3, 1874; and an infant, born June 17, 1882.

H. T. WARNER, Deputy Sheriff, Morris, was born in Chicago, February 16, 1853; son of Hiram Warner, who is a native of New York State, born about 1813. He came to Chicago when a young man, and engaged in the grain business, which he followed some twenty years, and has since engaged in various other occupations, but mainly farming, which he has pursued for the past twenty years in this county, where he still resides. Sarah F. (Taylor) Warner, the mother of our subject, was also born in New York, about the year 1824, and is still living in this county. The parents have six children, three sons, of whom our subject is the youngest, and three daughters. Our subject was educated in Chicago, and after roving around for a few years, sowing his wild oats, he finally settled in Morris, and served on the police force. In June, 1881, he was elected Deputy Sheriff of Grundy County, an office he holds at the present time. Mr. Warner was married in Morris, November 12, 1875, to Jeanie M., daughter of H. O. Ward; she was born in 1854. They have four children—one son and three daughters. Mr. Warner is a Republican.

JOHN WINTERBOTTOM, machinist Morris. John Winterbottom was born in Lancashire, England, June 30, 1842. He came to the United States in 1859, landing at Morris April 12. He is a machinist by trade, at which trade, together with engineering, he worked for several years in Morris. In 1870, he established a gunsmith shop on Liberty street, where he is still engaged. Mr. Winterbottom was married December 26, 1876, to Miss Mary Williams of Grundy County, Ill. She was born December 20, 1850. They have two sons —William R., born October 3, 1877; and Russell W., born August 30, 1880. Our subject enlisted in Company I, Sixty-ninth Illinois Volunteers, and when his term of service expired, he enlisted in the One Hundred and Thirty-eighth Illinois Volunteers. Mrs. Winterbottom is a member of the Methodist Episcopal Church. Mr. Winterbottom was raised by Quaker par-

AU SABLE TOWNSHIP.

ents. William Winterbottom, father of John, was born in England in 1821, and died in Olathe, Kan., in 1874. Martha Winterbottom, his mother, was born in 1821 in England, and is now living in that country. Jacob Williams, father of Mrs. Winterbottom, was born in Wales August 23, 1820, and is now living in Grundy County. Anne Williams, mother of Mrs. W., was born in Wales August 20, 1819, and died in this county, April 21, 1873. Mr. Winterbottom is a Republican.

FREDERICK A. WILLIAMS, house carpenter, Morris, is a native of New York, born February 13, 1847. At the age of nine, his parents moved to Illinois, and settled in Morris, Grundy County, where he was principally educated. His father, F. H. Williams, was a building-contractor, in which business he established himself, and followed it until his death, which occurred at Morris. In 1870, Mr. F. A. Williams went to Kansas, and engaged at building and contracting for four years. Returning on a visit, in 1874, he found it to his interest to remain, and in 1875 he began his present business in Morris. He ran a planing-mill and a general carpentering business, employing a large force of workingmen. He is having a very fair success. Mr. Williams is unmarried, assuming the responsibility of the family, which now consists of the mother, one brother and one sister. The children are our subject; Sarah L., born December 10, 1848, who is married to Thomas Shaw, of Morris; Charles H., born October 3, 1860; and Ida B., born November 6, 1863. Cynthia T. Williams, mother of the subject, was born September 28, 1825, in Herkimer County, N. Y., and is a member of the M. E. Church of Morris. The father, F. H. Williams, was a native of Oneida County, N. Y., born January 1, 1823, and died in Morris June 1, 1875. Mr. F. A. Williams is a conservative Republican.

CHARLES F. WASHBURN, Morris, is a native of Otsego County, N. Y., born November 25, 1827, was raised and educated in his native State. In the spring of 1855, he settled in Saratoga Township, Grundy County, where he bought a farm. Here he lost his wife, Mrs. Mary (Austin) Washburn, and his three children. On the 7th of September, 1858, he was married to Miss Martha Lyon, of Jefferson County, N. Y. She was born August 22, 1830, and came to Kendall County in 1848. The family consists of three children—George, born December 16, 1859; Frank M., September 30, 1861; and Adelbert, May 22, 1863. Mr. Washburn was for several years engaged in the grocery business on Liberty and Canal streets. He is now owner of a boat and team on the Illinois & Michigan Canal, spending much of his time on the line from Chicago to La Salle. Residence, northwest part of city. He is a Republican.

AU SABLE TOWNSHIP.

CHARLES W. BARKER, hardware and implements, Minooka, senior member of the firm of Barker & Stauffer, hardware merchants and dealers in agricultural implements, the leading interest of the kind in the town. He was born in Lisbon, Kendall Co., Ill., in March, 1851, eldest son of William M. Barker, who was born in Oneida County, N. Y., May, 1825, who was a son of Samuel and Susana (Rogers) Barker, he a native of Vermont, she of Massachusetts, and of Scotch descent. Samuel Barker, the grandsire of our subject, was one of the first settlers in Kendall County; his son William came with him when a young man, and succeeded his father on the homestead; afterward purchased a farm in the same county, where he made his permanent location, and remained on the same until his death, September, 1858. Two sons were born him—Charles William, who bears his name, and George H., who resides in Iowa. His widow is now the wife of Joseph Buckley, of this township. Charles W. came to this township in 1865; remained here three years, and, returning to Kendall County, lived there until the spring of 1876. In the fall of 1877, he associated in business with Adam Stauffer, under the firm name of Barker & Stauffer, which copartnership still exists. They keep a general hardware stock and handle farm implements, making a specialty of Weir and John Deere plows, Union and Deere planters, McCormick's harvesting machines, Webber wagons and Abbott's carriages. In 1872, he was married to Priscilla Coop, daughter of Samuel Coop, of this township; no children. He is a member of Minooka Lodge, No. 528, A., F. & A. M., Orient Chapter, R. A. M., and Blaney Commandery (Knights Templar).

JOSEPH BUCKLEY, farmer, P. O. Minooka; emigrated from Lancashire, England, to this county in the spring of 1849; he was born February 3, 1831, son of John and Mary Buckley, both natives of Lancashire, England. Mr. Buckley's early boyhood was spent in school and in the drug store of his father, who was an apothecary and who died in 1851, at which time Joseph returned to England to settle up his father's estate, remaining there four years and a half. Upon his return to the State, he located in Kendall County, in Lisbon Township, and engaged in farming. August 11, 1862, he responded to the Nation's call, and, although not a full-fledged citizen at that time, he promptly answered to the call to arms, and enlisted as a private in Company H, Eighty-ninth Illinois Volunteer Infantry, and continued in service and participated in all the engagements in which his regiment took part, beginning with Stone River and ending with that of Kenesaw Mountain, June 21, 1864, where he was shot through the shoulder, the ball passing down and out of the forearm. This ended his usefulness as a soldier, and, after several months in hospitals, was discharged, January 20, 1865, on account of disability, and returned to Kendall County. In the spring of 1866, he located in this township, on the southwest quarter of Section 5, upon land that he had purchased in 1863, and has since remained here. He has a good farm of 100 acres, with excellent buildings thereon. February 23, he married Mrs. Mary Barker, relict of William M. Barker; she was born in Derbyshire, England, daughter of Samuel and Martha (Milner) Naden, the latter a daughter of John and Mary Milner. The Naden family emigrated from England in 1846, locating in Lisbon, Kendall County. Mr. Buckley has one son. Both he and wife are members of the Au Sable M. E. Church.

PETER H. BRISCOE, farmer, P. O. Minooka. Among the representative young men and farmers of this township is Peter H. Briscoe. He was born May 23, 1853, at Dresden, this township, youngest son of Nicholas and Mary (Byrns) Briscoe. Nicholas Briscoe was born in Kings County, Ireland, in September, 1795, and came to America in the spring of 1830. The family consisted of himself, wife and nine children—Richard, Patrick, Allen, Maria, Eliza, James, John, Nicholas and Bridget. Those since born that lived are Peter H. and William. Nicholas Briscoe came to Dresden first, and lived there about two years; then moved to Section 24, where he rented land, and, several years after, purchased 360 acres, 160 acres on Section 13, balance on Section 24, and remained on the same until his death, which occurred August 1, 1882. He was a member of the Catholic Church and highly respected in the community in which he lived. His widow and five children now survive him, viz., Patrick, Ellen, Maria, Eliza and Peter H. Patrick resides in Will County, Ill., in Channahon. Ellen is the wife of Thomas Daly, and resides in Lynn County, Mo. Maria resides in this township, wife of James Mead, and Eliza resides in Minnesota, wife of William Harrison. Peter H. Briscoe, the subject of these lines, came to this farm with his parents, and remained with them until the year 1879, when, on November 3, that year, he married Margaret Burke, who was born in this township, daughter of Thomas Burke. After his marriage, he located on the farm he now owns, and has since remained there, engaged in farming, his farm consisting of 200 acres, on Section 24. He has always been identified with the Democratic party; he served the township as Collector in 1878 and 1879, and served two terms and was re-elected Supervisor of the township in the spring of 1882. Mr. and Mrs. Briscoe have two children—John and Eliza. He is a member of the Catholic Church at Minooka.

THOMAS BURKE, farmer, P. O. Minooka. Of the highly respectable citizens of Au Sable Township, Thomas Burke ranks among the first. He was born December 22, 1824, in County Clare, Ireland, in the same house that his ancestors for three generations were born. His father, Garrett Burke, was born in 1804; his wife, who bore our subject, (Thomas, the only son), was Sarah Kleine. Garrett Burke, the youngest, was a son of Patrick, who was a son of Michael Burke, who settled in County Clare prior to the Revolution. In 1847, the subject of this sketch left the old country and came to America, landing in New York in the spring of that year. He lived in New York about one year, then came to Pike County, Ind., where he lived until the fall of 1851, when he came to this township, and, for about six years, rented land, after which he made a purchase of eighty acres of unimproved land, paying for it $9 per acre, and has since added to the same, and now has 160 acres and some timber. In 1851, he married Elizabeth Welch, a native of Kings County, Ireland, daughter of William Welch; they have two children—Margaret and Elizabeth; the former is the wife of Peter Briscoe, of this township.

MICHAEL BRANNICK, Channahon, was born October 17, 1825, in County Mayo, Ireland, fourth son of Patrick and Mary (Carey) Brannick. Patrick Brannick was the son of William Brannick. Subject was raised on a farm, and, in April, 1846, he landed at New York; came to this county and to Morris in May, same year; worked awhile on the canal, then went out to Lisbon, Kendall Co., Ill., and stayed there four years, altogether, and, in the spring of 1850, he went the overland route to California; engaged in mining one year, then returned here, in 1851, and made a purchase of 100 acres, where he now resides, which cost $9 an acre cash, there being some little improvement on the land, fifteen acres broken and small log house on the place. He has now 514 acres in this county, including eighty acres given his son, and he has made all he has by hard labor. He was married, November 10, 1851, to Mary Ann Sterling, who was born in York State, daughter of John Sterling, who came West prior to 1848. Mr. Brannick has ten children—John, Ambrose, William, Mary E., Michael, Thomas, Kate, Patrick H. and Margaret, all living. He carries on general farming and stock raising. He is a member of the Catholic Church.

GEORGE COMERFORD, farmer and general business, P. O. Minooka. Among the representative men of Au Sable Township, George Comerford stands among the first. He was born August 3, 1826, in County Wexford, Ireland, eldest son of William and Honora (Nolan) Comerford, both natives of same county. His paternal grandsire was Pierce Comerford, whose wife was Mary Roche. Our subject was reared at home to agricultural pursuits, and received a collegiate education in the land of his birth, and, in the spring of 1850, emigrated to America, in company with his parents and family of six children, George being the first; then in order came Pierce, Mary, Charles, Nicholas and William. The family arrived in April, 1850; the father purchased land soon after his arrival, in the northeast part of the township, his purchase amounting to 560 acres of land, which he subsequently divided up among his children. His death occurred October 11, 1866; his wife preceded him, November 1, 1854. Of the Comerford family, George is the only one residing in the county; in fact, only one of the family is yet living aside from George, and that is his brother Charles, who resides in Brule, Chamberlain Co., Dak. When our subject came to this county, he engaged in railroading and helped locate and survey the Rockford & Rock Island Railroad, which runs through this county, and helped lay the first rail that was laid in the State. After the survey of the road, he assisted in building the same, and remained in the employ of the railroad company until 1856. He was the first railroad agent and the first Postmaster in the town of Minooka. He served consecutively as Postmaster nine years, and was station agent several years. He built some of the first business houses in the place, and has, perhaps, contributed more toward advancing and building up the town than any other one man. Soon after the establishment of the place, he engaged in commercial business, keeping station, post office and store in one small building. Afterward, he built what is now known as the Comerford Block and engaged in running a general store, and subsequently to this and other buildings, and did what he could to encourage the prosperity and the success of the town. During this time, he has been carrying on his farm, consisting of 160 acres, which is situated adjacent to the town on the west; the farm is well improved, its owner being a thorough, practical farmer. In justice to Mr. Comerford it can be said that he has been more prominently identified with the interests of this portion of the county than any other man living in the township. He has filled every office of trust in the township within the gift of the people, and served repeatedly in several official stations. In church matters he has borne a conspicuous part, assisting in the formation of the Catholic Church, and giving liberally to the establishment of the M. E. society at this place, also. In school matters, he has been prominently identified, being aware of the advantages of education; he has done all in his power toward the advancement of the interests of the same in this township, and is now President of the Board of Education here. September 16, 1855, he was united in wedlock to Catharine Smith, who was also a native of the same county as himself, daughter of Thomas and Mary Smith, all of Wexford, Ireland. Four children have been born to them, three of whom are living—Thomas S., Nicholas J. and Mary C., all of whom are receiving the advantages of a liberal education at the University at Notre Dame. In politics, Mr. Comerford is Democratic, and has proven true to its principles. He has recently returned from a visit to the home of his birth, and was received by his friends and acquaintances with ovations of a flattering character.

WILLIAM COMERFORD, Minooka, was born in this township September 15, 1859, eldest son of Pierce and nephew of George Comerford, of this township. Pierce Comerford was born January, 1828, in County Wexford, Ireland, and came to this country with his father, William, at the time of his settlement here. He settled on land given him by his father, and engaged in farming on Section 2, in this township, and remained on the farm until his death, which occurred in January, 1868. His widow yet survives him and resides on the homestead. She was born in County Kildare, Ireland, in 1832, daughter of Dennis Dempsey; she came to this county in 1855. To Pierce Comerford was born William, Honora, Nicholas, Mary E. and Anna, all residents of this township, living on the homestead of which William has had charge since 1881. February 11, 1881, he married Katie Kinney, who was born in Morris July 26, 1860, daughter of Patrick Kinney. They have one child—Mary E.

EDWARD CANTWELL, farmer, P. O. Minooka; has been a resident of the county since 1850; he is the eldest son of Michael Cantwell, who was born in Kings County, Ireland, in 1816, son of Edward and Bridget (Hoolen) Cantwell. The paternal grandsire of Michael was Matthew Cantwell. Michael Cantwell, the father of our subject, came to America in 1836, landing in Albany same year, and, having nothing when he came to this country, hired out to work, and continued in and about the city for about four years. In February, 1839, he married Margaret Feehan, a native of Kings County, daughter of Cornelius and Mary (Deegon) Feehan. About the year 1840, Mr. Cantwell removed to Michigan, where he had purchased land; there he remained until the spring of 1850, when he came to Chicago and engaged in the lumber business, but discontinued it and came to this township the fall of that year, and located here and since remained. He first bought forty acres of land at $3 an acre; afterward bought 160 acres near the canal, now owned by the Boyle family. He has five children—Edward, John, Margaret, James and Thomas, all residents of the township. Margaret is the wife of William Woods. Edward, the eldest of the family, was born in Albany County in 1840, removed with his parents to Michigan and returned with them to this county, in 1850. At the outbreak of the war, or soon after, he responded to the call to arms, and enlisted, in February, 1862, in Company I, Sixtieth Regiment Illinois Volunteer Infantry, and served until the close of the war. His first engagement was at Stone River. Afterward, Chickamauga, Mission Ridge, Lookout and Kenesaw Mountains, Resaca, Peach Tree Creek, Atlanta, Jonesboro and all the engagements of the campaign. At Bentonville, he was taken prisoner, April 19, 1864, and was transferred from different points until he was finally discharged, in June, 1865, having been a true and brave soldier during his period of enlistment. Upon his return home, he resumed work at home, where he remained until his marriage. Since then, he has been on his own land. He was married, August 15, 1875, to Josephine Gordon, a native of Massachusetts, daughter of George Gordon; they have four children—Edward, Thomas, Louisa and May. His farm is located on the northeast quarter of Section 10.

ISRAEL CRYDER, farmer, P. O. Minooka, born in Huntingdon County, Penn., March 11, 1835, fourth child of Jacob and Elizabeth Cryder. Jacob Cryder was a son of Israel Cryder, whose wife was a Miss Carpenter. Jacob Cryder was a farmer by occupation; he died in 1839, when subject was four years of age; he had six children, two sons and four daughters, all of whom lived to be grown, save one—Hannah M., Henry, Amanda, Israel, Sarah A. Those living are Israel and Sarah A., now Mrs. James Reardon, in Vienna Township, this county; all of the above came West and all first settled in this township. Hannah M. married N. H. Tabler. Henry died in November, 1872. Amanda married Jonas Bartlett; they settled in Saratoga Township; she died about the year 1854. Our subject came West in the fall of 1844, with his mother and the family; they lived with Henry Cryder a few years. Mr. Cryder remained with his grandfather until he reached the age of maturity, and engaged in farming. He bought 190 acres where he now lives, and has since lived here. September 14, 1862, he married Mary Hampson, born June 7, 1839, in Jefferson County, N. Y., daughter of George and Maria (Cash) Hampson, both of England, who settled in Jefferson County, then removed West, to Kendall County, in 1858, where the father yet lives; the mother died in 1867. Mrs. Cryder has four brothers and two sisters—Edward and Henry, in Kendall County; also, Hannah, wife of Thomas Newsom; Thomas, in Decatur County, Iowa; Jane, in same county, wife of Thomas Reardon, and Joseph, in Newark, N. J. Since Mr. Cryder located here, he has been a constant resident, engaged in farming and stockraising, keeping some fine Durham stock on the farm of 385 acres, on which he has put all the substantial improvements. Mr. and Mrs. Cryder have four children—Emma E. Edith M., Henry E. and Jessie B. He is a Republican and a member of the Masonic fraternity—Blue Lodge, Royal Arch, and Blaney Commandery.

GEORGE COLLEPS, book-keeper, Minooka, was born March 16, 1848, in Buffalo, N. Y., son of John W. and Margaret (Schroder) Colleps, both natives of Hesse-Darmstadt, and who came to the United States the same year that our subject was born. When young, he removed with his parents to Michigan, where they remained until 1853, when he came with them to this place. At the age of sixteen, he volunteered in the service of his country, enlisting in the spring of 1864, in Company G, Sixty-fourth Regiment of Illinois Volunteer Infantry, and, after participating in several of the engagements of the Atlanta campaign, was taken prisoner, July 22, at Atlanta, and taken to Andersonville Prison, where he was incarcerated for nearly ten months, and for nearly one month he stood, and laid on the ground in the rain, with no clothing or covering for his body but a shirt and pair of drawers. At the time of his capture, he weighed 130 pounds; at the time of his release, had dwindled down to fifty-six. His sufferings were indescribable, and the horrors of that den and the remembrances of the cruelties enacted there will ever remain vividly impressed upon his mind as long as reason holds her sway. Upon his release at the termination of the war, he returned to Minooka and engaged as clerk in the dry goods and grocery store of R. Gardiner, where he continued until 1870. Then, for three years, he was associated in the hardware business with W. A. Worthing, after which the partnership was dissolved by mutual consent; he then clerked again for R. Gardiner, continuing in his employ for two years, after which he was for two years and a half in copartnership with L. Smith in the grocery business; he then disposed of his interest to S. W. Smith, and remained with him as clerk until 1880, when he took charge of the books in the grain and elevator office of A. K. Knapp, and has since served in that capacity. September 14, 1869, he married Jennie Van Horn, who was born in Essex County, N. J., daughter of John and Maretha (Terhune) Van Horn; they have no children living. He is a member of Minooka Lodge, A., F. & A. M., Orient Chapter and Blaney Commandery.

THOMAS CARROLL, farmer, P. O. Minooka. Of the representative men of this township who came from Erin's Isle, none are more highly esteemed or more deserving than Thomas Carroll. He was born August 15, 1814, in County Lovel, Ireland. His parents were Thomas and Mary (Tafe) Carroll, and to them were born the following children: Patrick, John, James, Thomas, William, Edward, Maria, Alice and Bridget. None of the family came to this county save Thomas, who emigrated to America in June, 1837, landing in New York. When he came he had nothing but his hands and a willing heart, but he made good use of his opportunities, though few they were. He hired out to work as teamster, and turned his attention to whatever employment was the most remunerative to him. He remained in New York four or five years, then came to this State prior to the building of the canal. The first work he did upon his arrival to this State was for Mr. Kimball, at Marseilles, where he stayed some two years or more. Then he worked about three years on the canal. Afterward went to Ottawa, where he worked on the canal, and afterward worked for William Armstrong about two years. Prior to 1850, he located on the land he now owns. Having accumulated some money, he invested first in forty acres of land, which cost him $7 per acre, the land being unimproved. He afterward purchased eighty acres in Will County, for which he paid $13 per acre, and he has now 210 acres, all of which he has worked for and obtained by great industry. His wife before his marriage was Mrs. Mary Ann Freckleton, a native of County Tipperary, Ireland; her maiden name was Conn and her mother's maiden name was Ann Heakey, now eighty-eight years old; by this union, there have been born eight children, whose names, according to the order of births, are John, Thomas, Andrew, Michael, Edward, William, Maria and Mary A. Mr. Carroll is a Democrat and member of the Catholic Church.

JOHN CASS, farmer, P. O. Channahon. Among the old settlers and self-made men of this township is Mr. Cass, who was born in Queen's County, Ireland, in 1828, only son of William and Bridget (Kenihan) Cass. Subject was raised on the farm; left home May 19, 1849, and after five weeks and four days' voyage, landed in New York, July 2, same year. When he came to Chicago, he had but 33 cents in his pocket, all he possessed. He worked a short time at Blue Island, and came to Au Sable that harvest; worked through the season, then went to Iowa and worked on the public works until the spring, and returning here, he worked on the State boat until harvest. He then hired out at $10 per month on a farm about thirteen months, losing but one and one-half days in that time, for John Adams. He then took the farm and rented the same on shares for two years, after which he rented land of the Lewis heirs, on the land which Briscoe now owns, for about five years. After he had been here three years, he bought eighty acres, where he now lives, paying $30 per acre; no improvements on the land whatever. He remained on the Lewis farm until December, 1856, when he moved on his eighty acres, and has since lived there, having now 220 acres of land with good improvements. April 3, 1852, he married Nora Delaney, born in

Queen's County, Ireland, daughter of James and Bridget Lynch Delaney. Mrs. Cass came here in 1850. When Mr. Cass located on this farm, he had but little in the way of comforts. They had a hard time for several years, but by hard labor, diligence and great industry, they have acquired the home and property they now have. They are members of the Catholic Church. Mr. Cass also owns some property in Joliet.

SAMUEL COOP, farmer, P. O. Minooka, born August 20, 1827, in Lancashire, England, second son of James and Mary (Birtwistle) Coop. At the age of fourteen, he went to learn the machinists' trade, and served seven years in the shop. December 25, 1853, he married Ann, daughter of John and Mary (Holden) Ball. In the spring of 1855, he emigrated to this county and purchased eighty-five acres of Mr. Longworth, on the west half of the northwest quarter of Section 5, paying $9 per acre. There were no improvements on the same whatever when he located here, yet, by hard work and economy, he has succeeded in making a good home and a competence for himself. He has but one child Priscilla, wife of Charles W. Barker, of Minooka. Mr. Coop is a Republican, and has always voted that ticket.

PATRICK CLENNON, farmer, P. O. Minooka, was born in Queen's County, Ireland, 1825, son of Patrick and Judah (Scott) Clennon. Mr. Clennon emigrated to America in 1849, landing in New Orleans in December the same year. From there he went to Fayette County, Ohio, where he hired out among the farmers by the month, taking his pay in scrip, and remained there until the fall of Buchanan's election, when he located in this township, where he now resides upon land that he purchased two years prior to his leaving Ohio, said land being unimproved at the time of his purchase, and costing him $4.50. He has now a good farm, well improved and plenty of stock, all of which has been the fruits of his own earnings. He was married, in 1848, to Margaret Phalen, daughter of Daniel and Catharine (Campen) Phalen. This marriage has been crowned by the birth of one son—James Patrick, who resides with his parents on the homestead. He was born in Fayette County, Ohio, and removed to this county with his parents and since remained. May 3, 1860, he married Jennie Kinsley, who was born in this township, daughter of Andrew and Eliza (Smith) Kinsley; they have one son—James Patrick, born December 25, 1881. Mrs. Clennon, Jr., is a grand-daughter of Andrew Kinsley, one of the pioneers of this township, who was prominently identified with this portion of the county; he was a contractor on the canal at the time of its building; was one of the founders of the Catholic Church at Dresden, one of the first Supervisors in the township and one of the leading and representative men of his time in Au Sable Township. He had three sons - James, Michael and Andrew, none of whom are now living in the county. Andrew Kinsley died in August, 1872; Eliza, his wife, in August, 1862; she was a daughter of Thomas Smith, of County Wexford, Ireland, who came to Lockport, N. Y., in 1852, and there died in 1854. He has one son in this township—George T., a merchant in Minooka. Mr. and Mrs. Andrew Kinsley had two children—Jennie and Mary.

GERHARD DAHLEM, Postmaster and store, Minooka. The present efficient Postmaster of Minooka came to this township in 1855, and since that time has been a constant resident of the place and identified with its interests. He was born July 16, 1832, in Bavaria, Germany, son of John and Kate (Ruth) Dahlem. In 1852, Gerhard emigrated to America and spent three years in Lee

County, Iowa, at a place called Denmark, where he worked in a cheese factory. In September, 1855, he came to this State and township, and engaged as a farm hand in the employ of R. Gardiner for one year, after which he worked on a railroad section one year; then was switchman two years, after which he was in charge of the section as foreman on the railroad for three years. August 29, 1862, he enlisted as private in Company D, Fourth Illinois Cavalry, and served until the close of the war; was advanced to Corporal, then to Sergeant, and participated in many of the stirring and thrilling engagements of the war, and was at times Orderly on Gens. Grant's, McPherson's and Thomas K. Smith's staff. After his discharge, in May, 1865, he returned to this place and resumed work for the railroad company, as switchman and baggageman, until the spring of 1867, when he engaged as clerk for Daniel Ferguson, one year after which he was appointed night store-keeper in the Au Sable distillery. In 1868, Daniel Ferguson having resigned as Postmaster, Mr. Dahlem was appointed in his stead and engaged in the grocery business, afterward adding dry goods. October 9, 1870, he was burned out, but rebuilt and associated in business with his nephew, Adam Stauffer, under the firm name of Dahlem & Stauffer, which copartnership lasted three years, when, owing to ill health, he sold out his interest to Samuel Persells, but retained the post office, where he continued. In August, 1876, he engaged with William Shepley, in general merchandise business, which association has since been kept up, the firm name being Dahlem & Shepley, the post office being still kept by Mr. Dahlem; he has been twice married—first, in 1854, to Susan Webber, daughter of John and Mary (Ruth) Webber; she died August 13, 1862, leaving one child —Jacob J.; his present wife is Mary Stauffer, daughter of Jacob and Catharine Stauffer; they were married October 28, 1865, and four children have blessed this union—Adam, Katie, Daniel and Mary. Mr. Dahlem has a snug home, a good business and is well and favorably known throughout the entire county. He is a member of the Minooka Lodge, No. 528, A., F. & A. M., and served several years as the Worshipful Master of that lodge; is also a member of the Chapter at Morris, and of the Commandery at that place. Has always been a stanch Republican.

FLETCHER DIRST, farmer and stock-raiser, P. O. Minooka, is one of the leading farmers and stock-raisers in Grundy County. He was born August 10, 1835, near the town of Galena, Berkshire Township, Delaware Co., Ohio; he is the eldest son of John and Caroline (Searles) Dirst. John Dirst was a son of Paul Dirst, a native of Pennsylvania, who emigrated to Ohio in an early day, settling near Chillicothe, Ohio, where he died. The father of our subject when a young man came to Berkshire Township, Delaware County, and there married and engaged in farming. In 1858, the Dirst family came to this State, the family consisting of the parents and four children—Fletcher, Howard, Albert and Sylva. Fletcher began for himself at the age of twenty-two, and while he remained in Ohio was engaged in farming and stock-trading. Since he came to this county, he has given his attention to farming and stock-raising, and has done much to encourage the growth and introduction of fine stock in the county. When he came here, he purchased 480 acres, part of which was in Seward Township, in Kendall County, adjoining. He has resided in the meantime in Au Sable Township, where he has a fine farm, well adapted for farming and general stock purposes. He has given especial attention to thoroughbred Cotswold and Leicestershire sheep, importing the same from Canada; he is engaged, also, in breeding Durham cattle, and in his business has been successful, being a thorough and progressive farmer. He was married, December 7, 1857, in Delaware County, Ohio, to Ann Dustin, a native of that county, daughter of Nathan Dustin, one of the early settlers and prominent men of that county; his wife was Almira Buzwell, both natives of New Hampshire. Mr. Dirst has now 240 acres of land; his residence is on Section 3, on the banks of the Au Sable, two miles west of Minooka. He has filled the office of Supervisor and other positions of trust in that township. He is a member of Minooka Lodge, No. 528, A., F. & A. M., of Orient Chapter and Blaney Commandery. He has three children—Ann A., John F. and Charles F.

THOMAS DEMPSEY, butcher, Minooka. Among the interests of the town of Minooka that is deserving of especial mention is that of Thomas Dempsey, who supplies the people of this town and locality with the best of meats, and thereby contributes not only to the comfort and happiness of the people in this direction, but is filling a need that is indispensable in the way of refreshing the "inner man." He has been carrying on this business since 1873. He was born in the town of Lee, Oneida Co., N. Y., June 20, 1835, the second son of Thomas and Margaret (Taylor) Dempsey, natives of Ireland, he born in County Kildare, she in County Down; they emigrated to New York about 1834, locating there, and came West, to Kendall County, Ill., about 1845; stayed there one year, then moved to Will County, Ill. Subject's father is still living; his mother died in 1863; they had a family of five sons and one daughter—John (deceased), Thomas, William, James, Hugh and Jane, wife of M. Hinsler, of Chicago. Our subject left home at the age of twenty-one, and engaged in farming; in 1864, he bought eighty acres of land in Will County, where he remained a few years, then came to Minooka. In June, 1857, he married Miss C. Tyrrel, a native of Connecticut and daughter of James T. Tyrrel; they have nine children—Mary J., Maggie, Nellie, Elizabeth, Lydia, William, Edward, Burton and Vincent. Mr. Dempsey is a Democrat.

HARRISON ENEIX, farmer, P. O. Minooka; is of Virginia stock, and was born in Marshall County, near Wheeling, Va., February 28, 1825. His father, Brice Eneix, was a native of Fayette County, and married Leah Mace, a native of England. Mr. Eneix was reared to agricultural pursuits; at the age of twenty-two, he started in life to do business upon his own account. March 16, 1848, he wedded Lovina, daughter of Clemeth Leech, and engaged as a tiller of the soil. In 1855, he came West, to this State, locating in Lisbon, Kendall County, remaining there two years, when he sold his interests and removed to Saratoga Township, this county, and purchased a farm of 200 acres. In the spring of 1877, he sold his farm, and has since been located in Minooka, and is yet farming, having 162½ acres in Will County, Ill. Since 1859, Mr. Eneix was engaged in stock trading, his field of operations extending over a large extent of country; he continued in the stock business with varied success up to within the past two years, but since that time has abandoned the business, and given his personal attention to the management of his farm. Of a family of twelve children borne him, ten are now living—Corbley, John, Rachel, Clara, Franklin, Amanda, Martha, Eliza, Mary and Harrison. Rachel resides in Iroquois County, wife of Thomas Riggs. Clara resides in Minooka, wife of Jacob Dahlem. Amanda is also a resident of this place, wife of Oliver Sadler. The other children are residents of the town. In 1864, Mr. Eneix made a trip to Idaho, and driving an ox-team and being four months on the road, having no idea at that time of the marked improvements that have since taken place in that waste of country over which he traveled with his ox-team. Mr. Eneix is a member of Minooka Lodge, No. 528, A., F. & A. M., and was one of the charter members of the establishment of the lodge at Lisbon, Kendall County.

PATRICK FEEHAN, farmer, P. O. Morris, was born in Queen's County, Ireland, March 17, 1824, son of Patrick and Mary (Boland) Feehan, she a daughter of Owen Boland. Mr. Feehan came to America in 1850, arriving in New York on New Year's eve, and immediately after came to this State, and, having nothing but his hands to make a living, he immediately set to work. He hired out by the month on a farm at low wages, and after saving sufficient means, purchased a team, and, for eighteen months, followed the fortunes of the railroad. After this, he sold his outfit for $240, came to this township, purchased some cows and engaged in stock-raising; at the same time, he worked among the farmers; all this time he was supporting his mother and one sister. After a time, his stock having accumulated, he made a cash sale and purchased a team and engaged in farming, on the land which Henry Newman now owns, remaining there about two years. About this time, he purchased eighty acres of canal land, on Section 21, paying therefor $6.75, but still continued renting land for about four years, when he purchased eighty acres additional, which cost him $9 per acre, making him 160 acres in one body. He then located on this land, and has since remained, and has put on all the improvements. In 1860, he married Ann O'Mara, a native of County Tipperary, Ireland, daughter of Jerry and Kittie (Whalen) O'Mara, who came to America in 1849, landing in St. Louis, and finally locating in Cincinnati. Mr. and Mrs. Feehan have but one child—Joseph—who resides with them at home, and who was born January 15, 1861. Mr. Feehan owes his success in life to his own energy and industry.

S. A. FERGUSON, blacksmith, Minooka, one of the thorough-going and successful mechanics of Grundy County is S. A. Ferguson; he came to Minooka and set up in business in February, 1880; he was born July 15, 1855, in Lisbon, Kendall Co., Ill., eldest son of Gardiner and Almira (Lamb) Ferguson, he a native of Maine, she of New York State. They came West, to Kendall County, about the year 1848. The subject of these lines was brought up on the farm, but, being of a mechanical turn of mind, at the age of twenty-one, he went to Millington, Ill., where he worked three years at the blacksmith's trade. After the completion of his trade, he came to Minooka, set up in business and has been well patronized, and is doing a thriving trade. November 18, 1880, he married Belle Thayer, a native of Kendall County, who has borne him one child—Guy T. In connection with his blacksmith shop, he carries on a wagon and general repair shop, and also painting in his line.

JAMES HARVEY, farmer, P. O. Morris. One of the old-time residents and honored pioneer representatives of Au Sable Township, is Esquire Harvey, who came here in 1838, and has since been a continued resident of the township. He was born on "Erin's Green Isle," Roscommon County, about the year 1809, son of Michael and Bridget (McDermot) Harvey, she a daughter of Charles McDermot, a mechanic and wheelwright. The paternal grandsire of our subject was

John Harvey, of same place. In 1834, our subject bid good-bye to his native land, and set sail for America, leaving in April and arriving at Quebec, Canada, in June. He began work on the St. Lawrence Canal, where he continued until October, 1837, when he made his way to this State, coming from Detroit by land and arriving in Chicago in February, 1838. He came on to the county, and engaged at once at work on the canal here, continuing for three years; he then came down to Au Sable and purchased land, where he now resides, and has since been a constant resident of this township. In September, 1843, he was first elected Justice of the Peace, and was subsequently re-elected. He has been twice married—first, when in Canada, in 1837, to Ellen Kinsey, who died in April, 1845, having borne him five children, three sons and two daughters—John, Michael, James, Bridget and Mary. The boys are deceased; all of them went forth at the nation's call, and enlisted in the Fifty-third Regiment, Illinois Volunteer Infantry, and were true and valiant soldiers. John and James lost their lives while in the service. Michael served three years and "veteraned," and served through the entire war and died, since his return home, from the effects of his exposure, etc., while in the service. Bridget resides in Traverse City, Mich., wife of Daniel Matison. Mary is the relict of Samuel Burgess. In 1847, Mr. Harvey married his present wife, Mary Kehoe, of same county as himself, and by her has one son—Thomas—who resides with them on the homestead.

MATTHEW KICKELS, farmer, P. O. Channahon, whose residence is on Section 25 overlooking the surrounding country on the south, is one of the most commanding and beautiful that can be found in this, or, in fact, any other portion of the State. His residence is on the high bank, or rather plateau, overlooking the head of the Illinois River at the junction of the Kankakee and Des Plaines Rivers, at an elevation of about 150 feet above the level of the surrounding country. In Felix Township, immediately at the foot of this plateau, courses the canal and river, running parallel with each other. Upon this beautiful site stands the residence of Mr. Kickels, where a view of a score of miles or more can be easily had. Braidwood and Wilmington lying off to the southeast in full view, while immediately south a vast expanse of country, upon which can be seen thousands of cattle grazing. To those who have not seen this enchanting spot, a visit to this point will not be in vain. Matthew Kickels, proprietor of this place, was born December 2, 1823, on the Rhine, in the "Fader Land," and emigrated to this country to seek his fortune in 1852. His parents, Peter and Lucy (Mitchell) Kickels never came to America. Matthew came alone and penniless, to Kendall County, where he hired out by the month, where he remained until the fall of Buchanan's election, when he came to Au Sable Township, and purchased ninety-nine acres of land, which cost him $8 per acre, there being no improvements on the land at the time. He has since extended his domain, having now 155 acres, and 132 in Will County, all of which, with the assistance of his noble wife, he has gained by active industry. February 20, 1854, he married Margaret Adgey, who was born March 11, 1831, in County Antrim, Ireland, daughter of Robert and Sarah E. (Cunningham) Adgey. Mrs. Kickels came to this country alone in 1849. Six children have been born of this marriage, but two of whom are living: Mary E., residing at Lockport, wife of James Duddage, and John, at home with parents. The children deceased were James P., Matthew R. and Joseph F. Mr. Kickels is a member of the Catholic and Mrs. K. of the Presbyterian Church.

L. K. KEOGH, Justice of the Peace, Minooka. Among the substantial residents of the village of Minooka is Esquire Keogh, who came here in the fall of 1856 and has since resided. He is a son of Patrick and Margaret (Keary) Keogh, the Kearys being of Welch extraction. He was born in 1827, in County Wexford, Ireland, where he received a liberal education and engaged in teaching at eighteen, and continued shaping the direction of the "young idea" in that country until he emigrated to America, in the fall of 1852. He stopped first at Syracuse, N. Y., where he taught for three years, then, coming to this State, in 1855, he taught one year in Joliet and until his coming to this place, where he was at once employed as a teacher in the public school, and continued very successfully for about ten years in all. For three years, he was engaged in the grocery business with Mr. Kinsley, under the firm name of Kinsley & Co. He has served the township as an officer in all the offices of trust, as Justice of the Peace, Commissioner of Highways, Town Clerk, Assessor and Treasurer, and is now serving as Justice of the Peace, which office he has held since 1874; he attends to the duties of his office, and also accommodates his neighbors with the use of his money at a reasonable rate of interest. September 26, 1866, he was married to Martha Weston, of Staffordshire, England; they have no children.

JACOB H. MURPHY, Minooka, was born in Belmont County, Ohio, September 18, 1830, eldest son of Horatio and Hannah (Beam) Murphy. Horatio Murphy was born about 1792 in Virginia; his wife was born in Belmont County, Ohio, and was a daughter of Benjamin Beam, who was a native of Germany and came to Ohio when the country was in its infancy. Horatio Murphy was of Scotch-Irish parentage, and came to Belmont County, Ohio, when a young man, and there married. He was a jeweler by trade, and, settling in Belmont, engaged in his business, remaining there until 1856, when he removed to this State, when he came to this county and lived among his children until his death, which occurred in the fall of 1865; his wife died in Ohio several years previous to his coming to this State. They raised a family of seven children, all of whom lived to raise families—Jacob H., Benjamin, John, Mary, Joanna, Ann E. and William. Benjamin lives in Livingston County, near Dwight, and is a farmer. John resides in Dwight, same county. Mary lives at Nevada, Ill., wife of Mitchell Thompson. Joanna lives in Joliet, wife of Caleb Thayer. Ann in same county, wife of Charles Smith. William resides in Champaign County; is a farmer. Jacob H. left home when nearly of age, and worked three years by the month, receiving $10 per month the first two years, and the third year his wages were increased to $11 per month. He then came to Illinois, bringing some stock through to this place for a Mr. Bradshaw, with whom he hired, remaining with him until his health failed, when he engaged in trading in horses for nearly two years, then engaged in farming by renting on the farm now owned by Israel Cryder; then he and his brother Benjamin opened up a farm for John B. Davidson, in Erienna Township, and stayed there about seven years. August 29, 1863, he purchased the farm he now owns, which was then owned by H. Bradshaw, for whom he worked when he first came here, and, with the exception of two years, when he lived in Minooka, he has remained on the farm, and all the time in the township. He has 200 acres of land,

and put the substantial improvements on the farm, and has been engaged in farming and stock-raising, keeping good graded stock. He was married, October 18, 1859, to Mary B. Pumphrey, born in Belmont County, Ohio, December 30, 1838, daughter of Ridley Pumphrey; she died April 9, 1875, leaving three children—Laura, Willie and Nettie, the latter deceased; Laura and Willie are at home. January 27, 1876, he married Mrs. Franceelia Whittington, born in Whitehall, Washington Co., N. Y., daughter of Thaddeus and Eunice M. (Reynolds) Curtis, natives of Vermont. By the last marriage, two children have been born, one of whom is living--Freddie, born December 27, 1876, and Jessie, died young, October 27, 1881, aged two years, five months and seventeen days. Mr. and Mrs. Murphy are members of the M. E. Church, and of the Mutual Aid Society. He is a supporter of the Republican party. Mrs. Murphy's grandfather, Nicholas Reynolds, was born in West Rutland, Vt.; he was a son of Jonathan Reynolds, who lived to be one hundred years old (lacking fourteen days), and who was a great hunter; when eighty-three years old, he stood in his own door and killed a deer with his rifle.

HENRY NEWMAN, farmer, P. O. Minooka. Among the self-made men of Grundy County who came from Germany, there are none who have more fully developed the truth of the adage, that wherever "there is a will" a way will be forthcoming, than Henry Newman. Coming to this country as he did, poor and destitute of friends, he, by steady industry and rigid economy, has become one of the opulent and independent farmers of the county. He was born January 6, 1825, near Frankfort, in Hesse-Darmstadt, third son of Casper and Margaret Newman. In 1850, he came to America, landing in New York, and, for three years, worked out by the month in New York State, sometimes on the railroad and at other times on a farm, making $8 per month, and receiving such wages as the times justified. In 1853, he came to this county, and, for several years, worked about Morris and the surrounding country. During this time, he was saving his money, while it came slowly, yet it was sure, and it was not squandered. At the beginning of the war, he made his first purchase, on Section 9, in Au Sable Township, buying 190 acres, at $14.50 per acre; here he located, and has since lived, and has been prosperous. He has now about 400 acres of land, well stocked with cattle, all of which, with the assistance of his faithful wife, he has made by his own industry and good management. In addition to his land here in this township, he has recently purchased several hundred acres in Dakota. He was married, in 1855, to Lena Meyers; they have five children—Mary, George, Henry, Lizzie and Adaline. Mary is the wife of Al Patten and resides in this township.

WILLIAM H. RANDALL, farmer, P. O. Minooka, was born in this township, where old Dresden now is, November 25, 1840, the only son of Samuel S. and Nancy L. (Perkins) Randall. Samuel S. Randall was born in Massachusetts March 3, 1809, son of Joshua Randall, of Massachusetts, who married Sally Skeel, who bore him a family of nine children, six sons and three daughters, all of whom lived to be grown—Bethany, Samuel S., Hannah, Dinnah, Henry H., Louisa, William A. and Adaline A. Bethany married Frances H. Butler, in Kansas. Hannah married Geo. W. Dealing, settled in Chautauqua County, N. Y., and there died. Dinnah now residing in New York, Oneida County, married a Mr. Fox. Henry H., in Minnesota. Louisa settled in Wisconsin, now deceased; she married L. McMaster. William A. resides in Kansas. Adaline resides in Marseilles, wife of S. K. Danley. Samuel S., the father of William H., emigrated West, to this State, locating in this township, in June, 1837, and lived some time at Dresden. He was a carpenter by trade, which occupation he followed for several years, and assisted in building the first frame house in Morris, the old American House. He finally located on Section 15, west half of the southwest quarter, where he built a house in 1844, and remained there until his death, which occurred June 14, 1877; his wife "passed over" the year previous, in August, 1876. He was a Whig, and later, a Republican, and, in early days, was one of the first Constables; subsequently, he served consecutively as Justice of the Peace for fourteen years, and Supervisor and other official stations of trust in the township. He was a successful man in business, and, by adding to his first purchase, he had, at the time of his death, about 400 acres of land. To him and wife were born five children, three of whom lived to marry—W. H., Mary J. and Helen. Mary J. is the wife of George W. Collins; she died March 3, 1873, leaving four children—Edward L., Hattie and Kate A. Helen married Ezra Tabler, and resides in this township. Elizabeth died in 1864, aged 15. Harriet died in infancy. William Henry now succeeds his father on the homestead, and has since his birth been a resident of the township, where he received the home school advantages. At twenty-three years of age, he began business for himself, engaged in farming. November 12, 1866, he married Harriet M. Gifford, who was born in Lorain County, Ohio, daughter of John N. and Martha (Messenger) Gifford. Immediately after the death of his father, Mr. Randall located on the homestead, and has since resided there. He has two children—Libbie May and Henry G. They are members of the M. E. Church. Mr. Randall is a member of Minooka Lodge, No. 528, A., F. & A. M.

WILLIAM SHEPLEY, hotel, Minooka, was born in Lancashire, England, September 3, 1821, and was raised in Cheshire, England. He is the oldest son of William Shepley, who was a son of John Shepley. His mother's maiden name was Elizabeth Lindley, daughter of John Lindley. Subject was raised at home; his father died when he was sixteen years old, and William then remained with his mother until twenty-five years of age; during this time, he assisted in maintaining the family; at the age of nine years, he went to work in a cotton factory, and worked at the same business until twenty-six years of age; he then went into a foundry, at Staleybridge, and worked there until he came to America. In 1855, he came to this State and stopped in Yorkville, Kendall County, and stayed there one year, working out by the month among farmers. The year following, he came to Plainfield, and worked there in a foundry, for Dillman. He stayed in Plainfield about ten years. In 1866, he left Plainfield, and went to Troy, in Will County, and stayed there four years, carrying on a grocery store. In February, 1868, he came to Minooka and engaged in the hotel business, which he has since continued; he has been in partnership in the mercantile business, with G. Dahlem, which partnership still exists. He was married, July 7, 1844, at Stockport, England, at the "Old Church," to Fannie Kay, who was born in Lancashire December 5, 1816, daughter of John and Lucy (Assen) Kay. Mr. and Mrs. Shepley have four children living—Matthew, Edward, Elizabeth A. and John. Matthew, on the farm in Kendall County; Edward, living with parents; Elizabeth, wife of Oliver Paul, who served four years in the army, and who died in 1879. Mr. Shepley has eighty acres in Will and eighty acres in Kendall County, Ill., and has valuable property in Minooka. He keeps a good hotel on Main street, having a bar in connection, stocked with best wines and liquors; he also, in connection with the hotel, runs a good livery and feed stable. He is a Republican.

THOMAS SCHIEK, proprietor of the Union Hotel, Minooka, was born February 11, 1827, in the Kingdom of Wittenberg, Germany, eldest son of Thomas Schiek, whose father was likewise named Thomas. His mother's maiden name was Margaret, daughter of George Reuben. During the early life of our subject, he was raised in a vineyard and upon a farm. In November, 1849, he left the old country, and was upon the ocean until April 12, the following year, before he landed in New York. For five years, he lived at Mt. Vernon and the adjacent cities, working during this time at farm labor and learning the carpenter's trade, and coming West, to this State, soon after, he continued at his trade as builder and contractor in Chicago and other places, and, being a thorough workman, his services were always in demand. He continued at his trade until 1881, since which time he has been engaged in the hotel business at this place, having rebuilt the hotel and fitted the same in excellent order; the house is situated near the depot, and is three stories high, containing about twenty rooms, with a dancing-hall in the third story. There is a bar in connection with the hotel, which is well stocked with liquors, wines and cigars, all of the most approved brands, while his table is well supplied with all the substantials that cheer and refresh the "inner man." He has been thrice married—first, to Margaret Palmer, who died four years after, leaving one daughter—Sophia. His second wife, Louisa Lentz, died, leaving four children—Augusta, Emma, Ida and Lizzie. His present wife was Mrs. Julia Schmidt; who is a valuable aid to his business.

D. C. TABLER, farmer, P. O. Morris, is the second son of Nathaniel Tabler, one of the pioneers of Grundy County; was born July 12, 1833, in Delaware County, Ohio, and was brought to this county when a babe by his parents, who settled on Section 8 in this township. At the age of nineteen, he left home and hired out to his uncle, Michael Cryder, for whom he worked some time. Soon after, he purchased a horse and a shovel plow, and, with an unbroke horse that his uncle Cryder let him have, he made out his team, and with it planted his first crop of corn. He remained with his uncle until the spring, and, at the age of twenty-two, he married Julia E. McCloud, who was born in 1834, in Clinton County, N. Y., daughter of John and Paulina (Ricketson) McCloud, who settled in Kendall County in 1836. After his marriage, he resided two years on his uncle's place, in Saratoga Township, and, October 13, 1863, he purchased his first land, he and his brother Nathaniel buying 120 acres of land in partnership, paying $20 per acre; there were no improvements on the land. March 27, 1865, they purchased twenty-five acres of J. E. Mathers. November 7, 1872, the brothers, by mutual consent, dissolved partnership, giving each quitclaims, after dividing up their land. October 28, 1873, subject bought of George Collins twenty acres of the west half of the southwest quarter of the northeast quarter on Section 17, paying $37.50 per acre for it. December 26, 1881, he purchased of Jeremiah Collins eighty acres of the northwest quarter of Section 17, and has now 155 acres, all of which lies on the 17th section. Mr. Tabler is the present Commissioner of Highways, and has served in that capacity eight years in all. He is one of the representative members of the Au Sable M. E. Church. Of five children born him, but one—Minnie M.—is living.

N. L. TABLER, farmer, P. O. Morris, was born on the old homestead July 4, 1838; he is the fourth child now living by his father's marriage to Mary Ann Cryder; he remained on the homestead until his twenty-third year, then associated with his brother David C. in farming; purchasing land together, they continued together for nine years, after which he located on the land he now owns, which he improved, the buildings thereon being built by his own hands. Though he never worked at the carpenter's trade, yet it runs in the Tabler family to be of a mechanical turn; all of them can construct anything they desire. February 2, 1870, he married Hannah Mary Caldwell, who was born in Huntingdon County, Penn., December 6, 1831, fourth child and second daughter of Samuel and Mary (Cryder) Caldwell; her paternal grandfather was David Caldwell; her mother, Mary Cryder, was a daughter of Israel Cryder, whose wife was Mary Seibert. To Samuel Caldwell and his wife Mary were born three daughters and two sons, Mrs. Tabler being the only one who came West. Mr. and Mrs. Tabler have three children—Ella, Rebecca and Mary. He is a member of the Au Sable M. E. Church, and class leader of the same. In school matters, he takes an active part, and is School Director of the same.

EZRA TABLER, farmer, P. O. Minooka. Among the thorough-going young farmers in Au Sable Township is Ezra Tabler, who was born in the township October 21, 1843, on Section 8; he is the sixth son now living that was born to Nathaniel and Mary Ann (Cryder) Tabler; he left home in the spring of 1864, when he was married to Cynthia Kellogg, who died the same year of her marriage, leaving no issue; his last marriage was in 1869, to Helen Randall, who was born in this township on the farm adjoining, only daughter of S. S. Randall, one of the early settlers and prominent men in the township, now deceased. After his marriage, Mr. Tabler located on a portion of his father's land. In 1873, he located where he now resides, on Section 16, which was formerly owned by his brother Joseph, who improved it. Mr. Tabler has one of the finest locations in the township; he has a good brick house, and is making improvements of a substantial character on his premises; he has three children by his last marriage—Alice, Henry and Elizabeth; he is independent in political matters and liberal in religion.

JEROME R. TABLER, farmer, P. O. Morris, is the eldest son of Nathaniel Tabler by his second wife, Hannah Mary Cryder; he was born on the homestead March 2, 1853, and has since been a resident of the township, and now resides within a short distance of the place where he was born. He was married, July 27, 1876, to Mary A. Bradshaw, who was born October 14, 1854, in this county and township, eldest daughter of Hamilton Bradshaw, now deceased. After his marriage, Mr. Tabler lived one year on the homestead, but, since February, 1877, has been a resident of the farm he now owns, consisting of 100 acres. He is a progressive young man, an intelligent farmer and a successful one. They have one child—Albert Roy, born April 2, 1877.

LEWIS WESLEY TABLER, farmer, P. O. Minooka, is the third son of Nathaniel Tabler by his wife, Hannah M. Cryder; he was born November 8, 1856, on the farm where he now lives and where he has since resided. February 14, 1877, he was married to Anna L. Bradshaw, who was born December 28, 1859, on Section 8, in this township, daughter of Hamilton and Mrs. Hannah Bean Bradshaw, the latter's maiden name being Davis. Hamilton Bradshaw was born July 16, 1811, in Guernsey County, Ohio, son of William Bradshaw. Hamilton was married to Mrs. Bean, on December 21, 1853; she was born in the town of Woodsfield, Monroe Co., Ohio, July 8, 1822, only daughter of Dr. Ezekiel and Elizabeth (Large) Davis; she was born in Chester County, Penn., daughter of Robert and Sarah (Whittaker) Large. Dr. Davis was born in Boston, Mass., son of Levi and Hannah (Shepherd) Davis. Dr. Davis removed with his family West, to Muskingum County, Ohio, in 1826, and two years later was drowned, while crossing the river on his horse, on his way to see a patient. Hamilton Bradshaw removed West, to this county, in 1854, and located on the farm now owned by J. H. Murphy, on Section 8, where two children were born—Anna L., wife of C. W. Tabler, and Mary A. now wife of Jerome Tabler, both of this township. Mr. Bradshaw resided on that farm about fifteen years, when he located at Channahon, Will County, Ill., where he died July 31, 1868; his widow yet survives him; her first husband was Landon Bean, born April 17, 1817, in Belmont County, Ohio, son of Levi Bean; by Mr. Bean she had two sons and one daughter—Wesley R., David T. and Sarah E. Wesley is now a Methodist minister in Nebraska City, Neb. David T. is in the employ of a railroad company at Omaha. Sarah E. married Brainard Curtis, and resides in Russell County, Kan. Mr. Tabler resides on the homestead; he has two children—Hattie May and Oliver Wesley. He is a member of the M. E. Church.

JOHN T. VAN DOLFSON, farmer, P. O. Minooka. Of the early settlers in this township that have risen from small beginnings, making their commencement by hard months and continued years of manual labor on a farm at low wages, is Mr. Van Dolfson. His ancestors originally came from Holland, and settled in the Mohawk Valley, in New York State. His paternal grandfather was John T. Van Dolfson, only son of his father's family; he married a Miss Brunk; to them was born Tunis Van Dolfson, the father of our subject. Tunis married Elizabeth Ten Eyck, who bore him five children—Charlotte, Conrad Garritie, Elizabeth and John T., all of whom lived to attain the years of manhood and womanhood, and are yet living, save Charlotte, who married Ephraim Brunk, who first settled in this county, but afterward removed to Kendall County, where she died. Conrad resides in Chicago, and has three children. Garritie resides in Labette County, Kan., wife of Theran Collins, and Elizabeth resides in Kendall County, wife of W. H. Perkins. John T. was the youngest of the family, and is the only one of the name in the county; he was born April 5, 1822, in Albany County, N. Y.; his mother died when he was quite young. In 1838, he came to the West, and directly to this county; the following year, he went to Kendall County, where he hired out by the month. In the spring of 1843, he returned to this township, and, with his accumulated earnings, he purchased land where he now resides, paying therefor $3 per acre; there was a log cabin and about seventeen acres broken; here he settled and has since been a constant resident and a safe and successful business man, having accumulated a handsome property; he has been twice married—first, to Rachel Widney, December 7, 1848; she was born June 28, 1825, in Miami County, Ohio, daughter of John Widney; she passed to her rest in the "beyond" September 11, 1858, having given birth to two children, both of whom are now living —Mary E., wife of William H. Smith, of Will County, and William, residing near his father's, in this township. In 1864, Mr. Van Dolfson married Miss Sarah E. Ross, also a native of Miami County, daughter of Charles Ross, of Ohio; no children by last marriage; he is a member of Minooka Lodge, No. 528, A., F. & A. M., and was one of the charter members.

ZACHARIAH WALLEY, farmer, P. O. Morris. Among the old pioneers of this township is Mr. Walley, who was born November 1, 1807, in Washington County, Md., and son of Conrad and Catharine (Beard) Walley. Conrad Walley was a native of Germany; came to America when small, and settled in Maryland, where he married Catharine Beard, a native of that State, daughter of Zackariah and Mary Beard. Our subject removed with his parents, when ten years of age, to the vicinity of Zanesville, Muskingum Co., Ohio, and remained there about fifteen years; then removed to Delaware County, on the Scioto River; here, on attaining his majority, he run a saw-mill on the river for five years; then engaged in farming by renting. He married, September 22, 1831, Catharine, daughter of Henry and Mary Ann (Hess) Cryder. Mrs. Walley was born in Delaware County, Ohio, December 12, 1814. In the fall of 1833, Mr. Walley removed West, to this township, in company with Nathaniel H. Tabler and Henry Cryder, his father-in-law, all of whom settled in what is now this township. Mr. Walley settled first on Section 17, where he squatted, and, not liking the situation, lived there only one year, when, in the fall of 1834, he removed to his present place, took a pre-emption claim of 160 acres, and has since resided here and been engaged in farming. His wife died February 4, 1849, leaving seven children—Elizabeth, Susan, Maria, William and Sarah, all of whom raised families Emily deceased, aged twenty-two years, unmarried; Mary (deceased), married William Walker, now deceased. Those living now are Susan, wife of John McHanna, of Seward, Kendall Co., Ill., and Maria, in same county, wife of Peter Davis; William, residing in this township, and Sarah, resides seven miles south of Chatsworth, Ill., married Henry Netherton. February 6, 1851, Mr. Walley married Mrs. Eunice Kellogg, born in Madison County, town of Nelson, June 3, 1814, daughter of Daniel Warren and Sarah Lord, both of the State of Maine and who finally settled in New York. By this marriage three children have been born—Le Roy A., Catharine A., Antis Z. Le Roy died young; Antis Z. died, aged sixteen years nine months, and Catharine, at homestead, wife of Thomas Hague; they have two children—Ira Z. and an infant, unnamed. Mr. Walley has been identified with the M. E. Church since 1842; he was originally a Democrat, and first voted for Gen. Jackson, but since Buchanan's term has been a Republican. Mrs. Walley came to this State in 1830; settled first on the Vermillion, and came to this county and township in 1851; she has only one brother living —Nathan Warren, who lives in LaSalle County; her father died in LaSalle County, in September, 1831; her mother died September 20, 1834. Mrs. Walley has been a member of the M. E. Church since 1834.

WILLIAM A. WALLEY, farmer, P. O. ————, is the only son of Zachariah Walley, one of the pioneers of the county, and was born May 3, 1842, on the homestead, where he was raised to the years of manhood. February 23, 1868, he married Lonisa Pyle, a native of Belmont County, Ohio, daughter of Enos and Matilda C. (Harry) Pyle. Enos Pyle was born October 10, 1815, and, November 8, 1838, he married Miss Harry, who was born in Harrison County, Penn., June 28, 1816. The Pyle family came West in 1844, and settled in this county. Enos Pyle died May 9, 1877; his wife died September 4, 1859; they had seven children, among whom was one son who was a member of Company D, Thirty-sixth Regiment, of Illinois Volunteer Infantry, and was killed at the battle of Perryville. After Mr. Walley's marriage, he located in Saratoga Township, this county, where he purchased land and remained until the spring of 1882, when he purchased the Urich farm; he has three children—Bertha E., William Cryder and a babe unnamed. They lost Freddie November 7, 1877, five years and ten months old, and a promising child. Mr. Walley is a member of the M. E. Church, and is one of the Trustees and president of the board; is also a member of the prohibition society of this township. He is a Republican.

W. A. WORTHING, banking, Minooka, the proprietor and founder of the Exchange Bank at Minooka, was born in Mt. Pleasant, Iowa, in 1842, and removed with his parents to Kendall County, Ill., the year of his birth, and remained there until his location in Minooka, in the spring of 1866, where he has since resided. His father was Solon Worthing, whose father was a minister. The Worthing family trace their ancestry to England, from which place their progenitors emigrated at an early day, locating in the Eastern States. Solon Worthing, the father of our subject, was a native of New Hampshire and a farmer by occupation, to which vocation our subject was raised; he received the advantages afforded at the common district schools, and took a course at Oberlin College, where he graduated in the Commercial Department. Soon after his coming to Minooka, he engaged in the hardware business, and continued that business for fourteen years, and during this time was associated with several different parties in the business; he has 160 acres of land in Kendall County, and sixty-five acres in the corporation of Minooka. In the spring of 1880, he started the Exchange Bank at this place, and has since given it his especial attention, and is doing a good business, the bank being a great accommodation to the business men and farmers of the surrounding country, collections being attended to and remittances made promptly. In connection with his bank, he deals in agricultural implements, and does a good insurance business, representing some of the best companies, such as the Ætna, Hartford, Phœnix, Springfield, Mass., etc. He is also identified with the M. E. Church at this place; has been a member twenty-five years; also a Sunday school worker, and has been Superintendent of the school here several years. In the fall of 1864, he married Mary E. Avery, of Pittsfield, Lorain Co., Ohio, daughter of Carlos Avery.

E. N. WEES, blacksmith, Minooka. Among the representative business men of the town of Minooka, and who were among the first to become established in business here, is E. N. Wees, who came here in February, 1862, and immediately began the completion of his trade, which he had begun prior to his coming here. He was born May 9, 1843, in Upper Canada, son of John M. and Laura M. (Howell) Wees, both natives of Canada. His paternal grandsire was William Wees, who was of German stock; at the age of nineteen, Mr. Wees left Canada for the United States; he had been reared upon a farm, but had commenced learning the blacksmith trade prior to his leaving Canada; he arrived at Minooka in February, 1862, and worked in Wilmington and Platteville until the final completion of his trade, and, in the fall of 1865, he came to this town and set up in business on his own account, and has since continued, removing to his present place of business in 1868. In connection with his shop, he carries on the wagon-making business, and also a paint shop, and, being a thorough mechanic, he has been well patronized and has been successful in business. His inclinations toward stock-raising, farming and its attendant minutiæ, and he contemplates in the near future to give his attention to this enterprise. In April, 1864, he married Eliza Andrews, a native of Kendall County, Ill., daughter of Ambrose and Sarah A. (Wire) Andrews; they have had four children—Charles, Fred, Lottie and Allie. He is a member of the several Masonic organizations from the Blue Lodge to the Commandery, Minooka Lodge, No. 528, Orient Chapter and Blaney Commandery.

S. S. WATSON, merchant, Minooka, is located on the corner that was formerly occupied by Daniel Ferguson, a former business man of this place, now deceased. The subject of these lines was born January 25, 1848, in Ottawa, Canada; he is the third son of Southwell Watson, who was a native of County Down, Ireland, and who emigrated to Canada when a young man; he married Jane Strong, and by her raised a family of children, but two of whom are residents of Grundy County—Dr. I. S. and S. S. In 1866, Mr. Watson came to Chicago from Canada, and, three years later, to Minooka, where he engaged in business for a time, then returned to Chicago and engaged in the drug business with his brother. In 1878, he came back to Minooka and associated in business with H. T. Wheeler, under the firm name of Wheeler & Watson. This copartnership lasted but six months, when he purchased his partner's interest and has since conducted the business himself; he keeps a good stock of groceries, canned fruits, boots and shoes, ready-made clothing and furnishing goods, and is doing a successful business, being well patronized. July 28, 1880, he married Mrs. Libbie Ferguson, daughter of A. C. Worthing; she was the relict of Daniel Ferguson, one time a prominent business man of this place. Mr. Watson and wife are members of the M. E. Church. He is a member of Minooka Lodge, No. 528, A., F. & A. M.

H. T. WHEELER, merchant, Minooka, is the senior member of the firm of Wheeler & Sadler, the leading business firm of the town, and is one of the self-made young men of the county; he was born in Wiltshire, England, Jan. 13, 1852, son of Thomas and Ann (Dyer) Wheeler, both natives of the same place. Mr. Wheeler came to this country in the spring of 1870; came the same year to this county and located in this town. He worked for his uncle, John Dyer, on the farm in this county for two years; then engaged as clerk with D. Ferguson, with whom he stayed until Mr. Ferguson's death. Mr. Wheeler and Alex Ferguson bought this stock and carried on business under the firm name of Ferguson & Wheeler, about three years, when Mr. Wheeler bought out Mr. Ferguson's interest and carried on the business himself, for about one year, when, on account of ill health, he sold out and retired from business for a year. In September, 1881, he entered into partnership with Oliver B. Saddler, with whom, under the firm name of Wheeler & Saddler, he has since carried on business, and doing a good trade in dry goods, groceries, boots and shoes, hats, caps, clothing, notions, glassware and crockery, their business, which is the best in the town, having increased fully 50 per cent since they began business in 1881. Mr. Wheeler married Artie Greenly, a native of Will County, Ill., who has borne him two children—Elsie and Jessie.

MAZON TOWNSHIP.

JOHN ANTIS, physician and surgeon, Mazon, was born in Montgomery County, N. Y., in 1817, and early in life commenced the study of medicine, graduating from the College of Physicians and Surgeons of the Western University of New York, in the year 1838. He practiced his profession in North Brookfield, Madison County, N. Y., four years, and during that time, in 1840, married Miss Nancy A. Sweet, youngest daughter of Samuel G. Sweet. In 1841, they had born to them their eldest daughter, Eudora A. The same year (1841), Dr. Antis moved to Mixville, Allegany County, N. Y., and lived there four years, during which time his youngest daughter, Mary L., was born. In 1845, the Doctor moved to Morris, where he resided until 1879, when he moved out to his farm in Mazon Township, where he has enjoyed the full possession of health and happiness, and a large circle of friends and acquaintances. Thus have been chronicled the dates of the births and marriage of the Doctor and his estimable wife, whose lives have been intimately blended and moulded into the interests of the county and city of their adoption. They have lived to see their daughters married to cherished husbands, and they, surrounded by children, the pride of their parents. The lives of this aged pair have been a series of experiences from which they have learned to judge wisely and live properly, and are now looking forward to that great change when the man proper will separate from the man physical, and stand out in its own pristine worth, untrammeled by matter and its laws.

ABBOTT BARKER, farmer, P. O. Mazon, is a native of Washington County, N. Y., born January 12, 1823, son of Leonard and Hannah Barker, of New Hampshire. He was raised and educated in the common schools of his native State, came to Illinois and settled in Putnam County, about 1857. Here he lived until 1861, when he moved to his present residence in Mazon Township, Grundy Co. He took the trade of carpenter and joiner after coming to Illinois. He was married on March 5, 1856, to Miss Malinda Hopkins, of Putnam County, Ill. She was born May 1, 1830, and died in Mazon Township May 22, 1865. They had two children—Joel H., born January 31, 1860, and H. J., born January 16, 1857, and married, December 28, 1876, to Rev. A. D. Beckhart. April 17, 1866, Mr. Barker married the second time. They own a farm of 235 acres of improved land in Sections 5 and 8, of Mazon Township, land worth $50 per acre. Mr. and Mrs. Barker are members of Wauponsee Grove Congregational Church.

J. F. BURLEIGH, farmer, P. O. Mazon, was born in Livingston County, N. Y., March 24, 1824, and took an academic course of study in his native State. He is a son of John and Sarah E. Burleigh, of New Hampshire. He was married in the State of New York, October 28, 1847, to Miss Hannah J. Maynard of Wayne County, N. Y. She was born February 5, 1826, and died August 9, 1854. They had two children—Willis C., born July 29, 1848, died February 28, 1850 ; and Ella, born June 26, 1854. August 27, 1856, our subject married Miss Susan D. Underwood, who was born March 27, 1831 ; by this union there were born four children—Arthur, born July 24, 1860 ; Alice G., June 4, 1862 ; Ida J., December 6, 1863 ; and Irving C., April 22, 1870. Mr. and Mrs. Burleigh and the two older children are members of the Congregational Church of Wauponsee Grove. Our subject owns a farm of 240 acres of improved land in Section 4, Mazon Township, worth $60 per acre. He is a Republican, and has been repeatedly elected to the offices of his township. He is a member of the Masonic fraternity. The two elder children were educated at the Cook County Normal Institute. John and Sarah (Fellows) Burleigh, parents of J. F., were married at Salisbury, N. H., December 14, 1810; he was born in New Hampshire April 26, 1789, and died in the State of New York May 27, 1866; she was born in New Hampshire December 4, 1794, and died in the State of New York July 18, 1865. They raised a family of five children—John L., Catherine, Harriet, Joseph F. and Elizabeth A.

ISAAC N. CLITHERO, farmer, Mazon, was born in Monroe County, Ohio, January 13, 1833, and was raised and educated in his native State; he is a son of John D. and Jemima Clithero. He was first married, March 5, 1856, to Miss Sarah Taylor, who was born in Ohio September 24, 1835, and died April 2, 1858. They had one daughter—Mary V., born July 27, 1857, and died June 14, 1858. Mr. Clithero came to Illinois, and settled in Mazon Township, Grundy County, in December, 1862. He now has a farm of 140 acres of improved land, worth $60 per acre, in Sections 28 and 29. January 28, 1869, Mr. Clithero married Miss Jane E., daughter of William and Jane Pool, of Ohio. She was born December 23, 1843, in Monroe County, Ohio; the result of this union was three children—William T., born April 16, 1872; Addie V., born February 5, 1876, and an infant, born August 8, 1882. The family are members of the Methodist Episcopal Church of Mazon. Mr. Clithero is a Republican. John D. Clithero, father of our subject, was born November 25, 1803, and died March 9, 1880; Jemima Clithero, mother of our subject, was born March 6, 1806, and died June 14, 1881.

MELVIN CARTER, farmer, P. O. Mazon. The family of Abraham C. and Margaret A. Carter came to Illinois from Ohio in June, 1851, and settled in Mazon Township, Grundy County. The family consists of ten children—Abraham Carter, born in Belmont County, Ohio, October 17, 1818, and died in Mazon Township, March 2, 1876; his wife, Margaret Ann (Preston) Carter, a native of Tuscarawas County, Ohio, born June 14, 1826, is now living with her sons on the old homestead, which is controlled by the eldest son, Melvin, who was born in Guernsey County, Ohio, November 17, 1845; Sarah M., was born March 27, 1849, married to Alex Lee, November 11, 1867; Martha A., born October 21, 1851, died December 24, 1854; Lora and Flora were born March 29, 1854—Lora E. was married, June 27, 1876, to George W. Satterlee. Flora B. married September 1, 1879, to Marion Mecham; Amanda J., born August 27, 1857, married to Elwood Randal, October 9, 1880; Douglas P., born June 29, 1860; William H., born February 6, 1863; Amos A., born March 11, 1865; Frank B., born August 17, 1867. The Carter estate consists of 354 acres of valuable land in Sections 26, 27, 34 and 35, of Mazon Township, his residence being situated two and a half miles southeast of Mazon. Melvin Carter owns a farm consisting of a quarter section, in Sections 22 and 27, including dwelling house and other improvements, the land being valued at $60 per acre. He is among the solid farmers of Grundy County, and is engaged in stock-raising.

JOHN DRESSER, farmer, P. O. Mazon, was born in Stockbridge, Mass., December 12, 1813. While he was quite young, his parents, Samuel and Nancy Dresser, removed to Portage County, Ohio, where John was raised and received a common school education. At an early age he learned the trade of carpenter and joiner, at which he worked for several years. He was married in February, 1841, to Miss Betsey Morse; she was born in Massachusetts March 16, 1816, and died in Mazon Township

September 28, 1854. Soon after they were married, Mr. and Mrs. Dresser moved to Miller County, Mo., where they lived till 1851, when they came to Illinois, and located in Mazon Township, Grundy Co.; there in Section 4. Mr. Dresser owns eighty acres of improved land valued at $50 an acre. Mr. Dresser's second marriage occurred May 6, 1855, when he married Mrs. Betsey Jones, of Missouri, formerly of Ohio. She was born March 13, 1829. Mr. Dresser had by his first wife two children—Jacob, born in October, 1843, died in September, 1848; Mary, born May 7, 1849, died in October, 1871. By his second wife Mr. Dresser had the following children—Isaac M., born May 13, 1857; Martha E., born August 20, 1860 (married in November, 1877, to William Holmes); John E., born April 30, 1865, and Alma B., born September 5, 1867, died March 10, 1882. John Dresser cast his first vote for Andrew Jackson and has adherred to the same principles since.

S. H. DEWEY, farmer, P. O. Mazon Center, was born in Lewis County, N. Y., August 21, 1821; was raised and educated in New York, from whence, in 1855, he came to Illinois, and settled on the present site of the village of Verona, Grundy Co. In May, 1851, he married Miss Malissa Fisk, of Booneville, Oneida Co., N. Y. She was born November 24, 1828. At Verona Mr. Dewey bought a farm of eighty acres to which he added extensively in after years, owning at the present time 485 acres of farm land, worth $50 an acres in the townships of Mazon and Goodfarm of this county. Mr. Dewey is now a resident of the thriving village of Mazon Center, where he has lately erected a substantial dwelling. From 1872 to 1877, he was a resident of Morris, and being an ardent advocate of temperance, he was run for Mayor on the temperance ticket. In politics, he is a Republican, and has taken an active part in the business of the county. He served from 1873 to 1877, on the State Board of Equalization; also served several terms as Supervisor, and is now Justice of the Peace. Mr. and Mrs. Dewey have a family of six children—Ellen N., born in New York, (married to Horace H. Overocker); Alice E., born in New York, (married to Rev. D. W. Frances, of Pennsylvania); Milton S., born in New York (married to Miss Maggie Dewey, of Grundy County); Mary J., born in Grundy County; Lester S., born in Grundy County (married to Miss Dora Smith), and Flora born in Grundy County.

G. W. DANIELS (deceased) was born in Vermont June 8, 1818, and was married in New York January 9, 1843, to Miss Fidelia Belding, a native of Vermont, born August 17, 1816. By this union five children were born—Charles E., born November 6, 1846, married January 1, 1873; Sarah A., born April 20, 1849 (married June 10, 1873, to James Foster, of Indiana); L. E., born March 4, 1851; Ellen A., born December 1, 1854 (married February 8, 1875, to DeWitt Hinkle, of Iroquois County, Ills.), and William A., born March 5, 1856. The second son, L. E., has a farm in Section 16, Mazon Township. Mr. Daniels died October 20, 1882, from paralysis of the heart; he was a man highly esteemed in the community in which he resided, and figured prominently in the enterprises of his county. At the time of his death he owned a farm in Section 16, Mazon Township, worth $75 an acre, a portion of the village of Mazon Center being on his land. Mr. Daniels taught school for some time, and held the office of School Treasurer. He was a Democrat and a member of the Masonic fraternity, Blue Lodge and Knights Templar.

J. K. ELY, farmer, P. O. Mazon, son of James G. and Rebecca E. Ely, was born in Oneida County, N. Y., December 2, 1837. He was educated in Rock River Seminary, became qualified for teaching, which he followed in LaSalle and Grundy Counties for seven years. He enlisted at Chicago on the 12th of August, 1862, in Company H, Eighty-eighth Illinois

Volunteer Infantry, with which he continued until discharged at the close of the war. Took part in the battles of Stone River, Chickamauga, Chattanooga, Mission Ridge and Dalton, and marched with Sherman to Atlanta, Ga., where he was wounded July 20, 1864, after which he saw no more field service. September 5, 1864, he married Miss Lovina J. Mossman, daughter of William and Mary Mossman, of Iowa. She was born April 12, 1845. They have a family of two sons and four daughters—Rubie M., Lena G., May R., Nellie V., John M. and William Ray. Mr. Ely owns 320 acres of valuable land in Sections 4 and 5, of Mazon Township. His father, James Ely, died in 1844, his mother, Rebecca, is now living with our subject. He is a Republican and Justice of the Peace of Mazon Township. Mrs. Ely is a member of the Congregational Church. Mr. Ely first settled in Nettle Creek Township in 1847.

OWEN H. FULLER, grain and lumber, Mazon Center, is a native of Onondaga County, N. Y., born January 19, 1834, and came to the town of Mazon with his parents in 1839, they being among the first settlers of the county. His father, Hiram Fuller, took an active part in the early history of this county. He died at the home of O. H. Fuller, in Mazon Township, April 13, 1872. Our subject was married, July 31, 1853, to Miss Weltha Isham, daughter of G. Isham. Mrs. Fuller was born in Vermont October 23, 1836, and has borne five children—Olney B., born December 18, 1860; Alta A., born November 1, 1863; R. Dale, born December 10, 1865; Olin M., born December 30, 1867; and Erlan G., born December 25, 1875. Alta A. was married June 11, 1882, to O. S. Viner of Mazon Township. Mr. Fuller is associated with A. O. Murray in the grain and lumber trade at Mazon Center; they own an elevator near the Chicago, Peru & South Western Railroad. Mr. Fuller is a Democrat, and has been repeatedly elected to the offices of the township. He is now Notary Public.

V. L. FULLER, farmer, P. O. Mazon, was born in Onondaga County, N. Y., May 10, 1836. His parents, Hiram and Mary Ann Fuller, settled in Mazon Township, Grundy County, when our subject was but three years old, and three years before the organization of the county; at that time there were but three or four families in the township. Mr. V. L. Fuller was raised a farmer, and now owns a farm of eighty acres of improved land in Section 17, of Mazon Township, the land being worth $55 per acre. Mr. Fuller was married, February 13, 1859, to Miss Sofrona, daughter of Josiah and Lavina Tuck, of Maine. She was born February 13, 1830, and is the mother of five children—Will C., born January 11, 1860; Cora L., March 23, 1862; George W., April 26, 1865; Frank E., June 20, 1867; and Mary A., May 2, 1872. Mr. Fuller is a Republican; is Deputy Sheriff of the county, and has served the county as Constable for seventeen years. Josiah Tuck, father of Mrs. (Tuck) Fuller, was born in Maine June 19, 1799, and died in Grundy County February 6, 1875; his wife, Lavina Tuck, was born in Maine April 19, 1807, and died at the home of her daughter, Mrs. Fuller, November 25, 1881.

PERLEY E. FULLER, farmer, P. O. Mazon, was born in Grundy County January 6, 1847, and was raised and educated in this county. He is a son of Richard and Cornelia Fuller, natives of Ohio; the father died in Mazon Township in November, 1880; the mother was born in September, 1824, and is now living in Mazon Township, with her daughter, Mrs. Hough. Our subject was married September 24, 1871, to Miss Mary A., daughter of John and Margaret Hough. She was born in Newport, R. I., July 6, 1852, and is the mother of two daughters—Mabel A., born August 18, 1872, and Valley V., born January 20, 1879. Mr. Fuller has a farm of eighty acres of improved land, in Section 22, of Mazon Township, worth $65 per acre. Both Mr. and Mrs. Fuller are members of the Methodist Episcopal Church of Mazon. He is a Republican and an ultra temperance advocate.

SILAS W. GIBSON, farmer, P. O. Mazon. S. W. Gibson was born in Saratoga County, N. Y., February 24, 1842, and came to Grundy County, Ill., with his parents when less than one year old. He attended the first school organized in Mazon Township, in the old Fuller Schoolhouse, Constance Hulse and Lafayette Doud being among his first teachers. He is the second of a family of four children of Robert C. and Elizabeth (Largent) Gibson. His father was born in the Green Mountains of Vermont, in 1811, and died in Morris May 10, 1882. The mother was a native of Ohio, and died in Grundy County March 29, 1867. Our subject was married, October 2, 1866, to Miss Clarissa C. Lattimer, daughter of Silas and Mary Lattimer. She was born in Indianapolis, Ind., November 22, 1848. They have a family of four children —Orrel B., born November 27, 1867; Robert S. G., December 20, 1869; Burton I.; Clara E.; Mr. Gibson enlisted in Company I, Sixty-ninth Illinois, and served three months, then enlisted in 100-day service in Company H, One Hundred and Thirty-eighth Illinois Regiment; was detailed on garrison duty, principally in Missouri and Kansas. He is a Republican, a member of the I. O. O. F. and one of the leading farmers of Grundy County. He owns the old Robert Gibson farm, consisting of 300 acres in Sections 10 and 11; his residence is three and a half miles northeast from Mazon. He is engaged in stock-raising and general husbandry. Mrs. Gibson's parents are living in Felix Township, Grundy County.

OREN GIBSON, farmer, P. O. Mazon, was born in Grundy County, Ill., September 24, 1846; son of Robert and Elizabeth Gibson, who are among the earliest settlers of this county, coming here in 1836. His mother was among the number whose lives were spared by the timely warning of the friendly chief, Shabona. His father was born in Landgrove, Vt., May 4, 1811, and died in Morris May 4, 1881; the mother was born in Urbana, Champaign Co., Ill., October 19, 1821, and died March 29, 1868, in Mazon Township. Our subject was educated at Aurora, and afterward took a course at Bryant & Stratton's Business College, Chicago. He was married October 6, 1869, to Miss Mary R., daughter of William Fuller, of Mazon Township. She was born August 10, 1852, and is the mother of five children—Orma, born December 11, 1870; Enid, July 16, 1872; William R., June 5, 1874; Stella M., May 9, 1876; and Vivian born December 17, 1881. Mr. Gibson owns 385 acres of improved land in Sections 3, 10, 22 and 27 of Mazon Township; also two houses in Mazon. He is filling some of the offices of the township, and is a member of the Masonic brotherhood and I. O. O. F.; he is a Republican. Mrs. Gibson is a member of the Methodist Episcopal Church.

ROBERT GLENN, farmer, P. O. Verona, is a native of County Antrim, Ireland, and a son of Robert and Mary Glenn. He was born September 12, 1835; came to the United States, June, 1857, in the vessel "Empire State," and settled in this county the same year. He now owns 335 acres of improved land, including one dwelling and 175 acres in Sections 30 and 31 of Mazon Township, and 160 acres in Section 21 of Vienna Township, the land being worth $55 per acre. He was married in Grundy County, December 31, 1866, to Miss Catherine Thomas, daughter of Thomas and Jane Thomas. She was born in Wales September 20, 1845, and came to the United States in 1860. They have a family of three children, all born in this county—Mary, born September 27, 1867; Anna E., born December 1, 1870; Robert James, born March 11, 1875. Robert Glenn, father of our subject, is now living in Vienna Township, Grundy County.

HENRY HOLDER, farmer, P. O. Verona, is a son of Henry and Sarah Holder, born March

MAZON TOWNSHIP.

24, 1839, in Manchester, England. His parents emigrated to the United States in 1848, and settled in Pittsburgh, Penn., where they remained two and a half years, then removed to Illinois, and located in Kendall County, near Plattville, where they lived until they came to Grundy County in 1862. His mother died in Mazon Township February 13, 1866, and his father in February, 1877; both are buried in the Ward Cemetery. Our subject was educated in the common schools of Pennsylvania and England. He now owns a farm of 160 acres of land in Section 19, Mazon Township, valued at $50 per acre, his residence being located two miles west from Mazon. He has a younger brother, William, who was a soldier from Will County, Ill., in the late war. Mr. Holder is Independent in politics.

TURNER B. HOUGH, farmer, P. O. Mazon Center, is a native of Newport, R. I., and was born April 14, 1850. When he was seven years old, his parents, John and Margaret Hough, emigrated to Illinois, and settled in Kendall County. In the spring of 1863, they removed to Grundy County, and the next year settled in Mazon Township, where they are now living on their farm of 160 acres, in Section 20. Our subject received a common school education, and September 18, 1872, married Miss Eda A. Fuller, born in Mazon Township April 1, 1855. They have two sons and a daughter—George T., born July 7, 1873; Nettie C., March 30, 1875; and Harrie L., May 27, 1876. Mr. Hough owns a farm of 115 acres of cultivated land in Section 22, Mazon Township, adjoining the village of Mazon, valued at $75 per acre. Mrs. Hough is a member of the Methodist Episcopal Church. Mr. Hough is a Republican.

M. ISHAM, merchant, Mazon, is the fourth of a family of nine children, and was born June 7, 1829, in Chittenden County, Vt. When he was young, his parents, Gersham and Annie Isham, removed to St. Lawrence County, N. Y., where they lived until 1844, when they came to Illinois, and settled in Mazon Township, this county. Our subject was married, March 4, 1855, to Miss Ellen, daughter of George Jenkings, of Michigan. She was born September 13, 1834, and is the mother of six daughters—Rosa, born October 20, 1856, married to George W. Clow, March 19, 1876; Alice J., born March 14, 1858, married to Frank Myers, December 25, 1877; Nellie V., born February 22, 1860, married to John Wilkinson, March 8, 1881; Almyra, born May 22, 1863; Laura M., born March 6, 1865; and Katie V., born April 17, 1869. Mr. Isham has a farm of eighty acres of improved land in Section 28, Mazon Township, worth $50 per acre. He is engaged in the general mercantile business in the village of Mazon, in which he resides. He is a Democrat.

ZACH ISHAM, farmer, P. O. Mazon Center, is a native of Vermont, and was born February 11, 1831. When he was seven years old, his parents removed to the State of New York, and settled in St. Lawrence County, where they lived until 1844, when they came to Illinois. They first settled in McHenry County, where they lived one year, then came to Grundy County, and have been residents of Mazon Township since. G. Isham, father of our subject was was born in Vermont March 3, 1801, and died in Mazon Township October 6, 1878. Mr. Isham was married, November 30, 1854, to Miss Susan S. Viner, of Mazon Township. She was born November 22, 1835. They have a family of eight children, of whom but three are living. Mr. Isham now owns 240 acres of land in Section 21, Mazon Township, the town of Mazon Center being laid out on his land. The value of his farm land is $75 per acre. Mrs. Isham is a member of the Methodist Episcopal Church of Mazon. Mr. Isham is one of the solid business men of his township, combining the interests of farming with business of a general character connected with the village of Mazon Center. He manifests a public spirit in the enterprises of his community, giving liberally to the fund for the erection of the Methodist Episcopal Church building of the village. His mother, Eliza Isham, was born in Hinesburg, Vt., February 22, 1802, and is now living in Mazon with her son, Jehial Isham. The mother raised a family of nine children, our subject being the fifth child.

SALEM IRONS, farmer, P. O. Mazon, is a native of Worcester County, Mass., born October 18, 1823. When he was fourteen years old, his parents, James and Phœbe Irons, removed to Rhode Island, where they remained several years. Subject came to Grundy County, Ill., in 1854, and bought land in Mazon Township, where he now owns 145 acres of cultivated land, in Sections 9 and 10, worth $50 per acre. He was married, in Rhode Island, to Miss Harriet, daughter of James Yaw, of Rhode Island; she was born in Rhode Island December 15, 1823. They have a family of three children—Henry A., born in Rhode Island June 14, 1850, married to Miss May Keith; Maria, born in Grundy County May 4, 1855, married to T. H. Roseman, of Mazon Township; and Clara L., born October 26, 1858, married to Fred Keith, of Mazon Township. Mr. Irons is a member of the Masonic fraternity, and is a township official. His residence is one and one-quarter miles north of Mazon. He is a Republican.

D. C. JACKSON, farmer, P. O. Mazon, is a son of John and Elizabeth Jackson, of the State of New York, and was born in Schoharie County, N. Y., April 4, 1819, in which State he was raised and educated. He was married, in 1844, to Miss Rhoda, daughter of James and Nancy Brown; she was born in 1823, and died in Albany County, N. Y., in April, 1846. The result of this union was one son, John, born August 4, 1845; killed at the battle of Cold Harbor. In 1865, Mr. Jackson came to Illinois and settled in Mazon Township, where he owns a farm of eighty acres of land, worth $50 per acre, in Section 29. Subject was married to Mrs. Elizabeth Traver, widow of David Traver, August 27, 1865; she is a native of Schoharie County, N. Y., born February 25, 1830. This union has blessed them with four children—Annie E., born February 6, 1867; Laura M., born July 3, 1872, died March 17, 1874; Frank, born April 10, 1873; and Minnie B., born March 25, 1875. The family are members of the Wauponsee Grove Congregational Church. Mr. Jackson is a Democrat.

J. C. KELTNER, grain, Mazon Center, was born near Dayton, Ohio, December 10, 1832. When he was quite young, his parents, John and Nancy Keltner, removed to Indiana and settled in Elkhart County, where they lived until the time of their death, and where James C. was raised and received a common school education. He came to Illinois and to Grundy County in October, 1854, and engaged at his trade as carpenter and joiner, which he had acquired in Indiana, and at which he worked for ten years. He was married, in Grundy County, February 17, 1858, to Miss Sarah A., daughter of James and Elizabeth McKeen, of this county; she was born April 20, 1839, and is the mother of six children, two of whom are deceased—Benjamin F., born February 17, 1859; Columbus, July 8, 1862; Lulu M., June 18, 1864; William C., January 2, 1866; James A., August 7, 1870; and Venice, January 3, 1881. Mr. Keltner owns a farm of eighty acres, worth $50 an acre, in Section 23 of Mazon Township; his residence is one mile east of Mazon Center. He is engaged in the grain trade at the village of Mazon, also in the stock business, in which he is associated with Charles H. Overocker.

PERRY F. LANDPHERE, farmer, P. O. Mazon, was born in Cayuga County, N. Y., April 23, 1834. He is a son of Silas and Nancy Landphere, of Cayuga County, N. Y., where his father died in 1837. His mother subsequently married a Mr. Hyslop, and is now living in Morris, this county, and is sixty-six years old. Subject came with his mother and step-father to this county in 1845; they settled in the town of Vienna. Mr. Landphere was married, April 28, 1867, to Miss Rhoda Jackson, born in Guilderland, Albany Co., N. Y., September 15, 1849, and came to Illinois in March, 1867. They have lost one child in infancy, born February 21, 1874; the second child, Allen DeWitt, was born August 22, 1882. They have two adopted children. Mr. Landphere owns a farm of 240 acres of valuable land in Sections 18 and 29 of Mazon Township and Section 11 of Vienna Township. They are members of the Congregational Church at Wauponsee Grove. In politics, he is Republican.

HIRAM MENAUGH, farmer, P. O. Mazon. During the war of 1812, Mr. Menaugh's parents were living in the southern part of what is now Indiana, then Indiana Territory. They were compelled to flee into a fort, near Frankfort, Ky., for protection against the Indians, and in this fort our subject was born December 25, 1812. In the year 1811, his brother, Col. John L. Menaugh, was captured by the Delaware Indians, and was afterward retaken from them at Vincennes, Ind.; he died in June, 1879, after serving the country in various capacities for many years. Hiram Menaugh was married, near Salem, Ind., October 4, 1832, to Miss Martha Patlock, who was born in South Carolina November 25, 1813. Mr. and Mrs. Menaugh came to Grundy County in the spring of 1844, when there were but few families in their township. They have a family of five children—Robert; Elizabeth, married to Charles Nance; James, who died October 11, 1878; Martha, born in Grundy County, married Henry Baird, died April 20, 1876; and Ferriday, born in Grundy County, and married to William Howe, of this county. Mr. Menaugh owns a farm of eighty-eight acres, worth $55 an acre, in Section 27 of Mazon Township; his residence is one and one-half miles southeast of Mazon.

ROBERT D. MENAUGH, farmer, P. O. Mazon, was born in Washington County, Ind., July 21, 1833, son of Hiram and Martha Menaugh. They came to Illinois in the spring of 1844, and settled in Mazon Township, where they are still living. Robert was married July 24, 1856, to Miss Harriet J., daughter of Daniel Rowen; she was born in Ohio, December 4, 1833. Their family consists of nine children—Lora E., born August 1, 1857; O. L., August 27, 1859; Laura A., March 17, 1861; Lida B., June 3, 1863; James M., March 12, 1865; Robert R., May 12, 1867; Luella A., September 1, 1869; Hiram A., October 20, 1873; and Volany W., December 17, 1878. Mr. Menaugh owns a farm of 240 acres of improved land, worth $45 an acre, in Section 33 of Mazon Township. He is a Democrat.

AUGUSTUS O. MURRAY, grain and lumber, Mazon Center, was born February 9, 1832, in Oswego County, N. Y. When he was three years old, his parents, Jonathan C. and Permelia M. Murray, removed to Illinois and settled in Mazon Township, Grundy County, seven years before the organization of the county. The father is remembered as one of the first men in the early enterprises of the county. He was drowned in the month of June, 1844; the mother died in Ottawa, Ill., in February, 1870. Subject was married, October 18, 1852, to Miss Lydia A. Isham, of Vermont, born May 15, 1835. They have a family of two sons and five daughters—Louis R., born March 6, 1859, married to Sarah E. Riggall December 25, 1881; Ella L., born December 16, 1860, married to Fred Kingman December 31, 1879; Hettie P., born August 24, 1862; Frank A., July 10, 1864; Gertie E., September 4, 1868; Eva W., February 16, 1871; and Maud, May 22, 1876. Mr. Murray owns 430 acres of cultivated land in Sections 23, 25, 26 and 33 of Mazon, also 110 acres in Black Hawk County, Iowa. He is associated with O. H. Fuller in the grain and lumber trade at Mazon Center, of which place he is a resident. Mrs. Murray is a member of the Methodist Episcopal Church of the village of Mazon. Mr. Murray is an ultra temperance advocate.

CHARLES H. OVEROCKER, stock-dealer, Mazon, was born in Oneida County, N. Y., October 21, 1838, and educated at Whitestown, N. Y. He was married, November 1, 1859, to Miss Amanda M. Roscoe, of New York. She died in New York October 9, 1864. Subject enlisted, August 13, 1862, in Company A, Tenth New York Artillery, with which he was connected until mustered out in May, 1865. He was engaged at Cold Harbor and Petersburg. Was in the hospital at Albany, from November, of 1864, until mustered out. His second marriage occurred December 31, 1867, when he espoused Miss Sarah E. Allison, of Grundy County. Subject has one son by his first wife, and three children have blessed his present union—Milton, born in New York; John H., Freddie H. and Lenora B., all three born in Grundy County. Subject is a member of the Masonic fraternity and Knights Templar. He cast his first vote for A. Lincoln in 1860.

HORACE H. OVEROCKER, farmer, P. O. Mazon, is a son of Jacob Overocker, born in Oneida County, N. Y., September 28, 1850. In that State he was raised until sixteen years old, during which time he received a common school education. He is the youngest of a family of six children, and was left an orphan when quite young, after which he was reared by an aunt. With this aunt and his brother C. H. Overocker, he came to Illinois in the fall of 1866, after which he was employed as a farm hand until he attained his majority, since which time he has farmed for himself. He was married, November 26, 1874, to Miss Nellie M. Dewey, daughter of S. H. Dewey, of Mazon Township. She was born in Lewis County, N. Y., May 30, 1852. They have one son, Berton H., born in Grundy County December 11, 1875. He owns a farm of 220 acres of improved land in Sections 9 and 10, of Mazon Township, worth $55 per acre. His residence is located seven miles south from Morris and one and three-quarters north from Mazon. In politics, he is a Republican.

JAMES PAXTON, farmer, P. O. Mazon, is a son of Samuel and Sarah Paxton, was born in Guernsey County, Ohio, December 3, 1819, and came to Illinois in the spring of 1848, having married, September 28, 1843, Miss Phœbe A. Keepers, daughter of Joseph and Hannah (Jordan) Keepers. They settled in Mazon Township, Grundy County, and bought eighty acres of land, which Mr. Paxton at once improved. To this he added from time to time, and now owns 400 acres—240 in Section 32 of Mazon Township and 160 acres in Section 5, of Goodfarm Township. This land is worth $60 per acre. Mr. and Mrs. Paxton have a family of eleven children—Sarah B., born June 13, 1844, died August 4, 1846; Joseph K., August 18, 1846; Hannah M., born February 26, 1849, died August 18, 1851; Samuel J., born September 9, 1851; Harriet L., born February 23, 1854, married November 23, 1875, to James M. Warnock, of Ohio—he died December 16, 1877; Philena J., born July 13, 1856, died August 20, 1859; Phœbe E., born February 7, 1859, married November 27, 1879, to Nathan Klinefelter; James E., born February 7, 1859; William E., born July 23, 1861; George M., born October 13, 1866; and Mary E., born October 13, 1866. Mr. and Mrs. Paxton and daughter Harriet L. are members of the Church of God, of Goodfarm Township. Their residence is situated three and three-quarter miles southwest of Mazon.

GEORGE PAXTON, farmer, P. O. Verona. The subject of these lines is a native of Guernsey County, Ohio, born June 8, 1834, son of Samuel and Sarah Paxton, formerly of Pennsylvania. When he was fourteen years old, his father moved to Illinois, his mother having died in Ohio. His father settled in Mazon Township, Grundy County, about 1849, educat-

MAZON TOWNSHIP.

ed in Ohio, married November 15, 1855, to Miss Martha A. Preston, daughter of Elijah and Martha Preston. She was born in Guernsey County, Ohio, May 9, 1839. They have a family of one son—Elmer E. Paxton, born in Grundy County, Ill., May 13, 1865. Mr. Paxton now owns a farm of eighty acres in Section 31; residence, five miles southwest from Mazon. Samuel Paxton, father of our subject, died in Mazon Township, Grundy County, October 22, 1852. Mrs. Paxton's father, Elijah Preston, died in Grundy County, only two months after their arrival, August 15, 1851. Martha A. Preston died in Grundy County, December 17, 1867.

WILLIAM PRESTON, retired, Mazon, is a native of Ohio, born November 6, 1825; was raised principally in Guernsey County, Ohio; is a son of Elijah and Martha Preston, and is the second of their family of nine children. Was married, in Ohio, May 18, 1847, to Miss Phœbe Randall, daughter of Hunter and Margaret Randall, of Guernsey County, Ohio. Mrs. Preston was born July 30, 1825. They have a family of five children—Sparks, born June 1, 1848, died May 13, 1858; Nancy Jane, born April 24, 1852, died June 2, 1853; Alexander, born November 19, 1854, married to Annie Kagan; Harlin, born February 23, 1856, married to Susan Hamilton April 29, 1877; Marion, born June 16, 1858, died August 22, 1860. Mr. Preston came to Illinois, settling in Grundy County in 1849, and bought land in the township of Wauponsee. He has since sold this and bought 213 acres of cultivated land located in Section 5, of Goodfarm Township, and Section 32, of Mazon Township, valued at $50 per acre. He owns two lots and a handsome residence in the village of Mazon. Mrs. Preston is a member of the Methodist Episcopal Church. Elijah, father of William Preston, was born April 16, 1799, and died of cholera taken at Chicago when hauling lumber for his buildings, August 15, 1851. Subject's mother, Martha (Wheatley) Preston, was born October 3, 1799, and died in Mazon December 17, 1867. The father and mother were married March 22, 1820.

GEORGE B. ROBINSON, farmer, P. O. Morris. The subject of this sketch is a son of Mitchell and Maria Robinson, formerly of Michigan, born July 18, 1833, in Cass County, Mich. His father, Mitchell Robinson, was a native of Virginia, and died in Michigan, where he had moved from Ohio, in 1832. His mother, Maria (Colwell) Robinson, a native of Kentucky, also died in Michigan. Subject was raised and educated in Michigan. Married, in Mazon Township, January 8, 1858, to Miss Margaret E. Roseman, daughter of Joseph and Tabitha Roseman, born in Guernsey County, Ohio, May 16, 1838. The family consists of ten children, all living with parents, as follows: Vena B., born December 1, 1858; Joseph E., December 16, 1859; Rosa M., September 22, 1860; Hettie E., March 15, 1862; Maud E., September 28, 1865; Mamie A., April 6, 1869; Eva S., April 12, 1872; Tracy L., March 2, 1876; Clarence M., April 27, 1878; Ernest, May 31, 1882. Mr. Robinson owns a farm of 160 acres of improved farm land, in Sections 7 and 8 of Mazon Township, and 160 acres in Section 13, of Vienna Township, valued at $60 per acre. His residence is located four miles northwest from Mazon, eight miles southwest from Morris. In politics, he is a Democrat. Mrs. Robinson's parents are dead.

CHARLES ROBINSON, farmer, P. O. Mazon, was born in Chenango County, N. Y., April 12, 1837. Was raised and educated principally in Michigan and the State of New York. He is a son of Dow A. and Betsey Robinson, who settled in Kankakee County, Ill., in 1859. They removed, four years after, into this county, and located in Felix Township, where the father died in February, 1876. After the death of his father, Charles took charge of the business of the family. His mother died at his residence in Mazon Township September 30, 1880. He was married, March 15, 1871, to Miss Elizabeth Flanders, of Vermont. She was born February 22, 1841. Bore him five children—Eugene, born February 15, 1872, died January 27, 1880; Frank, born October 3, 1873; Millie, October 10, 1874; Alice, November 12, 1876, and Cora A., December 16, 1877. Subject owns a farm of eighty acres in Section 10 of Mazon Township. His land is valued at $55 per acre. His residence is seven miles south of Morris, and one and three-fourths miles north of Mazon. Mr. Robinson is a Republican.

T. W. ROYAL, farmer, P. O. Mazon, was born in Miami County, Ohio, January 25, 1823; is a son of Charles and Mary Royal, formerly of Virginia. On coming to Illinois, they settled near Newark, now Kendall County, and there our subject was raised and received his education. Mr. Royal was married, March 22, 1845, to Miss Amanda Goodrich, born in Chenango County, N. Y., March 4, 1824; she is the daughter of Gardner and Nancy Goodrich, who came to this county in 1844. Mr. and Mrs. Royal have five children—G. C., born September 16, 1848, married February 14, 1869, to Miss Sarah Hinkley, of Massachusetts; George F., born July 25, 1851, died August 23, 1851; A. B., born December 26, 1853, married, September 17, 1879, to Miss Belle C. Jaqnith, of Michigan, she was born May 10, 1856, and is the mother of one child—Henry J., born July 6, 1880; E. Royal was born December 17, 1857, and was married April 27, 1880, to A. D. Wood, formerly of New York. A. B. Royal was educated in the classical schools of Newark and Morris, is a graduate of Rush Medical College of Chicago, and is practicing in Lyon County, Kan. Mr. and Mrs. Royal and their son Dr. A. B., are members of the M. E. Church, in which T. W. Royal has been a local preacher for sixteen years; he is also a member of the Masonic fraternity.

A. J. ROBB, farmer, P. O. Mazon. The subject of this sketch is a native of Brown County, Ohio, born October 10, 1825, son of James and Rosana Robb, who settled in Wauponsee Township, in 1834, being among the first dozen families in the county. Subject was then nine years of age, and for many years had no school privileges. The father had a family of six children, of whom A. J. was the oldest; sometimes employed a teacher to come to his house to teach his children. James Robb, subject's father, died in Wauponsee Township in 1855; his wife is still living at Marseilles, Ill., in her seventy-sixth year. Mr. Robb was married, October 18, 1846, to Miss Betsey Hulse, daughter of Henry Hulse. She was a native of Trumbull County, Ohio, born in 1815 and died at their home in Mazon Township January 10, 1880. Mr. Robb has a family of four children—Emery and Emeline, born August 21, 1848; Emery was married in November, 1878, to Miss Sadie Pummell, of Grundy County; Henry W., born February 13, 1850, died December 14, 1856; Wesley W., born February 13, 1857, married February 16, 1879, to Miss Dora Clow, of Grundy County. Subject has a farm of eighty acres of improved land in Section 3, of Mazon Township, two and one-half miles north from Mazon and six and one-half miles south from Morris. Engaged in general husbandry. There is but one other settler now living who has been in the county as long as Mr. Robb; that one is Mr. L. W. Claypool, who came here at the same time.

THOMAS RANKIN, merchant, Mazon, is a son of Duncan and Elizabeth Rankin, and was born December 15, 1857, in De Kalb County, Ill. When he was nine years old, he removed with his parents to Morris, where he was principally educated. His father afterward moved to Braidwood, where he is still engaged in business. Subject was married, April 24, 1878, to Miss Ada Lish, daughter of John and

MAZON TOWNSHIP.

Susan Lish, of Essex, Ill. She was born January 7, 1859. They have one son—William F., born November 11, 1881. Mr. Rankin came to Mazon, February 14, 1879. and engaged in general mercantile business. One year after, he established the Mazon Creamery, with which he is doing a flourishing business. He is a Republican.

WILSON SMALL, hardware, Mazon Center, is a native of Somerset County. Maine, born January 1, 1843. When he was twelve years old, his parents, Harris and Sophrona Small, moved to Illinois and settled in Highland Township, Grundy County, where our subject was educated in the common schools. He enlisted July 31, 1861, in Company G. Thirty-sixth Illinois Volunteer Infantry, in which he served three years. He was mustered out September 23, 1864. at Atlanta, Ga.; he participated in the battles of Pea Ridge, Perryville, Stone River and Jonesboro. He was married, December 23, 1868, to Miss Philena C. Mooney, daughter of H. B. and Mary L. Mooney, of Grundy County. Mrs. Small was born in Essex County, N. Y., May 5, 1848, and is the mother of seven children—Ira M., born in Grundy County June 29, 1870 ; Guy W., born in Grundy County October 11, 1871 ; Clarence H., born in Grundy County March 3, 1873 ; G. Winnefred, born in Grundy County May 27, 1875 ; Ina V., born in Grundy County August 27, 1876 ; Raymond, born August 28, 1878, died August 12, 1882 ; and Ida May, born July 21, 1882. Mr. Small owns a farm of eighty acres of cultivated land, valued at $50 per acre, in Section 2. of Highland Township. He is engaged in the hardware trade at Mazon Center ; is a Republican and a member of the Masonic fraternity. Blue Lodge, of Verona, No. 757.

MILLARD SMALL, farmer, P. O. Verona. The subject of this sketch, Mr. Millard Small, is a native of Somerset County, Me., born July 31, 1850, and came to Grundy County, Ill. when four years old. He is the fifth of a family of six children of Harris and Sophrona Small ; was educated in Grundy County, and raised on the farm. He was married, July 4, 1875, to Miss Imogene Ward, daughter of Samuel and Harriet Ward, born on the farm now occupied by Mr. Small, in Mazon Township, March 3, 1852. They have two sons—George H., born March 19, 1876 ; Byron C., October 24, 1880. They own a farm of 113 acres in Section 30 of Mazon Township, valued at $50 per acre. Mrs. Small's parents came to Grundy County spring of 1849, and settled in Mazon Township, where they lived. until the time of their death. Her father, Samuel Ward, was born in July, 1825 ; died in Mazon Township June 17, 1881, from injuries received on the railroad near his home. He was struck by the engine while attempting to reach a crossing, seeming not to realize the near approach of the train from the fact of his being somewhat deaf and lame. Harriet Ward, mother of Mrs. Small, died in this county on the 27th of August, 1881, after suffering as an invalid for fourteen years.

SAMUEL G. SINCLAIR, farmer, P. O. Mazon, was born in Canada June 6, 1822, son of Jonathan and Betsey (Warner) Sinclair, who moved to Franklin County, N. Y., when Samuel G. was quite young. They afterward removed to St. Lawrence County of the same State, in which our subject received a common-school education. May 22, 1845, he married Miss Rhoda, daughter of Silas and Paulina Daniels ; she was born August 27, 1824, in Westport, N. Y. Mr. and Mrs. Sinclair have a family of nine children : Celestia, born July 31, 1846, married January 10, 1866, to George Eells ; Sophia, April 24, 1848, married September 19, 1875, to William Bennett ; Lefa P., April 18, 1854, married December 22, 1871, to Henry Burnam ; Emma, July 26, 1850, died in infancy ; Adelia M., April 18, 1854, married March 22, 1879, to Robert Howe ;

Francis I., March 16, 1858; Henrietta A., August 9, 1861; George E., June 2, 1865, and Artie W., October 29, 1866. Mrs. Sinclair is a member of the Methodist Episcopal Church. Mr. Sinclair owns eighty acres of land in Section 21, Mazon Township, adjoining the village of Mazon. This land is worth $50 an acre.

THOMAS SYMONS, farmer, P. O. Mazon, is a native of Devonshire, England, born December 13, 1818, and was raised and educated in England. He was married March 1, 1853, to Miss Elizabeth, daughter of John Vale, of England; she was born March 1, 1821. Mr. Symons came to the United States and to Grundy County in 1857. He settled in Nettle Creek Township and bought eighty acres of land, which he has since sold. He removed into Mazon Township, where he owns a farm of five hundred and twenty-five acres of improved land in Sections 2, 5 and 15, valued at $50 an acre. Mr. and Mrs. Symons have a family of four children—J. W., born in England February 11, 1854, and died in England May 15, 1855; W. H., born in England March 28, 1855; Charles, born in England May 7, 1856, died in Grundy County December 28, 1874, and S. B., born in Grundy County December 18, 1857. Mr. and Mrs. Symons and oldest son are members of Wauponsee Grove Congregational Church.

GEORGE P. THOMAS, farmer, P. O. Mazon, is a native of Oneida County, N. Y., born September 14, 1835, and was raised and educated in the State of New York. He was married in Oneida Co., N. Y., July 4, 1860, to Miss Sarah J. Richardson, who died in New York in 1861. Mr. Thomas enlisted in Company F, Twenty-sixth New York Volunteer Infantry, April 26, 1861, and served about four years, having re-enlisted in the Eleventh New York Cavalry. He participated in the battles of Cedar Mountain, Rappahannock Station, second battle of Bull Run, Chantilly, South Mountain, Antietam and others; he was discharged in July, 1865, and then came to Illinois, and located in Mazon Township, Grundy County. Mr. Thomas was married, September 22, 1868, to Mrs. Sarah A. Preston, born September 23, 1838, widow of Asbury Preston, of Grundy County, by whom she had one daughter—Abbie, born in February, 1864. Mr. and Mrs. Thomas have one son—Benjamin N., born November 21, 1869. Subject has 120 acres of improved land in Section 8, of Mazon Township, valued at $50 per acre; his residence being located seven and one-half miles south of Morris. Benjamin N. Thomas, father of our subject, was born in 1809, and is living in Oneida County, N. Y. His mother, Luraney R. (Burlingame) Thomas, was born November 19, 1811, and died in June, 1856. Mr. Thomas is a member of the Masonic fraternity.

ANN WALKER, farmer, P. O. Mazon, is the widow of Lazenby Walker, born in Ohio, August 4, 1829. She is a daughter of John D. and Jemima Clithero, married March 18, 1852. The family consists of six children— William D., born January 7, 1853, died July 15, 1859; Isaac B., born January 18. 1855; Harriet J., born March 8, 1857, died June 30, 1858; Thomas W., born April 16, 1859; Eddie W., born October 31, 1861, and Oliver L., born December 8, 1863. They have a farm of 200 acres in Section 28, of Mazon Township. The following is the notice of the death of her husband, Lazenby Walker, one of Grundy County's noblest soldiers:

"How sleep the brave, who sink to rest
By all their country's wishes blest!
When spring, with dewy fingers cold,
Returns to deck their hallowed mold;
She then shall dress a sweeter sod
Than fancy's feet hath ever trod.

"By fairy hands their Rude is rung,
By forms unseen, their dirge is sung;
There, honor comes, a pilgrim gray,
To bless the sod that wraps their clay;
And Freedom shall awhile repair
To dwell a weeping hermit there."

Died, at Post Hospital, in the city of Brownsville, Cameron Co., Texas, Lazenby Walker, of Company D (Capt. Fosha's), Ninety-first Illinois Volunteer Infantry.

The deceased was born at Belleville, in the State of Ohio, A. D. 1826, and was, at the time of his death, thirty-seven years of age. He enlisted on the 11th day of August as a volunteer soldier in response to the call of the President of the United States for the purpose of aiding in putting down the rebellion. At the time of his enlistment, he resided at Mazon, in the county of Grundy, Ill. Brother Walker was a good and faithful soldier, always ready to do his duty as a soldier in every particular. He had only one fault, and that cost him his life. That was his zeal in the cause in which he had cast his all. For three months, the disease of which he died, chronic diarrhœa, had been preying on his system, before he reported himself on the sick list; and when he did, he was so exhausted and so ill that, our regimental hospital tent not having been brought up from Brazos Island, I sent him to the post hospital at Brownsville, where he could get comfortable quarters for his enfeebled body. There he continued over four weeks. Part of the time he seemed to improve until the 13th, when he failed rapidly in strength, and expired on the morning of the 14th of December. He was buried with military honors in the soldiers' burying ground, of Fort Brown, December 15, 1863.

"Then let him like a warrior sleep,
The green turf on his breast;
And where the summer roses bloom,
They laid him down to rest."

Brother Walker was a good citizen and neighbor, beloved and respected by all who were acquainted with him. At home, he was the same as in the regiment. He had no enemies. As a father and husband, he was always at his post, kind, warm-hearted and affectionate. To mourn his loss, he leaves a wife and four children, besides an aged father and mother. No more will they behold his manly form No more with smiles of pleasure will they be greeted on his return from the labors of the day. No more will she hear his voice, so pleasant and agreeable to her he loved so well. No more will his dear children, for whose enjoyment he could sacrifice so much, see their noble father again. He is gone!

"He'll come no more as once he came,
A partner's heart to cheer,
To bring the smiles of pleasure back,
Or stay the falling tear."

Brother Walker was not only a good citizen and soldier, but he was more. He was a good man and a Christian. Following in the footsteps of his worthy father, years ago he was converted to God, joined the Methodist Church, and by his Godly walk and conversation convinced all that he was what he professed, a meek and humble follower of the Lamb.

Although the summons came in early manhood, it did not find him unprepared. A few hours before he breathed his last, he became satisfied that his hour of departure had come. He gave some directions to Capt. Fosha about his funeral, which he requested should be carried out, spoke of his dying far away from home, from wife and children, from father and mother, expressing a wish to see them all once more on earth. But saying it was impossible (as he felt the cold damp of death on his brow) "I yield to Him who doeth all things well. I go to my Father's house, a house not made with hands, eternal in the heavens."

"Behold the Christian warrior stand,
In all the armor of his God;
The Spirit's sword in his right hand,
His feet are with the Gospel shod.
 *   *   *   *   *
"Thus strong in his Redeemer's strength,
Sin, death and hell he trampled down;
Fights the good fight, and wins at length,
Through mercy, an immortal crown."
DAVID LEROY,
Surgeon Ninety-first Illinois Volunteers.

J. C. WHITMORE, farmer, P. O. Mazon, was born in Middletown, Conn., April 25, 1831, son of D. C. and Sarah Whitmore, who moved from Connecticut to Ohio when John C. was but three years old. Here he was soon deprived of the care of his mother, who died in December, 1837. Mr. Whitmore was first married, August 27, 1859, to Mrs. Emma T. Sitterly, widow of Silas Sitterly, of Connecticut; she was born December 13, 1822, and died in Mazon Township March 13, 1877; she blessed Mr. Whitmore with two children—Hattie E., born November 19, 1861, married February 1, 1882, to Irvin F. Traver, of Grundy County; and Harry C., born October 2, 1866. Mr. Whitmore was again married, June 6, 1882, to Mrs. Mary M. Moore, of Brookfield, N. Y., born April 3, 1839. She was the widow of Frank Moore, of the State of New York. She has one daughter—Marian F. Moore, born in Brookfield, N. Y., May 15, 1869. Subject has 120 acres of finely improved land, valued at $60 per acre, in Section 9, of Mazon Township; his residence is situated two miles north of Mazon and seven miles south of Morris. Mr. Whitmore is a Republican and a member of the Wauponsee Grove Congregational Church.

GEORGE WHEELER, farmer, P. O. Mazon, was born in Grundy County February 20, 1851. Raised on the farm and educated in the common schools of the county. He was married, October 11, 1871, to Miss Jennie Keepers, of Ohio, who was born March 16, 1854. They have one daughter—Effie P. Wheeler, born March 11, 1877. Residence three and one-half miles southeast from Mazon. Mr. Wheeler is a son of H. H. and Amanda R. Wheeler, of Morris; they own 160 acres of valuable land in Section 35, of Mazon Township. Mr. Wheeler owns a farm of 160 acres of improved land in Section 2, of Goodfarm Township, and Section 35, of Mazon, valued at $45 per acre.

WAUPONSEE TOWNSHIP.

JOSEPH ASHTON, farmer, P. O. Morris, was born in Delaware County, Penn., in September, 1820, and lived there until he became twenty-two years of age, when he, with his parents, moved to Kendall County, Ill., and settled near Lisbon, where they bought a farm. Mr. Ashton now owns a farm of 190 acres, in Sections 19 and 20, of Wauponsee Township. This land is worth $45 an acre; 150 acres of the farm is under cultivation. On the 21st of February, 1865, Mr. Ashton married Miss Rachel Hager, daughter of Godfrey Hager, of Virginia. Mrs. Ashton was born June 12, 1840, in Illinois, and is the mother of three children, viz., William E., Sarah L. (deceased) and John A. Mr. Ashton is a Republican.

MICHAEL BERRY, farmer, P. O. Morris, was born in Ireland in 1829, and came to this country with his parents in 1837. They first settled in Athens County, Ohio, but, in the fall of 1840, removed to Grundy County, Ill., where the father of our subject assisted in the construction of the Illinois & Michigan Canal. Mr. Berry was married, in June, 1851, to Miss Mary Harney, a native of Ireland, born in 1828. She is the mother of four children, viz., Bridget B., born in 1854, and married, February 12, 1878, to William Foley; Kate E., born in 1856, and married, November 25, 1879, to William McCabe; Anna A., born April 25, 1858, and married, February 13, 1882, to Michael Moran; Ella M., born February 26, 1861, unmarried. The entire family are members of the Catholic Church at Morris. Mr. Berry owns a farm of eighty acres in Section 17, all under cultivation. In February, 1862, Mr. Berry enlisted in Company K, Fifty-third Illinois Volunteers, and served three years; was taken prisoner at Jackson, Miss., and held at Richmond prisoner until he was exchanged, when he returned to his regiment, after an absence of about ten months. He was twice reported among the killed, and initial steps were taken to recover his back pay. In politics, Mr. Berry is Republican.

JOHN CLAYPOOL, farmer, P. O. Morris, was born in Wauponsee Township January 5, 1837, son of Perry A. and Mary (Foster)

Claypool. Our subject was the third white child born in this county, his father settling here in 1834; the latter, while hauling logs from Chicago to Morris, was kicked by his horse, from the effects of which he died October 15, 1846. Mary (Foster) Claypool, the mother of our subject, is still living. Mr. John Claypool received his education in Morris, where he attended the first day school ever organized there. He was married, April 7, 1859, to Miss Elizabeth Hume, born in England May 15, 1837, daughter of Edward Hume, who came from England with his family and settled in New York State, where they remained until about 1858, when they came to Wauponsee Township, Grundy County, Ill. Here Mrs. Claypool's father died, in January, 1859, and her mother September 17, 1879. Mr. and Mrs. Claypool have three children, as follows: Jennie M., born May 2, 1860; Abel, born April 11, 1862, and John E., born July 11, 1868. Mr. C. owns 408 acres of land. He is a Republican, and has filled a number of offices in his township.

P. G. COSGROVE, farmer, P. O. Morris, was born in County Roscommon, Ireland, March 17, 1811, and was raised on a farm. He came to the United States in April, 1840, and worked in Pennsylvania for two years on canal and railroad; he then went to Canada, where he was engaged on public works for the following two years; then came to Chicago, where he worked until August 15, 1846, when he began steamboating on the Mississippi River. In the spring of 1853, he went to California, where he worked in the mines for three years. Returning to Illinois, he settled in Wauponsee Township, Grundy County, on his present farm of 160 acres, which is all under cultivation, and valued at $50 an acre. Subject was married, February 17, 1833, to Miss Annie Kattican, of County Roscommon, Ireland, born October 22, 1808, and died in Wauponsee October 15, 1874. She bore him one son—Redman, born November 10, 1837. He was married, February 27, 1869, to Miss Mary Nolen, who was born July 10, 1849; they have had seven children—Mary Ann, born April 21, 1871; Martin, June 5, 1872; Margaret, April 16, 1874; Catherine, November 1, 1875; Seva, February 24, 1877; Pabuck, March 18, 1879; Nellie, November 10, 1882. Our subject has an adopted son—Daniel, born in 1855.

HENRY CLAPP, horticulturist, Morris, was born April 7, 1825, in Addison County, Vt. When our subject was six years old, his parents moved to St. Lawrence County, N. Y., where he received a common-school education. In October, of 1846, he settled in McHenry County; coming to Grundy County in 1847. he located in Mazon Township, where for four years he engaged in farming. He next lived upon a small farm in Greenfield Township, which, after five years, he sold, and made purchase of his present farm of eighty acres, situated in Section 15, of Wauponsee Township, two and one-half miles southeast of Morris. Here he carries on a very lucrative business in small fruits and market gardening. November 22, 1857, in Pontiac, Ill., he married Mrs. Pyrena Dugan, born May 15, 1817. She was the widow of Robert Dugan, of Wauponsee Township. Mr. Clapp is a Republican.

ORSON BINGHAM GALUSHA, P. O. Morris, was born December 2, 1819, in Shaftsbury, Bennington Co., Vt. His father, Jonas Galusha, Jr., lived at the time of the birth of the subject of this sketch on the estate of his father, Gov. Jonas Galusha, who was at that time serving his second term as Governor of the State. Orson was the youngest of three children, having one sister,

Eloisa Electa, and one brother, Joseph Hinsdale. He lived upon his grandfather's estate, his father having charge of the several large farms into which it was divided, until sixteen years of age, in the meantime receiving such educational advantages as the district school afforded, and also was sent one year to Union Academy, in Bennington. At the age of fourteen, he united with the Baptist Church, and continued in the communion of this denomination until 1844, when he united with the Congregational Church, in Grand Rapids, Mich., and is now a member of that church. In 1834, his father removed to Rochester, N. Y., where he lived four years, for the purpose, mainly, of giving his children better facilities for education, and at the same time have them at home, and here Orson was placed under the tuition of Chester Dewey, D. D., of the Rochester Collegiate Institute. He also taught one year under Prof. Nathan Brittan, his brother-in-law, in the Fitzhugh Street Seminary. Owing to the failing health of his mother, his father resolved to try a Western climate, in 1839, and removed to a farm near Grand Rapids, Mich. Soon after the arrival of the family there, the mother died, and the father and brother returned to Rochester, while he remained in Michigan about fifteen years, during which time he occasionally taught school in winters, working upon the farm during summers. In this period, he served almost constantly, after attaining his majority, in the capacity of School Inspector and Township Clerk. March 9, 1843, he was married to Mary J., third daughter of Judge Mitchell Hinsdale, of Kalamazoo, who is now living. In the year 1849, he exchanged his real estate in Michigan for a small farm in Grundy County, Ill., situated on the north line of the county, and two miles from Lisbon, Kendall County; he soon engaged in the nursery business, which he carried on there until his removal to his present residence, where it was at once resumed. During his residence at Lisbon, the agitation of the plan for a system of agricultural colleges took place, and in this project he took a deep interest, frequently writing and talking upon the subject. When the plan was finally adopted by the Congress of the United States, he was the first man appointed by the Governor of Illinois as a member of its Board of Trustees, to take charge of the 480,000 acres of land which fell to the share of the State, and to found a college and to start it in operation. He was elected Recording Secretary of the board, which position he held until after the inauguration of the enterprise and the college was in successful operation, and remained a member of this board for the term of six years, and until the number of the members of the board was considerably reduced, by act of the Legislature. In 1864, he was elected a member of the State Board of Agriculture, and re-elected in 1866, holding the position for four years, during which time and for several years, both previous and afterward, he was Superintendent of the Horticultural Department at the State fairs. But the principal and most valuable public services rendered by Mr. Galusha were within the Illinois State Horticultural Society. This society was organized in Decatur in 1856, and Mr. Galusha elected Corresponding Secretary, which position he held till December, 1861, when he was elected to the Presidency of the society. He continued in the gratuitous service of the society, traveling thousands of miles annually as member of the "Ad-interim Committee," collecting horticultural information for publication in the annual volume; was re-elected Corresponding and Recording Secretary in 1869, and has continued in this position until the present time, with the exception of one year, when he declined re-election, on account of severe illness at the time of the annual meeting. During these years, he has annually edited and published a volume of the transactions of the society, about 400 pages each. In 1868, he sold his farm on the county line and purchased where he now lives, three miles southeast from Morris, to which place he removed a large portion of his nursery stock, and continues in this business, gradually reducing it, however, and planting and raising fruits for market. This eighty-acre fruit farm is known as the Evergreen Fruit Farm. Mr. and Mrs. Galusha have had two children—one a son, buried in Paris, Kent Co., Mich., who died at the age of four years; the other, a daughter, Nellie H., born October 4, 1849, and now the wife of Prof. W. H. Smith, of Peoria, Ill.

JOSEPH D. HILL, farmer, P. O. Morris, was born in Franklin County, Ohio, August 26, 1822, but spent most of his boyhood in Delaware County. When twenty-one years of age, he came to Illinois, and bought some land in Pike County. At this time, he also entered a tract of land in Mazon Township, Grundy County. After returning to Ohio and remaining there about seven years, Mr. Hill, September 24, 1854, married Mrs. Margerotta Nicholas, born September 29, 1827, when he moved to his land in Mazon Township, which land he sold in 1865, and moved into Wauponsee Township, where he now owns 280 acres of improved land, in Sections 21 and 22, situated four miles southeast of Morris. This land is valued at $65 an acre, and produces fine crops of corn, oats and hay. Mr. and Mrs. Hill have but one child—Homer D. Hill, born in Adams County, Ind., June 5, 1856, who was married, January 7, 1880, to Miss Flora Case, born March 24, 1856, daughter of Morris and Caroline Case, of Delaware County, Ohio. Our subject is one of the stalwarts of Grundy County. He enlisted a company of men for the ranks, in the early part of the rebellion, but, owing to physical disability, was obliged to place them in charge of Capt. Fosha. Mr. Hill and his son are both Republicans.

HORACE HOYT, gardener, Morris, was born in New York in April, 1811; was raised and educated in Oneida County, N. Y., where he engaged in mercantile pursuits until 1857, when he came to Morris. Here he continued the mercantile business for five years, when he sold out and went to Mexico, where he was engaged for one year in buying, compressing and shipping cotton. After a trip East, he came back to Morris, where for the past six years he has been engaged in market gardening. He is located one mile south of Morris, on sixty acres of well-cultivated land, the soil of which is well adapted to the raising of such produce as he handles. He has one son—Harris Hoyt, born in New York September 17, 1841; has buried two sons and one daughter. Mrs. Hoyt is a member of the Congregational Church of Morris. Mr. Hoyt is a member of the Society of Friends, of Rochester, N. Y., and belongs to the Republican party.

PETER A. JOHNSON, farmer, P. O. Morris, was born in Sweden March 24, 1843, son of John and Hannah Johnson, both natives of Sweden. In the spring of 1853, John Johnson started with his family for the United States. On his voyage, he and two of his sons died of cholera. Peter and the rest of the family reached New York City safely and came immediately to Morris, where the subject received his education, principally in the Morris Normal and Scientific Institute. At the age of eighteen, he enlisted in Company D, Thirty-sixth Illinois Volunteer Infantry, Capt. W. P. Pierce; term of service, three and one-fourth years. He participated in the battles of Pea Ridge, Shiloh, Perryville, Stone River and Chickamauga. At the last-named battle, he received a wound, resulting in permanent injury. May 7, 1864, he married Miss Elizabeth Claypool, daughter of Perry A. Claypool. She was born August 18, 1845. They have a family of four children—Perry A., Frederick S., Frank A. and Nellie. Mr. Johnson's farm is situated three miles south of Morris, and consists of 240 acres of well-improved land, upon which he has erected a handsome residence. He is one of the prominent men of Wauponsee Township, being a first-class farmer and an active Republican. Mr. and Mrs. Johnson are both members of the M. E. Church at Morris.

WILLIAM JACKSON, farmer, P. O. Morris, was born in Norfolk, England, November 17, 1829, where he was raised and educated. He came to Grundy County, Ill., while quite a young man, and located in Morris. The year following, he bought a farm of 120 acres, in Section 1, of Mazon Township, which he still owns. He has since purchased 240 acres in Section 36 of Wauponsee Township, where he now lives. His entire farm of 360 acres is valued at $50 an acre. Subject was married, November 14, 1864, to Amelia, daughter of George Lane, of Canada; she was born in 1847, and is the mother of three children—John W., born in 1869; Walter, 1873; Freddie, 1875. Mrs. Jackson is a Methodist.

MOSES PANGBURN, farmer, P. O. Morris, was born in New York State November 30, 1802, and lived there until 1855, when he moved into Wauponsee Township, Grundy County, where he bought eighty acres of land in Section 14, which he has since traded for 120 acres in Sections 15 and 27. In 1856, he bought the forty acres on which he now lives. He was married, September 25, 1828, to Miss Kate Sitterley, of New York State, born March 3, 1805. She died in Wauponsee Township March 19, 1865. They raised a family of eight children, viz., Martin, Stephen, James M., Clarissa A., Charlotte, Eliza M., John H. and Caroline A. Mr. Pangburn is now living with his daughter, Caroline A., now Mrs. Spencer, who was married August 30, 1871, to David E. Spencer, of Grundy County; he was born October 25, 1842. They have five children—Charles O., Edna M., Walter W., Clarence E. and Kate M. David E. Spencer was a soldier in the late war, serving two years and ten months. He enlisted April 1, 1862, in Company M, First Illinois Artillery, and was transferred, after ten months, to another battery; he served six months on vidette duty for Brig. Gen. A. W. Elliott, and participated in the siege of Vicksburg and battle of Port Gibson; he was discharged February 1, 1865.

JOHN A. SUMMERS, farmer, P. O. Morris, was born in Freetown, Cortland Co., N. Y., March 11, 1824, son of Nicholas and Mary Summers. When our subject was four years old, his parents moved to Onondaga County, N. Y., where they remained nine years; they then came to Illinois and settled in Wauponsee Grove, where the father died in October of 1839. Mr. Summers came to this county some years before it was organized as such, and attended the first school taught here. It was held in the house of the teacher, Mrs. Dewey. In 1838, subject's father built the first house of the county; it was situated south of the river, and was roofed with joint shingles. John Summers began the trade of carpenter and joiner, under the instruction of his father, at which trade he worked for several years, in and around Morris. He has a vivid recollection of having to grind the breadstuffs for the

WAUPONSEE TOWNSHIP.

family in a common coffee-mill, the severe freezing weather rendering the grist-mill useless for weeks at a time. In 1852, he bought eighty acres of farm land in Section 21, of Wauponsee Township, which he sold in the spring of 1882; has recently bought 320 acres in Douglas County, Dakota Territory, where he will soon move his family. Mr. Summers was married, May 25, 1854, to Miss Matilda R. Summers, of Ohio, born in March, 1835. They have a family of eight children —Clara C., born in 1855; Fred E., 1857; Hortense J., 1858; Edgar D., 1860; Emily M., 1862; Harry M., 1866; Helen M., 1869; John G., 1872.

OWEN SWEENEY, farmer, P. O. Morris, was born in County Cork, Ireland, in 1817, and was raised a farmer. In 1846, he came to the United States, and settled in Boston, where he was engaged in day labor for four years. In 1851, he came to Kendall County, Ill., Lisbon Township, where he bought eighty acres of land. Here he remained about four years, when he rented his farm and moved to Morris, Grundy County, where he remained eleven years; while living here, he sold his farm in Kendall County. He next bought a farm of 103 acres in Wauponsee Township, on which he lived three years; selling this, he bought a farm of 120 acres in Section 33, of the same township. This land, upon which he now lives, is valued at $50 an acre. Mr. Sweeney was married in Boston, in 1850, to Miss Mary Carey, a native of Ireland, born June 25, 1825. This union has resulted in six children, viz., Ellen, born August 26, 1856; Alice, born September 23, 1854, and married, April 11, 1882, to Edward Higgins, of Mazon Township; Mary Jane, born December 17, 1859; John W., born June 27, 1861; Dennis J., born July 12, 1864, and Annie S., born May 8, 1867. The entire family are members of the Catholic Church of Morris. Mr. Sweeney is a Democrat.

HENRY THUM, farmer, P. O. Morris, was born July 9, 1848, in Chautauqua County, N. Y., and was the son of Melchart and Oret (Clark) Thum; he was born in Herkimer County, N. Y., December 31, 1804, and died in Wauponsee Township August 29, 1872. The subject's mother, Oret Thum, was born in Ellery, Chautauqua Co., N. Y., August 16, 1817, and is now living with her son Henry. The parents of Henry Thum settled in Grundy County, Saratoga Township, when he was nine years old; here they remained four years, when they moved into Wauponsee Township, and, in 1864, purchased a farm of eighty acres, which the subject now owns and lives upon. He was married, December 27, 1876, to Mrs. Jennie Wagner, of Pennsylvania. She was born July 6, 1849, and is the daughter of Samuel and Nancy Miller, the former born December 10, 1820, died June 11, 1878; the latter was born in 1823, and died April 17, 1856. Miss Ella C. Thum, sister of Henry Thum, and a member of his family, was born in Chautauqua County, N. Y., May 26, 1854. Mr. and Mrs. Thum are the parents of two children—Laura A., born October 21, 1877, and George H., born January 3, 1879.

JOHN THOMPSON, farmer, P. O. Morris, was born in Canada July 4, 1835, son of James and Hannah Thompson. About 1838, his parents moved to Dresden, Grundy Co., Ill., where they lived for some years, and where the mother of our subject died the first year after their arrival. John's father next bought a farm in Wauponsee Township, to which they removed, and where the father died April 12, 1880. Mr. John Thompson was married, March 10, 1856, to Miss Mary Jane Thompson, daughter of David Thompson, of Ireland. She was born in 1835, and died at their residence, in Wauponsee Township, May 12, 1882. The family consists of three children, viz., James, born August 29, 1857; Susan, born October 12, 1859, and Samuel, born August 2, 1865. Mr. Thompson owns 120 acres of good farm land, in Sections 17 and 30, of Wauponsee Township. This land is valued at $50 an acre, 100 acres of which are under cultivation. He is a member of the Episcopal Church, and a Republican in politics.

SAMUEL WOOD, farmer, P. O. Morris, was born in England January 4, 1824, and lived there until 1850, when he came to the United States, and settled in Pennsylvania, near the Ohio line. Here he worked one year in a brick-yard and in a coal-bank. He next went to Canada and worked in the copper mines for some months. From Canada he came to Peoria, where he worked for two years at mining, at the end of which time, the spring of 1854, he settled in Morris, where he and Daniel Williams opened the first coal bank ever started in the vicinity of Morris. For the next ten years, he worked at farming in the summer and mining in the winter. April 24, 1855. Mr. Wood married Miss Maria Claypool, born February 2, 1840, daughter of Perry A. and Miss (Foster) Claypool, who were among the first families to settle in Grundy County. Mr. Claypool was born in Ohio, June 5, 1815, and died October 15, 1846. Mrs. Claypool was born April 24, 1819, and is still living. Soon after his marriage, Mr. Wood bought eighty acres of land in Section 17, Wauponsee Township, which he has added to until he now has 195 acres, valued at $50 per acre, and all under cultivation. Mr. and Mrs. Wood have a family of five children—David, born November 26, 1862; Charles, born December 9, 1865; Sarah, born October 25, 1868; James, born December 13, 1872, and Mary, born May 17, 1875. They have also buried four children. Mr. and Mrs. Wood are members of the Methodist Episcopal Church.

GREENFIELD TOWNSHIP.

ZELOTES J. ANDREWS, farmer, P. O. Gardner, was born in Oneida County, N. Y., July 7, 1840, son of William S. and Amanda (Convis) Andrews, natives of New York State; the father was a farmer by occupation, and died in 1878, aged seventy-eight years; the mother, who is still living, was born in 1814, and had four children, of whom our subject was the youngest child; he received a common-school education and followed the occupation of farming; came to Illinois in 1857, and located in Kendall County; came to Grundy County in 1874, and now carries on a general farming business. December 22, 1870, he married Miss Alice Convis, who was born in Oneida County, N. Y., in 1851; she is the daughter of Andrew and Rachel Convis, natives of New York State, he living, she dead. Mr. and Mrs. Andrews have four children, viz., Ralph, Arthur, May and Mate, the two last being twins. Our subject has been Street Commissioner several terms, and also School Director; he is a Republican.

H. C. ATKINSON, blacksmith, Gardner. Mr. Atkinson ranks among the leading blacksmiths of this county. He began learning his trade with H. Hart, of this village (Gardner), with whom he remained for two years. October 19, 1877, he opened a shop on his own resources, and is

GREENFIELD TOWNSHIP.

now making a specialty of horse-shoeing. It is only justice to say that but few are his equal in this branch of smithing. He is a son of R. Atkins, a popular coal dealer of this village, who started life in this country with only $15. The father is a native of Ireland, and came to America May 3, 1839.

O. J. BOOTH, retired farmer, P. O. Gardner. The subject of this sketch, whose portrait appears in this history, was born in Trumbull County, Ohio, April 8, 1824; his father and mother were natives of Connecticut, the former born in 1794; followed farming for a livelihood; died in June, 1842. The latter was born March 16, 1794; is still living, but feeble with age. Their names were Truman and Rebecca (Percey) Booth; to them were born nine children, eight of whom grew to maturity. O. J. received such education as the common school of his native town afforded. In the spring of 1840, when in his sixteenth year, he visited Illinois; then railroads were not built, and young Booth took stage from Warren to Wellsville, and then a boat down the Ohio and up the Mississippi to St. Louis, where he arrived in eight days; his finances were now reduced to $1 good money, and a $2 bill that he had received unsuspectingly on a broken bank; he invested his $1 in crackers and cheese and reshipped for Peru, offering all he had left, the poor note, to the Captain in payment of fare; his note was refused, and he was threatened with being "put ashore" but was finally allowed to stay aboard, nibbling sparingly the while, about five days, on his crackers and cheese; he helped a man carry his baggage from Peru to Ottawa, and for his service received dinner, supper and lodging. He started from Ottawa at 3 o'clock the following morning, and walked to his uncle's, at Georgetown, now Newark, twenty-five miles, before breakfast. This line from life's record shows something of the push and courage that have ever characterized the man, and given him in business more than ordinary success. Returning to Ohio upon the death of his father, he took charge of the farm and looked after the interests of the family. Mr. Booth was married, January 4, 1844, to Miss Sarah Hulse, native of the same county, born May 5, 1824, dying August, 1876. He came with his family to Illinois in the spring of 1846, and located in Mazon Township, buying forty acres of Government land. By industry and economy, he added to this from time to time, until he owned over 500 acres. His fields were well cultivated, and his thoroughbred stock of cattle and hogs were admired by all who saw them. In the spring of the present year, he sold his farm and moved to Gardner, where he now resides. Mr. and Mrs. Booth had nine children, three of whom, viz., Rocelia, Wesley and Amelia, are dead; the latter grew into womanhood, and was engaged in teaching when she contracted her fatal disease. Permelia, Judson and Frank are in Kansas, the two former being married. Emma, Adora and Minnie are at home. Mr. Booth, while he has looked carefully to his finances, has been given to hospitality, not turning the worthy poor empty away. Mrs. Booth was a careful, devoted wife and mother, and to her the family are indebted largely for its success. Mr. Booth has been a Republican since the organization of the party, and was delighted with the overthrow of American slavery; he has watched over his children with zealous care, in every way guarding them from temptation and wrong, and has the satisfaction of seeing them grown up, esteemed for their virtues by all, and to him a solace in his declining years.

BENJAMIN BOOKWALTER, farmer, P. O. Gardner, was born July 31, 1831, in

Pennsylvania, is the son of Abraham and Elizabeth (Witmer) Bookwalter, also natives of Pennsylvania, and the parents of ten children, nine of whom grow up—Mary, John, Daniel, David, Samuel, Anna, Benjamin, Elizabeth and Michael. The family came to Greenfield Township in 1854, where they bought a large tract of land at $9 per acre, a portion of which had been entered by Dr. Abbott, an early settler. The father died on this farm, in June, 1872, and the mother in July, 1882. They were Mennonites. Mr. B. attended the country schools, obtaining but a slight education; he has always devoted his time to rural labors. He was married, in 1859, to Susan Barkey, a daughter of Enos and Eve (Sigler) Barkey, early settlers of Mazon Township; she was one of five children—Susan, Sigler, John, Enos and Jude. Mr. B. now has 660 acres of well-improved land, well adapted to stock-raising, to which he is applying his personal attention; he has raised some of the fastest horses in this country, among which is Troubadour and Chicago Maid; he is also raising Durham cattle. He has served the township as Trustee and Road Commissioner, and votes the Republican ticket. He is the father of four children, two of whom are living—Emma and Abraham, each of whom has received a good education, having attended the Normal, McLean County. Miss Bookwalter ranks among the best musicians in this county, and is giving instruction to many.

MICHAEL BOOKWALTER, farmer, P. O. Gardner, was born in Pennsylvania April 7, 1835; is a brother of Benjamin, whose sketch appears elsewhere; his life has also been spent on the farm. He was married, in 1861, to Sarah, a daughter of George B. and Rebecca (Somers) Kulp, natives of Pennsylvania; her parents came to this county about 1854; their children were four — Joseph, Sarah, Jacob and Alvin; the mother survives, living in Iowa. Our subject has five children as a result of his marriage, three of whom are living—Rebecca, wife of John Robertson; Minerva E. and Alice C. Mr. B. settled for awhile after his marriage on his father's farm. In 1874, he located on his present farm of eighty-four acres; he has in all 240 acres of fine land, on which he is raising fine stock; his first wife died, and, in 1873, he was again married, to Mary Konline; he took an interest in educating his children. He votes the Republican ticket.

ELIZABETH BAUMGARDNER, teacher, Gardner. The father of our subject, John Baumgardner, was born in the Canton of Glarus, Switzerland, May 1, 1825. He started for America April 15, 1849, landing at New Orleans. The mother, Magdalena (Bahr Baumgardner, was born near Wurzburg, Kingdom of Bavaria, Germany, July 30, 1832, leaving her native land for this September 20, 1848, landing at Baltimore. They were married in Galena, Ill., July, 1853; are the parents of ten children, eight of whom are now living—Elizabeth, next to the oldest, was born in Thompson Township, Jo Daviess County, January 14, 1856; arriving at sufficient age, was sent, for a time, to the public schools of Galena, and in the fall of 1875, entered the Illinois State Normal University, from which she graduated in May, 1880. Two of the five years were spent earning the means with which to complete her course. She received her "degree" with nineteen others, and was chosen "valedictorian." Upon the completion of her studies, she accepted the position of teacher of the Gardner Primary School, for the school year commencing September 1, at $45 per month. Her services in this department were so acceptable to the patrons, that she was gladly retained for another year, at an advance of $10 per month. She is now Principal of the Gardner Public Schools, at a salary of $75 per month. She is offered the position, as "teacher of the primary training department" of the State Normal School at Carbondale. As a teacher, she is eminently successful, gaining already a reputation as wide as the State, and for her the future appears rich with promise.

CHARLES BLANEY, farmer, P. O. Gardner, was born in Pennsylvania August 17, 1804; is a son of John and Mary Blaney, natives of Pennsylvania and early residents of Licking County, Ohio; they were the parents of four children that grew up—George, Maria, Charles and Benjamin. Our subject received schooling in a pioneer cabin; he has always been a farmer. He was married, in 1833, to Rebecca Kimpton, the result being three children that attained their majority—Vincent, Benjamin and Mary; his wife died in 1873, and he has since kept house with his niece, Mrs. Mary Latta, a daughter of Joseph and Elizabeth Cox; she was born in 1823, and had a like chance with Mr. B in the pioneer schoolroom; she was married, in 1842, to John Latta, and has one child—Anna—living, of a large number. Mr. B. came to Illinois in 1865, and settled on the farm where he now resides, consisting of 160 acres, which he has under good cultivation; his two sons, Benjamin and Vincent, were in the late war. He votes the Republican ticket.

BARTON W. BARBER, farmer, P. O. Gardner, was born in Rutland County, Vt., August 31, 1828, son of James W. and Lorain (Parker) Barber, natives of Vermont, he born in 1797, died in July, 1875; was a farmer by occupation; she was born in 1802, and died in 1874; she was the mother of five children, of whom our subject was the second child; he received a common-school education and worked upon the farm; he came to Grundy County in 1869, and located on his present farm of 160 acres. In connection with general farming, he handles some stock and carries on a dairy. January 8, 1861, Mr. Barber married Marietta E. Farwell, born at Castleton, Rutland Co., Vt., March 23, 1833; she is the daughter of Salomon and Louise (Pond) Farwell, natives of Vermont, both dead. This marriage has been blessed with four children, viz., Carrie L., Adelbert F., Frederick D. and Edith L.; the latter died in infancy. Mr. Barber is a member of the A., F. & A. M. Although he commenced as a poor man, he is now in comfortable circumstances, as a result of his own labors.

CLOVER BROTHERS, lawyers, Gardner. Edward Clover, the junior member of this firm, was born in Hardin County, Iowa, January 25, 1861; he came to Illinois with his parents in 1864, they locating in Mazon Township, where they remained fourteen years; they lived in Kansas three years, after which they settled in Gardner. The parents of our subjects are Gerettus and Susan (Maddox) Clover, natives of Indiana, he born February 22, 1836; is a retired farmer; she was born February 7, 1840, and is the mother of three children—Bartlette, deceased; Thomas F. and Edward, who compose the firm of Clover Bros. Edward received a good education, and, after reading law with N. M. Purviance, of Kansas, was admitted to the bar, November 26, 1881, when he was but twenty years of age. Thomas, the senior member of the firm, was born in Leavenworth County, Kan., January 23, 1859; he received a good education, and, after studying law with Webb & Glass, of Oswego, Kan., was admitted to the bar June 10, 1880. He served as City Attorney of Oswego, Kan., one year, and then entered into partnership with his brother, at Gardner, Ill., April 22, 1882. In connection with their law practice, the Clover Bros. are extensively engaged in the insurance business. They are men of ability, and have thus far been successful; they are identified with the Democratic party.

AMOS CLOVER, stock-dealer, Gardner, was born November 25, 1822, in Hamilton County, Ohio; is a son of John M. and Mary (Williams) Clover, natives of Pennsylvania. The mother was of German and Welsh descent, and died about 1840; she was the mother of eleven children. When our subject was an infant, his parents removed to Vermillion County, Ind., where he attended school and worked on the farm until twenty-one years of age. In 1843, he came to Grundy County, where he now owns about 600 acres of farm land. Subject was married, in 1848, in Grundy County, to Martha J. Fayler, who was born in 1832, in McLean County, Ill., and died August 15, 1878; she was the daughter of John and Cynthia (Smith) Fayler, and left four children—Emma J., John L., Flora C. and Mary B. Mr. Clover has retired from active labor; he represented Grundy County in the Thirtieth General Assembly of Illinois; has held the offices of Justices of the Peace and Supervisor; he is a member of the A., F. & A. M., and of the National Greenback party.

THADDEUS P. CRANE, farmer, P. O. Gardner, was born in Middlebury, Vt., September 9, 1820, son of Mahlon and Abigail (Reed) Crane, he a native of New York, born January 3, 1791; is a farmer, living in Grundy County; she a native of Vermont, died in November, 1873, aged about seventy years. They were the parents of nine children, of whom our subject was the fifth child. When two years of age, he, with his parents, removed to New York State, where he was educated in the common schools. In 1862, he came West, locating in Grundy County, where he engaged in farming. In the fall of 1864, he removed to his present place of residence; his first purchase consisted of forty acres of unimproved land, to which he has added until now he has 200 acres, all under a state of cultivation that stamps Mr. Crane as a first-class, practical farmer; his buildings and general surroundings betoken neatness and thrift. He makes no specialties in farming, but grows the usual crops and handles some stock. June 12, 1855, in Steuben County, N. Y., he married Phebe Thompson, born in New York State November 16, 1831, a daughter of Robert and Dolly (Skinner) Thompson, natives of Connecticut, both deceased. This union resulted in five children, viz., Fred, Nellie, Harry, Frank and Charles, the last two deceased. Mr. Crane is something of a traveler, having spent three years in that pleasant recreation in South America. During one term of three years, he held the office of County Commissioner of Grundy County. He is a member of the A., F. & A. M. at Gardner.

JOHN H. COLES, shoemaker, Gardner, was born in Delaware County, Penn., February 5, 1822; son of Enoch and Margaret (Henderson) Coles. The father, a native of New York State, was a shoemaker, born in 1792, and died in 1854. The mother, a native of the State of Delaware, was born in 1802, and died March 17, 1879. Our subject received a common-school education, and at the age of twenty-one learned the trade of a shoemaker. In September, 1857, he came to Gardner, and continued at his trade. In September, 1848, he was married, in Pennsylvania, to Miss Mary E. Hart, born in that State January 23, 1823; she died January 22, 1861, and was the mother of five children —George, Henry A. (both deceased), Mary E., John A. and William F. Mr. Coles was again married, April 10, 1862, to Mrs. Martha J. Dunmore, born March 1, 1826; she has four children, viz., Jessie M., Elwood

A., Herbert M. and Nathan E. Mr. Coles was the first President of the Board of Trustees of Gardner, and was also the first Police Magistrate of that place; has been Town Clerk about twelve years, and Township Trustee four terms; has had the commission of Notary Public about seventeen years, and is now serving his fifth term as Justice of the Peace; he has always been a strong temperance man; has been a member of the M. E. Church forty years, and has belonged to the Republican party since its foundation; his wife is a Presbyterian.

SAMUEL CHRISTY, farmer, P. O. Gardner, was born in Ireland November 5, 1833; is a son of James and Mary Graham Christy, the parents of eight children—Robert, Ellen, John, Joseph, Thomas, Samuel and one deceased. Mr. C. spent but three weeks in the schoolroom. In 1853, he came to New York City, where he engaged at weaving, and afterward in a dry goods factory. In 1860, he came to Kankakee County, Ill., where he rented a farm for nine years; in the meantime, he bought forty-three acres, and kept adding until he owned 125 acres in Kankakee County, which he sold in 1875, and bought forty acres in Grundy County, where he now lives. He was married, in 1856, to Sarah McConnell; they have no children. He is making a specialty of breeding Norman horses and fast stock, having at this time two fine stallions of the above-named breed. When he settled in New York he had about $500, which, by frugality, has been increased until he ranks among those of excellent circumstances; he has reared two boys—Christopher and Michael Daily.

CYRUS M. EASTON, physician, Gardner, was born in Trumbull County, Ohio, October 23, 1842, to Alexander and Hannah (Lee) Easton, he born in Franklin County, Mass., September 25, 1801, a local preacher by profession and also a farmer; his death occurred November 1, 1880; she, born in Oppenheim, N. Y., January 5, 1811, died December 7, 1843; she was the mother of six children, of whom the Doctor was the youngest child. During his early childhood, his time was employed in rendering what assistance he could to his parents upon the homestead farm and in attending the common schools of the county, where he received the foundation of his subsequent education. At the age of fifteen years, he emigrated to the then far West, and eventually located in Grundy County, where he was engaged about three years as a farm hand; he then returned to Ohio and entered the Western Reserve Seminary, with a view of fitting himself for school teaching, which occupation he followed a part of the three years following, when not engaged with his studies. His literary education was completed at the Illinois Wesleyan University at Bloomington; commenced the study of medicine with Dr. J. D. Curl, of Mazon; attended his first course of lectures at Ann Arbor, Mich.; completed his studies and received his diploma as an M. D. at Rush Medical College of Chicago, January 17, 1872, but had been practicing about five years previous; came to Gardner in August, 1874, where he has the satisfaction of conducting a very successful practice. Being ambitious to keep abreast of his profession, the Doctor attended the practitioners' course at Chicago, in the spring of 1882, where he also received a diploma. He was married in Kankakee County, August 20, 1867, to Miss Mary Ann Armstrong, who was born in Calhoun County, Mich., September 13, 1843, to Wellington G. and Grace (Glass) Armstrong, he a native of New York, born in 1814, March 27, died April 1, 1876; she a native of England, born July 6, 1811, still living. Mrs. Easton is the mother of three children, viz., Cora May, born July 10, 1869; Lena Almira, born August 19, 1870; Rufus Wellington, born February 11, 1875. During the rebellion, Dr. Easton entered the service, in Company F, One Hundred and Forty-fourth Illinois Infantry, Capt. Barber, and served on detached duty as Clerk and Warden of the military prison at Columbus, Ky., until mustered out in 1864. Politically, he is a stanch advocate of the principles of the Republican party.

ALCINOUS EASTON, farmer, P. O. Gardner, was born in Trumbull County, Ohio, July 25, 1837; is a son of Alexander and Hannah (Lee) Easton; his education was limited to the common school of his native county. When seventeen years old, he left the homestead farm and engaged in school teaching and farming. In 1854, he came to Grundy County, Ill., and the following year went to Minnesota, where he remained about three years. After spending three years in Iowa, he returned to Grundy County, where he has since been engaged in farming. In Wisconsin, April 23, 1857, Mr. Easton married Miss Mary Jane Doan, who was born in Lake County, Ohio, October 25, 1841, is a daughter of Seth and Lucy (Francis) Doan, natives of Ohio, both deceased. By this marriage there were ten children, viz., Hannah, wife of Daniel Showalter; Henry, Frederick, Allie, Howard, Minnie, Effie, Eva, Emery and Elmer; the three last mentioned are deceased. In 1875, Mr. Easton was granted a license to preach by the M. E. Church, and he is now one of the local preachers on the Gardner Circuit. Politically, he is a Republican.

HARVEY ELDRED, furniture dealer, Gardner, was born in Milford, Otsego Co., N. Y., September 3, 1830, son of Robert and Phebe (Swartwout) Eldred, natives of New York State. The father, who is dead, was a farmer and stock-dealer. Our subject is the eldest of six children, and received a common-school education; when eighteen years of age, he came with his parents to Illinois and located in Kendall County, where, November 25, 1848, he entered into partnership with his father and three brothers, and for six years they rented and worked land. Our subject then learned the trade of a mason, which trade he followed in Gardner from 1856 to 1871; he then purchased the furniture business of William F. Hastings; this he has since been engaged in. Our subject was married, in New York State, in October, 1848, to Miss Margaret Self, a native of England, born in 1828; she is the mother of seven children—Dr. C. C. Eldred, of Braidwood, Ill.; Mary A., wife of Charles Butler; Robert J.; Phœbe J., a school teacher; Hattie B.; Mary and Amy, both deceased. Mr. Eldred has held several town and county offices, such as Collector and member of the Town Board, of which he is now President. He commenced life as a poor boy, and is now in good circumstances; was formerly a Democrat, but voted for Garfield, and will remain in the Republican party.

ROBERT FOSTER, retired farmer, P. O. Gardner, was born July 8, 1812, in Old Virginia; he is a son of Vincent and Oma (Hickman) Foster, natives of Virginia, and the parents of three children—Sarah, Robert and Vincent. The father was in the war of 1812. Robert attended school in the pioneer cabins, walking a distance of five miles. His father was killed in the war spoken of above, and the son was reared by his grandfather Foster. At the age of seventeen, he began for himself in rural pursuits for some time, and then engaged in a brewery at Zanesville, Ohio; he was married, November 28, 1834, to Malina, a daughter of Jesse and Mary (Toben) Smith; she was born April 5, 1813, and was one of seven children—Maranda. Ann, Malina, John, William, Eliza and Emily. Mr. Foster's union gave him six children, five of whom survive—George, a farmer of Benton County, Ind.; Sarah E., wife of Josiah Foreman, farmer, of McLean County, Ill.; Mary A., the wife of Franklin Clark, she is deceased; Thomas J., in Colorado; James M., married to Sarah Daniels, the result being two children, viz., Ella B. and Anna F.; he is also a farmer in Benton County; the last son is Robert J., farmer in same county. After marriage, our subject settled in Muskingum County, Ohio, and subsequently in Belmont and Washington Counties. In 1852, he settled in Mazon Township, Grundy County, Ill., where he bought sixty acres of improved land, which he sold in 1870, and has since retired to Gardner, his present residence. He and wife have been members of the M. E. Church for forty-five years, in which he has held office and has been Superintendent of Sabbath school in said organization. He cast his first Presidential vote for Gen. Jackson, and is now identified with the Republican party.

BRIGGS FULLER, retired farmer, P. O. Gardner, was born January 27, 1824, in Seneca County, N. Y., is a son of Jesse and Rachel Allen Fuller, the former a native of Vermont, and the latter of New York; his great-grandparents, Allen, were of German descent, and emigrated at an early day, from Holland, to America; his parents had five children—Leroy, Abel B., William W., Sarah M. and Callista J.; the father was a ship carpenter; the parents were Methodists. Our subject attended school but little, and that in a log cabin. In his younger days, he worked at calking canal boats and ship-building. In 1860, he came West and engaged in farming, renting for three years, and then bought eighty acres in Grundy County, and has since added forty acres, all of which is well improved and the attainment of his own labors, together with that of his estimable consort, whom he married in 1851. Her maiden name was Maranda Vanhouten, born April 2, 1832, and is a daughter of Aaron and Mary (Daily) Vanhouten, the former a native of Holland and the latter of New York. Her parents came to Grundy County about 1854, settling in Goodfarm Township, where her father died August 20, 1880; her mother is still living; she was one of seven children — Betsey, Ann (deceased), Mary, Maranda, Jane (deceased), Sarah, William; her mother was a Methodist. Mr. and Mrs. Fuller have no children; they have reared Mary, a daughter of Thomas Campbell, whom they took when four years old; they are also rearing Samuel N. West, a son of Mrs. F.'s sister, Jane (deceased). The father of Samuel was an early settler of this county. The grandfather Allen was a blacksmith, and made the nails for the construction of the first house in the State of New York. Mr. F. votes the Republican ticket. Is now living in Gardner, retired from farm labors.

LEWIS C. FULLER, farmer, P. O. Gardner, was born in Trumbull County, Ohio, April 14, 1849, son of Alexander and Almira (Gates) Fuller, natives of Ohio. The father was born in 1814, came to Illinois in 1866; is a retired farmer, living at Streator, Ill. The mother was born about 1817, and has borne five children, all of whom are living. Our subject attended the colleges of Oberlin, Ohio, and Hillsdale, Mich.; he remained upon the home farm until twenty-seven years of age, when he came to his present place of residence. He was married, in Gardner, July 10, 1879, to Miss Maggie Allison, who was born in Illinois May 11, 1856. Mr. Fuller is extensively engaged in the raising of blooded stock, both horses and cattle. He is a member of the fraternity of A., F. & A. M., at Gardner, and belongs to the Republican party, of which he is a staunch supporter.

ROBERT GLASS, farmer. Mr. Glass was born in Monroe Township, Guernsey County, Ohio, June 29, 1824, seventh child of a family of thirteen children born to Thomas and Rebecca (Storer) Glass. Thomas Glass, who was a farmer by occupation, was born near Pittsburgh, Penn., in 1787; he lived in Guernsey County, Ohio, until May, 1852, when he moved with his family to Grundy County, Ill., where he died, near Gardner, on what is now known as the "Parker farm," March 22, 1853, his wife, who was born in Harrison County, Ohio, in 1793, died in Grundy County, Ill., February 22, 1853. Of their family of thirteen children, eight are deceased, six older and two younger than the subject of this sketch. Mr. Glass received a limited education, such as the subscription schools of that day afforded, attending from twenty to fifty days each winter season, until he attained his majority, when he began working the homestead farm on shares with his father, working in that way for about one and one-half years. November 12, 1846, he married Mary Little, a native of Guernsey County, Ohio, born December 17, 1828, eldest child of a family of eight children, born to Francis and Rebecca (McDonald) Little. Francis Little, a native of Ireland, born of Protestant parents, came to America with his parents when nine years of age, and is now living in Guernsey County, Ohio; his wife, who was of Scotch parentage, was born in Muskingum County, Ohio, and died in Guernsey County, Ohio. After his marriage, Mr. Glass rented a part of his father's farm, which he worked for two years, then, in the spring of 1849, moved to Grundy County, Ill., and settled on the farm near Gardner, now occupied by Mr. Blaney, which he located by a land-warrant for $130. In the spring of 1865, he sold this place to Mr. Blaney for $4,000, and bought the east half of the same section, where he lived for about sixteen years, and, in the fall of 1881, sold out for $14,000, and moved to Kansas, where he purchased 640 acres of land, on which he intends to locate permanently; his wife also owns 100 acres of land in Carroll County, Mo. Mr. and Mrs. Glass have been blessed with nine children, five of whom are deceased —Rebecca, born in Guernsey County, Ohio, January 21, 1848; Thomas Francis, born in Grundy County, Ill., June 16, 1850; George Little, born October 25, 1852, died April 21, 1874, Charles Wesley, born October 27, 1855, died April 5, 1871; Alice, born July 12, 1858, died January 22, 1859; Robert Lincoln, born September 3, 1862; William Mordecai, born October 23, 1865; Andrew Jackson, born June 5, 1868, died June 29, 1868, and an infant daughter, born February 3, 1861, died the same day. Of these nine children, all, save the eldest, were born in Grundy County, and all those deceased died in this county. Mr. and Mrs. Glass are members of the Methodist Church. He is a Republican.

LOUIS GERMAIN, stock and grain-dealer, Gardner, was born in Clinton County, N. Y., in the year 1836 to Peter and Julia (Christian) Germain; the former was a native of France, born in 1791; was an ore miner by occupation; died in Clinton County, N. Y., December 16, 1865; the latter was born in New York State in May, 1803, and died in 1863; they were the parents of nine children. Louis had to depend upon the common schools for his education, but with these chances and his natural ability, he was quite well prepared for business. He was a good accountant and an elegant writer. His first business for himself was that of clerk in

GREENFIELD TOWNSHIP.

a wholesale house at Goshen, Ind. Mr. Germain was married to Mary Adaline Stone, at Ligonier, Ind., March 29, 1859; she was born in Noble County, Ind., October 11, 1841; was the daughter of Richard and Mary (Higgins) Stone, natives of Pennsylvania, the former born in Harrisburg. Soon after the marriage of our subject, he moved to this county and rented a farm a half mile west of Gardner. Although his crops were good, yet owing to the low price of produce, his profits were small. In company with R. B. Huss, he kept, for a time, a dry goods and grocery store. For about fourteen years, he has been buying and shipping stock and grain. He has been financially successful by his own industry and economy, making himself well to do. Such has been his record, that he enjoys the confidence and esteem of all who know him. He has served the public as Constable and Deputy Sheriff, as Collector and Assessor, the latter for twelve years, and three years since, was elected Supervisor, which office he still holds. As a public servant, he has been faithful to every trust. He went into the army, in 1864, as a private, Company D, One Hundred and Forty-sixth Regiment Illinois Volunteer Infantry; was promoted to be First Lieutenant; was discharged at the close of the war. Mr. and Mrs. Germain have four children living— Eva, Mabel, Grace and Guy. Mr. Germain belongs to no secret society. In politics, he is an active Republican, and has been since the formation of the party.

GEORGE GOODSON, farmer, P. O. Gardner, is a native of England, born February 20, 1833; he had very limited educational advantages while young, but, after coming to America, in 1857, he taught himself to read and write, and acquainted himself with the common branches of education. The parents of our subject were John and Lucy (Howett) Goodson, natives of England; he was a day laborer, and died in 1864. She, born March 12, 1813, is still living in Gardner; she is the mother of eleven children, of whom subject is the oldest. He came to Grundy County in 1859; enlisted in Company A, One Hundred and Twenty-seventh Illinois Volunteer Infantry, in which he served eight months; he was disabled while building barracks in Chicago. In January, 1860, he married Margaret Snyder, born in 1840; she has borne him three children, viz., Mary, Frank and John. Mr. Goodson carries on a general farming business, and is a member of the Republican party.

E. W. HULSE, Postmaster, Gardner, was born April 3, 1842, in Trumbull County, Ohio; is a son of C. R. and Bethsheba (Foot) Hulse, natives of Ohio and parents of four children—Rosetta, E. W., Z. F, N. J.; the mother died in 1850, and the father came to Illinois in 1851, and was subsequently married to Mary Rice, the result being one child—Henry J. The father was married a third time, to Mary J. Rutledge, and by her was blessed with two children—Judson O. and Hattie; the father survived all his wives. Was a minister of the Protestant Methodist Church. Our subject began for himself at the age of nine, his mother having died about that time; he worked on a farm at $4 per month. When the war broke out, he offered his services, but was refused. Later, he enlisted in Company G, Thirty-sixth Illinois Volunteer Infantry, for three years, and was wounded at the battle of Pea Ridge, which caused his side to be paralyzed; he was discharged August 9, 1862. In 1865, he enlisted in Company F, One Hundred and Forty-first Illinois Volunteer Infantry, and remained till the close. In 1866, was married to Mary A. Currier, a daughter of John and Anna Currier, natives of Pennsylvania, and parents of James, I. Lewis, Arvilla, Amanda and two deceased. Mr. H. had three children as a result of his marriage—Nelson W., Eben R., Ira N.; his wife died May 14, 1877, and he was again married, in 1878, to Elizabeth A. Wartman, resulting in one child—Mary L. He engaged in the hardware business in Gardner under the firm name of Pratt & Hulse, for five years, and was successful. He has held several minor offices; has run for County Superintendent of Livingston County one term. He was appointed Postmaster at this place, November 10, 1879, which position he still holds. The life of Mr. H. has been one mixed with trials; he hobbled around on crutches for several years, and managed to attend the Western Reserve Seminary, at Farmington, Ohio, for two years; he is a Baptist, while his wife is of the Christian Church. He votes the Republican ticket.

ROBERT HOUSTON, retired farmer, P. O. Gardner, was born in Ireland August 14, 1809; he is a son of John and Jane (Gibson) Houston. The father died in Ireland and the mother in New York; they were the parents of nine children—Ellen, Jane, William, Robert, James, John, Mary, Alexander and Thomas; the parents belonged to the First Baptist Church of Ireland. Robert had but little chance of attending school; his father died when he was small, and, at the age of eleven, he had to take charge of the family; he came to America in 1831, settling in New York City, where he engaged in weaving, manufacturing cotton goods; he followed weaving for twenty years; he saved enough aside from keeping his family to have $1,000 left when coming to Illinois. He was married, in 1837, to Mrs. Elizabeth Murphey, a daughter of Thomas Shaw, which union blessed him with nine children— Eliza, the wife of D. Morris; John, who died in the late war; Robert, wounded on the Red River expedition, losing his right leg; Thomas, wounded in the shoulder at the battle of Shiloh, taken prisoner by the rebels and confined in the hospital at Mobile, Ala., and Andersonville for nine months; Ann, Mary, William, Ellen and Martha. Mr. H. bought 160 acres of land in Braceville Township on coming here, for $165, which he afterward traded for 160 acres in Greenfield Township, which he still owns; this land is located on Section 14; he has retired from the rural pursuits of life, being located in good property of his own in Gardner. He and wife are active members of the Baptist Church, in which he has always held office, and is now Deacon. The financial interests of said organization have always been blessed by the relationship of Mr. Houston, he having donated largely to the construction of two churches at this place, one of which was consumed by fire. He is an unfaltering believer in the Savior of mankind, and shows by his walks his faith. He votes the Republican ticket.

RICHARD B. HUSS, merchant, Gardner, was born June 24, 1836, in Hocking County, Ohio, son of Jacob and Ellen (Boyd) Huss, natives of Pennsylvania, he a farmer by occupation, dying in 1841, aged sixty-three years; she, in 1865, aged sixty-three years; she was the mother of nine children. When our subject was five years old, he was taken by his mother to Wells County, Ind., where he learned the trade of harness-making. He first commenced business in Newark, Kendall Co., Ill., where he remained seven years. In 1863, he removed to Gardner and continued in the harness business one year, and then enlisted in Company D, One Hundred and Forty-sixth Illinois Volunteer Infantry, Capt. Loveday; he remained in the service ten months, and then resumed his former

GREENFIELD TOWNSHIP.

trade, which he followed until 1866, when he commenced dealing in butter and eggs. In 1872, he, with a partner, commenced general merchandising, under the firm name of Germain & Huss. In 1874, he purchased Mr. Germain's interest, and continued the business on his own account. In 1870, he sustained a loss by fire of about $12,000; he does a business of about $60,000 per annum. Mr. Huss has been twice married—first, in 1856, to Miss Rachel A. Crumley, who died in January, 1872, leaving six children—Ellen E., Huldah A., Harriet J., Nora E., Cora A. and William S. Mr. Huss was again married, in 1874, to Miss Frances M. Waters, born in Grundy County in 1852, and two children have been born to them—Howard and Maggie. Mr. Huss is a member of the M. E. Church, and a Republican.

STACEY E. HARTLEY, farmer, P. O. Gardner, was born in Guernsey County, Ohio, June 1, 1839, son of Stacey and Mary (Wait) Hartley, natives of Ohio; he died in August, 1839; was a hotel-keeper; she was born in 1805, and is still living. Our subject was one of a family of nine children, and received such an education as the common schools of his native place afforded. In 1850, he came to Grundy County with George Willis, his brother-in-law, and engaged with him three years in farming, after which he labored on the railroad for one year. In 1855, he went to Iowa, where he remained three years, then settled in Gardner and engaged in farming. During the rebellion, our subject served for three years in Company D, One Hundred and Twenty-seventh Illinois Volunteer Infantry, with Capt. Chandler, the regiment being commanded by Col. Van Arnam. After returning from the war, Mr. Hartley resumed agricultural pursuits, near Gardner, where he has remained since, upon his farm of 190 acres of good land, all in a good state of cultivation. He makes no specialties, but grows the usual farm crops and raises some stock. Mr. Hartley was married, December 19, 1868, to Rose Butterfield, born in Pennsylvania April 3, 1847; she is the daughter of Joseph and Susan Butterfield, both deceased. By this marriage, there is one child—Carrie, born October 25, 1870. Mr. Hartley has been School Director, is a member of the Republican party.

GEORGE W. HIBNER, farmer, P. O. Gardner, was born in Richland County, Ohio, November 16, 1840, son of John and Nancy (Kurtz) Hibner, he a native of Ohio, born in 1814, a farmer by occupation, and lives near Joliet, Ill.; she, born in Pennsylvania in 1816, is still living and the mother of thirteen children, twelve of whom are living. Our subject came to Illinois with his parents in 1847, received a common-school education and assisted his parents on the farm. In 1870, he came to Grundy County, where he has since been engaged in raising stock and carrying on general farming. He was married, in Will County, Ill., April 12, 1866, to Almeda Eibe, born in Will County July 29, 1849; she is a daughter of George and Mary Ann (Zumault) Eibe. Mr. and Mrs. Hibner have been blessed with seven children, viz., Lewis A., Clara A., Mary A., George J., Emma A., Virginia I. and John A., the latter deceased. Mr. Hibner has been School Director about twelve years; he and wife are connected with the Wesleyan Methodist Church. Politically, Mr. Hibner has always been independent until latterly he has been identified with the Republican party. He commenced life a poor man, and, by his industry, has accumulated a property of 400 acres of land, well stocked and cultivated.

CHARLES V. HAMILTON, hardware merchant, Gardner, was born in Fulton, Oswego Co., N. Y., December 18, 1845, son of John V. and Charlotte H. (White) Hamilton, he born September 9, 1818, at Ira, Cayuga Co., N. Y.; was a ship builder by trade, and came to Illinois in 1860, where he followed the trade of a carpenter until 1869, when he removed to Wisconsin, and, in 1880, to Dakota, where he lives in retirement from actual labor. The mother, also a native of Ira, N. Y., was born May 23, 1826, and died in Wisconsin December 26, 1877; she was the mother of five children, three of whom are living—Charles (our subject), Helen H. and Edward E. Our subject availed himself of the educational privileges of the common schools of his native place, and, at the age of eighteen, commenced clerking in a store of general merchandise, which occupation he followed in different localities until 1876, when he came to Gardner, Ill., and opened a hardware store. June 17, 1874, he married Miss Ellen Hustin, who was born in Grundy County February 21, 1853, and is a daughter of Robert and Elizabeth Hustin, of Gardner. By this marriage there are three children, viz., Verner E., born April 9, 1875; Robert J., July 16, 1877, and Charlotte M., March 2, 1879. Mr. Hamilton has been more than ordinarily successful in his business as a hardware merchant, and his trade is steadily increasing. He has been Village Trustee one term, and is now serving his third term as Township Treasurer; is an active member of A., F. & A. M. His wife is a member of the Baptist Church.

HIRAM JONES, farmer, P. O. Gardner, was born in Somerset County, Me., May 4, 1840, son of Thomas J. and Harriet (Small) Jones, natives of Maine. The father was a farmer by occupation, and died in April, 1868. The mother died in August, 1870. Our subject availed himself of such educational advantages as his native place afforded, and, when the late war broke out, he enlisted in Company E, Seventeenth Maine Volunteer Infantry, under Capt. Sawyer, the regiment being commanded by Col. West. After serving two years and three months in the army, Mr. Jones engaged in farming. In 1867, he located in Highland Township, Grundy County, where he remained eight years; he then came to Gardner, where he has since engaged in general farming, occasionally drilling wells and sinking coal shafts. He was married, in Maine, August 20, 1863, to Hannah N. Collins, born in Maine October 28, 1839. This union has been blessed with five children, viz., Leland E., Bertrand P., Willie B., Byron C. and Luella M. Mr. Jones is a Republican.

C. M. KING, editor and proprietor of the Gardner News, Gardner, was born at Chambersburg, Penn., and is a son of Samuel and Elizabeth (Coffroth) King. Samuel King, subject's father, who is still living, is a merchant, and was born at Mercersburg, Penn., in 1803; his wife, who was born in 1804, died May 9, 1882; they had a family of seven children. Mr. King received his education in the common schools of Pennsylvania, and began the business of life as a teacher, which occupation he followed for four years, 1860 to 1864. In the latter year, he enlisted in the regular army was detailed to the Signal Service, and served till the close of the war. He married at Greencastle, Penn., July 1, 1874, to Minnie Hoke, and by this union they have one child—Samuel, aged four years. Mr. King learned the printer's trade, partly in Shirleysburg, in Huntingdon and Altoona, Penn. He has been engaged in the printing business for fifteen years, and established and owned the following papers: The Neponset *Gazette*, 1868, Prairie City (Ill.) *Herald*, 1870; Chenoa *Times*, 1872; Lexington *Enterprise*, 1872 to 1876; Altamont *Telegram*, 1876 to 1880, and in 1881 he established the Gardner *News*, which he now publishes.

GREENFIELD TOWNSHIP.

The Gardner *News* was established with the printing establishment of the late Altamont *Telegram*, moved to Gardner with fine equipment of material and power cylinder press. The size of the paper is 28x45, nine column folio. In 1882, Mr. King established the Braceville *Miner*, a Republican sheet, which is printed in the office of the Gardner *News*. This paper is 28x45 folio, thirty-six columns. Mr. King is a Republican, and is conservative in his religious views.

I. J. KEEPERS, farmer, P. O. Gardner, was born in Beaver County, Penn., in March, 1829, and settled on his present farm in April, 1866. When he was but a small boy, his father moved to Guernsey County, Ohio, and there he lived till he came to Grundy County. He received his education chiefly in Ohio, but attended school a short time in Pennsylvania. In Guernsey County, Ohio, August 22, 1850, he married Miss Mary Kimble, a native of that county, and by this union they have been blessed with six children, all of whom, save one, were born in Ohio. Mr. Keepers has made farming his chief occupation, but he followed saw-milling in Ohio for some time. In September, 1864, he enlisted in the One Hundred and Seventy-sixth Ohio Volunteer Infantry, and served till the close of the war, the regiment being stationed at Nashville, Tenn., the greater part of the time. He has lately sold his farm and bought another of 160 acres, located in the same township, three and one-half miles west of Gardner. He began life without any means, renting land at first, and by industry and economy has accumulated his present property. He and his wife are members of the Baptist Church; he is a Republican and been one ever since the organization of that party. Their children are William I., Mary J., Joseph H., Caroline O., Hannah Myrtle and Olive W. Mr. Keepers is a son of Joseph and Hannah Keepers, who were born in Chester County, Penn., where they remained for some years, and, after their marriage, moved to Beaver County, Penn. Joseph Keepers died in Guernsey County, Ohio, December 6, 1842; his wife came to Illinois and died at her daughter's house in Iroquois County, April 28, 1873. Subject's wife is a daughter of Adam and Mary Kimble, who were born in Pennsylvania; came to Ohio when young, and died in Guernsey County, that State.

JACOB C. LUTZ, general merchant and banker, Gardner. The subject of this sketch, whose portrait appears in this history, was born in Wurtemberg, Germany, February 13, 1844. He was the son of Jacob B. and Katharina (Kern) Lutz, the former a native of Germany, born January 27, 1812, the latter born in 1814. To them were born three children— Christina, wife of John Weber, of Kansas; Jacob C., subject; Carrie, wife of Henry Fey, of Morris. The family moved to this country in the summer of 1855, stopping in Cleveland, Ohio, six months, and in Chicago one year, when they moved to Minooka, this county. The father was a carpenter by occupation; limited in means; died in Morris in 1879; the mother is still living. Our lad Jacob was put to herding cattle for R. Gardner, an extensive farmer and merchant of Minooka. The second year, he hired to the same party to do chores for $70; was employed a part of the time in the store, where he soon became very efficient. So competent and faithful did he prove that his employer retained him as clerk for seven years. When twenty-one, he had accumulated $500, and with a partner opened a flour and feed store in Chicago. This proved unprofitable, and in six months he returned to Minooka with only $200. He took his old place in Gardner's store for a little time, when he went to Morris and clerked in the store for J. J. Irwin. In March, 1867, with $475 of his own and $1,000 borrowed money, he, in company with Charles Foote, opened a "general store" in Gardner. The first year's receipts were

$32,000, and Lutz paid his borrowed money in ten months. After four years, he was able to buy out his partner's interest, and, notwithstanding the increased competition, his first year's sales reached $62,000. Four years since, he took Eli Eldred as partner, and with a stock of $20,000 the firm is commanding a profitable business. A few years since, in company with C. K. Snyder and others, he went into the grain and lumber trade, and is now, in company with Louis Germain, buying and shipping grain. The business has been well conducted, and has been of considerable profit. With the means he had saved in his business, about five years ago he began buying real estate, adding from time to time, until, at this writing, he has 2,180 acres. His lands are in Greenfield and Braceville, and comprise some productive farms, which are being handsomely improved. Two years since, Mr. Lutz started the Bank of Gardner, making W. V. D. Bishop Cashier. The enterprise is yet young, but of goodly promise. J. C. Lutz was married to Annie Bowers at Minooka April 8, 1868, Leander Smith, Justice of the Peace, making the nuptial tie. She was born at Clifton Springs, N. Y., February 5, 1846; was the daughter of William and Martha (Weston) Bowers, of English nativity. He died near Vicksburg, while in the service of his country. She is still living at Minooka. Mr. and Mrs. Lutz have six children, all born in Gardner— Carrie Louisa, born January 27, 1869; Annie Katharina, January 10, 1871; Bernhardt Otto, November 23, 1872; Jacob Charles, August 12, 1874; Robert G. Ingersoll, March 18, 1879; Carl Henry, March 12, 1881. Owing to the financial condition of his parents, Mr. Lutz had early in life to depend upon his own labor for support, and consequently his chances for education were quite limited. Nature gave him a mind to think and a memory to retain. With these endowments, coupled with industrious habits, using his leisure moments for reading, he has gained a very thorough knowledge of business, and in the general news of the day he is well versed. Financially, he has been successful in an eminent degree. Beginning his career with nothing save a determination to win, he has, while yet but middle-aged, made an ample fortune. While desirous of adding to his estate, he is hospitably inclined, many a poor unfortunate receiving aid and comfort at his hands. In politics, he is a Republican, in religion, a Liberal. In his home, he is cheerful and affectionate, in health generously providing for every want of wife and children, and in sickness caring for them with devoted tenderness. Mrs. Lutz is a woman of pleasing address and good judgment, caring but little for society, but attached to husband and children by the strongest ties. The will of the father and the little ones is the mother's pleasure, and to sacrifice for their good is no discomfort. Her every-day life and record prove her worthy of the husband she has chosen and the children she has borne.

J. W. LEWIS, Superintendent coal mines, Gardner, was born October 24, 1844, in Pennsylvania, is a son of William and Catharine (Matthews) Lewis, natives of Wales. The parents emigrated to the United States about the year 1842. They had seven children, viz., Winifred, Margaret, James, J. W., Albert, Lewis and Thomas. The mother died in 1846, and the father was married to Catharine Harris. J. W. attended school in a log cabin in his boyhood days and labored on a farm. He began learning the machinist's trade in 1855, under Harry Waters, at Tamaqua, Penn, with whom he remained until August 15, 1861, when he enlisted in Company —, Twenty-eighth Pennsylvania Volunteer Infantry, and was afterward transferred to Company C, One Hundred and Forty seventh Pennsylvania Volunteer Infantry. He re-enlisted at Wauhatchie, Tenn., in 1863, and was honorably discharged July 15, 1865. He then began working at his trade as foreman of a shop at Patten's Valley, in Schuylkill County, Penn. November 9, 1867, he was married to Mary Bowen, and, in 1868 they moved to another part of the county, and later to another part of the State. In 1870, he moved his family to Iowa, where he was employed as an engineer for Ira Stockwell, a saw-mill man. Here he remained for four months, and engaged in the Chicago & North-Western Railway shops at Clinton, Iowa. Later, he was employed at Cleveland, Ill. November, 1870, he commenced working in a coal mine for Taylor Williams, and continued until 1871, when he transferred to the employ of the Davenport Coal Company at Dayton, Henry Co., Ill., putting up machinery. October 31, 1871, he left there and engaged as foreman of the coal mines for Taylor Williams at Rapids City, Rock Island Co., Ill. In 1874, he took charge of the machinery until 1878, at which time, he with Joseph Ramsey took a contract to run the Port Byron coal mines of Sterling, Whitesides Co., Ill, owned by T. Williams, at a stated sum per ton, until 1879, when he was engaged by Mr. W. as Assistant Superintendent of the mines, which position he held until January 31, 1880, at which time he went to Utah Territory. In February, 1880, he returned to Illinois, and the following May he was employed by the Carbondale Coal and Coke Company as machinist, which position he held until 1881, when he moved to Gardner, where he is superintending the coal interests of Taylor Williams. He has three children, viz., Ella, born September 7, 1869; Willie, November 23, 1872; John, March 28, 1874. Mr. Lewis has served the people as President of the Board of Trustees and School Director. He has good property at Murphysboro, Jackson Co., Ill. It is due to Mr. Lewis to say that as a mechanic he has but few equals, and as a Superintendent he is courteous and kind to his men, and is careful, seldom ever having any accidents.

HENRY LEACH, farmer, P. O. Gardner, was born in Kendall County, Ill., August 13, 1845, son of Henry and Sarah (Bacheshow) Leach, natives of England. The father was a merchant while in England, but pursued farming after emigrating to America; he was an early settler of Kendall County, Ill., and died in 1851, aged thirty-eight years. The mother died in 1880, at the age of sixty-seven. Our subject was one of five children; received his education at the common schools and at Fowler's Institute. At twenty-three years of age, he left home and worked at farming for six years, in Livingston County; he then removed to his present place of residence, where he is engaged in general farming and stock-dealing. He was married, January 19, 1869, to Miss Iona Howland, born in Wayne, N. Y., November 30, 1847, daughter of Stephen and Catharine Howland, natives of New York State, and early settlers of Grundy County, Ill.; he is deceased; she is still living. This marriage has resulted in four children—Henry C., Howard E., Roy B. and Arthur. Mr. Leach is a member of the order of A., F. & A. M., of Gardner; politically, he is a Republican.

ISAAC B. McGINNIS, Notary Public and Justice of the Peace, Gardner, was born in New Jersey August 31, 1815; is a son of John and Amelia (Woodruff) McGinnis, natives of New Jersey; the father was a carriage manufacturer, born in 1789, and died in 1868. The mother was born in 1795, and died in 1855; they had ten children, of whom our subject was the eldest. He attended the common schools of his native place until sixteen years of age, when he entered a tannery. This business he continued until twenty-seven years of age, when he came to Illinois, located at Joliet and engaged in buying and selling brick and lime. In 1864, he settled in Gardner and engaged in the lumber business. In 1869, he was elected Justice of the Peace, when he sold out his lumber business and gave his attention to the duties of his office, in connection with his agency for real estate. In 1876, he was appointed Notary Public, and has filled several town offices. He was married, in New Jersey, in 1837, to Miss Rachel Vanzandt, born in New Jersey May 1, 1820, and died June 7, 1879; she was a daughter of Richard and Rhoda (Kaywood) Vanzandt, natives of New Jersey, both deceased. This union resulted in eight children, viz., Eliza, Martha, John, Amelia, Edwin, Isaac, Kate W. and Augusta S.; five of them are still living. Mr. McGinnis is a stanch Republican.

A. S. MARTIN, agricultural implements, Gardner, was born October 4, 1836, in Ohio, is a son of Peter and Jane A. (Wells) Martin, natives of New York and Vermont, respectively; they were the parents of seven children—J. J., Maria, N. W., A. S., Catharine, Abigail and Isabella; the parents emigrated from Ohio to Beloit, Wis., in 1848, and thence to Green Bay, where they are living. Mr. Martin attended school and farmed during his younger days; at the age of fifteen, he was employed with his parents in a hotel at Kaukauna, Wis., until twenty years old, when he left for other parts of the State, for a short time, and then attended school at Aurora, Ill., afterward teaching until 1862, when he enlisted in Company D, One Hundred and Twenty-seventh Illinois Volunteer Infantry; was Sergeant, and served till the close. He then resumed teaching, and added real estate at Gardner. In 1875, he entered into the grocery and farming implement business. In 1879, he disposed of the grocery department and has since continued handling all kinds of farm implements at a small profit on the articles, yet aggregating a large amount of gain. He was married, in 1866, to Julia A. Petit, a native of New York, the result of this union being three children, two of whom survive—B. A. and L. A. He and wife are members of the Baptist Church. He votes the Republican ticket.

G. W. MELBOURN, plasterer, Gardner, was born in England March 23, 1835; is a son of Robert and Mary (Smith) Melbourn, also natives of England, where they died; they were the parents of seven children, viz., Thomas, William, G. W., James, John, Robert and Mary. Our subject had no chance to attend school in his native country, only Sunday school, his father having died when he was young. He came with his brother William to New York, landing April 23, 1853; he soon engaged with a farmer by the name of Remington, whose son taught him to read, write and cipher. In 1858, he rented a farm in Michigan, and two years later, he farmed a short time in Missouri, and was driven out by the war of the rebellion. He came directly to this county, and when he arrived, had but 50 cents. He early sought employment by the day and began to build up. In 1862, he enlisted in Company D, One Hundred and Twenty-seventh Illinois Volunteer Infantry, and served until the close of the war; he was slightly wounded in the face, the buck-shot yet remaining in his jaw-bone. On his return from the war, he labored in a coal mine in this county for sixteen months, after which he engaged with Henry Eldred in the mason and plastering business, which he has continued mostly since, and now ranks among the best plasterers in the county, his work always giving entire satisfaction. November 5, 1855, he was married to Lucy Day, the result of the union being seven children, viz., William, Katy (deceased), David, Charles, Hella, Hattie and Carrie. He is now Road Commissioner.

GREENFIELD TOWNSHIP.

By economy and frugality, he secured eighty acres of fine land in Greenfield Township, which he recently sold for $4,000. He votes the Republican ticket.

L. A. McCULLM, hair dresser, Gardner, was born in Magnolia, Putnam Co., Ill, May 20, 1852, son of John and Prudence (Shipley) McCullm, he born in Ireland in 1801, was a Constable for twenty-five years, and died in Wenona, Marshall Co., Ill., October 27, 1875; she was born in Kentucky December 2, 1820, and is living; the parents had ten children, of whom our subject was the eighth; he attended school in Magnolia, and began life as a farmer. In 1876, he located in Wenona, and worked at the trade of a barber. In December, 1881, he came to Gardner, where he has since carried on a first-class barber shop; he also deals in cigars, tobacco, candies and notions. January 28, 1875, in Wenona, Mr. McCullm married Emma L. Carson, born September 25, 1860, in Bethany, Harrison County, Mo.; she is the daughter of Charles and Nancy S. (Garner) Carson, natives of Ohio, he dead, she living. Mr. and Mrs. McCullm are the parents of two children—Clara B. and Mary L. Mr. McCullm is a member of the I. O. O. F. and a Republican.

TRUMAN PHELPS, general merchant, Gardner, was born in Herkimer County, N. Y., April 11, 1837, son of Isaac and Ruth (Vickery) Phelps, natives of New York State, both deceased. Our subject was the youngest of a family of five children, and, when eighteen years of age, went to Trumbull County, Ohio, where he finished his education; he was engaged in teaching school and various other occupations until 1863, when he came to Grundy County and engaged in farming; after following this occupation for about ten years, he located in Gardner and engaged in merchandising. In 1878, the firm of Pratt, Martin & Phelps was formed, and continued for two years, when Mr. Phelps withdrew his interest and formed a partnership with George Lewis. The firm of Phelps & Lewis has been very successful and their trade is steadily increasing. January 26, 1862, Mr. Phelps was married to Carrie Griswold, born in Trumbull County, Ohio, September 20, 1843; she is the daughter of Jesse Griswold, a native of Pennsylvania, who died about 1874. This union has been blessed with one child—William M., born February 9, 1876. The Phelps family are of English descent, and some of the ancestry came to this country in its early years. Mr. and Mrs. Phelps are Baptists; he is a Republican.

JOHN F. PECK, builder, Gardner. Mr. John F. Peck was born in Addison County, Vt., September 24, 1836; raised and educated in Vermont; learned the trade of carpenter and joiner, at which he has worked for many years as contractor, working in his native State, in Troy, N. Y., and in Grundy County, Ill. Besides, he has combined a thorough knowledge of moving buildings, which occupies most of his time of late years, moving more buildings, perhaps, than any other man in the State. Was in the Government employ during the war as foreman of a wrecking train. December 23, 1858, he was married to Miss Sarah E. Kellogg, of Ferrisburg, Vt.; she was born September 23, 1838, daughter of Reuben and Elizabeth Kellogg; they came to Grundy County in 1865; they have a family of four children—Frederick C. Peck, accountant in Chicago; Flora E. Peck; Edward J. Peck, jeweler by trade, and Walter F. Peck. He worked about two years as traveling agent for the Ruttan Heating and Ventilating Company. He is a member of the Masonic fraternity, Knights Templar. Residence on the corner of Dwight and Jackson streets, Gardner.

DENNIS PETIT, farmer, P. O. Gardner, was born in Schoharie County, N. Y., October 20, 1832, son of Chester W. and Nancy (Collins) Petit, natives of New York State; he is a farmer by occupation; she died in August, 1873. Our subject was one of ten children; received a common-school education and assisted on the home farm; came to Kendall County, Ill., in 1856, and to Grundy County in 1871; here he has since resided on a well-cultivated farm of eighty acres. Mr. Petit was married, November 4, 1852, to Catharine Baxter, who was born in Sharon, N. Y., June 14, 1827; this union has been blessed with three children—Charles, Nancy and Wesley. Mr. Petit is a Republican.

S. M. ROGERS, hardware, Gardner. Mr. Rogers was born January 27, 1823, in Rensselaer County, N. Y. His parents, S. G. and Tenny A. (Armstrong) Rogers, were natives of the same State, and came from Wayne, N. Y., to Illinois in 1845. Here the mother died, and the father died in California. They were blessed with ten children—Mary, S. M., William A., Phœbe K., Isaac P., Daniel, Martha, John H., George M. and Eugene. Mr. R. had some good school advantages and applied himself at rural labors in his younger days. He began for himself at the age of thirty running a farm, which he continued until 1875, when he began the sale and repairing of wagons at Gardner, which he still continues, together with a general stock of hardware. His partner is George Smith. He was married, November 9, 1847, to M. L. Pond, who died soon after, and he was again married, in 1852, to Lucy M. Powers, of this county, the result of which was four children—Ida, wife of J. H. Wheeler; Effie, wife of A. Spalding; Edith M. and one deceased when an infant. He has held office in Livingston County; was Deputy Sheriff in this and La Salle Counties. In 1880, was a candidate for Sheriff of this county.

Mr. Rogers possesses some excellent property in this county, the result of his own energy. He has seen some of the hardships that make up the life of the pioneer, such as hauling grain from here to Chicago, and plowing the soil with the ancient plows and ox teams. Votes the Greenback ticket.

CHESTER K. SNYDER, grain dealer, Gardner, was born in Red Creek, Wayne Co., N. Y., April 23, 1832; is the son of Amos and Sally (Enos) Snyder, natives of New York State; the former was born in 1801, and died in 1875; was a real estate dealer, Justice of the Peace and Judge of Wayne County, N. Y. The mother was born in 1806, and died in 1873; they had six children, of whom our subject was the fifth; he was educated in the common schools of his native place, and, at the age of nineteen, left home and learned telegraphy; for three years, he operated in New York State, Canada and Kentucky. In 1854, he came to Grundy County and located at Gardner, where he was the first telegraph operator. One and one-half years after coming here, he purchased a farm, and a year from this time went to Williamsville and engaged in the lumber and grain business. In 1861, he returned to Gardner, and farmed for one and one-half years; he then engaged in the railroad business for one and one-half years, when he again engaged in farming. The latter occupation he continued until 1874, when he once more engaged in the grain and lumber business at Gardner; this he still continues. While farming, he bought and shipped stock extensively; he now owns a farm of about 400 acres, all under cultivation, as well as some town property. Mr. Snyder was married, November 17, 1857, to Polly J. Holland, born in May, 1830, in Cayuga County, N. Y.; they have two children—Harry and Maggie. Mr. Snyder holds the position of Commissioner of Highways, and is independent in politics.

G. F. SPENCER, farmer, P. O. Gardner, was born December 7, 1822, in New York, and is the son of George and Laura Hatzel Spencer, natives of New Hartford, Conn., and parents of six children—Adaline, Lydia, G. F., Norton, Anna and one deceased. Mr. Spencer's mother died when he was eleven years old, and he was bound out to Joseph B. Roe until he was sixteen, when he was employed at a small salary by Mr. Roe. At eighteen, he hired out at $11 per month. In the fall of 1850, he came to Grundy County, Ill., and purchased his present farm of 160 acres, which was then mostly raw prairie. With logs from the grove he erected a cabin, about 16x24 feet, in which he lived. He began breaking the soil with an ox-team and the pioneer breaking-plow. With this same team, he hauled grain some distance. He was married, in 1851, to Eliza, daughter of Mahlon and Abigail Crane, she being one of nine children—Mary, William, Henry, Lucinda, Thaddeus, Edwin, Harriet, Howard, Eliza and Helen; her parents were Methodists; her father was in the war of 1812. Mr. Spencer has, as a result of the union, three children—Alice, the wife of Reed Keepers; Libbie; and Ida, the wife of Philip Southcomb, of Morris. The spring after his marriage, he was chosen one of the petit jurors for this county, and, after having been kept two weeks at Morris, when he would liked to have been cultivating his crops, he was dismissed at 4 o'clock on Saturday evening; he walked all the way home; when he came to the foot log across the stream near his home, at 10 o'clock, when all was dark, he found that the rain had raised the branch about two feet above the one log bridge; he knew from the channel that the water was over ten feet deep, and that, should he fall in, he would, in all probability, be drowned; he was bound for home, and at once "cooned" the log on all fours, his head only being above the water while passing over. This is only one of many such scenes which this pioneer experienced. When he built his cabin, he constructed a brick chimney, which was a curiosity to the neighbors, who often called out when passing, "take in the brick." In this building, the Methodists and other organizations held meetings. Near by Mr. Spencer's residence was located one of the first schoolhouses in this part of the county, the construction of which was largely due to the efforts of our subject. The father of Mrs. Spencer is residing with them, at the age of eighty-eight. Mr. S. has been Assessor and Justice of the Peace.

JOHN SPILLER, retired farmer. Gardner, was born in Devonshire, England, November 28, 1808, son of Robert and Ann (Applin) Spiller, natives of England; he was a farmer by occupation and died in 1872, at the age of eighty years. The mother died in 1848, aged about sixty. Our subject received a limited education, and assisted his parents upon the home farm, until he was thirty years of age, when he went to farming on his own account. In 1851, he emigrated to America, locating in Kendall County, Ill. October 31, 1839, Mr. Spiller was married, in England, to Miss Joanna Wakley, born in Devonshire June 24, 1819; she is the mother of six children, viz., Ann, William, Joel, Thomas, Mary Jane and John. For eight months after landing in this country, our subject was ill, and the entire support of the family devolved upon Mrs. Spiller. Upon regaining his health, Mr. Spiller engaged as a farm hand until, by his industry and economy, he had accumulated sufficient means to purchase eighty acres of farm land in Grundy County; this he added to until he had

168 acres, upon which he located in 1858. In the spring of 1875, he retired from active labor, and the farm is now managed by his son. Thomas Spiller, one of the sons of our subject, was born in England February 20, 1845. When six years of age, he came with his parents to America, and located in Kendall County, Ill.; received a common-school education and assisted on the home farm until twenty-one years of age. In 1876, he came to Gardner and engaged in harness-making, which he has since continued and at which he has been very successful. He was married, in Grundy County, January 9, 1868, to Elizabeth Allen, born in 1846; they have four children —Walter, Frank, Clarence and an infant. Mr. and Mrs. Thomas Spiller are members of the M. E. Church. He is a Republican; his father also a Republican; cast his first vote for Lincoln.

CHARLES H. SHERWOOD, dentist, Gardner, was born in Marshall County, Ill., October 15, 1853, is a son of Lycurgus and Rachel B. (Wilson) Sherwood, he born at Saratoga, N. Y., in August, 1824, a retired farmer, living at Normal, McLean Co., Ill.; the mother was born in Delaware County, Ohio, October 24, 1832, and has borne five children, of whom the subject is the eldest child. When ten years of age, he removed with his parents to the town of Wenona, where he received a common-school education; attended the Northwestern University at Evanston, one year, and spent four years at Wesleyan University, at Bloomington, where he completed the junior year. In addition to his other studies, our subject had studied medicine and dentistry, which subjects he continued prosecuting after leaving school, with Dr. S. C. Wilson, a prominent dentist and politician of Bloomington. In 1879, Dr. Sherwood entered the Philadelphia Dental College, from which he graduated with honors, March 26, 1881, as surgeon dentist. After nine months' practice at Galesburg, he came to Gardner, where he is nicely located and doing a good business. He is a supporter of the Republican party.

AARON SCOGGIN, farmer, P. O. Gardner, was born in Hamilton County, Ohio, February 23, 1809; is a son of Eli and Elizabeth (Meisner) Scoggin; the former was a native of Pennsylvania, a farmer by occupation, and died in 1852, at about the age of sixty-five. The mother, a native of Virginia, died in 1860, aged about sixty-seven years; she was the mother of seven children, of whom our subject was the third child. He received a common-school education and commenced his business career as a trader on the Mississippi River; this he continued seven years, and afterward, for about six years, ran a steam-mill, in Dearborn County, Ind. In 1856, he came to Grundy County, and for two years engaged in the lumber business at Gardner; he next located on his present farm. July 4, 1851, he married Miss Sarah Kirkpatrick, who died in 1853, leaving one child, which died April 26, 1863. Mr. Scoggin was again married, in 1857, to Anna B. Weaver, born in Juniata County, Penn., in 1827; they have had four children, one of whom is dead. Those living are Lizzie, Mary and John. Mr. Scoggin has a farm of 320 acres of choice land, all under cultivation; he handles stock as extensively as his farm will permit, and also carries on general farming. He has been a Republican since the organization of the party.

FRED G. THOMPSON, City Marshal, Gardner, was born March 29, 1844, in Somerset County, Me., son of Osgood and Hannah (Wentworth) Thompson, he born in Maine December 31, 1819, a farmer by occupation; she, also a native of Maine, born in 1821, and the mother of seven children, of whom subject was the second. He received a common-school education; enlisted in Company B, Seventh Maine Volunteer Infantry, under Capt. Albert A. Nickerson; regiment commanded by Col. F. C. Mason. Subject remained in the army two years and four months, when he again resumed farming, but, owing to injuries received in the war, was obliged to leave the service; for the ensuing fourteen years, he was engaged in photography. In the spring of 1866, he came to Grundy County, and, in 1867, located in Gardner. In 1880, Mr. Thompson was obliged to abandon photography, and at present is City Marshal, which position he has held about seven years. He has been twice married—first, in Grundy County, April 7, 1867, to Miss Nellie A. Locke, born at Harmony, Me., and died October 21, 1871, at the age of twenty-six years, leaving one child—Inez W. Mr. Thompson's second marriage occurred June 26, 1872, when he united with Lina W. Briggs, who was born in Wisconsin May 20, 1854, daughter of Enoch I. an Emma (Winslow) Briggs, of Gardner. By this second marriage there was one child—Emma Maud, born September 8, 1874, died October 20, 1880. Mr. Thompson held the office of Town Clerk one term, and has held other minor offices. He is an active member of the I. O. O. F., of Gardner, and is a Republican.

JAMES I. TURNER, farmer, P. O. Gardner, was born in Lake County, Ill., May 18, 1854, son of Richard and Sarah (Donne) Turner, natives of Maine. The father was born in 1817; is a stock-dealer, living in Kansas. The mother died in 1876, at the age of fifty five; she had two children—Nellie, who died at the age of twenty-seven, and James, our subject. He came to Cook County when four years of age, with his parents; attended the common schools and finished his education at Bryant & Stratton's Business College in Chicago. In 1872, he settled in Gardner, where he pursued the lumber business until 1877. In the fall of 1872, he erected the grain elevator now owned by Mr. Atkinson, and engaged in the grain business, in connection with his lumber trade. In 1876, he sold out his business to Mr. Atkinson, and the following year went to Sheldon, Ill., where he engaged in the grain business a year. He next went to Minnesota, where he engaged in farming until 1880, when he returned to Grundy County and settled on his present place. October 9, 1880, he married Miss Jessie Manegold, born in Kankakee County, Ill., in 1860; she is the daughter of John and Mary Manegold, he dead, she living in Gardner. This union has resulted in one child—Richard. Mr. Turner carries on general farming and stock-dealing; he has been School Director one year, and is a member of the order of A., F. & A. M. of Gardner.

ABRAHAM TINSMAN, farmer, P. O. Gardner, was born in Butler County, Penn., April 7, 1828, son of Adam and Elizabeth (Sigler) Tinsman, he born in October, 1802, and died in July, 1882, was a farmer by occupation. The mother was born March 2, 1806, and had twelve children, of whom our subject is the oldest. He attended the common schools and worked on the farm in his younger days. In 1858, he came to Grundy County, and located where he now lives. Mr. Tinsman was married, September 15, 1873, to Susan Williman, born in Stark County, Ohio, February 28, 1841; she is the daughter of Jonas and Barbara Williman, who live in Grundy County. This marriage has resulted in three children, viz., Forney, Adam J. and Marlin. Our subject carries on general farming, and has held the positions of Road Commissioner and School

Director. He and wife are members of the Church of God. He is a Republican.

J. B. TAXIS, physician and surgeon, Gardner, was born October 22, 1833, in Pennsylvania. Was married in 1860 to Virginia M. Hawley, the result being five children, three of whom survive, viz., Howard H., Herbert J. and Virginia I. He came to Gardner in 1859, and has built up a lucrative practice.

JOEL UNDERHILL, physician, Gardner. Prominently identified among the physicians of this county is the man whose name heads this article. He was born November 25, 1823, in Dutchess County, N. Y.; is a son of Henry N. and Julia A. (Carpenter) Underhill, natives of New York, and the parents of nine children—Caroline, Joel, Louisa, Henry P., Ida, only survive. The parents belonged to the Christian denomination known as Friends. The Doctor had but little chance of attending school in his younger days. At the age of twenty-one, he started for himself. While at New Orleans, he was taken with the yellow fever, and returned home when only partially recovered. He engaged some time after this in farming, renting of his father. He later met with another misfortune, that of the erysipelas, and after recovering he began reading medicine with Dr. Galord, and remained with him till 1849-50, at which time he attended lectures at a medical college, New York, transferring from there to Sodus Ridge, N. Y., where he bought a drug store with Dr. Galord, and remained there for two years, when he sold out and went to Buffalo, and continued his studies with Dr. Hill for about three years, after which he attended three courses of lectures at Buffalo, at which city he opened up an office for three years. At this period, he gave up his practice on account of poor health. He made some changes in locality, and finally engaged in a flouring mill at Dwight, this State. In 1864, he bought a farm in Greenfield Township, this county, and has farmed the same since until 1872, when he resumed practice, taking up the homœopathic system. Was married, in 1862, to Caroline Crouthers. His wife is a member of the Presbyterian Church. The Doctor votes the Democratic ticket.

JAMES S. WILSON (deceased) was born in Niagara County, N. Y., December 12, 1821, son of William and Maggie (Callard) Wilson. Our subject came to Illinois when eighteen years of age, having but 50 cents in his pocket, but he was energetic, and wished to make his own way in the world. In 1854, he came to Gardner and engaged in farming; previous to this time, he had made two trips overland to California, and had improved two farms. At one time, Mr. Wilson had over 1,000 acres of farm land, all under a high state of cultivation, and on the homestead farm, which contained about 600 acres, he sunk a coal shaft, which he managed for two years. In 1871, he sold out his entire business interests in this line. He next purchased the Commercial House and its surroundings, to which he made several additions by way of improvement. In connection with his duties as landlord, he did a general real estate and broker business. His death occurred January 1, 1877; he was married twice, his first wife being Jane Freelove; she died in 1863, leaving seven children—Andrew, Mary, Achsah, Maria, La Fayette, Ida and Frank. Mr. Wilson was again married, September 1, 1864, to Nancy Ann (Thatcher) Wheeler, born in Essex County, N. Y., July 27, 1830; she had by her first husband five children—Nancy, Julius H., Jennie, Hattie and Frederick. Mrs. Wilson has by her second husband, our subject, two children—Lucy A. and Charles J. S. At Mr. Wilson's death, Mrs. Wilson became administratrix of the estate of her husband, and assumed full control of the Commercial House.

DR. A. H. WRIGHT, dentist, Gardner, was born in La Porte County, Ind., December 16, 1857, son of Gideon L. and Sarah E. (Concannon) Wright, natives of Indiana. Our subject passed through the common and high school of his native place, and spent two years in college; afterward studied dentistry two years at Valparaiso, Ind., where he started in business and remained one year. He then went to Joliet, where he remained a year, and, in January, 1882, came to Gardner, where he has a lucrative practice. He votes the Republican ticket. Dr. Wright is the eldest of three children born to his parents. One sister, Millie, is living; the other, Hattie, is dead.

EDWIN B. YOUNG, editor of the Gardner *Enterprise*, is the eldest son of William B. and Ellen A. Young; he was born in the town of Chatham, Middlesex Co., Conn., May 22, 1858, and was educateed at the high school in his native town. He has one brother, Howard P. Young, born October 12, 1870. In the spring of 1874, the family moved West, and settled in Clifton, Iroquois County, this State. Here the *Enterprise* was started by the present publisher in October, 1876. The family wishing a change of country, moved to Gardner, in the fall of 1878, where the paper has since been published. The *Enterprise*, which started as a four-column folio, has been enlarged from time to time, and is now a large sheet of eight, columns to the page, enjoying a good run of advertising and a large subscription list. Its editor is unmarried, and resides with his parents and brother.

BRACEVILLE TOWNSHIP.

GEORGE P. AUGUSTINE, Postmaster, Braceville, was born December 28, 1811, in Stark County, Ohio; is a son of John and Margaret (Wishard) Augustine, natives of Pennsylvania, and the parents of John, George P., Mary, Joseph, Matilda, Margaret and Oliver P. The mother died in 1844, and the father came West in 1852, locating 640 acres in Braceville Township, this county, as a land warrant for services in the war of 1812. The father was a Justice of the Peace here, Supervisor, and held other minor offices. While in Ohio, the father was Sheriff of Stark County, and was eight years in the State Legislature; he died in 1871. Our subject closed his school days at the age of twelve years, at which time he was actively engaged on a farm. When he reached his majority, he begin boating on the Ohio Canal, at which he was successful. In 1844, he entered the mercantile business at Waynesburg, Stark County, Ohio, and in 1861 he closed out his business there and applied his time in Grundy County, erecting the first house in what is now the present site of the village of Braceville. The old building is now known as the Milwaukee Hotel. He used this building as a warehouse and for store room; he bought corn at that time for 9 cents per bushel, and eggs at 3 cents per dozen. In 1876, he closed out said business, and also his coal interests, in which he had been interested since 1865. At the latter, he sustained a severe loss. By economy, he had accumulated a fortune, of probably $300,000, the greater portion of which he lost in the coal business. In 1862, he was commissioned Postmaster at Braceville, which position he holds to-day. Was married, in 1847, to Julia Fisher, the result being one child—Elizabeth, who married S. B. Holly (deceased). His wife died in 1872 and since then he has resided with his daughter. In the spring of 1882, he was chosen Justice of the Peace, which position he now holds. He was identified with the Whig party, and since then has been a strong Republican.

GEORGE W. BOOTH, farmer and stockbreeder, P. O. Gardner. Among the leading farmers and stock-dealers of Illinois, the gentleman whose name heads this article ranks second to none. He is a native of Trumbull County, Ohio, and was born January 13, 1837. His parents, Moses and Myra (Hubbell) Booth, were natives of Connecticut, and came to Ohio at an early day, where the father died February, 1856, and the mother in this county in 1882. The parents were blessed with three children by their union, viz., George W.; Theresa, the wife of Henry Waters; Emma, the wife of Robert Briscoe, of Marseilles, Ill. The mother of our subject was the second wife of Moses Booth, he having married Sarah Judson, the result being several children—Truman, Moses, Samuel, Eliza, Laura, Sallie, et al. Moses B. was in the war of 1812, and he and wife were Presbyterians. George had the chance to attend the district schools in his younger days. At the age of fourteen, he began driving cattle, and at sixteen, he was engaged with F. N. Andrews, of Trumbull County, Ohio. At the age of twenty, he had saved some means, and invested the same in hogs and cattle, which proved successful. April, 1863, he took charge of a stock farm for Elias Trumbo, of La Salle County, Ill., with whom he remained five years, after which he bought 160 acres of land in Greenfield Township, this county. He owned this but a short time, and made several changes before he finally settled on his present farm in Braceville Township. Here he began to widen in his stock dealing, and, in 1877, he took in full partnership his son-in-law, Lyman Hawley, which firm name of Booth & Hawley still exists. Their herd of cattle now consists of the following noted families: Rose of Sharon, Pansy, Dulci Bella, Arabella and Seventeens, a class of the first importation from Europe by the Clays. They are also breeding the registered Poland-China hogs, which they ship to different parts of Illinois, Iowa, Kansas, Nebraska, Ohio and Indiana. They are stocking about eight hundred acres of land. Mr. Booth was married, April 9, 1856, to Caroline Rainy, a daughter of William and Mary (Taylor) Rainy, natives, the father of Ireland, and the mother of Pennsylvania. The parents were blessed with three children—Nancy, Mary and Caroline. Her parents were members of the Seceder Church. Mrs. B. was born May 3, 1838, and her union has given her two children—Warren (deceased) and Mary, who has one child by her marriage with Lyman Hawley—Maud. Mr. Booth has served his township as Supervisor for eight years, of which board he was Chairman seven years. He has also been chosen Town Treasurer of Schools for nine years, and other minor offices. His estimable lady is a member of the Baptist Church of Gardner. He votes the Republican ticket.

JOHNSON BABCOCK, farmer, P. O. Coal City, was born August 12, 1800, in Rensselaer County, N. Y., is a son of Johnson and Zilpa (Green) Babcock, natives, the father of Connecticut, and the mother of New York. The parents had eleven children, six of whom are living. Johnson attended school awhile during his younger days. He emigrated to Ohio in 1831, and in 1846 he removed to a farm near Aurora, Ill., where he rented for three years. In 1848, he bought land where he now lives, and settled on the same in 1849, where he has since remained. Was married October 29, 1826, to Dorcas Messinger, who blessed him with twelve children, six of whom survive—Martin, Mary L., Eleanor, Frederick, Albert and Henry. His wife died January 20, 1872. He has served as Justice of the Peace, Assessor, Town Clerk and other smaller offices with credit to himself and his friends. He was a Democrat until Buchanan's campaign, since when he has been a stanch Republican. His son Albert married Almira Stallman, the result being Minnie E. and Orin E. and one deceased. This son lives with his father and farms the old homestead. Another son, T. J., was born October 29, 1837, in Ohio, and was married December, 1862, to Martha E. Laymon, the result being four children, viz., William A. (deceased), Ralph S., Maranda A. and Thomas T. This son has eighty acres of good land, which he is farming.

SAMUEL BRADBEER, farmer, P. O. Gardner. This representative pioneer is a native of England, and was born April 3, 1821. His parents, Samuel and Jane (Lake) Bradbeer, emigrated to Kendall County, Ill., in 1853, where the father died in 1856. The parents were blessed with eight children, viz., Robert, Mary, Elizabeth, Samuel and James, and three deceased. They were members of the Congregational Church. The father was one time in excellent circumstances financially, but was made to sustain quite a loss by some illegal proceedings. He was therefore unable to give his children much chance to obtain an education. Our subject had the advantage of the country schools until he was eight years old, at which time he engaged on a farm, herding cattle, gathering stones, etc., for which he received only his board for two years. At the age of ten, he was called home to take his older brother's place, he having hired out for long time. In two years, he was set free again to care for himself, and engaged to a farmer for his board and clothing. Later, he was rewarded with £2 of English money per year. In one year more, he received £8, or $40, per year. Two years later, he withdrew from active labor and prospected for awhile in London, and finally returned to his parents, and soon engaged to a doctor for about six months. He was then employed as a waiter in a private family at Exmouth for ten years, receiving from $80 to $100 per year. He was married, April 11, 1851, to Sarah Carter, the result being three children—Susan J., Alice and Sarah. Mrs. B. was born in Somerset County, England, January 20, 1815; is a daughter of Robert and Susannah (Diment) Carter, natives of the same country, and the parents of three children—Sarah, John and William. Our subject lived in Kendall County, Ill., for nine years, and then came to Braceville Township, this county, in 1863, where they have since remained. They possess now 100 acres of fine land, the result of their own labors. He is a member and Pastor of the Old School Baptist organization, holding at present the pastoral charge of the Verona church. His wife and daughter Sarah are Methodists. In the person of Mr. B. we have the character of a remarkable self-made man. The first penny he ever had in his life was given him by a cattle driver whom he helped transfer his herd a short distance. This he spent for two English songs, "Farmer's Boy" and "On Fox Hunting." When twelve years old, he would slip books from the library where he was working, and sit by his bed at the barn and read nearly all night. At another place where he worked, he had an alarm clock which he arranged to strike at three o'clock, at which time he would light a candle and sit up in bed and read some book or paper. So earnest was he in the pursuit of knowledge that he and his brother James gathered old bones and broken glass from the fields, which they sold in order to secure the *Saturday Magazine*, which cost 6 d. per month.

W. D. BRIDEL, farmer, P. O. Mazon, was born June 5, 1826, in England. Is a son of Robert and Mary (Diment) Bridel, who came to Pennsylvania in 1841, and in 1845 to Kendall County, Ill.; the father is living with his second wife, Alice Sutliff. Our subject is one of five living children from a family of eight;

William D., Isabella, Mary, Rachel, Robert are the names of those living; their mother died about the year 1858. Mr. Bridel was married, in 1862, to Caroline R. Towns, a daughter of Aaron and Mary (Green) Towns, natives of New York, and the parents of six children, viz., Joshua, Clarinda, Edward, Sarah, Caroline and William. Mr. Bridel has six children—William, Mary R., George W., Robert S., Belle and Lillie E. He settled on his present farm about 1854; he has now 316 acres of fine land; has been in small offices; was drafted and hired a substitute; he is a Democrat.

WILLIAM CAMPBELL, Superintendent Wilmington Star Mining Company, Coal City. Mr. Campbell was born April 3, 1848, in Scotland; is a son of William and Susan (Melroy) Campbell. William began mining when quite young, and had followed the same the greater portion of his life. He mined at Braidwood as early as 1867, and, in 1879, he was appointed Superintendent of the Wilmington Star Mining Company at Coal City, which position he holds, and through his management these mines are turning out about 500 tons daily. He was married twice, the first time to Isabel Clombie (deceased), and the second time to Agnes Patterson, the latter union resulting in four children—Ellen, Arthur, Laura and Fannie.

ALEXANDER CAMERON, farmer, P. O. Braceville, was born April 12, 1820, in Scotland. Is a son of William and Jane Cameron, natives of the same country, and parents of ten children, four of whom are living, viz., Alexander, William, Isabel and Archibald. The parents emigrated to Peoria County, Ill., in 1833, and farmed in said county. The father died in 1864, and the mother in 1867; they were Methodists. Our subject never attended school a single day in his life, yet he has picked up a fair business education. Was married, June 3, 1846, to Julia A. Morrison, a daughter of William H. and Barbara (Usong) Morrison. Mrs. Cameron was born March 28, 1825, in Pike County, Ill. She and her husband settled the present farm in 1856; they have 250 acres of fine land, the result of their own efforts; they have no children. Mrs. Cameron's father left his family in Pike County when she was very small, and traveled along the river looking up land to purchase, and never returned. The party who went with him said he died with fever. She lived for some time with Dr. Henry Ross, of Pike County, until twelve years old, and returned to her mother, she having married Ira Ackley, the result being one child—Lydia E., and by the former union two children—Julia A. and William. Mrs. Cameron's education is also limited, she having been unable to attend school in her younger days. Mr. Cameron votes the Republican ticket.

REUBEN CARTER, farmer, P. O. Gardner, was born February 18, 1855, in England. Is a son of William and Elizabeth (Chick) Carter, natives of the same country, and parents of nine children, eight of whom survive, viz., Sarah, Susan, Mary, Elizabeth, Alice, William, Reuben and George. Our subject had but little advantage of school. At the age of ten, he took active labor in the rural pursuits of of life, at 16 cents per day. He came to America in 1871, settling in Grundy County. Was married in April, 1880, to Alice, a daughter of Samuel Bradbeer, whose sketch appears elsewhere in this work. His union has resulted in one child—Mabel. When on his way from his native country to this county, the train on which he was traveling through Michigan was wrecked, and he barely escaped from sudden death, with the loss of the right little finger. He owns eighty acres of well-improved land, which he bought in 1881 of James Smith. This is the result of his own labors, he having only one shilling left when arriving in this county. He votes the Republican ticket.

HENRY CASSINGHAM, farmer, P. O. Gardner; born October 8, 1815, in England; son of Thomas and Phœbe (Ford) Cassingham, natives of England. The parents emigrated to Muskingum County, Ohio, where they died, the mother in October, 1838, and the father in 1845. They had twelve children, all of whom grew up and were married, nine are living—Thomas, Richard, James, George, John, Henry, Phœbe (deceased), Elizabeth, Sophia (deceased), William, Ford and Mary (deceased). The parents belonged to the Methodist Church. Our subject attended the subscription schools in the country, getting a fair business education. He worked with his father until the age of twenty-one, when he began learning the carpenter trade, which he continued for fourteen years. He moved to Kendall County, Ill., in 1845, where he carpentered until 1849, at which time he came to his farm of eighty acres, in what is now Mazon Township, which he had purchased of the Government a little while prior to his moving. Here in this neighborhood he has lived and now possesses 240 acres, the result of their own labors. When locating in Kendall County, they had about $300. They settled on raw prairie, and witnessed the scenes of the early pioneers. Was married, in 1839, to Jane Osler, a daughter of George and Jane (Hollenback) Osler, the father a native of Maryland and the mother of Virginia, and the parents of four children—Jane, George, John and Nancy. The mother was married, prior to that with Mr. Osler, to Nathan Devore, and the result was two children—Elizabeth and David. Mr. Devore was drafted in the war of 1812, in which service he died. Her mother was married, after the death of Mrs. Cassingham's father, to John Hartford, the result being two children—Eliza A. and Sarah E. Mrs. Cassingham's mother was a church member of the Methodist Episcopal organization for sixty years before her decease, to which the father belonged. Mr. and Mrs. Cassingham have been blessed with eleven children, viz., David H., deceased; Marshall, physician at Roberts, Ford Co., Ill.; Ellen, deceased; David, deceased; Mary E., deceased; Elvira, the wife of Thomas Foster; Arvilla, the wife of Dr. W. H. Watson, of Caberey, Ill.; Alice, deceased; Ora W., druggist, Ford County, Ill.; Clinton, married Melissa La Force; and E. W. Mr. Cassingham was Supervisor for eight terms, Justice of the Peace several years, and other small offices; was once solicited and was run for County Judge, and was only sixteen votes behind. He and wife have been connected with the Methodist Church for over forty-four years. He was once Whig, and joined the Republican party at its organization. A brother of Mr. Cassingham came from Ohio to this county on horseback, bringing with him a dog to hunt. The first chase was a wolf, which they caught. Ford, the brother, took the hide from the animal, and started home without his dog, which he thought was either dead or stolen. When he arrived at his home, he found his faithful dog awaiting him.

E. H. COTTON, farmer, P. O. Coal City, was born December 3, 1835, in Montgomery County, N. Y.; is a son of Nicholas and Elizabeth (Sweet) Cotton. The parents were married January 15, 1815; they removed from New York to Braceville Township in 1854, at which time the father erected a blacksmith shop, on the present site of the village of Braceville; he lived for awhile with his son-in-law, Braugham, who had settled here about 1852. The father died in this county in 1870, and the mother in 1872; were the parents of Mary, Sallie, John R., Nicholas, Garrett, Lucinda, James P., David G., Calvin H. and E. H. The father served in the war of 1812. Our subject attended school some during his younger days, and has always been a farmer; he hauled all the lumber from Morris by ox team, from which his father constructed his first house in this county; he was married September 15, 1855, to Elizabeth J. Mitchell, a daughter of John and Lucy (Patterson) Mitchell; she was one of seven children, viz., Lydia, James, Elizabeth, Margaret, John

Lucy and Mary. Mr. Cotton settled on his present farm in 1867, buying eighty acres of James Barrett, and has since added until he has 240 acres of fine land. His union gave him seven children — Mary E. (the wife of James Sherry, of Iowa), Sarah J., Lida (the wife of Jesse Slutter, of Chicago), John J., Nicholas, Anna and Lillie; his wife died August 20, 1879. He has been Assessor; is now Supervisor of Braceville Township; votes the Democratic ticket; his father was a member of the A., F. & A. M., and was buried by that fraternity.

GEORGE H. CRAGG, farmer, P. O. Gardner, was born April 5, 1840, in Grundy County, Ill.; is a son of John and Agnes (Litchhult) Cragg, natives of New Jersey; they came to this county about the year 1832, and erected a log cabin 20x20, which is still standing; here they witnessed the scenes that make up the life of the actual pioneer, such as going to church in a wagon or sled, drawn by ox teams. The father was consumptive, and the greater portion of the labor depended upon Mrs. Cragg, which she performed readily. The father was of English descent, and early learned a trade. It has been said he could make almost anything; he was born March 6, 1803, and was the father of seven children, three of whom survive, viz., Martin, George H. and Louisa. The mother is living; was born January 7, 1813, in New Jersey; she yet weaves, having a loom which she used about the time she settled here. George H. had some chance to attend school in a pioneer cabin. At the death of his father, he was sent to school at Wilmington for six months; was married, February 17, 1861, to Rachel Bridel, the result being four children — Alice, Robert, Cora B. and Emma. He has fifty-five acres of well-improved land, and is farming seventy-five acres which belongs to his mother; he enlisted in Company —, One Hundred and Fifty-six Illinois Volunteer Infantry; he votes the Republican ticket. Further notice is given of the Cragg family in the township history.

MARTIN CRAGG, farmer, P. O. Gardner. Martin Cragg is probably the first white child born in Braceville Township, the date of his birth being January 21, 1836; he is a brother of George H., whose biogrophy appears in this book. His early days were spent as much as was convenient in the log school cabin; he was very fond of chasing the wild animals that were so numerous when he was a boy. On one occasion the grey-hounds caught a deer, and Martin was a little swifter on foot than the other boys who were with him on the chase, and on arriving, he bounced the wild animal, and the dogs thinking their master could manage it, let loose, and as soon as they did, the deer made a leap with Martin on its back, and away it went for the thicket. The gritty little fellow was going backward, and hung on until the brush forced him off. He was married, December 17, 1861, to Helen N. Caverly, a daughter of Isaac and Hannah (Newell) Caverly, natives of New Hampshire, and parents of four children; Helen only survives; her mother died when she was six years old, and her father was married a second time to Kate Kipp, of Philadelphia, Penn., the result being two children — William and Louisa; her father died in 1856, and Helen lived with her uncle, Robert Newell, of Boston, until she was fourteen, when she came to Gardner, Ill., to live with her uncle and aunt, Sawyer; her marriage with Mr. Cragg has resulted in four children, two of whom are living, viz., Edward C. and Jennie. Mr. Cragg has been Constable of Braceville Township two terms; he owns 170 acres of fine land, the most of which is the reward of his own labors. He is raising many plants for sale, having an excellent hot garden; grows entirely for the Braidwood market; votes the Republican ticket.

OLIVER DROWN, farmer, P. O. Coal City, was born October 23, 1823, in Canada; is a son of Hiram and Susannah (Stinson) Drown, natives, the father of Connecticut and the mother of Ireland, and parents of ten children—Oliver, Mary A., Susannah, Margaret, James, Jane, Rebecca, John, Thomas and one died young; his parents were Methodists. Our subject attended the district schools; has always worked on the farm; was married in 1849, to Harriet A. Thayer, a daughter of Ebenezer and Julia Thayer, natives of New York, and the parents of five children, viz., Harriet, Alonzo, Eliza, Emma and one deceased young. His union gave him seven children, six of whom are living—Julia, Hiram, Melvin, Emma, Frank, Ella and Jane (deceased). He came to Illinois in 1858, settling for awhile near Morris, where he engaged in a brick-yard and other vocations for some time. In 1869, he bought eighty acres where he now lives, of L. Crossley, where he has since resided. He is now School Trustee. He votes the Republican ticket. His brother Thomas died in the late war, member of Indiana Volunteer Infantry.

JOHN F. DUNLEAVY, farmer, P. O. Coal City, was born November 22, 1845, in England; is a son of Michael and Sarah Dunleavy, natives of Ireland and the parents of seven children—Martin, Michael, William, Daniel, Mary, John F. and Ann. The parents emigrated to Wisconsin in 1846, and in 1855 to Illinois, settling where our subject now lives, where they died, the father in 1874 and the mother in 1876; they were Catholics. Our subject obtained a fair education; enlisted in Company B, Fourth Illinois Volunteer Cavalry, on January 1, 1864, and remained until its close; was never married; has a family keeping house for him; owns 160 acres of fine land. He is raising the Holstein cattle, Poland-China hogs and Clydesdale horses. He votes the Greenback ticket. He lost his health to some extent in the war.

CASSIUS C. EASTON, farmer, P. O. Gardner, was born in Trumbull County, Ohio, March 21, 1845, was the youngest son of Alexander and Rhoda Easton. His father was a carpenter and farmer, born in Franklin County, Mass., September 25, 1801. Spent his last years with our subject, where he died November 1, 1880. His mother, whose maiden name was Rhoda Plumb, was born March 10, 1805 ; was married when seventeen years old to Joseph Lee, who died in 1843, and on March 27. 1844, she was again married to Alexander Easton. She died in Trumbull County, Ohio June 20, 1851 ; such was her life, that none knew her but to love her. C. C. received his education at the common schools of his native town. Working at carpenter work some with his father, he became quite skilled in the business, so that he has since constructed several houses. When sixteen, he came to Illinois and hired out as a farm hand. In the spring of 1868, he bought a farm of 100 acres in Norton, Kankakee County. In 1874, he rented his farm and moved to Gardner, where he lived a year or so, when he bought 120 acres, where he now lives ; has since added forty acres more and all is under a good state of cultivation. C. C. Easton was married in 1866, to Mary Jane, daughter of John Spiller, whose sketch appears elsewhere in the work. Mr. and Mrs. Easton have three children, two boys and one girl—Addison M., Rowland J. and Rhoda Belle. C. C. is a man of correct habits and uncompromising integrity, warmly attached to home and its environments, for which he amply provides. Mrs. Easton is a frugal, industrious woman, skillfully conducting her household affairs, always ready to do her part to make a home and make it happy.

REV. G. R. EVANS, Braceville, born May 20, 1821 in North Wales ; son of Richard and Ellen (Pryse) Evans, the parents of G. R. Sydney, William, Elizabeth, Ellen, Rees and Richard. Our subject attended school in the country and city, aside from his labors on the farm. At the age of twenty, he closed his school days and engaged actively in farming until 1850, when he was married to Ellen Jones, a native of Wales, and soon after engaged in buying grain on his own resource at Anglesea, Wales, for ten years, at which he was successful for awhile, and then sustained some losses. In 1861, he came to Racine, Wis., where he bought wheat for two years; transferred from there to Arena, same State, where he built a warehouse and purchased grain for two years. In 1849, he began in the ministry, and from Arena he went to Milwaukee, where he took charge of the Welsh Congregational Church for one year; then to Watertown, Wis., Ixonia and Emmet, and was pastor of a church at each place. In 1871, he located in Braceville, Ill., taking charge of the Braidwood and Braceville churches, and is still pastor of the former. In 1872, he was appointed agent for the American Express Company at Braceville, which he still holds. He is Police Magistrate of this village. His marriage gave him ten children—Sydney, Griffith, Ellen, Kate, Jennie, Richard (sea captain in Wales), Eliza, Susie, Lydia and Zula. He was Supervisor for Braceville Township in 1878. Votes the Republican ticket.

SOLOMON HARRIS, boots and shoes, Braceville, was born November 30, 1824, in South Wales, is a son of Isaac and Ann Harris, who came to this country in 1863; the father died in 1876. The parents had thirteen children, ten of whom grew up—Solomon, Joseph, Eliza, Enoch, Mary, Thomas, Jemima, Isaac (deceased), Leah and Isaac. Our subject attended school but little. When quite young, he began mining, which he followed in the old country until May 16, 1851, when he landed at Philadelphia, where he dug coal till January 24, 1862, when he came to Illinois and resumed his labors in a coal mine. In 1881, he engaged in his present business, that of boots and shoes, at which he is succeeding well. Was married, February 14, 1845, to Martha Watkins, a native of Wales, the union resulting in thirteen children—Isaac, Valentine, Jane, Solomon, William, Thomas, William W., Martha A., Eliza, Hannah, Ann and Annie, Rebecca. He and wife are members of the Baptist Church. Votes the Republican ticket.

C. E. HASTINGS, merchant, Braceville. Prominent among the leading young business men in Braceville is C. E. Hastings, of the firm of Trotter & Hastings. He was born in 1862, in Pennsylvania; is the son of Eli and Rachel (Karr) Hastings, natives of the same State, and the parents of Laura, Catharine, S. M., C. E., Jessie M. and Cora B. The parents came to Illinois in 1866, settling in Gardner and afterward in Morris. Our subject attended the schools of Gardner and Morris. He clerked for about three years in Braidwood. August 2, 1881, he formed the partnership named above, and is meriting a fine trade, having at this time a general line of dry goods, etc. September 21, 1882, he was married to Lizzie B., a daughter of Capt. L. A. Baker, of Wilmington. He is a pleasant, genial fellow, and has the respect and confidence of all with whom he does business.

TALCOTT HAWLEY, deceased. Mr. Talcott was born in 1800 in the State of New York; was a farmer, and married Elizabeth Mulford, and came to Lockport, Ill., about 1852, and a few months later they bought 160 acres of land in Braceville Township, on which farm the father died in 1859, and the mother in 1874; they were blessed with six children—Ellen and Lyman living, and Catharine, William, Daniel and Davis deceased. The deceased and companion had but little means when they located in this county; they used ox teams and all the old farming implements. Ellen owns the old homestead, and is living with William Vanhouton and family, who rents the farm. Mr. V. married Brittanna Cullen.

JOSEPH HOMAN, hardware, Coal City, was born October 26, 1852, in Union County, Ohio, is a son of William and Martha (Hill)

Homan. The father is a native of Virginia and the mother of Ohio. They were the parents of three children—Joseph, Emma (deceased, was the wife of W. S. Keay) and W. E. Joseph attended the country schools as much as was convenient. At the age of fifteen, he engaged actively on the farm, which avocation he continued until 1879, when he entered his present business, and is carrying a fine line of hardware. In 1880, his father took a half-interest in the same, and is still a member of the firm. Our subject was married September 14, 1881, to Isabel, a daughter of John and Ellen (Keay) Chadwick, by whom he has one child—Herbert W. He was at one time Treasurer of the village. Votes the Republican ticket.

WILLIAM HOMAN, farmer, P. O. Coal City, was born August 22, 1824, in Virginia; is a son of Joseph and Martha M. Homan, natives of the same State. The parents settled in Muskingum County, Ohio, in 1832, where they reared nine children, five of whom are living—William, John, Walter, Ira and Allen. The parents were Presbyterians. Mr. Homan had some school advantages. Was married, in 1849, to Martha Hill, a daughter of John and Esther (Marsh) Hill, natives of, the father Pennsylvania and the mother New York; she was one of eleven children, eight of whom survive—Joseph, Martha, H. D., Clarinda, Lucinda, William, Hugh M. and Esther. Mrs. Homan was born May 22, 1824, and has blessed her husband with two children living and one deceased—Joseph and William E.; Emma, deceased. Mr. Homan settled where he now lives in 1868; has 160 acres of fine land; has held some small offices; he is a Democrat.

FRANK HORAN, farmer, P. O. Gardner, was born September 9, 1851, in Chicago; is a son of Owen and Mary (Kernan) Horan, natives of Ireland. They emigrated to Chicago between 1833 and 1840; the mother was one of ten children, four living—Mary, Catharine (Mrs. P. A. Fennerty, of Chicago), B. F. and Ellen, the wife of A. G. Willard, of Chicago. Our subject was one of five children—P. A., Frank, Ellen, John and Lettie. The father followed engineering of lakes and farming, having located where Frank now lives in 1859. At his death, he owned 240 acres of well-improved land, which the family still owns. Frank had some school advantages, and early embarked in farm life. Was married, 1878, to Hannah Walsh, a daughter of Richard and Catharine (McNamara) Walsh, natives of Ireland. Her father came to La Salle County, Ill., in 1848, and her mother in 1837. Hannah and Ellen are the only ones living from a family of six children. Mr. Horan is now Commissioner of Highways. His union has blessed him with three children—Frank, Henry and Lester J. He and wife are Catholics; he votes the Republican ticket. His father died August 20, 1862, and his mother is living in Ottawa, Ill.

O. T. HOUSE, grocer, Braceville, was born June 19, 1857, in Bristol, Conn., is a son of Alfred and Ellen (Taylor) House, natives of the same State, and the parents of four children—Ralph O., Nettie, Minnie and O. T. The parents came to Beloit, Wis., in 1864, and are now residing in Wilmington, Ill. O. T. attended school at Rockton, Ill. He began the grocery business at Braceville November 20, 1881, and has a large stock of everything that constitutes a first-class retail grocery. Was married June 19, 1882, to Lillian Quackenbush. He worked for some time in the paper mills of M. D. Keeney, of Wilmington, by which he obtained the means to start his present fine business. Was a member of the I. O. O. F. of Wilmington, but severed his connection on account of moving away.

GEORGE LITTLEJOHN, farmer, P.O. Gardner. Mr. Littlejohn was born January 17, 1845, in Scotland; is a son of Hugh and Elizabeth (Wilson) Littlejohn, natives of Scotland and parents of three children—George, Susan and Jeanie; the father died August 18, 1869;

the mother was born February 12, 1810, and is living with the subject; she and her husband helped to organize the first Presbyterian Church in Ottawa, La Salle County, and Gardner, this county, and he was Elder in the latter. Their children were sent to school at a pioneer building beyond the river, and were compelled to cross the same with a boat, or on the chunks of ice. George was married, January 15, 1871, to Isabel Smith, a daughter of James and Jean (Menzies) Smith, natives of Scotland; her parents emigrated to this country in 1854, and in 1858 they settled in Greenfield Township, this county; they were blessed with six children—James, Isabel, Alexander, Robert, Emeline and Albert. Her mother died in 1861, and her father was subsequently married to Mrs. Mary Gleghorn. The parents are Presbyterians. Mr. and Mrs. Littlejohn have three children as a result of their union—Hattie, Mabel and Hugh; they have 120 acres of fine land. He enlisted in Company F, One Hundred and Fifty-sixth Illinois Volunteer Infantry; votes the Republican ticket. Mrs. L. was born May 24, 1848.

JAMES M. LAYMON, farmer, P. O. Coal City, was born September 4, 1807, in Clermont County, Ohio; is a son of Abraham and Elizabeth (Goodpaster) Laymon, natives of Tennessee, and the parents of ten children—James M., Elias, David, Will, Cynthia, John, Rachel, Frank, Cornelius and Jesse. The parents were Baptists. Our subject took chances at subscription schools, and worked on a farm. Was married, in 1825, at the age of eighteen, to Maria Sloan, a daughter of George and Sarah (Story) Sloan, natives of Pennsylvania and the parents of seven children—Nellie, Thomas, Mary, Margaret, John, William and Maria; her parents were Methodists. At marriage, they settled in Ohio, and thence to Indiana in 1842, settling near Crawfordsville, where they farmed for about four years, and then continued the same in Bartholomew County, the same State, and from there to Miami County. In 1859, they left Lee County, Ind., and came to Grundy County, Ill., settling where they now live. Their union gave them fifteen children, eight living—George, Elizabeth, Will, John, Thomas, David, Martha, Lida J. He and wife are members of the Methodist Church. He votes the Republican ticket. Thomas, the fifth child, was born May 15, 1840, in Bartholomew County, Ind.; was married, April 10, 1861, to Esther Morrison, the result being one child—Elva J. He was in Company K, Illinois Light Rifles and Company K, Illinois Light Artillery, etc. Lida J. married Thomas R. Curran, the result being Margaret A., Lydia M. and James H. Mr. C. has been Township Clerk.

LLOYD & REES, merchants, Braceville. Prominently identified with the business firms of Braceville are the gentlemen whose names head this article. John Lloyd was born December 30, 1849, in Wales. Is a son of David and Sarah (Buttrey) Lloyd, natives of Wales, and the parents of fourteen children, seven of whom survive, viz., Mary, Richard, John, Elizabeth, Ann, Davy and Abraham. The parents emigrated to America in 1861, settling in Pennsylvania. In 1863, the family came to Grundy County, Ill., where the father purchased eighty acres of land lying within the corner of Will, Kankakee and Grundy Counties, after having mined for many years. The parents are living in Braceville, retired from the active pursuits of life. John, of whom we write, mined until about twenty-one years old, when he engaged in other vocations. He began his present business in July, 1881, and on March 13, 1882, he accepted Mr. R. Rees as a full partner, which firm name still exists, having at this time a full line of groceries, dry goods and notions. He was married April 5, 1873, to Sarah A. Rees, a sister of his partner, which resulted in four children, two of whom are living, viz., John and Daniel. Mr. Lloyd was a Justice of the Peace in Braidwood; is a member of Braidwood Lodges, A., F. & A. M. and U. O. F., and of Braceville Lodge K. of P., and is D. D. G. C. in the latter. Rees Rees, the junior member of the firm, was born November 28, 1854, in Wales, and is a son of William and Sarah Rees, natives of the same country, and the parents of a large family. His parents emigrated to Illinois in 1864, and in 1865 they came to Braceville, and are now residing at Braidwood. At the age of nine, our latter subject of this sketch began mining, which he has worked at more or less since. He had some experience as a clerk in a grocery store before forming his present partnership. He had some good school advantages. Was married, January 27, 1877, to Mary Oliver, of Braidwood, Will County, which union has resulted in two children—Lillie and Emma H. He is a member of the Braceville Lodge, K. of P.

A. J. LAGERQUIST, contractor and builder, Braceville, was born January 8, 1840 in Sweden. Is a son of Jonas and Corrie Lagerquist, natives of Sweden, and parents of five children, viz., Jonas, Katy, Elias, A. J. and Corrie. Mr. Lagerquist attended school but little, and at the age of thirteen he began the tailor's trade, and soon after worked at carpentering at very small wages. At the age of twenty-two, he engaged in farming, together with his trade. Was married, in 1859, to Caroline Lagerquist, and in the same year he came to America, settling in Kansas, where he farmed until 1864, when he engaged in carpentering in Gardner, this county. In 1875 he settled in Braceville, where he has since carpentered, and has added the lumber trade and house-moving. He owns some good property here. His union blessed him with four children—Anna, Anders (furniture dealer at this place), Charles and Caroline L. He votes the Republican ticket.

JESSE MILL, Justice of the Peace, Coal City, was born January 10, 1840, in England. Is the son of John and Jane (Fulford) Mill, the parents of James, John, Joshua, Jonathan, Jesse, Jemima, Julia, Jethro, Jabez, Josiah and Joce. It is a remarkable fact that this entire family of eleven children possesses a name commencing with J. Our subject attained an excellent education. He graduated in a law school in his native country, and came to Wisconsin in 1864, and in 1865 to Braceville Township, this county, where he farmed and mined for several years. In 1863, he was married to Kate Pomeroy, resulting in seven children—William, Jerome, Augustus, Jessie, Bertie, Charles and Sealey. He was elected Justice of the Peace in 1877, which position he holds yet, together with Township Clerk and Treasurer, Village Clerk, and about ten other minor offices.

THOMPSON MARTIN, retired farmer, P. O. Gardner, was born August 28, 1832, in New York City. Is son of Alfred and Hannah (Cox) Martin, natives of New Jersey, and the parents of nine children—John, Mary, Thompson, Henry L., William K., Harriet D., Jane M., George W. and James P. Our subject attended school considerably. At the age of six, he fell from a mill and injured his skull, which impaired his mental powers. Was with his parents till nineteen, when he came to Illinois on a hunting spree, and finally made a settlement, his father buying him eighty acres of land in Braceville Township, which was mostly timbered. Was married to Amanda Cairns, the result being two children—William and Charlie. In 1873, he left his farm and came to Gardner on account of poor health, where he has since remained. He enlisted in Company I, Fifty-eighth Illinois Volunteer Infantry, in 1861, and was out over three years. His wife died June 28, 1858, and he was again married, November 14, 1865, to Huldah Sutton, the result being six children—Harriet A., Alberta, Alfred N., John B., Helen E. and Llewellyn. The present Mrs. Martin is a daughter of Nathan and Martha Sutton, settlers here about

1861; her mother is living with them, and is hale and hearty at eighty-seven years. He has served in some small township offices; was Deputy Postmaster once, and carried the mail from Braceville to Craigs. Our subject owned the first log cabin ever built on the prairies in this part of the country; it was built by Woodward in 1847. The building was used for firewood and hitching-posts in Gardner.

JAMES McKINLEY, boarding, livery and undertaking, Coal City, was born October 1, 1830, in Scotland, is a son of John and Margaret (Brown) McKinley, also natives of Scotland. The parents had ten children—June, Margaret, Mary, James, John, Elizabeth, William, Robert, Jesse, Elam. Mr. McKinley began coal mining when ten years old. In 1852, came to Pennsylvania, where he mined for four years, transferring then to La Salle, La Salle Co., Ill, and following the same avocation. In the fall of 1856, he was employed for a few months at Morris, Grundy County, after which he farmed in De Kalb County for five years. He abandoned farming there, and after laboring a few months at Morris, he went to Belleville, St. Clair Co., Ill., and mined for two years, and from there to Vermillion County, where he mined and bossed the miners for about three years. His next transfer was to Braidwood, Will County, at which place he took an interest in some mines, which proved unsuccessful, and he invested what means he had in a restaurant, which, with other property, he traded for land in Braceville Township, where he farmed until 1882, when he left his farm of 240 acres and engaged in his present business, that of boarding, livery and undertaking, having the only establishment of the latter two businesses in the village. Was married August, 1856, to Margaret Haughy, which resulted in six children, four of whom are living—John, James, Margaret and Nellie. Has served as Commissioner of Highways and School Director. Votes the Republican ticket.

THOMAS MORGAN, blacksmith and wagon shop, Braceville, was born October 15, 1825, in Wales, is a son of Thomas and Margaret (Evans) Morgan, also natives of Wales, and the parents of seven children, viz., Thomas, Evan, Jacob, John, Mary, Margaret and William. Mr. Morgan attended school until eleven years old, when he took sick with a fever, and was unable to labor until he was twelve, at which time he commenced learning the trade of a blacksmith, which he has followed during the remainder of his life. In 1868, he emigrated to New York, and there worked at his trade. In one year, he transferred to a shop near Akron, Ohio, and from there to Racine, Wis., where he was employed by Mitchell Bros. in the manufacture of wagons for six years. He came to Dwight, Ill., in 1880, and a little later, to Braceville, where he is doing a good business. Was married, October 5, 1850, to Maria Williams, who blessed him with eight children, namely, John, Thomas, Evan, William (deceased). Catharine, William (deceased), Maggie and Jane. He has been no office-seeker, and has given his time to his business. He and wife are members of the Welsh Methodist Church, in which he is Treasurer and Superintendent of the Sunday School. He votes the Republican ticket.

E. J. MYERS, livery, Braceville, was born January 29, 1844, in Du Page County, Ill. He is a son of Jacob and Elovina (Rhodes) Myers, natives of Lancaster County, Penn. The family came to Du Page County at an early day. Our subject is one of seven children, viz., Mary, the wife of F. Benter; E. J.; Albert; Eliza, the wife of George Hullinger; Maria, the wife of B. T. Harley; Jacob and Oscar. Mr. M. attended school some after twenty-one years of age, paying his way by taking care of horses for Dr. Bell, of Naperville. After leaving the Northwestern College, he engaged as a clerk for Kline & Rickert, commission merchants of 156 and 158 South Water street

Chicago. At the expiration of six months, he began farming for his uncle, Elias Myers, of Will County, which he continued for two years, and then rented a farm in De Kalb County. One year later, he rented south of Joliet. January 26, 1881, he was married to Frantie Ramer, of De Kalb County, Ill., which resulted in one child—Floyd. He came immediately after marriage to Braceville, and opened up a livery business, renting an old building. He has continued the same, and has lately constructed a fine stable, to which he has added a fine line of buggies and first-class driving horses. He votes the Republican ticket.

JOHN MATHIAS, saloon, Braceville, was born in 1839, in Wales, is a son of James and Mary (Lewis) Mathias. The parents came to this country, the father in 1862, and the mother in 1863. They were the parents of four children, viz., Ann, John, Margaret and Martha. Our subject attended school until thirteen years old, when he began mining, which he followed the greater portion of his life since. He came to Youngstown, Ohio, in 1860, where he mined for one year, and then came to Morris, Ill., and there engaged with Steel in a mine. He worked at the same business at Braceville for some time. He settled here when there were but three houses to be seen on the present site of the village. He took an interest in mines in Kankakee County. In 1868, he closed his mining career at Gardner, Ill. Was married January 31, 1869, to Elizabeth Williams, a native of Wales, which union resulted in five children—John, Mary, Thomas, Lottie and Elizabeth. The latter two only survive. He was Police Magistrate of this village for two years, and is now in his second term as Tax Collector. He is a member of Braceville Lodges, I. O. O. F. and K. of P., and A., F. & A. M., of Gardner. He is holding office in the first-named lodge.

J. E. PAGE, farmer, P. O. Mazon, was born June 21, ——, in Cook County, Ill.; is a son of T. N. and Selinda (Noyes) Page, natives of New Hampshire. They came to Illinois between 1833 and 1837; they emigrated West with a wagon; the mother died March 6, 1880, having blessed her husband with eight children, seven of whom are living, viz., J. E., Elizabeth, Ellen, Hannah L., Hiram A., Fred W. (deceased), Mattie and George R. The father is living in Cook County, where he first settled; is a Methodist, to which organization his consort belonged; he was Postmaster at Elk Grove for many years. Our subject attended school some in the country. Was married, December 28, 1859, to Laura J. Thomas, a daughter of Josephus and Affy (Dyer) Thomas. Her parents came to Illinois in June, 1850, settling in Elgin. Her father died January 18, 1882, and her mother is living in Chicago. Laura J. and Milo are the only children living. Mrs. P.'s parents united early with the Methodist Episcopal Church. The great-grandfather Thomas was born in 1736, in Providence, R. I.; was married to Sarah Emerson, of Uxbridge, Mass. He was one of the first legislators of Vermont. Mr. P.'s grandfather Page was Governor of New Hampshire two terms, and his uncle, John Page, was Treasurer of said State for ten years. Our subject made a few different settlements during his sojourn, until 1882, when he located on his present farm of 160 acres in Braceville Township. His union has blessed him with seven children, six of whom are living, viz., Helen M. (graduated at the grammar schools of Chicago, and has taught ten terms), John, Ed L., Charles D., Fred W. and Gracie A. He is an active Republican.

CHARLES PRICKETT, farmer, P. O. Coal City, was born October 16, 1829, in Logan County, Ohio; is a son of James and Rebecca Prickett. The parents came to Kendall County, Ill., in 1833. They had seven children, viz., Elijah, Joel, Charles, John, Aaron, Elizabeth, Jane. He has always been a farmer. Was married,

February 6, 1858, to Adaline A. Holderman, the result being twelve children, viz., Jane E., George, Byron, Jacob, Rhua, Melissa, Joel, Nellie, Burton C., Rose, Elizabeth, Anthony. He settled at his marriage near Morris, this county, and in 1864 he bought his present farm of 160 acres, and has lived on the same since. He has been Highway Commissioner, Tax Collector and Constable; votes the Republican ticket; takes an interest in educating his children.

RICHARD RAMSEY, Superintendent coal mines, Braceville, was born November 22, 1842, in England; is a son of William and Ann (Hackles) Ramsey, the parents of seven children—Margaret, William T., Richard, George, Mary A., Joseph, John. The subject attended school until eleven years old, and then began laboring in coal mines. He came to America in 1863 with his mother, settling in Morris, this county. He soon after began mining at Pekin, Tazewell County. In 1873, he located at Braidwood, and was made general pit boss, and in 1881 he was appointed Superintendent of the mines at Braceville, which position he now occupies, having under his charge about a thousand men and three shafts. Was married in 1867, to Mary A. Barly, of Morris, the result being six children—Z. B., William, Sarah, Laura L., Clara M. and Richard. He is a member of the Braidwood Lodge, A., F. & A. M., and Knights Templar of Joliet. Votes the Republican ticket. As a Superintendent, Mr. Ramsey has but few superiors; he is careful, and is respected by his entire class of men.

H. C. RICHEY, clerk coal company, Braceville, was born January 7, 1841, in La Salle County, Ill., and is a son of W. W. and Maria (Thompson) Richey, natives, the father of Ohio and the mother of Norway. The father settled in La Salle County in 1829, and the mother in 1838. The parents had but one child—H. C. The father was married a second time to Eliza Horton, the result being two children—William F. and Cora A. Our subject attended school in the pioneer cabins, with slab seats, slab writing-desks, etc. When fifteen, he began clerking in a store for his father at Marseilles, and in 1862 he enlisted in Company C, Seventy-seventh Illinois Volunteer Infantry, and was out until the close. Was in the Quartermaster's Department. Was captured at La Grange, Tenn., and taken to St. Louis, and was afterward exchanged. On his return from the war, he was with his father for two years, and then built bridges with Alex Bruce, of Marseilles, for four years. Came to Braceville in 1871, and kept books for the Braceville Coal Company; thence to Henry, Marshall County, engaging with Nicholson & Bruce for three and one-half years; from there to Florida for two years, to recruit his health. In 1878, he returned to Braceville, where he engaged as Superintendent of the Braceville Coal Mines until the company sold out, when he was retained as clerk for the present Superintendent. Was married in 1861 to S. A. Day, the result being three children—F. L., A. D. and Gertie. His wife died in 1868, and he was again married in 1871, to M. E. Tremaine, the result being two children—Hattie and Belle. Is a member of Marseilles Lodge, No. 418, A., F. & A. M. Votes the Republican ticket.

E. H. ROBINSON, farmer, P. O. Coal City, was born April 11, 1834, in Brooklyn, N. Y., is a son of John and Elizabeth (Hayes) Robinson, who came from an English ancestry. They were natives of England, and landed in America the day before the falling of the meteors in the year 1833. They remained in Brooklyn, N. Y., till June, 1834, when they settled in Delaware County, Ohio, on the line between that and Union County. Here the mother died May 10, 1879, and the father is still surviving. The parents reared seven children—E. H., Alfred J., Reuben, Arthur, Mary, Edward and Guido. The father was a wood-carver, and left his farm under the management of his energetic sons, who received for their industry about one hundred acres of land. E. H., of whom we write, received a liberal education from his father, who was a graduate of the Old French College of London, England, founded by the French Huguenot refugees in that city after their escape from the massacre of St. Bartholomew, of whom the Robinsons are descendants. Our subject was married, September 16, 1858, to Lucinda, a daughter of John and Esther Hill. Her parents are of German origin, their ancestors having emigrated to Pennsylvania some time before the American Revolution, in which struggle they figured prominently. A pair of the second and a pair of the third generation removed from Westmoreland County, Penn., to Ohio about the year 1811. The younger pair, Stephen and Mariam, reared a large family, the descendants of whom are scattered over many States. The Hills noted in Braceville and Wauponsee Townships are descended from this pair mentioned above. Mr. and Mrs. Robinson have two sons as the result of their union, viz., Alfred D. and William R., both of whom are at home. They came to Grundy County March 21, 1865, and bought a farm in Braceville Township, where they are located, and are the possessors of a beautiful home, containing 240 acres. His rare business talent soon won for him the confidence of the people, who soon placed him in their service as Assessor, Trustee of Schools, and other offices, all of which he has held several terms with honor to himself and those who placed him there. He votes the Republican ticket.

FREDERICK SEEK, farmer, P. O. Gardner, was born September 7, 1843, in Baden, Germany; is a son of Michael and Catharine Seek, natives of Germany. The parents came to Louisiana in 1853, where the father died, and the mother is living in La Salle County, Ill. Our subject worked upon a farm when quite young. Enlisted in Company C, Eighty-eighth Illinois Volunteer Infantry, and remained in the service two years, a part of which time he was a sharpshooter. He was shot through the top of the skull. He helped to capture Mission Ridge, and was with Gen. Sheridan nearly one year. Was married, October 27, 1866, to Louisa Colwell, and has six children—Lillie, Frederick, Willie, Minnie, Louisa and Arthur. He settled on his present farm of eighty acres in 1876; came to this county in 1868, and rented for several years of Cameron. He votes the Republican ticket.

JAMES SHORT, merchant, Coal City. Mr. Short was born November 14, 1874, in Grundy County, Ill. Is one of five children by Lemuel and Sarah (Burr) Short, viz., James, W. B., Alvina, Lemuel and William. Mr. Short had but little advantage of school, owing to the scarcity of school-buildings in his younger days. At the age of nine, he was put to herd cattle on the wild, unbroken prairie, which was covered with stones. This he followed until about twenty-one years old. He can recall many interesting reminiscences of his early "cow-boy" life. On one occasion, he scared up a wolf, and made chase with his pony, and finally drove the wild animal to a thicket. When he alighted from his horse, he noticed that the wolf had bitten the pony's legs, which were bleeding freely. This sad sight aroused Mr. Short's temper, and awakened his love for his prairie companion, which he mounted, and returned to the thicket with a full determination to destroy the beast that had so shamefully lacerated his horse's forelegs. He either found the same wolf or another, and chased him for about four hours over the prairie, whipping and lashing him with his large cow-whip until he had put out one eye of the wild animal, and cut his head so badly that it was covered with blood, and it lay down to rest, at which juncture of the race our little hero alighted, and with stones beat the wolf to death. From this time on the faithful horse would run any wolf that aroused from his lair. This was not all that our subject amused himself at. Every cattle dealer that came along had with him a fast horse, which he would bet on, and every wager was promptly accepted by Mr. Short, and his pony always won the race. Over the prairie, where rocks were as thick as hail after a hard storm, would this wiry little chap run his horse and secure the booty. In 1875, he engaged in cattle dealing for himself, which he has continued since with good success; he was for awhile in the meat business at Coal City, and in 1880 he opened up a line of dry goods, which he is still running. Was married, in 1874, to Frances Lattimer, the result being one child—Frances. His wife died in 1876, and in 1881 he was married a second time to Mrs. Caroline Clark, a daughter of William Moore, an old settler of this county. She was married to Loren G. Clark, resulting in four children—Ettie, Gertrude, Henry and Alla. Mr. Short was President of the Board of Trustees when the village of Coal City was organized. He votes the Republican ticket.

T. T. SMITH & CO., hardware merchants, Braceville. Mr. T. T. Smith of the above firm, was born September 8, 1846, in Michigan, is a son of T. and Esther A. (Bashford) Smith, natives of New York, and the parents of five children—Oliver N., Harriet A., T. T. and two deceased when young. Our subject obtained a fair education, and spent his younger days on a farm. In 1864, he enlisted in Company G, One Hundred and Thirty-fourth Illinois Infantry, and remained until the war closed. On his return from the war, he engaged in the grocery business, together with dry goods, at Braidwood, with L. H. Goodrich. After severing his connection with Goodrich, he engaged with C. W. & V., at same village for two years; afterward he managed a farm for Homes & Cody for two years, and then was with J. L. Swanburg in the hardware business, which he bought April 4, 1882, and has since continued the same at Braceville, having at this time a full line of hardware, etc. He has a fine business room with a good hall above, which is used for general meetings. Was married, in 1870, to Jennie Bennett, of Wilmington. She lived but a short time, and he was again married, in 1874, to Lucy Leatherman, the result being Roy L., Zula M. and Oliver T. He is now President of the Village Board, and is Trustee of the Methodist Church; is a member of the A. O. U. W., and is Master of the same; is a member of the Braidwood Lodge, A., F. & A. M.; votes the Republican ticket.

ALFRED VINCENT, blacksmith, Braceville. Mr. Vincent was born July 5, 1861, in Montreal, Can., and is a son of Julian and Asena (La Rock) Vincent, natives of Canada. The family came to Illinois in 1865, settling at Manteno, Kankakee County. The parents had nine children—Frank, Will, Ed, Julian, Alfred, Lillie, Agnes, Lina and Napoleon. Our subject attended school but little, and learned the carpenter's trade, beginning it when about ten years old. At the age of sixteen he began learning the blacksmith's trade with Thomas O'Neal, of Braidwood, with whom he remained for about three years. In 1882, he began his present business, that of a general blacksmith and wagon, buggy and repair shop, at which he is succeeding admirably, having in his employ two men of experience.

F. S. WATKINS, attorney at law, Braceville, born September 13, 1810, in Maryland; son of Lafayette and Lydia (Stringer) Watkins, natives of Maryland and parents of six children—Richard G., George W., John G., Edward, Rachel and our subject, who attended the district schools until ten years old, when he engaged as a clerk for J. Merrill at $10 per month; here he remained for five years, after which he farmed. In 1831, he came to Pekin, where he clerked, and afterward worked on a farm in Tazewell County, thence to La Salle

County, engaging in farming, and from there into the same business in De Kalb County, thence to Grundy County in 1846, and has lived the greater portion of the time since in Morris. In 1851, he was elected Treasurer of this county, which position he filled with credit. Was a member of the committee on building the court house. He moved to Heyworth, McLean County, in 1866, where he remained until 1877, at which period he returned to Morris, or rather to his fine farm near Morris, which he sold in 1882, and has since been located at Braceville, where he applies his time in some legal business. Was married, in 1832, to Augusta Young, the result being five children—Frederick, Richard G., Augusta, Sarah and Lydia. His wife died in 1844, and he was again married, in 1846, to Mrs. Joannah Phinney, the mother of eight children by her first marriage—Lydia, Joseph, Chester, William, Martha, Adelia, Emerson and James L. Mr. W. has been a Justice of the Peace for many years, and has served as Town Supervisor. Votes Democratic ticket.

JONAS WATERS, farmer, P. O. Mazon, was born February 22, 1851, in Mazon Township, Grundy County, Ill.; is a son of William and Bethemia (Booth) Waters, who came to this county in 1848, settling in Mazon Township, where they remained until death. Henry, Jonas and George are the only ones living from their large family of children. Jonas was left without parents when quite young, and was compelled to work for his own sustenance. Was married, December 3, 1872, to Alvaretta, a daughter of John N. and Susannah (Truby) Whitsel, natives of Pennsylvania, and residents of Goodfarm Township, this county. Her parents have seven children living from a family of ten, viz., Mary E., Labona C., Jonathan L., Joannah, Alvaretta, Melinda E., Jane, Christopher T., John E., and William C. Our subject has one child, the result of his union, Clarence B. He has 100 acres of land lying in Braceville and Mazon Townships, the result of his own labors. He bought the same in 1874 of B. A. Crister, who entered it from the Government. He votes the Republican ticket.

A. G. WATSON, agent for Allen Bros, lumber dealers, Braceville, was born October 4, 1855, in Center County, Penn.; is a son of James B. and Elizabeth (Hess) Watson, natives of Pennsylvania, and the parents of four children, three of whom are living, viz., A. G., Belle and R. L.; Blanche, deceased. The mother died in 1865, while the father was in Company G, Pennsylvania Volunteer Infantry; he was Orderly in Company B, Forty-eighth Pennsylvania Volunteer Infantry, at the beginning of the war. The father died in 1878; he and consort were Presbyterians. Our subject, by applying his spare moments to his books, became able to teach in the country schools, and with the means obtained in that way he was enabled to attend the Millersville Academy, where he received a good grade. After closing his school days, he began learning car-building at Altoona, Penn., which he continued for five years. He then came West, and worked at house carpentering at Joliet for six months. In 1879, he did some carpentering at Braceville for D. Winters, a contractor of Joliet. In January, 1881, he took charge of the lumber business of Allen Brothers at this place, which he still continues. He is serving the people as Village Trustee, and is a Notary Public; is a charter member of the A. O. U. W., of Braceville; is a stanch Republican. He was married January 18, 1881, to Kittie W. Thornton, of Joliet.

S. J. WARNER, boot and shoe dealer, Braceville. This energetic young man was born in 1858, in Kankakee County, Ill. He is a son of Jerome and Helen M. (Ladd) Warner, the former a native of Massachusetts, and the latter of Vermont. They emigrated from Pennsylvania to Will County. They were blessed with three children who grew up and three who are deceased. Those living are Jay, Adelbert and S. J. The latter attended school at Wilmington and Naperville. He clerked some before coming here; was in the post office at Wilmington, Ill., for some time, and was employed in the fire insurance business at Chicago. February 1, 1882, he opened up a line of boots and shoes at Braceville, and is doing a fine business, giving his own personal attention, and, like all who love their vocation, is successful.

T. A. YOUNG, merchant, Braceville, was born January 19, 1837, in Pennsylvania. Is a son of Aaron and Martha (Harrison) Young, natives of England, and the parents of six children—T. A., John, Mary, Martha, Joseph and Albert. In 1862, subject came to Braceville, where he engaged in the mines. In 1866, he opened the first coal shaft in Kankakee County, on what is known as the "Hook farm;" he later engaged in the mercantile business, under the firm name of Young & Price. In three years Price withdrew, and our subject has continued the same since, having now a full line of dry goods, notions, groceries, etc. Was married, in 1865, to Martha Williams, the result being five children—John, William, Thomas, George and Mary. He was once a Justice of the Peace here; is now a member of the Town Board. Is a member of Braceville Lodge, No. 679, I. O. O. F., and Gardner Lodge A., F. & A. M.; votes the Republican Ticket.

FELIX TOWNSHIP.

JOSHUA R. COLLINS, farmer, P. O. Morris. The subject of this sketch is a native of Grundy County, born November 13, 1854; son of Jeremiah and Maggie (Widley) Collins. Raised and received the elements of an English education at the common schools of the county; took a course at the Morris Classical Institute. Afterward graduated at the Grand Prairie Seminary and Commercial College. Married, November 27, 1879, in Grundy County, to Miss Anna Holroyd, daughter of Benjamin and Susan Holroyd, of Grundy County, living in Wauponsee Township. Mrs. Collins, born in Will County, Ill., April 3, 1855, and educated in Will County. They have one son—Frank W. Collins, born in Grundy County February 26, 1882. Mr. Collins is among the leading stock-raisers of the county, and has a vast farm of valuable land in Felix Township known as the Samuel Holderman farm, residence four and a half miles southeast from Morris.

SILAS LATTIMER, farmer, P. O. Wilmington. The subject of this sketch is a native of Athens County, Ohio, born April 17, 1821; son of Isaac and Jane Lattimer. Raised and educated principally in Mercer County, Ohio. In 1845, he with his mother removed to Marion County, Ind., his father having died in Ohio. Subject was married, in Indiana, April 30, 1846, to Miss Mary Schroyer, daughter of Joseph and Eliza Schroyer. She is a native of Wayne County, Ind., born October 3, 1826. They remained in Indiana until 1854, engaged in farming. At this time, he removed to Illinois and settled in Felix Township, near where he now lives. He here owns a farm of 280 acres in Sections 15 and 22 of Felix Township, residence nine miles southeast from Morris. Value of land, $30 per acre. They have ten children—Eliza J. Lattimer, born in Indiana April 28, 1847, married to C. C. Massey in December, 1866; Clarissa C. Lattimer, born in Indiana November 22, 1848, married to Silas W. Gibson, of Mazon Township; Malinda F. Lattimer, born in Indiana December 17, 1850, married June 11, 1874, to James Short, died July 1, 1876; Charity C. Lattimer, born No-

FELIX TOWNSHIP.

vember 6, 1853, and died November 5, 1855; James N. Lattimer, born in Grundy County, Ill., March 31, 1856, married Miss Caroline Rodee April 23, 1879; Laura A. Lattimer, born in this county February 7, 1858, married to Horace Severns December 22, 1880; Johnson W. Lattimer, born in Grundy County November 23, 1860; Tedee Lattimer, born in Grundy County January 12, 1863, died at the home in Felix Township December 17, 1866; Sarah E. Lattimer, born in Grundy February 21, 1865; Ida May Lattimer, born in Grundy County March 19, 1869. Mr. Lattimer is a Democrat politically, and has been a Justice of the Peace and Township official for many years. Engaged in stock raising and general farming.

DAVID MACKIE, miner, Diamond. The subject of these lines is a native of Ayrshire, in Scotland, born within eighteen miles of Glasgow, January 1, 1837; son of David and Janet (Barkley) Mackie. Raised and educated in Scotland, and came to the United States in 1869. Mr. Mackie is a practical miner, having worked at this business since nine years old. At the age of twenty-two, he was put in charge of a series of mines as assistant superintendent, which position he held until coming to this county in 1869. First located in Wisconsin and engaged to a farmer during his harvest, afterward employed in the Prairie du Chien Machine Shops as a machinist. In October, 1869, he came to Braidwood, Will County, and engaged his services to Messrs. Bennett & Turner, working at dumping mud from shaft about the time of the completing of the sinking of No. 1 shaft; afterward ran the engine for about six months. Afterward took position as mining boss; was then promoted to the position now held, that of Superintendent of Wilmington Coal Mining & Manufacturing Company. Married in Scotland, October 18, 1860, to Miss Elizabeth Kerr, daughter of Thomas and Jane (Pringle) Kerr. She was born in Scotland June, 1841. They have a family of four sons and two daughters—David Mackie, born in Scotland June 20, 1862; Thomas Mackie, born in Scotland November 9, 1869; Janet Mackie, born in Scotland September 6, 1865; George B. Mackie, born in Scotland December 3, 1868; Jane P. Mackie, born in Felix Township, Grundy County, July 25, 1872; John W. Mackie, born in Grundy County December 9, 1877. Mr. Mackie is superintending a force of about 400 men, the monthly pay-roll amounting to $17,931 for the month ending October 31, 1882. Their average capacity is about 500 tons per day. The company own a tract of 1,040 acres of coal land in Felix and Braceville Townships.

THOMAS PATTISON, farmer, P. O. Coal City. The subject of this sketch is a native of Grundy County, Ill., born April 8, 1847; son of William and Martha Pattison, who were among the first settlers of this county. Subject was educated in Grundy County, and at the Fowler Institute of Kendall County, and married, March 24, 1870, to Miss Martha E. Struble, daughter of Elias Struble. She was born in New Jersey September 10, 1850, and came to Grundy County when about sixteen years old. They have a family of two children—Bertha E. Pattison, born in Grundy County September 6, 1872; Eva M. Pattison, born in Grundy County June 13, 1878. Mr. Pattison owns a farm of 120 acres of improved land in Section 31 of Felix Township, residence nine and a half miles southeast from Morris. Value of land, $40 per acre. Mr. Pattison's father, William Pattison, died in Grundy County March 8, 1882. His mother has been dead since he was a mere boy. Has one brother in the county—J. H. Pattison, present County Treasurer. Politics, Republican.

LEMUEL SHORT, Sr., farmer, P. O. Wilmington. The subject of these lines is a native of Allegheny County, Penn., born August 15,

1819; son of James and Ellen (McFarland) Short, natives of Pennsylvania. When subject was five years old, his parents removed to what is now Ashland County, Ohio, where his mother died. His father died in the same county in 1863. In 1836, subject came to Michigan and spent one summer, then returned to Ohio, but came to Illinois in 1838, and located in Lake County. Here he soon purchased land and engaged in farming, hunting and trapping, the latter business affording money to pay on land. Subject first came to Grundy County for permanent residence in 1856. He was married, December 31, 1845, to Miss Sarah Burr, daughter of Warham and Nancy (Cummins) Burr, her father formerly of New York, and her mother formerly of Ohio. Mrs. Short was born in Shelby County, Ind., February 10, 1826, and came to Will County, Ill., with her parents in 1833. They have a family of five children—James Short, born in Will County, Ill., November 14, 1847—married to Miss Malinda F. Lattimer June 11, 1874, his second wife was a Widow Moore, married, August 3, 1881; Warham B. Short, born in Will County August 9, 1849—married, January 1, 1878, to Miss Mary Heydecker; Alvina Short, born in Lake County May 25, 1852—married, July 4, 1871, to M. Gassny; Lemuel Short, born in Lake County January 24, 1855—married, May 1, 1876, to Miss Clara Heydecker; William Short, born in Lake County July 17, 1856, died in same county February 1, 1859. Mr. Short now owns about 2,400 acres of land in Felix Township of Grundy County, and a farm of 373 acres in Lake County, Ill. His residence is ten miles southeast from Morris. He has been among the leading stock-raisers of the county, and is too well known as a thorough business man to need especial mention in that particular. Politics, Republican. Mrs. Short's father died in Will County Sep. 6, 1861, and her mother in the same county March 31, 1862.

SARATOGA TOWNSHIP.

WILLIAM H. AYRES, farmer, P. O. Morris, was born in New Canaan, Conn., June 17, 1811, son of Frederick and Rebecca (Seymour) Ayres. Frederick was born in New Canaan in 1781, and died in 1853. Rebecca was born in same place in 1783, and died in 1845. After obtaining his education in his native place, William learned the trade of tanner and currier. In 1834, he married Eliza J. Benedict, who was born in New Canaan October 12, 1813. She is a daughter of Caleb and Alice Benedict, natives of New Canaan. In 1846, the subject of our sketch moved to Grundy County, since which time he has been engaged in agricultural pursuits. He is a Republican and a member of the Congregational Church. Has been School Director in Saratoga Township. Mr. and Mrs. Ayres are the parents of six children, of whom Henry G., James S., Rebecca A. and William E. are dead. Louvica and Frederick H. are living.

JERRY COLLINS, farmer, P. O. Morris, was born in Albany, N. Y., in September, 1820, son of Joshua and Margaret (Row) Collins, the former born in Rhode Island about 1776; was well educated, served in the war of 1812, and was one of the pioneers of this township. Margaret, his mother, a native of New York, was the mother of nine children, of whom the subject of our sketch was the fifth. His first business enterprise was the purchase of 80 acres of land in this township, which he has added to until he now owns 800 acres of good farming land, well improved. He was married in this county, in 1848, to Miss Hannah Cryder, who lived but eighteen months after her marriage. His second wife, Margaret Widney, was born about 1833, and is the mother of three children. Joshua, the eldest, is married, and a man of family; Hannah May, the second, is dead; Oscar, the youngest, lives with his parents. Mr. Jerry Collins was but thirteen years of age when brought to this township. His mother and the children came from Chicago in a wagon driven by Charlie Smith. Our subject handled the logs for the first house erected in the town of Morris, so he has been the witness and assistant of vast improvements in this part of the country. His political faith is Republican.

CRYDER COLLINS, farmer, P. O. Morris, was born in Saratoga Township, Grundy County, April 13, 1855. He is the son of Joshua and Harriet (Cryder) Collins; his mother is still alive; his parents had six children. Our subject received his schooling in Morris, this county, and commenced life as a farmer. He has been and is at present engaged in stock-raising. In March, 1880, he was married in this township to Lilly Nelson, who was born in Norway. They have one child—Isaac. Mr. Collins has 948 acres of land. He is a Republican.

JOSHUA E. COLLINS, farmer, P. O. Morris, was born in Grundy County, Ill., October 7, 1859, and is the youngest son of Joshua Collins, Sr., and Harriet Cryder. He received his early education in the common schools of the country, and finished at the high school at Morris. He took charge of the home place after the death of his father, which he now owns, and from surroundings, it would impress one that he is quite energetic and practical in all his operations. He handles a great deal of stock and raises large crops of grain. His mother still lives with and keeps house for him, as he is still unmarried. Politically, a Republican. His father started quite poor and accumulated quite a large and valuable property, which his widow and children are now enjoying, and his grandfather was one among the earliest settlers of the county.

HENRY R. CONKLIN, farmer, P. O. Morris, was born in New York in 1823; son of Henry and Emma (Bristol) Conklin, the former was born in New York about 1793; a farmer by occupation, and was engaged in the war of 1812; he died about 1872; his wife was born in New York in 1803, and was the mother of four children, of whom our subject was the second. During his boyhood, Mr. Conklin worked on his father's farm, and attended the common country schools. In 1851, he moved to this State, and settled on his first purchase of 160 acres of land. This was unimproved, and had no buildings upon it, excepting one small shanty, which would hardly warrant the name of a house. He now owns 200 acres of good tillable land, upon which he has erected good, substantial buildings of all kinds, necessary for a well-regulated farm. In New York State, in the year 1848, he married Miss Mahala Westfall, a native of New York, born in June, 1821, and a daughter of John and Polly (Turner) Westfall; the former was born in New York in 1797; he is still living and engaged in farming. The latter was born in Massachusetts in 1799, she died in May, 1871. The subject and his wife are the parents of two living children —Etta, the oldest daughter, is married to a Mr. McGrath, and resides in Kansas; they have two children, Henry, the only son, was born in this county about 1857, and has one child. Mr. Conklin and his family are members of the Congregational Church.

M. H. CRYDER, farmer, P. O. Morris, was born in Ohio March 21, 1820, son of Henry and Mary A. (Hess) Cryder. Henry, his father, was born in Pennsylvania about 1779; was a farmer by occupation, and died in 1835. Mary, his mother, was born in Pennsylvania about 1777, and is the mother of eight living children, the subject being the sixth. He received a good common-school education, which was commenced in Ohio and finished in this county, to the latter of which his parents came October 25, 1833. His marriage, which was one of the first on the records of this county, occurred March 7, 1847, when he was united to Miss Rachael Thomas, a native of Ohio, born about 1818. Her parents came to this county from Ohio. She is the mother of three children— Edwin T., Mariett and Eugene. The daughter is married. The sons are engaged in farming on the home place. Mr. Cryder is a man of more than ordinary intelligence, and has served the public in a number of important capacities, such as Assessor, Commissioner, Supervisor and Collector for Au Sable Township. He is influential and highly respected in the community where he lives.

K. M. J. GRANVILLE, farmer, P. O. Morris, was born in Norway May 17, 1827, son of John and Belle (Mulster) Granville. He was born in Norway in 1804, and died in 1857; was County Clerk in his county, and followed the occupation of a farmer. His wife was born in Norway in 1806, and died in 1881. Our subject received his education in Norway, and taught school there. He there married his first wife, Carrie Kythe, by whom he had two children. After his removal to this country, he taught school in Kendall County, Ill., where, in 1858, he married his second wife, Martha Anderson, who was born in Norway December 16, 1840. She is the mother of nine children, viz., Caroline J., Christina, Isabella, Andrew, Edward, Albert, Malinda Ann, Franklin and Martha. Mr. Granville taught school in Grundy County, and was afterward School Director. He has been interested in the erection of churches in both Kendall and Grundy Counties, and is a member of the Lutheran Church. Politically, he is a Republican.

PELEG T. HUNT, farmer, P. O. Morris, was born in New Lebanon, N. Y., August 10, 1823, son of William F. and Betsy (Tabor) Hunt. He was born in Columbia County, N. Y., February 25, 1798. Was a farmer, and died March 22, 1869. His mother, Betsy, was born in Rensselaer County, N. Y., September 22, 1801, and died August 26, 1879. Mr. Peleg Hunt received his education in Nassau, N. Y., and began life as a farmer. In 1855, March 15, he came to Grundy. He has filled the position of School Director. His wife, Mary S. Cummings, a native of New York, was born February 9, 1827. She is the daughter of Russell D. and Sophia Cummings. Her father was born April 28, 1801, and died August 29, 1856. Her mother was born April 5, 1803, and is still living. They are both natives of New York. Mr. and Mrs. Hunt have four children as follows—George W., Lenora J., Fannie M. and Emma L. Mr. P. F. Hunt's paternal grandfather, William Hunt, was born in Norwich, Conn., November 5, 1768, and died October 8, 1852. His paternal grandmother, Susanna Hunt, was born at Long Point, Conn., May 9, 1768, and died August 18, 1854. Mr. Peleg Hunt is a Republican.

GERSHOM HUNT, farmer, P. O. Morris, was born in New Lebanon, N. Y., January 18, 1828, son of William F. and Betsy (Tabor) Hunt. The former was born in New York February 25, 1798, and died March 22, 1869. The latter was born in New York September 22, 1801, and died August 26, 1879. His grandparents were William and Susanna Hunt. The former was born in Norwich, Conn., November 5, 1768, and died October 8, 1852. The latter was born at Long Point, Conn., May 9, 1768, and died August 18, 1854. Gershom Hunt obtained his education in Rensselaer County, N. Y. Began to till the soil in New York, which occupation he continues in Illinois, to which latter State he came in February, 1856. He was married in Columbia County, N. Y., September 15, 1855, to Miss Hannah Smith, born in Columbia County, N.

SARATOGA TOWNSHIP.

Y., April 30, 1826. She is the daughter of Frederick and Catharine Smith, natives of Columbia County, N. Y. Her father was born in 1790, and her mother in 1799. Our subject has, since his residence here, held the positions of Township Supervisor, Township Clerk and School Director. He belongs to the Republican party.

JAMES A. HUNT, farmer, P. O. Morris, was born in New Lebanon, Columbia Co., N. Y., September 10, 1838, and is the son of William F. and Betsey (Tabor) Hunt. He was born in Columbia County, N. Y., February 25, 1798, and died March 22, 1869; his occupation was farming. The mother of our subject was born in Rensselaer County, N. Y., September 22, 1801, and died August 26, 1879. Mr. James Hunt's grandfather, William Hunt, was born in Norwich, Conn., November 5, 1768, and died October 8, 1852. His grandmother, Susanna Hunt, was born at Long Point, Conn., May 9, 1768, and died August 18, 1854. Mr. Hunt obtained his schooling in New York State, and there commenced farming. He removed to Illinois in April, 1859, and in Morris on August 20, 1862, was married to Laura Bristol, a native of Rensselaer County, N. Y., born February 2, 1838. Her parents, Asa and Maria Bristol, are both natives of New York. Mr. and Mrs. Hunt have one child, William E., born June 14, 1864. Mr. Hunt has been School Director and Township Trustee. In politics, he is a Republican.

FRANK HUNT, farmer, P. O. Morris, was born in Nassau County, N. Y., November 12, 1843, son of William F. and Betsy (Tabor) Hunt. The former was born in Columbia County, N. Y., February 25, 1798, and died March 22, 1869; was a farmer by occupation. Betsy Hunt, his mother, was born in Rensselaer County, N. Y., September 22, 1801, and died August 26, 1879. His grandfather, William Hunt, was born in Norwich, Conn., November 5, 1768, and died October 8, 1852. His grandmother, Susanna Hunt, was born at Long Point, Conn., May 9, 1768, and died August 18, 1854. Mr. Frank Hunt received his education in Nassau County, N. Y. While in New York, he followed the occupation of farming, which he has continued to good advantage since his settlement in Illinois. January 16, 1868, he married Frances A. Waterbury, born in Nassau County, N. Y., August 26, 1846. Her parents, Sylvester and Permelia Waterbury, are natives of the same place. From this marriage, there are two children—William W., born May 18, 1872, and Alice M., September 10, 1876. Mr. Hunt has filled the position of School Director. He is a Republican.

JOHN JOHNSON, farmer, P. O. Morris, was born in Norway in 1806, son of John and Sarah (Benson) Johnson. His father, who was a farmer, was born in Norway, and died there in 1849. Sarah, his mother, was born in Norway in 1783, and died in 1879. Our subject availed himself of such educational privileges as were at hand and worked at farming while in Norway. He there married his first wife, Gustie Nutson, who died before he came to this country. By her he had two children—Sarah, deceased, and John, who still survives. He next married Annie Larson, a native of Norway, born in 1807. Her parents, Lewis and Tena Larson, were also natives of Norway. As a result of this second union, there are four children—Lewis, Gostey, Tena and John. Since his residence in this country, Mr. Johnson has continued his occupation of farming. He is a Republican, and a member of the Lutheran Church.

ADMOND JOHNSON, farmer, P. O. Morris, was born in Norway June 24, 1818, son of John and Sarah (Benson) Johnson. The former was a native of Norway, where he died in 1849. The latter, also a native of Norway, was born in 1783, and died in 1879. Our subject received his education in the common schools of his native country, and worked at farming until he came to America. In 1858, at Lisbon, Ill., he was married to Sarah Halgeson, a native of Norway, born in 1837. She is the daughter of Henry and Carrie Halgeson, both natives of Norway. Mr. and Mrs. Johnson have had eight children, of whom Carrie is dead. Sarah, Henry, John, Carrie, Halver, Thomas A. and Anna H. are living. The subject of this sketch has acted in the capacity of School Director. He is a Republican in political tenets, and a member of the Lutheran Church.

ERIK JOHNSON, farmer, P. O. Morris, was born in Norway July 21, 1828, the youngest of three children, son of John and Anna (Swensen) Olston. He was born in Norway about 1788, and died about 1830. His mother, a native of Norway, was born in 1786, and died in 1862. Mr. Johnson was educated in the common schools of his native country; worked for a time at shoemaking. He came to this country when twenty-six years of age; landed first at Quebec; remained there a short time and then came to this county. Settled first in Nettle Creek Township, where he worked on a farm eighteen months. He then moved to Saratoga Township and continued farming a few years. Although he commenced without a dollar, he had sufficient means to purchase sixty-six acres of unimproved land, a part of his present homestead. This he has added to and improved until now he has a fine farm of one hundred and thirty-two acres. In 1852, in Norway, he was married to Tennie Michleson, who was born in that country January 1, 1829. Her father and mother were natives of the same place. By this union, there were seven children. Mr. Johnson, in 1864, joined the Thirty-sixth Illinois Regiment, Company A, and was in the battles of Columbia, Spring Hill, Franklin and Nashville, Tenn. During the war, he received a wound from which he has never recovered, being now unable to work. He contributes toward the support of the Gospel, is a faithful Christian and respected citizen. He belongs to the Lutheran Church, and is a Republican.

GUNNER JOHNSON, farmer, P. O. Morris, was born in Norway December 19, 1835, son of John Peterson and Annie Gunderson, both of Norway. The former was born about 1790, and was a farmer until his death, which occurred in 1865. The mother of our subject was born in 1794, and died in 1876. In Morris, Ill., August 16, 1870, Mr. Johnson married Caroline Johnson, a native of Norway, born in 1850. She is the daughter of John and Julia Peterson, and the mother of four children, viz., John O. and Annie, deceased; George and Annie J. still living. Mr. Johnson is a member of the Lutheran Church and a Republican.

STORY MATTESON, farmer, P. O. Morris, was born in Michigan February 15, 1838, and is the second son of Beriah H. and Susan (Jones) Matteson. Beriah, who resides at Morris, Grundy County, was born in New York in 1812. Susan was born in New York in 1812, and is the mother of nine children, our subject being the second. Our subject attended the country schools and worked at farming until he became twenty-two, when he started for Illinois. He arrived here without friends or money, but was soon employed by a farmer named Bartlett, for whom he worked industriously three years. His employer then allowed him to work on shares, which opportunity he eagerly improved. As he cleared $1,200 the first year, this enabled him to do business for himself. His first purchase was 160 of land, for which he gave $40 per acre; he now owns 1,500 acres of finely improved land. In 1866, he married Miss Virginia Collins, who was born in this county September 3, 1846, and is the daughter of Joshua and Harriet (Cryder) Collins. The former was born in New York September 19, 1802, died June 19, 1879. The latter was born in Ohio August 4, 1822, and is the mother of six children, of whom Mrs. Matteson is the eldest. Mr. and Mrs. Matteson are the parents of six children, viz., William, Story, Gracie, Cora, Cryder and Hattie. Mr. Matteson is a Republican.

HALVER OSMONSEN, farmer, P. O. Morris, was born in Norway May 26, 1825, his parents being natives of that country. In his youth, he assisted on the home farm, and attended the common schools. In 1849, he emigrated to this country, arriving in New York July 3. He first went to Morris, where he remained but a short time, soon settling near Lisbon, where he engaged in farming for a period of eight years, although he started without a dollar, he now had sufficient means to purchase sixty acres of land; after adding one hundred acres to this, and improving the whole, he sold it for a good profit. He then came to Grundy County and purchased lands about three miles north of Morris, here he resided about ten years, making great improvements. He next bought land a few miles further north, where he now resides; owns in all, 924 acres of well-improved land. He is a large grain-raiser and dealer, also raises some stock. In the fall of 1849, in Kendall County, he married Miss Engeri Olsen, a native of Norway, born in 1822, her parents being natives of the same country. There are two children by this marriage, viz., Halver Osmonsen, Jr., and Ole H. Osmonsen, both married. Mr. Osmonsen and family are members of the Lutheran Church, he being one of the leading men who raised funds for the erection of the fine structure of that denomination which they attend. He espouses the Republican cause.

OLIVER H. OSMONSON, farmer, P. O. Morris, was born in Lisbon, Kendall Co., Ill., January 14, 1850. His parents had two children, of whom he was the elder. He received his education in the schools of Saratoga Township, and began life as a farmer. Mr. Osmonson is a School Director. He was married in Saratoga Township, March 1, 1870, to Susan A. Johnson, who was born June 10, 1852. She is the daughter of Oscar and Annie Johnson. Mr. and Mrs. Osmonson have had six children—Halver, Oscar, Annie, Severt, Joseph (deceased), and Joseph. Mr. and Mrs. Osmonson are members of the Lutheran Church. Mr. Osmonson belongs to no secret societies. He votes the Republican ticket.

OLIE OSMONSON, farmer, P. O. Morris, was born in Otter Creek Township, La Salle Co., Ill., December 1, 1852. His parents had two children, of whom he was the younger. Mr. Osmonson received his education in the normal school at Morris, Ill. He was married in Saratoga Township January 27, 1878, to Maggie E. Craig, who was born June 25, 1858, in Lisbon, Kendall County. Mrs. Osmonson's father, Samuel Craig, was born November 7, 1824, in County Antrim, Ireland. Her mother was born in Oneida County, N. Y., May 22, 1833. Mr. and Mrs. Osmonson are members of the Lutheran Church. Mr. Osmonson votes the Republican ticket.

WIER PETERSON, farmer, P. O. Lisbon, was born in Norway May 28, 1829. His father, Wier Peterson, was a farmer, and was born in Norway in 1789, and died March 4, 1871. His mother, whose maiden name was Julia Nelson, was born in Norway in 1791, and died February 28, 1873. Our subject received his education in the schools of Norway, and began life as a farmer. He came to Grundy County in 1856, and has been School Director. He was married in Lisbon, Ill., on July 4, 1857, to Annie Thompson, who was born in Norway January 6, 1837. She is the daughter of Torkel and Julia Thompson. Mr. and Mrs. Peterson have nine children—William P., born September 12, 1858; Julia A., October 18, 1860; Sarah, July 18, 1862; Mary E., January 1, 1865; Thomas O., July 2, 1868; Edwin F., September 16, 1870; Eli F., August 13, 1871; John, November 20, 1874, and Annie M., April 22, 1877. Mr. and Mrs. Peterson are members of the Lutheran Church. Mr. Peterson is a Republican.

ANDREW SOREM, farmer, P. O. Morris, was born in Norway March 25, 1830; son of Nels Michaelson and Brita Larsdottor. Nels, by occupation a farmer, was born in Norway in 1784, and died in the same place in 1874. Brita was born in that country in 1796, and died there in 1871. Andrew attended school in Norway, and was married there June 24, 1861, to Carrie Gregoriusdotter, who was born in Norway February 2, 1825. Her parents, Gregorious and Brita Anderson, were both natives of Norway. Andrew was a farmer in Norway, and since his residence in this country has followed the same pursuit. Andrew and his wife Carrie are the parents of eight children—Nels, Andrew, Betsy, Tena, Bell, Carrie, Michael and Emma. Mr. Sorem has been School Director in Saratoga, Grundy County. He is a Republican, and a member of the Lutheran Church.

MONS. N. SOREM, farmer, P. O. Morris, was born in Norway May 12, 1840. His education was received in the schools of that country. He was married in Norway May 6, 1861, to Sarah Ostrom, a native of that country, who was born March 28, 1838. They have had nine children—Nels N., born September 11, 1864; Severt, born September 30, 1866; Nels Michael, born December 12, 1868, deceased; Nels Michael, born June 4, 1870; Isabel S., born May 22, 1872; Ben L., born April 16, 1874; Lonnis, born February 29, 1876; Mons. O., born October 31, 1878; and Betsy E., born July 30, 1881. Mr. Sorem began life as a farmer. In politics he is a Republican. Mr. and Mrs. Sorem are members of the Lutheran Church. They came to this county in 1867.

WALTER S. SMITH, farmer, P. O. Morris, was born in Jefferson County, N. Y., August 24, 1843. He is the fifth child of Eleazer and Maria (Derby) Smith, who were the parents of ten children. His father, who is still alive, is a farmer, and was born in Rutland County, Vt., September 21, 1807. His mother was born in Chittenden County, Vt., August 28, 1815. Our subject went to school in New York, and afterward in Morris, Ill., and began life as a farmer. He has been School Director and Road Supervisor. In 1862, he enlisted in the militia, but did not enter into action. He was married, in Morris, Ill., June 9, 1875, to Annie Colwell, born in England in 1854, the daughter of William and Ann Colwell. They have had four children—Mabel A. (deceased), Clara, Jessie (deceased) and Irwin. They are members of the Presbyterian Church. Mr. Smith is a Republican in politics.

JOHN STEEL, coal miner, Morris, was born near Durham, England, March 16, 1812; son of Joseph and Elizabeth (Enns) Steel. Joseph was born in Cumberland, Eng., in 1812, and died in 1866. He was a gardener. Elizabeth was born in Stockton, Eng., in 1812, and died in 1851. John attended school in England for a time, and then went to work in the coal mines. About 1850, he married Elizabeth Humble at Lockport, Ill. She was born July 6, 1813. Mr. Steel is a member of the Church of England.

NATHANIEL H. TABLER, retired farmer, P. O. Morris, was born March 13, 1809, in Berkeley County, Va. He is the son of Henry and Mary (Oller) Tabler. Our subject's grandfather, George Tabler, was one of the early settlers in that country, having come from Germany and settled in Berkeley County, Va., shortly after the the Revolution. He had five children—Michael, Henry (subject's father), Christian, William and one daughter, whose name is unknown, all of whom settled in Virginia. To our subject's grandfather, on his mother's side, were born John, Jacob, George, Peter, Betsey, Catherine, Mary, and another daughter whose name is unknown, all of whom were born in Virginia. The children of our subject's parents were Nathaniel H., Joshua, Levi Harrison, Peter, Mary and Anna. His father was a farmer, and Mr. Tabler remained under the parental roof until he was twenty-one years of age, when he started alone for Delaware County, Ohio, and settled on the Scioto River about the year 1830. His father bought 200 acres of land, but did not himself come. Subject moved on to this land which was mostly wooded, and immediately commenced improvements. While here, in November, 1830, he was married to Mary Cryder, daughter of Henry Cryder. In October, 1853, he came to this county, and settled on Section 8, in Au Sable Township. At that time there were no improvements on the place. Three families—the Wollys, Cryders and N. H. Tabler—constituted the population of the county at that time. Remaining on his farm until 1876, he went to Minooka, this county, and lived there till the fall of 1882. His children by his first wife were Joseph, David C., Elias, Matthew, Ezra, and Mary, who was the wife of John McCloud. His second marriage was with Hannah Marie, daughter of Jacob and Betsey Cryder. Their children were Jerome, William, Lewis and Anna. He was married a third time to Susan Paulding, who was born near Waynesboro, Franklin Co., Penn. She was the daughter of Frank M. and Sarah (Rogers) Paulding. Joseph, Mr. Tabler's son by his first wife, lives in Florida, and the others are in Au Sable Township. Edward was all through the war, afterward coming home, and was killed in 1866 by the kick of a mule. Mr. Tabler was for the fourth time united in marriage, this time to Mrs. William Johnson, by whom he has one child—Farada, born July 4, 1881. Mr. Tabler has been a member of the M. E. Church for about fourteen years. He was a Democrat up to the time of Lincoln, since which he has voted the Republican ticket. Since coming to Morris, Mrs. Tabler has been running the Cottage Hotel, and boards the students attending the Normal School.

SENECA TUPPER, farmer, P. O. Morris, was born in Genoa, Cayuga County, N. Y., October 6, 1826; his father, Benjamin Tupper, was a farmer, and was born in Bennington County, Vt., August 28, 1790, and died October 21, 1874; his mother's maiden name was Philinda Cutter. They had eight children. The subject came to this county in February, 1857; he received his education at the Genoa Academy, N. Y., and began life as a farmer; he has filled many and various offices, having been Sheriff, Township Treasurer, School Director, and Township Supervisor. November 21, 1854, Mr. Tupper was married, in Venice, Cayuga County, N. Y., to Sarah Nelson, who was born May 5, 1833, in Sing Sing, Westchester Co., N. Y.; she was the daughter of Joseph G. and Pamela Nelson. Her father was born in Westchester County, N. Y., in 1792, and died in the fall of 1863; her mother was born in New York City in 1804, and died in 1859. Mr. Tupper is a member of the Baptist Church, and votes the Republican ticket.

ALEXANDER TELFER, miner, Morris, was born at Musselburg, Scotland, November 1, 1826; raised and educated in his native country. In 1852 (September), he came to the United States; located at Pittston, Penn., working in the mines of the Pennsylvania Coal Company until January, 1855; he then came to Morris, Grundy Co., Ill., and wrought in the mines of Oliver and Alexander Telfer (the latter a cousin of subject), for three years. In 1858, he bought some land and opened a mine for himself, and has been in the business ever since; he is also engaged in farming, having a farm of 200 acres, besides his coal lands, valued at $50 per acre. Since 1865, he has been in the brick business in connection with coal, and in this department is associated with Henry Burrell. Subject was married June 18, 1849, to Miss Agnes Kerr, of Scotland. She was born

October 6, 1826. They have six children—Christina, born in Scotland; Janet, born in Pennsylvania; William, born in Morris; Alexander, born in Morris; John, born in Morris; Mary Jane, born in Morris. Subject and wife are members of the Presbyterian Church ; he is also a member of the I. O. O. F. and Masonic fraternities and Knights Templar; residence one and a half miles northeast of Morris.

JOHN TREDINNICK, farmer, P. O. Morris, was born in Ashwater Parish, Devonshire, England, January 15, 1831, son of Thomas and Susan (James) Tredinnick. Thomas, who pursued farming, was born in Devonshire in 1801, and died in 1871. Susan, mother of subject, was born in the same place about 1804, and died about 1868. Our subject attended school in Saratoga Precinct, where he has since been School Director. At Morris, Ill., October 18, 1863, he married Ann Horrie, by whom he had three children—Franklin R., James F. and Wm. C., all of whom are dead. Mrs. Tredinnick was born in the Orkney Islands, Scotland, about 1831; she was the daughter of Robert and Jane Horrie, natives of the same place. Mr. Tredinnick came to Grundy County in April, 1856, since which time he has pursued his occupation of farming. He is a member of the Republican party.

A. F. WATSON, farmer, P. O. Morris, was born in Northumberland, England, February 17, 1833, son of George and Ann (Foster) Watson; his father, who was a coal miner, was born in Northumberland, England, in 1809, and died in 1875. His mother was born in the same place in 1811, and died April 10, 1857. Our subject was one of a family of nine children, and received his education in England. While in that country, he was a farmer and coal miner. In Statsworth, Durham, England, October 29, 1855, he married Nellie A. Humble, who was born in Durham, England, October 24, 1832 ; she was the daughter of George and Mary Ann Humble; her father was a native of England, born July 17, 1805, and died July 17, 1870; her mother of the same place, was born in 1807, and died December 18, 1871. Mr. Watson and wife are the parents of ten children—Susana, George, Elizabeth, Ann, Mary J., John, Alice, Isabella, Sarah and Margaret. Mr. Watson settled in Grundy County in 1853; has been School Director. Politically, he is a Greenbacker, and is connected with the Methodist Church.

NETTLE CREEK TOWNSHIP.

ISAAC N. BROWN, farmer, P. O. Nettle Creek, was born in Saratoga County, N. Y., August 15, 1817; he is the son of David and Mary (Brownell) Brown. Our subject was among those who came to this township in 1849; his father was born in Queensbury Township, Washington Co., N. Y., in 1794; his mother was born in Pittstown, Rensselaer Co., N. Y., and was the daughter of Simeon and Sarah (Hoag) Brownell. Our subject's grandfather, Justus Brown, married Desire Mosher, who bore him eleven children of whom our subject's father was the ninth. To Simeon and Sarah Brownell were born fifteen children, all of whom save one, lived to raise families. The great-grandfather of our subject was Benedict Brown; he was the father of nine children, all of whom lived to good age. Justus was his second child, and was born March 5, 1749. The family were great hunters, and were remarkably large men, weighing as high as 300 pounds. His wife was born in 1757. They had eleven children—Stephen, Phebe, Deborah, Lydia, Hannah, Abigail, Benjamin, Richard, David,

Annie and Justus. Of these, David and Justus are living. Simeon Brownell was born in 1759, and his wife, Sarah Hoag, in 1764. Their fifteen children were Alice, Joseph, Stephen, Daniel, Simeon, Meria, Sarah, Benjamin, Mary, Nathan, Isaac, John, Supham, Phebe and Henry H. To David and Mary Brown were born Isaac N. (our subject), Simeon, Sarah, Mary A., Edwin and Phebe. These lived and raised families. Mr. David Brown is still living, his wife died February 15, 1877. Our subject lived with his parents until coming West. In 1818, he removed to Chautauqua County, N. Y., and settled there with his parents, living there until the spring of 1844, when he came and settled in Big Grove Township, Kendall Co., Ill., where he remained until 1849, when he came to this county; he began by renting land in Kendall County. When he arrived in this county, he bought eighty acres, where he now lives, in January, 1846. It was situated on Section 4, and cost 10 shillings per acre; he soon added forty acres more, at a cost of $6.25 per acre; there were no improvements on it. In 1857, he purchased eighty acres at $15 per acre, and forty acres more in 1866, at a cost of $37.50 per acre; he has now 240 acres of well improved land. In 1849, he built his first house. March 22, 1840, he married Phebe Ann, daughter of Seth and Content (Ingraham) Clark. She was born May 13, 1819, in Chautauqua County, N. Y. Mr. and Mrs. Brown have had nine children, of whom six are living —David N., Mary C., Harriett A., Edie A., Phebe I. and Edwin L. Isaac C. died, aged eighteen, and the other two died when young. Mr. Brown was first elected Justice of the Peace in 1849, and has, with the exception of a year or two, served continuously ever since, having held a commission from *every* Governor since that time; he has been Supervisor, Collector and School Trustee for fourteen years, and has been Township Treasurer since 1875; he taught school for ten terms. Mr. Brown and wife have been members of the Congregational Church for over twenty years; he is at present Postmaster of Nettle Creek, which office has been running about three years.

OLIVER DIX, farmer, P. O. Nettle Creek, was born in Oneida County, N. Y., January 5, 1822; he was the only child of Ara and Lydia (Richards) Dix; his father was born in Pittsfield County, Conn., July 14, 1793, and was the son of Charles Dix, also a native of Connecticut, and who married a Miss Wells. The Dix family were of Welsh descent. Mr. Ara Dix was married, December 31, 1816, and died September 4, 1826, in Vernon, Oneida Co., N. Y. Our subject's mother was born in Litchfield, Conn., June, 1792, and died September 19, 1881. Mr. Ara Dix emigrated from Connecticut to Oneida County, N. Y., about the year 1808; he was a tanner and currier. Our subject was about four years old when his father died, and he still lived with his mother until he was fourteen. She had married some time previously, John E. Waterman, and they came out and settled in Lisbon, Kendall Co., Ill. Mr. Dix stayed with them until he was of age, when he started and worked for himself; he came to this township in 1845, having purchased land here in the spring of 1843, for about $12 per acre; he also bought 160 acres for $300. In the fall of 1844, he entered eighty acres of Government land, on which he still resides, having built on it during the summer of 1845. February 2, 1848, he married Lydia, daughter of Thomas and Sarah (Brownell) Wing. She was born in Chautauqua County, N. Y.; her father, Thomas Wing, was born in Dutchess County, N. Y., April 27, 1789, and died in 1856, in Kendall County; he married Sarah Brownell, July 29, 1810, who was born January 15, 1792, in Rensselaer County, N. Y., and who died March 4, 1827, in Chautauqua County. Mr. Thomas Wing came to Kendall County, Ill., about the year 1845. Our subject's wife died December 23, 1857. By her he had two children—Ara W. and Orville E. Ara W. resides on Section 9, this township, and Orville lives near Cresent City, Iroquois Co., Ill.; January 5, 1860, he married Louisa McKinzee, born in Alleghany County, Md., daughter of William and Ann S. (Spellman) McKinzee, natives of the same State. Mr. McKinzee was born February 2, 1798, and died March 25, 1874; his wife died April 1, 1874. They removed to Shelby County, Ind., in 1838, where they lived till the fall of 1851, when they came and settled in La Salle County, Ill., where they resided for three years, afterward removing to the town of Manlius, Ill., and finally coming to this township in 1865, where they both died. They were the parents of five girls, all living and married—Mary A., wife of S. A. Summers, of Iowa; Louisa (Mrs. Dix); Susanna M., wife of J. W. Small, of Iowa; Harriet, wife of James Ashton, of this county, and Nancy, wife of Peter Eckersley, of this county. Mr. and Mrs. Dix have five children—Lydia B., William Ettie M., Susan L. and George R. Lydia B. is now the wife of John W. Johnson, of this county. Mr. Dix taught school for three terms in Kendall County, Ill.; he was elected Justice of the Peace about 1849; he owns 700 acres of land ; he is Republican in politics.

SEVERT OSTROM, farmer, P. O. Morris, was born in Norway July 14, 1848. He is the fifth child of Severt and Engebor J. (Rygh) Ostrom. His parents had nine children. His father was born in Norway, in March, 1810, and was a farmer by occupation. His mother was born in Norway in January, 1817. Our subject received his schooling in his native land, started in life as a soldier, and afterward turned his attention to farming. At one time he was a Sheriff in Norway, and he has been Township Collector for Saratoga Township, this county. March, 14, 1874, he was married in Saratoga Township to Julia, a daughter of Tollef and Magele Thompson. She was born in Norway, 11, 1848. They have six children—Eliza O., Joseph, Maggie, Louis, Isabel and Theodore. Mr. and Mrs. Ostrom are members of the Lutheran Church. He votes the Republican ticket.

ERIENNA TOWNSHIP.

ABRAHAM HOLDERMAN, Sr., Seneca. The subject of this sketch, Abraham Holderman, is a son of Abraham and Charlotte Holderman, who came to what is now Grundy County in the fall of 1831, the year before the Black Hawk war. Subject was then nine years old, being born in Ross County, Ohio, January 22, 1822. At the time of his first recollection of this county there were but two houses between the Holderman Grove and Chicago, and no house from them to Bloomington. Went to mill over thirty miles. Nearest trading point was Chicago. Their first school was taught in the winter of 1834, obtaining a teacher for $10 per month. At this time there was not a sawed board nor a nail in any of their buildings. Some years they lost all their hay and grain from prairie fires. Subject was married in Grundy May 4, 1847, to Miss Mary E. Hoge, daughter of William and Rachael Hoge. She was born in Loudoun County, Va., August 17, 1827, and came with her parents to this county the fall of 1831. They were the first family in the county. Her brother James Hoge being the first white child born in the county. Subject has a family of eight children, three of whom are dead—William Holderman, born July 3, 1848; Joseph, February 11, 1850, and Hendley, December 11, 1851, all deceased ; Abram J. Holderman, whose biography appears on another page; Albert H. Holderman, April 19, 1856; Martha J. Holderman, born March 16, 1858; Landy S. Holderman, born November 8, 1859, and Samuel D. Holderman, born July 21, 1865. Mr. Holderman now owns about 5,000 acres of land, principally in one body, besides giving his children 2,000 acres. Engaged in farming and stock-raising. Politics, Republican; seventy-three voters in the township when organized, seventy-one of whom were Irish canal hands; subject being the only one left in the township.

ABRAM J. HOLDERMAN, farmer, P. O. Morris. The subject of this sketch is a native of Grundy County, Ill., born May 17, 1853, son of Abram and Mary E. Holderman, who are among the first settlers of the county. Educated in his native county, and married, March 6, 1876, to Miss Josephine V. Bashaw, daughter of Robert and Virginia Bashaw. She was born in Rappahannock County, Va., September 14, 1855, and came to this county in 1873. Her mother is dead, the father living in Virginia. They have a family of three children—Mary V. Holderman, born in Grundy County March 28, 1877; Walter T. Holderman, born in Grundy County September 29, 1878; Robert J. Holderman, born in Grundy County, February 11, 1882. Subject now owns a farm of 640 acres in Sections 11, 12, 13 and 14, of Erienna Township; residence four and one-half miles west from Morris. Engaged in stock-raising; politics, Republican.

JOSHUA HOGE, JR., farmer, P. O. Morris, the subject of this sketch is a native of the county of Grundy, Ill., born July 25, 1850, son of Samuel and Matilda Hoge, of Nettle Creek Township. Raised in Grundy County and educated in the State Normal Lombard University, and took a course in Bryant & Stratton's Commercial College of Chicago. Married, February 19, 1876, in Morris, to Miss Lora E. Quigley, daughter of Henry and Matilda Quigley, formerly of Pennsylvania. Mrs. Hoge was born in the vicinity of Meadville, Crawford Co., Penn., December 11, 1859. They have a family of two children—Samuel Hoge, born in Grundy County, August 12, 1877; unnamed, born August 25, 1882. Subject owns a farm of 560 acres of valuable land in the town of Erienna. Sections 1 and 6, of Erienna; residence, four miles west from Morris. Value of land, $50 per acre; engaged in stock-raising and mixed husbandry; politics, Republican. Mrs. Hoge's father was a native of Pennsylvania, born 1812, and died in Crawford County, Penn., 1866. Her mother is now living with her son, E. H. Quigley, of Morris, in her fifty-seventh year.

WILLIAM KENNEDY, farmer, P. O. Morris; the subject of this sketch is a native of county of Queens, Ireland, born December 14, 1820, son of John and Hanora Kennedy; raised and educated in his native country. Came to United States in 1839, landing at New York City August 9, of that year; vessel, "Margaret Scott, of Liverpool." Located in Ohio, 1840; engaged on public works for about eighteen months and came to Illinois in the fall of 1841; assisted in the construction of the Illinois & Michigan Canal; was book-keeper for Walter D. McDonald. Subject was married in May, 1842, to Miss Mary Kenrick, of Ireland, County Limerick. About 1849, he bought canal land and engaged in agriculture which he has followed since. He now owns a farm of 280 acres in Sections 1 and 2 of Erienna Township; residence four miles west from Morris; land valued at $50 per acre. Subject also owns a handsome store building and residence houses on Washington street, in Morris; they have no family. Politics, Democrat, and is among the standard element' of Grundy County. They are members of the Catholic Church of Morris.

NORMAN TOWNSHIP.

HENDERSON BUNCH, farmer, P. O. Morris. The subject of this sketch is a native of Tennessee, born July 27, 1825. He is the second of a family of four children of David and Nancy Bunch. David Bunch was a native of Tennessee, and his mother, Nancy (Hart) Bunch, was a native of Virginia. When subject was quite young his parents removed to Kentucky, where they lived but few years, and came to Illinois, and settled in what is now Grundy County, Norman Township, about 1834. Subject remembers vividly the Indians that were camped within one mile of his father's house for two years, 500 in number. They often trafficked with them, exchanging pork for honey, etc. David Bunch located on Section 27, of Norman Township, where he lived until his death, which occurred June 29, 1873, in his seventy-eighth year. His mother died in August, 1875, in her sixty-eighth year. The first school attended by H. Bunch was conducted in a log house, built where Jonas Newport settled, built by an Englishman named Ford; the first house erected in Vienna Township. The school was composed of the children of David Bunch and Jonah Newport. Subject remembers when there was but one house where Ottawa now stands. Mr. Bunch was married, March 30, 1850, to Miss Mary A. Doty, daughter of John and Sarah (Williams) Doty, who were among the pioneers of Grundy County. John Doty died February 19, 1872, in his seventy-ninth year, and her mother October 24, 1874, in her seventy-second year. They have a family of seven children living, having buried two. Martha J. Bunch, born June 10, 1852, married to Lemuel Quincy January 12, 1869; Cornelia M. Bunch, born October 25, 1854, married to Reuben Hollenbeck March 6, 1872; William H. Bunch, born December 1, 1856, married to Miss Ellen Boyette, October 18, 1878; Esther A. Bunch, born December 27, 1858, married to David Humphrey, July 7, 1882; Perry E. Bunch, born February 28, 1860, died March 17, 1863; Ida I. Bunch, May 9, 1863, died March 4, 1864; Frances L. Bunch, born April 24, 1865; Marinda I. Bunch, born June 21, 1868; Sherman W., born October 24, 1870.

PERRY GOSS, farmer, P. O. Morris. The subject of these lines, P. Goss, is a native of Portage County, Ohio, born August 7, 1823, son of Beder and Phydelia (Cross) Goss. Subject's father was born in Connecticut February 28, 1796, and moved to Ohio in 1804; died in Ohio May 3, 1879; his mother, a native of Vermont, was born September 30, 1800; she is still living in Wisconsin. Subject came to Indiana from Ohio in 1847; was married, in Montgomery County, Ind., March 7, 1850, to Miss Mary Frances Spillman, daughter of William and Dorcas J. Spillman, Kentucky. She was born in Kentucky April 18, 1827; her parents died in Crawfordsville, Ind., father March 20, 1876, mother March 8, 1879. Mr. Goss and family came to Grundy County September, 1854, and settled in Norman Township. Their family consists of nine children, seven sons and two daughters. Their names are Albert B. Goss, born in Indiana April 12, 1851, married to Ellen A. Kimball August 10, 1882; William E. Goss, born in Indiana January 10, 1854; Charles B. Goss, born in Grundy County, October 14, 1856; Mary Frances Goss, born January 22, 1858; George P. Goss, born July 31, 1860; John F. Goss, born April 9, 1863; Edwin Lincoln, born May 7, 1865; Eva Jane Goss, December 14, 1866; Julius Goss, born December 19, 1870. Mr. Goss now owns a farm of 213 acres, 200 of improved farm land in Section 27, of Norman Township, value $60 per acre; valuable improvements eight and a half miles southwest from Morris. Mr. and Mrs. Goss are members of the M. E. Church (Zion), of Norman Township. Mrs. Goss' father, William Spillman, was born in Kentucky December 15, 1803; mother, Dorcas (Garrison) Spillman was born in Kentucky September 22, 1802.

JUSTUS HOLLENBECK, farmer, P. O Seneca. The subject of these lines. Justus Hollenbeck, is a native of Greene County, N. Y., born January 6, 1821; was raised and educated in his native county. When at the age of twenty-two, he went to East Troy, Wis., having married, August 31, 1843, to Miss Rebecca Bennet, daughter of William and Hannah Bennet. She was born in Schoharie County, N. Y., August 25, 1816. Soon after marrying they went to Wisconsin, where they lived nine years, and came to Illinois in 1852, settling in Grundy County, Vienna Township; now lives in Section 33 of Norman Township, where he owns a farm of 160 acres, all in Section 33, valued at $40 per acre; his residence is nine miles southwest from Morris, and five miles southeast from Seneca; Hog Run divides his farm from north to south. They have a family of seven children—Emma E. Hollenbeck was born in East Troy, Wis., March 25, 1844; was married to Alphonso Diebold, of Seneca; Louisa Hollenbeck was born November 9, 1845; was married to John Barker, of Seneca; George Hollenbeck was born February 28, 1847, and died December 13, 1865; Isabelle Hollenbeck was born February 17, 1849, and died by drowning in a well April 22, 1855; Julius F., and Julia A. Hollenbeck, born June 11, 1852; Julia A. is married to Spencer Cox, of Seneca; Julius F. is married to Frances Kelsoe; Adeline Hollenbeck was born September 5, 1855; was married to John Nott, of East Troy, Wis. Our subject is a son of John and Elizabeth Hollenbeck, of Greene County, N. Y.; his mother, Elizabeth (Bennett) Hollenbeck, died at their home in Wisconsin March 7, 1852, in her fifty-third year; his father is still living in Wisconsin, in his eighty-eighth year. Mrs. Hollenbeck's parents died in Greene County, N. Y.

G. H. HULL, farmer, P. O. Wauponsee. The subject of this sketch is a native of Rensselaer County, York State, born February 25, 1827; he is the third of a family of five, Samuel and Hannah (Green) Hull. The father was a native of New York, born April 29, 1795, and died at his home in Rensselaer County, N. Y., September 12, 1882. His mother, Hannah Green, was born in New York February 28, 1803, and died in New York March, 1874. Subject was married in New York August 17, 1850, to Miss Elizabeth A. Shaw, daughter of Samuel and Elizabeth Shaw, of New York. She was born in Rensselaer County October 24, 1831. They came to Illinois in March, 1854, and settled in Grundy County, 1856, where they now live; he owns a farm of 400 acres of improved farm land, 240 acres in Section 35, of Norman Township, eighty acres in Section 33, of Norman Township, and eighty acres in Section 12 of Vienna Township; splendid residence and improvements on Section 35, nine miles southwest from Morris; value of farm land $50 per acre; engaged in mixed husbandry and stock-raising. They have a family of three—Doer C. Hull, born in York State December 9, 1851, married to Miss Lizzie D. Wilson, December 24, 1873; Earl J. Hull, born in Illinois July 26, 1856, married to Miss Ettie Brown January 25, 1882; Cora E. Hull, born May 11, 1867. Mrs. Hull's parents, Samuel Shaw and Elizabeth Wilkey, were married February 9, 1808; she is the youngest of a family of six children. Her father was born March 25, 1780, and died January 7, 1864; her mother, Elizabeth Wilkey, was born December 16, 1787; and died September 14, 1845.

WILLIAM JOHNSON, farmer, P. O. Morris. The subject of this sketch is a native of Knox County, Ky., born April 1, 1827. Subject is the third of a family of seven children of John and Charlotte Johnson; parents were both natives of Ashe County, N. C. When subject was but two years old, his parents removed to Indiana, where they lived one and a half years, coming to Illinois in 1831, and settled in Iroquois County. Here subject was raised until nineteen years old, when he, with his mother, came to Grundy County in 1845, his father having died in Iroquois County April 7, 1842. He has lived in Grundy County ever since; first settled in Hog Run, near the settlement of David Bunch. Subject now lives in Norman Township, where he now owns a farm of 160 acres of land, eighty acres in Section 13 of Norman, and eighty acres in Section 18, of Wauponsee Township; residence four and a half miles southwest from Morris. Subject was married in Grundy County December 14, 1850, to Miss Harriet Dean, daughter of John and Maria Dean; she is a native of England, born September 20, 1833. They have a family of five children, all born in Grundy County—John W. Johnson, born August 9, 1852, married to Miss Lydia B. Dix, of Nettle Creek Township; Maria Johnson, born October 10, 1854, married to Malbone W. Bennett; Scott Johnson, born June 4, 1857, married to Miss Emma Helman; Elrae Johnson, born April 20, 1861; Willie Johnson, born November 17, 1867; politics, Republican, and one of the organizers of Republicanism in Wauponsee Township. His mother, Charlotte (Hart) Johnson removed to Minnesota in 1854 with two sons and two daughters, where she died September 8, 1878. Mrs. Johnson's parents were formerly of England, and residents of Grundy County for over twenty years, and now living in Macon County, Mo.

CHARLES M. PIERCE, farmer, P. O. Morris. Charles M. Pierce, the subject, is a native of Worcester County, Mass., born March 5, 1817; son of William and Lydia (Lincoln) Pierce; raised and educated in Franklin County, Mass., town of Wendell. Here his parents died; his father in the fall of 1827; his mother was cousin to Gov. Lincoln, of Massachusetts. She died in Wendell in 1873, in her eighty-ninth year. In early life subject learned the trade of tanner and currier, which trade he followed in his native State for twenty-three years; was burned out in 1850, and moved to Illinois in 1855 (January), and settled in Norman Township of Grundy County, having married in Massachusetts, November 24, 1841, to Miss Clarinda Browning, of Massachusetts, born in Worcester County (Rutland), May, 1817; died in Massachusetts November, 1847. By this union he has two children—Edwin L. Pierce, born in Massachusetts November 19, 1842, living in Missouri; Clarinda G. Pierce, born in Massachusetts October 4, 1844, married to Thomas Brackley, of La Salle County. Subject was married to his present wife May 20, 1848, to Miss Charlotte Clapp, daughter of Oliver and Adelia Clapp, born in Massachusetts, March 4, 1830. They have a family of six children as the result of second marriage—Mary E. Pierce, born May 4, 1849, married to Fred M. Green March 17, 1872, now a resident of Green County, Kan.; Hetta Ella, born June 22, 1850, died June 27, 1865; George A. Pierce, born May 10, 1852, married to Mary B. Slosson January 1, 1880; Walter M. Pierce, born May 30, 1861, educated at Morris and Ann Arbor, and teaching in Kansas; Charles M. Pierce, born October 11, 1866; Minnie B., born October 3, 1868. Subject owns a farm of 160 acres in Section 27 of Norman Township; resides eight miles southwest from Morris; engaged in mixed husbandry. He is a member of the Masonic fraternity.

LORENZO KENIFF, farmer, P. O. Wauponsee. The subject of this sketch is a native of Massachusetts, born July 24, 1819; son of

Daniel and Rhoda (Cummins) Reniff; raised and educated in Franklin County, Mass.; by trade a carpenter. He came to Illinois in 1842, and located in Putnam County, where he lived twelve years. Here he was married, December 25, 1848, to Miss Lutheria E. Chittenden, daughter of Daniel and Mary Chittenden; she was born in the State of New York, March 19, 1831, and came to Illinois when six years old. They have a family of five children—Lucius M. Reniff, born in Putnam County July 22, 1850, married to Miss Jennie Lord, daughter of Abram Lord, of Morris, September 29, 1872; Grace E. Reniff, born February 22, 1853, married to Bruce Cooper, February 22, 1874, died in Norman Township May 2, 1875; Clara A. Reniff, born April 2, 1856, and married to Eugene Van Atta, March 3, 1878; Ida M. Reniff, born February 21, 1859; Herman G. Reniff, born March 28, 1865. Subject moved to Grundy County in December, 1853, and settled in Norman Township, where he now lives. He owns a farm of 120 acres in Sections 14 and 26. Residence, eight miles southwest from Morris; land valued at $50 an acre. Mr. Reniff's father died in this county in August, 1861, and his mother in February, 1864. Mrs. Reniff is a member of the Zion Methodist Episcopal Church, of Norman Township. Her mother, Mary A. (Lowel) Chittenden, was born in Vermont January 24, 1806, and died in Grundy County July 13, 1881. Her father was a native of York State, where he died in 1837.

THOMAS WINSOR, farmer, P. O. Morris. The subject of this sketch is a native of Devonshire, Ipplepen, near Torquay, England, born April 21, 1816; son of James and Elizabeth Winsor. Subject is the seventh of a family of eleven children; raised and educated in the elements of an English education in his native country. Married, February 12, 1843, in England, to Miss Martha Thomas, daughter of William and Mary Thomas, born in Devonshire, near Torquay, July 15, 1819. They came to the United States in the sailing vessel "Agnes," landed at New York and came by canal and lakes to Joliet, settled in Kendall County for two years, and then removed to Grundy County in 1850 and located in Saratoga Township, where he bought land and lived until 1864, when he removed to Norman Township, where he now lives. Here he owns a farm of 160 acres in Section 24, residence five and a half miles southwest from Morris. They have a family of eleven children, two of whom are dead, one son dying in England, and one daughter in Grundy County. Mr. Winsor is a Republican, and has served Norman Township as Justice of the Peace for eleven consecutive years.

VIENNA TOWNSHIP.

JAMES ANDERSON, retired, Verona, is a native of Huntingdon County, Penn., born May 27, 1817, son of Andrew and Elizabeth Anderson, of Ireland, who came to the United States in 1793, he being then but three years old. When subject was nine years old, his parents moved from Pennsylvania to Harrison County, Ohio, where they lived until 1840, when they removed to Illinois, and settled in Pike County. There our subject was married, March 25, 1841, to Miss Lydia Marshall, daughter of David and Elizabeth Marshall, born in Huntingdon County, Penn., May 16, 1804. Mrs. Anderson has been blind since the fall of 1874. They came to Grundy County in June, 1855, and settled in Section 13, of Vienna Township, where he owned 330 acres of land, including 168 acres in Section 18 of Mazon

Township, where he lived until 1873; he has lately sold his farms and bought property in the village of Verona, where they have lived for the past two years. his father died in this county February 19, 1857; his mother died in Macon County, Ill.; in 1867. Mr. and Mrs. Anderson are members of the Presbyterian Church of Verona. Since selling his farms he has retired, and they expect to spend the remainder of their days in the quiet of the village of Verona.

A. H. BRUCE, farmer, P. O. Verona, is a native of Westford. Mass., born September 29, 1828. When he was two years old, his parents removed to Oneida County, N. Y., where subject was raised and educated; he was married in Oneida County, N. Y., May 31, 1850, to Miss Malvina Janes, daughter of David and Elizabeth Janes; she was born in Oneida County, N. Y., September 17, 1827. In the spring of 1852, they came to Illinois and settled in Vienna Township, Grundy County, where they own a farm of sixty acres, improved land, in Section 26, worth $50 per acre; their residence is one mile northeast from Verona. They have a family of ten children, three of whom are dead: Lucy A., born March 11, 1851, married to O. Johnson September 11, 1869; Mary E. born September 12, 1852, married to William Dewey June 18, 1873; Leroy A., born November 25, 1854, married to Christina Coles January 24, 1878; Elizabeth M., born June 16, 1856, married to James Bennett February 6, 1876; Fred J., born March 21, 1858, died June 1, 1858; Ada A., born June 16, 1859, died March 12, 1864; Eddie L., born May 19, 1861, died March 11, 1862; Katie M., born June 16, 1864; Herman A., born March 17, 1866; and Sarah E., born October 23, 1869. Mr. Bruce is one of the early settlers of the county, and remembers when the wolves were very plentiful, and has had them jump at his horse as he rode along. Mr. and Mrs. Janes, parents of Mrs. Bruce, died at the residence of Mr. Bruce in this county; her father in August, 1855, and her mother in March, 1856.

GEORGE W. CARPENTER, grain, Verona, is a native of West Greenwich, R. I.; he was born April 15, 1826, son of Amos and Mary (Bailey) Carpenter, he being the sixth of a family of nine children. When he was about six years old, his father moved to Eastern Connecticut, where george W. was raised and educated. In 1854, he came West and settled in Grundy County, Ill.; bought 160 acres of land in Section 9, of Mazon Township, where he lived twelve years, and then moved to Morris, where he engaged in the implement and grain business. He remained there in business until 1878, when he came to Verona and engaged in the grain trade, which he still carries on. He shipped, in 1880, 153,638 bushels of corn. He was married first, in 1854, to Miss Sarah Underwood, born in Woodstock, Conn., in 1830, who died while on a visit at Binghamton, N. Y., in 1878. They had three children, one of whom is dead—Ella A., born in Grundy County April, 1857, married in 1876 to Mr. A. H. Gage, of New York; Mary B., born in 1861, died in 1863; and Mary Lilian, born December 26, 1866. He married in March, 1881, Mrs. Rebecca Murphy, formerly of Ohio. They have a farm of eighty acres of improved land in Section 12, of Vienna, worth $55 per acre. He is a Republican, and has frequently been elected to the offices of his township. He has an elevator and a nice residence in the village of Verona.

THOMAS S. COLMAN, farmer, P. O. Wauponsee, is a native of Putnam County, Ill., born August 2, 1838, son of John and Mary A. Colman, who moved into Putnam County, Ill., from the State of New York, in 1835. His father was born in Vermont in 1797 and died in La Salle County May 2, 1849, and his mother in New Hampshire, in January, 1806; she died at the residence of her son, in Norman Township, Grundy County, July 13, 1881. Our subject was raised and educated principally in La Salle County, Ill. He married, November 25, 1864, Miss Catharine Nelson, daughter of Miles and Adeline Nelson of New York. She was born in Steuben County, N. Y., December 15, 1838, and is the eldest of a family of five children. Their family consists of three children— John N., born October 1, 1865; Guy A., born September 12, 1869; William T., born August 22, 1871. Mr. Colman now owns 160 acres of improved farm land in Section 12, of Vienna Township, valued at $55 per acre; he resides one half mile south of Wauponsee Station. He is a member of the Masonic fraternity; in politics, he is a Republican, and has been elected to the offices of his township. He has one brother, John T. Colman, living in Norman Township, Grundy County.

MATTHEW DIX, farmer, P. O. Verona, is a native of Berkshire, England, born May 4, 1831, son of Charles and Martha Dix, of England. He is the fifth of a family of eight children, and was raised and educated in England. He came to the United States in 1856, in the vessel "Amazon," being six weeks on the passage. He came immediately to Illinois and settled in Kendall County, where he engaged in farming for eight years; came to Grundy County in the spring of 1865. Here he located in Section 22, of Vienna Township, where he owns a farm of 160 acres of well-improved land, and resides one and one-half miles northwest from Verona; the land is valued at $50 per acre. Mr. Dix was married in Kendall County, September 21, 1864, to Miss Gertrude Cody, daughter of Thomas and Harriet Cody, born in Oneida County, N. Y., July 8, 1843. They have a family of seven children, three of whom are dead—Freddy L., born in Grundy County December 26, 1868; Lewis M., December 24, 1870, died of diphtheria December 22, 1880; Clara A., born November 2, 1872; Mina G., January 20, 1876, died June 12, 1877; Sadie E., born February 3, 1878; and Effie J., born August 27, 1879. George T., Mr. Dix's eldest son, born January 21, 1865, drowned by falling into a tub of water in October, 1866. They are members of the Methodist Episcopal Church of Verona.

THOMAS B. GRANBY, farmer, P. O. Verona, is a native of Greene County, N. Y.; born September 10, 1840, son of James A. and Eliza A. Granby, our subject being the eldest of a family of eight children. His parents came to this county in 1855, from New York; his mother, Eliza A. (Carter) Granby, died in Grundy County in the fall of 1877; his father died December 23, 1879. Mr. Granby was educated in his native State. He enlisted August 10, 1862, in Company D, Seventy-second Illinois Volunteer Infantry, and participated in the Vicksburg campaign, under Grant, in 1862, and in the seige of Vicksburg in 1863; battle of Raymond. Miss.; Champion Hills; Black River Bridge; Fort Hill (charge); Franklin, Tenn., where he was captured November 30, 1864, by Gen. Hood's force and held in Andersonville and other prisons until March 10, 1865, and was then paroled and in August was mustered out at Springfield, Ill. He married November 10, 1872, Miss Mary E. Cooper, daughter of William Cooper. She was born in Indiana July 12, 1846. They have one son—Edgar A., born in Grundy County, August 16, 1873. Mr. Granby owns 100 acres of improved land; eighty acres in Section 10 of Vienna, and twenty acres in Section 29 of Norman Township. He is a Republican.

HENRY G. GORHAM, farmer and grain merchant, Wauponsee, is a native of Putnam County, Ill., born November 5, 1848, son of Gardner T. and Elizabeth A. Gorham, who settled in this county in 1849. His mother is a daughter of Jesse and Jane Newport, who settled in Vienna Township in 1834. Mr. Gorham was educated in the common schools of Grundy County, and, at the Lombard University of Galesburg, Ills. He was married, November 6,

1878, to Miss Clara Lord, daughter of L. M. Lord, of Morris. She was born in Kendall County, Ill., November 7, 1852. They have one daughter, Mabel, born in Grundy County December 31, 1870. Mr. Gorham is engaged in the grain trade at Hill Park, and has control of the Gorham estate, consisting of 860 acres of farm land in Section 1 of Vienna Township, and Section 6 of Mazon Township. He is a member of the Masonic fraternity, Morris Commandery. His father, who was a native of New York, born in 1804, died in Grundy County October 1, 1872.

AARON HARFORD, Verona, is a son of Harry and Maria (Tyler) Harford, was born in South Salem, Westchester Co., N. Y., July 2, 1822, and was raised and received the elements of English education in his native State. His mother and President John Tyler were first cousins; she died in San Francisco, Cal., March 10, 1881, in her eighty-eighth year; his father, Harry Harford, died in the same city December 25, 1874; he was a soldier through the war of 1812, and was in his ninetieth year at the time of his death. Our subject came to Illinois with his father, and located four miles east of Lisbon, in Kendall County, coming the entire distance from the Hudson River with a team. Here he remained with his father until twenty-four years old, at which time, November 1, 1847, he married Miss Francis Dewey, daughter of John and Mary Dewey, born in Ketton, Rutlandshire, Eng., December 4, 1825, and came to the United States with her parents when about eleven years old. They settled at Wauponsee Grove, in Grundy County, on the farm now occupied by A. Newport, in the spring of 1839, being among the pioneers of Grundy County. Mr. Harford began life for himself by settling in Vienna Township, where he now lives on land then owned by his wife's father (Dewey). His taxes for first year were about 75 cents; he now owns a tract of land consisting of 620 acres in Sections 14 and 23, of Vienna Township. They have had a family of seven children, three of whom are dead : Cornelia D., born August 9, 1848; married, April 8, 1872, to Mr. Edwin C. Slosson, of Vienna Township; Mary, born February 4, 1850, died June 4, 1851; Fannie M., born November 24, 1852; married, March 28, 1877, to James Mulvanie; Frederick, born September 27, 1854; married to Clara Pomeroy. April 4, 1876; Addison, born March 14, 1857, died May 25, 1875; Olive, born July 7, 1861; died June 7, 1870, and Ellen, born April 12, 1864. Mr. Harford has for many years been an extensive stock-raiser, but of late years has turned his attention to blooded horses, having first introduced the English draft, Norman and Clydesdale breeds into the county. Politically, he was formerly what was known as an abolitionist; was a Republican during the war, and at present an Independent Greenbacker.

FRED HARFORD, farmer, Vienna, is a son of Aaron and Frances Harford, was born in Grundy County September 27, 1854, and educated in the schools of this county. He married, at Benton Harbor, Mich., April 4, 1876, Miss Clara A. Pomeroy, daughter of Alexander and Hannah E. Pomeroy. She was born in Portage County, Ohio; was educated at Niles, Mich., and Morris, Ill., and taught school during twelve years, from 1864 to 1876, principally in Grundy County, where she enjoys an enviable reputation as a teacher. They have two children: Leland F., born February 15, 1878, died February 23, 1878, and Aaron C., born September 5, 1880. Mr. Harford now owns a farm consisting of 240 acres of valuable land; 160 acres in Section 13, and eighty acres in Section 13 of Vienna Township; his residence is situated two and a half miles northeast from Verona. In politics, he is a Greenbacker, and has served his township officially.

CHARLES A. HILL, farmer, P. O. Wauponsee, is a native of New Hampshire, born September 18, 1836; son of Capt. Alfred and Ann (Lea) Hill. He is a descendant of Peter

Hill, one of the passengers of the Mayflower in 1620. His father, Capt. Alfred Hill, was a seaman, being a captain from the time he was twenty-one years old until the time of his death, which occurred at the wreck of the steamship Rhode Island, when four days out from New York, bound for San Francisco, Cal. His mother's ancestry dates back to the nobility of England. She was lost at sea in the wreck of the steamship Home, seven miles off the coast of Charleston, S. C., her husband saving his life on this occasion by swimming ashore. Subject was raised in Oneida County, N. Y., by his grandparents (Lea). He married at Verona, Oneida County, N. Y., March 5, 1856, Miss Sarah E. Overocker, daughter of Jacob E. and Betsey Overocker. She was born in New York January 8, 1832. They have a family of three children—Annie L., born October 20, 1866, married to E. W. Overocker November 11, 1878; Clara A., born August 18, 1867, and Ada B., born July 20, 1869. Mr. Hill came to Grundy County in March, 1859, and has since been a resident of the county. Since 1866, he has lived in Vienna Township, where he owns a farm of 160 acres in Sections 2 and 11, his residence being Hill's Park Station. Mrs. Hill is a member of the Congregational Church of Waupansee Grove.

JOSEPH HUTCHINGS, farmer, P. O. Verona, is a native of Lincolnshire, Eng., born October 26, 1827; son of William and Mary Hutchings, and was raised and educated in the old country. He came to the United States in 1851, and located in the State of New York for four years, engaged in farming. In the fall of 1855, he came to Illinois and settled in Norman Township, Grundy County, where he lived six years. In the winter of 1861, he bought a farm of Aaron Harford, in Vienna Township, upon which he has lived since. He now owns a farm of 320 acres of improved land in Sections 11 and 14, valued at $50 per acre, his residence being two and a half miles north of Verona. He married in Buffalo, N. Y., November 4, 1855, Miss Bridget Clark, of Ireland, born December 25, 1833. They have a family of five children, one of whom is dead—Francis M., born November 4, 1856; Mary E., born September 29, 1859; Margaret W., born February 9, 1863, died December 6, 1881; John J., born April 27, 1866, and James W., born January 1, 1871. They are members of the Catholic Church of Highland. He is a Democrat.

ALBERT HOLLENBECK, farmer, P. O. Verona, is a son of Abram and Jane A. Hollenbeck, and is a native of Dutchess County, N. Y., born August 22, 1845. His parents came to Illinois and settled in Vienna Township, Grundy County. His father, Abram Hollenbeck, was born in New York June 23, 1809, and died in Vienna Township, Grundy County, October 10, 1854. His mother is now living in Morris, wife of William H. Curtis, one of the pioneers of the county. Mr. Hollenbeck is the third of a family of five children. He received the elements of an English education in Grundy County, and January 1, 1880, married Miss Imogene Reed, of La Salle County, Ill., born in Freedom Township, La Salle County, July 5, 1860. They have a son—Marion A., born in this county December 6, 1880. Mr. Hollenbeck now owns a farm of 130 acres of land in Section 18 of Vienna Township, besides controlling a farm of 190 acres in Sections 17 and 18, owned by William H. Curtis. His residence is seven miles southeast from Seneca and five miles northwest from Verona. Mr. Hollenbeck is among the substantial farmers of Vienna Township. In politics, he is Republican, and he is a member of the Central Committee. His mother, Jane A. Hinchman, was born in New York February 13, 1817, and was married to Abram Hollenbeck January 15, 1835.

M. G. HAYMOND, farmer, P. O. Waupansee, is a native of Shelby County, Ind., born November 9, 1836; son of William and Anna

Haymond, he a native of Virginia, she of Kentucky. When subject was only one year old, his parents removed to Illinois, and settled in Kendall County in 1837, where he received his education principally. He came to this county in 1855, and in 1864 bought a farm in Section 2 of Vienna Township. Here he still lives owning a farm of 122 acres of valuable land with splendid improvements, situated on the west side of Section 2, the land being worth $60 per acre. He was married in Grundy County October 10, 1861, to Miss Eliza M. Pangburn, daughter of Moses Pangburn, of Wauponsee Township, she was born in Onondaga County, N. Y., September 22, 1841. They have a family of two children, one living—Freddie, born in Grundy County December 25, 1865, died May 10, 1866, and Katie May born in this county February 24, 1868.

J. W. MARTIN, Verona, was born in Brown County, Ohio, November 7, 1840; son of Benjamin M. and Elizabeth Martin. When he was six years old, his parents removed to Illinois in 1846, and settled in La Salle County, where they lived about ten years, engaged in farming. They then removed to Highland Township, Grundy County, where his father died in September, 1866. His mother now lives in Dwight, Livingston Co., Ill., aged seventy years. Mr. Martin enlisted August 15, 1862, in Company D, One Hundred and Twenty-seventh Ill. Vol. Infantry (Capt. Chandler), in which he served during the war, and was discharged at Washington in June, 1865. He participated in the siege of Vicksburg, and was with Sherman through his entire career. He married, March 7, 1877, Miss Emily J. Crozier, daughter of Christopher Crozier, of Grundy County; born in Ross County, Ohio, May 18, 1846. They have a family of five children—Carrie J., born in Grundy County January 13, 1868; Ira L., born in Grundy County May 14, 1869; Early William, born in Grundy County February 9, 1871; Nellie, born in Grundy County July 8, 1876, and Maud, born in Grundy County January 13, 1881. Mr. Martin has a farm of 160 acres of improved farm land in Section 18, of Highland Township. He is now engaged in mercantile business in the village of Verona, and owns two store-rooms stocked with a general stock. He came here in the spring of 1876. In politics, he is a Republican.

WILLIAM PETERSON, Verona, was born in Ross County, Ohio, August 6, 1816, where he was raised on a farm, and educated in South Salem Academy. He followed the profession of teaching for fifteen years, principally in Ross County. He was married March 13, 1843, in Ross County to Miss Louisa Fearrell, born April 23, 1820, daughter of James and Elizabeth Fearrell, of Ohio. They came to Illinois and settled in Wauponsee Grove, Grundy County, in the fall of 1853. He remained there for three years, then sold his farm and moved to Vienna Township, where he now owns a farm of 320 acres of improved land in Section 35, of Vienna Township, valued at $50 per acre, on which he is engaged in stock-raising. They have a family of three sons—Hamilton C., the eldest, was born in Ross County, Ohio, January 13, 1844. His first official work was that of teacher; he afterward entered the army, and served through the war; was then commissioned Second Lieutenant in the regular army, subsequently promoted to First Lieutenant, and after serving four years resigned to engage in the practice of law. He died at Laredo, Tex., in April, 1878. John H., the second son, was born in Ross County, Ohio, December 25, 1846, and is now living in Verona. The youngest son, Rufus A., was born in Highland County, Ohio, February, 1849. Mr. and Mrs. Peterson are members of the Presbyterian Church of Verona. He is a Republican. Their residence is situated one mile south of Verona.

JAMES REARDON, farmer, P. O. Wauponsee, is a native of Franklin County, N. Y., born March 11, 1834, son of William and

Catharine Reardon, who were born in Ireland; his father died in Morris, this county, and his mother, Catharine (Curtis) Reardon, died in Au Sable Township, this county. Subject came with his parents to Illinois in 1851. They settled in Grundy County and remained until their death. Mr. Reardon received the elements of an English education principally in York State; he was married, November 12, 1856, in Grundy County to Miss Sarah A. Cryder, daughter of Israel and Elizabeth Cryder; she was born in Pennsylvania November 13, 1837. Mr. Reardon began life for himself in the town of Au Sable, where he lived about eight years; he then sold his farm and removed to Saratoga Township, where he followed farming for one year, when he sold out and moved to Morris where he resided three years. Since then he has lived in Vienna Township, where he has a farm of eighty acres of improved land in Section 2, his residence being ten miles southwest from Morris, and one mile west from Wauponsee Station. He engages in general farming on his place which is valued at $60 per acre. He is a supporter of the Republican party.

WILLIAM RANSLEY, farmer, P. O. Verona, is a native of the county of Kent, Parish of Frindsbury, England, born February 22, 1817, son of William and Sarah Ransley, of England, and was raised and educated in his native country. September 17, 1854, he landed at New York City, and remained in New York until January, 1855, then came to Illinois and settled in Grundy County, February 7, 1855, he located in Vienna Township, where he now owns a farm of 290 acres of improved land including four dwelling houses in Section 26 of Vienna Township, the land being valued at $55 per acre. His residence is situated one-half mile north of Verona. He was married November 19, 1869, in Milton, Ulster Co., N. Y., to Miss Dinah Susans, born at Gravesend, England, in 1844. They have a family of three children—William, born in Grundy County, August 28, 1870; Beatrice, born in Grundy County June 2, 1872, and Frank, born in Grundy County March 17, 1875. Mr. Ransley has crossed the ocean five times; first on the Yorktown, thirty-eight days; second, City of Antwerp, eleven days; third, City of Brooklyn, ten days; fourth, City of Brooklyn, ten days; fifth, City of Richmond, ten days. He is a supporter of the Republican party.

NICHOLAS AND DANIEL RAGAN, farmers. P. O. Verona, are sons of Timothy and Bridget Ragan, of Ireland. Daniel was born in Grundy County August 31, 1849; Nicholas also was born in Grundy County April 5, 1853. Their father, Timothy Ragan, assisted in the construction of the canal and was one of the early settlers of this county; he died in Grundy County in April, 1853. They first settled in Erienna Township, where they lived until 1867, when the family consisting of Nicholas, Daniel, their mother and one sister, removed to Vienna Township. Their sister, Fannie, was born in La Salle County March 7, 1848, and was married, February 27, 1870, to Mr. John Fitzpatrick, who died in Grundy County September 21, 1873. Mrs. Fitzpatrick has a daughter Mary A., born in Grundy County November 27, 1870. The brothers have a farm of eighty acres in Section 34, of Vienna Township, and eighty acres in Section 3, of Highland Township, including two dwelling houses, their present residence being situated one mile southwest from Verona. The land is valued at $50 per acre. They are all members of the Catholic Church of Highland Township. Daniel Ragan is Assessor for Vienna Township. They are engaged in stock-raising and general husbandry; in politics, they are Independent.

D. S. RENNE, hardware, Verona, is a son of Justin and Maria Renne, formerly of New York State. He was born in Dutchess County, N. Y., October 27, 1845. The fifth of a family of seven children; he received the elements of an English education in his native county, and engaged in farming until 1875, when he was employed as station agent of the Chicago, Pekin & South-Western Railroad, in which office he remained five years. In September, 1881, he associated himself with D. Beal in the hardware, stove and implement trade, on Division street, Verona, where they keep on hand an extensive stock of general hardware. Mr. Renne was married, February 16, 1879, to Miss Anna M. Ryder, born in Ottawa, Ill., February 4, 1857, daughter of John and Adelia Ryder, of this county. Mr. Renne is a member of the Masonic fraternity; in politics, he is a Democrat. The biography of his parents appears elsewhere in this work.

HARRIS SMALL, retired, Verona, is a native of Somerset County, Me., born May 24, 1817, son of Nathan and Susan Small. He was raised and educated in his native State. He married, November 29, 1838, Miss Sophrona Lombard, born in Somerset County, Me., February 19, 1819, daughter of Nathaniel and Abigail Lombard, of Maine. He came to Illinois in 1854, and settled in Grundy County, Highland Township, where they lived until the spring of 1877, when he retired from farm life and moved to Verona, where he now lives. They rent their farm of eighty acres in Section 12, of Highland Township. They have a family of eight children, five of whom are still living: Franklin S., born September 26, 1839, died February 19, 1842; Daniel, born May 27, 1841, died June 13, 1842; Wilson, born January 1, 1843; Emily J., born February 15, 1844; Shepherd D., born January 6, 1846; Livona, born May 19, 1848; Millard F., born July 31, 1850, and Ellen M., born May 9, 1857. All except the last named were born in Maine; Ellen M. was born in Grundy County; Livona died January 25, 1878. Mrs. Small is a member of the Congregational Church of Verona. When Mr. Small came to Grundy County, Highland Township had about twelve voters.

AARON SMALL, mechanic, Verona, is a son of Alvin and Anna Small, formerly of Maine, and was born October 6, 1837, in Athens County, Me. His parents moved to Illinois when he was about six years old; settled for about one year in Kane County; thence moved to Highland Township, Grundy County, where his father is still living, in his seventy-ninth year; his mother, Anna (Stephens) Small, born in Maine, died in Highland Township, Grundy County, November 22, 1858. Mr. Small was raised and educated in Grundy County; began learning the trade of a blacksmith when eighteen years of age, and has followed that business ever since. For six years, he has been manufacturing wagons and buggies, and handling farm implements in the village of Verona. He married, June 6, 1860, Miss Sarah Hart, daughter of Rev. William and Jane Hart. She was born in Delaware County, Penn. They have a family of four children, two sons and two daughters—Ella, born in Gardner, Grundy County, April 11, 1862, married to Walter Ward, of Grundy County; William A., born in Grundy County, February 8, 1865; Verdett, born in Grundy County, August 19, 1867, and Lula, born in Grundy County, December 7, 1873. Mr. Small is a member of the Masonic fraternity (Knights Templar). He owns forty acres of improved farm land in Section 1 of Highland Township, valued at $50 per acre, and also owns the shops and residence in Verona, Grundy County. In politics, he is Republican. Mrs. Small's parents are now living in Mazon Township.

JAMES SEAMARKS, farmer, P. O. Verona, is a native of England, born in the county of Kent February 15, 1810; was raised on a farm and educated in England, and came to the United States in 1839, landing at New York City. He came over in the sailing vessel Quebec. He first settled in Mahoning County, Ohio, where he lived for fifteen years, coming to Illinois in the spring of 1854, where he had previously bought land in Vienna Township, Grundy County. He still lives upon the same farm, which consists of 240 acres of splendid farming land, including three dwelling houses, situated in Section 27, the residence being three-quarters of a mile northwest from the village of Verona. The land is valued at $50 per acre. Mr. Seamarks was married, in England, May 22, 1835, to Miss Mary Ransley, of England, born September 4, 1814, and who died at their home in Vienna Township, December 21, 1881. They had a family of two children—Charlotte, born in England September 11, 1837; married, March 31, 1856, to Richard Hughes, of England, now living in Marseilles, Ill., and Fannie, born in England August 21, 1839, married, March 31, 1856, to Mr. Levi Barner—she died April 10, 1874, in Livingston County, leaving a family of eight children, three of whom are with their grandfather, Mr. Seamarks; Anna, born March 6, 1864; Fannie, born October 19, 1868; Frank, born October 10, 1870. Mr. S. also owns 240 acres in Livingston County, Ill., with two dwellings, also a dwelling house in Verona.

EDWIN C. SLOSSON, manufacturer, Verona, is a son of Rufus K. Slosson, M. D., and Hannah G. (Brown) Slosson, and was born in Cayuga County, N. Y., February 25, 1843. In the spring of 1854, his parents came to Illinois, and settled in Vienna Township, Grundy County, where our subject received the elements of an English education. He enlisted August 22, 1862, in Company C, Seventy-sixth Illinois Volunteer Infantry, in which he served during the war and was discharged in Chicago in August, 1865. During his term of service he participated in the siege of Vicksburg, Jackson; siege of Fort Blakely, where he was shot through both thighs. April 8, 1872, he married Cornelia D. Harford, daughter of Aaron and Frances Harford, of Vienna Township, born August 9, 1848. They then went to California where he engaged in the lumber trade for five years, then returned to Grundy County, and has since been in Verona, engaged in manufacturing the "Slosson Cultivator." He is associated in business with his brother, Eugene Slosson. Mr. and Mrs. Slosson have one child now living, and have lost two—Vallie, born in Oregon February 2, 1873, died died in Grundy County August 25, 1880; Fannie May, born in Oregon August 11, 1875, died in Grundy County September 1, 1880, and Ellen, born in Grundy County, August 14, 1881. He is a Republican.

JOHN C. SCHROEDER, farmer, P. O. Seneca, is a native of Mechlenburg-Schwerin, Germany, born October 8, 1830; raised and educated in Germany; came to the United States in 1858; landed at New York City, and came immediately to Marseilles, Ill. He lived in La Salle County for about five years, then settled in Vienna Township, Grundy County, where he now owns 200 acres of valuable improved farm land in Section 4; residence three miles west from Wauponsee Station. Our subject was married, in La Salle County, October 31, 1863, to Miss Mary Schroeder, daughter of Christian and Eva Schroeder, of Germany. She was born January 1, 1833; they have a family of five children, one dead—Wilhelmina, born born January 19, 1865; Caroline, December 19, 1869; Dorothea, April 29, 1872; Mary, February 17, 1875; also one son who died in infancy. The entire family are members of the German Lutheran Church. Mrs. Schroeder's father died in Grundy County, November 27, 1881. Her mother is now living with them in her seventy-third year. Mr. Schroeder is engaged in stock-raising and general husbandry.

JACOB STONER, farmer, P. O Verona, is a native of Cumberland County, Penn., born January 15, 1824; son of George and Mary Stoner, of Pennsylvania. In 1835, his parents removed to Summit County, Ohio, where subject resided until 1845, when he came West, spent some time in Illinois, and, until 1849, was traveling in Louisiana, Wisconsin and Michigan. In 1849, he settled in Grundy County, Ill., and has been a resident of the county ever since. He now owns a farm of 173 acres of improved land in Section 22 of Vienna Township, and resides two and three-quarter miles northwest from Verona. His land is valued at $50 per acre. He was married, in Grundy County, July 4, 1855, to Miss Caroline Nance, daughter of Eaton and Mary Nance, formerly of Kentucky. She was born in Sangamon County, Ill., January 24, 1838. They have a family of seven children, all born in Grundy County—Charles E., born August 2, 1857; De Alton, born January 24, 1859, died February 14, 1859; J. Irwin, born October 5, 1861; Lulu, born February 29, 1864; Ulysses G., born July 20, 1865; Mary C., born December 14, 1867; and Sarah M., born September 6, 1876. Mr. Stoner is engaged in general husbandry.

ALLEN S. TILDEN, farmer, P. O. Verona, is a native of Addison County, Vt., born December 25, 1822; son of Isaac and Minerva Tilden. When about thirteen years old his parents removed to St. Lawrence County, N. Y., where he remained until 1852, then came to Grundy County, Ill. When subject became of age, he went to North Leverett, Franklin Co., Mass., where he engaged at his trade (that of a blacksmith); worked there four years, and afterward three in the northern part of New Hampshire, and came to Illinois in 1852 and settled in Vienna Township, where he now owns a farm of 560 acres of land, 400 in Sections 9 and 16 of Vienna Township. His residence with extensive improvements being located five miles northwest from Verona. He was married, in May, 1852, to Miss Elvira Willis, daughter of Ezra Willis, born in Franklin County, Mass., in 1831. They have three children—Eva E., born in Grundy County, September 24, 1853; Lucy C., born in Grundy County October 17, 1860, married to E. Willson December 3, 1879; and Frank C., born December 20, 1872. Mr. Tilden's mother is now living with him. She is now eighty-two years of age. His father, Isaac Tilden, died at subject's residence in August, 1866.

I. C. TILDEN, farmer, P. O. Verona, is a native of Addison County, Vt., born June 15, 1830; son of Isaac and Minerva (Sherwood) Tilden, who removed to St. Lawrence County, N. Y., where our subject was principally raised and educated. In 1852, they came to Illinois and settled in Vienna Township, Grundy County, where the sons purchased land. Our subject is the fifth of a family of eight children. He was married, February 10, 1859, to Miss Roxana Porter, daughter of Arza and Jane Porter, of Vienna Township. Mrs. Tilden was born in Livingston County, N. Y., April 2, 1836. They have a family of three children, all born in this county—Mary E., born June 4, 1864; Frances M., March 10, 1868; and Katie L., November 6, 1872, died when within one hour of being one year old, November 6, 1873. Mr. Tilden has a farm of 320 acres of improved land in Section 21 of Vienna Township. His residence, with all valuable improvements, lies two and one-half miles west from Verona. The land is valued at $62.50 per acre. They are members of the Methodist Episcopal Church of Verona. He is engaged in stock-raising as a specialty. Mrs. Tilden's father, Arza Porter, for some years a resident of Vienna Township, died in January, 1858; her mother is still living in Vienna Township.

L. H. TILDEN, farmer, P. O. Wauponsee, is a native of Stockholm, St. Lawrence Co., N. Y., born April 23, 1841, son of Isaac and Minerva Tilden, subject being the youngest of a family of eight children. He came to Illinois with his parents, and settled in Grundy County, where he has since lived, and where he was educated principally. He enlisted, September 6, 1862, in Company D, One Hundred and Twenty-seventh Illinois

VIENNA TOWNSHIP.

Volunteer Infantry, in which he served two years, afterward detailed to Battery A, First Illinois, and mustered out at Chattanooga, Tenn., June 19, 1865. He participated in the following engagements: Chickasaw Swamp, Arkansas Post, Black Bayou, Resaca, Dallas, Kenesaw Mountain, Chattahootchie River, Atlanta and Jonesboro. He married, April 10, 1866, Miss Lucy E. Willis, daughter of Ezra and Electa Willis. She was born in Leverett, Franklin Co., Mass., January 20, 1842. They have a family of four children, all born in Grundy County, named as follows: Lillian E., born September 27, 1870; Guy W., born October 9, 1873; Mary E., born August 14, 1877; and Roy E., born July 2, 1879. Mr. Tilden owns 120 acres of improved farm land in Section 3 of Vienna Township, Grundy County. His residence is one mile west from Hill's Park Station. Value of farm land, $50 per acre. In politics, he is a Republican.

JONATHAN WILSON, farmer, P. O. Verona, is a native of Union County, Ky., born December 3, 1810. When about fourteen years old, his parents, Thornton and Elizabeth Wilson, moved to Illinois and settled in Sangamon County for one year, after which they lived near Tremont, in Tazewell County, for two years. In the fall of 1827, they moved into Putnam County, where they purchased a farm; there the father died, March 9, 1835; the mother had previously died in Tazewell County, in February, 1826. Subject remained in Putnam County till 1850, and while there was married, January 24, 1839, to Miss Elma Hoyle, daughter of William and Edith Hoyle; her father was a native of England, and her mother a native of Pennsylvania; her mother died in Putnam County August 5, 1840, and her father died in the same county January 9, 1876. Mrs. Wilson was born in Jefferson County, Ohio, August 27, 1824. Since 1850, Mr. Wilson has resided in Vienna Township, of Grundy County, Ill. They now own the "Old Jonah Newport" farm, consisting of 326 acres, in Sections 4 and 9 of Vienna, their residence being situated twelve miles southwest from Morris. Mr. and Mrs. Wilson are parents of ten children—William A., born March 3, 1840, died February 28, 1871; Edith E., born October 4, 1843; Mary E., born March 18, 1845, married to Albert Hollenbeck on February 18, 1875, and died August 22, 1875; Joseph A., born February 20, 1849, married Hattie E. Collins March 5, 1879; Oliver T., born January 1, 1852, died January 31, 1852; Sabina M., born April 6, 1854; Edward F., born April 6, 1856, married December 3, 1879, to Miss Lucy M. Tilden; Marshall B., born March 11, 1859; Charley E., born March 29, 1864, and Orville T., born June 15, 1868. Mr. Wilson is engaged in general husbandry.

EDWARD WILSON, farmer, P. O. Wauponsee, is a native of Grundy County, Ill., born April 6, 1856, the seventh of a family of ten children born to Jonathan and Elenor Wilson. He was educated in the schools of his native county, and took a commercial course at Grand Prairie Seminary. He was married, December 3, 1879, to Miss Lucy Tilden, born October 17, 1860, daughter of A. S. and Alvira Tilden, of Vienna Township; they have one daughter—Eva May, born in Grundy County May 8, 1881. Mr. Wilson owns a farm of 160 acres of improved land, in Sections 9 and 10 of Vienna Township, and resides two and a half miles west from Wauponsee Station; his land is valued at $50 an acre. He is a Republican.

JOHN WELDON, farmer, P. O. Verona. The subject of this sketch is a son of John and Bridget (Mede) Weldon, formerly of Ireland, who emigrated to the United States in

1832 and settled in New York, where subject was born November 18, 1837. When he was six years old (in 1843), his parents moved to Illinois and settled in Will County, where they remained, engaged in farming, until 1849. They then moved to Grundy County and bought land in Vienna Township. Subject enlisted, August 4, 1861, in Company I, Fifty-fifth Illinois Volunteer Infantry, in which he served three years, and was discharged at Nashville, Tenn., November 1, 1864. He participated in the battles of Shiloh, siege of Vicksburg, Chattanooga, Tenn., battle of Nashville, and others; was taken prisoner at or near Memphis by Richardson's guerrillas, from whom he escaped three days after, and returned to his regiment. His brother, Lieut. James Weldon, of Company H, Fifty-fifth Regiment, was killed in the battle of Shiloh. Thomas Weldon, another brother, was a member of the One Hundred and Twenty-seventh Illinois Regiment, in which he served three years; wounded. After returning, Mr. Weldon was married, October 11, 1865, to Miss Ellen Slattery, daughter of William Slattery, of Ireland. She was born in County Tipperary, in December, 1841, and came to the United States in 1853. Their family consists of seven children, three of whom are dead—Dora E., born September 26, 1868; William J., born January 30, 1872; Eveleon M., born February 23, 1876; and Clara A., born April 26, 1879. They own a farm of 268 acres of improved land in Sections 33 and 27 of Vienna Township, valued at $50 per acre, their residence being two miles southwest of Verona. They are members of the Catholic Church. He is a member of the Masonic fraternity, and, in politics, is a National Greenbacker.

PHILIP WAIT, Verona, was born in Montgomery County, N. Y., June 5, 1819, son of Walter and Margaret Wait, of New York State. He remained till ten years old in New York, when his parents moved to Genesee County, N. Y., where they lived about nine years. They then went to Ohio and settled in Hancock County for a few years, and afterward moved to Muskingum County, Ohio, where subject was married, November 10, 1844, to Miss Nancy Bryant, born in Muskingum County, Ohio, May 4, 1827, daughter of Joseph and Nancy Bryant, of Virginia. By this union they have a family of six children—Alwilda M., born in Ohio March 10, 1847, married, March 12, 1866, to Henry Jones, of Grundy County; Romando W., born January 20, 1848, married, in the spring of 1868, to Miss Martha A. Allison, of Grundy County; Alice M., born March 26, 1851, married to Rhonelle Thompson in 1871; Edgar B., born January 11, 1856, married, in September, 1877, to Miss Zelma Paxton, of Grundy County; Emma T., born September 11, 1853; and Newton, born November 11, 1858. Mr. Wait removed from Ohio to Kane County, Ill., in 1848, and, the year following, moved to Grundy County, and settled in Mazon, where he lived one year, then moved on a farm, which he had previously bought, in Highland Township, upon which they lived until 1876, when they removed to the village of Verona. Mr. Wait now owns two farms in Highland Township—111 acres in Section 14, and eighty acres in Section 2, including two dwelling houses, the land being valued at $50 per acre. He also owns a desirable property in the village of Verona. While living in Mazon, Mr. Wait sustained the loss of his only team by a violent storm, which occurred on May 28, 1851. After this, he lost, on an average, one horse each year for twenty-seven years.

THOMAS WALSH, farmer, P. O. Verona, was born in the Province of Quebec, Canada, in December, 1835; was educated in Canada, and came to the United States in 1860, settling in Kendall County, where he remained one year. He came to this county in 1861, and farmed on rented land until 1864. He then bought 340 acres of land in Vienna Township, Section 22, and has since bought eighty-eight and one-half acres in Section 19, of Mazon Township, valued at $60 per acre. He is engaged in raising stock. He married, March 31, 1868, Miss Priscilla Ward, daughter of Samuel Ward, late of Mazon Township.

She was born in New York State, January 11, 1845; they have six children, one of whom is dead—Elizabeth, born September 19, 1869; William C. C., born February 5, 1871; Margaret M., born December 20, 1873; Mary E., born August 12, 1876, died February 14, 1878; Jessie, born September 1, 1878, and Hugh, born February 25, 1878. Mr. and Mrs. Walsh are members of the Presbyterian Church.

HIGHLAND TOWNSHIP.

JOHN CURTIN, farmer. P. O. Verona, was born in Ireland in 1828. He came alone to America in 1840. Having a brother and two sisters living in Ottawa, Ill., he came to that place. He remained in La Salle County for about thirteen years, seven years of which he was with Mr. Joel Armstrong. From La Salle County, he came to Grundy County, settling on his present farm, which consisted of 240 acres. He was married in La Salle County, in 1855, to Miss Catharine Maloney, who was also a native of Ireland. They have six children, three boys and three girls. Mr. Curtin is a member of the Catholic Church, and is Democratic in politics. All his schooling he received in Ireland. His occupation has always been that of farming.

JOSEPH DONDANVILLE, farmer, P. O. Verona, settled in this county in February, 1867; he moved on to the place formerly settled by Simon Wait, who sold it to T. Hibbard, who in turn sold to Mr. Dondanville. He was born December 20, 1840, in Alsace, France. Emigrated to America in the fall of 1851, and settled with his parents in La Salle County, Ill. In 1859, he went to Pike's Peak, and in 1864–65 he went to the northern mines. During these years, Mr. Dondanville was through most of the Western country. He was married, September 22, 1865, to Miss Mary E. Beal, a native of Ohio, but who came to Kendall County at an early date. They have five children, three boys and two girls. His farm consists of 205 acres, all of which he has made since coming here. He was brought up in the Catholic Church, and is Democratic in politics. Neither of his parents are living.

MRS. JOHN T. EMPIE, farming, P. O. Verona, came to Grundy County in March, 1851, and has lived on the same place since. She was born and raised in Columbia County, N. Y.; her parents moved to Kane County, Ill., in the spring of 1845, where they lived for three years, afterward going to Cook County, where they remained for two years. It was then that Mrs. Empie was married to John T. Empie, and they both settled on the farm where Mrs. Empie now lives. Her father, Samuel O. London, is still living, and is eighty-three years old. He is a native of New York State. Mrs. Empie's mother also came from New York, and is seventy-eight years old. Both the parents were born near Lebanon Springs, in Columbia County. Mr. Empie was born in Jefferson County, N. Y., and came from Watertown to Chicago. He died in March, 1867. Mrs. Empie has four children living—two sons and two daughters. The sons still remain in the county, but the two daughters are living in Kansas. John D. and William A. are the names of her two sons. These four children are all that remain of a family of ten. Mr. Empie bought a Mexican land-warrant, and laid it here, the quarter-section costing $72, including the expenses connected with the purchase. He then put up a shanty, which cost $32. By trade, Mr. Empie was a clothier, but his health failing him, he went to farming. Mrs. Empie's father, Mr. Loudon moved from Columbia County to Buffalo, N. Y., when Mrs. Empie was about five years old; from there they went to Broome County, where they remained for three years, afterward going to Cattaraugus County, where they lived for seven years, when they came to Illinois. Mrs. Empie saw some pretty hard times when first settling, owing to failure of crops, etc. There was not a schoolhouse in the township at that time, and Morris was the nearest trading point.

FATHER JOHN A. HEMLOCK, Kinsman, was born in Cedarburg, Wis., in 1851; he is the second youngest child of William Hemlock, a native of Ireland, who follows the occupation of a farmer at Cedarburg, Wis., and who has a family of four sons and two daughters. The subject of this sketch received his elementary education at St. Joseph's College, Bardstown, Ky., afterward finishing his studies at St. Francis Seminary, Milwaukee, Wis. His first charge was St. Bridget's Church, Chicago, from which he was transferred to St. Columbkill's, and thence came to his present charge, in October, 1880; he has been in the ministry since June, 1878. Since he has come here, he has established a new mission in Norman Township, which already consists of at least thirty families, and a church will be built there in a short time. Father Hemlock has also built their parsonage since he came here, and has done much to advance the welfare of the people.

JOHN W. HINCH, farmer, P. O. Verona, was born in Huntingtonshire, England, in 1831. He came to America in 1841, and settled with his parents in Oneida County, N. Y. He lived there until twenty-one years of age, when he came to Illinois and settled in Lisbon, Kendall County, remaining there for four years, when he moved to Saratoga, Grundy County. Here he lived until 1863, after which he resided in Livingston County one year, then came back to this county. In 1865, he moved on to his present farm of 160 acres, and has remained on it ever since. A good dwelling is among the attractive features of the place. Mr. Hinch was married, in Kendall County, in 1858, to Agnes Fulton; she was born in Scotland, and came to this country when she was twenty years of age. They have had eleven children, nine of whom—five boys and four girls—are still living. Mr. Hinch's occupation has always been that of farming. His father, William Hinch, who is dead, was also a farmer. Mr. and Mrs. Hinch are members of the Presbyterian Church. Mr. Hinch is a Republican.

WILLIAM PIERCE, farmer, P. O. Verona, is a native of New York, born in Monroe County, that State, in 1815; his father moved into Genesee County, N. Y., when subject was but seven years old. In 1838, Mr. Pierce came to Kane County, Ill., and remained there till the spring of 1851, when he moved to his present farm, taking his family with him. This farm consists of 320 acres of well-improved land. Mr. Pierce was raised on a farm, and has made farming his occupation ever since coming to the State. He is the oldest settler in the township, and has always taken an active part in its affairs. He received his education in the schools of his native State. He was married in New York in 1838. Mrs. Pierce was born in Genesee County, N. Y., to which place her parents had emigrated from Vermont. Her maiden name was Julia Burr; she is the daughter of Salmon and Azuba (Thomas) Burr; her grandfather Thomas served seven years as musician in the Revolutionary war. Gen. Thomas, of rebellion fame, is Mrs. Pierce's cousin. Seth Thomas, of world-wide reputation as a clock manufacturer, was her great-uncle. Mr. and Mrs. Pierce have had twelve children, five of whom are still living. The eldest son was killed in the army. Of the children now living, there are three in McPherson County, Kan., one is living in Joliet, Ill., and one is at home. When Mr. Pierce came to this county, it was in its wild state, deer, wolves and other wild animals being plentiful. In politics, Mr. Pierce is a Republican.

SYPREON P. SMALL, farmer, P. O. Verona, was born in Somerset County, Me., in 1841; he came to Illinois in 1861, and has lived in this county most of the time since. He is a son of Harrison Small, who is now living in Kansas. Mr. Small received his education mostly in Maine. In 1862, he enlisted in Company A, Twelfth Illinois Cavalry, Col. Voss, in which he served three years and never got a scratch. This company was an escort to Gen. Slocum for some time, and then were sent back to their regiment, after which they did duty as provost guards. In 1867, he returned to Maine, and was there married shortly afterward to Miss Mary Corson; he returned to Illinois, staying three years, when he went back to Maine on a visit, and while there his wife died, July, 1876. He was married a second time, in Maine, this time to Miss Lizzie Whitman, whereupon he returned to Illinois, and has since resided in this State. He has had five children, three by his first wife, one of whom, a boy, is living, and two boys by his second wife, who are living. Mr. Small's farm consists of eighty acres. He votes the Republican ticket.

D. S. SMALL, farmer, P. O. Verona, came to Grundy County when only nine years old, and has remained here ever since. He was born in Somerset County, Me., in 1846. He is the son of Harrison Small, who now lives in Verona. The first year after coming to the county, they lived in Vienna Township, but have ever since lived in this township. The first place they settled on, an unimproved farm, is now owned by John Young. Mr. Small is one of a family of six children, three boys and three girls. One girl is dead and the other two live in Streator. Two of the boys are in Mazon Township, and the remaining one, our subject, still remains in Highland Township. His present farm consists of eighty acres. Mr. Small received his education in this county. In 1872, he was married to Miss May Hamilton; she was born in Canada. Her father, Robert Hamilton, died when she was small, and her mother moved to this State in 1863 or 1864. Mr. and Mrs. Small have two children—one boy Burton, and a girl, Myrtle. Mr. Small's occupation has always been that of farming. He votes the Republican ticket.

FREMONT VICKERY, farmer and stock-raiser, Dwight, was born in Vienna Township, this county, in 1856. His father, John Vickery, moved to the subject's present farm when Fremont was two years old. Here they lived for about thirteen years, and then moved to Livingston County, where the father still lives. Mr. Vickery was married, in January, 1877, in Lee County, to Miss Nettie Johnson.

a daughter of Rev. William Johnson, a Presbyterian minister, who was born in Edinburgh, Scotland. Mrs. Vickery was born in Lee County. Mr. and Mrs. Vickery have one child—Paul. Mr. Vickery received his education in the common schools of this county, attended the Dwight schools, and afterward was, for fifteen months, a student at the Wesleyan University at Bloomington. After he was married, he moved to the old homestead, in Highland Township. His farm consists of 355 acres. Raising stock and feeding sheep, hogs and cattle is his main business. He is a member of the Masonic fraternity, and also, with his wife, a member of the M. E. Church. In politics, Mr. Vickery is a Republican.

GOODFARM TOWNSHIP.

WILLIAM CONSTANTINE, farmer, P. O. Dwight, was born in Wurtemberg, Germany, in 1841. He came to America in 1857, and lived for two years near Aurora, Ill., afterward coming to Grundy County. In 1861, he enlisted in Company I, Fifty-fifth Illinois Infantry, serving three years. In 1864, he re-enlisted, and served till the close of the war. In March, 1865, he was taken prisoner in North Carolina, near Goldsboro. Being paroled in July, 1865, he returned home. He was with Sherman's army, and helped open the Mississippi River, and in the memorable march through Georgia. During all the time that he served, he received not even a wound. After the war, he returned to Grundy County, where he has since remained. He bought his present farm, which consists of eighty acres of well-improved land, in 1869. In 1866, he was married to Miss Mary Klughart, who was born in Kendall County, this State. They have five children, two boys and three girls—Emma, Edward J., Clara, Martha and William. Mr. Constantine received his education mostly in Germany, but he attended English schools in Illinois for some time. Mr. Constantine has held several township offices, and is a member of the Evangelical Association. He votes the Republican ticket.

L. NATHAN LEWIS, deceased, was a native of Vermont, but, when a young man, moved to St. Lawrence County, N. Y., where his children were born. In 1845, he came to Illinois, and lived in Kane and McHenry Counties for about four years, when he came to this county and settled on a place on Mazon Creek. Mr. Lewis died in December, 1853, at his old homestead. He organized the first church in the township, at the residence of David Gleason, and was their first minister. This was a Free-Will Baptist Church, and there were six members at the organization. Mrs. Nathan Lewis is still living in this township, with her daughter, Mrs. E. B. Stevens. Mrs. Lewis was born December 25, 1800. In 1858, Miss Fannie Lewis (now Mrs. Stevens) was married to Dr. John F. Trowe, of New Hampshire. They lived in Dundee, Ill., till 1860, when Mr. Trowe died. They had one son, Frank.

GEORGE PRESTON, farmer, P. O. Mazon, was born in Tuscarawas County, Ohio, in September, 1822. He moved to Grundy County in 1851, and settled on his present farm. His father, Elijah Preston, came at the same time, but died soon afterward. At that time, there were but few settlers between Mazon Creek and Johnny Creek, both north and south, and the grass was so high that two persons on horseback could scarcely discern each other, if only separated but by a short distance. The subject's brother, William Preston, had already come and settled about two years previous. Mr. Elijah Preston entered an eighty-acre tract of Government land, which was the only Government land near him at that time. Mr. Preston's farm now consists of 400 acres, besides property in Mazon. He was married, in Virginia, in 1840, to Elizabeth Carnes, who was born in Tuscarawas County, Ohio. She died about 1854. He has three children living by this wife, two sons and one daughter—William C., George W. and Mary E. Mr. Preston was married a second time, in this county, a short time before the war, to Jane Johnson, born in Ashland County, Ohio, but raised in Guernsey County, Ohio. When Mr. Preston first came here, he came together with several other families, all of whom moved in wagons. At that time, it was about three miles to any school. There were no bridges, roads, or anything to make hauling easy, so that twenty bushels of corn were all that could be hauled most of the year. There was a small boat at the river, which could carry two teams across at a time. Mr. Preston is now building a new residence in Mazon, to which he will shortly move, having sold his old homestead. He is a Republican.

DANIEL ROEDER, farmer, P. O. Dwight, was born in Prussia, Germany, and came to America in 1857, and lived in La Salle County, Ill., for nearly four years, when he returned to Germany, coming back to America in 1861, bringing his family with him. He rented land and farmed in La Salle County until 1869, when he moved onto his present farm, which he had bought the year before. He now has 240 acres of well-improved land, which represents the result of his industry and frugality since coming to America. He was educated in the German schools, and is Republican in politics. He is a member of the Lutheran Church. His father, Henry Roeder, was a farmer in Langenstein, R. G. B. Z., Cassel, Germany. Mr. Roeder has nine children—seven boys and two girls. Those by his first wife, whom he married in Germany, are Stephen, born in 1843; and Henry, born in 1851. The remaining seven are by the present wife, viz., John, born in 1855; Balcer, in 1857; Elizabeth, in 1861; Lena, in 1864; William, in 1866; Leonard, in 1870; and George, in 1873.

E. B. STEVENS, farmer, P. O. Dwight, moved to Goodfarm Township April 22, 1850, having been there and purchased land the year previous. The place which Mr. Stevens had bought had a log cabin on it, 12x16 feet, into which seven people moved. Mr. John Henry and family had moved there at the same time. Mr. Stevens had bought a Mexican land warrant, for which he paid $120, which was at the rate of $1 per acre, as he received 120 acres. He also bought forty acres of a settler who had entered it. Mr. Stevens came to this county from Kalamazoo County, Mich., and his was the ninth family to settle in this township. The first school in the township was in session when he moved in. It was in a log house, with puncheon floors, etc., and was situated on Mazon Creek. The first crop of wheat and oats which Mr. Stevens raised could not be threshed until a machine came from Wilmington, a distance of eighteen miles, and what bread they had in the meantime was made from grated corn. His farm now consists of 270 acres. He is the son of Levi Stevens, a native of Vermont, who moved from Vermont to New York, afterward to Pennsylvania, and finally to Michigan, where he died. Mr. E. B. Stevens, our subject, is a native of Vermont, and was married, in February, 1850, to Miss Betsy A. Cullen, a native of Canada, but whose parents were from the old country- her father from Ireland and her mother from London, England. Mrs. Stevens died December 26, 1866. Her mother, Mrs. Cullen, lived to be ninety-one years old. Mr. Stevens has three children by his first wife, living—Charlie, Darwin and Eddie. Mr. Stevens married the second time, to Mrs. Fannie (Lewis) Trowe, in the fall of 1867. They have one little girl living, named Fannie Luella. Mr. and Mrs. Stevens are members of the Methodist Episcopal Church.

ADISON WOOD, farmer, P. O. Dwight, came to Grundy County in 1849, and has lived in Goodfarm Township all the time since. In the township now there are but two older settlers living—Mrs. Holtz and Mrs. L. V. Wood. Mrs. Wood is a native of Otsego County, N. Y., and his wife is from Schoharie County, N. Y. When they first moved into the township, there were but eleven houses in it, and they could cross the prairie, going southeast, to the State of Indiana, and not come across a house. Wolves and deer abounded in plentiful numbers. In 1843, Mr. Wood came to Lake County, Ill., from New York, and was there about six years, when he sold out and went to Cook County, staying there one season before coming to this county. Mr. Wood is the son of Newcomb Wood, and was born in 1822. He was married, in Dundee, Kane Co., Ill., December 16, 1847, to Miss Catharine Bute. When he first came to this county, Mr. Wood bought 160 acres of Government land, for which he paid but $112, having bought a land warrant. His present farm consists of eighty acres. When the township was first organized, which was the year following Mr. Wood's arrival, he was elected the first Justice of the Peace, in which capacity he served three years. He has been a Republican since the party was organized, before which he was a Whig. Mr. and Mrs. Wood are members of the Methodist Episcopal Church of Dwight. Their children are eight in number—four boys and four girls. Their names are as follows: Levi, Mary J., Charles M., Lucretia, Erma A., Barney A., Sarah L. and Henry A. Mrs. Wood is the daughter of Lewis B. Bute, who came to Lake County in 1846.

L. V. WOOD, farmer, P. O. Dwight, was born in Oneida County, N. Y., in 1829. His father was Russell Wood, a native of New York, but who had moved to Michigan in 1845, and was accidentally killed while felling trees. In the spring of 1846, his mother moved to Illinois, on the Fox River, in Kane County. Mr. Wood lived in Kane and Kendall Counties until 1851, when he came to this county, where he has remained ever since, and his present farm is the same one on which he first settled. In June, 1852, he was married, in this county, to Miss Pluma A. Gleason, daughter of David Gleason, who had settled in this township in 1849, and lived here till his death. He was one of the earliest settlers in the township. Mrs. Wood is at present, with a single exception, the oldest resident in this township. Mrs. Wood is a native of New York. Mr. and Mrs. Wood have four children—two sons and two daughters—all of whom are married—Russell O., Allie L., Henry O. and Alma. Mr. Wood received his early education in the State of New York. When he first came here, he located on the open prairie, by laying a Mexican land warrant. In politics, Mr. Wood is a Republican, and he and his wife are members of the Methodist Episcopal Church of Dwight. His farm consists of eighty acres of land.

www.ingramcontent.com/pod-product-compliance
Lightning Source LLC
Chambersburg PA
CBHW021418300426
44114CB00010B/544